SOMETHING ABOUT THE AUTHOR®

Something about
the Author *was named
an "Outstanding
Reference Source,"
the highest honor given
by the American
Library Association
Reference and Adult
Services Division.*

ISSN 0276-816X

something ABOUT THE AUTHOR®

**Facts and Pictures about Authors
and Illustrators of Books for Young People**

volume 185

GALE
CENGAGE Learning™

Detroit • New York • San Francisco • New Haven, Conn • Waterville, Maine • London

GALE
CENGAGE Learning™

Something about the Author, Volume 185

Project Editor: Lisa Kumar

Editorial: Dana Ferguson, Amy Elisabeth Fuller, Michelle Kazensky, Jennifer Mossman, Joseph Palmisano, Mary Ruby, Robert James Russell, Amanda D. Sams, Marie Toft

Permissions: Mollika Basu, Barb McNeil, Tracie Richardson

Imaging and Multimedia: Leitha Etheridge-Sims, Lezlie Light

Composition and Electronic Capture: Amy Darga

Manufacturing: Drew Kalasky

Product Manager: Peg Knight

For product information and technology assistance, contact us at
Gale Customer Support, 1-800-877-4253.
For permission to use material from this text or product,
submit all requests online at **www.cengage.com/permissions**.
Further permissions questions can be emailed to
permissionrequest@cengage.com

While every effort has been made to ensure the reliability of the information presented in this publication, Gale, a part of Cengage Learning, does not guarantee the accuracy of the data contained herein. Gale accepts no payment for listing; and inclusion in the publication of any organization, agency, institution, publication, service, or individual does not imply endorsement of the editors or publisher. Errors brought to the attention of the publisher and verified to the satisfaction of the publisher will be corrected in future editions.

EDITORIAL DATA PRIVACY POLICY: Does this product contain information about you as an individual? If so, for more information about our editorial data privacy policies, please see our Privacy Statement at www.gale.cengage.com.

Gale
27500 Drake Rd.
Farmington Hills, MI, 48331-3535

LIBRARY OF CONGRESS CATALOG CARD NUMBER 62-52046

ISBN-13: 978-0-7876-9934-5
ISBN-10: 0-7876-9934-9

ISSN 0276-816X

This title is also available as an e-book.
ISBN-13: 978-1-4144-3837-5
ISBN-10: 1-4144-3837-0
Contact your Gale sales representative for ordering information.

Printed in the United States of America
1 2 3 4 5 6 7 12 11 10 09 08

Contents

Authors in Forthcoming Volumes

Below are some of the authors and illustrators that will be featured in upcoming volumes of *SATA*. These include new entries on the swiftly rising stars of the field, as well as completely revised and updated entries (indicated with *) on some of the most notable and best-loved creators of books for children.

Ibtisam Barakat ∎ Born in Palestine, Barakat experienced a childhood shadowed by war: at age three, with the outbreak of the Six-Day War, she fled with her family to Jordan to escape the terror, then returned to live under Israeli occupation. In addition to working as an activist to end racial discrimination, Barakat has produced the young-adult memoir *Tasting the Sky: A Palestinian Childhood.*

*Nicholas Debon ∎ French-born writer and illustrator Debon leads a dual life. In addition to working for the French consulate in Toronto, Ontario, Canada, he has also developed a reputation as a children's book illustrator. Although much of his more recent work appears in books for French-language readers, Debon's art can be found in Virginia Walton Pilegard's "Warlord" fantasy novels, as well as in picture books such as Jean E. Pendziwol's *Dawn Watch* and Dominique Demers' *Every Single Night.*

K.L. Denman ∎ Denman's memories of her own childhood, spent living and working on a ranch in Alberta, Canada, as well as the experiences of her teen children, inspire her books for young adults. Her first novel, *Battle of the Bands,* focuses on the life of an ambitious teen musician, while *Mirror Image* and *Rebel Tag* also address common teen concerns within the context of a compelling story. Realizing the need for books that entice reluctant readers, Denman makes a special effort to give her novels elements that will appeal to teen boys.

*Jackie French ∎ One of the most beloved authors in her native Australia, French is inspired by her love of the Australian landscape, and her stories resonate with her good-natured humor and her passionate concern for the environment. The Australian bush serves as the backdrop of her acclaimed story collection *Rainstones,* while the unique creatures that live Down Under star in picture books such as *Diary of a Wombat* and *Josephine Wants to Dance.* French's reputation as a self-sufficiency guru has been firmly cemented with works such as *New Plants from Old* and *Plants That Never Say Die.*

Gris Grimly ∎ Grimly is an artist, author, and filmmaker who is known for his macabre yet whimsical creations. Working primarily in ink and watercolor, his illustrations reflect the influences of film designer Tim Burton and author/illustrators Edward Gorey and Dr. Seuss. In addition to creating artwork for books such as Marilyn Singer's *Monster Museum* and Carolyn Crimi's *Boris and Bella,* he has created the self-illustrated *Gris Grimly's Wicked Nursery Rhymes,* which pairs ghoulish poems satirizing traditional nursery rhymes with his macabre art.

Conor Kostick ∎ The young-adult novels of Kostick were inspired by the work of fantasy writers such as J.R.R. Tolkien and Andre Norton. Kostick, a professor of medieval history at Trinity College, Dublin, worked as a designer for one of the first live-action role-playing games. His first teen novels, such as *Epic, Saga,* and *The Book of Curses,* address a provocative question: What would the world be like if one's successes in online fantasy games actually impacted real life?

*Pat Mora ∎ One of the most distinguished Hispanic writers working in the United States, Mora also works to advance literacy and multiculturalism. Designed to promote the recognition and preservation of Mexican-American culture and often set in the American Southwest, her books for children inspire young Latinos with pride in their ethnic heritage. Mora's picture books, biographies, concept books, and retellings of Mayan folktales include *A Birthday Basket for Tia, The Gift of the Poinsettia,* and *The Desert Is My Mother.* A poet for adults, she has also compiled verse anthologies for both children and teens.

Jerry Pallotta ∎ A former insurance salesman, Pallotta began his writing career in 1985 after becoming frustrated by the lack of interesting, informative alphabet books available for his own children. Known in literary circles as the "Alphabet Man," he has published such innovative abcedariums as *The Icky Bug Alphabet Book, The Skull Alphabet Book,* and *The Airplane Alphabet Book.* In addition, Pallotta explores basic math concepts in such works as *The Hershey's Kisses Addition Book* and *Twizzlers Shapes and Patterns.*

René Saldaña, Jr. ∎ A first-generation American of Mexican descent, Saldaña is the author of a number of critically acclaimed works for young adults, including *The Jumping Tree* and *The Whole Sky Full of Stars.* His short stories and novels are loosely based on his own experiences growing up in southern Texas near the U.S.-Mexico border. A native of McAllen, Texas, Saldaña was raised in nearby Nuevo Peñitas, a town that often serves as the setting for his tales.

*Eileen Spinelli ∎ The mother of seven children, poet and teacher Spinelli has a good idea of what works and what does not work in the arena of children's picture books. Her picture-book contributions to children's literature include *Somebody Loves You, Mr. Hatch, The Perfect Thanksgiving,* and *Summerhouse Time,* and her rhymes are featured in *The Giggle and Cry Book, City Angel,* and *Polar Bear, Arctic Hare: Poems of the Frozen North.* Cats often make an appearance in Spinelli's stories, and they occupy center stage in the books *Moe McTooth: An Alley Cat's Tale, Hero Cat,* and *Callie Cat, Ice Skater.*

Introduction

Something about the Author (*SATA*) is an ongoing reference series that examines the lives and works of authors and illustrators of books for children. *SATA* includes not only well-known writers and artists but also less prominent individuals whose works are just coming to be recognized. This series is often the only readily available information source on emerging authors and illustrators. You'll find *SATA* informative and entertaining, whether you are a student, a librarian, an English teacher, a parent, or simply an adult who enjoys children's literature.

What's Inside *SATA*

SATA provides detailed information about authors and illustrators who span the full time range of children's literature, from early figures like John Newbery and L. Frank Baum to contemporary figures like Judy Blume and Richard Peck. Authors in the series represent primarily English-speaking countries, particularly the United States, Canada, and the United Kingdom. Also included, however, are authors from around the world whose works are available in English translation. The writings represented in *SATA* include those created intentionally for children and young adults as well as those written for a general audience and known to interest younger readers. These writings cover the entire spectrum of children's literature, including picture books, humor, folk and fairy tales, animal stories, mystery and adventure, science fiction and fantasy, historical fiction, poetry and nonsense verse, drama, biography, and nonfiction. Obituaries are also included in *SATA* and are intended not only as death notices but also as concise overviews of people's lives and work. Additionally, each edition features newly revised and updated entries for a selection of *SATA* listees who remain of interest to today's readers and who have been active enough to require extensive revisions of their earlier biographies.

Autobiography Feature

Beginning with Volume 103, many volumes of *SATA* feature one or more specially commissioned autobiographical essays. These unique essays, averaging about ten thousand words in length and illustrated with an abundance of personal photos, present an entertaining and informative first-person perspective on the lives and careers of prominent authors and illustrators profiled in *SATA*.

Two Convenient Indexes

In response to suggestions from librarians, *SATA* indexes no longer appear in every volume but are included in alternate (odd-numbered) volumes of the series, beginning with Volume 57.

SATA continues to include two indexes that cumulate with each alternate volume: the Illustrations Index, arranged by the name of the illustrator, gives the number of the volume and page where the illustrator's work appears in the current volume as well as all preceding volumes in the series; the Author Index gives the number of the volume in which a person's biographical sketch, autobiographical essay, or obituary appears in the current volume as well as all preceding volumes in the series.

These indexes also include references to authors and illustrators who appear in *Gale's Yesterday's Authors of Books for Children, Children's Literature Review,* and *Something about the Author Autobiography Series.*

Easy-to-Use Entry Format

Whether you're already familiar with the *SATA* series or just getting acquainted, you will want to be aware of the kind of information that an entry provides. In every *SATA* entry the editors attempt to give as complete a picture of the person's life and work as possible. A typical entry in *SATA* includes the following clearly labeled information sections:

PERSONAL: date and place of birth and death, parents' names and occupations, name of spouse, date of marriage, names of children, educational institutions attended, degrees received, religious and political affiliations, hobbies and other interests.

ADDRESSES: complete home, office, electronic mail, and agent addresses, whenever available.

CAREER: name of employer, position, and dates for each career post; art exhibitions; military service; memberships and offices held in professional and civic organizations.

MEMBER: professional, civic, and other association memberships and any official posts held.

AWARDS, HONORS: literary and professional awards received.

WRITINGS: title-by-title chronological bibliography of books written and/or illustrated, listed by genre when known; lists of other notable publications, such as plays, screenplays, and periodical contributions.

ADAPTATIONS: a list of films, television programs, plays, CD-ROMs, recordings, and other media presentations that have been adapted from the author's work.

WORK IN PROGRESS: description of projects in progress.

SIDELIGHTS: a biographical portrait of the author or illustrator's development, either directly from the biographee—and often written specifically for the *SATA* entry—or gathered from diaries, letters, interviews, or other published sources.

BIOGRAPHICAL AND CRITICAL SOURCES: cites sources quoted in "Sidelights" along with references for further reading.

EXTENSIVE ILLUSTRATIONS: photographs, movie stills, book illustrations, and other interesting visual materials supplement the text.

How a *SATA* Entry Is Compiled

SATA editors examine a wide variety of published sources to gather information for an entry. Biographical and bibliographic sources are consulted, as are book reviews, feature articles, published interviews, and material sometimes obtained from the biographee's family, publishers, agent, or other associates. Whenever possible, the author or illustrator is sent a copy of the entry to check for accuracy and completeness.

Entries that have not been verified by the biographees or their representatives are marked with an asterisk (*).

Contact the Editor

We encourage our readers to examine the entire *SATA* series. Please write and tell us if we can make *SATA* even more helpful to you. Give your comments and suggestions to the editor:

Editor
Something about the Author
Gale, Cengage Learning
27500 Drake Rd.
Farmington Hills MI 48331-3535

Toll-free: 800-877-GALE
Fax: 248-699-8070

Something about the Author Product Advisory Board

The editors of *Something about the Author* are dedicated to maintaining a high standard of excellence by publishing comprehensive, accurate, and highly readable entries on a wide array of writers for children and young adults. In addition to the quality of the content, the editors take pride in the graphic design of the series, which is intended to be orderly yet inviting, allowing readers to utilize the pages of *SATA* easily and with efficiency. Despite the longevity of the *SATA* print series, and the success of its format, we are mindful that the vitality of a literary reference product is dependent on its ability to serve its users over time. As literature, and attitudes about literature, constantly evolve, so do the reference needs of students, teachers, scholars, journalists, researchers, and book club members. To be certain that we continue to keep pace with the expectations of our customers, the editors of *SATA* listen carefully to their comments regarding the value, utility, and quality of the series. Librarians, who have firsthand knowledge of the needs of library users, are a valuable resource for us. The *Something about the Author* Product Advisory Board, made up of school, public, and academic librarians, is a forum to promote focused feedback about *SATA* on a regular basis. The nine-member advisory board includes the following individuals, whom the editors wish to thank for sharing their expertise:

Eva M. Davis
Youth Department Manager,
Ann Arbor District Library,
Ann Arbor, Michigan

Joan B. Eisenberg
Lower School Librarian,
Milton Academy,
Milton, Massachusetts

Francisca Goldsmith
Teen Services Librarian,
Berkeley Public Library,
Berkeley, California

Susan Dove Lempke
Children's Services Supervisor,
Niles Public Library District,
Niles, Illinois

Robyn Lupa
Head of Children's Services,
Jefferson County Public Library,
Lakewood, Colorado

Victor L. Schill
Assistant Branch Librarian/Children's Librarian,
Harris County Public Library/Fairbanks Branch,
Houston, Texas

Caryn Sipos
Community Librarian,
Three Creeks Community Library,
Vancouver, Washington

Steven Weiner
Director,
Maynard Public Library,
Maynard, Massachusetts

SOMETHING ABOUT THE AUTHOR

BARTH-GRÖZINGER, Inge 1950-

Personal

Born 1950.

Career

Writer; high school teacher in Ellwangen, Germany.

Writings

Etwas bleibt (novel), Thienemann (Stuttgart, Germany), 2004, translation by Anthea Bell published as *Something Remains: A Novel*, Hyperion Books for Children (New York, NY), 2006.

Sidelights

Inge Barth-Grözinger's *Something Remains: A Novel* grew out of an exercise she developed with her high school class in Ellwangen, Germany. Over a period of eighteen months she led a research project attempting to trace the history of the town's tiny Jewish community during the 1930s, a period when Germany was dominated by Nazis who promoted persecution of Jews. The changes in Ellwangen are seen through the eyes of schoolboy Erich Levi, one of only three young Jews in the town's school. "A mixture of fiction and historical fact," declared a *Publishers Weekly* reviewer, "this chilling story asks readers to speculate how the Holocaust could have happened."

From Erich's point of view, the changes in Ellwangen are small, but their effects are devastating. "Hitler's genius," wrote *Kliatt* contributor Myrna Marler, "lay in depriving Jews of their rights little by little so that each loss seemed bearable until the Final Solution." "A teacher leads bullying and insults; classroom exercises label Jews 'bloodsuckers'; the Hitler Youth run things," explained Hazel Rochman in *Booklist*. "Erich endures," a *Kirkus Reviews* contributor stated, "quietly celebrating his bar mitzvah, keeping a low profile in school and briefly falling in love." "This story of a boy who tried to live an ordinary life in an extraordinary, terrible time," Carlie Webber wrote on *TeenReads.com*, "is both hopeful and saddening."

Biographical and Critical Sources

PERIODICALS

Booklist, September 1, 2006, Hazel Rochman, review of *Something Remains: A Novel*, p. 108.
Kirkus Reviews, September 1, 2006, review of *Something Remains*, p. 900.
Kliatt, November, 2006, Myrna Marler, review of *Something Remains*, p. 6.
Publishers Weekly, November 27, 2006, review of *Something Remains*, p. 51.

ONLINE

TeenReads.com, http://aol.teenreads.com/ (April 1, 2007), Carlie Webber, review of *Something Remains*.*

BENDALL-BRUNELLO, John

Personal

Born in England; married; wife's name Tiziana. *Education:* Completed college, 1981. *Hobbies and other interests:* Playing piano, snooker, badminton, chess, travel.

Addresses

Home and office—Cambridge, England; Cannes, France. *Agent*—Shannon Associates, 630 9th Ave., New York, NY 10036. *E-mail*—contact@johnbendall-brunello.com; john@glasspencil.demon.co.uk.

Career

Illustrator.

Writings

SELF-ILLUSTRATED

The Seven-and-one-half Labors of Hercules, Dutton (New York, NY), 1991.

ILLUSTRATOR

Martin Waddell, *The Big Bad Mole's Coming,* Walker (London, England), 1993.
Trish Cooke, *When I Grow Bigger,* Candlewick (Cambridge, MA), 1994.
June Crebbin, *Into the Castle,* Candlewick (Cambridge, MA), 1996.
Martin Waddell, *Yum, Yum, Yummy,* Candlewick (Cambridge, MA), 1998.
John Farndon, *Weather,* Dorling Kindersley (New York, NY), 1998.
Trudi Braun, *My Goose Betsy,* Candlewick (Cambridge, MA), 1998.
Catherine Bruzzone, *Puppy Finds a Friend/Cachorrito encuentra un amigo//Le petit chien se trouve un ami,* Barron's (Hauppauge, NY), 2000.
Lois Rock, *God Bless Me, God Bless You,* Baker (Grand Rapids, MI), 2001.
Lynn Hodges and Sue Buchanan, *I Love You This Much: A Song of God's Love,* Zonderkidz (Grand Rapids, MI), 2001.
Linda Ashman, *The Tale of Wagmore Gently,* Dutton (New York, NY), 2002.
A.H. Benjamin, *Mouse, Mole, and the Falling Star,* Dutton (New York, NY), 2002.
Shutta Crum, *Fox and Fluff,* Albert Whitman (Morton Grove, IL), 2002.
Jamie Rix, *Looking after Murphy,* Barron's (Hauppauge, NY), 2002.
Claire Freedman, *Hushabye Lily,* Orchard (New York, NY), 2003.

Claire Freedman, *The Naughtiest Piglet,* Pinwheel, 2003.
Abby Levine, *Daddies Give You Horsey Rides,* Albert Whitman (Morton Grove, IL), 2004.
Stuart J. Murphy, *100 Days of Cool,* HarperCollins (New York, NY), 2004.
Lynn Hodges, *Count Yourself to Sleep,* Zonderkidz (Grand Rapids, MI), 2005.
Malachy Doyle, *Big Pig,* Simon & Schuster (New York, NY), 2005.
Jacqueline Mitchard, *Rosalie, My Rosalie: The Tale of a Duckling,* HarperCollins (New York, NY), 2005.
Lynn Hodges, *Dear God, It's Me: A Song of God's Love,* Zonderkids (Grand Rapids, MI), 2005.
Sue Buchanan, *Angels Watching over Me: A Song of God's Love,* Zonderkidz (Grand Rapids, MI), 2006.
Gillian Harker, *Little Elephant's Clever Trick,* Parragon, 2006.

Also illustrator of *Babe* by Dick King Smith, and texts by Martin Waddell.

Sidelights

British illustrator John Bendall-Brunello grew up drawing. As the youngest of nine children, he was raised in a household full of pets, and he learned about other animals while visiting his aunt's farm. During school, Bendall-Brunello often doodled images of teachers and other creatures in the margins of his notebooks. Eventually attending a local college, he studied design and illustration, and got his first job illustrating a picture book from London's Orchard Books in 1985.

Bendall-Brunello usually uses water color in his illustrations, sometimes combining them with pencil lines, and he has created images to pair with texts by well-known authors such as Martin Waddell and Jacqueline Mitchard. His work has been praised for containing "fluid, airy lines and [a] sunny palette," as a *Publishers Weekly* critic wrote in a review of *Looking after Murphy* by Jamie Rix. "Pencil and watercolor artwork enhances each satin soft page" of A.H. Benjamin's *Mouse, Mole, and the Falling Star,* according to a *Kirkus Reviews* contributor. Judith Constantinides, in a review of the same title for *School Library Journal,* made note of Bendall-Brunello's "soft, uncluttered illustrations."

Bendall-Brunello's illustrations are often said to "add humor to the understated text," as *Booklist* reviewer Kay Weisman wrote of *When I Grow Bigger* by Trish Cook. In *Daddies Give You Horsey Rides,* his art "provides an extra layer of humor" to Abbie Levine's story, according to Ilene Cooper in *Booklist.* Writing about the lively dog, who stars in *The Tale of Wagmore Gently,* a *Kirkus Reviews* contributor wrote that Bendall-Brunello's "exuberant watercolor illustrations bring Wagmore to life." Helen Rosenberg, writing in *Booklist,* also noted the comedy in Bendall-Brunello's drawings when she commented that the book's "humorous illustrations capture all of the tail-wagging motion and ensuing chaos" in Levine's tale. Reviewing Bendall-

John Bendall-Brunello's scratchy, warmhearted art enhances Linda Ashman's story in **The Tale of Wagmore Gently.** (Illustration © 2002 by John Bendall-Brunello. Reproduced by permission of Dutton Children's Books, a division of Penguin Putnam Books for Young Readers.)

Brunello's contribution to Shutta Crum's picture book *Fox and Fluff,* Lauren Peterson wrote in *Booklist* that the "lively, loose-lined watercolor-and-pencil artwork . . . reflects the humor of the goings-on."

Although often cited for their humor, Bendall-Brunello's illustrations have also been praised for the depth they add to each story's character. "Chiffon textures and openhearted characterizations meld beautifully," wrote a *Publishers Weekly* critic in describing the artist's work

for Claire Freeman's *Hushbye Lily.* "The characters' postures speak volumes," noted Linda Staskus in her review of Irish storyteller Malachy Doyle's *Big Pig* for *School Library Journal.* As in *Big Pig,* many of Bendall-Brunello's illustration projects feature farm animals, and for these he draws on childhood memories of time spent at his aunt's. His artwork for Trudi Braun's picture book *My Goose Betsy* "features extreme close-ups and delightful action poses" of a goose and her family, noted Carolyn Phelan in *Booklist.* Phelan also commented on Bendall-Brunello's "quiet precision," and a *Horn Book* critic noted that *My Goose Betsy* features "an abundance of large yet cozy illustrations."

Biographical and Critical Sources

PERIODICALS

Booklist, September 1, 1994, Kay Weisman, review of *When I Grow Bigger,* p. 49; April 1, 1999, Carolyn Phelan, review of *My Goose Betsy,* p. 1408; October 1, 2002, Helen Rosenberg, review of *The Tale of Wagmore Gently,* p. 330; October 15, 2002, Lauren Peterson, review of *Fox and Fluff,* p. 411; March 15, 2004, Ilene Cooper, review of *Daddies Give You Horsey Rides,* p. 1308; April 1, 2004, Hazel Rochman, review of *100 Days of Cool,* p. 1367; July, 2005, Abby Nolan, review of *Rosalie, My Rosalie: The Tale of a Duckling,* p. 1925.

Horn Book, May, 1999, review of *My Goose Betsy,* p. 311; January-February, 2003, Betty Carter, review of *Fox and Fluff,* p. 54.

Irish writer Malachy Doyle's barnyard story comes to life in Bendall-Brunello's gentle paintings for **Big Pig.** (Illustration © 2005 by John Bendall-Brunello. Reproduced by permission.)

Kirkus Reviews, June 1, 2002, review of *Mouse, Mole, and the Falling Star,* p. 800; August 1, 2002, review of *Fox and Fluff,* p. 1125; September 15, 2002, review of *The Tale of Wagmore Gently,* p. 1383; August 1, 2003, review of *Hushabye Lily,* p. 1016; January 1, 2004, review of *100 Days of Cool,* p. 39; March 1, 2005, Jacquelyn Mitchard, review of *Rosalie, My Rosalie,* p. 292; September 15, 2006, Malachy Doyle, review of *Big Pig,* p. 951.

Publishers Weekly, July 4, 1994, review of *When I Grow Bigger,* p. 61; April 12, 1999, review of *My Goose Betsy,* p. 73; June 3, 2002, review of *Looking after Murphy,* p. 87; June 2, 2003, review of *Hushabye Lily,* p. 50; May 9, 2005, review of *Rosalie, My Rosalie,* p. 71.

School Library Journal, August, 2002, Judith Constantinides, review of *Mouse, Mole, and the Falling Star,* p. 146; November, 2002, Elaine Lesh Morgan, review of *The Tale of Wagmore Gently,* p. 110; December, 2002, Kristin de Lacoste, review of *Fox and Fluff,* p. 86; November, 2003, Andrea Tarr, review of *Hushabye Lily,* p. 93; March, 2004, Gloria Koster, review of *100 Days of Cool,* p. 198; May, 2004, Be Astengo, review of *Daddies Give You Horsey Rides,* p. 117; June, 2005, Christine McGinty, review of *Rosalie, My Rosalie,* p. 122; November, 2006, Linda Staskus, review of *Big Pig,* p. 90.

ONLINE

Harper Collins Web site, http://www.harpercollins.com/ (December 1, 2007), "John Bendall-Brunello."
John Bendall-Brunello Home Page, http://www.johnbendall-brunello.com (December 1, 2007).
Shannon Associates Web site, http://www.shannon associates.com/ (December 1, 2007), "John Bendall-Brunello."*

*   *   *

BENTLEY, Karen
See TASCHEK, Karen

*   *   *

BERGER, Carin

Personal
Female.

Addresses
Home—New York, NY. *E-mail*—carinbergerdesign@ hotmail.com.

Career
Illustrator and author. Graphic artist; designer and illustrator of book covers for various publishers.

Awards, Honors
Bank Street College of Education Best Children's Books of the Year designation, and Chicago Public Library Best of the Best designation, both 2004, both for *Not So True Stories and Unreasonable Rhymes;* Founder's Award, Society of Illustrators, 2006; New York Public Library 100 Titles for Reading and Sharing, 2006, and Scandiuzzi Children's Book Award, Seattle Public Library, 2007, and Best of Show award, 3 x 3 Magazine Children's Book Show, all for *Behold the Bold Umbrellaphant, and Other Poems..*

Writings

SELF-ILLUSTRATED

Not So True Stories and Unreasonable Rhymes, Chronicle Books (San Francisco, CA), 2004.
All Mixed Up, Chronicle Books (San Francisco, CA), 2006.
The Little Yellow Leaf, Greenwillow Books (New York, NY), 2008.
Ok Go!, Greenwillow Books (New York, NY), 2009.

ILLUSTRATOR

Jack Prelutsky, *Behold the Bold Umbrellaphant, and Other Poems,* Greenwillow Books (New York, NY) 2006.
Bobbi Katz, *Trailblazers: Poems of Exploration,* Greenwillow Books (New York, NY), 2007.

Sidelights
"Channeling Hieronymus Bosch, but with a smile," is how a *Kirkus Reviews* contributor described the work of author and illustrator Carin Berger. Crafted from scraps of paper torn from mail-order catalogues, bits of newspapers, and even the odd ticket stub, Berger's art for *Not So True Stories and Unreasonable Rhymes,* which features a collection of original nonsense poems, "exert[s] an immediate pull" due to her use of "intricate" cut-paper-collage images featuring elongated shapes and dramatic contrasts, in the opinion of a *Publishers Weekly* contributor. "The imagination at work here marks this author-artist as one to watch," the critic added. Berger's work for children includes the interactive picture book *All Mixed Up,* a spiral-bound volume in which the pages are cut in three segments to allow readers to remix art and text in nonsensical and humorous fashion.

As an illustrator, Berger has seen her work paired with poetry by notable children's writer Jack Prelutsky. In a review of the collaboration resulting in *Behold the Bold Umbrellaphant, and Other Poems,* Donna Cardon dubbed the work "whimsical" in her *School Library Journal* review. The critic added that the illustrator's mixed-media collage art "create[s] a rich visual treat well suited to the poetry." "Berger's . . . inventive, tex-

Carin Berger creates a unique interactive reading experience in the tri-cut pages of **All Mixed Up.** (Illustration © 2006 by Carin Berger. Reproduced by permission of Chronicle Books, LLC., San Francisco. Visit www.ChronicleBooks.com.)

tured collages add up to a visual treat," concluded a *Publishers Weekly* critic of the same volume, calling *Behold the Bold Umbrellaphant, and Other Poems* kid-friendly and "fantastically silly." Noting that Prelusky's work has been brought to life by some of the most talented illustrators working in contemporary children's books, J. Patrick Lewis concluded in the *New York Times Book Review* that "Berger's cut paper and collage art complements" Prelutsky's "galloping zaniness."

Biographical and Critical Sources

PERIODICALS

Booklist, September 1, 2006, Gillian Engberg, review of *Behold the Bold Umbrellaphant, and Other Poems,* p. 123.

Horn Book, November-December, 2006, Susan Dove Lempke, review of *Behold the Bold Umbrellaphant, and Other Poems,* p. 730.

Kirkus Reviews, March 15, 2004, review of *Not So True Stories and Unreasonable Rhymes,* p. 266; September 15, 2006, review of *Behold the Bold Umbrellaphant, and Other Poems,* p. 964.

New York Times Book Review, February 11, 2007, J. Patrick Lewis, review of *Behold the Bold Umbrellaphant, and Other Poems,* p. 17.

Publishers Weekly, March 29, 2004, review of *Not so True Stories and Unreasonable Rhymes,* p. 63; August 28, 2006, review of *Behold the Bold Umbrellaphant, and Other Poems,* p. 52.

School Library Journal, June, 2004, Kathleen Whalin, review of *Not So True Stories and Unreasonable Rhymes,* p. 123; October, 2006, Donna Cardon, review of *Behold the Bold Umbrellaphant, and Other Poems,* p. 142; July, 2007, Lee Bock, review of *Trailblazers: Poems of Exploration,* p. 117.

ONLINE

Carin Berger home page, http://www.carinberger.com (December 15, 2007).

ISpot Web site, http://www.theispot.com/ (December 15, 2007), "Carin Berger."

* * *

BLYTHE, Gary 1959-

Personal

Born 1959, in England. *Education:* Attended college until 1980.

Addresses

Home—Wirral, England.

Career

Illustrator.

Awards, Honors

Kate Greenaway Medal, 1990, for *The Whales' Song* by Dyan Sheldon.

Illustrator

Dyan Sheldon, *The Whales' Song,* Hutchinson (London, England), 1990, Dial (New York, NY), 1991.

Dyan Sheldon, *The Garden,* Hutchinson (London, England), 1993, published as *Under the Moon,* Dial (New York, NY), 1994.

Joyce Dunbar, *This Is the Star,* Harcourt (San Diego, CA), 1996.

Geraldine McCaughrean, *Beauty and the Beast,* Doubleday (London, England), 1999, Carolrhoda (Minneapolis, MN), 2000.

Bram Stoker, *Bram Stoker's Dracula,* edited by Jan Needle, Candlewick Press (Cambridge, MA), 2004.

Nicola Davies, *Ice Bear: In the Steps of the Polar Bear,* Candlewick Press (Cambridge, MA), 2005.

Michael Morpurgo, *I Believe in Unicorns,* Candlewick Press (Cambridge, MA), 2006.

(With others) Mary-Jane Knight, *Vampyre: The Terrifying Found Journal of Dr. Cornelius Van Helsing and Gustav de Wolff, His Trusted Companion,* HarperCollins (New York, NY), 2007.

Sidelights

Despite his standing as an award-winning illustrator, British artist Gary Blythe takes his greatest pleasure from living a quiet life and painting. His detailed art effortlessly adapted itself to book illustration, and shortly after leaving college Blythe was able to support himself by creating cover art for paperback book editions. It was one of these covers, an image for *The Goose Boy* by A.L. Barker that in 1989 attracted the notice of an editor at London's Hutchinson Children's Books. Shortly thereafter, Blythe received his first and most well-known book illustration project: creating art for Dyan Sheldon's picture book *The Whales' Song*. In praise of this work, which won the Kate Greenaway Medal in 1990, a *Publishers Weekly* reviewer dubbed Blythe's illustrations "extraordinary," adding that the artist's "vibrant panoramas" of the story's coastal setting "possess a rare luminosity and beauty that should not be missed."

Other books that feature Blythe's illustrations include *Ice Bear: In the Steps of the Polar Bear* by nonfiction writer Nicola Davies, Geraldine McCaughrean's retelling of Beauty and the Beast, and Michael Morpurgo's *I Believe in Unicorns*. Praising *Ice Bear* as an "inviting picture book," *Booklist* contributor Jennifer Mattson had special praise for Blythe's "impressionistic oil paintings of stunning polar settings," while in *School Library Journal* Amelia Jenkins remarked that the "realistic" and "often lovely" paintings contribute substantially

to the "quiet, thoughtful book." Morpurgo's story, which finds a narrator remembering a scene from his boyhood, benefits from what Susan Helper described in *School Library Journal* as "sensitive crosshatched pencil, black wash, and full-color watercolors," the critic adding that Blythe's art injects the book with "enough drama to entice second and third graders." A holiday-inspired work, Joyce Dunbar's *This Is the Star,* stands as "an exquisite rendition of the Nativity," according to a *Publishers Weekly* reviewer who credited Blythe for contributing detailed images in "awe-inspiring oils."

Discussing his art—and his work for *The Whales' Song* in particular—Blythe explained to an interviewer for *Publishers Weekly:* "I enjoy doing dreamlike images, where you try to incorporate realism into fantasy—not so much where you have a dream and you know it's a dream, but where you have fantasy images that somehow look real. For example, I've got no access to whales, nor to whales jumping across the moon as such. Trying to make an image like that appear as though it could be feasible, as though it actually does exist, is what I've always enjoyed trying to achieve."

Biographical and Critical Sources

PERIODICALS

Booklist, June 1, 1994, Mary Harris Veeder, review of *Under the Moon,* p. 1845; September 1, 1996, Shelley

Gary Blythe was awarded the Kate Greenaway Medal for his illustrations for Dyan Sheldon's picture book **The Whales' Song.** (Illustration © 1990 by Gary Blythe. Reproduced by permission of Puffin Pied Piper Books, a division of Penguin Putnam Books for Young Readers.)

Townsend-Hudson, review of *This Is the Star,* p. 136; December 1, 2005, Jennifer Mattson, review of *Ice Bear: In the Steps of the Polar Bear,* p. 66; December 1, 2006, Ilene Cooper, review of *I Believe in Unicorns,* p. 47.

Bulletin of the Center for Children's Books, May, 1991, review of *The Whales' Song,* p. 226.

Horn Book, January-February, 2006, Betty Carter, review of *Ice Bear,* p. 97.

Kirkus Reviews, November 15, 2005, review of *Ice Bear,* p. 1230; October 15, 2006, review of *I Believe in Unicorns,* p. 1075.

Publishers Weekly, September 30, 1996, review of *This Is the Star,* p. 88; October 9, 2000, review of *Beauty and the Beast,* p. 87; July 5, 1991, "Flying Starts," p. 38; May 10, 1991, review of *The Whales' Song,* p. 281.

School Library Journal, December, 2000, Susan Scheps, review of *Beauty and the Beast,* p. 134; February, 2006, Amelia Jenkins, review of *Ice Bear,* p. 95; December, 2006, Susan Helper, review of *I Believe in Unicorns,* p. 110.

ONLINE

Walker Books Web site, http://www.walkerbooks.co.uk/ (December 15, 2007), "Gary Blythe."*

*   *   *

BOWERS, Tim

Personal

Born in Troy, OH; married. *Education:* Columbus College of Art and Design, B.F.A.

Addresses

Home—OH. *E-mail*—info@timbowers.com.

Career

Illustrator and author of children's books. Graphic illustrator in Dayton, OH; Hallmark Cards, Kansas City, MO, cofounder of "Shoebox Greetings" line and illustrator for five years. Visiting artist to schools.

Writings

SELF-ILLUSTRATED

A New Home, Harcourt (San Diego, CA), 2002.

ILLUSTRATOR

John C. Souter, *What's the Good Word?: The All New Super Incredible Bible Study Book for Junior Highs,* Zondervan (Grand Rapids, MI), 1983.

Charles Ludwig, *Susanna Wesley, Mother of John and Charles,* Mott Media (Medford, MI), 1984.

Jan Wahl, *The Toy Circus,* Harcourt (San Diego, CA), 1986.

Livingston Taylor and Maggie Taylor, *Pajamas,* Harcourt (San Diego, CA), 1988.

Jan Wahl, *The Adventures of Underwater Dog,* Grosset & Dunlap (New York, NY), 1989.

Jan Wahl, *The Rabbit Club,* Harcourt (San Diego, CA), 1990.

Marilyn Kaye, *A Day with No Math,* Harcourt (San Diego, CA), 1992.

Kim Henry, *Two Prayers for Patches,* Standard Pub. (Cincinnati, OH), 1994.

Clare Mishica, *A Friend for Fraidy Cat,* Standard Pub. (Cincinnati, OH), 1994.

Laura Numeroff, *Sometimes I Wonder If Poodles Like Noodles,* Simon & Schuster (New York, NY), 1999.

Amy Axelrod, *The News Hounds in the Great Balloon Race: A Geography Adventure,* Simon & Schuster (New York, NY), 2000.

Alex Moran, *Sam and Jack: Three Stories,* Harcourt (San Diego, CA), 2001.

Amy Axelrod, *The News Hounds Catch a Wave: A Geography Adventure,* Simon & Schuster (New York, NY), 2001.

Cynthia Rylant, *Little Whistle,* Harcourt (San Diego, CA), 2001.

Cynthia Rylant, *Little Whistle's Dinner Party,* Harcourt (San Diego, CA), 2001.

Cynthia Rylant, *Little Whistle's Medicine,* Harcourt (San Diego, CA), 2002.

Laura Numeroff and Nate Evans, *Sherman Crunchley,* Dutton Children's Books (New York, NY), 2003.

Cynthia Rylant, *Little Whistle's Christmas,* Harcourt (San Diego, CA), 2003.

Deborah Wiles, *One Wide Sky: A Bedtime Lullaby,* Harcourt (San Diego, CA), 2003.

Deborah Heiligman, *Fun Dog, Sun Dog,* Marshall Cavendish (New York, NY), 2005.

Shutta Crum, *The Bravest of the Brave,* Alfred A. Knopf (New York, NY), 2005.

Lynn Downey, *Matilda's Humdinger,* Knopf (New York, NY), 2006.

Andrew Clements, *Dogku,* Simon & Schuster (New York, NY), 2007.

Bernard Lodge, *Surprise,* HarperCollins (New York, NY), 2007.

Lisa Findlay, *Puss in Boots,* Random House (New York, NY), 2008.

Margie Palatini, *Gorgonzola,* Katherine Tegen Books (New York, NY), 2008.

Biographical and Critical Sources

PERIODICALS

Booklist, February 15, 2001, Ilene Cooper, review of *Little Whistle,* p. 1142; March 1, 2002, Gillian Engberg, review of *Little Whistle's Medicine,* p. 1144; August,

2003, Shelle Rosenfeld, review of *One Wide Sky: A Bedtime Lullaby,* p. 1991; May 1, 2005, Julie Cummins, review of *Fun Dog, Sun Dog,* p. 1590; October 15, 2006, Hazel Rochman, review of *Matilda's Humdinger,* p. 54; May 1, 2007, Julie Cummins, review of *Dogku,* p. 92.

Kirkus Reviews, September 1, 2001, review of *Little Whistle's Dinner Party,* p. 1300; January 15, 2002, review of *Little Whistle's Medicine,* p. 108; March 1, 2003, review of *One Wide Sky,* p. 401; September 15, 2006, Lynn Downey, review of *Matilda's Humdinger,* p. 951.

Publishers Weekly, June 14, 1999, review of *Sometimes I Wonder If Poodles Like Noodles,* p. 69; February 7, 2000, review of *The New Hounds in the Great Balloon Race: A Geography Adventure,* p. 86; April 2, 2001, review of *Little Whistle,* p. 63; January 27, 2003, review of *One Wide Sky,* p. 257; October 13, 2003, review of *Sherman Crunchley,* p. 77; June 4, 2007, review of *Dogku,* p. 49.

School Library Journal, April, 2000, Jill O'Farrell, review of *The New Hounds in the Great Balloon Race,* p. 90; May, 2001, Marlene Gawron, review of *Little Whistle,* p. 134; October, 2001, Sharon McNeil, review of *Little Whistle's Dinner Party,* p. 130; November 1, 2001, Alice Casey Smith, review of *Sam and Jack: Three Stories,* p. 124; April, 2002, Heather E. Miller, review of *Little Whistle's Medicine,* p. 122; June, 2002, Susan Lissim, review of *A New Home,* p. 88; December, 2003, Sheilah Kosco, review of *Sherman Crunchley,* p. 122; April, 2005, Lisa Gangemi Kropp, review of *The Bravest of the Brave,* p. 96; May, 2005, Catherine Callegari, review of *Fun Dog, Sun Dog,* p. 85; October, 2006, Catherine Callegari, review of *Melinda's Humdinger,* p. 109; July, 2007, Gloria Koster, review of *Dogku,* p. 89.

ONLINE

Tim Bowers Home Page, http://www.timbowers.com (December 15, 2007).*

*　　　*　　　*

BRINDLE, Max
See FLEISCHMAN, Sid

*　　　*　　　*

BUCKLEY-ARCHER, Linda 1957(?)-

Personal

Born c. 1957, in Sussex, England; married; children: two. *Education:* Undergraduate degree; studied for a doctorate at London University.

Addresses

Home—London, England.

Career

Has worked as a freelance journalist for London *Independent* and other newspapers, and as a French teacher.

Writings

Gideon the Cutpurse: Being the First Part of the Gideon Trilogy (novel; for children), Simon & Schuster Books for Young Readers (New York, NY), 2006.

Also author of radio scripts, including *Gideon the Cutpurse, Pearls in the Tate, One Night in White Satin,* and *Brief Encounters.*

Adaptations

Gideon the Cutpurse was adapted as an audiobook, Simon & Schuster, 2006.

Sidelights

Linda Buckley-Archer initially intended her first children's novel, *Gideon the Cutpurse: Being the First Part of the Gideon Trilogy,* to be a radio play; but her own children's enthusiastic response to readings in progress led her to develop it as a novel. The time-travel story takes Peter and Kate, two modern-day twelve year olds, back to 1763 England via a mishap with an antigravity device being developed by Kate's father. Fortunately, the device went back in time with them. As a result, Peter and Kate have high hopes of returning to their own time, until the machine is stolen by the nefarious thief known as the Tar Man. Gideon, a former thief himself, helps Kate and Peter track down the Tar Man as the children's parents frantically search for them. "Readers will be eager for the sequel to this exciting time travel adventure," asserted Paula Rohrlick in *Kliatt.* Jennifer Mattson, writing in *Booklist,* commented that the author proves herself skilled at portraying "the pistol-waving encounters with highwaymen and chases through London's underbelly." Melissa Moore concluded in *School Library Journal* that *Gideon the Cutpurse* "is a rare gem."

Biographical and Critical Sources

PERIODICALS

Booklist, August 1, 2006, Jennifer Mattson, review of *Gideon the Cutpurse: Being the First Part of the Gideon Trilogy,* p. 63.
Kirkus Reviews, June 1, 2006, review of *Gideon the Cutpurse,* p. 569.
Kliatt, September, 2006, Paula Rohrlick, review of *Gideon the Cutpurse,* p. 8.
Publishers Weekly, June 19, 2006, review of *Gideon the Cutpurse,* p. 63.

School Library Journal, July, 2006, Melissa Moore, review of *Gideon the Cutpurse,* p. 97.

ONLINE

Authortrek.com, http://www.authortrek.com/ (December 17, 2006), brief profile of Linda Buckley-Archer.
BookLoons.com, http://www.bookloons.com/ (December 17, 2006), Hilary Williamson, review of *Gideon the Cutpurse.*
Gideon Trilogy Web site, http://www.thegideontrilogy.com (December 17, 2006).
London Times Online, http://www.timesonline.co.uk/ (December 17, 2006), Amanda Craig, review of *Gideon the Cutpurse.**

* * *

BUELL, Janet 1952-

Personal

Born April 20, 1952; daughter of William F. Buell, Sr. (owner of an insurance agency). *Education:* Carthage College, B.A., 1974; Notre Dame College, M.Ed., 1993. *Politics:* "Independent." *Hobbies and other interests:* Reading, anthropology, archaeology, indoor soccer, softball, hiking, health, "possibilities."

Addresses

Home—Goffstown, NH.

Career

Writer and educator. Round Lake School District, Round Lake, IL, grade-school teacher, 1974-76; Timberlane Regional School District, Atkinson, NH, grade-school teacher, 1976-86; Londonderry School District, Londonderry, NH, gifted program teacher and advanced math teacher, 1986—. Londonderry Cable Television, creator, producer, and host of *The Cosmic Learning Roadshow,* 1990-92.

Member

Derry Regional Writers' Group.

Awards, Honors

Anna Cross Giblin nonfiction work-in-progress grant, Society of Children's Book Writers and Illustrators, for "Time Travelers" series; Outstanding Children's Book designation, New Hampshire Writers' Project Literary Awards, for *Bog Bodies.*

Writings

NONFICTION; "TIME TRAVELERS" SERIES

Bog Bodies, Twenty-first Century Books (Brookfield, CT), 1997.

Janet Buell (Reproduced by permission.)

Ice Maiden of the Andes, Twenty-first Century Books (Brookfield, CT), 1997.
Ancient Horsemen of Siberia, Twenty-first Century Books (Brookfield, CT), 1998.
Greenland Mummies, Twenty-first Century Books (Brookfield, CT), 1998.

OTHER

Sail away, Little Boat (picture book), illustrated by Jui Ishida, Carolrhoda (Minneapolis, MN), 2006.

Contributor to *The Guinness Book of Records* and to periodicals including *Cobblestone, Cricket, Special Reports, New Hampshire Editions, Writer,* and *Horse Digest.*

Sidelights

Janet Buell, who teaches gifted students for the Londonderry, New Hampshire public schools, is the author of *Bog Bodies, Greenland Mummies,* and other works in her "Time Travelers" series for middle-grade readers. In 2006 Buell published her first picture book, *Sail Away, Little Boat.*

Buell once told *SATA:* "Lots of kids dream about being authors when they grow up. I don't remember ever wanting that for myself. Mostly, when I bothered to think about growing up, I thought about being a veterinarian. I became a teacher instead—a stroke of luck, as it turns out, for my future as a writer.

"Back in the early 1980s, I was teaching third grade in Atkinson, New Hampshire. A man named Don Graves from the University of New Hampshire came to our school to study how children learn to write. I was really happy when he picked some students in my class as the subjects of his study.

"Don and his assistants spent lots of time watching these students. As they watched, the researchers saw how the children searched for ways through the writing process. For example, my kids always hoped their first drafts would be neat and clean so they wouldn't have to rewrite. They soon found out that neat and clean first drafts don't exist—at least not those that go on to be good pieces of writing.

"First drafts are ways to explore what you want to say. They can be very messy. All writers I know tug at their first words in some way or another. They change their minds. They rearrange. They cross out. They shuffle entire paragraphs from one place to another or annihilate them altogether. It's this tugging and rearranging—this hard work—that sets a writer apart from others who merely *want* to write.

"Don told me the only way I'd be able to teach my students to write well is to write. So I did. I wrote when my kids wrote—just like they wrote. I wrote drafts. I revised. I edited. I struggled to find words for the ideas buzzing about in my head. If you write, you know that struggle. I discovered that I *really* liked it.

"Then, as now, I was being open to possibilities. It's a philosophy that has stuck with me my whole life and has helped me to experience lots of different things. I've traveled different parts of the United States, camping along the way. I've gone moth collecting at night with the Nature Conservancy. I've taught courses to adults. I've acted in a play and I started a show on a local cable network, with my students and me as hosts.

"Being open to possibilities launched me into a writing career. Around the time my students and I were learning to write, I went to a seminar for writers. Two women, who had recently started a history magazine for kids called *Cobblestone,* led one of the sessions. Later when I talked with them, they encouraged me to query the magazine. A query is a letter telling the editors about the article you'd like to write for them. It's the way a lot of magazine articles get written in this country.

"I figured I had nothing to lose by trying, so I sent the editors a query for an upcoming issue they were doing about cowboys and the old west. I had done a little research into the subject and discovered the interesting history of cattle branding. The editors thought it was interesting, too. They gave me a 'go-ahead' to write the article on speculation. When editors assign an article on speculation, it means they're not going to commit to buying it until they see if it's any good or not. Editors often give new writers assignments on speculation.

"As you can imagine, I was thrilled. Those feelings were dampened a bit by a few doubters. They warned me that my piece might not be accepted after all. I think they were trying to soften my disappointment if the article didn't get accepted. I didn't let that stop me. I knew that I could write a good article and I did. *Cobblestone* accepted it.

"I wrote more articles for *Cobblestone* and for other magazines. Then, one day I visited a local bog. After my visit, I wanted to learn more about this fascinating wetland. At the library I discovered the strange, grim secret buried in bogs. That secret is the bodies buried in some of them. These bodies are so old, yet so beautifully preserved, that they defy belief. It's very weird to see the face of a two thousand-year-old person, beard stubble and all. I also learned that technology has become so advanced that scientists can learn a lot about these ancient humans—even what they ate for their last meal!

"Right away I knew I had to write a book about it. No one I knew had ever heard about bog bodies, and I wanted to tell everyone about them. Before I could start, though, I learned about other ancient human remains. Some of these remains were frozen on mountain tops or in arctic graves or on the high plateaus of Siberia. Instead of writing one book, I decided to write a series of books called 'Time Travelers.'

"The next step was to write a proposal. A lot of people think you always write the book first and then look for a publisher. That's not the case with nonfiction. My proposal explained to publishers what I wanted to do. I sent it to five different publishers before Twenty-first Century Books accepted it.

"It took a little less than two years to write the four books in 'Time Travelers.' Mostly I wrote during my summer break from teaching, but I also wrote during the school year—in the evenings or on weekends. For a long time it seemed like the books would *never* get done!"

In the first two volumes in Buell's "Time Travelers" series, *Bog Bodies* and *Ice Maiden of the Andes,* she discusses the techniques used by scientists who study ancient societies. Reviewing both works in *Booklist,* Helen Rosenburg observed that "the well-written texts provide insight into an intriguing topic." In *School Library Journal,* Cathryn A. Camper described *Greenland Mummies* as "useful to students studying Inuit life and sure to interest mummy enthusiasts." In the book, Buell explores evidence provided by the 500-year-old mummified Inuit remains discovered in Greenland by Hans and Jokum Gronvold. As she pieces together information from these rare scientific finds, Buell details the lives of the primitive Inuit people for her young readers. Camper praised the author's "fascinating details about how these people hunted with harpoons, constructed igloos and sod huts, battled frostbite, and gave themselves tattoos with needle and thread."

Ancient Horsemen of Siberia describes the ancient burial site of a Pazyryk woman that was found preserved in an icy tomb along with her horses and possessions. Buell also examines what the site reveals about a people who lived long ago. In her review for *School Library Journal,* Elizabeth Talbot praised the author for going "beyond the [burial site] discovery to examine how Russian archeologist Natalya Polosmak and her colleagues made educated guesses about the lives and culture of [these] individuals who rode horses and tended other animals." Talbot also applauded Buell for clearly presenting a complex and interesting subject, and for further assisting the reader with the "valuable additions" of a glossary, a timeline, and suggestions for further reading.

Buell made the jump from nonfiction to fiction with *Sail away, Little Boat,* a rhyming tale inspired by her walks along a brook near her New Hampshire home. After two children launch a red toy boat down a babbling brook, it encounters a variety of animals on its voyage, including whirligig beetles, otters, and a bear cub. As the tiny vessel reaches the open sea, it is found by another group of children who are playing on the beach. *Sail away, Little Boat* received strong reviews. "Delightful sounds, rich language, imagery, and buoyant verse characterize the writing," observed *School Library Journal* contributor Teresa Pfeifer. A *Kirkus Reviews* critic stated that, "deeply respectful of the places where man and nature meet," Buell's tale "is a serene journey of beauty." A *Publishers Weekly* critic praised the work of illustrator Jui Ishida, stating that her "compositions feel bracing and bold—every spread conveys the energy of the water coursing inexorably through the landscape." According to Rebecca Rule, writing in New Hampshire's *Portsmouth Herald,* "this simple, beautiful story is as New Hampshire as can be—and as universal as well."

Biographical and Critical Sources

PERIODICALS

Booklist, February 1, 1998, Helen Rosenberg, reviews of *Bog Bodies* and *Ice Maiden of the Andes,* p. 912.
Kirkus Reviews, February 15, 2006, review of *Sail away, Little Boat,* p. 178.
Portsmouth Herald (Portsmouth, NH), May 14, 2006, Rebecca Rule, review of *Sail away, Little Boat.*
Publishers Weekly, March 6, 2006, review of *Sail away, Little Boat,* p. 74.
School Library Journal, March, 1998, Ann G. Brouse, reviews of *Bog Bodies* and *Ice Maiden of the Andes,* p. 229; October, 1998, Elizabeth Talbot, review of *Ancient Horsemen of Siberia,* pp. 151-152, and Carolyn A. Camper, review of *Greenland Mummies,* p. 152; April, 2006, Teresa Pfeifer, review of *Sail away, Little Boat,* p. 97.

ONLINE

New Hampshire Mirror Online, http://www.thenhmirror.com/ (December 20, 2006), Holly Bedard, "Janet Buell: Children's Author."*

*   *   *

BURTINSHAW, Julie 1958-

Personal

Born 1958.

Addresses

Home and office—Vancouver, British Columbia, Canada. *Agent*—Transatlantic Literary Agency, 72 Glengowan Rd., Toronto, Ontario M4N 1G4, Canada. *E-mail*—jburtinshaw@gmail.com.

Career

Young-adult writer. Editor for *suite101.com*; member of part-time staff in an independent book store. Writer-in-residence in Dawson City, Yukon Territory, 2007.

Member

Children's Writers and Illustrators of British Columbia, Vancouver Children's Literature Roundtable.

Awards, Honors

Red Cedar Award nomination, Chocolate Lily Award nomination, and Diamond Willow Award nomination, all for *Dead Reckoning*; Canadian Library Association Book of the Year nomination, 2002, Chocolate Lily Award nomination, Langley Book of the Year Award nomination, and Manitoba Young Reader's Choice Award nomination, all 2004, all for *Adrift*; Stellar Book Award nomination, British Columbia's Teen Readers' Choice Award, 2008, for *The Freedom of Jenny*.

Writings

YOUNG-ADULT NOVELS

Dead Reckoning, Raincoast Books (Vancouver, British Columbia, Canada), 2000.
Adrift, Raincoast Books (San Diego, CA), 2002.
The Freedom of Jenny, Raincoast Books (Berkeley, CA), 2005.
The Perfect Cut, Raincoast Books (Berkeley, CA), 2008, published as *Being Brian,* Raincoast Books (Vancouver, British Columbia, Canada), 2008.

OTHER

Romantic Ghosts (adult short fiction), Lone Pine, 2003.

Sidelights

Canadian writer Julie Burtinshaw is the author of novels for young adults. Her first book for teens, *Dead Reckoning,* earned critical praise and was nominated for several awards for its retelling of the nautical disaster of the *Valencia,* a ship that sunk on its way from San Francisco, California, to Vancouver, British Columbia. "The descriptions of the sea, the storm, the boys' final moments aboard ship, and their struggles ashore create a vivid picture of that stretch of coast," wrote a reviewer for *Resource Links* in a review of the book.

Although its focus is contemporary rather than historical, like *Dead Reckoning*, *Adrift* is also set along the Canadian coast. David and Laura have effectively been abandoned by their parents: their mother has fallen into depression, and their father, unable to cope, has left his family behind. David takes on the role of caring for younger sister Laura, a responsibility that only eases when his father sends the children to stay with their aunt on Fern Island. There, David learns to relax again, but when his father returns to take the children home again, the boy explodes with anger and puts himself and his sister in a dangerous situation wherein they must battle nature to survive. "Burtinshaw is at her best as she describes a West Coast landscape and [rural] lifestyle," wrote Cora Lee in *Resource Links.* Susan Cooley, reviewing *Adrift* in *School Library Journal,* concluded that, "with its quick pacing and interesting detail about island life," Burtinshaw's novel "will be popular" with teen readers.

Drawing on historical events in British Columbia in the mid-1800s, *The Freedom of Jenny* is the story of former slaves who journey from Missouri to British Columbia after they gain their freedom. Their road is a treacherous one, however, and along with the challenges of finding a place to belong, they must also tame their environment. The result is a mix of pioneer survival and African-American history as told through the eyes of ten-year-old Jenny. Burtinshaw's story of a girl forced to carry the responsibility for her family after her mother dies "dramatizes the heartache and backbreaking work that sometimes made the newly free feel 'more a slave [than] ever,'" wrote Jennifer Mattson in *Booklist.* While noting that Burtinshaw's authorial voice sometimes overwhelms her young heroine's narrative, Pat Leach acknowledged in *School Library Journal* that *The Freedom of Jenny* "successfully reflects the complexity of the times." A *Kirkus Reviews* contributor felt that "Jenny proves a resilient heroine and her story is jam-packed with the stuff of history." In *Resource Links,* Victoria Pennell concluded that *The Freedom of Jenny* "is a great addition to the collection of literature concerning blacks in Canada."

Alongside her work as a writer, Burtinshaw offers creative-writing workshops for middle-school and high-school students in her native Vancouver. She also holds a part-time job that allows her to engage in an important writer's hobby: watching people interact. "I work

Cover of Julie Burtinshaw's middle-grade novel The Freedom of Jenny, *which draws readers back to the mid-nineteenth century and the trials of American's former slaves.* (Raincoast Books, 2005. Reproduced by permission.)

part-time in a bookstore where I can indulge my second passion—listening, watching and observing human behaviour," she explained on the *Suite 101* Web site. "Like all writers, I am curious almost to the point of [being] nosy."

Biographical and Critical Sources

PERIODICALS

Booklist, February 1, 2006, Jennifer Mattson, review of *The Freedom of Jenny,* p. 61.

Canadian Review of Materials, April 13, 2001, review of *Dead Reckoning.*

Kirkus Reviews, February 15, 2006, review of *The Freedom of Jenny,* p. 179.

Resource Links, February, 2001, review of *Dead Reckoning,* p. 11; October, 2002, Cora Lee, review of *Adrift,* p. 27; February, 2006, Victoria Pennell, review of *The Freedom of Jenny,* p. 42.

School Library Journal, January, 2003, Susan Cooley, review of *Adrift,* p. 134; May, 2006, Pat Leach, review of *The Freedom of Jenny,* p. 120.

Voice of Youth Advocates, December, 2002, review of *Adrift,* p. 374.

ONLINE

Book Rapport Web site, http://www.bookrapport.com/ (December 1, 2007), profile of Burtinshaw.
Children's Writers and Illustrators of British Columbia Web site, http://www.cwill.bc.ca/ (December 1, 2007), profile of Burtinshaw.

International Readings at Harbourfrontcentre Web site, http://www.readings.org/ (December 1, 2007), profile of Burtinshaw.
Julie Burtinshaw Web log, http://burtinshaw.wordpress. com/ (November 22, 2007).
Stellar Award Web site, http://www.stellaraward.ca/ (December 1, 2007), profile of Burtinshaw.
Suite 101 Web site, http://www.suite101.com/ (December 1, 2007), profile of Burtinshaw.
Transatlantic Literary Agency Web site, http://www.tla1. com/ (December 1, 2007), profile of Burtinshaw.

C

CAREY, Janet Lee 1959(?)-

Personal

Born c. 1959, in NY; married; children: three sons. *Hobbies and other interests:* Hiking, reading, family, meditation, yoga, and music.

Addresses

Home—WA. *E-mail*—janetleecarey@hotmail.com.

Career

Writer and educator. Teaches writing workshops.

Writings

YOUNG ADULT NOVELS

Molly's Fire, Atheneum Books for Young Readers (New York, NY), 2000.
Wenny Has Wings, Atheneum Books (New York, NY), 2002.
The Double Life of Zoe Flynn, Atheneum Books for Young Readers (New York, NY), 2004.
The Beast of Noor, Atheneum Books for Young Readers (New York, NY), 2006.
Dragon's Keep, Harcourt (Orlando, FL), 2007.

Sidelights

Janet Lee Carey began writing as a young girl and has since produced books for both children and young adults. In her first book, *Molly's Fire,* Carey introduces thirteen-year-old Molly, who refuses to believe that her father was shot down over Holland during World War II. Molly forms a friendship with Jane, who is half-Japanese, and along with her and another friend, Peter, sets out to discover if Molly's father is alive. The childrens' investigation leads them to visit a nearby Ger-

man prisoner of war camp. A *Publishers Weekly* contributor noted that "the details about food ration coupons, victory gardens and Japanese internment camps breathe life into an important period of history."

Wenny Has Wings finds young Will writing letters to his dead sister Wenny, who was killed when both were hit by a truck. Will's near-death experience is mixed with a story of a family struggling to survive after a tragedy. Ilene Cooper, writing in *Booklist,* commended the book for illustrating "sibling relationship and its unique capturing of the phenomenon of heading into the light." In a review for *School Library Journal,* B. Allison Gray called the work "a useful meditation on death and guilt," and *Kirkus Reviews* contributor referred to *Wenny Has Wings* as "a gentle epistolary novel requiring at least three hankies."

In *The Double Life of Zoe Flynn,* Carey tells the story of Zoe's coming to terms with homelessness after her dad loses both his teaching job and his bookstore. As the family struggles, with both parents only able to get part-time work, Zoe finds herself living out of a van with her mother and father and attending a new school 500 miles away from the beloved beloved California town she once called home. A *Kirkus Reviews* contributor called *The Double Life of Zoe Flynn* "thought-provoking." Hazel Rochman, writing in *Booklist,* commented that "there's plenty of drama in the hardship of the middle-class kid," and Miriam Lang Budin wrote in the *School Library Journal:* "The struggles of this middle-class family to keep their heads above water are realistically and sympathetically presented."

The Beast of Noor tells the adventure story of fifteen-year-old Miles and thirteen-year-old Hanna Sheen. The Sheen family has long been outcast in the local area due to a legend that asserts they brought a monster dog called the Shriker to the area when they arrived there 300 years before. As they set out to break the family curse, Miles and Hanna soon find themselves in the Otherworld trying to capture the Shriker. Sally Estes, writing in *Booklist,* noted that the author "delivers an eerie, atmospheric tale, full of terror and courage." *School Library Journal* contributor Saleena L. Davidson wrote that "the novel reads almost like a fairy tale, with the same rhythms and the same etiquette," and a *Kirkus Reviews* contributor referred to *The Beast of Noor* as "an engaging tale, with just the right touch of terror to make a good story."

Biographical and Critical Sources

PERIODICALS

Booklist, July, 2002, Ilene Cooper, review of *Wenny Has Wings,* p. 1841; September 1, 2004, Hazel Rochman, review of *The Double Life of Zoe Flynn,* p. 120; August 1, 2006, Sally Estes, review of *The Beast of Noor,* p. 65.

Kirkus Reviews, June 1, 2002, review of *Wenny Has Wings,* p. 801; June 1, 2004, review of *The Double Life of Zoe Flynn,* p. 534; June 15, 2006, review of *The Beast of Noor,* p. 632.

Publishers Weekly, May 29, 2000, review of *Molly's Fire,* p. 83; July 15, 2002, review of *Wenny Has Wings,* p. 74.

School Library Journal, May, 2000, Faith Brautigan, review of *Molly's Fire,* p. 170; July, 2002, B. Allison Gray, review of *Wenny Has Wings,* p. 114; August, 2004, Miriam Lang Budin, review of *The Double life of Zoe Flynn,* p. 116; November, 2006, Saleena L. Davidson, review of *The Beast of Noor,* p. 130.

ONLINE

BookLoons, http://www.bookloons.com/ (February 20, 2007), J.A. Kaszuba Locke, review of *The Double Life of Zoe Flynn;* Ricki Marking-Camuto, review of *The Beast of Noor.*

Janet Lee Carey Home Page, http://www.janetleecarey. com (February 20, 2007).

Kidsreads.com, http://www.kidsreads.com/ (February 20, 2007), Carlie Webber, review of *The Double Life of Zoe Flynn.*

SimonSays.com, http://www.simonsays.com/ (February 20, 2007), "Q&A: A Conversation with Janet Lee Carey."*

*   *   *

CHRISTIE, Gregory
See CHRISTIE, R. Gregory

*   *   *

CHRISTIE, R. Gregory 1971-
(Gregory Christie)

Personal

Born July 26, 1971; son of Gerard A. (a pharmacist) and Ludria V. (a dietician) Christie. *Education:* School of Visual Arts (New York, NY), B.F.A. (media arts), 1993.

R. Gregory Christie (Photograph by Gary Spector. Reproduced by permission of Lee & Low Books, Inc.)

Addresses

Office—Gas-Art Studios, 320 7th Ave., Brooklyn, NY 11215. *E-mail*—Christie@gas-art.com.

Career

Illustrator. Commercial Art Supply, Plainfield, NJ, worked in sales and stock, 1985-89; *Newark Star Ledger,* Newark, NJ, intern/spot illustrator, 1989; Solomon R. Guggenheim Museum, New York, NY, worked in stock and book store sales, 1989, security, 1991-98. Freelance illustrator, creating art for covers of CD-ROMs, posters, and brochures, beginning 1993; children's book illustrator, beginning 1996.

Awards, Honors

Coretta Scott King Honor Book designation, American Library Association, 1997, for *The Palm of My Heart,* and 2001, for *Only Passing Through* by Anne F. Rockwell; *New York Times Book Review* Ten Best-Illustrated Children's Books selection, and New York Public Library One-Hundred Recommended Book Titles selection, both 2000, both for *Only Passing Through;* Coretta Scott King Illustrator Award Honor Book designation, 2006, for *Brothers in Hope* by Mary Williams; Schneider Family Book Award, 2007, for *The*

Deaf Musicians by Pete Seeger and Paul Dubois Jacobs; Theodore Seuss Geisel Award, 2008, for *Jazz Baby* by Lisa Wheeler.

Illustrator

America, My Land, Your Land, Lee & Low Books (New York, NY), 1996.

(Under name Gregory Christie) Davida Adedjouma, editor, *The Palm of My Heart: Poetry by African-American Children,* introduction by Lucille Clifton, Lee & Low Books (New York, NY), 1996.

William Miller, *Richard Wright and the Library Card,* Lee & Low Books (New York, NY), 1997.

Anne F. Rockwell, *Only Passing Through: The Story of Sojourner Truth,* Knopf (New York, NY), 2000.

Barbara M. Joosse, *Stars in the Darkness,* Chronicle Books (San Francisco, CA), 2001.

Tony Medina, *DeShawn Days,* Lee & Low Books (New York, NY), 2001.

Tonya Bolden, *Rock of Ages: A Tribute to the Black Church,* Knopf (New York, NY), 2001.

Tony Medina, *Love to Langston,* Lee & Low Books (New York, NY), 2002.

Rukhsana Khan, *Ruler of the Courtyard,* Viking (New York, NY), 2003.

Jeron Ashford Frame, *Yesterday I Had the Blues,* Tricycle Press (Berkeley, CA), 2003.

Lisa Wheeler, *Jazz Baby,* Harcourt (Orlando, FL), 2004.

Barbara M. Joosse, *Hot City,* Philomel Books (New York, NY), 2004.

Tonya Bolden, *The Champ: The Story of Muhammad Ali,* Knopf (New York, NY), 2004.

Pat Sherman, *The Sun's Daughter,* Clarion Books (New York, NY), 2005.

Steve Seskin and Allen Shamblin, *A Chance to Shine,* Tricycle Press (Berkeley, CA), 2005.

Mary Williams, *Brothers in Hope: The Story of the Lost Boys of Sudan,* Lee & Low (New York, NY), 2005.

Peet Seeger and Paul DuBois, *The Deaf Musicians,* Putnam's (New York, NY), 2006.

Carole Boston Weatherford, *Dear Mr. Rosenwald,* Scholastic (New York, NY), 2006.

Beah E. Richards, *Keep Climbing, Girls,* Simon & Schuster (New York, NY), 2006.

Anne Rockwell, *Open the Door to Liberty!: A Biography of Toussaint L'Ouverture,* Houghton Mifflin (Boston, MA), 2007.

Contributor of illustrations to periodicals, including *New Yorker, Village Voice, Madison, Los Angeles, Rolling Stone, Parenting, Travel & Leisure, Golf, Vibe, Cigar Aficionado, Teaching Tolerance, Atlantic Monthly,* and *Philadelphia Inquirer.*

Sidelights

In addition to his work for high-profile magazines such as the *New Yorker,* R. Gregory Christie is an artist whose intensely colored paintings filled with elongated figures have graced the pages of a number of award-winning children's books. In *DeShawn Days,* a collection of poems by Tony Medina that focuses on life from the per-

Christie's folk-style illustrations bring to life Tony Medina's **DeShawn Days,** *the story of a close-knit African-American family.* (Illustration © 2001 by R. Gregory Christie. Reproduced by permission of Lee & Low Books, Inc.)

spective of a ten-year-old African-American boy, Christie provides illustrations that are suffused with the warmth and joy of a close-knit family scene, and are alternately "bleak and sophisticated," according to a *Publishers Weekly* reviewer. Wanda Meyers-Hines also praised Christie's work in *School Library Journal,* writing that the artist's acrylic and gouache paintings "beautifully capture the cultural and artistic aspects" of a young boy's home life in the pages of *Yesterday I Had the Blues,* by Jeron Ashford Frame. Reflecting the sultry mood of Barbara M. Joosse's summertime story in *Hot City,* Christie cools his palette of hot pinks, reds, and bright oranges with clear yellows to create "quirky acrylic paintings [that] take playful liberties with perspective and scale," according to a *Publishers Weekly* reviewer. His "vivacious, artfully distorted" images for the book "sizzle along with the rhythmic, smooth-as-melted-butter" text, according to a *Kirkus Reviews* writer.

Anne F. Rockwell's *Only Passing Through: The Story of Sojourner Truth,* a biography of the African-American abolitionist, orator, and freedom fighter, is expressively illustrated by Christie, his choice of hues and his manipulation of the human figure working together to give "a powerful sense of Sojourner Truth's . . . compelling personality," in the opinion of *Book* critic Kathleen Odean. Another biography, Tonya Bolden's *The Champ: The Story of Muhammad Ali,* was described by a *Kirkus Reviews* writer as "picture-book biography at its best" due in part to Christie's "strongly hued" and "eye-catching" illustrations.

In his work for *Ruler of the Courtyard* Christie exhibits his versatility by drawing on images from a Middle Eastern aesthetic. Set in Pakistan, Rukhsana Khan's story focuses on a young girl who is terrorized by the chickens running wild outside her family's rural home. Christie's "vigorous and slightly naive" art warms the story with what *School Library Journal* reviewer Dona Ratterree described as "hot bright backgrounds" and "attentive detail." While his art "provide[s] the balance between ambiguity and realism that the text requires," Christie also astutely captures the girl's "feelings through her facial expressions and body language," a *Kirkus Reviews* writer observed of *Ruler of the Courtyard.* Another multicultural picture book, Pat Sherman's *The Sun's Daughter,* features a Native-American porquoi story that is enhanced by dramatic illustrations by Christie that "intensify the sense of abstraction from reality common to folklore," according to *Booklist* contributor Jennifer Mattson.

Returning to his own culture, Christie contributes what a *Publishers Weekly* contributor deemed "stylized,

Christie's illustrations for Carole Boston Weatherford's **Dear Mr. Rosenwald,** *a picture book that captures a little-known piece of early-twentieth-century history.* (Illustration © 2006 by R. Gregory Christie. Reprinted by permission of Scholastic, Inc.)

boldly hued gouache and colored pencil art" to Carole Boston Weatherford's *Dear Mr. Rosenwald.* Based on the true story of the way one man's vision and the aspirations of a poor rural community combined to create a school for black children during the 1920s, *Dear Mr. Rosenwald* presents "a heartening sliver of American history," according to the *Publishers Weekly* critic. In *Booklist* Hazel Rochman wrote that Christie's "exuberant gouache and colored-pencil illustrations" bring to life the "vibrant family and community" at the center of Weatherford's tale, and *School Library Journal* reviewer Catherine Threadgill deemed the book's art a "good complement" to the "rough-around-the-edges" account of its young narrator.

Christie once told *SATA:* "I began painting when I was thirteen, drawing even before I could speak. My art has naturally taken a leading role in my life and the creation of it is the form of a conversation that I feel the most comfortable executing. Painting is a personal endeavor that serves as an outlet for my emotions. I feel that a painting is only half done until it's viewed by others. Therefore, I see art and painting as a type of conversation between the creator and viewer. Not an audible word needs to be uttered during this exchange, but in order for there to be a learning process or for an image to be appreciated the two participants must speak the same visual language.

"Often I receive questions regarding the exaggerated body proportions and color choices of my paintings. The answer simply lies in my use of the compositional elements as a directional device. The same way an orator will use highs, lows, and iambic pentameter to keep the listener's interest, I use color, form, and shape to appeal to one's visual sense. Everything beyond that is a matter of rhythm and instinct.

"I enjoy showcasing my images in the form of the children's book format. I am comfortable with it and I feel as though it is making a difference in the world. I usually spend one to three months painting the books, then, once they're published, one to three weeks in order to forget about them. I move on to the next project with a full focus. Although I may appreciate the accolades and the challenges presented from previous projects, moving on to a new job keeps me humble. In the end the books are more for the children than for my ego."

Biographical and Critical Sources

PERIODICALS

Book, May, 2001, Kathleen Odean, review of *Only Passing Through: The Story of Sojourner Truth,* p. 80.
Booklist, October 1, 2001, Hazel Rochman, review of *Rock of Ages: The Story of the Lost Boys of Sudan,* p. 334; November 1, 2003, Jennifer Mattson, review of *Yesterday I Had the Blues,* p. 500; March 15, 2005, Jen-

Cover of Janet McDonald's novel **Chill Wind,** *which features an illustration by Christie.* (Illustration © 2002 by R. Gregory Christie. Reproduced by permission of Frances Foster Books, a division of Farrar, Straus & Giroux, LLC.)

nifer Mattson, review of *The Sun's Daughter,* p. 1292; May 1, 2005, Hazel Rochman, review of *Brother in Hope: The Story of the Lost Boys of Sudan,* p. 1584; February 1, 2006, Carolyn Phelan, review of *Keep Climbing, Girls,* p. 70; October 1, 2006, Hazel Rochman, review of *Dear Mr. Rosenwald,* p. 61.

Christian Parenting Today, March, 2001, review of *Only Passing Through,* p. 62.

Horn Book, March-April, 2003, Susan P. Bloom, review of *Ruler of the Courtyard,* p. 204; January-February, 2004, Susan Dove Lempke, review of *Yesterday I Had the Blues,* p. 69; January-February, 2005, Kathleen Isaacs, review of *The Champ: The Story of Muhammad Ali,* p. 106.

Kirkus Reviews, December 15, 2002, review of *Ruler of the Courtyard,* p. 1851; August 15, 2003, review of *Yesterday I Had the Blues,* p. 1072; May 15, 2004, review of *Hot City,* p. 493; March 1, 2005, review of *The Sun's Daughter,* p. 295; December 15, 2004, review of *The Champ,* p. 1198; December 1, 2005, Beah E. Richards, review of *Keep Climbing, Girls,* p. 1279; August 15, 2006, review of *Dear Mr. Rosenwald,* p. 853.

New York Times Book Review, November 19, 2000, Linda Villarosa, "Serving No Master but the Truth," p. 61.

Print, January, 2001, Ariana Donalds, "Home and Away," p. 104.

Publishers Weekly, May 21, 2001, review of *DeShawn Days,* p. 107; January 6, 2003, review of *Ruler of the Courtyard,* p. 59; July 12, 2004, review of *Hot City,* p. 63; March 21, 2005, review of *The Sun's Daughter,* p. 51; October 23, 2006, review of *Dear Mr. Rosenwald,* p. 51.

School Library Journal, July, 2001, Patti Gonzales, review of *DeShawn Days,* p. 96; February, 2003, Dona Ratterree, review of *Ruler of the Courtyard,* p. 114; October, 2003, Wanda Meyers-Hines, review of *Yesterday I Had the Blues,* p. 119; June, 2005, Mary N. Oluonye, review of *Brothers in Hope,* p. 131, and Cris Riedel, review of *The Sun's Daughter,* p. 144; February, 2006, Julie Roach, review of *Keep Climbing, Girls,* p. 124; October, 2006, Catherine Threadgill, review of *Dear Mr. Rosenwald,* p. 129; November, 2006, Genevieve Gallagher, review of *The Deaf Musicians,* p. 112.

ONLINE

R. Gregory Christie Home Page, http://www.gas-art.com (December 15, 2007).

* * *

COLLISON, Linda 1953-

Personal

Born 1953, in Baltimore, MD; married Bob Russell; children: three. *Education:* Laramie County Community College, A.D.N., 1982; attended Metropolitan State College. *Hobbies and other interests:* Outdoor sports, sailing, maritime history.

Addresses

Home—Kamuela, HI. *E-mail*—starcrossed@lindacollison.com.

Career

Freelance writer. Presbyterian/St. Luke's Medical Center, Denver, CO, registered nurse, 1982-92; Skydive Colorado, Loveland, instructor and jumpmaster, 1989-93; Skydive St. Louis, Jonesburg, MO, drop zone assistant manager, 1991. Has also worked as a volunteer firefighter and a first aid/CPR instructor.

Awards, Honors

Grand prize, Maui Writers Conference, 1996; Books for the Teen Age selection, New York Public Library, 2007, for *Star-crossed;* awards from National Student Nurses Association, *Honolulu* magazine, and Southwest Writers Workshop.

Writings

(With husband, Bob Russell) *Rocky Mountain Wineries: A Travel Guide to the Wayside Vineyards,* Pruett Publishing (Boulder, CO), 1994.

(With Bob Russell) *Colorado Kids: A Statewide Family Outdoor Adventure Guide,* Pruett Publishing (Boulder, CO), 1997.

Star-crossed (young-adult novel), Knopf (New York, NY), 2006.

Contributor of essays, short stories, articles, and poetry to periodicals.

Sidelights

Linda Collison is the author of *Star-crossed,* a critically acclaimed young-adult novel. An award-winning writer of articles, essays, poems, and short stories, Collison has led an adventurous life, working as a registered nurse, a skydiving instructor, a volunteer firefighter, and a first-aid instructor. Her first two books, *Rocky Mountain Wineries: A Travel Guide to the Wayside Vineyards* and *Colorado Kids: A Statewide Family Outdoor Adventure Guide,* were coauthored with her husband, Bob Russell.

"Writing has played an important part in my life ever since grade school," Collison told *SATA.* "Through writing I've managed to connect the piece of my life; my victories and failures, my obsessions, heartbreaks, hard lessons, and hopes. And I can explore what it might be like to be someone else entirely. Or to have lived in another age."

Star-crossed, a work of historical fiction, was published in 2006. An avid sailor, Collison also has an interest in maritime history, and she based the tale on one of her most memorable experiences at sea. In 1999 she and Russell helped crew the H.M. *Bark Endeavour,* an Australian-built replica of Captain Cook's eighteenth-century square-rigged, three-masted ship. "Aboard *Endeavor* we had a taste of what a sailor's life was like in those days," the author explained on her home page. "We heave-ho'ed the eighteenth century way, climbing the tarred ratlines to make and furl sail. We took turns steering the square-rigged vessel, we scrubbed the deck and everything in sight to pass the captain's ruthless inspections, and we took our turns toiling in the galley." The idea for *Star-crossed* came to Collison one night while she was manning the ship's helm. As she commented on the *Author's Den* Web site, "I knew the setting, because I was living it. I was enthralled with it. And I wanted to explore what it might have been like to be a girl, a young woman, aboard a ship much like this one, back in the mid-eighteenth century."

Star-crossed centers on Patricia Kelley, a prim and proper seventeen year old seeking her fortune in the West Indies. While attending an English boarding school, Patricia learns that her father has died, leaving her penniless. Determined to claim his plantation in Barbados, Patricia stows away aboard a merchant vessel bound for the Caribbean. After she is discovered, the young woman becomes part of the ship's crew, training as an assistant to the ship's surgeon by day and

learning to climb the rigging by night. Though Patricia falls in love with Brian Dalton, a kindly bosun's mate who teaches her valuable survival skills, he cannot support her financially, and instead she enters a marriage of convenience with the surgeon. Together they combat yellow fever in Barbados, but when her husband dies, Patricia disguises herself as a man and returns to sea as a surgeon's mate aboard a frigate, where she is reunited with Dalton.

Star-crossed garnered generally strong reviews, as critics compared the book to Avi's *The True Confessions of Charlotte Doyle* and Tanith Lee's *Piratica.* A contributor in *Kirkus Reviews* called Collison's novel a "well-researched, riveting adventure that brings to light an overlooked part of women's history," and Claire Rosser, reviewing the work in *Kliatt,* stated that the "details of life on ship, diseases, injuries and treatments, battles and politics, women who sailed with the men—these details are copious and realistic." Other critics focused on Collison's portrayal of her main character. According to Cheri Dobbs, reviewing *Star-crossed* for *School Library Journal,* the author "does an excellent job of allowing her protagonist to develop." Dobbs added that although Patricia is at first self-centered, "ultimately she

Cover of Linda Collison's historical novel Star-crossed. (Illustration © 2006 by Griesbach and Martucci. Reproduced by permission of Alfred A. Knopf, a division of Random House, Inc.)

matures and becomes free of the shackles of convention." As Carolyn Phelan noted in *Booklist*, "this seafaring saga features a heroine who longs for both independence and love."

Biographical and Critical Sources

PERIODICALS

Booklist, September 15, 2006, Carolyn Phelan, review of *Star-crossed*, p. 69.
Children's Bookwatch, review of *Star-crossed*.
Kirkus Reviews, October 15, 2006, review of *Star-crossed*, p. 1068.
Kliatt, November, 2006, Claire Rosser, review of *Star-crossed*, p. 6.
School Library Journal, December, 2006, Cheri Dobbs, review of *Star-crossed*, p. 134.
Voice of Youth Advocates, February, 2007, Patti Sylvester Spencer, review of *Star-crossed*, p. 522.

ONLINE

Author's Den Web site, http://www.authorsden.com/ (September 27, 2007), Linda Collison, "Heave-ho, Me Bully Boys!"
Linda Collison Home Page, http://www.lindacollison.com (December 1, 2007).
Upon Further Review, http://amateurdelivre.tripod.com/id2.html/ (December 1, 2007), review of *Star-crossed* and interview with Collison."

*   *   *

CONSTANTIN, Pascale

Personal
Born in Montréal, Québec, Canada.

Addresses
Home—Montréal, Québec, Canada. *Agent*—Ronnie Herman, Herman Agency, 350 Central Park W., New York, NY 10025. *E-mail*—pascale@pascaleconstantin.com.

Career
Illustrator.

Awards, Honors
Governor General's Award for Illustrations for Children's Literature nomination, and Grafika Design competition finalist, both 2000, both for *Gulp!* by Lucie Papineau; Alcuin Society Award honorable mention, Mr. Christie's Book Awards shortlist, and Governor General's Award for Illustrations for Children's Literature

nomination, all 2001, all for *Alexis, chevalier des nuits* by Andrée-Anne Gratton; Governor General's Award for Illustrations for Children's Literature nomination, 2004, for *Jurlututu rien ne va plus*, by Sylvie Roberge Blanchet; Great Books for Children designation, Canadian Toy Testing Council, 2007, for *Camilla Chameleon* by Colleen Sydor.

Illustrator
Jean-Pierre Davidts, *Le chat gris raconte*, Éditions Boréal (Montréal, Québec, Canada), 1996.
Lucie Papineau, *Gloups! Bébé-vampire*, Dominique et cie. (Saint-Lambert, Québec, Canada), 1999, translation published as *Gulp!: Baby Vampire*, 1999.
(With others) Henriette Major, *Mil comptines*, Édition Fides, 1999.
Andrée-Anne Gratton, *Alexis, chevalier des nuits*, Les 400 Coups (Montréal, Québec, Canada), 2001.
Sonia Sarafati, *Quand le monstres se montrent*, Les 400 Coups (Montréal, Québec, Canada), 2001.
Sylvie Roberge Blanchet, *Jurlututu rien ne va plus: un conte d'Afrique de l'ouest*, Le 400 Coups (Montréal, Québec, Canada), 2003.
Mara Rockliff, *Next to an Ant*, Children's Press (New York, NY), 2004.
Colleen Sydor, *Camilla Chameleon*, Kids Can Press (Toronto, Ontario, Canada), 2005.
Gilles Tibo, *La vie compté de Raoul Lecompte*, La Courte échelle (Montréal, Québec, Canada), 2005.
Harriet Ziefert, *Danny's Bad Dream*, Sterling Publisher (New York, NY), 2006.
Colleen Sydor, *Raising a Little Stink*, Kids Can Press (Toronto, Ontario, Canada), 2006.
Sylvie Jones, *Go Back to Sleep*, Blue Apple Books (Maplewood, NJ), 2006.
Sylvie Jones, *Who's in the Tub?*, Blue Apple Books (Maplewood, NJ), 2007.
Jason Carter Eaton, *The Facttracker*, HarperCollins (New York, NY), 2008.
Harriet Ziefert, *Mother Goose Manners*, Blue Apple Books (Maplewood, NJ), 2008.

Books featuring Constantin's illustrations have been translated into Spanish.

Biographical and Critical Sources

PERIODICALS

Kirkus Reviews, September 15, 2005, review of *Camilla Chameleon*, p. 1035; September 15, 2006, review of *Go Back to Sleep*, p. 956.
Resource Links, February, 2006, Zoe Johnstone, review of *Camilla Chameleon*, p. 13; April, 2006, Linda Ludke, review of *Raising a Little Stink*, p. 12; December, 2006, Adriane Pettit, review of *Go Back to Sleep*, p. 4.
School Library Journal, March, 2000, Martha Topol, review of *Gulp!: Baby Vampire*, p. 210; June, 2006, JoAnn Jonas, review of *Camilla Chameleon*, p. 128.

ONLINE

Herman Agency Web site, http://www.hermanagency.com/ (December 10, 2007), "Pascale Constantin."
Pascale Constantin Home Page, http://www.pascaleconstantin.com (December 10, 2007).*

*　　*　　*

CORNISH, D.M. 1972-

Personal

Born 1972. *Education:* Attended University of South Australia.

Addresses

E-mail—david@daviddraws.com.

Career

Writer and illustrator.

Writings

(Self-illustrated) *Foundling* (Book 1, "Monster Blood Tattoo" series), Putnam (New York, NY), 2006.

Sidelights

D.M. Cornish is an Australian author of young adult fantasy novels. Beginning as an art student in 1993, he spent a decade meticulously filling twenty-three notebooks with the facts, figures, histories, definitions, and pictures of a mythical world, Half-Continent, which he was happily creating. Then in 2003 a children's book publisher encouraged him to put these notebooks to use in creating fantasy juvenile fiction. The result was *Foundling,* the first of three planned novels in the "Monster Blood Tattoo" series.

This initial novel in the series features the foundling named Rossamund who was raised in Madam Opera's Estimable Marine Society for Foundling Boys and Girls. Possessing a girl's name does not make life any easier for this young boy, who finally sets out to report to his new job as a lamplighter for the emperor. Thus he is launched into a medieval-style world and has adventures fighting monsters and meets strange and curious people as he comes of age. Writing in *SFFWorld,* Rob H. Bedford felt that "the detail and thought put into his world is indeed extensive, [and] Cornish's many years of building up the world are evident throughout." Bedford also went on to praise the narrative viewpoint Cornish employs. "By placing the story at Rossamund's level," the critic noted, "Cornish allows the reader to discover his richly detailed world along with . . . Ros-

samund." Similar praise came from *Booklist* contributor Cindy Dobrez, who called *Foundling* a "Dickensian orphan story [with] an original spin." Dobrez also commended Cornish's original and "impressive black-and-white portraits." Likewise, *School Library Journal* contributor Christi Voth dubbed *Foundling* was an "inventive debut novel," as well as a "delightful, refreshing standout in a sea of cookie-cutter fantasy worlds." However, with its hundred pages of glossary and appendices, the book is also "overblown," in the opinion of a *Kirkus Reviews* critic. A *Publishers Weekly* reviewer had no such reservations, concluding of *Foundling* that "from the pre-industrial English feel to the sprawling setting and backstory" Cornish's debut "feels every bit as substantial as its heft implies."

Biographical and Critical Sources

PERIODICALS

Booklist, April 1, 2006, Cindy Dobrez, review of *Foundling,* p. 42.
Bulletin of the Center for Children's Books, July-August, 2006, April Spisak, review of *Foundling* p. 493.
Kirkus Reviews, May 1, 2006, review of *Foundling,* p. 455.
Publishers Weekly, June 19, 2006, review of *Foundling,* p. 63; July 10. 2006, Michelle Kung, "Hot-Blooded," p. 16.
School Library Journal, July, 2006, Christi Voth, review of *Foundling,* p. 100.

ONLINE

D.M. Cornish Home Page, http://www.monsterbloodtattoo.com (March 3, 2007).
SFFWorld.com, http://www.sffworld.com/ (June 2, 2006), Rob H. Bedford, review of *Foundling.*
Wantz upon a Time Book Reviews Web site, http://www.wantzuponatime.com/ (July 21, 2006), Christina Wantz Fixemer, review of *Foundling.**

*　　*　　*

CROCKER, Nancy 1956-

Personal

Born February 20, 1956; married Dan Roettger; children: one son. *Education:* Columbia College, B.A.

Addresses

Home and office—Minneapolis, MN. *E-mail*—nancycrocker1@mac.com.

Career

Singer, actor, radio announcer, and writer.

Writings

Betty Lou Blue, illustrated by Boris Kulikov, Dial (New York, NY), 2006.
Billie Standish Was Here, Simon & Schuster (New York, NY), 2007.

Contributor to anthology *My Brush with History: By 95 Americans Who Were There,* Black Dog & Leventhal (New York, NY), 2001.

Sidelights

While Nancy Crocker was performing as a singer, studying music in college, and working as a radio announcer and an actor, she was also writing. "Poetry, short stories, personal essays (some of which were actually published), songs . . . you name it," Crocker quipped on her home page. Her essay "What She Wore," published in *American Heritage* magazine in 1992 and later anthologized, describes the week infamous fan dancer Sally Rand came to live in Crocker's college dorm.

Although she wrote her first novel in 1993 during a trip with her now-husband, Dan, Crocker did not become a published author of fiction until over a decade later, when her picture book *Betty Lou Blue* was released. The novel *Billie Standish Was Here* followed close on its heels, bringing all of Crocker's years of writing into the public eye.

Betty Lou Blue began when Crocker imagined what the largest feet in the world must sound like. After the first line of the story popped into her head, it was not long until Crocker had set down the rhyming tale of young Betty Lou, who is cursed with the largest feet in the world. The girl is teased by bullies because of her extraordinary shoe size, but when she is able to stay on the surface of mounds of snow while the bullies sink down into the chilly drifts, she must confront a choice: whether to let them stay neck deep in snow or do the right thing and help them. Piper L. Nyman, writing in *School Library Journal,* called *Betty Lou Blue* "a fun seasonal selection and a great starting point for conversations about bullies."

Set in 1968-73 Missouri, an area similar to that where Crocker herself grew up, *Billie Standish Was Here* focuses on a young girl who, neglected by her family, finds support and love from an elderly neighbor. During a town emergency, however, Miss Lydia's adult son assaults Billie. Although Billie says nothing, Miss Lydia realizes what has happened and becomes the girl's protector. The novel follows the relationship between the girl and the older woman through Billie's teen years, showing how the girl heals from years of abuse and neglect and eventually becomes protector and caregiver to the elderly woman. Crocker's novel "is beautiful, painful, and complex, and the descriptions of people, events,

The characters introduced in Nancy Crocker's picture book **Betty Lou Blue** *are portrayed with appealing warmth by illustrator Boris Kulikov.* (Illustration © 2006 by Boris Kulikov. Reproduced by permission of Dial Books for Young Readers, a division of Penguin Putnam Books for Young Readers.)

and emotions are graphic and tangible," wrote Nancy P. Reeder in a *School Library Journal* review of *Billie Standish Was Here.*

When asked by an online interviewer for *Seven Impossible Things before Breakfast* about her writing process, Crocker explained: "I do not outline. I know the beginning and end when I start, and have learned to trust that the route will become apparent—and to get out of the way when it does."

"My grade school had no kindergarten, which led my parents to start piano lessons when I was five," Crocker told *SATA.* "I learned to read music before words. Once I could read both, books and music became my passports to the world beyond our town of around one hundred people. I was lucky to have far-sighted parents who told me I was capable of reaching any goal I set; I think my varied career has come about partly because I never believed anything was impossible.

"Except maybe juggling live chickens. While wearing roller skates.

"When aspiring writers ask for advice, I tell them the only way to become a writer is to write. That sounds so simple—yet, everyone wants to be a writer; nobody wants to do the work. Write whenever you can, and read everything you can get your hands on. You can learn even from bad writing. Sometimes *especially* from bad writing."

Biographical and Critical Sources

PERIODICALS

Booklist, August 1, 2006, Ilene Cooper, review of *Betty Lou Blue,* p. 84.

Kirkus Reviews, September 15, 2006, review of *Betty Lou Blue,* p. 950; April 15, 2007, review of *Billie Standish Was Here.*

School Library Journal, December, 2006, Piper L. Nyman, review of *Betty Lou Blue,* p. 96; July, 2007, Nancy P. Reeder, review of *Billie Standish Was Here,* p. 100.

ONLINE

Nancy Crocker Home Page, http://www.nancycrocker.com (December 1, 2007).

Seven Impossible Things before Breakfast Blog site, http://blaine.org/sevenimpossiblethings/ (August 30, 2007), interview with Crocker.

Simon & Schuster Web site, http://www.simonsays.com/ (December 1, 2007), "Nancy Crocker."

* * *

CUMMINGS, Mary 1951-

Personal

Born 1951.

Addresses

Office—Sparkling Press, 137 E. Curtice St., St. Paul, MN 55107. *E-mail*—sparklingpress@peoplepc.com.

Career

Children's book writer.

Writings

Three Names of Me, illustrated by Lin Wang, Albert Whitman (Morton Grove, IL), 2006.

And the Baker's Boy Went to Sea, Sparkling Press (St. Paul, MN), 2006.

Also author of *The Lives of the Buddha in the Art and Literature of Asia* (academic paper), 1982. Contributor to periodicals, including *Cricket.*

Biographical and Critical Sources

PERIODICALS

Bulletin of the Center for Children's Books, December, 2006, Deborah Stevenson, review of *Three Names of Me,* p. 165.

Kirkus Reviews, September 15, 2006, review of *Three Names of Me,* p. 950.

School Library Journal, October, 2006, Margaret R. Tassia, review of *Three Names of Me,* p. 109.

ONLINE

Mary Cummings Home Page, http://www.thebakersboywenttosea.com (December 5, 2007).

Children's Literature Network, http://www.childrensliteraturenetwork.org/ (December 5, 2007), "Mary Cummings."

* * *

CURRY, Tom

Personal

Born in Coleman, TX; married; wife's name Susan. *Education:* North Texas State University, B.A. (art).

Addresses

Office—Tom Curry Studio, 901 W. Sul Rd., Alpine, TX 79830. *E-mail*—contact@tomcurrystudio.com.

Career

Painter, illustrator, and political cartoonist. Taylor Publishing, Dallas, TX, graphic artist; University of Texas, Austin, designer and illustrator; Sagebrush Studio, Austin, freelance illustrator; Prickly Pear Studio, Austin, illustrator, 1987-93; Tom Curry Studio, Alpine, TX, founder and illustrator, 1993—. *Exhibitions:* Artwork featured in solo shows and included in collections in the United States, Europe, and Japan.

Awards, Honors

Story Teller Award for best illustrated children's book, Western Writers of America, 1998, for *The Bootmaker and the Elves;* illustration awards from Communication Arts, New York Art Directors Annual, Print Regional Annual, and Society of Illustrators.

Illustrator

PICTURE BOOKS

Jim Latimer, *Snail and Buffalo,* Orchard Books (New York, NY), 1995.

Susan Lowell, *The Bootmaker and the Elves,* Orchard Books (New York, NY), 1997.

Linda Arms White, *Comes a Wind,* DK Publishing (New York, NY), 2000.

J. Patrick Lewis, *Galileo's Universe,* Creative Editions (Mankato, MN), 2003.

Susan Wojciechowski, *A Fine St. Patrick's Day,* Random House (New York, NY), 2004.

Ellen A. Kelley, *Buckamoo Girls,* Abrams Books for Young Readers (New York, NY), 2006.

Contributor of illustrations to periodicals, including *Time, Newsweek, Rolling Stone, Atlantic Monthly,* and *Texas Monthly.*

Sidelights

Tom Curry has illustrated a number of highly regarded children's books, among them Susan Lowell's *The Bootmaker and the Elves* and Ellen A. Kelley's *Buckamoo Girls.* A native of West Texas, Curry began drawing as a child, influenced by his mother, a fine-arts painter. After graduating from North Texas State University, he performed design work for Taylor Publishing and the University of Texas before turning to freelancing. His illustrations have appeared in such publications as *Time, Newsweek, Rolling Stone,* and *Mother Jones.*

In 1993 Curry moved to Alpine, Texas, and began focusing on his paintings, which often incorporate Southwestern themes. "Most noticeable in Curry's work is a wry, sometimes slightly twisted sense of humor," noted a contributor on the Kiowa Gallery Web site. Describing his artistic style on the Kchisos Gallery Web site, Curry stated, "I guess I would call it 'humorous despair' because I see humor and despair in everything. It's just the way our culture is, blending good and bad qualities."

Tom Curry's energetic illustrations bring to life Susan Lowell's picture book **The Bootmaker and the Elves,** *which retells a traditional story for new generations.* (Illustration © 1999 by Tom Curry. Reproduced by permission of Scholastic, Inc.)

Curry illustrated his first children's book, Jim Latimer's *Snail and Buffalo*, in 1995. The work concerns the unlikely friendship between an energetic, talkative bison and a tiny, unassuming snail. According to a reviewer in *Publishers Weekly,* "Curry's stylized illustrations . . . offer some playful perspectives on the characters' relative sizes."

In *The Bootmaker and the Elves,* which garnered the 1998 Western Writers of America Story Teller Award, Lowell offers her take on the classic fairy tale "The Shoe Maker and the Elves." When a struggling bootmaker retires for the night, leaving some scraps of leather about his shop, two elves transform the scraps into a pair of spectacular cowboy boots which are ultimately purchased by a wealthy rancher. Curry's "brassy illustrations sashay across the page in blazing, southwestern colors with zany, toe-tickling details," noted *Horn Book* contributor Marilyn Bousquin, and a *Publishers Weekly* critic stated that the illustrator's "acrylic dry-brush technique lends an adobe texture to the shop walls, and the outdoor shots capture the unique quality of Southwestern light."

In *Comes a Wind,* written by Linda Arms White, two ornery brothers constantly attempt to one-up each other. When their mother asks them to tone down the competition on her birthday, Clement and Clyde head to the front porch just as the wind picks up. As the duo swap stories about the biggest storm they ever encountered, a huge gust of wind swoops up their mother and deposits her on the roof of her house, prompting a rescue effort. "Curry depicts the blustery day in American primitive style, with a deliberately flattened perspective and Western details," noted a *Publishers Weekly* contributor. *School Library Journal* critic Ginny Gustin noted that "Curry's folk-art style acrylic paintings . . . make a perfect accompaniment to White's witty tall tale." Curry also provided the illustrations for *Galileo's Universe,* a pop-up verse biography of mathematician and astronomer Galileo Galilei by J. Patrick Lewis. In the words of *Booklist* reviewer Carolyn Phelan, "Curry's excellent paintings give a sense of the era as well as dramatically portray people and events."

In Susan Wojciechowski's *A Fine St. Patrick's Day,* the rival towns of Tralee and Tralah prepare for the annual holiday festivities. When a wee man asks the townspeople of Tralah for help with his cows, they turn him away; the folks in Tralee, however, set aside the competition to offer their assistance, thus earning the villagers an unexpected reward. "Curry's drolly mock-primitive paintings practically glow with color and bristle with texture," wrote Kitty Flynn in *Horn Book,* and *School Library Journal* critic Grace Oliff stated, "The folk-art style complements the folktale feel of this pleasant story about the rewards of kindness and community."

Joanna and Susanna, a pair of ordinary cows, transform themselves into cowgirls for one exciting day in *Buckamoo Girls,* "a flight of sublime silliness," remarked

Curry's quirky art takes center stage in the pages of Ellen A. Kelley's picture book **Buckamoo Girls.** (Abrams Books for Young Readers, 2006. Illustration © 2006 by Tom Curry. Reproduced by permission.)

Christopher Porterfield in *Time.* After donning skirts, vests, and boots, the twosome spend their time roping steers and dancing at a hoedown. According to a *Publishers Weekly* reviewer, "Curry's illustrations depict the kinetic motion," and Susan E. Murray, writing in *School Library Journal,* observed that Curry's artwork "gives the book a strong flavor of the West."

Biographical and Critical Sources

PERIODICALS

Booklist, September 15, 1997, Julie Corsaro, review of *The Bootmaker and the Elves,* p. 242; March 15, 2000, Susan Dove Lempke, review of *Comes a Wind,* p. 1390; December 15, 2003, Karin Snelson, review of *A Fine St. Patrick's Day,* p. 242; December 1, 2005, Carolyn Phelan, review of *Galileo's Universe,* p. 59.

Horn Book, November-December, 1997, Marilyn Bousquin, review of *The Bootmaker and the Elves,* p. 691; January-February, 2004, Kitty Flynn, review of *A Fine St. Patrick's Day,* p. 77.

Kirkus Reviews, December, 2003, review of *A Fine St. Patrick's Day,* p. 1455; September 15, 2006, review of *Buckamoo Girls,* p. 957.

Publishers Weekly, October 16, 1995, review of *Snail and Buffalo,* p. 61; September 22, 1997, review of *The Bootmaker and the Elves,* p. 80; February 21, 2000, review of *Comes a Wind,* p. 86; January 5, 2004, review of *A Fine St. Patrick's Day,* p. 61; November 6, 2006, review of *Buckamoo Girls,* p. 60.

School Library Journal, May, 2000, Ginny Gustin, review of *Comes a Wind,* p. 158; January, 2004, Grace Oliff, review of *A Fine St. Patrick's Day,* p. 108; January, 2007, Susan E. Murray, review of *Buckamoo Girls,* p. 98.

Time, December 11, 2006, Christopher Porterfield, review of *Buckamoo Girls,* p. 92.

ONLINE

Kchisos Gallery Web site, http://www.kchisosgallery.com/ (December 1, 2007), "Tom Curry."
Kiowa Gallery Web site, http://www.kiowagallery.com/ (December 1, 2007), "Tom Curry."
Tom Curry Studio Web site, http://www.tomcurrystudio. com (December 1, 2007).*

*   *   *

CURTIS, Jennifer Keats

Personal

Children: two. *Education:* University of Maryland, B.A., 1991, M.A., 1993. *Hobbies and other interests:* Boating and any activity on the water, running, basketball, reading.

Addresses

Home—Annapolis, MD. *E-mail*—jcurtis@cablespeed. com; jenniferkcurtis@gmail.com.

Career

Author, editor, and educator. Presenter at schools and workshops; editor-at-large, *Maryland Life* magazine.

Awards, Honors

Frederick Douglass Award, Maryland Council of Teachers of English Language Arts, 1999, for *Oshus and Shelly Save the Bay;* ASPCA Henry Bergh Children's Book Award finalist, 2006, for *Turtles in My Sandbox.*

Writings

Oshus and Shelly Save the Bay, illustrated by Christie Sauer Fifer, Captain Caleb Communications, 1999.
Turtles in My Sandbox, illustrated by Emanuel Schongut, Sylvan Dell (Mount Pleasant, SC), 2006.
Osprey Adventure, illustrated by Marcy Dunn Ramsey, Cornell Maritime Press, 2007.
Baby Owl, Sylvan Dell (Mount Peasant, SC), 2008.

Contributor to periodicals, including *It's Your Life* and *Corridor, Inc.*

Sidelights

Although her books have universal appeal, Jennifer Keats Curtis focuses her writing on teaching children about the wildlife and ecology of the Maryland coastal region where she lives. An outgrowth of her workshops and school presentations, her books *Oshus and Shelly Save the Bay, Turtles in My Sandbox,* and *Osprey Adventure* focus on the animals that live in the complex Chesapeake Bay estuary ecosystem, where freshwater flows into the Atlantic and mixes with the ocean's salt water. Since 1983, scientists have worked to restore and preserve the Chesapeake Bay ecosystem.

Curtis's award-winning first book, *Oshus and Shelly Save the Bay,* tells the story of two oysters as they try to keep pollution from destroying the bay. As part of her environmental efforts, Curtis dedicated a portion of the profits from sales of this book to the Severn River Association, where it was used to help restore the area's dwindling oyster population.

Other books include *Turtles in My Sandbox,* a finalist for the ASPCA Henry Bergh Children's Book Award, and *Osprey Adventure,* a fact-based story about a boy who joins his biologist father to saves a young osprey from certain death. Inspired by an ongoing educational program that introduces children to the life cycle of the native terrapin, *Turtles in My Sandbox* focuses on a young girl named Maggie, who discovers that a mother diamond-backed terrapin has laid her eggs in Maggie's backyard sandbox. With the help of her mom, the girl meets a woman known as the Turtle Lady, and she learns how to care for the ten eggs, keeping them safe from predators as she waits for the tiny turtles to hatch. A portion of the royalties from this book are donated to

Jennifer Keats Curtis weaves a lesson about the resilience of nature into Turtles in My Sandbox, *a picture book featuring artwork by Emanuel Schongut.* (Illustration © by Emanuel Schongut. Reproduced by permission.)

a nonprofit organization dedicated to preserving terrapins in their natural habitat. Citing the "detailed watercolors" by illustrator Emanuel Schongut, a *Kirkus Reviews* writer predicted that *Turtles in My Sandbox* will be "sure to spark an interest in these amazing creatures, and to increase participation in Maryland's turtle project."

By thoroughly researching her topic and interviewing real experts, including children working to help preserve and protect the local wildlife, Curtis has developed a knack for teaching young children about important ecological issues. Although, because of her journalism background, she loves the investigation and process of writing that goes into creating her picture books, Curtis is most tickled by the delightful response she gets from students when she visits schools with book in hand, live animal in another. "Rascal, my three-year-old turtle, never fails to elicit a grin from the kids,"

Curtis told *SATA* "It's such a pleasure to introduce children to the creatures who live in their backyards."

Biographical and Critical Sources

PERIODICALS

Kirkus Reviews, October 15, 2006, review of *Turtles in My Sandbox,* p. 1068.
School Library Journal, December, 2006, Daisy Porter, review of *Turtles in My Sandbox,* p. 96.

ONLINE

Children's Literature Web site, http://www.childrenslit.com/ (December 15, 2007), "Jennifer Keats Curtis."
Turtles in My Sandbox Web site, http://www.terrapinbook.com/ (December 15, 2007), "Jennifer Keats Curtis."

D

DePALMA, Mary Newell 1961-

Personal

Born August 20, 1961, in Pittsburgh, PA; daughter of Francis and Joan Newell; married Alphonse DePalma III; children: Kepley Therese, Alphonse IV. *Education:* Rochester Institute of Technology, B.F.A. (medical illustration), 1983. *Hobbies and other interests:* Gardening, knitting, reading.

Addresses

Home and office—Boston, MA. *E-mail*—mary@marynewelldepalma.com.

Career

Freelance illustrator, Boston, MA, beginning 1984. Has worked as an interpreter for the deaf, a calligrapher, and a hand-knitter of designer sweaters. *Exhibitions:* Work included in Society of Illustrators Annual Exhibition 42, 2000; Original Art Exhibition, 2001; Huntington House Museum, Windsor, CT, 2002; Concord Museum, Concord, MA, 2002; Chemer's Gallery, Tustin, CA, 2004; and Elizabeth Stone Gallery, Alexandria, VA, 2007. Work included in permanent collection at Mazza Museum of International Art from Picture Books, Findlay, OH.

Member

Society of Children's Book Writers and Illustrators.

Writings

SELF-ILLUSTRATED

The Strange Egg, Houghton Mifflin (Boston, MA), 2001.
A Grand Old Tree, Arthur A. Levine (New York, NY), 2005.

The Nutcracker Doll, Arthur A. Levine (New York, NY), 2007.

Author's work has been translated into French and Korean.

ILLUSTRATOR

Ilona Kemeny Stashko and Carol Whiting Bowen, retellers, *Goldilocks and the Three Bears,* Come Alive Publications (Concord, MA), 1992.
Miriam Aroner, *Giraffes Aren't Half as Fat,* Millbrook Press (Brookfield, CT), 1995.
Matt Curtis, *Six Empty Pockets,* Children's Press (New York, NY), 1997.
Patricia Hubbell, *Black Earth, Gold Sun* (poems), Marshall Cavendish (New York, NY), 2001.
Susan Blackaby, *Rembrandt's Hat,* Houghton Mifflin (Boston, MA), 2002.
Marc Harshman, *Roads,* Marshall Cavendish (New York, NY), 2002.
Betsy James, *My Chair,* Arthur A. Levine (New York, NY), 2004.
Eileen Spinelli, *Now It Is Winter,* Eerdmans (Grand Rapids, MI), 2004.
Jan Wahl, *Knock! Knock!,* Henry Holt (New York, NY), 2004.
Jill Esbaum, *Estelle Takes a Bath,* Henry Holt (New York, NY), 2006.
Margaret Read MacDonald, *The Squeaky Door,* HarperCollins (New York, NY), 2006.
Susan Milord, *Happy School Year!,* Scholastic (New York, NY), 2008.

Sidelights

Mary Newell DePalma was not always an author and illustrator for young children. Discussing her less-than-traditional career path with Elaine Magliaro in the *Wild Rose Reader Blog Spot,* DePalma went on to describe some of her previous occupations: knitting sweaters, addressing envelopes and creating signs using calligraphy, interpreting for the deaf in classrooms, and brain-

Mary Newell DePalma's illustrations have appeared in picture books such as Patricia Hubbell's **Black Earth, Gold Sun.** (Illustration © 2001 by Mary Newell DePalma. Reproduced by permission of Marshall Cavendish.)

storming ideas for scented stickers. When she decided she wanted to be an illustrator, DePalma worked in a number of fields, from advertising to textbook illustration, before becoming a children's book illustrator. "I had never even given it a thought because I was kind of in awe of children's book illustration, I guess. I imagined that some separate species of illustrator—geniuses—illustrated children's books," she told Magliaro.

DePalma's brightly colored, unusual illustrations first began appearing in books written by others. One of her early titles, *Rembrandt's Hat* by Susan Blackaby, is a story about a bear who loses his hat. While *Rembrandt's Hat* would make a fine choice for read-aloud time, according to Robin L. Gibson in *School Library Journal,* "children will want to take a closer look, as the illustrations deserve careful inspection." A contributor to *Publishers Weekly* concluded that, "all in all," the book is "simply fedorable." In *Roads,* Marc Harshman's story of a family road trip, DePalma's illustrations were noted for their realism. According to Roxanne Burg, they "have a two-dimensional look to them, almost like still photographs." Noting the growing number of children that populate the illustrations in *My Chair* from first page to last, a *Kirkus Reviews* contributor predicted that "young viewers will pore over the actively posed figures and sometimes-surprising details" illustrating Betsy James' story.

Accompanying Jan Wahl's spooky folk-tale picture book *Knock! Knock!,* DePalma's "illustrations are filled with creepy details and atmospheric shadows," wrote Susan Weitz in *School Library Journal.* A *Kirkus Reviews* contributor felt that, "with their exaggerated perspectives and spooky shadows," DePalma's characters "seal the deal." Margaret Read Macdonald's retelling of a traditional tale in *The Squeaky Door* features animals in pajamas as a grandmother tries to comfort her grandson in his new bed. DePalma's artwork, "diminutive and detailed, envision[s] a cozy home and loving grandma," wrote Stephanie Zvirin in *Booklist,* while a *Kirkus Reviews* contributor noted that the "full-color illustrations highlight the hilarity." Equally silly pictures adorn *Estelle Takes a Bath,* as Estelle interrupts her bubble bath to chase a mouse around her house. Calling the illustrations for Jill Esbaum's story "lighthearted," Blair Christolon noted in *School Library Journal* that the pictures are "filled with humor as bubbles, steam, and an assortment of strategically placed household objects" preserve the young girl's modesty.

Featuring the combination of a naive bird and a wise little monkey, DePalma's first self-illustrated children's book, *The Strange Egg,* focuses on the joy of new friends and the value in sharing dreams and ideas. "These are the ingredients for many wonderful adventures," DePalma once told *SATA.* With few words and short sentences, the book describes the antics of a small black bird that finds a round, orange object and tries to determine what it is. Finally, deciding that the object must be an egg, the bird sits on it, to the great amusement of a monkey, who shows the bird how to peel and eat the orange. They enjoy the fruit and the bird returns the favor by teaching the monkey how to plant the orange's seeds. Soon, the two are friends, and they enjoy many oranges together.

A contributor to *Kirkus Reviews* dubbed *The Strange Egg* "an odd little tale of fruit and friendship," and Susan Marie Pitard pointed out in *School Library Journal*

Cover of DePalma's picture book **A Grand Old Tree,** *a gentle nature story featuring her colorful graphic art.* (Illustration © 2005 by Mary Newell DePalma. Reproduced by permission of Scholastic, Inc.)

that the story "underlines issues important to children: cooperation, friendship, using your individual talents," and others. Both reviewers noted that the exuberance of DePalma's mixed-media illustrations provide much of the humor and fun of the story. "There is real humor in the illustrations," the *Kirkus Reviews* critic observed, while a contributor to *Publishers Weekly* credited much of the book's success to the author/illustrator's "quirky" and "postmodern" illustrations. "This offbeat riff on the joys of the unexpected as well as the give-and-take of friendship is eggs-actly right," the critic concluded.

DePalma's self-illustrated *A Grand Old Tree* is the story of a tree's life cycle. The illustrations show the many creatures that live in the tree while it is alive and healthy, as well as those living there after it has died. Carolyn Phelan, writing in *Booklist,* commented that DePalma's "well-chosen words . . . are poetic in the economy of their expression and the precision of their imagery." Maura Bresnahan, reviewing the book for *School Library Journal,* wrote that the "art superbly complements the writing." Noting the variety of collage materials that accompany DePalma's watercolors, a *Kirkus Reviews* contributor found the illustrations "winningly simple," adding that "her big-eyed animals are sweetly comical." Also favorably reviewing *A Grand Old Tree,* a *Publishers Weekly* critic felt that "the stylized shapes of the watercolor and torn-paper art emanate a carefree, childlike feel."

The inspiration for *The Nutcracker Doll,* DePalma's third original story, was found close to home: "My daughter Kepley and everyone involved with Boston Ballet's *The Nutcracker,*" as she explained to an online interviewer for *Book Page.* The tale is based on Kepley's experiences as part of the Boston Ballet's production of *The Nutcracker* as a third grader. Both text and illustrations "incorporate the details that authenticate the story and make readers feel like insiders," wrote a contributor to *Publishers Weekly.* In *Horn Book,* Jennifer M. Brabander concluded that *The Nutcracker Doll* is "a book that's as sweet and delectable as a Christmas cookie."

When asked by Magliaro on the Wild Rose Reader Web log whether she prefers illustrating original stories or the texts by other authors, DePalma admitted to enjoying both for different reasons. "I enjoy the freedom and flexibility of writing my own text. Sometimes the story evolves in surprising ways and I'm free to follow my ideas and change my text if I want to. Illustrating other writers' works helps me to stretch out of my comfort zone and has helped me to learn new things."

Biographical and Critical Sources

PERIODICALS

Booklist, April 15, 2002, Kay Weisman, review of *Rembrandt's Hat,* p. 1405; October 15, 2002, Helen Rosenberg, review of *Roads,* p. 412; September 15, 2004, Karin Snelson, review of *My Chair,* p. 250 October 15, 2004, Julie Cummins, review of *Now It Is Winter,* p. 411; December 1, 2004, Karin Snelson, review of *Knock! Knock!,* p. 664; November 15, 2005, review of *A Grand Old Tree,* p. 51; December 1, 2005, Stephanie Zvirin, review of *The Squeaky Door,* p. 54; January 1, 2007, Janice Del Negro, review of *Estelle Takes a Bath,* p. 114.

Bulletin of the Center for Children's Books, September, 2004, Deborah Stevenson, review of *My Chair,* p. 23, and Timnah Card, review of *Knock! Knock!,* p. 43; March, 2006, Elizabeth Bush, review of *The Squeaky Door,* p. 319.

Horn Book, November-December, 2007, Jennifer M. Brabander, review of *The Nutcracker Doll,* p. 628.

Kirkus Reviews, March 15, 2001, review of *The Strange Egg,* p. 406; June 15, 2004, review of *My Chair,* p. 577; July 15, 2004, review of *Knock! Knock!,* p. 695; August 15, 2004, review of *Now It Is Winter,* p. 813; November 1, 2005, review of *A Grand Old Tree,* p. 1183; December 15, 2005, review of *The Squeaky Door,* p. 1325; September 15, 2006, review of *Estelle Takes a Bath,* p. 952.

Library Media Connection, February, 2006, Barbara B. Freehrer, review of *A Grand Old Tree,* p. 82.

Publishers Weekly, February 19, 2001, review of *The Strange Egg,* p. 90; January 14, 2002, review of *Rembrandt's Hat,* p. 59; December 19, 2005, review of *A Grand Old Tree,* p. 62; January 16, 2006, review of *The Squeaky Door,* p. 63; October 22, 2007, review of *The Nutcracker Doll,* p. 53.

School Library Journal, April, 1995, Lisa Wu Stowe, review of *Giraffes Aren't Half as Fat,* p. 121; May, 2001, Susan Marie Pitard, review of *The Strange Egg,* p. 114; November, 2001, Nina Lindsay, review of *Black Earth, Gold Sun,* p. 146; July, 2002, Robin L. Gibson, review of *Rembrandt's Hat,* p. 83; September, 2002, Roxanne Burg, review of *Roads,* p. 193; July, 2004, Marianne Saccardi, review of *My Chair,* p. 78; August, 2004, Susan Weitz, review of *Knock! Knock!,* p. 97; September, 2004, Kathleen Kelly MacMillan, review of *Now It Is Winter,* p. 181; December, 2005, Maura Bresnahan, review of *A Grand Old Tree,* p. 126; January, 2006, Elaine Lesh Morgan, review of *The Squeaky Door,* p. 108; November, 2006, Blair Christolon, review of *Estelle Takes a Bath,* p. 92.

Tribune Books (Chicago, IL), May 13, 2007, Maria Pontillas, review of *The Squeaky Door,* p. 6.

ONLINE

Mary Newell DePalma Home Page, http://www.marynewelldepalma.com (December 3, 2007).

Book Page Web site, http://www.bookpage.com/ (July 12, 2007), "Mary Newell DePalma."

Scholastic Web site, http://content.scholastic.com/ (December 3, 2007), profile of DePalma.

Wild Rose Reader Web log, http://wildrosereader.blogspot.com/ (November 15, 2007), interview with DePalma.

* * *

DOWER, Laura 1967-
(Jo Hurley)

Personal

Born March 12, 1967, in MA; married; children: one daughter, one son. *Hobbies and other interests:* Collecting glass bottles and writing instruments.

Addresses

Home—NY.

Career

Writer. Scholastic, Inc., New York, NY, former creative director; full-time writer, 1999—.

Awards, Honors

YALSA Quick Pick for Reluctant Readers designation, 1999, for *Real Teens;* National Parenting Center Seal of Approval, 2002, for "From the Files of Madison Finn" series.

Writings

(Published anonymously) *Real Teens: A Diary of a Junior Year,* six volumes, 1999.

I Will Remember You: What to Do When Someone You Love Dies: A Guidebook through Grief for Teens, introduction by Elena Lister, Scholastic (New York, NY), 2001.

Rewind, Scholastic (New York, NY), 2006.

The Boy Next Door, Scholastic (New York, NY), 2006.

For Girls Only: Everything Great about Being a Girl, Feiwel & Friends (New York, NY), 2008.

Also author of "Celebrity Quiz-o-Rama" series, and of activity books.

"FROM THE FILES OF MADISON FINN" SERIES; MIDDLE-GRADE NOVELS

Only the Lonely, Hyperion (New York, NY), 2001.

Boy, Oh Boy!, Hyperion (New York, NY), 2001.

Play It Again, Hyperion (New York, NY), 2001.

Caught in the Web, Hyperion (New York, NY), 2001.

Thanks for Nothing, Hyperion (New York, NY), 2001.

Lost and Found, Hyperion (New York, NY), 2002.

Save the Date, Hyperion (New York, NY), 2002.

Picture Perfect, Hyperion (New York, NY), 2002.

Just Visiting, Hyperion (New York, NY), 2002.

Give and Take, Hyperion (New York, NY), 2002.

Heart to Heart, Hyperion (New York, NY), 2003.

Light's Out!, Hyperion (New York, NY), 2003.

Sink or Swim, Hyperion (New York, NY), 2003.

Double Dare, Hyperion (New York, NY), 2003.

Off the Wall, Hyperion (New York, NY), 2004.

Three's a Crowd, Hyperion (New York, NY), 2004.

On the Case, Hyperion (New York, NY), 2004.

To Have and to Hold: Super Edition 1 (anthology), Hyperion (New York, NY), 2004.

Give Me a Break, Hyperion (New York, NY), 2004.

Keep It Real, Hyperion (New York, NY), 2005.

All That Glitters, Hyperion (New York, NY), 2005.

Forget Me Not, Hyperion (New York, NY), 2005.

All Shook Up, Hyperion (New York, NY), 2006.

2c4w: Bind-up 1 (anthology), Hyperion (New York, NY), 2006.

Bf4e: Best Friends Forever: Bind-up 2 (anthology), Hyperion (New York, NY), 2006.

Hit the Beach: Super Edition 2 (anthology), Hyperion (New York, NY), 2006.

Friends till the End: Super Edition 3 (anthology), Hyperion (New York, NY), 2007.

ADAPTOR; BASED ON "POWERPUFF GIRLS" TELEVISION CARTOON BY CRAIG MCCRACKEN

Mojo Jojo's Rising, Scholastic (New York, NY), 2000.

Monkey See, Doggy Do, Scholastic (New York, NY), 2000.

Paste Makes Waste, Scholastic (New York, NY), 2000.

Bubble Trouble, Scholastic (New York, NY), 2000.

Fishy Business, illustrations by Christopher Cook, Scholastic (New York, NY), 2001.

Beat Your Greens, illustrations by Ken Edwards, Scholastic (New York, NY), 2001.

The Powerpuff Girls Save Valentine's Day!, illustrations by Don Bishop, Scholastic (New York, NY), 2001.

Bought and Scold, Scholastic (New York, NY), 2001.

Three Girls and a Monster, illustrations by Ken Edwards, Scholastic (New York, NY), 2002.

The Valentine's Day Mix-up, Scholastic (New York, NY), 2002.

Let the Fur Fly, Scholastic (New York, NY), 2002.

'Twas the Fight before Christmas, Scholastic (New York, NY), 2003.

Bubbles Bedazzled!, Scholastic (New York, NY), 2003.

Not-so-Awesome Blossom, Scholastic (New York, NY), 2004.

UNDER NAME JO HURLEY

Celebrity Quiz-o-Rama Pop Party: Pop Quizzes, Party Ideas, and More!, Scholastic (New York, NY), 2000.

Secret Spy Superear!, illustrated by Marty Baumann, Tangerine Press (New York, NY), 2002.

Every Girl Can Be a Princess!: Storybook Dress-up, and Party Fun, illustrated by Zina Saunder, Tangerine Press (New York, NY), 2003.

Scooby-Doo! and the Phantom Prankster, Scholastic (New York, NY), 2005.

Firehouse Fun, illustrated by Tino Santanach, Scholastic (New York, NY), 2006.

Friendship 101: Quizzes and Questions, illustrated by Taia Morley, Scholastic (New York, NY), 2006.

(Adaptor) *New Truck on the Block* (based on *Firehouse Tales* television program), illustrated by Tino Santanach, Scholastic (New York, NY), 2006.

(Adaptor) *Help's on the Way!* (board book; based on *Firehouse Tales* television program), illustrated by Artful Doodlers, Scholastic (New York, NY), 2006.

Perfect Parties, Sleepovers, and More, Scholastic (New York, NY), 2007.

Also author of unauthorized biographies *Pop People: Britney Spears* and *Hangin' with Hilary Duff.*

Sidelights

A former creative director for New York City publisher Scholastic, Inc., Laura Dower is a prolific writer whose books are geared for preteen girls. Sometimes writing under the pen name Jo Hurley, she is best known to preteen readers for her "From the Files of Madison Finn" series, about a girl who has difficulty dealing with the changes that life brings. Dower has also created picture-book adaptations of an animated television series featuring the adventures of a trio of kindergarten girls with super powers who are known as the Powerpuff Girls. Created by Craig McCracken, *The Powerpuff Girls* series aired on cable television's Cartoon Network beginning in 2000.

As readers meet Madison in *Only the Lonely,* the Internet-savvy sixth-grade graduate is dealing with the aftershock of her parents' divorce. Described by a *Pub-*

Cover of Laura Dower's Just Visiting, *an installment in the "From the Files of Madison Finn" series that features artwork by Stephanie Power.* (Illustration © 2002 by Stephanie Power/Reactor Art + Design. Reproduced by permission of Hyperion Books for Children.)

lishers Weekly contributor as a "high-strung and contemplative heroine who pronounces herself 'allergic' to change," Madison weathers the transition to middle school with best pals Egg and Aimee. Noting that Dower's prose is salted with e-mail-ese, the *Publishers Weekly* reviewer added that in *Only the Lonely* preteen "issues are real enough and credibly handled." In *Thanks for Nothing,* the approach of the holidays forces Madison to choose between her parents, while *Heart to Heart* finds the twelve year old excited over the attentions of a secret fan. Other volumes find Maddie volunteering at a local animal shelter, competing in a Web-page design contest, babysitting, and traveling to New York City to share a friend's thirteenth birthday celebration. In a review of *Only the Lonely* for *School Library Journal,* Marilyn Payne Phillips predicted that the "From the Files of Madison Finn" books will be perfect as a "light summer read." *Booklist* critic Lauren Peterson also noted that humor takes center stage in Dower's preteen novels, writing that, "although some serious topics are raised" in Madison's computer-age chronicle, "they are handled mostly in a lighthearted way."

Biographical and Critical Sources

PERIODICALS

Booklist, June 1, 2001, Lauren Peterson, review of *Only the Lonely,* p. 1882; February 15, 2006, Hazel Rochman, review of *Rewind,* p. 91.
Publishers Weekly, April 16, 2001, review of *Only the Lonely,* p. 66.
School Library Journal, August, 2001, Marilyn Payne Phillips, review of *Only the Lonely,* p. 178.

ONLINE

Laura Dower Home Page, http://www.lauradower.com (December 20, 2007).
Madison Finn Web site, http://www.madisonfinn.com/ (December 20, 2007).*

*   *   *

DOWNEY, Lynn 1961-

Personal
Born 1961; married; children: three sons.

Addresses
Home—Hampstead, MD.

Career
Author and poet.

Writings

Sing, Henrietta! Sing!, illustrated by Tony Sansevero, Ideals Children's Books (Nashville, TN), 1997.
The Flea's Sneeze, illustrated by Karla Firehammer, Henry Holt (New York, NY), 2000.
This Is the Earth That God Made, illustrated by Benrei Huang, Augsburg Books (Minneapolis, MN), 2000.
Papa's Birthday Gift, illustrated by Stacey Schuett, Augsburg Books (Minneapolis, MN), 2003.
Most Loved Monster, illustrated by Jack E. Davis, Dial Books for Young Readers (New York, NY), 2004.
The Tattletale, illustrated by Pam Paparone, Henry Holt (New York, NY), 2006.
Matilda's Humdinger, illustrated by Tim Bowers, Knopf (New York, NY), 2006.

Contributor of poems to literary journals.

Sidelights
Lynn Downey is the author of several well-received picture books for young readers. Downey published her debut work, *Sing, Henrietta! Sing!,* in 1997. Gardening

aficionados Henrietta and George decide to combine their efforts and sell their own vegetables, which grow splendidly thanks to Henrietta's unconventional approach to horticulture: she sings to all the plants in their garden. Unfortunately, her off-pitch warbling also frightens the customers. When George asks her to remain quiet in order to encourage shoppers, the garden suffers and the business closes until the pair comes up with a unique solution to their problem. Susan Garland, writing in *School Library Journal,* called *Sing, Henrietta! Sing!* "a wonderful read-aloud choice."

In *The Flea's Sneeze,* a tale told in verse, a tiny flea with a bad head cold manages to wake a barn full of animals, including a frightened rat, an annoyed cat, a confused cow, and an equally sickly hog. A reviewer in *Publishers Weekly* complimented the "perky volume," offering praise for the "rollicking rhythms and kid-pleasing repetition" found in Downey's story. *This Is the Earth That God Made,* which is similar in style to

the popular nursery rhyme "This Is the House That Jack Built," celebrates humankind's relationship to the natural world. According to a contributor in *Publishers Weekly,* Downey's text "successfully conveys its message of gratitude, admiration and praise for the glory, bounty and benevolence of the Creator," and Patricia Pearl Dole, reviewing *This Is the Earth That God Made* in *School Library Journal,* remarked that the book's "simple, cheerful words gently remind readers of nature's wonders and are suitable for any faith recognizing a heavenly maker."

A young girl learns a valuable lesson about forgiveness in *Papa's Birthday Gift.* On Tessa's sixth birthday, a snowstorm delays her father's return home, despite the girl's prayers for his quick arrival. A disappointed Tessa receives a wonderful surprise later that evening, however, and realizes that God has answered her prayers in an unexpected way. Sibling rivalry is the theme of *Most Loved Monster,* another picture book by Downey. As

Lynn Downey introduces readers to a group of industrious animal entrepreneurs in her picture book **Matilda's Humdinger,** *featuring illustrations by* **Tim Bowers.** (Illustration © 2006 by Tim Bowers. Reproduced by permission of Alfred A. Knopf, a division of Random House, Inc.)

Mama Monster tucks her four monstrous offspring into bed, each one asks, "Who do you love most?" Mama points out that each of her fiends is special in his or her own way. Downey "freshens up a well-worn premise with genial grossness," wrote a critic in *Publishers Weekly,* and *School Library Journal* contributor Wanda Meyers-Hines noted that the book "truly captures the spirit of giving and appreciation."

Downey's story pairs with Pam Paparone's illustrations in *The Tattletale.* In this picture book William the pig constantly reports on the bad behavior of his older brother, Wembly. After their exasperated mother separates the pair, a lonely William watches as Wembly joins Iggy, a troublesome neighbor, to build a tree fort. When Iggy teases Wembly about his fear of heights, William comes to his brother's aid. Although a critic in *Kirkus Reviews* believed that Downey keeps her "focus . . . more on appreciating siblings than on tattling," Lucinda Snyder Whitehurst noted in *School Library Journal* that *The Tattletale* "will find a ready audience with siblings everywhere."

A messy, clumsy waitress prevents a heist in *Matilda's Humdinger,* another amusing tale by Downey. Matilda the cat is the worst waitress at Burt's Diner, but her funny, exciting stories keep the customers entertained. After a health inspector spots a number of violations, Matilda vows to clean up her act, but she also quits spinning her tales, much to the dismay of her patrons. When robbers enter the diner, however, Matilda's quick wit and storytelling skills return and ultimately save the restaurant. According to *Booklist* reviewer Hazel Rochman, Downey's narrative "reveals the strength of the small rebel and the power of the tales she tells."

Biographical and Critical Sources

PERIODICALS

Booklist, October 15, 2006, Hazel Rochman, review of *Matilda's Humdinger,* p. 54; November 1, 2006, Ilene Cooper, review of *The Tattletale,* p. 60.

Bulletin of the Center for Children's Books, July, 2000, review of *The Flea's Sneeze,* p. 397.

Children's Bookwatch, October, 2006, review of *The Tattletale;* January, 2007, review of *Matilda's Humdinger.*

Kirkus Reviews, July 15, 2004, review of *Most Loved Monster,* p. 683; September 15, 2006, reviews of *Matilda's Humdinger* and *The Tattletale,* p. 951.

Publishers Weekly, March 13, 2000, review of *This Is the Earth That God Made,* p. 81; September 4, 2000, review of *The Flea's Sneeze,* p. 106; August 9, 2004, review of *Most Loved Monster,* p. 250.

School Library Journal, July, 1997, Susan Garland, review of *Sing, Henrietta! Sing!,* p. 61; September, 2000, Patricia Pearl Dole, review of *This Is the Earth That God Made,* p. 215; August, 2004, Wanda Meyers-Hines, review of *Most Loved Monster,* p. 85; October, 2006, Catherine Callegari, review of *Matilda's Humdinger,* p. 109; November, 2006, Lucinda Snyder Whitehurst, review of *The Tattletale,* p. 90.*

E-F

EHRENHAFT, Daniel 1970-
(Erin Haft, Daniel Parker)

Personal

Born August 12, 1970, in Washington, DC; married; wife's name Jessica. *Education:* Attended Columbia University. *Hobbies and other interests:* Music, especially music composed from 1966 to 1982, reading, mob movies, ping-pong, volunteering for 826nyc (a nonprofit literacy and writing lab for children).

Addresses

Home—Brooklyn, NY. *E-mail*—dan@danielehrenhaft. com.

Career

Musician, composer, and author. Former worker in a cheese shop.

Awards, Honors

Edgar Award, Mystery Writers of America, for best young adult novel, 2003, for "Wessex Papers" trilogy; Best Books for the Teen Age selection, New York Public Library, 2005, for *10 Things to Do before I Die.*

Writings

FOR YOUNG ADULTS

Marc Andreessen: Web Warrior (nonfiction), Twenty-first Century Books (Brookfield, CT), 2001.
Larry Ellison: Sheer Nerve (nonfiction), Twenty-first Century Books (Brookfield, CT), 2001.
The Last Dog on Earth (novel), Delacorte Press (New York, NY), 2003.
10 Things to Do before I Die (novel), Delacorte Press (New York, NY), 2004.
Tell It to Naomi (novel), Delacorte Press (New York, NY), 2004.
Drawing a Blank; or, How I Tried to Solve a Mystery, End a Feud, and Land the Girl of My Dreams (novel), illustrated by Trevor Ristow, HarperCollins (New York, NY), 2006.
The After Life (novel), Razorbill (New York, NY), 2006.
Pool Boys (novel), Scholastic (New York, NY), 2006.

Contributor to *My Dad's a Punk: 12 Stories about Boys and Their Fathers,* edited by Tony Bradman, Kingfisher (Boston, MA), 2006.

YOUNG-ADULT FICTION; UNDER PSEUDONYM DANIEL PARKER

Trent, HarperTrophy (New York, NY), 2000.
Trust Falls (first novel in "Wessex" trilogy; supernatural fiction), Avon Books (New York, NY), 2002.
Fallout (second novel in "Wessex" trilogy; supernatural fiction), Avon Books (New York, NY), 2002.
Outsmart (third novel in "Wessex" trilogy; supernatural fiction), Avon Books (New York, NY), 2002.

"COUNTDOWN" SERIES; YOUNG-ADULT FANTASY FICTION; UNDER PSEUDONYM DANIEL PARKER

January, Aladdin Paperbacks (New York, NY), 1998.
February, Aladdin Paperbacks (New York, NY), 1999.
March, Aladdin Paperbacks (New York, NY), 1999.
April, Aladdin Paperbacks (New York, NY), 1999.
May, Aladdin Paperbacks (New York, NY), 1999.
June, Aladdin Paperbacks (New York, NY), 1999.
July, Aladdin Paperbacks (New York, NY), 1999.
August, Aladdin Paperbacks (New York, NY), 1999.
September, Aladdin Paperbacks (New York, NY), 1999.
October, Aladdin Paperbacks (New York, NY), 1999.
November, Aladdin Paperbacks (New York, NY), 1999.
December, Aladdin Paperbacks (New York, NY), 1999.

"WATCHING ALICE" SERIES; YOUNG-ADULT FICTION; UNDER PSEUDONYM DANIEL PARKER; WITH LEE MILLER

Break the Surface, Razorbill (New York, NY), 2004.
Walk on Water, Razorbill (New York, NY), 2004.
Seek the Prophet, Razorbill (New York, NY), 2004.
Find the Miracle, Razorbill (New York, NY), 2005.

Sidelights

Daniel Ehrenhaft is a prolific author of young-adult fiction who has penned tales ranging from the supernatural to mysteries to comedies and thrillers. Under the pen name Daniel Parker, for instance, he published the "Countdown" series about teenagers battling the Demon Lilith after a plague has killed off everyone over twenty years of age. The somewhat more realistic young adult novel *The Last Dog on Earth* is about a troubled teen named Logan, who finds comfort through the love of his dog. A mysterious plague is killing dogs around the world, however, and the disease can be passed along to people. Trying to protect his pet from murderous vigilantes, Logan flees his home and runs into his biological father, a scientist who has developed a vaccine for the disease. However, his father requires a dog who is immune to the disease to finish his work, and it turns out that Logan's pet is just such a dog. As a *Publishers Weekly* critic wrote, "If the bittersweet ending stretches credibility, this is still a smartly written, thoroughly engrossing tale." In the *Journal of Adolescent & Adult Literacy,* Rachel Seftel observed that the novel is basically "a traditional boy-and-his-dog story" that is weakened by its subplots and "somewhat heavy-handed" foreshadowing. However, Seftel concluded that the tale is "an interesting and absorbing variation on this somewhat conventional theme."

Ehrenhaft often employs situational comedy and humorous characters in his stories, even when they deal with serious themes. In *10 Things to Do before I Die,* for example, Ted Burger believes he has been fatally poisoned by a psychotic fast-food cook. The teen resolves to fulfill all his life goals in a single day, but his plans go humorously awry. *Kliatt* contributor Paula Rohrlick appreciated the realistic narrative and the main character's "self-deprecating" sense of humor, adding that the story is "lively fun." Francisca Goldsmith, writing in *School Library Journal,* considered the characters to be "engaging and likable."

Tell It to Naomi is the story of Dave Rosen, who writes an advice column for his high-school newspaper. When the paper's editor does not believe Dave could write with such a feminine voice, the sophomore attributes the column to his older sister, Naomi, an unemployed journalist. The advice column causes quite a stir, and might even help Dave win over the heart of a girl he loves from afar. The subterfuge eventually falls apart to reveal the truth, however, in "a typical and timeless story about a teenager and his unfulfilled love," as Daniela Kostadinovska described it in the *Journal of*

Adolescent & Adult Literacy. A *Publishers Weekly* contributor praised the "snappy dialogue and an impeccable sense of timing." "Hilarious, honest, and raw" is how Gillian Engberg characterized the novel in *Booklist,* while *Kliatt* writer Claire Rosser dubbed *Tell It to Naomi* "fun entertainment."

In a unique blend of mystery and graphic novel, *Drawing a Blank; or, How I Tried to Solve a Mystery, End a Feud, and Land the Girl of My Dreams* features Carlton Dunne, the son of a wealthy man who has been kidnapped. Resolving to rescue his father, Carlton must journey to Scotland and discover the meaning behind an old family feud. There he meets a mysterious woman who promises to help him. Carlton, who enjoys drawing comic books, turns her into a superheroine in an illustrated tale that in many ways parallels the plot in the main novel. A *Publishers Weekly* critic felt that the parallel comic book tale could have done more "to carry the plot points instead of simply mirroring the events of the narrative" but still found the book a "fun, light read." In *Kliatt,* Rohrlick considered it a "lighthearted entertainment." In *Booklist,* Carolyn Phelan concluded that *Drawing a Blank* is "a fresh, effervescent combination of mystery, adventure, and teen angst."

The After Life features another teenager, Will, who goes on an unexpected adventure. He has just learned about his biological father, who has left him a two-million-dollar inheritance provided Will can drive his father's car from Miami to New York City. The problem is that Will does not yet know how to drive. What follows is a wild road trip in which the characters indulge in drugs and alcohol while working through mixed emotions about their parents. "Readers will almost certainly feel compelled to finish this surreal trip, even if, at the end, they are nearly as exhausted as the protagonists," declared a *Publishers Weekly* reviewer.

Biographical and Critical Sources

PERIODICALS

Booklist, March 15, 2001, Carolyn Phelan, review of *Marc Andreessen: Web Warrior,* p. 1396; September 15, 2004, Gillian Engberg, review of *Tell It to Naomi,* p. 232; November 1, 2004, Debbie Carton, review of *10 Things to Do before I Die,* p. 475; May 1, 2006, Carolyn Phelan, review of *Drawing a Blank; or, How I Tried to Solve a Mystery, End a Feud, and Land the Girl of My Dreams,* p. 42.
Journal of Adolescent & Adult Literacy, November, 2003, Rachel Seftel, review of *The Last Dog on Earth,* p. 274; February, 2005, Daniela Kostadinovska, review of *Tell It to Naomi,* p. 440; April, 2005, Sara Ann Schettler, review of *10 Things to Do before I Die,* p. 624.
Kirkus Reviews, December 1, 2002, review of *The Last Dog on Earth,* p. 1767; May 15, 2004, review of *Tell It to Naomi,* p. 490; November 1, 2004, review of *10*

Things to Do before I Die, p. 1044; May 1, 2006, review of *Drawing a Blank,* p. 456; September 1, 2006, review of *The After Life,* p. 902.

Kliatt, May, 2004, Claire Rosser, review of *Tell It to Naomi,* p. 18; November, 2004, Paula Rohrlick, review of *10 Things to Do before I Die,* p. 8; May, 2006, Paula Rohrlick, review of *Drawing a Blank,* p. 8; September, 2006, Paula Rohrlick, review of *10 Things to Do before I Die,* p. 21.

Publishers Weekly, January 27, 2003, review of *The Last Dog on Earth,* p. 260; June 28, 2004, review of *Tell It to Naomi,* p. 51; June 5, 2006, review of *Drawing a Blank,* p. 65; October 30, 2006, review of *The After Life,* p. 63.

School Library Journal, July, 2001, Mary Mueller, review of *Marc Andreessen,* p. 122; December, 2001, Yapha Nussbaum Mason, review of *Larry Ellison: Sheer Nerve,* p. 153; February, 2003, Mary Ann Carcich, review of *The Last Dog on Earth,* p. 141; August, 2004, Angela M. Boccuzzi, review of *Tell It to Naomi,* p. 120; November, 2004, Francisca Goldsmith, review of *10 Things to Do before I Die,* p. 142; June, 2006, Francisca Goldsmith, review of *Drawing a Blank,* p. 154.

ONLINE

Armchair Interviews Web site, http://www.armchair interviews.com/ (February 14, 2007), Jenny Salyers, review of *Drawing a Blank.*

Daniel Ehrenhaft Home Page, http://www.danielehrenhaft. com (February 14, 2007).

YA Books Central Web site, http://www.yabookscentral. com/ (February 14, 2007), "Daniel Ehrenhaft."*

*   *   *

FIEDLER, Lisa

Personal

Female.

Addresses

Home—Monroe, CT.

Career

Writer.

Writings

YOUNG ADULT NOVELS

Curtis Piperfield's Biggest Fan, Clarion Books (New York, NY), 1995.

Lucky Me, Clarion Books (New York, NY), 1998.

The Case of the Cheerleading Camp Mystery, HarperEntertainment (New York, NY), 2000.

Mary-Kate and Ashley Starring in Switching Goals, HarperEntertainment (New York, NY), 2000.

Dating Hamlet: Ophelia's Story, Holt (New York, NY), 2002.

Know-It-All, Simon Pulse (New York, NY), 2002.

Romeo's Ex: Rosaline's Story, Holt (New York, NY), 2006.

Sidelights

Lisa Fiedler has written many novels for young adult readers, including some that take liberties with the classic dramas of William Shakespeare. In *Dating Hamlet: Ophelia's Story,* Fiedler retells Shakespeare's classic tragedy, *Hamlet,* from the point of view of Hamlet's love, Ophelia. She used the same approach to create another unique tale in *Romeo's Ex: Rosaline's Story,* which recounted the story of *Romeo and Juliet* from the perspective of one of Romeo's former girlfriends.

Fiedler created an original, contemporary heroine in her first novel, *Curtis Piperfield's Biggest Fan,* and its sequel, *Lucky Me.* The character is Cecily "C.C." Caruthers, an aspiring writer who attends a Catholic girls' school. C.C., who narrates both novels, is sincerely interested in her faith and spirituality, but she is also keenly interested in boys. In the first book, C.C. is in the ninth grade. She worries about enjoying kissing too much, struggles to express herself in her poetry, and relates it all in a voice that is "outrageous, irreverent, and also serious," according to Hazel Rochman in *Booklist.* Rochman found Fiedler's debut to be a "hilarious" book. C.C.'s story continued in *Lucky Me,* which continues on immediately after the events recounted in *Curtis Piperfield's Biggest Fan.* The themes are slightly more mature in this book, as is C.C. However, she still proves to be "an engaging commentator on the social life of young teens," and is both thought-provoking and funny, according to Lauren Adams in a review for *Horn Book.* Rochman, in another *Booklist* review, found the sequel to be "candid and hilarious."

Fiedler took considerable liberties with a Shakespearian classic with *Dating Hamlet.* In the Bard's original drama, Hamlet's love, Ophelia, is generally considered a weak and passive character, one who ends by committing suicide. In contrast, Fiedler's Ophelia is clear-thinking, strong-willed, and devoted to life. Her suicide is not even real, merely a staged event to help Hamlet avenge his father's murder. Fiedler uses excerpts of dialog from the real play and interweaves them with her own, and her additions are "aptly full of the wordplay Shakespeare's Hamlet is so fond of," according to Jennifer M. Brabander in *Horn Book.* Brabander felt that the "inventive" story will draw readers in and pique their interest in Shakespeare's original play, but she also believed that those dedicated to Shakespeare's version of the story would also enjoy and benefit from *Dating Hamlet.* "Those who have read *Hamlet* will get more from this book than those who have not," in the opinion of *Kliatt* reviewer Claire Rosser, who described Fiedler's novel as "a comedy, turning the tragedy of Hamlet upside down." Rosser also praised the author's inventive mingling of modern and Shakespearian language and her clever reinterpretation of classic lines from the play. "This is quite a lot of fun," Rosser concluded.

In *Romeo's Ex*, Fiedler takes the same approach as she did in *Dating Hamlet*. The narrator is Rosaline, a cousin of Juliet Capulet, who was briefly pursued by Romeo Montague. Having seen what disasters love can lead to, Rosaline has decided to remain chaste. She wants to focus on her career instead. Like *Dating Hamlet*, this story turns the original on its head, and freely uses new characters and interpretations to create a very different story, while at the same time incorporating much of the classic dialog and plotline. It is "extremely useful for students struggling with a first reading of Shakespeare's work," stated Johanna Lewis in *School Library Journal*. Claire Rosser, in a review for *Kliatt*, found Fiedler's revision of the tragedy to be funny and "often moving," and also recommended it as complementary to the study of Shakespeare's classic. *Romeo's Ex* was also recommended by a *Kirkus Reviews* writer, who credited Fiedler with "giving the timeless tale enough twists to engross Shakespearean fans and novices alike."

Biographical and Critical Sources

PERIODICALS

Booklist, September 15, 1995, Hazel Rochman, review of *Curtis Piperfield's Biggest Fan*, p. 152; November 15, 1998, Hazel Rochman, *Lucky Me*, p. 580; September 15, 2002, Hazel Rochman, review of *Dating Hamlet: Ophelia's Story*, p. 226; September 15, 2006, Ilene Cooper, review of *Romeo's Ex: Rosaline's Story*, p. 69.

Horn Book, November, 1998, Lauren Adams, review of *Lucky Me*, p. 727; January-February, 2003, Jennifer M. Brabander, review of *Dating Hamlet*, p. 70.

Kirkus Reviews October 15, 2002, review of *Dating Hamlet*, p. 1529; September 1, 2006, review of *Romeo's Ex*, p. 902.

Kliatt, November, 2002, Claire Rosser, review of *Dating Hamlet*, p. 9; September, 2006, Claire Rosser, review of *Romeo's Ex*, p. 10.

Publishers Weekly, November 25, 2002, review of *Dating Hamlet*, p. 69; October 16, 2006, review of *Romeo's Ex*, p. 55.

School Library Journal, November, 2002, Betsy Fraser, review of *Dating Hamlet*, p. 164; February, 2004, Nancy Menaldi-Scanlan, review of *Dating Hamlet*, p. 83; November, 2006, Johanna Lewis, review of *Romeo's Ex*, p. 134.*

*   *   *

FLEISCHMAN, Albert Sidney See FLEISCHMAN, Sid

FLEISCHMAN, Sid 1920- (Max Brindle, Albert Sidney Fleischman, Carl March)

Personal

Born March 16, 1920, in Brooklyn, NY; son of Reuben and Sadie Fleischman; married Betty Taylor, January 25, 1942; children: Jane, Paul, Anne. *Education:* San Diego State College (now University), B.A., 1949. *Hobbies and other interests:* Magic, gardening.

Addresses

Home—Santa Monica, CA.

Career

Writer for children and adults. Worked as a magician in vaudeville and night clubs, 1938-41; traveled with Mr. Arthur Bull's Francisco Spook Show (magic act), 1939-40; *Daily Journal*, San Diego, CA, reporter and rewrite man, 1949-50; *Point* (magazine), San Diego, associate editor, 1950-51; full-time writer, 1951—. Author of scripts for television show *3-2-1 Contact*, 1979-82. *Military service:* U.S. Naval Reserve, 1941-45; served as yeoman on destroyer escort in the Philippines, Borneo, and China.

Member

Authors Guild, Authors League of America, Writers Guild of America West, Society of Children's Book Writers and Illustrators.

Awards, Honors

Children's Spring Book Festival Honor Book, *New York Herald Tribune*, and Honor Book designation, *Boston Globe/Horn Book*, both 1962, both for *Mr. Mysterious & Company;* Spur Award, Western Writers of America, Southern California Council on Literature for Children and Young People Award, and Junior Book Award, Boys' Clubs of America, all 1964, Recognition of Merit Award, George C. Stone Center for Children's Books, 1972, and Friends of Children and Literature (FOCAL) Award, Los Angeles Public Library, 1983, all for *By the Great Horn Spoon!;* Juvenile Book Award, Commonwealth Club of California, 1966, for *Chancy and the Grand Rascal;* Lewis Carroll Shelf Award, 1969, for *McBroom Tells the Truth;* Children's Spring Book Festival Honor Book designation, *Book World*, and Notable Books selection, American Library Association (ALA), both 1971, both for *Jingo Django;* Southern California Council on Literature for Children and Young People Award, 1972, for "Comprehensive Contribution of Lasting Value to the Literature for Children and Young People"; Golden Kite Honor Book, Society of Children's Book Writers and Illustrators, 1974, for *McBroom the Rainmaker;* Mark Twain Award, Missouri Association of School Libraries, and Charlie May Simon

Sid Fleischman (Photograph by Damon Webster. Courtesy of Sid Fleischman.)

Children's Book Award, Arkansas Elementary School Council, both 1977, and Young Hoosier Award, Association for Indiana Media Educators, 1979, all for *The Ghost on Saturday Night;* National Book Award finalist, and *Boston Globe/Horn Book* Award for Fiction, both 1979, both for *Humbug Mountain;* Newbery Medal, ALA, and Children's Books of the Year selection, Child Study Association of America, both 1987, and Nene Award, 1992, all for *The Whipping Boy;* Paul A. Witty Award, International Reading Association, and Children's Picturebook Award, *Redbook,* 1988, both for *The Scarebird;* Parents Choice Award, 1990, for *The Midnight Horse,* and 1992, for *Jim Ugly;* Jo Osbourn Award for Humor in Children's Literature, 1997; Children's Literature Council of Southern California Award, 1997, for *The Abracadabra Kid;* Charley May Simon Children's Book Award, Arkansas Elementary School Council, and Black-eyed Susan Award (MD), both 1998, and California Young Reader Medal, 1999, all for *The 13th Floor;* John and Patricia Beatty Award, California Library Association, 1999, and FOCAL Award, Los Angeles Public Library, 2002, both for *Bandit's Moon;* Golden Dolphin Award, Southern California Children's Booksellers Association; Literary Fellowship, Magic Castle's Academy of Magical Arts, 2002; establishment of Sid Fleischman Humor Award, Society of Children's Book Writers and Illustrators, 2003.

Writings

FOR CHILDREN AND YOUNG ADULTS

Mr. Mysterious & Company, illustrated by Eric von Schmidt, Little, Brown (Boston, MA), 1962, reprinted, Greenwillow (New York, NY), 1997.

By the Great Horn Spoon!, illustrated by Eric von Schmidt, Little, Brown (Boston, MA), 1963, published as *Bullwhip Griffin,* Avon (New York, NY), 1967.

The Ghost in the Noonday Sun, illustrated by Warren Chappell, Little, Brown (Boston, MA), 1965, illustrated by Peter Sis, Greenwillow (New York, NY), 1989.

Chancy and the Grand Rascal, illustrated by Eric von Schmidt, Little, Brown (Boston, MA), 1966, reprinted, Greenwillow (New York, NY), 1997.

McBroom Tells the Truth, illustrated by Kurt Werth, Norton (New York, NY), 1966, illustrated by Walter Lorraine, Little, Brown (Boston, MA), 1981, illustrated by Amy Wummer, Price Stern Sloan (New York, NY), 1998.

McBroom and the Big Wind, illustrated by Kurt Werth, Norton (New York, NY), 1967, illustrated by Walter Lorraine, Little, Brown (Boston, MA), 1982.

McBroom's Ear, illustrated by Kurt Werth, Norton (New York, NY), 1969, illustrated by Walter Lorraine, Little, Brown (Boston, MA), 1982.

Longbeard the Wizard, illustrated by Charles Bragg, Little, Brown (Boston, MA), 1970.

Jingo Django, illustrated by Eric von Schmidt, Little, Brown (Boston, MA), 1971, reprinted, Dell (New York, NY), 1995.

McBroom's Ghost, illustrated by Robert Frankenberg, Grosset (New York, NY), 1971, illustrated by Walter Lorraine, Little, Brown (Boston, MA), 1981, illustrated by Amy Wummer, Price Stern Sloan (New York, NY), 1998.

McBroom's Zoo, illustrated by Kurt Werth, Grosset (New York, NY), 1972, new edition illustrated by Walter Lorraine, Little, Brown (Boston, MA), 1982.

The Wooden Cat Man, illustrated by Jay Yang, Little, Brown (Boston, MA), 1972.

McBroom's Wonderful One-Acre Farm (includes *McBroom Tells the Truth, McBroom and the Big Wind,* and *McBroom's Ghost*), illustrated by Quentin Blake, Chatto & Windus (London, England), 1972, Greenwillow (New York, NY), 1992.

McBroom the Rainmaker, illustrated by Kurt Werth, Grosset (New York, NY), 1973, new edition illustrated by Walter Lorraine, Little, Brown (Boston, MA), 1982, new edition illustrated by Amy Wummer, Price Stern Sloan (New York, NY), 1999.

The Ghost on Saturday Night, illustrated by Eric von Schmidt, Little, Brown (Boston, MA), 1974, new edition illustrated by Laura Cornell, Greenwillow (New York, NY), 1997.

Mr. Mysterious's Secrets of Magic (nonfiction), illustrated by Eric von Schmidt, Little, Brown (Boston, MA), 1975, published as *Secrets of Magic,* Chatto & Windus (London, England), 1976.

McBroom Tells a Lie, illustrated by Walter Lorraine, Little, Brown (Boston, MA), 1976, new edition illustrated by Amy Wummer, Price Stern Sloan (New York, NY), 1999.

Here Comes McBroom (includes *McBroom Tells a Lie, McBroom the Rainmaker,* and *McBroom's Zoo*), illustrated by Quentin Blake, Chatto & Windus (London, England), 1976, Greenwillow (New York, NY), 1992.

Kate's Secret Riddle Book, F. Watts (New York, NY), 1977.

Me and the Man on the Moon-eyed Horse, illustrated by Eric von Schmidt, Little, Brown (Boston, MA), 1977, published as *The Man on the Moon-eyed Horse,* Gollancz (London, England), 1980.

Humbug Mountain, illustrated by Eric von Schmidt, Little, Brown (Boston, MA), 1978.

Jim Bridger's Alarm Clock and Other Tall Tales, illustrated by Eric von Schmidt, Dutton (New York, NY), 1978.

McBroom and the Beanstalk, illustrated by Walter Lorraine, Little, Brown (Boston, MA), 1978.

The Hey Hey Man, illustrated by Nadine Bernard Westcott, Little, Brown (Boston, MA), 1979.

McBroom and the Great Race, illustrated by Walter Lorraine, Little, Brown (Boston, MA), 1980.

The Bloodhound Gang in the Case of the Flying Clock, illustrated by William Harmuth, Random House/Children's Television Workshop (New York, NY), 1981.

The Bloodhound Gang in the Case of the Cackling Ghost, illustrated by Anthony Rao, Random House (New York, NY), 1981.

The Bloodhound Gang in the Case of Princess Tomorrow, illustrated by Bill Morrison, Random House (New York, NY), 1981.

The Bloodhound Gang in the Case of the Secret Message, illustrated by William Harmuth, Random House (New York, NY), 1981.

The Bloodhound Gang's Secret Code Book, illustrated by Bill Morrison, Random House (New York, NY), 1982.

The Bloodhound Gang in the Case of the 264-Pound Burglar, illustrated by Bill Morrison, Random House (New York, NY), 1982.

McBroom's Almanac, illustrated by Walter Lorraine, Little, Brown (Boston, MA), 1984.

The Whipping Boy, illustrated by Peter Sis, Greenwillow (New York, NY), 1986, reprinted, HarperTrophy (New York, NY), 2003.

The Scarebird, illustrated by Peter Sis, Greenwillow (New York, NY), 1988.

The Ghost in the Noonday Sun, illustrated by Peter Sis, Greenwillow (New York, NY), 1989.

The Midnight Horse, Greenwillow (New York, NY), 1990.

Jim Ugly, illustrated by Joseph A. Smith, Greenwillow (New York, NY), 1992.

The 13th Floor: A Ghost Story, illustrated by Peter Sis, Greenwillow (New York, NY), 1995.

The Abracadabra Kid: A Writer's Life (nonfiction), Greenwillow (New York, NY), 1996.

Bandit's Moon, illustrated by Joseph A. Smith, Greenwillow (New York, NY), 1998.

A Carnival of Animals, illustrated by Marylin Hafner, Greenwillow Books (New York, NY), 2000.

Bo and Mzzz Mad, Greenwillow Books (New York, NY), 2001.

Disappearing Act, Greenwillow Books (New York, NY), 2003.

The Giant Rat of Sumatra; or, Pirates Galore, illustrated by John Hendrix, Greenwillow Books (New York, NY), 2005.

Escape!: The Story of the Great Houdini, Greenwillow Books (New York, NY), 2006.

The White Elephant, illustrated by Robert McGuire, Greenwillow Books (New York, NY), 2006.

The Entertainer and the Dybbuk, Greenwillow Books (New York, NY), 2007.

NOVELS; FOR ADULTS

The Straw Donkey Case, Phoenix Press (New York, NY), 1948.

Murder's No Accident, Phoenix Press (New York, NY), 1949.

Shanghai Flame, Fawcett Gold Medal (New York, NY), 1951.

Look behind You, Lady, Fawcett Gold Medal (New York, NY), 1952, published as *Chinese Crimson,* Jenkins (Austin, TX), 1962.

Danger in Paradise, Fawcett Gold Medal (New York, NY), 1953.

Counterspy Express, Ace Books (New York, NY), 1954.

Malay Woman, Fawcett Gold Medal (New York, NY), 1954, published as *Malaya Manhunt,* Jenkins (Austin, TX), 1965.

Blood Alley, Fawcett Gold Medal (New York, NY), 1955.

Yellowleg, Fawcett Gold Medal (New York, NY), 1960.

The Venetian Blonde, Fawcett Gold Medal (New York, NY), 1963.

SCREENPLAYS

Blood Alley, Batjac Productions, 1955.

Goodbye, My Lady (based on a novel by James Street), Batjac Productions, 1956.

(With William A. Wellman) *Lafayette Escadrille,* Warner Brothers, 1958.

The Deadly Companions (based on his novel *Yellowleg*), Carousel Productions, 1961.

(With Albert Maltz) *Scalawag,* Byrna Productions, 1973.

(Under pseudonym Max Brindle) *The Whipping Boy* (adapted from his novel), Disney, 1994.

OTHER

Between Cocktails, Abbott Magic Company (Colon, MI), 1939.

(Under pseudonym Carl March) *Magic Made Easy,* Croydon (New York, NY), 1953.

The Charlatan's Handbook, L & L Publishing (Tahoma, CA), 1993.

Contributor, Paul Heins, editor, *Crosscurrents of Criticism,* Horn Book (Boston, MA), 1977.

Fleischman's books have been translated into sixteen languages.

Adaptations

By the Great Horn Spoon! was filmed as *Bullwhip Griffin* by Walt Disney, 1967; *The Ghost in the Noonday Sun,* starring Peter Sellers, was filmed by Cavalcade Films, 1974.

Sidelights

Regarded as a master of the tall tale as well as one of the most popular humorists in American children's literature, Sid Fleischman is noted for writing action-filled adventure stories that weave exciting plots, rollicking wit, and joyous wordplay with accurate, well-researched historical facts and characterizations that reveal the author's insight into and understanding of human nature. He is perhaps best known as the author of *The Whipping Boy,* a Newbery Medal-winning story that features a spoiled prince and the stoical lad who takes his punishment, as well as a comic series of tall tales about blustery Iowa farmer Josh McBroom and his amazingly productive one-acre farm. Often compared to such writers as Mark Twain, Charles Dickens, and Leon Garfield, Fleischman has been praised for his ingenuity, vigorous literary style, polished craftsmanship, and keen sense of humor.

Fleischman's works, which often draw on American folklore and are set against historic backdrops such as the California Gold Rush, seventeenth-century piracy, and rural life from Ohio to Vermont, are consistently acknowledged for their diversity of subjects and settings. Formerly a professional magician, Fleischman fills his books with mystery, elements of surprise, and quick-witted characters. As Emily Rhoads Johnson noted in *Language Arts,* Fleischman's young protagonists often embark on quests "for land or treasure or missing relatives," and in doing so "meet up with every imaginable kind of trouble, usually in the form of villains and cut-throats, impostors and fingle-fanglers." In his book *Written for Children,* John Rowe Townsend asserted that, like Garfield, Fleischman "is fond of flamboyant, larger-than-life characters, and of mysteries of origin and identity; a recurrent Fleischman theme is the discovery of a father or father-substitute."

Although he frequently styles his stories as farces, Fleischman underscores his works with a positive attitude toward life and a firm belief in such values as courage, loyalty, and perseverance. The author's love of language—an attribute for which he is often lauded—is evident in the flamboyant names he gives to his characters, his use of wild metaphors and vivid images, and the colorful expressions that dot his stories. As Johnson explained, Fleischman's "words don't just sit there on the page; they leap and cavort, turn somersaults, and sometimes just hang suspended, like cars teetering at the top of a roller coaster." Acknowledged as exceptional to read aloud, Fleischman's works are often considered appropriate choices for reluctant readers.

Reviewers have consistently given Fleischman's books a warm critical reception. Johnson noted in *Language Arts* that the author has "produced some of the funniest books ever for children," while Jane O'Connor claimed in the *New York Times Book Review* that "when it comes to telling whopping tall tales, no one can match Sid Fleischman." Writing in the same publication, Georgess McHargue maintained that Fleischman "can put more action into thirty-two pages than some authors of 'explosive best sellers' can put into seventy-five turgid chapters." Writing in *Horn Book,* Mary M. Burns noted that although Fleischman's books are expectedly funny,

his "transforming setbacks into comic situations and seeing possible triumphs where others with lesser gifts see only disasters . . . [is perhaps] what makes his books so popular." Observing that Fleischman's characters care deeply about each other, Johnson noted, "this . . . is what gives his books their substance and strength. To know Sid Fleischman, in person or through his work, is to experience an affirmation of life."

Born in Brooklyn, New York, Fleischman was raised in San Diego, California. He credits his father Reuben, a Russian Jewish immigrant whom his son described as "an airy optimist with nimble skills," and his mother Sadie, a "crackerjack penny ante card player," with fostering his interest in storytelling. "My earliest literary memories were funny ones," Fleischman wrote in *Horn Book.* Although he recalled his mother reading *Aesop's Fables* and *Uncle Tom's Cabin* to him, the book that affected the future writer most profoundly was *Robin Hood,* which he described as "my first great reading experience, and my favorite of those early years."

As a member of a minority in San Diego due to his Jewish faith, the young Fleischman developed an identity with underdogs. He also developed a strong interest in magic, voraciously reading books on the subject, perfecting tricks to perform, and creating inventions of his own. As a teen, he decided to write a book of his original tricks, *Between Cocktails.* Published when Fleischman was nineteen, the book was still in print a half century later. "When I saw my name on the cover," Fleischman once recalled, "I was hooked on writing books."

After graduating from high school, Fleischman traveled around the country with stage acts such as Mr. Arthur Bull's Francisco Spook Show. His first-hand experience of the last days of vaudeville, traveling in small towns throughout America, gained Fleishman the exposure to folk tales and folk speech that inspired his son, Newbery Award-winning writer Paul Fleischman, to describe his father as a prestidigitator of words" in *Horn Book.* The author himself referred to his own writing as "sleight-of-mind" in an interview with Sybil S. Steinberg in *Publishers Weekly.*

During World War II, Fleischman served in the U.S. Naval Reserve on a destroyer escort in the Philippines, Borneo, and China. In 1942, he married Betty Taylor, with whom he raised his three children: Jane, Paul, and Anne. After the war, Fleischman began writing detective stories, suspense tales, and other pulp fiction for adults, learning "to keep the story pot boiling, to manage tension and the uses of surprise," as he later recalled. In 1949, he graduated from San Diego State College and began working as a reporter for the San Diego *Daily Journal.* A year later, Fleischman was hired on as associate editor of *Point* magazine, a position he held until 1951 when he became a full-time writer.

When his children were young, Fleischman recalled in *Publishers Weekly,* they "didn't understand what I did for a living. So one day I sat down and wrote a story for children and read it to them." This book, *Mr. Mysterious & Company,* which includes Fleischman and his family as characters, became his first published book for children. Describing the warm relationship of the Hackett family, *Mr. Mysterious & Company* includes the concept of Abracadabra Day, an annual event where children are allowed to be as bad as they want to be without fear of reproach. Dorothy M. Broderick wrote in her *New York Times Book Review* appraisal of the book that Abracadabra Day is "a marvelous institution that may well sweep the country." In *Horn Book,* Ruth Hill Viguers called *Mr. Mysterious & Company* "wholly delightful" and added: "It is hard to imagine a child who would not enjoy it."

The central premise of the author's popular "McBroom" series, about an Iowan and his fertile farmland, came to mind while Fleishman was writing *Chancy and the Grand Rascal,* a story about a young boy and his peripatetic uncle that *New York Times Book Review* contributor Jane Yolen dubbed a "perfect blend of one part quest story and two parts tall tale." "For all readers who adore braggadocio and consider Paul Bunyan and Pecos Bill the apogee of American humor," Yolen continued, "*Chancy and the Grand Rascal* is a godsend." While coming up with two tall tales for the book, Fleischman was so amused by his initial invention that he turned it into the first "McBroom" book, *McBroom Tells the Truth.* Although he did not intend to write another story about McBroom, Fleischman went on to pen several more books about the folksy character, a man who entertains young readers by describing a succession of wild impossibilities involving his farm and his eleven offspring. As Zena Sutherland described it in her *Bulletin of the Center for Children's Books* review, "the marvelous McBroom farm" is a place "where instantaneous growth from superfertile soil and blazing Iowa sun provide magnificent crops of food and stories."

Another popular book series by Fleischman features the Bloodhound Gang, a team of three multiethnic junior detectives. Based on Fleischman's scripts for the *3-2-1 Contact* television show, which aired on public television, the "Bloodhound Gang" stories are fast paced, fun-to-solve preteen mysteries that include short chapters filled wit plenty of action. In each book, as Judith Goldberger noted in *Booklist,* "a neatly worked out plot is based on simple, believable gimmicks."

With *The Whipping Boy,* Fleischman departs from his characteristic American settings to write a story that, according to *Horn Book* reviewer Ethel L. Heins, is styled in "the manner of Joan Aiken and Lloyd Alexander" and "set in an undefined time and place." Reminiscent of Mark Twain's *The Prince and the Pauper* and written in a style that harkens back to that of nineteenth-century melodramas, *The Whipping Boy* describes how spoiled Horace—nicknamed Prince Brat because of his behavior—runs away with Jemmy, a street-smart orphan who takes punishments for the

things the prince refuses to do, like learn to read. When the two boys are kidnapped by villains Cutwater and Hold-Your-Nose Billy, they switch identities. After escaping the scoundrels in an exciting chase through a rat-filled sewer, Horace and Jemmy return to the palace as friends: Jemmy has learned to sympathize with the prince's restricted life and admire the boy's courage while realizing his own desire for knowledge, and Horace discovers his personal strength and his ability to change. "Like much of the author's writing," maintained Heins, "beneath the surface entertainment, the story also speaks of courage, friendship, and trust." Janet Hickman, writing in *Language Arts* noted that, in addition to "its lively entertainment value and stylistic polish, [*The Whipping Boy*] . . . has much to say about human nature and the vagaries of justice." Writing in the *New York Times Book Review,* Martha Saxton deemed the book "a good, rollicking adventure," and Frances Bradburn wrote in the *Wilson Library Bulletin* that "the importance of education, the true meaning of friendship, and the need for understanding and compassion for all people are. . . . such an integral part of the story that there would be no story without them."

The initial idea for *The Whipping Boy* was inspired by historical research Fleischman was doing for another book, and it took almost ten years to write. In his Newbery Medal acceptance speech, as printed in *Horn Book,* Fleischman explained: "I stumbled across the catapulting idea for *The Whipping Boy.* . . . I checked the dictionary. 'A boy,' it confirmed, 'educated with a prince and punished in its stead.'" Fleischman thought he could write the book quickly, but "after about eighteen months I was still trying to get to the bottom of page five." Eventually, he realized the problem. "My original concept for the story was wrong," he explained. "Wrong, at least, for me. I saw *The Whipping Boy* as a picture book story." One day he read over the manuscript and discovered that his work needed to be much longer: "Once I took the shackles off, the story erupted. Scenes, incidents, and characters came tumbling out of a liberated imagination. Within a few months, I had it all on paper." When told that *The Whipping Boy* had won the Newbery Medal, Fleischman was elated. "I don't happen to believe in levitation, unless it's done with mirrors, but for a few days I had to load my pockets with ballast. The Newbery Medal is an enchantment. It's bliss. It should happen to everyone."

Following *The Whipping Boy,* Fleischman published *The Scarebird,* which contains illustrations by Peter Sis, an artist who has also provided the pictures for several of the author's other works. *The Scarebird* describe how Lonesome John, a man whose sole companion is the scarecrow in his yard, slowly makes friends with Sam, an orphan looking for work who comes to John's farm. In her review in the *Bulletin of the Center for Children's Books,* Betsy Hearne stated that, "in a period of thin picture books, this has much to teach about the substance of story and the complement of illustration."

With *The Midnight Horse,* Fleischman returns to the adventure story genre with what Ethel R. Twichell described in *Horn Book* as "a mixture of tall tale, folktale, and downright magic." Fleishman's story outlines how Touch, an orphan boy who comes to the small New Hampshire town of Cricklewood and ultimately reclaims his rightful inheritance from his wicked great-uncle with the help of a ghostly magician. "The enjoyment of the book," Twichell concluded, "lies in Fleischman's exuberant narrative flow and his ingenuity in dispatching his scoundrels." A *Publishers Weekly* critic called *The Midnight Horse* a "deftly told tale of innocence and villainy."

Fleischman's novel *Jim Ugly* is a parody set in the American West that includes such thinly disguised film stars of the early twentieth century as Mary Pickford, Douglas Fairbanks, Mae West, and W.C. Fields. In this story, twelve-year-old Jake discovers that the father he thought he had buried is, in fact, alive and an accused thief. Meanwhile, with his father's dog—an animal that is actually part wolf—as companion, Jake and Jim Ugly travel by baggage car from town to town, trying to escape a villainous bounty hunter. In a review of *Jim Ugly* for the *Bulletin of the Center for Children's Books,* Zena Sutherland wrote that Fleischman's "lively, clever, and humorous" novel "must have been as much fun to write as it is to read," and *School Library Journal* contributor Katherine Bruner added that, "with a little silent-movie piano accompaniment, this rollicking parody of Western melodrama would effortlessly unfold across any stage."

With *The 13th Floor: A Ghost Story* Fleischman makes his first contribution to the time-travel genre of fantasy literature. In this work, twelve-year-old Buddy and his lawyer-sister Liz are left penniless when their parents are killed in a plane crash. Liz disappears after meeting a client on the thirteenth floor of an old building, and the client turns out to be the siblings' ghostly ancestor, a young girl who had been accused of witchcraft in Puritan Boston. When Buddy goes after Liz, he is taken by magic elevator to a pirate ship captained by another ancestor. After being cast adrift, he is reunited with Liz, who defends—and acquits—ten-year-old Abigail in court. At the end of the book, the siblings return safely to the twentieth century with a valuable treasure in hand. As a *Publishers Weekly* critic advised: "Hold on to your hats—there's never a dull moment when Fleischman is at the helm." In *Horn Book* Ann A. Flowers described the book as "an easy, light-hearted adventure," noting that Fleischman's informative "author's note also points out the serious consequences of ignorance and superstition."

With *Bandit's Moon,* Fleischman spins a tale of a Mexican bandit and an orphan girl who live during the California Gold Rush. Annyrose Smith is left in the care of a man who turns out to be less than honorable. Disguised as a boy, she makes her escape, only to be swept up by the outlaw band of legendary Joaquin Murrieta.

Murrieta, it turns out, is badly in need of someone to teach him how to read, and he protects the young girl to that end. For her part, Annyrose is shocked by the behavior of the robber gang. Then she learns about the wrongs done to Murrieta and other Mexicans at the hands of the whites. Fleischman's plot includes his characteristic combination of fast pace and twists and turns, leading readers to a surprise ending. Writing in *School Library Journal,* Marlene Gawron called *Bandit's Moon* "classic Sid Fleischman: a quick read, with lots of twists, wonderful phrasing, historical integrity, and a bit of the tall tale thrown in." Calling the novel more than just "thundering hooves and gunfire," a *Publishers Weekly* contributor added that Fleischman "expertly crafts a fictionalized tale that takes a clear-eyed look at bigotry and racism, while steering away from the twin pitfalls of pedantry and sermonizing." Similarly, *Horn Book* contributor Ann A. Flowers concluded that the author managed to "clothe issues of loyalty and honesty in a roaring adventure story, smartly written and chock full of humor and derring-do."

A Carnival of Animals is a compilation of a half-dozen tall tales about the effects on various animals of a tornado that hits Barefoot Mountain. In "The Windblown Child," for example, a strange pink creature is blown in with the tornado; she turns out to be a hairless sheep whose fleece has been whisked away to take the place of missing hair on a bald farmer. "Emperor Floyd" tells of a rooster who develops a peculiar affliction as a result of the storm, and in "Stumblefrog," the amphibian in question gets jumping fever after eating the contents of a sack of Mexican jumping beans, torn open by the tornado. A reviewer for *Publishers Weekly* noted that "the glee with which [Fleischman] relates his outrageous yarns is infectious." In *Booklist* Gillian Engberg had similar praise for the stories, commenting that, "as usual, Fleischman writes about the fantastic and absurd with a captivating balance of casual assuredness and precise detail." Grace Oliff, reviewing the collection in *School Library Journal,* called Fleischman "a master of the tall tale."

Animals are also featured in Fleischman's picture book *The White Elephant.* With artwork by Robert McGuire, the book introduces a young elephant trainer named Run-Run, who lives in Siam where he works with ageing pachyderm Walking Mountain in removing stumps from farmer's fields. When Walking Mountain incurs the anger of a petulant prince, Run-Run is burdened with a white elephant who, while requiring the best of food, is prohibited from working. Fortunately, the white elephant, Sahib, is drawn to the older elephant and mimics its efforts pulling stumps from the ground. Although Run-Run worries that the prince will discover that his gift of Sahib is being misused, nature intervenes and Sahib ultimately proves his worth. While noting that *The White Elephant* features a slow-moving plot, a *Publishers Weekly* contributor praised Fleischman for creating "a rewarding portrayal of friendship and loyalty." In *Horn Book,* Robin Smith wrote that "the short chapters, evocative pencil sketches, and rich Siamese setting" in *The White Elephant* "will easily hold the interest of readers and listeners alike."

Returning to the novel with *Bo and Mzzz Mad,* Fleischman serves up another "classic . . . tale," according to a contributor for *Publishers Weekly.* When twelve-year-old Bo Gamage's parents die, the orphaned boy decides to visit long-lost relatives living in the Mojave Desert. Arriving in Queen of Sheba, California, Bo finds that the town is little more than a retired movie set, and its only residents are his relatives. A former actor in Westerns, great-uncle Charlie—alias Paw Paw—is now a full-time grump. Other relatives include an aunt and a cousin, Madeleine, a girl who prefers to call herself Mzzz Mad and who takes an immediate dislike to her new relative. Aunt Juna is the only one to take any interest in Bo; she talks him into tricking Paw Paw with a fake treasure map in order to restore the unhappy man's flagging spirits. The map is antiqued to mimic an old map showing the location of a gold mine that played a part in the family's original misfortunes. When a gang of modern bandits arrive in town, Bo and his feuding relatives get more adventure than they expected, and ultimately they team up and work together to survive. "The narrative speeds along with enough plot twists to keep readers flipping pages," observed Steve Clancy in a *School Library Journal* review of *Boo and Mzzz Mad.* A contributor to *Publishers Weekly* described the novel as a "thumping good page-turner spiced with humor, snappy descriptions . . . and a lickety-split plot," the critic noting that Fleischman seems to be "in top form." For a *Horn Book* critic, the novel is "a light-as-cotton-candy concoction," and *Booklist* critic Stephanie Zvirin pronounced it a "quick, enjoyable read that will fly off the shelves."

Orphans and adventure also figure in the plot of *Disappearing Act.* In this novel by Fleischman, Kevin and Holly Kidd have just lost their archaeologist mother in an earthquake in Mexico. When their home in Albuquerque, New Mexico, is subsequently targeted by burglars, the siblings suspect that someone is stalking them. Fleeing to Southern California, Kevin and Holly find a new home near the Venice boardwalk and rename themselves Gomez. Kevin becomes Pepe and takes up fortune-telling on the boardwalk, while his older sister, a fledgling opera singer, becomes Chickadee. The teens slowly establish themselves in this strange new life, making friends with such local characters as a juggling medical student, a human mannequin, a screenwriter with a penchant for bugs, and a benevolent landlady. Holly eventually lands a role in a production of *La Bohème,* but when the stalker from New Mexico shows up, all is put into jeopardy again.

In *Booklist* John Peters wrote that in *Disappearing Act* Fleischman mixes "themes both comic and serious" and is able to pull together the manifold plot lines of "his twisty, nail-biter to an untidy, but satisfying, conclusion." Other critics found that the novel's cast of sec-

Cover of Fleischman's middle-grade novel Disappearing Act, *featuring characteristically quirky artwork by Jane Wattenberg.* (Illustration © 2003 by Jane Wattenberg. Reproduced by permission of Jane Wattenberg and BookStop Literary Agency. All rights reserved.)

ondary characters is the primary draw of *Disappearing Act.* Betty Carter, writing in *Horn Book,* observed that the book "paints vivid character sketches" even as it "fails to sustain a coherent plot." For *School Library Journal* contributor Steven Engelfried, the "characters and the setting are the main draws," although "Fleischman neatly frames the conclusion into something more thoughtful and meaningful" than a mere potboiler. A critic for *Kirkus Reviews* also praised "the colorful assemblage of secondary characters," concluding of *Disappearing Act:* "Realistic fiction it's not, but good, quick, and smart fun—definitely."

Fleischman draws on the history of European Jewry in *The Entertainer and the Dybbuk.* In the novel, World War II is now over, but Freddie, an American ventriloquist and former GI, has remained on the continent and is performing his act throughout postwar Europe. Suddenly, Freddie becomes aware of the spiritual presence of Avrom Poliakov, a Jewish victim of the Holocaust. While Avrom, with his quick wit, helps Freddie improve his on-stage act, the spirit also has a mission. Possessed by the young ghost (or dybbuk), Freddie sets to work tracking down the Nazi colonel responsible for

Avrom's death, as well as the deaths of hundreds of other Jewish children. Noting the novel's serious themes, John Peters wrote in *Booklist,* that "Avrom's wisecracking will counterbalance matter-of-fact accounts of Nazi cruelty for young readers." Still, Peters added, more mature readers "will best appreciate the novel's eloquent 'inner voice' of conscience," and appreciate the sometimes horrible details Fleischman includes regarding the one and a half million Jewish children who were killed during the Holocaust. While Paula Rohrlick wrote in *Kliatt* that Avrom's "repartee with Freddie . . . is often very funny and affecting," she added that *The Entertainer and the Dybbuk* "mingles horror and humor," serving young readers as an "excellent and unusual addition to YA Holocaust literature." Noting that the novel stands out from "the plethora of mostly depressing Holocaust children's and YA literature," a *Kirkus Reviews* writer added that Fleischman's book is "quick, creative, clever and thoroughly entertaining."

The Abracadabra Kid: A Writer's Life is Fleischman's autobiography for young readers. Considered as lively and eminently readable as his fiction, the book includes personal information on the author as well as advice on writing; each chapter is introduced with quotes from children's letters to the author, ends with a cliff-hanging episode from Fleischman's eventful life, and features black-and-white family photographs. "Fleischman is a pro," asserted Betsy Hearne in her review of the book for the *Bulletin of the Center of Children's Books,* "and it shows in this autobiography as much as it does in his fiction." A *Kirkus Reviews* contributor claimed that Fleischman "offers a gold mine of interesting reflections of writing" from one who has "lived adventurously and thoughtfully." Mary J. Arnold, reviewing the book in *Kliatt,* called *The Abracadabra Kid* an "engaging memoir that serves as proof positive that writing flows from life experience." For Arnold, Fleischman's autobiographical sketch is "non-stop funny and entertaining," while in *Voice of Youth Advocates* Candace Deisley commented that "the reader is rewarded with an appreciation for the author's art, and spurred with the desire to read more of his works." Carolyn Phelan, writing in *Booklist,* concluded of the book that, "from cover to cover," *The Abracadabra Kid* serves up "a treat" to Fleischman's young fans.

"Novels are written in the dark," Fleischman commented in an essay for *Children's Books and Their Creators.* "At least mine are. Unlike many sensible authors, I start Chapter One with rarely a notion of the story that's about to unfold. It's like wandering down a pitch-black theater and groping around for the lights. One by one the spots and floodlights come on, catching a character or two against a painted backdrop. I sit back and enjoy the show. When the final curtain falls a year or two later, the stage is ablaze with lights, and I have a new novel."

Biographical and Critical Sources

BOOKS

Beacham's Guide to Literature for Young Adults, Volume 4, Beacham Publishing (Osprey, FL), 1990, Volume 11, Gale (Detroit, MI), 2001.

Cameron, Eleanor, *The Green and Burning Tree,* Atlantic/ Little, Brown (Boston, MA), 1969.

Children's Books and Their Creators, edited by Anita Silvey, Houghton Mifflin (Boston, MA), 1995.

Meigs, Cornelia, and others, editors, *A Critical History of Children's Literature,* revised edition, Macmillan (New York, NY), 1969.

St. James Guide to Children's Writers, fifth edition, St. James Press (Detroit, MI), 1999.

Townsend, John Rowe, *Written for Children: An Outline of English Language Children's Literature,* revised edition, Lippincott (Philadelphia, PA), 1974.

PERIODICALS

Booklist, September 15, 1976, Barbara Elleman, review of *McBroom Tells a Lie,* p. 174; April 15, 1981, Judith Goldberger, review of *The Bloodhound Gang in the Case of the Cackling Ghost* and *The Bloodhound Gang in the Case of Princess Tomorrow,* p. 1159; September 1, 1996, Carolyn Phelan, review of *The Abracadabra Kid: A Writer's Life,* p. 126; March 1, 1999, Sally Estes, review of *Bandit's Moon,* p. 1212; September 1, 2000, Gillian Engberg, review of *A Carnival of Animals,* p. 113; May 15, 2001, Stephanie Zvirin, review of *Bo and Mzzz Mad,* p. 1750; June 1, 2003, John Peters, review of *Disappearing Act,* pp. 1774-1775; February 1, 2005, Michael Cart, review of *The Giant Rat of Sumatra; or, Pirates Galore,* p. 957; September 1, 2006, Hazel Rochman, review of *The White Elephant,* p. 125; September 1, 2007, John Peters, review of *The Entertainer and the Dybbuk,* p. 114.

Bulletin of the Center for Children's Books, May, 1970, Zena Sutherland, review of *McBroom's Ear,* p. 143; September, 1988, Betsy Hearne, review of *The Scarebird,* pp. 6-7; March, 1992, Zena Sutherland, review of *Jim Ugly,* p. 179; October, 1995, p. 53; September, 1996, Betsy Hearne, review of *The Abracadabra Kid,* pp. 11-12; September 1, 2000, Gillian Engberg, review of *A Carnival of Animals, p. 113;* May 15, 2001, Stephanie Zvirin, review of *Bo and Mzzz Mad,* 1750; October, 2007, Elizabeth Bush, review of *The Entertainer and the Dybbuk,* p. 83.

Horn Book, June, 1962, Ruth Hill Viguers, review of *Mr. Mysterious & Company,* p. 279; May-June, 1986, Ethel L. Heins, review of *The Whipping Boy,* pp. 325-326; July-August, 1987, Sid Fleischman, "Newbery Medal Acceptance," pp. 423-428; July-August, 1987, Paul Fleischman, "Sid Fleischman," pp. 429-432; November-December, 1990, Ethel R. Twichell, review of *The Midnight Horse,* p. 744; November-December, 1995, Ann A. Flowers, review of *The 13th Floor: A Ghost Story,* pp. 741-742; November-December, 1996, Mary M. Burns, review of *The Abracadabra Kid,* p.

759; November, 1998, Ann A. Flowers, review of *Bandit's Moon,* p. 728; May, 2001, review of *Bo and Mzzz Mad,* p. 323; May-June, 2003, Betty Carter, review of *Disappearing Act,* p. 345; March-April, 2005, Betty Carter, review of *The Giant Rat of Sumatra,* p. 200; July-August, 2006, Betty Carter, review of *Escape@: The Story of the Great Houdini,* p. 463; November-December, 2006, Robin Smith, review of *The White Elephant,* p. 708.

Kirkus Reviews, October 1, 1972, review of *McBroom's Zoo,* p. 1144; July 1, 1996, review of *The Abracadabra Kid,* p. 967; March 1, 2003, review of *Disappearing Act,* p. 383; February 1, 2006, review of *The Giant Rat of Sumatra,* p. 176; June 15, 2006, review of *Escape!,* p. 632; September 15, 2006, review of *The White Elephant,* p. 952; August 1, 2007, review of *The Entertainer and the Dybbuk.*

Kliatt, September, 1998, Mary J. Arnold, review of *The Abracadabra Kid,* p. 35; January, 2005, Paula Rohrlick, review of *The Giant Rat of Sumatra,* p. 8; September, 2007, Paula Rohrlick, review of *The Entertainer and the Dybbuk,* p. 11.

Language Arts, 1982, Emily Rhoads Johnson, "Profile: Sid Fleischman," pp. 754-759; December, 1986, Janet Hickman, review of *The Whipping Boy,* p. 822.

New York Times Book Review, May 13, 1962, Dorothy M. Broderick, review of *Mr. Mysterious & Company,* p. 30; November 6, 1966, Jane Yolen, review of *Chancy and the Grand Rascal,* p. 40; September 11, 1977, Jane O'Connor, review of *Me and the Man on the Moon-eyed Horse,* p. 32; January 20, 1980, Georgess McHargue, review of *The Hey Hey Man,* p. 30; February 22, 1987, Martha Saxton, review of *The Whipping Boy,* p. 23.

Publishers Weekly, February 27, 1978, Sybil S. Steinberg, "What Makes a Funny Children's Book?: Five Writers Talk about Their Method," pp. 87-90; August 10, 1990, review of *The Midnight Horse,* p. 445; October 9, 1995, review of *The 13th Floor,* p. 86; August 3, 1998, review of *Bandit's Moon,* p. 86; August 28, 2000, review of *A Carnival of Animals,* p. 83; March 26, 2001, review of *Bo and Mzzz Mad,* p. 94; February 21, 2005, review of *The Giant Rat of Sumatra,* p. 176; July 10, 2006, review of *Escape!,* p. 83; November 6, 2006, review of *The White Elephant,* p. 61; September 24, 2007, review of *The Entertainer and the Dybbuk,* p. 73.

Reading Teacher, April, 1998, review of *The Ghost on Saturday Night,* pp. 588-589; October, 1999, review of *McBroom Tells the Truth,* p. 178; June-July, 2003, review of *Disappearing Act,* p. 32.

Reading Today, June-July, 2003, Lynne T. Burke, review of *Disappearing Act,* p. 32.

School Library Journal, April, 1992, Katherine Bruner, review of *Jim Ugly,* pp. 113-114; September, 1998, Marlene Gawron, review of *Bandit's Moon,* pp. 200-202; October 2000, Grace Oliff, review of *A Carnival of Animals,* p. 124; May, 2001, Steve Clancy, review of *Bo and Mzzz Mad,* p. 149; May, 2003, Steven Engelfried, review of *Disappearing Act,* pp. 150; August, 2006, Vicki Reutter, review of *Escape!,* p. 136; October, 2006, Lee Bock, review of *The White Elephant,*

p. 110; August, 2007, Elaine E. Knight, review of *The Entertainer and the Dybbuk,* p. 116.

Voice of Youth Advocates, April, 1997, Candace Deisley, review of *The Abracadabra Kid,* pp. 52, 54.

ONLINE

Sid Fleischman Home Page, http://www.sidfleischman. com (December 15, 2007).

OTHER

Good Conversation!: A Talk with Sid Fleischman (video), Tina Podell Productions, 2006.*

*   *   *

FOREST, Heather 1948-

Personal

Born September 19, 1948, in Newark, NJ; daughter of Manny (a teacher) and Fay (a nurse) Friedman; married Lawrence Foglia, September 27, 1981; children: Lucas, Laurel. *Education:* Douglass College, B.A. (art), 1970; East Tennessee State University, M.A. (storytelling), 2000; Antioch College, Ph.D. (leadership and change), 2007. *Politics:* Democrat. *Religion:* Jewish.

Addresses

Office—Story Arts, P.O. Box 354, Huntington, NY 11743. *E-mail*—heather@storyarts.org.

Career

Storyteller, beginning 1974; Story Arts Inc., Long Island, NY, executive director, 1975—.

Member

National Storytelling Association.

Awards, Honors

Notable Record Award, American Library Association, 1982, for *Songspinner;* Parents' Choice Gold Classic Award, 1993, for *Eye of the Beholder,* and Gold Award, 1994, for *The Animals Could Talk;* Storytelling World Anthology awards, 1996, for *Wonder Tales from around the World,* and 1997, for *Wisdom Tales from around the World;* Storytelling World Award, for recording *World Tales of Wisdom and Wonder*; Circle of Excellence Award, 1997, National Storytelling Association; Best Children's Books of the Year citation, Bank Street College of Education, for *Stone Soup*; American Bookseller Pick of the Lists citation, for *A Big Quiet House.*

Writings

RETELLER

The Baker's Dozen: A Colonial-American Tale, illustrated by Susan Gaber, Harcourt (New York, NY), 1980.

Heather Forest (Photograph by Peter Scheer. Reproduced by permission.)

The Woman Who Flummoxed the Fairies: An Old Tale from Scotland, illustrated by Susan Gaber, Harcourt (New York, NY), 1980.

Earthsong, Joyful Noise (Norwich, VT), 1988.

Wonder Tales from around the World, illustrated by David Boston, August House (Little Rock, AR), 1995.

Wisdom Tales from around the World: Fifty Gems of Story and Wisdom from Such Diverse Traditions as Sufi, Zen, Taoist, Christian, Jewish, Buddhist, African, and Native American, August House (Little Rock, AR), 1997.

A Big Quiet House: A Yiddish Folktale from Eastern Europe, illustrated by Susan Greenstein, August House (Little Rock, AR), 1997.

Stone Soup, illustrated by Susan Gaber, August House (Little Rock, AR), 1998.

Feathers: A Jewish Tale from Eastern Europe, illustrated by Marcia Cutchin, August House (Little Rock, AR), 2005.

The Little Red Hen: An Old Fable, illustrated by Susan Gaber, August House (Little Rock, AR), 2006.

The Contest between the Susn and the Wind, illustrated by Susan Gaber, August House (Augusta, GA), 2008.

RECORDINGS

Songspinner: Folktales and Fables Sung and Told, Weston Woods (Weston, CT), 1982.

Tales of Womenfolk, Weston Woods (Weston, CT), 1985.

Sing Me a Story, A Gentle Wind (Albany, NY), 1986.

Tales around the Hearth, A Gentle Wind (Albany, NY), 1989.

Eye of the Beholder, Yellow Moon Press (Boston, MA), 1990.

The Animals Could Talk: Aesop's Fables, August House (Little Rock, AR), 1994.

Wonder Tales, August House (Little Rock, AR), 1995.

Sidelights

Storyteller Heather Forest has entertained both young and old listeners for dozens of years with her retellings of stories from around the world. Through recordings as well as in books for young children such as *The Woman Who Flummoxed the Fairies: An Old Tale from Scotland, Stone Soup,* and *Wonder Tales from around the World,* Forest has expanded her audience to library story hours and "read me a story" bed times alike with tales that contain "phrasing and imagery [that] are consistently vivid," according to *School Library Journal* contributor Lee Bock. Her written stories contain "the same smooth, appealing cadence that she uses in her live performances," Susan Scheps noted in a review of *The Baker's Dozen: A Colonial-American Tale* for *School Library Journal,* the critic adding that "each comma and phrase [is] carefully placed to create a musical whole." In addition to her own story-telling, Forest has also founded Story Arts, a storytelling organization that presents concerts and workshops.

Forest became interested in storytelling while learning to play folk guitar as a teen. As she noted on her Story Arts Web site, she "especially enjoyed ballads because they had a plot," and when she began writing her own songs in her early twenties, she looked to the traditional ballad form for inspiration. She also turned to the folktale section of her local library for stories to set to music, and discovered that she "could wander the world reading plots from cultures around the globe and create songs out of them." From writing songs, Forest soon began to craft spoken tales, inspired by traditional stories that contained "a sense of familiarity . . . as though it was really about something that happened to me. Or maybe there was something I needed to learn from the tale. Maybe it healed me. Maybe it made me face myself, by telling it again and again. There is a freeing anonymity and at the same time, a revealing vulnerability in telling a folktale."

Since Forest began telling stories in the mid-1970s, invitations to perform have come from all over the country: "from concert halls to circus tents, to elementary school auditoriums," as the storytelling author once told *SATA.* She has been a featured storyteller at Jonesborough, Tennessee's National Storytelling Festival several times, and has also appeared at the Smithsonian Institute and the Museum of Modern Art, as well as at Edinburgh, Scotland's Festival Fringe, Austria's World Festival of Fairytales, and Rio de Janeiro's "Telebration." "As a storytelling artist, I am attracted to tell folk tales

Susan Gaber creates illustrations for Forest's **The Baker's Dozen,** ***which sets its entertaining story in a colorful and cozy kitchen.*** (Harcourt Brace & Company, 1988. Illustration ©1988 by Susan Gaber. Reproduced by permission.)

and fables from around the world that contain a kernel of wisdom passed down through the oral tradition," Forest once explained. "Spanning time and place, these ancient tales have a universality which is fresh and relevant in modern times. Although [their]. . . .plots . . .

come from diverse cultures, a common thread of joys, sorrows, hopes, dreams, and fears emerge as the colorful tapestry of human experience is presented in metaphor. In spite of our global differences, people everywhere share the same sky."

Forest combines a number of her retellings in larger collections such as *Wonder Tales from around the World* and its companion volume, *Wisdom Tales from around the World: Fifty Gems of Story and Wisdom from Such Diverse Traditions as Sufi, Zen, Taoist, Christian, Jewish, Buddhist, African, and Native American.* Each award-winning volume contains brief retellings meant for reading aloud and arranged by region of origin. *Wonder Tales from around the World* includes twenty-seven tales from around the globe, each of which is accompanied by Forest's source notes. The tales feature a repeating phrase to make it easy for audiences to join in with the storyteller in a group environment. Janice Del Negro, writing for *Booklist,* considered the collection "a good resource for storytelling and comparative research." *Wisdom Tales from around the World* features fifty tales, fables, and parables, both familiar and less-well-known. Noting both the humor and diversity of the cultures included, Karen Morgan predicted in *Booklist* that Forest's collection is "bound to please."

Other books contain only a single story. In *The Baker's Dozen,* for example, Forest describes the origins of the thirteen-item "baker's dozen," which takes readers back to New York City during the mid-1700s. A prominent baker who specializes in cookies shaped like St. Nicholas learns a bit about the Christmas spirit after he refuses to give one extra cookie to a mysterious customer who can only afford a dozen. When the customer returns the following year, a run of bad luck has made the baker realize what his stinginess has cost him; he gives her the thirteenth cookie free, completing the "baker's dozen."

Another stand-alone tale, *The Woman Who Flummoxed the Fairies,* retells a Scottish story about a sweet-toothed king of the fairies and the woman who outsmarts him. "Forest's graceful retelling perfectly captures the story's fairy-tale flavor," wrote Diane Roback in a *Publishers Weekly* review of the book. In *A Big Quiet House: A Yiddish Folktale from Eastern Europe,* Forest illustrates a clever solution to the problem of a complaining spouse who finds the house too small: slowly fill the home to overflowing with a host of noisy animals, then take the animals away and peace, quiet, and space are gained! In this version of the Yiddish tale "It Could Always Be Worse," Forest "hams up her telling with intermittent rhymes and refrains," noted another *Publishers Weekly,* who added that *A Big Quiet House* "invit[es] audience participation." Hazel Rochman, writing in *Booklist,* commented in particular on Forest's "rhythmic storytelling voice." Another Jewish folktale is the basis for *Feathers: A Jewish Tale from Eastern Europe.* The story, about the difficulty of taking back gossip once it has started, features a rabbi who releases all the feathers from a feather pillow into the wind, and instructs a gossiping woman to gather them all back. The story is "an entertaining tale, ably retold, with a timeless lesson" according to Lee Bock in *School Library Journal.*

Gaber and Forest again team up to create a new version of a traditional tale in **The Little Red Hen.** (August House LittleFolk, 2006. Illustration © 2006 by Susan Gaber. Reproduced by permission.)

A retelling of a familiar story, *Stone Soup,* finds two hungry travelers refused food when they stop at a small village. Finally, they convince the less-than-generous villagers that they can make soup from a stone. With contributions of various vegetables from curious—and hungry—onlookers, a wonderful collaborative soup is the result. Forest's "simple, direct telling is enhanced by the addition of several folkloric-style rhymes," noted *Booklist* contributor Kay Weisman. A reviewer for *Publishers Weekly* added that the author's "jolly prose simmers with energy. . . . Flavorful and nutritious, this classic tale is served up with a smile." The fable of *The Little Red Hen* shows that hard work should be valued. While in most accounts of this tale, the Little Red Hen is the only character who does any work, Feather's retelling offers the other animals a chance to redeem themselves and join in the work. Using one of the tale's repeated refrains, a *Kirkus Reviews* contributor asked, "Who will help read and enjoy this story? Everyone."

Forest lives with her family on a tree and perennial flower farm on Long Island, New York "As well as writing books, I share stories with over 40,000 children each year in the Long Island area in schools and community settings," the author/storyteller once explained to *SATA.* "I also travel to storytelling festivals and theaters throughout the United States to present my repertoire of world folk tales told in a minstrel style which interweaves original music, poetry, prose, and the sung and spoken word."

Biographical and Critical Sources

PERIODICALS

Booklist, May 15, 1995, Sandy Doggett, review of *The Animals Could Talk: Aesop's Fables,* p. 1662; November 15, 1995, Janice Del Negro, review of *Wonder Tales from around the World,* p. 551; October 1, 1996, Hazel Rochman, review of *A Big Quiet House: A Yiddish Folktale from Eastern Europe,* p. 353; March 1, 1997, Karen Morgan, review of *Wisdom Tales from around the World: Fifty Gems of Story and Wisdom from Such Diverse Traditions as Sufi, Zen, Taoist, Christian, Jewish, Buddhist, African, and Native American,* p. 1157; September 1, 1998, Kay Weisman, review of *Stone Soup,* p. 121.

Bulletin of the Center for Children's Books, February, 1997, review of *Wisdom Tales from around the World,* p. 204.

Kirkus Reviews, October 1, 2005, review of *Feathers,* p. 1079; September 15, 2006, review of *The Little Red Hen,* p. 953.

Publishers Weekly, March 16, 1990, Diane Roback, review of *The Woman Who Flummoxed the Fairies: An Old Tale from Scotland,* p. 68; October 7, 1996, review of *A Big Quiet House,* p. 74; December 2, 1996, review of *Wisdom Tales from around the World,* p. 62; May 25, 1998, review of *Stone Soup,* p. 89.

School Library Journal, December, 1983, "Heather Forest: Songspinner—Folktales and Fables Sung and Told," p. 47; April, 1989, Susan Scheps, review of *The Baker's Dozen: A Colonial-American Tale,* p. 96; June, 1990, Luann Toth, review of *The Woman Who Flummoxed the Fairies,* p. 112; April, 1996, Lee Bock, review of *Wonder Tales from around the World,* p. 144; November, 1996, Linda Greengrass, review of *A Big Quiet House,* p. 97; April, 1997, Judy Sokoll, review of *Wisdom Tales from around the World,* p. 169; May, 1998, Kathleen Whalin, review of *Stone Soup,* pp. 131-132; October, 2005, Lee Bock, review of *Feathers,* p. 138; November, 2006, Kathy Krasniewicz, review of *The Little Red Hen,* p. 120.

Voice of Youth Advocates, June, 1997, review of *Wisdom Tales from around the World,* p. 128.

ONLINE

August House Web site, http://www.augusthouse.com/ (December 3, 2007), "Heather Forest."

New England Library Association Web site, http://www.nelib.org/ (December 3, 2007), "Heather Forest."

Story Arts Web site, http://www.storyarts.org/ (December 2, 2007), "Heather Forest."

University of Calgary Web site, http://www.ucalgary.ca/ (December 2, 2007), "Heather Forest."

FRADIN, Dennis
See FRADIN, Dennis Brindell

* * *

FRADIN, Dennis Brindell 1945-
(Dennis Fradin)

Personal

Born December 20, 1945, in Chicago, IL; son of Myron (an accountant) and Selma Fradin; married Judith Bloom (an educator and author), March 19, 1967; children: Anthony, Diana, Michael. *Education:* Northwestern University, B.A., 1967; University of Illinois, graduate study, 1968. *Religion:* Jewish.

Addresses

Home—Evanston, IL. *E-mail*—yudiff@aol.com.

Career

Writer.

Awards, Honors

Flora Stieglitz Straus Award, Bank Street College of Education, Children's Books of Distinction Award, *Riverbank Review,* and *Smithsonian* Book of the Year designation, all 2001, all for *Ida B. Wells: Mother of the Civil Rights Movement;* Nonfiction Children's Book of the Year Award, Society of Midland Authors, 2001, for *Bound for the North Starlaves;* Golden Kite Honor Book for Nonfiction, Society of Children's Book Writers and Illustrators, 2004, and Carter G. Woodson Award, American Library Association, 2005, both for *The Power of One: Daisy Bates and the Little Rock Nine.*

Writings

FOR CHILDREN

Cara (fiction), Children's Press (Chicago, IL), 1977.

Cave Painter, Children's Press (Chicago, IL), 1978.

Bad Luck Tony, illustrated by Joanne Scribner, Prentice-Hall (Englewood Cliffs, NJ), 1978.

North Star, illustrated by William Neebe, Children's Press (Chicago, IL), 1978.

The New Spear, illustrated by Tom Dunnington, Children's Press (Chicago, IL), 1979.

Beyond the Mountain, beyond the Forest, illustrated by John Maggard, Children's Press (Chicago, IL), 1979.

Young People's Stories of Our States, Children's Press (Chicago, IL), 1980.

How I Saved the World (science fiction), Dillon Press (Minneapolis, MN), 1986.

Dennis Brindell Fradin (Photograph by Judith Bloom Fradin. Reproduced by permission.)

Remarkable Children: Twenty Who Changed History, Little, Brown (Boston, MA), 1987.

Medicine: Yesterday, Today, and Tomorrow, Enslow (Hillside, NJ), 1989.

Amerigo Vespucci, F. Watts (New York, NY), 1991.

The Nina, the Pinta, and the Santa Maria, F. Watts (New York, NY), 1991.

"We Have Conquered Pain": The Discovery of Anesthesia, McElderry Books (New York, NY), 1996.

Louis Braille: The Blind Boy Who Wanted to Read, Silver Press (Parsippany, NJ), 1997.

Maria de Sautuola: The Bulls in the Cave, Silver Press (Parsippany, NJ), 1997.

Mary Anning, the Fossil Hunter, Silver Press (Parsippany, NJ), 1997.

The Planet Hunters: The Search for Other Worlds, McElderry Books (New York, NY), 1997.

Searching for Alien Life: Is Anyone out There?, Twenty-First Century Books (New York, NY), 1997.

Sacagawea: The Journey to the West, Silver Press (Parsippany, NJ), 1998.

Samuel Adams: The Father of American Independence, Clarion Books (New York, NY), 1998.

Is There Life on Mars?, McElderry Books (New York, NY), 1999.

Bound for the North Star: True Stories of Fugitive Slaves, Clarion Books (New York, NY), 2000.

(With wife, Judith Bloom Fradin) *Ida B. Wells: Mother of the Civil Rights Movement,* Clarion Books (New York, NY), 2000.

My Family Shall Be Free! The Life of Peter Still, Harper-Collins (New York, NY), 2001.

(With Judith Bloom Fradin) *Who Was Sacagawea?,* Grosset & Dunlap (New York, NY), 2002.

Who Was Ben Franklin?, Grosset & Dunlap (New York, NY), 2002.

The Signers: The Fifty-six Stories behind the Declaration of Independence, Walker (New York, NY), 2002.

Who Was Thomas Jefferson?, Grosset & Dunlap (New York, NY), 2003.

Nicolaus Copernicus: The Earth Is a Planet, Mondo (New York, NY), 2003.

(With Judith Bloom Fradin) *Fight On!: Mary Church Terrell's Battle for Integration,* Clarion (New York, NY), 2003.

(With Judith Bloom Fradin) *The Power of One: Daisy Bates and the Little Rock Nine,* Clarion (New York, NY), 2004.

Let It Begin Here! Lexington and Concord: First Battles of the American Revolution, Walker (New York, NY), 2005.

The Founders: The Thirty-nine Stories behind the U.S. Constitution, Walker (New York, NY), 2005.

(With Judith Bloom Fradin) *Jane Addams: Champion of Democracy,* Clarion (New York, NY), 2006.

(With Judith Bloom Fradin) *5,000 Miles to Freedom: Ellen and William Craft's Flight from Slavery,* National Geographic (Washington, DC), 2006.

With a Little Luck: Surprising Stories of Amazing Discoveries, Dutton (New York, NY), 2006.

Tell Us a Tale, Hans! The Life of Hans Christian Andersen, Mondo (New York, NY), 2006.

(With Judith Bloom Fradin) *Volcanoes,* National Geographic (Washington, DC), 2007.

(With Judith Bloom Fradin) *Hurricanes,* National Geographic (Washington, DC), 2007.

Duel!: Burr and Hamilton's Deadly War of Words, illustrated by Larry Day, Walker (New York, NY), 2008.

(With Judith Bloom Fradin) *Earthquakes: Witness to Disaster,* National Geographic (Washington, DC), 2008.

"WORDS AND PICTURES" SERIES; UNDER NAME DENNIS FRADIN

Illinois in Words and Pictures, illustrated by Richard Wahl, Children's Press (Chicago, IL), 1976.

Virginia in Words and Pictures, illustrated by Richard Wahl, Children's Press (Chicago, IL), 1976.

Alaska in Words and Pictures, illustrated by Robert Ulm, Children's Press (Chicago, IL), 1977.

California in Words and Pictures, illustrated by Robert Ulm, Children's Press (Chicago, IL), 1977.

Ohio in Words and Pictures, illustrated by Robert Ulm, Children's Press (Chicago, IL), 1977.

Wisconsin in Words and Pictures, illustrated by Richard Wahl, Children's Press (Chicago, IL), 1977.

Alabama in Words and Pictures, illustrated by Richard Wahl, Children's Press (Chicago, IL), 1980.

Arizona in Words and Pictures, illustrated by Richard Wahl, Children's Press (Chicago, IL), 1980.

Arkansas in Words and Pictures, illustrated by Richard Wahl, Children's Press (Chicago, IL), 1980.

Colorado in Words and Pictures, illustrated by Richard Wahl, Children's Press (Chicago, IL), 1980.

Connecticut in Words and Pictures, illustrated by Richard Wahl, maps by Len Meents, Children's Press (Chicago, IL), 1980.

Delaware in Words and Pictures, illustrated by Richard Wahl, Children's Press (Chicago, IL), 1980.

Florida in Words and Pictures, illustrated by Richard Wahl, Children's Press (Chicago, IL), 1980.

Hawaii in Words and Pictures, illustrated by Richard Wahl, Children's Press (Chicago, IL), 1980.

Idaho in Words and Pictures, illustrated by Richard Wahl, Children's Press (Chicago, IL), 1980.

Indiana in Words and Pictures, illustrated by Richard Wahl, Children's Press (Chicago, IL), 1980.

Iowa in Words and Pictures, illustrated by Richard Wahl, Children's Press (Chicago, IL), 1980.

Kansas in Words and Pictures, illustrated by Richard Wahl, Children's Press (Chicago, IL), 1980.

Maine in Words and Pictures, illustrated by Richard Wahl, Children's Press (Chicago, IL), 1980.

Maryland in Words and Pictures, illustrated by Richard Wahl, Children's Press (Chicago, IL), 1980.

Michigan in Words and Pictures, illustrated by Richard Wahl, Children's Press (Chicago, IL), 1980.

Minnesota in Words and Pictures, illustrated by Richard Wahl, Children's Press (Chicago, IL), 1980.

Mississippi in Words and Pictures, illustrated by Richard Wahl, Children's Press (Chicago, IL), 1980.

Missouri in Words and Pictures, illustrated by Richard Wahl, Children's Press (Chicago, IL), 1980.

Nebraska in Words and Pictures, illustrated by Richard Wahl, Children's Press (Chicago, IL), 1980.

New Jersey in Words and Pictures, illustrated by Richard Wahl, Children's Press (Chicago, IL), 1980.

North Carolina in Words and Pictures, illustrated by Richard Wahl, Children's Press (Chicago, IL), 1980.

Oklahoma in Words and Pictures, illustrated by Richard Wahl, Children's Press (Chicago, IL), 1980.

Oregon in Words and Pictures, illustrated by Richard Wahl, Children's Press (Chicago, IL), 1980.

Pennsylvania in Words and Pictures, illustrated by Richard Wahl, Children's Press (Chicago, IL), 1980.

South Carolina in Words and Pictures, illustrated by Richard Wahl, Children's Press (Chicago, IL), 1980.

Tennessee in Words and Pictures, illustrated by Richard Wahl, Children's Press (Chicago, IL), 1980.

Utah in Words and Pictures, illustrated by Richard Wahl, Children's Press (Chicago, IL), 1980.

Vermont in Words and Pictures, illustrated by Richard Wahl, Children's Press (Chicago, IL), 1980.

Washington in Words and Pictures, illustrated by Richard Wahl, Children's Press (Chicago, IL), 1980.

West Virginia in Words and Pictures, illustrated by Richard Wahl, Children's Press (Chicago, IL), 1980.

Wyoming in Words and Pictures, illustrated by Richard Wahl, Children's Press (Chicago, IL), 1980.

Georgia in Words and Pictures, illustrated by Richard Wahl, Children's Press (Chicago, IL), 1981.

Kentucky in Words and Pictures, illustrated by Richard Wahl, Children's Press (Chicago, IL), 1981.

Louisiana in Words and Pictures, illustrated by Richard Wahl, Children's Press (Chicago, IL), 1981.

Massachusetts in Words and Pictures, illustrated by Richard Wahl, Children's Press (Chicago, IL), 1981.

Montana in Words and Pictures, illustrated by Richard Wahl, Children's Press (Chicago, IL), 1981.

Nevada in Words and Pictures, illustrated by Richard Wahl, Children's Press (Chicago, IL), 1981.

New Hampshire in Words and Pictures, illustrated by Richard Wahl, Children's Press (Chicago, IL), 1981.

New Mexico in Words and Pictures, illustrated by Richard Wahl, Children's Press (Chicago, IL), 1981.

New York in Words and Pictures, illustrated by Richard Wahl, maps by Len Meents, Children's Press (Chicago, IL), 1981.

North Dakota in Words and Pictures, illustrated by Richard Wahl, Children's Press (Chicago, IL), 1981.

Rhode Island in Words and Pictures, illustrated by Richard Wahl, maps by Len Meents, Children's Press (Chicago, IL), 1981.

South Dakota in Words and Pictures, illustrated by Richard Wahl, Children's Press (Chicago, IL), 1981.

Texas in Words and Pictures, illustrated by Richard Wahl, Children's Press (Chicago, IL), 1981.

"DISASTER!" SERIES

Volcanoes, Children's Press (Chicago, IL), 1982.

Tornadoes, Children's Press (Chicago, IL), 1982.

Earthquakes, Children's Press (Chicago, IL), 1982.

Fires, Children's Press (Chicago, IL), 1982.

Floods, Children's Press (Chicago, IL), 1982.

Hurricanes, Children's Press (Chicago, IL), 1982.

Blizzards and Winter Weather, Children's Press (Chicago, IL), 1983.

Droughts, Children's Press (Chicago, IL), 1983.

Famines, Children's Press (Chicago, IL), 1986.

"ENCHANTMENT OF THE WORLD" SERIES

The Netherlands, Children's Press (Chicago, IL), 1983.

The Republic of Ireland, Children's Press (Chicago, IL), 1984.

Ethiopia, Children's Press (Chicago, IL), 1988.

"A NEW TRUE BOOK" SERIES

Astronomy, Children's Press (Chicago, IL), 1983.

Archaeology, Children's Press (Chicago, IL), 1983.

Farming, Children's Press (Chicago, IL), 1983.

Movies, Children's Press (Chicago, IL), 1983.

Comets, Asteroids, and Meteors, Children's Press (Chicago, IL), 1984.

Explorers, Children's Press (Chicago, IL), 1984.

Olympics, Children's Press (Chicago, IL), 1984.

Pioneers, Children's Press (Chicago, IL), 1984.

Skylab, Children's Press (Chicago, IL), 1984.
Hailey's Comet, Children's Press (Chicago, IL), 1985.
Moon Flights, Children's Press (Chicago, IL), 1985.
Space Colonies, Children's Press (Chicago, IL), 1985.
Space Lab, Children's Press (Chicago, IL), 1985.
The Voyager Space Probes, Children's Press (Chicago, IL), 1985.
Voting and Elections, Children's Press (Chicago, IL), 1985.
Continents, Children's Press (Chicago, IL), 1986.
Heredity, Children's Press (Chicago, IL), 1987.
Nuclear Energy, Children's Press (Chicago, IL), 1987.
Radiation, Children's Press (Chicago, IL), 1987.
Space Telescope, Children's Press (Chicago, IL), 1987.
The Search for Extraterrestrial Intelligence, Children's Press (Chicago, IL), 1987.
Cancer, Children's Press (Chicago, IL), 1988.
Drug Abuse, Children's Press (Chicago, IL), 1988.
The Cheyenne, Children's Press (Chicago, IL), 1988.
The Declaration of Independence, Children's Press (Chicago, IL), 1988.
The Flag of the United States, Children's Press (Chicago, IL), 1988.
The Pawnee, Children's Press (Chicago, IL), 1988.
The Shoshoni, Children's Press (Chicago, IL), 1988.
The Thirteen Colonies, Children's Press (Chicago, IL), 1988.
Earth, Children's Press (Chicago, IL), 1989.
Pluto, Children's Press (Chicago, IL), 1989.
Uranus, Children's Press (Chicago, IL), 1989.
Jupiter, Children's Press (Chicago, IL), 1989.
Saturn, Children's Press (Chicago, IL), 1989.
Mars, Children's Press (Chicago, IL), 1989.
Venus, Children's Press (Chicago, IL), 1989.
Neptune, Children's Press (Chicago, IL), 1990.
Mercury, Children's Press (Chicago, IL), 1990.

"THE THIRTEEN COLONIES" SERIES

The Virginia Colony, Enslow (Hillsdale, NJ), 1986.
The Massachusetts Colony, Enslow (Hillsdale, NJ), 1987.
The New Hampshire Colony, Enslow (Hillsdale, NJ), 1988.
The New York Colony, Enslow (Hillsdale, NJ), 1988.
The Pennsylvania Colony, Enslow (Hillsdale, NJ), 1988.
The Rhode Island Colony, Enslow (Hillsdale, NJ), 1989.
The Connecticut Colony, Enslow (Hillsdale, NJ), 1990.
The Georgia Colony, Enslow (Hillsdale, NJ), 1990.
The Maryland Colony, Enslow (Hillsdale, NJ), 1990.
The New Jersey Colony, Enslow (Hillsdale, NJ), 1991.
The North Carolina Colony, Children's Press (Chicago, IL), 1991.
The Delaware Colony, Enslow (Hillsdale, NJ), 1992.
The South Carolina Colony, Children's Press (Chicago, IL), 1992.

"COLONIAL PROFILES" SERIES

Abigail Adams: Advisor to a President, illustrated by T. Dunnington, Enslow (Hillsdale, NJ), 1989.
John Hancock: First Signer of the Declaration of Independence, illustrated by T. Dunnington, Enslow (Hillsdale, NJ), 1989.

Anne Hutchinson: Fighter for Religious Freedom, illustrated by T. Dunnington, Enslow (Hillsdale, NJ), 1990.
King Philip: Indian Leader, illustrated by T. Dunnington, Enslow (Hillsdale, NJ), 1990.
Patrick Henry: "Give Me Liberty or Give Me Death," illustrated by T. Dunnington, Enslow (Hillsdale, NJ), 1990.
Hiawatha: Messenger of Peace, Margaret McElderry Books (New York, NY), 1992.

"BEST HOLIDAY BOOKS" SERIES

Columbus Day, Enslow (Hillsdale, NJ), 1990.
Hanukkah, Enslow (Hillsdale, NJ), 1990.
Christmas, Enslow (Hillsdale, NJ), 1990.
Valentine's Day, Enslow (Hillsdale, NJ), 1990.
Halloween, Enslow (Hillsdale, NJ), 1990.
Thanksgiving Day, Enslow (Hillsdale, NJ), 1990.
Lincoln's Birthday, Enslow (Hillsdale, NJ), 1990.
Washington's Birthday, Enslow (Hillsdale, NJ), 1990.

"FROM SEA TO SHINING SEA" SERIES

Georgia, Children's Press (Chicago, IL), 1991.
Illinois, Children's Press (Chicago, IL), 1991.
Massachusetts, Children's Press (Chicago, IL), 1991.
California, Children's Press (Chicago, IL), 1992.
Florida, Children's Press (Chicago, IL), 1992.
Michigan, Children's Press (Chicago, IL), 1992.
(With Judith Bloom Fradin) *Montana,* Children's Press (Chicago, IL), 1992.
New Hampshire, Children's Press (Chicago, IL), 1992.
North Carolina, Children's Press (Chicago, IL), 1992.
South Carolina, Children's Press (Chicago, IL), 1992.
Tennessee, Children's Press (Chicago, IL), 1992.
Texas, Children's Press (Chicago, IL), 1992.
Virginia, Children's Press (Chicago, IL), 1992.
Washington, DC, Children's Press (Chicago, IL), 1992.
Wisconsin, Children's Press (Chicago, IL), 1992.
Alabama, Children's Press (Chicago, IL), 1993.
Alaska, Children's Press (Chicago, IL), 1993.
Arizona, Children's Press (Chicago, IL), 1993.
Colorado, Children's Press (Chicago, IL), 1993.
Iowa, Children's Press (Chicago, IL), 1993.
Kentucky, Children's Press (Chicago, IL), 1993.
New Jersey, Children's Press (Chicago, IL), 1993.
New Mexico, Children's Press (Chicago, IL), 1993.
New York, Children's Press (Chicago, IL), 1993.
Ohio, Children's Press (Chicago, IL), 1993.
Utah, Children's Press (Chicago, IL), 1993.
Vermont, Children's Press (Chicago, IL), 1993.
(With Judith Bloom Fradin) *Arkansas,* Children's Press (Chicago, IL), 1994.
(With Judith Bloom Fradin) *Connecticut,* Children's Press (Chicago, IL), 1994.
(With Judith Bloom Fradin) *Delaware,* Children's Press (Chicago, IL), 1994.
Hawaii, Children's Press (Chicago, IL), 1994.
(With Judith Bloom Fradin) *Indiana,* Children's Press (Chicago, IL), 1994.
Maine, Children's Press (Chicago, IL), 1994.

(With Judith Bloom Fradin) *Maryland,* Children's Press (Chicago, IL), 1994.

Missouri, Children's Press (Chicago, IL), 1994.

(With Judith Bloom Fradin) *North Dakota,* Children's Press (Chicago, IL), 1994.

Pennsylvania, Children's Press (Chicago, IL), 1994.

(With Judith Bloom Fradin) *Washington,* Children's Press (Chicago, IL), 1994.

(With Judith Bloom Fradin) *West Virginia,* Children's Press (Chicago, IL), 1994.

(With Judith Bloom Fradin) *Wyoming,* Children's Press (Chicago, IL), 1994.

Idaho, Children's Press (Chicago, IL), 1995.

(With Judith Bloom Fradin) *Kansas,* Children's Press (Chicago, IL), 1995.

(With Judith Bloom Fradin) *Louisiana,* Children's Press (Chicago, IL), 1995.

(With Judith Bloom Fradin) *Minnesota,* Children's Press (Chicago, IL), 1995.

(With Judith Bloom Fradin) *Mississippi,* Children's Press (Chicago, IL), 1995.

Nebraska, Children's Press (Chicago, IL), 1995.

(With Judith Bloom Fradin) *Nevada,* Children's Press (Chicago, IL), 1995.

(With Judith Bloom Fradin) *Oklahoma,* Children's Press (Chicago, IL), 1995.

(With Judith Bloom Fradin) *Oregon,* Children's Press (Chicago, IL), 1995.

(With Judith Bloom Fradin) *Puerto Rico,* Children's Press (Chicago, IL), 1995.

(With Judith Bloom Fradin) *Rhode Island,* Children's Press (Chicago, IL), 1995.

(With Judith Bloom Fradin) *South Dakota,* Children's Press (Chicago, IL), 1995.

"TURNING POINTS IN AMERICAN HISTORY" SERIES

The Assassination of Abraham Lincoln, Benchmark (New York, NY), 2006.

The U.S. Constitution, Benchmark (New York, NY), 2007.

The Trail of Tears, Benchmark (New York, NY), 2007.

Mayflower Compact, Benchmark (New York, NY), 2007.

Jamestown, Virginia, Benchmark (New York, NY), 2007.

The Emancipation Proclamation, Benchmark (New York, NY), 2007.

The Declaration of Independence, Benchmark (New York, NY), 2007.

Custer's Last Stand, Benchmark (New York, NY), 2007.

The Boston Tea Party, Benchmark (New York, NY), 2007.

The Battle of Gettysburg, Benchmark (New York, NY), 2007.

The Alamo, Benchmark (New York, NY), 2007.

(With Judith Bloom Fradin) *The Lewis and Clark Expedition,* Benchmark (New York, NY), 2007.

The Battle of Yorktown, Benchmark (New York, NY), 2008.

The Boston Massacre, Benchmark (New York, NY), 2008.

The Underground Railroad, Benchmark (New York, NY), 2008.

OTHER

Contributor to periodicals, including *Highlights for Children, Scholastic, St. Anthony Messenger,* and *Chicago Sun-Times.* Some of Fradin's work has also been published in Spanish.

Sidelights

The author of more than two hundred books for young readers, Dennis Brindell Fradin specializes in writing nonfiction titles dealing with historical topics, science, and contemporary discussions of the states of the Union. Contributing to several reference-book series, he examines the territorial makeup of the United States in the "From Sea to Shining Sea" and "Words and Pictures" series, while his books for the "Colonial Profiles" and "Thirteen Colonies" series turn to the nation's political development. With his "Best Holiday Book" series Fradin turns his inquisitive eye to such important days as Christmas and Hanukkah. If such series work were not enough, he has also produced some sixty stand-alone titles dealing with scientific, historical, and biographical topics.

A man who clearly loves his work, Fradin once explained: "I have the time of my life as a children's author. Each day I take about five steps from my bedroom into my office, where I spend my time reading, writing, rewriting, and phoning people for information. Often I travel to do in-person research." In the course of just a couple of weeks in his busy research schedule, for example, he interviewed the ninety-year-old discoverer of the planet Pluto, Clyde Tombaugh, for *The Planet Hunters: The Search for Other Worlds,* and then went to Puerto Rico, where he saw the biggest radio telescope in the world, for a book on the search for extraterrestrial (ET) intelligence. There he talked to a scientist who was taking part in a program listening for signals that ET's may be sending us. "Can you imagine getting to visit places like that and actually making a living at it?" Fradin once remarked. "Every day I'm thrilled when I think that I became what I dreamed of becoming: a children's author."

Born in Chicago, Illinois, in 1945, Fradin started writing in junior high school and learned early on to trust his own instincts. "When I was a freshman in high school," the author once noted, "I wrote a science-fiction story that my English teacher said was the best story by a freshman he had ever seen. But then when I was a junior and showed my English teacher some of my stories, he advised me to forget about becoming an author. That was when I realized that if I wanted to become an author I couldn't live and die by other people's opinions but should do it out of my own desire and need to write." Attending Northwestern University, Fradin majored in creative writing, and went on to do graduate study at the University of Illinois. While in college, he married Judith Bloom, herself a writer and English teacher, and from 1968 to 1979, he worked as an elementary school teacher in the Chicago public schools.

$5.95

from SEA TO SHINING SEA

ARIZONA

Cover of Fradin's nonfiction picture book* Arizona, *which introduces readers to one of the most beautiful states in the American southwest. (Illustration
© 1993 by Scholastic Library Publishing, Inc. Reproduced by permission.)

While working as a school teacher, Fradin finally began to use his writing skills, penning six titles in the "Words and Pictures" series before giving up teaching to become a full-time writer. In these series titles Fradin provides a brief history of each state blended with geography and travelogue in forty-eight pages of text and pictures. Reviewing several titles in the series, Gail L. Gunnesh commented in *School Library Journal* that "the books are easy to follow and comprehend (color photographs and maps help), and there is no other series for beginning readers." Reviewing the Spanish-language version of the books on California and Texas in the same series, another reviewer for *School Library Journal* reiterated the fact that Fradin's books are unique for not only the age group but also the language group.

Publishing largely with Children's Press in Chicago, Fradin soon gained assignments to write for numerous series. His work on the states of the Union led also to his "From Sea to Shining Sea" books. Reviewing one installment, *Hawaii,* Marcia S. Rettig noted in *School Library Journal* that the book presents a "clear and concise overview" containing a "readable text" that "holds readers' interest and provides useful information." Reviewing *Georgia, Illinois,* and *Massachusetts* for *Booklist,* Denise Wilms predicted that the books "will be very useful and especially welcome by middle-grade reluctant readers." Critiquing Fradin's *New York* in the pages of *School Library Journal,* Cheryl Cufari found it to be a "simple overview of the Empire State that includes discussion of its history, industries, sites of interest, and short biographies of prominent New Yorkers."

Focusing on colonial America, Fradin has written books on notable Americans of that era as well as books about each of the original colonies. In *The Pennsylvania Colony,* for example, he manages to include history, personalities, and individual topics such as Native American relations. "This title is a rare treat," wrote Pamela K. Bomboy in a *School Library Journal* review, adding that the author writes "with vigor and strength" to provide "an accurate recollection of those exciting days before independence and statehood." In other works, Fradin tackles the founding of the nation, in one example providing an hour-by-hour account of the confrontations that began the War for Independence in *Let It Begin Here! Lexington and Concord: First Battles of the American Revolution.* The book "presents quick summaries of the two battles, highlighting a few interesting facts and individuals in the exciting narrative," noted Elaine Fort Weischedel in *School Library Journal.*

In *The Signers: The Fifty-six Stories behind the Declaration of Independence* Fradin profiles the men who risked their lives in pursuit of freedom, pairing such celebrated individuals as Thomas Jefferson, John Adams, and Benjamin Franklin with lesser-known figures like Robert Morris, the Revolutionary War's primary

fundraiser, and Oliver Wolcott, who melted down a statue of King George to make bullets. In the words of *New York Times Book Review* contributor Wilborn Hampton, "there are fifty-six stories behind the Declaration, and Fradin turns each into a miniature portrait with background information, anecdotes, family history and personal idiosyncrasies." A companion volume, *The Founders: The Thirty-nine Stories behind the U.S. Constitution,* was described by *Booklist* reviewer GraceAnne A. DeCandido as "another compelling collective biography."

Preparing *Samuel Adams: The Father of American Independence,* Fradin did a large amount of historical research. "For one thing," the author explained, "I read a very-hard-to-find three-volume, 1,000-page biography of Samuel by his great-grandson. The books were so old that the pages crumbled as I read them. Every day when I was done reading I had to get up pieces of the book with a vacuum cleaner! I also visited many historic sites associated with Samuel in the Boston, Massachusetts, area. For example, I tracked down the site where his house once stood and found out that a skyscraper now stands on the spot. I got to the point that I felt Samuel was an old friend. I just loved doing that book." Reviewers responded well to Fradin's enthusiasm about his subject. "Fradin's carefully researched and detailed account . . . does much to clarify the importance of Adams's role in history," wrote Shirley Wilton in a *School Library Journal* review of the biography. Wilton concluded, "This much-needed biography focuses on Samuel Adams as an astute politician, able propagandist, and inspired patriot." Writing in *Booklist,* Carolyn Phelan commented favorably upon Fradin's "unusually personal and readable afterword," noting that, although the author "clearly admires Adams, he doesn't shrink from pointing out the man's flaws." "In this literary portrait," Phelan continued, "Adams emerges as a complex man."

Turning to another of the founding fathers of America, in *Who Was Ben Franklin?* Fradin chronicles the amazingly varied career of a man whose achievements in government, science, and publishing are still considered remarkable. Franklin invented bifocal glasses, the lightning rod, and the Franklin stove. He helped to write the Declaration of Independence and the U.S. Constitution. He served as America's ambassador to France. He founded the country's first public library and first volunteer fire brigade, and established the postal system. "Few historic figures have led a life as varied and interesting," concluded Susan Dove Lempke in *Booklist.* Noting that Franklin's accomplishments are well presented in Fradin's biography, Edward Sullivan wrote in *School Library Journal:* "Fradin's anecdotal presentation describes all of the important contributions and inventions the man gave to the world," resulting in "a fun, informative introductory biography that will inspire many readers to learn more about this fascinating man."

Often collaborating with his wife, Judith Bloom Fradin, who sometimes coauthors the works and does the pic-

Fradin delves into the history of the American Revolution in his picture book **Let It Begin Here!,** *featuring artwork by Larry Day.* (Illustration © 2005 by Larry Day. Reproduced by permission.)

ture research, Fradin is highly professional in his methods. "Each [book] I research extremely carefully and rewrite about five to six times," he once explained. "I also check over all my facts line by line to make sure everything is accurate. So all that keeps me pretty busy. I try not to let a day of the year go by without working. Even when I fly on a plane I'm sure to bring along a book to read, just so the day doesn't go by without me doing any work. Not everything always [goes] smoothly, though. I love colonial history—a topic not too many people seem concerned about today." After all his work on the Adams biography, Fradin initially had trouble placing it, but it was eventually picked up by Clarion and published successfully. "One thing about being a writer," Fradin cautioned, "you often have to keep trying to have success because manuscripts often get rejected." "When I was in school I didn't much like history," Fradin further commented, "but now I *love* history—maybe because I'm so old that I feel I'm part of history."

Slave escapes have also piqued Fradin's curiosity, resulting in the book *Bound for the North Star: True Stories of Fugitive Slaves,* a compilation of over a dozen "compelling narratives of slaves' flight[s] to freedom," as *Horn Book* critic Anita L. Burkam noted, listing among them the story of heroic Harriet Tubman. A critic

for *Publishers Weekly* described the accounts as "riveting," and went on to comment that Fradin's use of such stories "will likely send many readers on to further volumes." *Booklist* critic Hazel Rochman found the book to be an "inspiring history of those who escaped slavery and their rescuers," and also praised Fradin for crafting a "direct" narrative "with no rhetoric or cover-up." Critiquing *Bound for the North Star* in the *New York Times Book Review,* Theodore Rosengarten thought that Fradin's "gifts for concision, for suspenseful pacing and for pushing his story to the edge of plausibility before drawing it back and letting the reader catch a breath make the stories feel new even to someone well versed in the sources."

Fradin tells the story of one slave in *My Family Shall Be Free!: The Life of Peter Still.* In the early nineteenth century, Peter Still and his brother were abandoned in the South when their slave mother escaped and fled North. After enduring some forty years of slavery, Peter himself escaped, found his family again, and raised enough money from lectures he gave about slavery to buy the freedom of his wife and children. Reviewing this title in *Booklist,* Roger Leslie felt that Fradin's book "is an engrossing saga that is both sweeping and intensely personal," and one that "remains strong to the very last page." Toniann Scime, writing in *School Library Journal,* found the same book "compelling."

In collaboration with his wife, Fradin published *5,000 Miles to Freedom: Ellen and William Craft's Flight from Slavery,* which recounts an amazing true story from 1848. By disguising herself as a white man, Ellen Craft, a light-skinned African American, traveled to Boston, bringing with her her husband, William, disguised as her slave. The fugitive couple made their way to England, where they worked for abolitionist causes and eventually returned to the United States in 1869. Patricia Ann Owens, writing in *School Library Journal,* noted that the work "presents the events in [the Crafts'] lives in an exciting, page-turner style that's sure to hold readers' attention."

The Fradins have also produced a biography of the great civil rights leader Ida B. Wells, an outspoken African-American journalist and reformer who was involved in the founding of the National Association for the Advancement of Colored People (NAACP) and who resisted racism of all sorts. *Ida B. Wells: Mother of the Civil Rights Movement* is a book John Peters, writing in *Booklist,* found to be "by far the most moving and complete" of several contemporary biographies. Leah J. Sparks, reviewing the same title in *School Library Journal,* called it a "stellar biography of one of history's most inspiring women," and one that offers "an excellent overview of Wells' life and contributions." Sparks concluded, "The Fradins' compelling book is one that most libraries will want." *Horn Book* contributor Anita L. Burkam called the biography "well-substantiated," and also felt that the Fradins "have remained constant to Wells as a person amidst the history."

In *The Power of One: Daisy Bates and the Little Rock Nine,* the Fradins examine the life of another important civil rights activist. Bates cofounded the *Arkansas State Press,* a weekly newspaper for African Americans, served as president of the Arkansas chapter of the NAACP, and helped counsel the Little Rock Nine, a group of African-American students who braved harassment to integrate Little Rock's Central High School in 1957. Jennifer Mattson, writing in *Booklist,* observed that the couple's "scrupulously documented storytelling and poignant journalistic photos sharply evoke the experiences" of the individuals at the center of the controversy. According to *School Library Journal* critic Jennifer Ralston, the Fradins' "compelling biography clearly demonstrates that one person can indeed make a difference."

The Fradins have also partnered on *Jane Addams: Champion of Democracy,* a biography of the famed humanitarian and peace activist. Addams founded the social settlement Hull House, which provided educational and social services to the needy, on Chicago's West Side in 1889. An outspoken critic of the nation's role in World War I, Addams became the first president of the Women's International League for Peace and Freedom and was awarded the Nobel Peace Prize in 1931. Janet S. Thompson, writing in *School Library Journal,* complimented the authors' ability to establish a context for

their subject's accomplishments, "placing Hull House and the activism of Addams and her friends within the sphere of the history they so clearly influenced." In the words of *Horn Book* contributor Margaret A. Bush, "the Fradins present a complex woman whose ideas are enduring and particularly timely in our day."

Fradin once explained that his favorite kinds of writing are history and science. In the latter category, the author has penned numerous volumes, astronomy and outer space being among his favorite topics. Reviewing his book *Astronomy* in *School Library Journal,* Frances E. Millhouser noted that Fradin uses a "personal style" to introduce the many scientists and their important discoveries in the field, adding information about "current research, theories, and trends." Looking into space, Fradin examines planets as well as comets, the colonizing of space, and the possibility for intelligent life elsewhere in the universe. For young readers, he provides brief overviews of the planets, including the titles *Uranus* and *Jupiter,* which are "very basic introductions to the planets," according to Margaret Chatham in *School Library Journal.* "The familiar format, with large type and lots of color photos, may appeal to reluctant readers who must do a report," Chatham further noted.

In *Nicolaus Copernicus: The Earth Is a Planet* Fradin looks at the fifteenth-century mathematician and astronomer who proposed that the earth revolves around the sun. "Readers will come away grasping the concept of intellectual history," a contributor stated in *Publishers Weekly.* In *The Planet Hunters,* which contains biographies of stargazers from Copernicus and Isaac Newton through Tombaugh of Pluto fame, the author "makes planetary discovery into an intriguing story with a surprising amount of human interest," in the opinion of *Booklist* reviewer Carolyn Phelan.

Fradin has also tackled the question of the existence of other life forms elsewhere in space in several titles. *Is There Life on Mars?* is a "fascinating, well-researched book," according to Linda Wadleigh, writing in *School Library Journal,* as well as a book in which the "author's genuine enthusiasm for his subject is contagious." "This fusion of science, history, and popular culture says at least as much about life on Earth as it does about the red planet," observed Randy Meyer in a *Booklist* review of the same title. For much younger readers, *The Search for Extraterrestrial Intelligence* "fills the gap between the simplest of introductions and more sophisticated, scientific treatments of this intriguing subject," according to *School Library Journal* contributor Ann G. Brouse. Brouse also felt that Fradin's "solid introduction to the topic . . . will lead budding astronomers to more advanced works."

From the laws of the land to the laws of outer space, Fradin has covered a wealth of historical and scientific topics in his works. Writing for both beginning readers and middle graders, he has helped keep young readers informed as well as entertained with his books. "One of the great things about writing is that you can do it at any age," Fradin has remarked. "I plan to be still writing when I'm 100 years old!"

Biographical and Critical Sources

PERIODICALS

Booklist, February 1, 1992, Denise Wilms, reviews of *Georgia, Illinois,* and *Massachusetts,* p. 1023; December 1, 1997, Carolyn Phelan, review of *The Planet Hunters: The Search for Other Worlds,* p. 621; July, 1998, Carolyn Phelan, review of *Samuel Adams: The Father of American Independence,* p. 1877; December 1, 1999, Randy Meyer, review of *Is There Life on Mars?,* p. 698; February 15, 2000, John Peters, review of *Ida B. Wells: Mother of the Civil Rights Movement,* p. 1105; March 1, 2000, Stephanie Zvirin, review of *Ida B. Wells,* p. 1248; January 1, 2001, Hazel Rochman, review of *Bound for the North Star,* p. 950; February 15, 2001, Roger Leslie, review of *My Family Shall Be Free!:The Life of Peter Still,* p. 1147, and Hazel Rochman, review of *Ida B. Wells,* p. 1152; March 1, 2002, Susan Dove Lempke, review of *Who Was Ben Franklin?,* p. 1132; April 1, 2004, Carolyn Phelan, review of *Nicolaus Copernicus: The Earth Is a Planet,* p. 1361; February 1, 2005, Jennifer Mattson, review of *The Power of One: Daisy Bates and the Little Rock Nine,* p. 967; October 15, 2005, GraceAnne A. DeCandido, review of *The Founders: The Thirty-nine Stories behind the U.S. Constitution,* p. 45; March 15, 2006, Hazel Rochman, review of *5,000 Miles to Freedom: Ellen and William Craft's Flight from Slavery,* p. 43; October 15, 2006, GraceAnne A. DeCandido, review of *Jane Addams: Champion of Democracy,* p. 46; January 1, 2007, Carolyn Phelan, review of *Jamestown, Virginia,* p. 88.

Book Report, November-December, 1998, Polly Fanus, review of *Samuel Adams,* p. 63.

Buffalo News, February 13, 2001, review of *My Family Shall Be Free!,* p. N12.

Cobblestone, October, 2005, review of *The Signers: The Fifty-six Stories behind the Declaration of Independence,* p. 45.

Horn Book, May-June, 2000, Anita L. Burkam, review of *Ida B. Wells,* p. 331; January-February, 2001, Anita L. Burkam, review of *Bound for the North Star,* p. 108; March-April, 2005, Roger Sutton, review of *The Power of One,* p. 214; November-December, 2006, Margaret A. Bush, review of *Jane Addams,* p. 732.

Kirkus Reviews, April 1, 2005, review of *Let it Begin Here!: Lexington and Concord. First Battles of the American Revolution,* p. 416; January 1, 2005, review of *The Power of One,* p. 51; October 15, 2006 review of *Jane Addams,* p. 1070.

New York Times Book Review, November 19, 2000, Theodore Rosengarten, review of *Bound for the North Star,* p. 62; September 29, 2002, Wilborn Hampton, review of *The Signers.*

Publishers Weekly, December 13, 1999, review of *Ida B. Wells,* p. 50; November 20, 2000, review of *Bound for the North Star,* p. 69; March 3, 2003, review of *Fight On!,* p. 77; February 16, 2004, review of *Nicolaus Copernicus,* p. 172; November 6, 2006, review of *Jane Addams,* p. 63.

School Library Journal, March, 1981, Gail L. Gunnesh, review of *Arkansas in Words and Pictures,* p. 131; December, 1987, Frances E. Millhouser, review of *Astronomy,* p. 93; January, 1989, Ann G. Brouse, review of *The Search for Extraterrestrial Intelligence,* p. 70; March, 1989, Becky Rosser, review of *The Declaration of Independence,* p. 173; April, 1989, Pamela K. Bomboy, review of *The Pennsylvania Colony,* p. 111; March, 1990, Margaret Chatham, review of *Jupiter and Uranus,* p. 206; February, 1994, Cheryl Cufari, review of *New York,* p. 108; November, 1994, Marcia S. Rettig, review of *Hawaii,* p. 114; July, 1998, Shirley Wilton, review of *Samuel Adams,* p. 105; January, 2000, Linda Wadleigh, review of *Is There Life on Mars?,* p. 144; April, 2000, Leah J. Sparks, review of *Ida B. Wells,* p. 148; November, 2000, Ginny Gustin, review of *Bound for the North Star,* p. 168; April, 2001, Toniann Scime, review of *My Family Shall Be Free!,* p. 158; March, 2002, Edward Sullivan, review of *Who Was Ben Franklin?,* p. 212; June, 2002, Nancy Collins-Warner, review of *Who Was Sacagawea?,* p. 120; May, 2003, Jennifer Ralston, review of *Fight On!,* p. 169; April, 2005, Jennifer Ralston, review of *The Power of One,* p. 150; July, 2005, Elaine Fort Weischedel, review of *Let It Begin Here!,* p. 89; May, 2006, Patricia Anne Owens, review of *5,000 Miles to Freedom,* p. 145; June, 2006, Jodi Kearns, review of *With a Little Luck: Surprising Stories of Amazing Discoveries,* p. 174; November, 2006, Janet S. Thompson, review of *Jane Addams,* p. 158; March, 2007, Esther Keller, review of *The Alamo,* p. 195.

ONLINE

Society of Children's Book Writers and Illustrators Web site, http://www.scbwi.org/ (December 1, 2007), "Judith Bloom Fradin and Dennis Fradin."

Society of Children's Book Writers and Illustrators—Illinois, http://www.scbwi-illinois.org/ (December 1, 2007), "Dennis Fradin."*

*   *   *

FRADIN, Judith Bloom 1945-

Personal

Born January 8, 1945, in Chicago, IL; daughter of Harold J. (a postal supervisor) and Elsie R. (a secretary and homemaker) Bloom; married Dennis Brindell Fradin (a writer), March 19, 1967; children: Anthony, Diana, Michael. *Education:* Northwestern University, B.A., 1967; Northeastern Illinois University, M.A., 1975. *Politics:* "Local." *Religion:* Jewish. *Hobbies and other interests:* "Trying to grow daisies."

Addresses

Home—Evanston, IL. *E-mail*—yudiff@aol.com.

Judith Bloom Fradin (Reproduced by permission of Richard A. Bloom Photography.)

Career

High school English and history teacher, 1967-75 and 1982-90; Northeastern Illinois University, Chicago, writing instructor, 1975-82; photo researcher, 1985—; researcher and writer, 1990—. Author-in-residence, Luther Burbank Elementary School, Chicago, IL. President, Southwest Evanston Associated Residents (SWEAR).

Awards, Honors

With husband, Dennis Brindell Fradin: Flora Stieglitz Straus Award, Bank Street College of Education, Children's Books of Distinction Award, *Riverbank Review,* and *Smithsonian* Book of the Year designation, all 2001, all for *Ida B. Wells;* Golden Kite Honor Book for Nonfiction, Society of Children's Book Writers and Illustrators, 2004, and Carter G. Woodson Award, American Library Association, 2005, both for *The Power of One.*

Writings

WITH HUSBAND, DENNIS BRINDELL FRADIN

Ida B. Wells: Mother of the Civil Rights Movement, Clarion Books (New York, NY), 2000.
Who Was Sacagawea?, Grosset & Dunlap (New York, NY), 2002.

Fight On!: Mary Church Terrell's Battle for Integration, Clarion (New York, NY), 2003.
The Power of One: Daisy Bates and the Little Rock Nine, Clarion (New York, NY), 2004.
Jane Addams: Champion of Democracy, Clarion (New York, NY), 2006.
5,000 Miles to Freedom: Ellen and William Craft's Flight from Slavery, National Geographic (Washington, DC), 2006.
Volcanoes, National Geographic (Washington, DC), 2007.
The Lewis and Clark Expedition, Benchmark (New York, NY), 2007.
Hurricanes, National Geographic (Washington, DC), 2007.
Earthquakes: Witness to Disaster, National Geographic (Washington, DC), 2008.

"FROM SEA TO SHINING SEA" SERIES; WITH DENNIS BRINDELL FRADIN

Montana, Children's Press (Chicago, IL), 1992.
Arkansas, Children's Press (Chicago, IL), 1994.
Connecticut, Children's Press (Chicago, IL), 1994.
Delaware, Children's Press (Chicago, IL), 1994.
Indiana, Children's Press (Chicago, IL), 1994.
Maryland, Children's Press (Chicago, IL), 1994.
North Dakota, Children's Press (Chicago, IL), 1994.
Washington, Children's Press (Chicago, IL), 1994.
West Virginia, Children's Press (Chicago, IL), 1994.
Wyoming, Children's Press (Chicago, IL), 1994.
Kansas, Children's Press (Chicago, IL), 1995.
Louisiana, Children's Press (Chicago, IL), 1995.
Minnesota, Children's Press (Chicago, IL), 1995.
Mississippi, Children's Press (Chicago, IL), 1995.
Nevada, Children's Press (Chicago, IL), 1995.
Oklahoma, Children's Press (Chicago, IL), 1995.
Oregon, Children's Press (Chicago, IL), 1995.
Puerto Rico, Children's Press (Chicago, IL), 1995.
Rhode Island, Children's Press (Chicago, IL), 1995.
South Dakota, Children's Press (Chicago, IL), 1995.

OTHER

Contributor of articles and photographs to *Footsteps* and *Cobblestone.*

Sidelights

Judith Bloom Fradin has partnered with her husband, writer Dennis Brindell Fradin, to create a number of award-winning nonfiction works, including *The Power of One: Daisy Bates and the Little Rock Nine.* A former educator who has taught both high-school and college writing courses, Fradin began her literary career in the 1980s as a researcher for a nonfiction book series her husband was producing on America's thirteen colonies. The Fradins subsequently collaborated on the informational "From Sea to Shining Sea" series. Focusing on the unique history and geography of many states in the union, the series also presents famous people who hail from each state, and the state's current developments and future trends as well.

Fradin once commented that when she and her husband began the "From Sea to Shining Sea" books, she did most of the research and he wrote them. "I spent hours each day in local and university libraries seeking information about recent events in each state. I also gathered biographical material for the 'Famous People' section of each book. Dennis and I often disagreed about which people and events should be included. Finally he said, 'If you think you could do better, why don't you write those sections?'" Since 1994 she has contributed a significant portion of the writing to each of their collaborative projects.

Expanding their writing focus in 2000, the Fradins started penning nonfiction biographical accounts of successful female activists. *Ida B. Wells: Mother of the Civil Rights Movement* was the first such work, and this award-winning biography was followed by *Fight On!: Mary Church Terrell's Battle for Integration.* Drawing on actual diaries, letters, and autobiographical information, as well as on other accumulated research, in *Ida B. Wells* the Fradins convey the passionate crusade of journalist Ida B. Wells as she struggles to fight against the racially segregating Jim Crow laws, which finally came to an end in the 1930s. After her friend was killed by a white mob because his grocery store was apparently too successful, Wells boldly spoke out against the atrocities taking place around her. Because *Ida B. Wells* contains photographs of actual lynching victims, some reviewers found it to be excessively graphic, while others maintained that such pictures convey the severe reality of a brutal period in U.S. history. "This stellar biography of one of history's most inspiring woman offers an excellent overview of Wells' life and contributions," stated Leah J. Sparks in *School Library Journal,* and *Booklist* contributor John Peters wrote: "Of the several recent biographies of this colorful reformer for young readers, this is by far the most moving and complete."

The Fradins made a fresh impact on young readers when they chronicled the fight of integration activist Mary Church Terrell in *Fight On!* Born prior to emancipation, Terrell attended Oberlin College, was the first black woman on the Washington, DC, Board of Education, and dedicated her life to promoting civil rights. At the age of eighty-nine she won a monumental 1953 U.S. Supreme Court decision to desegregate eating places in the nation's capital. As with their biography of Wells, in *Fight On!* the Fradins utilize Terrell's own writings and words to clearly impart the passion behind her crusade, and photographs of the period enhance readers' understanding of the events being discussed. In a *School Library Journal* review, Jennifer Ralston described the book as a "carefully researched" and "inspiring picture of a woman who fought for the rights awarded every American." Calling the work "very readable and handsomely designed," Carolyn Phelan added in *Booklist* that *Fight On!* "presents the life of an educated, energetic, and determined African American woman within the context of her times."

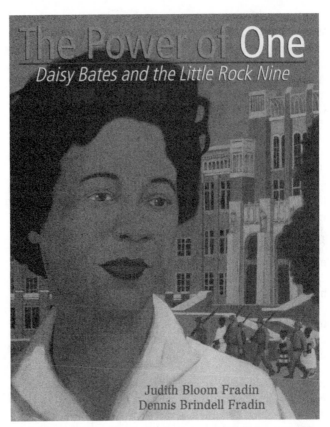

Cover of Fradin's civil-rights-era history **The Power of One,** *featuring artwork by Jim Burke.* (Illustration © 2004 by Jim Burke. Reproduced by permission of Clarion Books, an imprint of Houghton Mifflin Company. All rights reserved.)

In *The Power of One,* the Fradins examine the life of another important civil rights activist. Raised by foster parents after the murder of her birth mother, Daisy Bates cofounded the *Arkansas State Press,* a weekly newspaper for African Americans, served as president of the Arkansas chapter of the National Association for the Advancement of Colored People (NAACP), and helped counsel the Little Rock Nine, a group of black students who braved hatred and insults to integrate Central High School in Little Rock in 1957. *The Power of One* was named a Golden Kite Honor Book for Nonfiction and garnered the Carter G. Woodson Award. Readers will have "a clear-eyed appreciation for the Little Rock Nine's characters and accomplishments," noted a critic in *Kirkus Reviews.* "The Fradins have a lively style . . . and a smooth way of bringing a large cast of persons to life," remarked *Horn Book* contributor Roger Sutton, and Jennifer Mattson observed in her *Booklist* review that "the scrupulously documented storytelling and poignant journalistic photos sharply evoke the experiences" of the individuals at the center of the controversy. According to Ralston, "this compelling biography clearly demonstrates that one person can indeed make a difference."

The Fradins have also teamed up to write *Jane Addams: Champion of Democracy,* a biography of the humanitarian, peace activist, and Nobel Prize winner. A graduate of Rockford Female Seminary, Addams founded the social settlement Hull House on Chicago's West Side in 1889. Hull House provided educational and social services to the needy, including child-care facilities, an employment bureau, and citizenship classes. Addams also played a major role in several national organizations, serving as vice president of the Campfire Girls and voicing her support for the NAACP. A pacifist, Addams attended the International Congress of Women in 1915, hoping to prevent World War I, and later became the first president of the Women's International League for Peace and Freedom. She was awarded the Nobel Peace Prize in 1931. "A fascinating and rich life is related in strong, unfussy prose by the Fradins," noted GraceAnne A. DeCandido in a review of *Jane Addams* for *Booklist,* and Janet S. Thompson wrote in *School Library Journal* that the authors effectively establish a context for their subject's accomplishments by "placing Hull House and the activism of Addams and her friends within the sphere of the history they so clearly influenced." In the words of *Horn Book* contributor Margaret A. Bush, "the Fradins present a complex woman whose ideas are enduring and particularly timely in our day."

In *5,000 Miles to Freedom: Ellen and William Craft's Flight from Slavery* the Fradins recount an incredible true story. In 1848 Ellen Craft, a light-skinned African American, disguised herself as a wealthy white gentleman and traveled by train and steamboat to Boston with her husband, William, who was disguised as her slave escort. The fugitive couple made their way to England, where they worked for abolitionist causes, and eventually returned to the United States in 1869. In *Booklist,* Hazel Rochman praised "the carefully documented narrative," and Patricia Ann Owens, writing in *School Library Journal,* noted that the work "presents the events in [the Crafts'] lives in an exciting, page-turner style that's sure to hold readers' attention."

Biographical and Critical Sources

PERIODICALS

Booklist, February 15, 2000, John Peters, review of *Ida B. Wells: Mother of the Civil Rights Movement,* p. 1105; March 1, 2000, Stephanie Zvirin, review of *Ida B. Wells,* p. 1248; February 15, 2001, Hazel Rochman, review of *Ida B. Wells,* p. 1152; June 1, 2003, Carolyn Phelan, review of *Fight On!: Mary Church Terrell's Battle for Integration,* p. 1789; February 1, 2005, Jennifer Mattson, review of *The Power of One: Daisy Bates and the Little Rock Nine,* p. 967; March 15, 2006, Hazel Rochman, review of *5,000 Miles to Freedom: Ellen and William Craft's Flight from Slavery,* p. 43; October 15, 2006, GraceAnne A. DeCandido, review of *Jane Addams: Champion of Democracy,* p. 46.

Horn Book, May, 2000, Anita L. Burkam, review of *Ida B. Wells,* p. 331; July-August, 2003, Anita L. Burkam, review of *Fight On!,* p. 478; March-April, 2005, Roger

Sutton, review of *The Power of One,* p. 214; November-December, 2006, Margaret A. Bush, review of *Jane Addams,* p. 732.

Kirkus Reviews, January 1, 2005, review of *The Power of One,* p. 51; October 15, 2006 review of *Jane Addams,* p. 1070.

Publishers Weekly, March 3, 2003, review of *Fight On!,* p. 77; November 6, 2006, review of *Jane Addams,* p. 63.

School Library Journal, August, 1995, p. 146; April, 2000, Leah J. Sparks, review of *Ida B. Wells,* p. 148; June, 2002, Nancy Collins-Warner, review of *Who Was Sacagawea?,* p. 120; May, 2003, Jennifer Ralston, review of *Fight On!,* p. 169; April, 2005, Jennifer Ralston, review of *The Power of One,* p. 150; May, 2006, Patricia Anne Owens, review of *5,000 Miles to Freedom,* p. 145; November, 2006, Janet S. Thompson, review of *Jane Addams,* p. 158.

ONLINE

Society of Children's Book Writers and Illustrators Web site, http://www.scbwi.org/ (December 1, 2007), "Judith Bloom Fradin and Dennis Fradin."

Society of Children's Book Writers and Illustrators—Illinois Web site, http://www.scbwi-illinois.org/ (December 1, 2007), "Judith Bloom Fradin."*

*   *   *

FREEDMAN, Claire

Personal

Born in England.

Addresses

Home and office—Essex, England.

Career

Children's writer. Previously worked at Harrods and at British Broadcasting Corporation.

Awards, Honors

Richard & Judy Book Club Award, 2007, for *Aliens Love Underpants!*

Writings

An Ark Full of Activities, HarperCollins UK (London, England), 2001.

Where's Your Smile, Crocodile?, illustrated by Sean Julian, Peachtree (Atlanta, GA), 2001.

Tiggy Tiger: Brave Explorer, illustrated by Cecilia Johansson, Orchard (London, England), 2001, Barron's (Hauppauge, NY), 2002.

Good Night, Sleep Tight, illustrated by Rory Tyger, Harry N. Abrams (New York, NY), 2003.

Gooseberry Goose, Tiger Tales (Wilton, CT), 2003.

Hushabye Lily, illustrated by John Bendall-Brunello, Orchard (New York, NY), 2003.

Night-Night, Emily!, Tiger Tales (Wilton, CT), 2003.

Dilly Duckling, Margaret K. McElderry (New York, NY), 2004.

By My Side, Little Panda, illustrated by Rory Tyger, Tiger Tales (Wilton, CT), 2004.

Oops-a-Daisy!, Tiger Tales (Wilton, CT), 2004.

Snuggle up, Sleepy Ones, illustrated by Tina Macnaughton, Good Books (Intercourse, PA), 2005.

One Magical Morning, illustrated by Louise Ho, Good Books (Intercourse, PA), 2005.

New Kid in Town, illustrated by Kristina Stephenson, Good Books (Intercourse, PA), 2006.

Squabble and Squawk, illustrated by Leonie Shearing, Simon & Schuster UK (London, England), 2006.

A Kiss Goodnight, illustrated by Alison Edgson, Good Books (Intercourse, PA), 2007.

One Magical Day, illustrated by Tina Macnaughton, Good Books (Intercourse, PA), 2007.

Good Night, Sleep Tight, illustrated by Rory Tyger, Tiger Tales (Wilton, CT), 2007.

Aliens Love Underpants, Barron's (Hauppauge, NY), 2007.

I Love You, Sleepyhead, illustrated by Simon Mendez, Good Books (Intercourse, PA), 2008.

Follow That Bear If You Dare!, illustrated by Alison Edgson, Good Books (Intercourse, PA), 2008.

Sidelights

Author Claire Freedman discovered that she had a knack for writing children's books while attending a local writing group in her native England. She began submitting short works to magazine publishers, and in 2001 graduated to children's books when her first picture-book text appeared in *Where's Your Smile, Crocodile?* and *An Ark Full of Activities.* Freedman's work has won her recognition from parents and children alike, as well as earning a Richard & Judy Book Club Award in 2007.

Many of Freedman's picture books utilize animal characters to tell very human stories. In *Where's Your Smile, Crocodile?* Kyle the crocodile wakes up grumpy, and none of his friends are able to cheer him up, no matter how silly they act. When the grouchy Kyle meets a young lion cub who is lost, he tries to cheer the frightened creature up as they search together for the cub's mama lion. In the process, Kyle learns that he had his smile all along. A *Kirkus Reviews* contributor noted the "worthwhile lesson" in the tale, and a *Publishers Weekly* contributor wrote that, while the message is not new, "it's lightly proffered and colorfully imagined."

The young gosling in *Goosberry Goose* also thinks he is missing something: while his friends are all busy getting ready for winter, Gooseberry feels the need to practice flying. Worried, he asks his parents what he should do differently, and they explain that because geese fly south for the winter, he is doing everything right. "Read-

Claire Freedman's engaging characters are brought to life by illustrator Vanessa Cabban in the pages of **Gooseberry Goose.** (Illustration ©2003 by Vanessa Cabban. Reproduced by permission.)

ers will be captivated by this irrepressible gosling's infectious charm," wrote Martha Topol in a *School Library Journal* review of *Goosberry Goose,* and a *Publishers Weekly* contributor had special praise for Freedman's "vivacious and assured storytelling."

Hushabye Lily finds a young rabbit having trouble falling asleep, until the bunny's mother convinces her that all the farm yard noises are part of a lullaby. A *Publishers Weekly* contributor commented on the "lilting prose" Freedman uses in telling her simple tale, and Andrea Tarr wrote in *School Library Journal* that *Hushabye Lily* would make "a grand storytime choice." Another bed-time tale, *Good Night, Sleep Tight* begins as Grandma Bear tries to convince little Archie to fall asleep. Finally, she finds success when she tells the young cub stories of his own parents, which quickly lull Archie off to dreamland. "Freeman's . . . language, with its familiar words and rhythms, resonates with security and affection," wrote a *Publishers Weekly* contributor in a review of *Good Night, Sleep Tight.* "The language has a gentle cadence that is relaxing and soothing," Carolyn Phelan noted in *Booklist,* and a critic for *Kirkus Reviews* predicted that Freedman's story will provide "a real bedtime treat for both parents and children alike." *Snuggle up, Sleepy Ones* is filled with exotic animals who drift off to sleep. The "flowing cadences of [Freedman's] . . . rhyming couplets will lull young sleepyheads pleasantly into la-la land," predicted a *Kirkus Reviews* contributor, and a *Publishers Weekly* critic noted that the book's "rhymes have a comforting lilt."

Dilly Duckling, another of Freedman's animal-centered picture books, finds a young duck losing a feather while playing. Although the duckling worries that his mother will be mad, Mother Duck explains that losing feathers is just part of life. A *Kirkus Reviews* contributor called the *Dilly Duckling* "a breezy look at the changes of growing up." *Oops-a-Daisy!* is also a tale of growing up; this time: Daisy the rabbit is frustrated because she cannot learn to hop. However, with effort and the help of her friends, she builds confidence and is sure that, someday, she will hop as well as her mother. A *Publishers Weekly* critic noted that Freedman's "crisp, descriptive prose, and evocative nonsense phrases" will engage readers in *Oops-a-Daisy!*

Night-Night, Emily! is one of Freedman's stories that features a human child as the protagonist. In the story, Emily cannot fall asleep without her favorite bear, and as she searches the house for her toy, she gradually fills her bed with a menagerie of other stuffed animals. Sally R. Dow, writing in *School Library Journal,* called *Night-Night, Emily!* "a good choice for nighttime sharing."

Freedman leaves Planet Earth altogether in *Aliens Love Underpants!,* a beginning reader that received the Richard & Judy Book Club Award in 2007. "I first sent in a story about aliens, but the publishers came back to me saying that they wanted a different spin on it," Freed-

man explained to Candice Krieger in the *Jewish Chronicle.* "So I sent in something that was completely mad, but they seemed to really like it. I am really pleased to have won the award."

Biographical and Critical Sources

PERIODICALS

Booklist, May 1, 2001, Shelley Townsend-Hudson, review of *An Ark Full of Activities,* p. 1676; December 15, 2003, Carolyn Phelan, review of *Good Night, Sleep Tight,* p. 753; March 1, 2004, Ilene Cooper, review of *Dilly Duckling,* p. 1194.

Kirkus Reviews, August 15, 2001, review of *Where's Your Smile, Crocodile?,* p. 1212; July 15, 2003, review of *Good Night, Sleep Tight,* p. 963; August 1, 2003, review of *Hushabye Lily,* p. 1016; December 15, 2003, review of *Dilly Duckling,* p. 1450; May 15, 2005, review of *Snuggle up, Sleepy Ones,* p. 588; October 1, 2006, review of *New Kid in Town,* p. 1013; October 15, 2006, review of *Squabble and Squawk,* p. 1070.

Magpies, November, 2001, review of *Where's Your Smile, Crocodile?,* p. 27.

Publishers Weekly, August 20, 2001, review of *Where's Your Smile, Crocodile?* p. 78; June 2, 2003, review of *Hushabye Lily,* p. 50; October 6, 2003, review of *Good Night, Sleep Tight,* p. 82; November 10, 2003, review of *Gooseberry Goose,* p. 60; February 9, 2004, review of *Oops-a-Daisy!,* p. 79; June 20, 2005, review of *One Magical Morning,* p. 75; June 27, 2005, review of *Snuggle up, Sleepy Ones,* p. 61.

School Librarian, spring, 2002, review of *Tiggy Tiger Brave Explorer,* p. 18; spring, 2004, Janet Fisher, review of *Going on the Loose,* p. 19; autumn, 2004, Joyce Banks, review of *Oops-a-Daisy!,* p. 131; summer, 2005, Emma Doman, review of *By My Side, Little Panda,* p. 74.

School Library Journal, November, 2001, Patti Gonzales, review of *Where's Your Smile, Crocodile?,* p. 122; November, 2003, Andrea Tarr, review of *Hushabye Lily,* p. 93; December, 2003, Linda M. Kenton, review of *Good Night, Sleep Tight,* and Martha Topol, review of *Gooseberry Goose,* both p. 113; January, 2004, Sally R. Dow, review of *Night-Night, Emily!* p. 98; April, 2004, Judith Constantinides, review of *Dilly Duckling,* p. 110; May, 2004, Be Astengo, review of *Oops-a-Daisy!,* p. 110; May, 2005, Sheilah Kosco, review of *One Magical Morning,* p. 83; July, 2005, Sally R. Dow, review of *Snuggle up, Sleepy Ones,* p. 72; June, 2007, Jayne Damron, review of *A Kiss Goodnight,* p. 96.

ONLINE

Jewish Chronicle Online, http://www.thejc.com/ (November 1, 2007), Candice Krieger, "Claire Freedman Wins a Richard & Judy Book Award."

Simon & Schuster Web site, http://www.simonsays.com/ (December 1, 2007), "Claire Freedman."*

G

GARBER, Esther
   See LEE, Tanith

*   *   *

GILBERT, Anne Yvonne
   See GILBERT, Yvonne

*   *   *

GILBERT, Catherine
   See MURDOCK, Catherine Gilbert

*   *   *

GILBERT, Yvonne 1951-
(Anne Yvonne Gilbert)

Personal

Born April 7, 1951, in Wallsend, Northumberland, England; daughter of Anne Doreen Gilbert; married David Edward Owen (deceased); married Danny Nanos (a graphic designer and art director); children: Thomas Edward Gilbert Owen. *Education:* Attended Newcastle College of Art, 1969; Liverpool College of Art, B.A., 1973.

Addresses

Office—6A Belle Grove Ter., Spital Tongues, Newcastle upon Tyne NE2 4LL, England. *E-mail*—yvonne.gilbert@dsl.pipex.com.

Career

Illustrator and graphic artist. Freelance illustrator of book covers, picture books, greeting cards, postage stamps, and china, beginning 1978. Teacher at workshops; lecturer in art at a technical college, 1973-78; Manchester Polytechnic, Manchester, England, external assessor for CNAA course in illustration, 1981-85. *Exhibitions:* Work exhibited at Bluecoat Gallery, Liverpool, England; Hamilton's Gallery, London, England; Neville Gallery, Bath, England; London Illustrators Art Gallery; in European Illustration annual exhibitions; and for Scottish and Welsh Art Council. Work included in permanent collections.

Awards, Honors

Golden Stamp Award, 1985; Revel Cumberland Award for Best Use of Colored Pencils; British Philatelic Bureau, commissioned artist for British Christmas stamps, 1984, 1994.

Illustrator

Katharine Mary Briggs, *Abbey Lubbers, Banshees, and Beggars: An Illustrated Encyclopedia of Fairies,* Pantheon Books (New York, NY), 1979.

(And selector) *Baby's Book of Lullabies and Cradle Songs,* Dial Books (New York, NY), 1990.

Miriam Chaikin, reteller, *Children's Bible Stories: From Genesis to Daniel,* Dial Books (New York, NY), 1993.

Rebecca Hickox, *Per and the Dala Horse,* Doubleday (New York, NY), 1995.

Vivian French, *A Christmas Star Called Hannah,* Candlewick Press (Cambridge, MA), 1997.

M.C. Helldorfer, *Night of the White Stag,* Doubleday (New York, NY), 1999.

(Under name Anne Yvonne Gilbert) *The Night before Christmas: Classic Stories and Poems with a Christmas Message,* Candlewick Press (Cambridge, MA), 2000.

Billy Joel, *Goodnight, My Angel: A Lullaby* (includes audiocassette), Scholastic (New York, NY), 2004.

(Under name Anne Yvonne Gilbert) Hans Christian Anderson, *The Wild Swans,* Barefoot Books (Cambridge, MA), 2005.

(With others) Dugald Steer, editor, *Wizardology,* Candlewick Press (Cambridge, MA), 2005.

George R.R. Martin, *The Ice Dragon,* new edition, Starscape (New York, NY), 2006.

(With Helen Ward and Ian Andrew) Dugald Steer, editor, *Pirateology,* Candlewick Press (Cambridge, MA), 2006.

Kathy-Jo Wargin, reteller, *Frog Prince* (based on the story by the Brothers Grimm), Ann Arbor Media Group (Ann Arbor, MI) 2007.

Contributor of illustrations to books, including *The Iron Wolf,* Allen Lane (London, England), 1980, published as *The Unbroken Web: Stories and Fables,* Crown (New York, NY), 1980; and *DK Discoveries: Tutankhamun: The Life and Death of a Pharaoh,* DK Publishing (New York, NY), 1998.

Sidelights

Yvonne Gilbert's work as an illustrator ranges over a wide spectrum of advertising and design projects, including hundreds of book covers as well as greeting cards, limited-edition collectibles, and stamps issued by the British Post Office. Gilbert has been praised for her detailed, decorative images, and her pastel-hued artwork is exhibited at galleries throughout her native England. Inspired by artists such as Arthur Rackham, Maxfield Parish, and other artist at work during the late 1800s, Gilbert's media of choice is a challenging one: colored pencil.

While Gilbert's work first appeared in the pages of British children's books in the late 1970s, 1990's *Baby's Book of Lullabies and Cradle Songs* was the book that introduced her to an American readership. Since providing this work, which Gilbert illustrated and also edited, her art has graced picture books such as Rebecca Hickox's *Per and the Dala Horse,* Vivian French's *A Christmas Star Called Hannah,* M.C. Helldorfer's *Night of the White Stag,* and Billy Joel's *Goodnight, My Angel: A Lullaby.* Other books featuring her artwork include a new edition of Hans Christian Andersen's *The Wild Swans,* which *Booklist* contributor Carolyn Phelan praised as a "graceful, dramatic version" of the classic work due to Gilbert's "detailed" and "beguiling" colored-pencil art.

In *Per and the Dala Horse* three brothers inherit gifts from their father and each benefits from his as his character allows. While the oldest brother receives a farm, complete with a work horse and plow, and the second brother receives a fine horse, the youngest brother inherits a gift that seems minor by comparison: the painted wooden horse of the title. Though the youngest brother appears to have been short changed, the dala horse saves the day when trolls steal an important religious treasure. Cynthia K. Richey, writing in *School Library Journal,* likened Gilbert's use of intricate details and borders in *Per and the Dala Horse* to that of artist Jan Brett, and added that Gilbert's choice of color "effectively evoke[s] the setting" of the Eastern European tale.

Gilbert's work for *A Christmas Star Called Hannah* brings to life a young girl's experience being cast as an evening star in her school's Christmas pageant. When it is discovered that the doll that was to represent Baby Jesus has been forgotten, Hannah comes to the rescue with her own baby brother and becomes the true star of the production. In *Booklist,* Ilene Cooper remarked on the "photographic quality" of Gilbert's art, and a *School Library Journal* reviewer concluded that the illustrations "enliven [French's] . . . story and lend personality to its characters."

Set in medieval times, Helldorfer's *Night of the White Stag* tells the story of a boy hunting rabbits in the king's woods. When the boy encounters a mysterious blind man who is forlorn over the death of his son in the same war that orphaned the boy, man and boy become companions. When they join together to hunt for a legendary white stag, miraculous changes follow. As Tracy Taylor noted in *School Library Journal,* Gilbert's illustrations for the book are "realistically and gracefully rendered."

When pop musician Billy Joel wrote his first picture book, Gilbert was selected to illustrate the text. *Goodnight, My Angel* is actually a song Joel wrote for his young daughter, and Gilbert pairs it with "idealized images of the long-lashed heroine and luminous landscapes [that] echo the unabashedly sentimental strains of Joel's song," according to a *Publishers Weekly* reviewer.

Gilbert talked with Logan Kaufman of *Adventures Underground* online regarding her technique. "I love history and costume, arms, armour, etc. so I have a lot of books on related subjects," she explained. "Wherever I go I visit castles, palaces and museums, storing the information for when I may use it." In addition to collecting books, Gilbert also collects costumes and props, which she use when friends, family members, and sometimes even the odd passer-by model before the camera. "They have to be prepared to dress up in bits of material fashioned into costumes, holding bin-lids and broom-handles as shield and sword," she explained. "I have a collection of photographs of people looking very strange—lying on the floor to appear to be flying, sitting astride sofa backs to appear to be horse-riding." Although her choice of colored pencil as a medium is unusual, it is one Gilbert gravitated to early on. She continues to be devoted to colored pencil because of the velvety texture that results by using hard leads on smooth paper. "Even as a very small child I couldn't abide mess," she admitted to Kaufman. "Hence the pencils even though they do make me tear my hair out."

Biographical and Critical Sources

PERIODICALS

Booklist, November 15, 1995, Carolyn Phelan, review of *Per and the Dala Horse,* p. 564; November 1, 1997, Ilene Cooper, review of *A Christmas Star Called Han-*

*In addition to her work as a fine artist, Yvonne Gilbert creates cover art for numerous books, including Peter S. Beagle's **A Dance for Emilia.** (Reproduced by permission of Penguin Group (USA), Inc.)*

nah, p. 480; December 1, 1999, Marta Segal, review of *Night of the White Stag,* p. 711; April 1, 2005, Carolyn Phelan, review of *The Wild Swans,* p. 1364.

Kirkus Reviews, October 15, 2004, review of *Goodnight, My Angel: A Lullaby,* p. 2004; September 15, 2006, review of *The Ice Dragon,* p. 961.

Publishers Weekly, October 6, 1997, review of *A Christmas Star Called Hannah,* p. 55; October 11, 2004, review of *Goodnight, My Angel,* p. 78.

School Library Journal, January, 1996, Cynthia K. Richey, review of *Per and the Dala Horse,* pp. 84-85; October, 1997, review of *A Christmas Star Called Hannah,*

p. 41; November, 1999, Tracy Taylor, review of *The Night of the White Stag;* October, 2000, Tracy Taylor, review of *The Night before Christmas: Classic Stories and Poems with a Christmas Message,* p. 61; February, 2005, Jane Marino, review of *Goodnight, My Angel,* p. 104; February, 2007, Eva Mitnick, review of *The Ice Dragon,* p. 92.

ONLINE

Yvonne Gilbert Home Page, http://www.yvonnegilbert.com (December 10, 2007).

Adventures Underground Web site, http://www.adventures underground.com/ (January 1, 2007), Logan Kaufman, interview with Gilbert.

*   *   *

GOLDFINGER, Jennifer P. 1963-

Personal

Born February 1, 1963; married (husband a radiologist); children: two daughters. *Hobbies and other interests:* Cross-country skiing, playing squash, mountain biking.

Addresses

Home and office—Lexington, MA. *E-mail*—evaesme@ rcn.com.

Career

Author and illustrator of books for children. Abstract painter, working in oils, acrylics, and encaustic paints.

Member

Society of Children's Book Writers and Illustrators, Children's Book Council, Picture Book Artists Association.

Writings

SELF-ILLUSTRATED

A Fish Named Spot, Little, Brown (Boston, MA), 2001.
My Dog Lyle, Clarion Books (New York, NY), 2007.

ILLUSTRATOR

Eleanor Florence, *The Mystery of the Ancient Coins,* Guild Press Emmis Books (Zionsville, IN), 2003.
Charlie Thomas, *I Need Glasses,* Children's Press (New York, NY), 2005.
Linda Hayward, *The King's Chorus,* Clarion Books (New York, NY), 2006.

Sidelights

In her work as an author and illustrator, Jennifer P. Goldfinger entertains young readers with fun artwork and engaging stories. In addition to creating artwork for her original stories in *My Dog Lyle* and *A Fish Named Spot,* Goldfinger has also created illustrations for text by other writers, as in *The King's Chorus,* written by Linda Hayward, *I Need Glasses,* by Charlie Thomas, and *The Mystery of the Ancient Coins* by Eleanor Florence. In *The King's Chorus* a cocky rooster named Kadoodle loves to hear himself crow. Crowing day and evening, he keeps the rest of the barnyard awake all night. Hoping to silence the noisy rooster, Honketta the goose tells Kadoodle a story about a king who owns some of the world's most renowned roosters—roosters who only crow at dawn. Kadoodle, in his pride, wants to be considered among these premier roosters and appropriately crows only at dawn. Shelle Rosenfeld, writing in *School Library Journal,* commented of the book that Goldfinger mirrors the energy of Hayward's text in "charming, richly hued and textured illustrations [which] incorporate plenty of playful perspectives." According to a *Kirkus Reviews* critic, the illustrations for *The King's Chorus* "radiate colorful, quirky appeal."

In *My Dog Lyle* Goldfinger creates art to pair with her original story about a little girl who boasts proudly about all the wonderful and unusual characteristics of her beloved dog Lyle. *My Dog Lyle* includes "vibrant illustrations" that help give the story's doggy hero "a well-defined personality," according to a *Kirkus Reviews* critic. Rachel Kamin, in her *School Library Journal* review of *My Dog Lyle,* applauded the book's child-friendly story and wrote that Goldfinger's "lively text matches perfectly with [her] . . . vibrant, playful illustrations."

"I think my biggest advantage as a writer is the ability to see things the way children do," Goldfinger told *SATA.* "I feel like I can really connect with children when I read them my books, and also in talking to them about funny stories that I remember as a child. I bring this attitude to everything I do. I love to create in all ways, although originally I did so as an artist."

Biographical and Critical Sources

PERIODICALS

Booklist, July, 2001, review of *A Fish Named Spot,* p. 2019; February 15, 2007, Shelle Rosenfeld, review of *The King's Chorus;* June 1, 2007, Julie Cummins, review of *My Dog Lyle,* p. 83.
Bulletin of the Center for Children's Books, September, 2007, Deborah Stevenson, review of *My Dog Lyle,* p. 25.
Kirkus Reviews, June 1, 2007, review of *The King's Chorus,* p. 1072; June 15, 2007, review of *My Dog Lyle.*

13

Jennifer P. Goldfinger tells the story of a loyal pup in **My Dog Lyle,** *a picture book featuring the author's engaging art.* (Illustration © 2007 by Jennifer P. Goldfinger. Reproduced by permission of Clarion Books, an imprint of Houghton Mifflin Company. All rights reserved.)

Publishers Weekly, April 9, 2001, review of *A Fish Named Spot,* p. 74.

School Library Journal, June, 2001, Shawn Brommer, review of *A Fish Named Spot,* p. 114; June, 2007, review of *My Dog Lyle,* p. 100.

ONLINE

Jennifer P. Goldfinger Home Page, http://www.jennifer-goldfinger.com (November 17, 2007).

Children's Bookwatch Web site, http://www.midwest bookreview.com/ (January 1, 2007), review of *The King's Chorus.*

Picture Book Artists Association Web site, http://www.pic turebookartists.org/ (January 2, 2008), profile of Goldfinger.*

* * *

GORE, Leonid

Personal

Born in Union of Soviet Socialist Republics (now Russia); immigrated to United States, 1990. *Education:* Attended Art College of Minsk.

Addresses

Home and office—Oakland, NJ.

Career

Illustrator.

Awards, Honors

An Izard Storyteller's Choice Award and Rhode Island Children's Book Award, both 1994, both for *Jacob and the Stranger.*

Writings

SELF-ILLUSTRATED

Danny's First Snow, Simon & Schuster (New York, NY), 2007.

ILLUSTRATOR

Mary Packard, *I Am King!,* Children's Press (Chicago, IL), 1994.

Sally Derby, *King Kenrick's Splinter,* Walker (New York, NY), 1994.

Sally Derby, *Jacob and the Stranger,* Tichnor & Fields (New York, NY), 1994.

L.G. Bass, *The Pomegranate Seeds: A Classic Greek Myth,* Houghton Mifflin (Boston, MA), 1995.

Norma Simon, *The Story of Hanukkah,* HarperCollins (New York, NY), 1997.

Alma Flor Ada, *The Malachite Palace,* translated by Rosa Zubizarreta, Atheneum (New York, NY), 1998.

Philip Pullman, *Clockwork; or, All Wound Up,* Arthur A. Levine (New York, NY), 1998.

Janice Del Negro, *Lucy Dove,* Dorling Kindersley (New York, NY), 1998.

Sonia Craddock, *Sleeping Boy,* Atheneum (New York, NY), 1999.

Eve Bunting, *Who Was Born This Special Day?,* Atheneum (New York, NY), 2000.

Sue Alexander, *Behold the Trees,* Arthur A. Levine (New York, NY), 2001.

Robert Burleigh, *The Secret of the Great Houdini,* Atheneum (New York, NY), 2002.

Sue Stauffacher, *The Angel and Other Stories,* Eerdmans (Grand Rapids, MI), 2002.

Aaron Shepard, *The Princess Mouse: A Tale of Finland,* Atheneum (New York, NY), 2003.

Mary Packard, *I Am King!,* Children's Press (New York, NY), 2003.

Bruce Coville, *William Shakespeare's Hamlet,* Dial (New York, NY), 2004.

Monique de Varennes, *The Sugar Child,* Atheneum (New York, NY), 2004.

Kate Hovey, *Voices of the Trojan War,* Margaret K. McElderry (New York, NY), 2004.

Fran Manushkin, *The Little Sleepyhead,* Dutton (New York, NY), 2004.

Cynthia Zarin, *Saints among the Animals,* Atheneum (New York, NY), 2005.

Marianna Mayer, *The Boy Who Ran with the Gazelles,* Dial (New York, NY), 2005.

Anette Griessman, *The Fire,* Putnam's Sons (New York, NY), 2005.

Miriam Chaikin, *Angel Secrets: Stories Based on Jewish Legend,* Henry Holt (New York, NY), 2005.

Mary Quattlebaum, *Why Sparks Fly High at Dancing Point: A Colonial American Folktale,* Farrar, Straus & Giroux (New York, NY), 2006.

Jodi Lynn Anderson, *May Bird among the Stars,* Atheneum (New York, NY), 2006.

Sidelights

Leonid Gore was already a successful illustrator of children's book in his native USSR when he immigrated to the eastern United States in 1990. His familiarity with Eastern European culture combined with his training at the Art Institute of Minsk to make Gore a popular choice for illustrations and advertising campaigns that featured Russian landscape and culture. Along with such titles as *Jacob and the Stranger,* a story by Sally Derby that is set in the small town of Slavda, Gore also designed the art for the 1996 Stolichnaya vodka advertising campaign, which was "centered on Russian imagery" according to Stuart Elliott of the *New York Times.* In the years since, his ornate style has been featured in numerous other books, among them Mary Packard's *I Am King!,* Anette Griessman's picture book *The Fire,* Miriam Chaikin's *Angel Secrets: Stories Base on a Jew-*

ish Legend, and an illustrated adaptation of Shakespeare's *Hamlet* by Bruce Coville. In 2007, Gore released his first self-illustrated book for children, *Danny's First Snow,* which was described by a *Kirkus Reviews* writer as "a treat for wintry story times" due to Gore's "simple, well-written text, original plot, and perceptive illustrations."

Published in 1994, *Jacob and the Stranger* is the tale of Jacob, a lazy man who prefers leisure to work. He puts out a sign stating that he will do work as long as it is not too hard. When a stranger answers his sign and leaves Jacob a potted plant to care for while he is away, the lazy man soon finds that plant-tending is not as easy a job as he had hoped. Then the plant starts to bloom and cats of all sorts bud from the leaves. One of these cats, a black panther, captures Jacob's heart. When the stranger returns, he refuses to pay Jacob the agreed-upon wage, and Jacob must outsmart the stranger to keep the panther and collect his payment. "Gore's eerie black-and-white pictures [are] full of mystery and danger," wrote Ilene Cooper in a *Booklist* review of *Jacob and the Stranger*, and Anne Deifendeifer wrote in *Horn Book* that the illustrations "admirably reflect the folkloric mood."

Gore moves from Russia to ancient Greece in his illustrations for L.G. Bass's *The Pomegranate Seeds: A Classic Greek Myth.* The artist's "ink-and-acrylic illus-

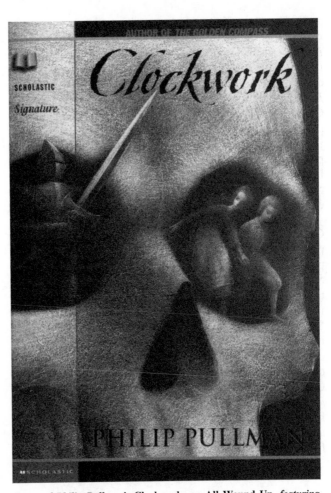

Cover of Philip Pullman's **Clockwork; or, All Wound Up,** *featuring Gore's soft-edged artwork.* (Illustration © 1998 by Leonid Gore. Reprinted by permission of Scholastic, Inc.)

Leonid Gore's unique art is featured in picture books such as Sally Derby's **Jacob and the Stranger.** (Illustration © 1994 by Leonid Gore. Reprinted by permission of Houghton Mifflin Company. All rights reserved.)

trations offer a feathery, dreamlike view of this classical world," wrote Kay Weisman in *Booklist.* For Norma Simon's *The Story of Hanukkah,* Gore's "organic and softly lit" illustrations of the Jewish story of the Maccabees "are both reverent and fresh," according to a *Publishers Weekly* contributor. Of Alma Flor Ada's original fairy tale, *The Malachite Palace,* Hazel Rochman commented in *Booklist* on "Gore's full-page, acrylic-and-ink pictures, in rich, shimmering shades of green and red."

For Janice Del Negro's retelling of a Scottish fairy story in *Lucy Dove,* Gore drew on members of his family. "As I created the character of Lucy, I drew inspiration from my Aunt Tanya and Aunt Fira in Russia," he explained on the *Embracing the Child Web site.* "Lucy is a combined portrait of these two aunts, and I dedicated the book to them." Susan Dove Lempke, writing in *Booklist,* wrote that the "luminescent, scratchy paintings" in *Lucy Dove* "capture the eerie quality well," and "are as bewitching as they are haunting," in the opinion of Mary M. Burns in *Horn Book.*

Among his work creating art for books, Gore has provided illustrations for Philip Pullman's short gothic novel *Clockwork; or, All Wound Up.* Here his "soft-edged drawings, full of light and shadow are extremely well crafted and satisfyingly strange," in the opinion of *Booklist* critic Ilene Cooper. A tale that combines fairy tales, an historic setting, and Gore's art is Sonia Craddock's *Sleeping Boy,* a picture book about which *Horn Book* contributor Roger Sutton wrote: "Only Leonid Gore's acrylic paintings, by turn tender and threatening, pitched at unsettling angles to the text, do the theme justice." His illustrations for Griessman's *The Fire* were praised by Julie Cummins, the *Booklist* contributor writing that Gore's "acrylics and pastels in intense, fiery reds, oranges, and golds viscerally convey the children's fright and the vicious heat of the blaze."

Gore's illustrations have continued to be successfully paired with fairy and folk tales. The "pastel and acrylic paintings" he contributes to Monique Varennes's *The Sugar Child* hold "all the colors of marzipan and the translucence of sugar candy," according to a *Kirkus Reviews* contributor. Catherine Threadgill, writing in *School Library Journal,* found Marianna Mayer's telling of *The Boy Who Ran with the Gazelles* weak, and commented that "Gore's sand-swept, evocative pastels deserve the accompaniment of a better story." In Mary Quattlebaum's *Sparks Fly High: The Legend of Dancing Point,* "Gore's depiction of colonial times with feathery backgrounds, pointy-chin-and-nosed people and gossamer overlays on fabric" is based on American folk art, according to a *Kirkus Reviews* contributor.

Biographical and Critical Sources

PERIODICALS

Booklist, September 1, 1994, Ilene Cooper, review of *Jacob and the Stranger,* p. 40; February 1, 1996, Kay Weisman, review of *The Pomegranate Seeds: A Classic Greek Myth,* p. 934; May 15, 1998, Hazel Rochman, review of *The Malachite Palace,* p. 1629; September 1, 1998, Susan Dove Lempke, review of *Lucy Dove,* p. 120; September 15, 1998, Ilene Cooper, review of *Clockwork; or, All Wound Up,* p. 229; February 1, 2000, Michael Cart, review of *Sleeping Boy,* p. 1024; March 1, 2001, review of *Behold the Trees,* p. 1276; October 1, 2005, Julie Cummins, review of *The Fire,* p. 62, and Ilene Cooper, review of *Angel Secrets,* p. 67; October 15, 2005, review of *May Bird and the Ever After,* p. 48; October 15, 2006, Gillian Engberg, review of *Sparks Fly High: The Legend of Dancing Point,* p. 52; December 1, 2006, Ilene Cooper, review of *Saints among the Animals,* p. 44.

Bulletin of the Center for Children's Books, December, 2006, Deborah Stevenson, review of *Sparks Fly High,* p. 185, and Elizabeth Bush, review of *Saints among the Animals,* p. 194.

Horn Book, September-October, 1994, Anne Deifendeifer, review of *Jacob and the Stranger,* p. 583; September-October, 1998, Mary M. Burns, review of *Lucy Dove,* p. 615; November, 1998, Ann A. Flowers, review of *Clockwork,* p. 740; January, 2000, Roger Sutton, review of *Sleeping Boy,* p. 63; September-October, 2005, Susan P. Bloom, review of *Angel Secrets,* p. 592; September-October, 2006, Joanna Rudge Long, review of *Sparks Fly High,* p. 601; January-February, 2007, Lauren Adams, review of *Saints among the Animals,* p. 87.

Kirkus Reviews, July 1, 2004, review of *Voices of the Trojan War,* p. 631; October 1, 2004, review of *The Sugar Child,* p. 959; June 15, 2005, review of *The Boy Who Ran with the Gazelles,* p. 686; August 1, 2005, review of *Angel Secrets,* p. 845; September 15, 2005, review of *The Fire,* p. 1026; September 15, 2005, review of *May Bird and the Ever After,* p. 1019; September 15, 2006, review of *Sparks Fly High,* p. 964, August, 2007, review of *Danny's First Snow.*

New York Times, October 15, 1996, Stuart Elliott, "The Future, according to the Marketer of Stolichnaya, Will Be Filled with Flavored Vodka."

Publishers Weekly, October 6, 1997, review of *The Story of Hanukkah,* p. 53; October 18, 1999, review of *Clockwork,* p. 86; November 1, 1999, review of *Sleeping Boy,* p. 56; September 25, 2000, Elizabeth Devereaux, review of *Who Was Born this Special Day?* p. 68; May 28, 2001, review of *Behold the Trees,* p. 85; December 20, 2004, review of *The Sugar Child,* p. 58.

School Library Journal, October, 2004, review of *William Shakespeare's Hamlet,* p. S50; November, 2004, Rachel G. Payne, review of *The Sugar Child,* p. 96; August 2005, Catherine Threadgill, review of *The Boy Who Ran with the Gazelles,* p. 103; November, 2005, Judith Constantinides, review of *The Fire,* p. 93; December, 2005, Tasha Saecker, review of *May Bird and the Ever After,* p. 136; December, 2006, Lucinda Snyder Whitehurst, review of *Sparks Fly High,* p. 127; January, 2007, Linda L. Walkins, review of *Saints among the Animals,* p. 121.

ONLINE

Arthur A. Levine Web Site, http://www.arthuralevinebooks.com/ (December 3, 2007), "Leonid Gore."

Embracing the Child Web site, http://www.embracingthechild.org/ (December 3, 2007), "Leonid Gore."

Simon & Schuster Web site, http://www.simonsays.com/ (December 3, 2007), "Leonid Gore."

H

HACKER, Randi 1951-
(Randi Dawn Hacker)

Personal

Born 1951; children: Juliana. *Education:* University of Michigan, B.A. (English); St. Michael's College, M.A. (English as a Second Language).

Addresses

Office—Center for East Asian Studies, Bailey Hall, Rm. 200, 1440 Jayhawk Blvd., Lawrence, KS 66045-7574. *E-mail*—rhacker@ku.edu.

Career

Author and educator. Former editor for in New York, NY, including at Children's Television Workshop; teacher at elementary schools in northern VT; former children's librarian; Kansas Consortium for Teaching about Asia, University of Kansas, outreach coordinator. Creator, editor-in-chief, and publisher of *P3* (environmental magazine for children), 1990.

Awards, Honors

New York Public Library Books for the Teen Age designation, 2007, for *Life as I Knew It;* featured author at Kansas Book Festival, 2007.

Writings

(With Jackie Kaufman) *Habitats: Where the Wild Things Live,* J. Muir Publications (Santa Fe, NM), 1992.

(With Sylvia S. Hacker) *What Every Teenager Really Wants to Know about Sex: With the Startling New Information Every Parent Should Read,* Carroll & Graf (New York, NY), 1993.

How to Live Green, Cheap, and Happy: Save Money! Save the Planet!, Stackpole Books (Mechanicsburg, PA), 1994.

Detective and Spy Science: Experiment Log, Scholastic (New York, NY), 2001.

Life as I Knew It, Simon Pulse (New York, NY), 2006.

Author of six titles in "Jim Henson's Bedtime Stories" series; and titles in "Magic Schoolbus" and "Pony Pals" activity-book series. contributor to television series "Windy Acres," 2004; and programs for Nickelodeon. Contributor of parenting articles to *Sesameworkshop.org.* Co-author, with Jackie Kaufman, of satirical essays published in *New York Times Book Review, Spy, Premier,* and *Punch.*

Sidelights

Writer and educator Randi Hacker has written both fiction and nonfiction titles, often focusing on educational topics. She has contributed to the "Jim Henson's Bedtime Stories" series, featuring the popular Muppets characters; has written scripts for television; and is the founder of *P3,* an environmental magazine geared for young readers. With her partner, Jackie Kaufman, Hacker created *P3*—the name refers to the fact that Earth is the third planet from the sun—to encourage activism in older elementary-grade children. Within a year of its 1990 launch the periodical boasted a circulation of 20,000 copies. Hacker and Kaufman also teamed up to write the book *Habitats: Where the Wild Things Live.* Also with Kaufman, she wrote teleplays for Nickelodeon programming as well as satirical essays that have been published in major periodicals. In addition to writing, Hacker works as outreach coordinator for the University of Kansas Center for East Asian Studies, located in Lawrence. In this capacity, she works with children ranging from preschool-aged to third grade, and teaches introductory Chinese, sometimes helped by her twelve-year-old adopted Chinese daughter, Juliana.

In 2006 Hacker moved from juvenile nonfiction to young-adult fiction with *Life as I Knew It.* Narrated by sixteen-year-old Angelina Rossini, the novel describes the trials in Angelina's life after her world stops being normal. Her father, around whom her life has revolved, is much older than her mother, and when he has a stroke, everything in the teen's world changes. The stroke leaves her dad partially paralyzed and unable to speak, and leaves Angelina feeling that she has lost a parent. Lyn Seippel, reviewing the novel for *Book Loons* online, found *Life as I Knew It* to be "a touching story and worth reading."

Although *Kliatt* reviewer Amanda MacGregor described the supporting characters in *Life as I Knew It* as "vibrant" and praised the tale as a "compelling and emotional story," she noted that Angelina's narrative voice seems "uninspired" by comparison. In *Kirkus Reviews,* however, a critic maintained that "Hacker vividly sketches Andrea, with Italian gusto and bits of bittersweet wisdom." Suzanne Gordon, reviewing the novel in *School Library Journal,* wrote that Hacker creates "a handful of strong homosexual characters" in her story, one of whom is Angelina's best friend, Jax. Angelina's crush on Jax serves as one of the conflicts in the novel.

Biographical and Critical Sources

PERIODICALS

Bulletin of the Center for Children's Books, February, 2007, Deborah Stevenson, review of *Life as I Knew It,* p. 252.
Kirkus Reviews, September 15, 2006, review of *Live as I Knew It,* p. 954.
Kliatt, September, 2006, Amanda MacGregor, review of *Life as I Knew It,* p. 23.
Lawrence Journal-World and News, October 3, 2007, Nick Krug, "Language Program Designed to Whet Appetites for Chinese."
New York Times, May 3, 1990, "For Children, Tips on Rescuing the Planet"; September 27, 1990, Trish Hall, "A Magazine for Every Child."
People, May 27, 1991, "For Preteens Who Think Green, Two Vermont Editors Create an Environmental Magazine for Kids," p. 54.
School Library Journal, December, 2006, Suzanne Gordon, review of *Life as I Knew It,* p. 142.

ONLINE

Book Loons Web site, http://www.bookloons.com/ (November 21, 2007), review of *Live as I Knew It.*
Cynsations Web site, http://cynthialeitichsmith.blogspot.com/ (November 21, 2007), interview with Hacker.
Kansas University Center for East Asian Studies Web site, http://www.ceas.ku.edu/ (November 21, 2007), "Randi Hacker."
Outreach World Web site, http://www.outreachworld.org/ (November 21, 2007), "Randi Hacker."

* * *

HACKER, Randi Dawn
See HACKER, Randi

HAFT, Erin
See EHRENHAFT, Daniel

* * *

HAGUE, Michael 1948-
(Michael R. Hague)

Personal

Born September 8, 1948, in Los Angeles, CA; son of Riley Herbert (a truck driver) and Daisy Marie Hague; married Susan Kathleen Burdick (an artist and author of children's books), December 5, 1970; children: Meghan Micaela, Brittany Michael, Devon Heath. *Education:* Art Center College of Design, B.F.A. (with honors), 1972.

Addresses

Home—Colorado Springs, CO. *E-mail*—michael@michaelhague.com.

Career

Artist, author, and illustrator. Hallmark Cards, Kansas City, KS, illustrator, 1973-75; Current, Inc., Colorado Springs, CO, illustrator, 1975-77; author and illustrator of children's books, 1977—. *Exhibitions:* Work exhibited at Port Washington, Long Island, Public Library, 1986, and Children's Books Mean Business group show, 1984. Illustrations appeared on television series *thirtysomething,* 1989.

Awards, Honors

Dream Weaver chosen for American Institute of Graphic Arts Book Show (formerly Fifty Books of the Year), 1980; International Reading Association Children's Choices citation, 1982, for *The Man Who Kept House;* Colorado Children's Book Award, University of Colorado, 1984, and Georgia Children's Picture Storybook Award, University of Georgia, 1986, both for *The Unicorn and the Lake;* Parents' Choice Award, Parents' Choice Foundation, 1984, for *The Frog Princess; Aesop's Fables, The Legend of the Veery Bird,* and *Alice's Adventures in Wonderland* included among Child Study Association of America Books of the Year, 1985; Graphic Arts Award for Best Juvenile Book, Printing Industries Association, 1986, for *A Child's Book of Prayers;* Golden Quill Award, 2006.

Writings

SELF-ILLUSTRATED CHILDREN'S BOOKS

(Reteller, with wife, Kathleen Hague) *East of the Sun and West of the Moon,* Harcourt Brace Jovanovich (New York, NY), 1980.

Michael Hague (Reproduced by permission.)

(Reteller, with Kathleen Hague) *The Man Who Kept House,* Harcourt Brace Jovanovich (New York, NY), 1981.

(Editor) *Michael Hague's Favorite Hans Christian Andersen Fairy Tales,* Holt, Rinehart & Winston (New York, NY), 1981.

(Editor) *Mother Goose: A Collection of Classic Nursery Rhymes,* Holt, Rinehart & Winston (New York, NY), 1984.

(Editor) *Aesop's Fables,* Holt, Rinehart & Winston (New York, NY), 1985.

A Child's Book of Prayers, Holt, Rinehart & Winston (New York, NY), 1985.

Unicorn Pop-up Book, Holt, Rinehart & Winston (New York, NY), 1986.

Michael Hague's World of Unicorns, Holt, Rinehart & Winston (New York, NY), 1986, revised as *Michael Hague's Magical World of Unicorns,* Simon & Schuster Books for Young Readers (New York, NY), 1999.

(Editor) Robert Louis Stevenson, *The Land of Nod, and Other Poems for Children,* Holt, Rinehart & Winston (New York, NY), 1988.

My Secret Garden Diary, Arcade (New York, NY), 1990.

Magic Moments: A Book of Days, Arcade (New York, NY), 1990.

Our Baby: A Book of Records and Memories, Arcade (New York, NY), 1990.

A Unicorn Journal, Arcade (New York, NY), 1990.

Michael Hague's Illustrated "The Teddy Bears' Picnic," Holt, Rinehart & Winston (New York, NY), 1992.

(Selector) *The Rainbow Fairy Book,* Morrow (New York, NY), 1993.

(Selector) *Sleep, Baby, Sleep: Lullabies and Night Poems,* Morrow (New York, NY), 1994.

The Owl and the Pussy-Cat, and Other Nonsense Poems, North-South Books (New York, NY), 1995.

Michael Hague's Family Christmas Treasury, Holt, Rinehart & Winston (New York, NY), 1995.

(Selector) *The Book of Dragons,* Morrow (New York, NY), 1995.

Michael Hague's Family Easter Treasury, Holt, Rinehart & Winston (New York, NY), 1996.

The Perfect Present, Morrow (New York, NY), 1996.

(Selector) *The Book of Pirates,* HarperCollins (New York, NY), 2001.

(Selector) *The Book of Fairy Poetry,* HarperCollins (New York, NY), 2004.

(Reteller) E. Nesbit, *Lionel and the Book of Beasts,* HarperCollins (New York, NY), 2006.

(Selector) *Animal Friends: A Collection of Poems for Children,* Henry Holt (New York, NY), 2007.

(And selector) *The Book of Wizards,* HarperCollins (New York, NY), 2008.

In the Small (graphic novel), Little, Brown (New York, NY), 2008.

ILLUSTRATOR; CHILDREN'S BOOKS

Ethel Marbach, *The Cabbage Moth and the Shamrock,* Star and Elephant Books (La Jolla, CA), 1978.

(As Michael R. Hague) Beth Hilgartner, *A Necklace of Fallen Stars,* Little, Brown (Boston, MA), 1979.

Jane Yolen, *Dream Weaver,* Collins (New York, NY), 1979, revised edition, Philomel Books (New York, NY), 1989.

Deborah Apy, reteller, *Beauty and the Beast,* Green Tiger (New York, NY), 1980.

Eve Bunting, *Demetrius and the Golden Goblet,* Harcourt, Brace, Jovanovich (New York, NY), 1980.

Julia Cunningham, *A Mouse Called Junction,* Pantheon (New York, NY), 1980.

Kenneth Grahame, *The Wind in the Willows,* Holt, Rinehart & Winston (New York, NY), 1980.

Lee Bennett Hopkins, editor, *Moments: Poems about the Seasons,* Harcourt Brace Jovanovich (New York, NY), 1980.

Clement C. Moore, *The Night before Christmas,* Holt, Rinehart & Winston (New York, NY), 1981.

Marianna Mayer, *The Unicorn and the Lake,* Dial (New York, NY), 1982.

Margery Williams, *The Velveteen Rabbit; or, How Toys Became Real,* new edition, Holt, Rinehart & Winston (New York, NY), 1983.

Kenneth Grahame, *The Reluctant Dragon,* new edition, Holt, Rinehart & Winston (New York, NY), 1983.

C.S. Lewis, *The Lion, the Witch, and the Wardrobe,* new edition, Macmillan (New York, NY), 1983.

Nancy Luenn, *The Dragon Kite,* Harcourt Brace Jovanovich (New York, NY), 1983.

Jakob Grimm and Wilhelm Grimm, *Rapunzel,* Creative Education (Mankato, MN), 1984.

Kathleen Hague, *Alphabears: An ABC Book,* Holt, Rinehart & Winston (New York, NY), 1984, published with cassette, Live Oak Media, 1985.

Elizabeth Isele, reteller, *The Frog Princess: A Russian Tale Retold,* Crowell (New York, NY), 1984.

J.R.R. Tolkien, *The Hobbit; or, There and Back Again,* new edition, Houghton Mifflin (New York, NY), 1984.

Lewis Carroll, *Alice's Adventures in Wonderland,* new edition, Holt, Rinehart & Winston (New York, NY), 1985.

Kathleen Hague, *The Legend of the Veery Bird,* Harcourt Brace Jovanovich (New York, NY), 1985.

Kathleen Hague, *Numbears: A Counting Book,* Holt, Rinehart & Winston (New York, NY), 1986.

Kathleen Hague, *Out of the Nursery, into the Night,* Holt, Rinehart & Winston (New York, NY), 1986.

Frances Hodgson Burnett, *The Secret Garden,* new edition, Holt, Rinehart & Winston (New York, NY), 1987.

J.M. Barrie, *Peter Pan,* new edition, Holt, Rinehart & Winston (New York, NY), 1987, centennial edition, Henry Holt (New York, NY), 2003.

Carl Sandburg, *Rootabaga Stories, Part One,* new edition, Harcourt Brace Jovanovich (New York, NY), 1988.

Carl Sandburg, *Rootabaga Stories, Part Two,* new edition, Harcourt Brace Jovanovich (New York, NY), 1989.

L. Frank Baum, *The Wizard of Oz,* new edition, Holt, Rinehart & Winston (New York, NY), 1989, centennial edition, 2000.

Charles Perrault, *Cinderella, and Other Tales from Perrault,* Holt, Rinehart & Winston (New York, NY), 1989.

Marianna Mayer, *The Unicorn Alphabet,* Dial (New York, NY), 1989.

William Allingham, *The Fairies: A Poem,* Holt, Rinehart & Winston (New York, NY), 1989.

Kathleen Hague, *Bear Hugs,* Holt, Rinehart & Winston (New York, NY), 1989.

Thornton W. Burgess, *Old Mother West Wind,* Holt, Rinehart & Winston (New York, NY), 1990.

(With Joe Krush) Carl Sandburg, *Prairie-Town Boy,* Harcourt Brace Jovanovich (New York, NY), 1990.

Mary Norton, *The Borrowers,* new edition, Harcourt Brace Jovanovich (New York, NY), 1991.

Twinkle, Twinkle, Little Star, Morrow Junior Books (New York, NY), 1992.

South Pacific, Harcourt Brace Jovanovich (New York, NY), 1992.

The Fairy Tales of Oscar Wilde, Holt, Rinehart & Winston (New York, NY), 1993.

Teddy Bear, Teddy Bear: A Classic Action Rhyme, Morrow (New York, NY), 1993.

Hans Christian Andersen, *The Little Mermaid,* Holt, Rinehart & Winston (New York, NY), 1993.

Louisa May Alcott, *Little Women; or, Meg, Jo, Beth, and Amy,* Holt, Rinehart & Winston (New York, NY), 1993.

William J. Bennett, editor, *The Children's Book of Virtues,* Simon & Schuster (New York, NY), 1995.

William J. Bennett, editor, *The Children's Book of Heroes,* Simon & Schuster (New York, NY), 1995.

Hugh Lofting, *The Story of Doctor Dolittle,* Morrow (New York, NY), 1997.

William J. Bennett, editor, *The Children's Book of America,* Simon & Schuster (New York, NY), 1998.

The Twenty-third Psalm: From the King James Bible, Holt, Rinehart & Winston (New York, NY), 1999.

Ten Little Bears: A Counting Rhyme, Morrow (New York, NY), 1999.

William J. Bennett, editor, *The Children's Treasury of Virtues,* Simon & Schuster (New York, NY), 2000.

William J. Bennett, editor, *The Children's Book of Faith,* Doubleday (New York, NY), 2000.

A Wind in the Willows Christmas, SeaStar Books (New York, NY), 2000.

Beatrix Potter, *The Tale of Peter Rabbit,* SeaStar Books (New York, NY), 2001.

Kate Culhane, a Ghost Story, SeaStar Books (New York, NY), 2001.

Hugh Lofting, *The Voyages of Doctor Dolittle,* edited by Patricia C. McKissack and Fredrick L. McKissack, HarperCollins (New York, NY), 2001.

William J. Bennett, editor, *The Children's Book of Home and Family,* Doubleday Books for Young Readers (New York, NY), 2002.

Kathleen Hague, *Good Night, Fairies,* SeaStar Books (New York, NY), 2002.

Jimmy Kennedy, *The Teddy Bears' Picnic,* Henry Holt (New York, NY), 2002.

L. Frank Baum, *The Life and Adventures of Santa Claus,* Henry Holt (New York, NY), 2003, published with new introduction by Michael O. Riley and afterword by Max Apple, Signet (New York, NY), 2005.

Sarah L. Thompson, *The Nutcracker,* SeaStar Books (New York, NY), 2003.

Marianna Mayer, *Legendary Creatures of Myth and Magic,* Madison Park Press (New York, NY), 2006.

Jim Aylesworth, *Little Bitty Mousie,* Walker & Company (New York, NY), 2007.

ILLUSTRATOR; CHRISTMAS CAROLS

We Wish You a Merry Christmas, Holt, Rinehart & Winston (New York, NY), 1990.

Jingle Bells, Holt, Rinehart & Winston (New York, NY), 1990.

Deck the Halls, Holt, Rinehart & Winston (New York, NY), 1991.

O Christmas Tree, Holt, Rinehart & Winston (New York, NY), 1991.

OTHER

Unicorn Calendar, Holt, Rinehart & Winston (New York, NY), 1989.

Also illustrator of numerous other calendars, including a series based on C.S. Lewis's "Chronicles of Narnia" books.

Sidelights

One of the foremost illustrators of children's books in America, Michael Hague is perhaps best known for his work revisioning such classics as Kenneth Grahame's

The Wind in the Willows and L. Frank Baum's *The Wizard of Oz* for a new generation. Hague has also illustrated works by contemporary authors such as William J. Bennett and Jim Aylesworth, and he has published a number of self-illustrated collections of stories and verse, including *The Book of Fairy Poetry.*

Hague claims to have known he possessed the ability to draw as far back as kindergarten. "My mother had been to art school in England and encouraged me greatly by bringing home art books from which I could copy paintings and drawings," he once told *SATA.* "She never gave me lessons. I knew as a child that I wanted to illustrate books. I was always reading and rendering illustrations of my own creations for the King Arthur books as well as making portraits of such baseball heroes as Duke Snider of the Los Angeles Dodgers."

Books filled Hague's childhood home, and he willingly entered their fictional worlds. Comic books and Disney books were among his favorites, and his most treasured book demonstrated how to draw and animate the Disney characters. "I'm still a great Disney fan—I hold documents as one of the first Mickey Mouse Club members," Hague once admitted. "To this day I remember an enormous man named Roy, a Disney animator often featured on the *Mickey Mouse Club* television show. I used to think to myself, 'One day he'll retire, and then . . . .'" Hague also cites Asian printmakers Hiroshige and Hokusai, as well as illustrators Arthur Rackham, W. Heath Robinson, N.C. Wyeth, and Howard Pyle, as influences on his work. The artist who left the most lasting impression on Hague, however, was Hal Foster, who created the epic *Prince Valiant* comic strip. "The wealth of information he provided in each picture had a great impact on me," Hague noted in an essay on *BookPage Online.* As he also told *SATA,* "I *still* have a hard time accepting that Prince Valiant is not a real character from English history."

Hague had many friends while growing up and he was involved in numerous sports, his favorite being baseball. He continued drawing throughout high school and also dreamed of playing professional baseball, all the while realizing that he was not talented enough to do the latter. After high school Hague briefly attended junior college before transferring to the Art Center College of Design in Los Angeles. His original major was illustration and he hoped for a career in children's books. However, the college directed its illustration majors toward more promising careers, such as advertising, so Hague changed his major to painting. His wife, Kathleen, was also a painting major, and the two married while still students.

Although Hague retained a strong interest in doing children's books, by graduation he was convinced that he could not earn a living at it and decided to teach instead. When he discovered that teaching was not the career for him, Hague applied for a job at Hallmark Cards and worked for two years in their Kansas City studio. "It was great to get paid for drawing every day," he recalled. Although he was glad to have a job, Hague still refused to give up on the publishing industry. He put together a portfolio during his first week at Hallmark and sent it out to numerous publishers. "Many of the comments I received early were quite discouraging," he recalled. "Some editors said my work was 'too weird' for children. Many art directors sent back my portfolio with *no* comment. Silence was the worst response, and alas, the most frequent. How did I keep my morale up? I just assumed they were idiots. Dr. Seuss went to twenty-nine publishers before he had his first book published. After five years, I finally was offered illustration work and then it all seemed to come at once."

The first illustration job Hague earned was a cover and an inside story for *Cricket* magazine, and his first published book illustration was a pop-up book version of *Gulliver's Travels.* Meanwhile, Hague had begun working for Current, Inc., another greeting-card company located in Colorado Springs. "While I was working at Current I contacted Green Tiger Press," Hague once commented. "To my delight, they asked what *I* would like to illustrate. The first thing that came to my mind was *Beauty and the Beast,* which they agreed to. My illustrations for the book were influenced by the Cocteau film. It took a long time before I had another opportunity to propose what *I* wanted to illustrate to a publisher. When you're getting started, it's the publishers who make suggestions, and illustrators tend to accept everything and anything. It still takes me a long time to say 'no' to a project that doesn't interest me. But after the publication and success of *The Wind in the Willows* in 1980, I was in a position to suggest books I like to illustrate."

Hague's maternal grandmother was born in 1908, only two years before *The Wind in the Willows* was published for the first time. "She can recall with delight her father reading aloud to her about the adventures of Mr. Toad and his friends," related Hague. "The book was her father's favorite, and indeed became hers as well. My grandmother passed on a love of 'Willows,' as she refers to it, to my mother; and so when the story reached me it had already claimed three generations and captivated its fourth generation in me." The book's main characters include Mole, Ratty, Badger, and Mr. Toad; and they, along with their surroundings, have inspired an immense following over the years. "With such a loyal and affectionate following, from young children to their great-grandparents, I felt a great responsibility in illustrating the book," explained Hague.

The Wind in the Willows had also been illustrated by two of Hague's idols, Ernest Shepard and Arthur Rackham, so when he was first approached about the project he was "thrilled, honored, and a bit frightened," Hague once noted. "I love the book. I love the dependable Water Rat, the kindly Mole, the sturdy Badger, and especially Mr. Toad. And so it is, as when one is in love,

One of Hague's early illustration projects, **A Unicorn Journal** *was originally published in 1984.* (Illustration © 1984, 1986, 1987, 1988, 1990 by Michael Hague. Reproduced by permission.)

one forgets all obstacles and fears. That is what happened to me. I've not tried to create a new visual style or interpretation of the story," continued Hague. "I have instead tried to infuse my illustrations with the same spirit Kenneth Grahame's magic words convey. There is, I think, a bit of Toad in all of us. Certainly there

must have been some of Mr. Toad in me when I agreed to illustrate this book." Hague later published a slightly altered version of the fifth chapter of that book as *A Wind in the Willows Christmas,* pairing it with "vibrant, cozy, and charming" gouache paintings, according to a *School Library Journal* reviewer.

L. Frank Baum's *The Wizard of Oz* is another favorite story from Hague's childhood. "When I was a child, there were three places I would have given anything to visit," the author/illustrator once stated. "One was England in the days of King Arthur; another was the Wild West of Hopalong Cassidy; the third, quite different, was the Wonderful Land of Oz. Arthur's England and Hoppy's West were confined to earthly borders. The landscape of Oz was as large or as small as I wished it to be. And, like Alice's Wonderland, it was populated with such extraordinary creatures that I knew anything might happen there. It was a place where the laws of our universe seldom applied." His desire to visit the land of Oz never waned over the years, so it was with much enthusiasm and joy that he accepted the job of painting his own Oz. "I count myself as one of the most fortunate of beings," Hague once said. "For as an artist I have not only the pleasure but the duty to daydream. It is part of my work. I have been a contented daydreamer all of my life, often to the exasperation of those around me. While creating the illustrations for *The Wizard of Oz,* I would slip away. My hands went about their business while my mind walked among the Quadlings and the fierce Kalidahs." Reviewing the hundredth anniversary edition of that book, Lynne T. Burke wrote in *Reading Today* that "Hague's old-fashioned style and muted watercolor palette are the perfect foil for this full-length version of America's best-known fairy tale."

Hague has also illustrated other childhood classics, such as Beatrix Potter's *Peter Rabbit,* Frances Hodgson Burnett's *The Secret Garden,* Margery Williams's *The Velveteen Rabbit* and J.M. Barrie's *Peter Pan,* Carl Sandburg's *Rootabaga Stories,* Charles Perrault's *Cinderella,* and Edward Lear's *The Owl and the Pussy-Cat, and Other Nonsense Poems. Booklist* reviewer Shelley Townsend-Hudson declared that in *The Owl and the Pussy-Cat* "Hague plays off the sensual and grotesque elements of the poetry and uses rich texture and imagination to extend the text's foolishness." The illustrator also offers his own take on *The Book of Beasts,* a work by nineteenth-century writer E. Nesbit, in *Lionel and the Book of Beasts.* Kirsten Cutler, writing in *School Library Journal,* praised Hague's "signature, elaborately detailed art," noting that the "luxurious details" add to the fantastical setting of Nesbit's story. In Sarah L. Thompson's version of *The Nutcracker,* "Hague's illustrations in pen and ink, watercolor, and colored pencil set a dark and theatrical mood," remarked a *Kirkus Reviews* contributor.

Working with his wife, children's author Kathleen Hague, Hague has produced several story collections, including the popular idea books *Alphabears: An ABC Book, Numbears: A Counting Book,* and *Calendarbears.* Reviewing *Calendarbears* in *Booklist,* April Judge dubbed it a "playful collection of bouncy rhymes." Hague teamed with Bennett, a former U.S. secretary of education, on Bennett's anthologies *The Children's*

Cover of Hague's self-illustrated **Kate Culhane,** *which tells a tale that touches on the supernatural.* (Illustration © 2001 by Michael Hague. Reproduced by permission.)

Book of Virtues, The Children's Book of Faith, and *The Children's Book of Home and Family.* Based on Bennett's bestselling work for adults, *The Children's Book of Virtues* contains a wealth of stories and poems. "Hague's plentiful artwork adds enormously to the charm of the collection," noted *Booklist* critic Susan Dove Lempke. *The Children's Book of Faith* is a volume of Biblical tales, scripture passages, and prayers; *School Library Journal* reviewer Patricia Pearl Dole noted that Hague's paintings "give interest and drama to the text." Ilene Cooper, reviewing *The Children's Book of Home and Family* in *Booklist,* remarked that "Hague's golden-glow pictures are what give this a feel of warmth and love." Hague also contributed the artwork to Jim Aylesworth's *Little Bitty Mousie,* a rhyming alphabet book. The illustrator's "delicate plays of light and bright colors bring a visually arresting blend of realism and fancy" to the work, observed a critic in *Kirkus Reviews.*

Among the author-illustrator's more popular self-illustrated titles are books full of furry forest creatures

Hague joins his wife, Kathleen Hague, in retelling a traditional tale in **East of the Sun and West of the Moon.** (Illustration © 1980 by Michael Hague. Reproduced by permission of Harcourt, Inc. This material may not be reproduced in any form or by any means without the prior written permission of the publisher.)

and teddy bears. Many of these self-illustrated titles are compilations of works culled from nursery rhymes, Irish legends, and even the Bible, to which Hague adds his detailed signature drawings. In *Michael Hague's Family Easter Treasury,* for example, he selects from works including Mother Goose, the Bible, and from the poets William Blake and Emily Dickinson, among others. In *Teddy Bears' Mother Goose,* Hague compiles fifty-five nursery rhymes illustrated with "precise detail" that "adds to the charm" of the rhymes, noted Townsend-Hudson. *The Perfect Present* deals with the adventures of a rabbit named Jack in a shop full of old-fashioned toys. "Fans of Hague's extravagant, nostalgic style will have a feast," commented Susan Dove Lempke in a *Booklist* review of that book. Reviewing the same title, a contributor for *Publishers Weekly* concluded, "Hague's sumptuous wintry watercolors are among his strongest work." An Irish folktale is served up in *Kate Culhane: A Ghost Story,* and fairies take center stage in *The Book of Fairies,* a tale complemented by "Hague's lush, highly detailed artwork," according to Cooper. In a related work, *The Book of Fairy Poetry,* Hague collects verse from such esteemed authors as Walter de la Mare and Sir Walter Scott. Jane Marino, writing in *School Library Journal,* complimented the "stunning illustrations," adding that Hague's "beings, both beautiful and fearsome, beckon to children on every page."

In contrast with his approach to his original stories, Hague tries to imbue his illustrations for classic stories with the same essence that inspired the author of the story itself. "I begin with character studies and try to capture on paper what I see in my mind's eye," explained Hague. To avoid making a book repetitious, he places his characters in a variety of light sources. "Light is one of the elements which makes a painting real," he once commented, "especially when you are painting the fantastic. The more real a tree looks, or the light appears, the more believable the fantasy elements will be. One can't afford to be vague when illustrating fantasy. Ninety percent of a fantasy book should be based on the real world; you don't need many strange elements to make a story work. In a good illustration of a knight riding on a horse, for example, the viewer will ride over the next hill with him, even though the artist hasn't illustrated what's over there. It's not hard to animate or give gesture to fantasy creatures once you have principles of drawing. I try to make movement and gesture look believable, and one way to do that is to be sure that the backgrounds are realistic. It adds emphasis. Once again, I build a concrete world—not a fuzzy, dream-like place—where kids can see real sky or walls or cities. Then a dragon can become believable."

Hague claims to have no special tricks or secret answers when it comes to illustrating. If something does not look right, he tweaks it until it does. "Sometimes I'll have a bad day, when nothing seems to come easy," he once observed. "People ask me how long it takes to do a painting, and I can't really say because it changes from painting to painting from day to day. I've done some paintings in one day, others in two weeks. I couldn't say why that is." While working on his illustrations, Hague creates for himself, not for a particular audience: "When I illustrate, I don't think about kids, or what age group the book is aimed toward. I don't like to generalize or second guess my audience. I try to please myself. I am still in touch with my childhood, with the child that still exists in me."

Some three decades after entering the world of book illustrating, Hague shows no signs of slowing down. "I strive to create something from an empty canvas that becomes a whole 'other world' that people can visit for a while and totally believe in," he noted on the Henry Holt Web site. "That challenge of bringing a subject to life and making it believable—that's what is exciting to me as an artist." For Hague, the world of imagination is among "the only forms of magic left. "When I was a kid, I thought that magicians actually did work magic— the power to cut a woman in two and put her back together again. As I got older," he recalled to *SATA,* "I, of course, realized that these were optical illusions. After a while one draws a distinction between doing tricks and imagination. Our imagination is real magic. And while imagination may change in our increasingly technological world, it is still magic—it's what got us to the moon! Without it, we'd still be living in trees."

Biographical and Critical Sources

PERIODICALS

Booklist, December 1, 1995, Shelley Townsend-Hudson, review of *The Owl and the Pussy-Cat, and Other Nonsense Poems,* p. 638; January 1, 1996, Susan Dove Lempke, review of *The Children's Book of Virtues,* p. 838; September 1, 1996, Susan Dove Lempke, review of *The Perfect Present,* p. 136; March 15, 1997, April Judge, review of *Calendarbears: A Book of Months,* p. 1247; December 15, 2000, Ilene Cooper, review of *The Book of Fairies,* p. 812; July, 2001, Shelley Townsend-Hudson, review of *Teddy Bears' Mother Goose,* p. 2013; November 1, 2002, Ilene Cooper, review of *The Children's Book of Home and Family,* p. 486; December 1, 2006, John Peters, review of *Lionel and the Book of Beasts,* p. 53; October 15, 2007, Shelle Rosenfeld, review of *Little Bitty Mousie,* p. 51.
Kirkus Reviews, November 1, 2003, review of *The Nutcracker,* p. 1320; September 1, 2007, review of *Little Bitty Mousie.*
Publishers Weekly, September 30, 1996, review of *The Perfect Present,* p. 88.
Reading Today, December, 2000, Lynne T. Burke, review of *The Wizard of Oz, 100th Anniversary Edition,* p. 35.
School Library Journal, October, 2000, review of *A Wind in the Willows Christmas,* p. 59; December, 2000, Patricia Pearl Dole, review of *The Children's Book of Faith,* p. 130; October, 2003, Eva Mitnick, review of *The Life and Adventures of Santa Claus,* p. 60; May, 2005, Jane Marino, review of *The Book of Fairy Poetry,* p. 108; January, 2007, Kirsten Cutler, review of *Lionel and the Book of Beasts,* p. 100; July, 2007, Susan Scheps, review of *Animal Friends: A Collection of Poems for Children,* p. 91.

ONLINE

Bookpage Online, http://www.bookpage.com/ (April, 2001), "Meet the Illustrator: Michael Hague."
Henry Holt Web site, http://www.henryholtchildrensbooks.com/ (November 20, 2007), "Michael Hague."
Michael Hague Home Page, http://michaelhague.com (November 10, 2007).*

*   *   *

HAGUE, Michael R.
See HAGUE, Michael

*   *   *

HALSEY, Megan

Personal

Married; husband's name Marty. *Education:* Mary University, M.A. (studio art and illustration).

Addresses

Home and office—Lansdowne, PA. *E-mail*—megan@meganhalseyart.com.

Career

Author and illustrator. Ah!Ha! Studios, co-founder. Moore College of Art and Design, Philadelphia, PA, instructor; Marywood University, Scranton, PA, graduate instructor. Worked previously at Pratt Institute, Brooklyn, NY.

Awards, Honors

Oppenheim Toy Portfolio Gold Award, 2001, for *Circus 1-2-3;* NAPPA Gold Award, National Parenting, 2005, for *Changed the World.*

Writings

SELF-ILLUSTRATED

Garden Colors, Western Publishing (Racine, WI), 1993.
Three Pandas Planting, Bradbury Press (New York, NY), 1994.
Jump for Joy: A Book of Months, Bradbury Press (New York, NY), 1994.
Hounds around Town: A Guess-What-They-Do Flap Book, Little Simon (New York, NY), 1997.
Circus 1-2-3, HarperCollins (New York, NY), 2000.

ILLUSTRATOR

Barbara Brenner, *Rosa and Marco and the Three Wishes,* Bradbury Press (New York, NY), 1992.
M.C. Helldorfer, *The Darling Boys,* Bradbury Press (New York, NY), 1992.
Janice Boland, *Annabel,* Dial Books for Young Readers (New York, NY), 1993.
Ross Martin Madsen, *Stewart Stork,* Dial Books for Young Readers (New York, NY), 1993.
Sara Atherlay, *Math in the Bath (and Other Fun Places, Too!),* Simon & Schuster Books for Young Readers (New York, NY), 1995.
Janice Boland, *Annabel Again,* Dial Books for Young Readers (New York, NY), 1995.
Clare Hodgson Meeker, *Who Wakes Rooster?,* Simon & Schuster Books for Young Readers (New York, NY), 1996.
Anne Rockwell, *One Bean,* Walker & Company (New York, NY), 1998.
Anne Rockwell, *Pumpkin Day, Pumpkin Night,* Walker & Company (New York, NY), 1999.
Jules Older, *Telling Time: How to Tell Time on Digital and Analog Clocks!,* 2000.
Phyllis S. Busch, *Winter,* Benchmark Books (New York, NY), 2000.
Phyllis S. Busch, *Summer,* Benchmark Books (New York, NY), 2000.

Phyllis S. Busch, *Spring,* Marshall Cavendish (Tarrytown, NY), 2000.

Phyllis S. Busch, *Autumn,* Benchmark Books (New York, NY), 2000.

Dandi Daley Mackall, *Things I Do,* Augsburg Fortress (Minneapolis, MN), 2002.

Dandi Daley Mackall, *Rainbow Party,* Augsburg Fortress (Minneapolis, MN), 2002.

Dandi Daley Mackall, *One Lost Sheep,* Augsburg (Minneapolis, MN), 2002.

Kathi Appelt, *Where, Where Is Swamp Bear?,* HarperCollins (New York, NY), 2002.

Dandi Daley Mackall, *Made by God,* Augsburg (Minneapolis, MN), 2002.

Anne Rockwell, *Becoming Butterflies,* Walker & Company (New York, NY), 2002.

Anne Rockwell, *Four Seasons Make a Year,* Walker & Company (New York, NY), 2004.

Anne Rockwell, *Little Shark,* Walker & Company (New York, NY), 2005.

Cynthia Chin-Lee, *Amelia to Zora: Twenty-six Women Who Changed the World,* Charlesbridge Publishing (Waterstown, MA), 2005.

Patricia Hubbell, *Trains: Huffing! Puffing! Pulling!,* Marshall Cavendish (New York, NY), 2005.

Anne Rockwell, *Backyard Bear,* Walker & Company, 2006.

Patricia Hubbell, *Cars: Rushing! Honking! Zooming!,* Marshall Cavendish (New York, NY), 2006.

Patricia Hubbell, *Trucks: Whizz! Zoom! Rumble!,* Marshall Cavendish (New York, NY), 2006.

Cynthia Chin-Lee, *Akira to Zoltan: Twenty-six Men Who Changed the World,* Charlesbridge Publishing (Watertown, MA), 2006.

Sidelights

Megan Halsey was introduced to art and literature by her family at a young age; her father was a teacher and an artist, and he would take Halsey to the museum every year on her birthday. Her love of art was balanced by her love for reading, and this hobby was encouraged by her schoolteacher grandmother. Halsey discovered the world of children's book illustration in college, and she knew immediately that she had found her life's work. An award-winning book illustrator who has created art for writers such as Anne Rockwell, Patricia Hubbell, Dandi Daley Mackall, Cynthia Chin-Lee, and Jules Older, Halsey is also the co-founder of her own design company, Ah!Ha! Studios. Her design partner, Sean Addy, is an illustrator whom Halsey met while teaching art classes at the Pratt Institute.

Halsey's illustrations have been recognized by critics for their ability to enhance texts written by a variety of authors, as well as for their uniqueness. For instance, she sometimes uses cutouts to give illustrations a three-dimensional effect. Her self-illustrated title *Circus 1-2-3* incorporates such cutouts, creating what a *Publishers Weekly* critic described as an equally unique "spotlight" effect in which "animals and acrobats alike appear to be performing under bright lights." Halsey also uses this cutout technique in *Who Wakes Rooster?,* a picture-

book featuring a text by Clare Hodgson Meeker. The farm animals in *Who Wakes Rooster?,* rendered in warm tones, are accented by the technique in such a way that a "warm, homey, and visually very interesting" effect is produced, according to *Booklist* critic Leone McDermott.

Biographical and Critical Sources

PERIODICALS

Booklist, November 1, 1996, Leone McDermott, review of *Who Wakes Rooster?* p. 508; April 15, 1998, Hazel Rochman, review of *One Bean,* p. 1449; September 1, 1999, Ellen Mandel, review of *Pumpkin Day, Pumpkin Night,* p. 142; March 1, 2000, Kathy Broderick, review of *Telling Time: How to Tell Time on Digital and Analog Clocks!,* p. 1246; March 15, 2002, Shelle Rosenfeld, review of *Becoming Butterflies,* p. 1261; April 15, 2003, Kay Weisman, review of *Trucks: Whizz! Zoom! Rumble!,* p. 1478; May 1, 2003, Gillian Engberg, review of *Two Blue Jays,* p. 1606; February 15, 2004, Carolyn Phelan, review of *Four Seasons Make a Year,* p. 1061; April 1, 2005, Ilene Cooper, review of *Amelia to Zora: Twenty-six Women Who Changed the World,* p. 1358; June 1, 2006, Hazel Rochman, review of *Akira to Zoltan: Twenty-six Men Who Changed the World,* p. 97; October 15, 2006, Randall Enos, review of *Backyard Bear,* p. 55; November 1, 2006, Carolyn Phelan, review of *Cars: Rushing! Honking! Zooming!,* p. 60.

Bulletin of the Center for Children's Books, May, 2002, review of *Becoming Butterflies,* p. 338; July-August 2005, review of *Little Shark,* p. 509.

Kirkus Reviews, January 15, 2002, review of *Becoming Butterflies,* p. 107; February 15, 2003, review of *Trucks,* p. 308; February 15, 2003, review of *Two Blue Jays,* p. 316; February 1, 2004, review of *Four Seasons Make a Year,* p. 138; March 15, 2005, review of *Amelia to Zora,* p. 349; April 15, 2005, review of *Little Shark,* p. 480; August 1, 2005, review of *Trains: Steaming! Pulling! Huffing!,* p. 850; June 15, 2006, review of *Akira to Zoltan,* p. 632; August 1, 2006, review of *Cars,* p. 788; September 15, 2006, review of *Backyard Bear,* p. 53.

New Yorker, November 18, 1996, review of *Who Wakes Rooster?,* p. 101.

Publishers Weekly, September 27, 1999, review of *Pumpkin Day, Pumpkin Night,* p. 107; July 31, 2000, review of *Circus 1-2-3,* p. 93; November 26, 2001, review of *What Is Swamp Bear?,* p. 60; March 3, 2003, review of *Two Blue Jays,* p. 75; March 29, 2004, review of *True Companions,* p. 64.

School Library Journal, September, 1996, Virginia Opocensky, review of *Who Wakes Rooster?,* p. 185; May, 1998, Pamela K. Bomboy, review of *One Bean,* p. 136; October, 1999, Betsy Barnett, review of *Pumpkin Day, Pumpkin Night,* p. 124; March, 2000, Anne Chapman Callaghan, review of *Telling Time,* p. 230; November, 2000, Lisa Gangemi Krapp, review of *Cir-*

Megan Halsey's graphic art is a perfect match for Jules Older's text in Telling Time. (Illustration © 2000 by Megan Halsey. Reproduced by permission of Charlesbridge Publishing, Inc.)

cus 1-2-3, p. 142; March, 2002, Ellen Heath, review of *Becoming Butterflies,* p. 220; January, 2003, review of *One Lost Sheep,* p. 106; January, 2003, Olga R. Kuharets, review of *Made by God,* p. 106; January, 2003, review of *Things I Do,* p. 106; May, 2003, Susan Scheps, review of *Two Blue Jays,* p. 128; June, 2003, review of *Trucks,* p. 107; September, 2005, Genevieve Gallagher, review of *Trains,* p. 174; April, 2005, Patricia Manning, review of *Little Shark,* p. 126; April, 2005, Peg Glisson, review of *Amelia to Zora,* p. 147; March, 2006, John Peters, review of *Amelia to Zora,* p. 89; July, 2006, Ann Wellton, review of *Akira to Zoltan,* p. 118; October, 2006, Andrea Tarr, review of *Backyard Bear,* p. 124; November, 2006, Maren Ostergard, review of *Cars,* p. 96.

ONLINE

Ah!Ha! Studios Web site, http://ahhastudios.com/ (November 20, 2007), "Megan Halsey."

Megan Halsey Home Page, http://www.meganhalseyart. com (November 20, 2007).

Walker Young Readers Web site, http://www.walker youngreaders.com/ (November 20, 2007), "Megan Halsey."*

* * *

HART, Karen

Personal

Married; husband's name Gary; children: two sons. *Education:* Attended Illinois State University.

Addresses

Home—Santa Rosa, CA. *E-mail*—Karen.hart@earth-link.net.

Career

Freelance writer. Worked variously as both a creative and a technical writer, in both corporate communications and public relations.

Writings

Butterflies in May (novel), Bancroft Press (Baltimore, MD), 2006.

Contributor to various periodicals, including *Sonoma Family-Life* and *Enlightened Woman.*

Sidelights

Karen Hart began writing when she was a teenager, getting her start on her high school newspaper. Hart's first novel, *Butterflies in May,* began as a story idea when she was still in high school. Although Hart never experienced a teen pregnancy, she went to school with several girls who did, and their situations forced her to ask herself what she would do in similar circumstances. Hart abandoned the idea at the time, only to revisit it as an adult, once she had married and started a family of her own. The book tells the story of Ali, a high school senior in a middle-class Chicago suburb, who finds herself pregnant after she and her boyfriend forgo using protection a single time. Hart shows the reader Ali's point of view, following her through the realization of what has happened, and her decision-making process. Miranda Doyle, in a review for the *School Library Journal,* found the book to be "a rather ordinary tale of teen pregnancy." However, Olivia Durant, writing for *Kliatt,* considered Hart's work to be "a realistic look at the emotional process a young woman might go through if she became pregnant."

Biographical and Critical Sources

PERIODICALS

Kirkus Reviews, May 1, 2006, review of *Butterflies in May,* p. 460.

Kliatt, July, 2006, Olivia Durant, review of *Butterflies in May,* p. 19.

School Library Journal, October, 2006, Miranda Doyle, review of *Butterflies in May,* p. 156.

ONLINE

Bancroft Press Web site, http://www.bancroftpress.com/ (February 17, 2007), author biography and interview.*

* * *

HAYWARD, Linda 1943-

Personal

Born June 6, 1943, in Los Angeles, CA; married. *Education:* University of California, graduated, 1965. *Hobbies and other interests:* Bird-watching, alligator-spotting, stargazing, swimming.

Addresses

Home and office—Naples, FL. *E-mail*—PforPelican@ aol.com.

Career

Educator, editor, and author. Formerly worked as a teacher in New York, NY; worked as an editor for New York publishers.

Writings

FOR CHILDREN

Letters, Sounds, and Words: A Phonic Dictionary, illustrated by Carol Nicklaus, Platt & Munk, 1973, published as *A Phonic Dictionary,* 1981.

(Reteller) *Hansel and Gretel,* illustrated by Sheilah Beckett, Random House (New York, NY), 1974.

The Curious Little Kitten, illustrated by Maggie Swanson, Golden Press (New York, NY), 1982.

When You Were a Baby, illustrated by Ruth Sanderson, Golden Press (New York, NY), 1982.

The Curious Little Kitten: A Sniff Sniff Book, illustrated by Maggie Swanson, Golden Press (New York, NY), 1983.

The Curious Little Kitten's First Christmas, illustrated by Maggie Swanson, Golden Press (New York, NY), 1984.

(With David Prebenna) *The Simon & Schuster Picture Dictionary of Phonics: From A to Zh,* illustrated by Carol Nicklaus, Simon & Schuster (New York, NY), 1984.

I Had a Bad Dream: A Book about Nightmares, illustrated by Eugenie, Golden Books (New York, NY), 1985.

Snowy Day Bear, illustrated by Lucinda McQueen, Grosset & Dunlap (New York, NY), 1985.

Windy Day Puppy, illustrated by Lucinda McQueen, Grosset & Dunlap (New York, NY), 1985.

Story-a-Night, illustrated by Amye Rosenberg, Random House (New York, NY), 1985.

The Story of Violet Pickles (adapted from characters created by E.J. Taylor), illustrated by Pat Sustendal, Random House (New York, NY), 1986.

The Curious Little Kitten around the House, illustrated by Maggie Swanson, Golden Press (New York, NY), 1986.

Rainy Day Kitten, illustrated by Lucinda McQueen, Grosset & Dunlap (New York, NY), 1986.

Sunny Day Bunny, illustrated by Lucinda McQueen, Grosset & Dunlap (New York, NY), 1986.

(Reteller) *Bible Stories from the Old Testament,* illustrated by Katherine Dietz Coville, Grosset & Dunlap (New York, NY), 1987.

(Reteller) *Noah's Ark: A Story from the Bible,* illustrated by Freire Wright, Random House (New York, NY), 1987, reprinted, 2003.

(Adaptor) *Hello, House!* (based on the characters of Joel Chandler Harris), illustrated by Lynn Munsinger, Random House (New York, NY), 1988.

D Is for Doll, illustrated by Denise Fleming, Random House (New York, NY), 1988.

Tea Party Manners, illustrated by Denise Fleming, Random House (New York, NY), 1988.

This Is the House, illustrated by Denise Fleming, Random House (New York, NY), 1988.

(Reteller) *The Three Little Pigs,* illustrated by Madelaine Gill Linden, Random House (New York, NY), 1988.

The Runaway Christmas Toy, illustrated by Ann Schweninger, Random House (New York, NY), 1988.

(Reteller) *Goldilocks and the Three Bears,* illustrated by M.G. Linden, Random House (New York, NY), 1988.

(Reteller) *Little Red Riding Hood,* illustrated by M.G. Linden, Random House (New York, NY), 1988.

Alphabet School, illustrated by Ann Schweninger, Random House, 1989.

Baby Moses, illustrated by Barb Henry, Random House (New York, NY), 1989.

All Stuck Up, illustrated by Normand Chartier, Random House (New York, NY), 1990.

The First Thanksgiving, illustrated by James Watling, Random House (New York, NY), 1990.

I Spy, Random House (New York, NY), 1993.

(Reteller) *My First Bible,* illustrated by Maria Grazia Boldorini, Random House (New York, NY), 1994.

The Stupid Fish, Random House (New York, NY), 1994.

Wheels, Random House (New York, NY), 1996.

(Adaptor with Cathy Goldsmith) *Wet Foot, Dry Foot, Low Foot, High Foot: Learn about Opposites and Differences* (based on books by Dr. Seuss), Random House (New York, NY), 1996.

(Adaptor with Cathy Goldsmith) *Did I Ever Tell You How High You Can Count? Learn about Counting beyond One Hundred* (based on books by Dr. Seuss), Random House (New York, NY), 1996.

Cave People, illustrated by Gabriela Dellosso, Grosset & Dunlap (New York, NY), 1997.

Lambchop and Friends Band in a Book, illustrated by Chris Angelilli, Golden Books (New York, NY), 1998.

The Curious Little Kitten's First Christmas, illustrated by Maggie Swanson, Golden Books (New York, NY), 1999.

The Adventures of Cliff Hanger, illustrated by Joe Ewers, Golden Books (New York, NY), 2001.

A Day in the Life of a Builder, Dorling Kindersley (New York, NY), 2001.

A Day in the Life of a Dancer, Dorling Kindersley (New York, NY), 2001.

A Day in the Life of a Doctor, Dorling Kindersley (New York, NY), 2001.

A Day in the Life of a Firefighter, Dorling Kindersley (New York, NY), 2001.

A Day in the Life of a Musician, Dorling Kindersley (New York, NY), 2001.

A Day in the Life of a Police Officer, Dorling Kindersley (New York, NY), 2001.

A Day in the Life of a Teacher, Dorling Kindersley (New York, NY), 2001.

A Day in the Life of a TV Reporter, Dorling Kindersley (New York, NY), 2001.

(Adapter) *Pepe and Papa,* illustrated by Laura Huliska-Beith, Golden Books (New York, NY), 2001.

(Adapter) *Little by Little,* illustrated by Peter Grosshauer, Golden Books (New York, NY), 2002.

What Homework?, Kane Press (New York, NY), 2002.

All Stuck Up, Random House (New York, NY), 2003.

The First Thanksgiving, Random House (New York, NY), 2003.

I Am a Pencil, illustrated by Carol Nicklaus, Millbrook Press (Brookfield, CT), 2003.

It Takes Three, illustrated by Michal Koontz, Millbrook Press (Brookfield, CT), 2003.

Monster Bug, illustrated by Diane Palmisciano, Kane Press (New York, NY), 2004.

The King's Chorus, illustrated by Jennifer P. Goldfinger, Clarion (New York, NY), 2006.

"SESAME STREET MUPPET" BOOKS

The Sesame Street Dictionary, illustrated by Joe Mathieu, Random House, (New York, NY) 1980.

The Sesame Street Storybook Alphabet, illustrated by Tom Cooke, Western Publishing (Racine, WI), 1980.

Going Up! The Elevator Counting Book, illustrated by Tom Leigh, Western Publishing (Racine, WI), 1980, published as *Going Up with Grover,* 1992.

Early Bird on Sesame Street, illustrated by Tom Leigh, Western Publishing (Racine, WI), 1980.

Twiddlebugs at Work, illustrated by Irene Trivas, Western Publishing (Racine, WI), 1980.

The Case of the Missing Duckie, illustrated by Maggie Swanson, Western Publishing (Racine, WI), 1981.

The Sesame Street Sun, illustrated by Tim Kirk, Western Publishing (Racine, WI), 1981.

Sesame Seasons, illustrated by Rick Brown, Western Publishing (Racine, WI), 1981, published as *A Big Year on Sesame Street,* 1989.

Which One Doesn't Belong?, and Other Puzzles from Sesame Street, illustrated by Kimberly A. McSparran, Western Publishing (Racine, WI), 1981.

A Day in the Life of Oscar the Grouch, illustrated by Bill Davis, Western Publishing (Racine, WI), 1981.

The City Worm and the Country Worm, illustrated by Carol Nicklaus, Western Publishing (Racine, WI), 1983.

I Can Count to Ten and Back Again, illustrated by Maggie Swanson, Western Publishing (Racine, WI), 1985.

Look What I Can Do, illustrated by Richard Brown, Western Publishing (Racine, WI), 1985.

Mine: A Sesame Street Book about Sharing, illustrated by Norman Gorbaty, Random House, 1988.

Grover's Summer Vacation, illustrated by Ron Fritz, Random House, 1989.

The Biggest Cookie in the World, illustrated by Joe Ewers, Random House, 1989.

Elmo Goes to Day Camp, illustrated by Carol Nicklaus, Random House, 1990.

Big Bird Visits Granny Bird, illustrated by Carol Nicklaus, Random House, 1991.

Ernie and Bert's Summer Project, illustrated by Carol Nicklaus, Random House, 1991.

Baker, Baker, Cookie Maker, Random House (New York, NY), 1998.

The Sesame Street Dictionary, illustrated by Joe Mathieu, Random House (New York, NY), 2004.

"ON MY WAY WITH SESAME STREET" SERIES; WITH OTHERS

Colors and Shapes, illustrated by Tom Brannen and others, Western Publishing (Racine, WI), 1989.

I Can Count, illustrated by Tom Cooke and others, Western Publishing (Racine, WI), 1989.

In the City, illustrated by Cooke and others, Western Publishing (Racine, WI), 1989.

My Family, illustrated by Cooke and others, Western Publishing (Racine, WI), 1989.

People in My Neighborhood, illustrated by Richard Eric Brown and others, Western Publishing (Racine, WI), 1989.

Sidelights

Linda Hayward grew up knowing that she wanted to be a writer. When she was ten years old, she started a newspaper and sold it, for a nickel, to all the members of her family. She continued to create her solo publications until high school, when she was appointed editor of the school newspaper and won an On-the-Spot article-writing contest. After graduating from college, Hayward moved to New York City and worked there as a teacher. Later on she made a career shift to publishing, and in her editorial position began producing texts for children's books.

A prolific author of picture books and board books for the preschool set, Hayward has written many stories based on the popular *Sesame Street* television show. In addition to recounting the antics of Bert and Ernie, Elmo, the Cookie Monster, Big Bird, and the lovable but slightly confused Grover, she has also penned dozens of other stories, including a number of retellings of classic folk and fairy tales. Drawing on her experiences

as a teacher, she has also compiled dictionaries for young people, including the 1,300-word *The Sesame Street Dictionary* and *The Simon and Schuster Picture Dictionary of Phonics: From A to Zh*. The definitions in *The Sesame Street Dictionary* were described by a contributor to *Publishers Weekly* as "crisp and unmistakable," the critic predicting that the book will allow beginning readers to learn spelling "and have a good time to boot." Similarly, a *Publishers Weekly* reviewer termed Hayward's *Letter, Sounds, and Words: A Phonic Dictionary* "a mixture of pure fun and effective education."

Among Hayward's books based on Jim Henson's Muppet characters, which were made popular via *Sesame Street* are *The Case of the Missing Duckie, Going Up!: The Elevator Counting Book, The Biggest Cookie in the World*, and *A Day in the Life of Oscar the Grouch*. In *A Day in the Life of Oscar the Grouch* the curmudgeonly Oscar emerges from his trash can just long enough to tell readers what he dislikes most about his can, his street, and everyone else on Sesame Street. Suspense fills Sesame Street in *The Case of the Missing Duckie*, as Ernie becomes perplexed at the disappearance of his yellow plastic bath-time buddy. Fortunately, ace detective Sherlock Hemlock comes to his aid and the mystery is eventually solved. *The Biggest Cookie in the World* finds Cookie Monster daydreaming while waiting for his latest baking project—cookies, of course!—to pop from the oven. In *A Big Year on Sesame Street*, first published as *Sesame Seasons*, Hayward includes not only stories, but poems, games, and suggestions for fun activities to celebrate each of the four seasons of the year, and also features ideas for welcoming in the New Year.

Books featuring original characters by Hayward include *When You Were a Baby, Story-a-Night, The Curious Little Kitten: A Sniff Sniff Book*, and the humorous *The Runaway Christmas Toy*, the last which finds a toy train hoping to road-test its wheels by rolling out of Santa's workshop before the jolly old gentleman is ready to make his annual rounds. In *The Curious Little Kitten*, as well as in the book's two sequels, a young kitten decides to expand her world and almost (but not quite) ends up using one of her nine lives. In *Story-a-Night* Hayward does what the title suggests, presenting 365 short stories that can be used to entertain youngsters on their way to bed every night of the year.

Hayward has also adapted several popular folk and fairy tales into picture-book format, among them *Hansel and Gretel, Goldilocks and the Three Bears*, and *Little Red Riding Hood*. In *Hello, House*, which features illustrations by talented artist Lynn Munsinger, Hayward presents readers with a retelling of a Brer Rabbit tale that *School Library Journal* contributor Gale W. Sherman deemed "simple but delightful." Based on a story by Joel Chandler Harris that pits the wits of Brer Rabbit against the wily Brer Wolf, Hayward's adaptation was also praised by *Booklist* reviewer Phillis Wilson for retaining the "integrity" of the original story. *All Stuck*

Up also features the antics of Brer Rabbit as he attempts to become unstuck from a tarbaby—a big gob of sticky stuff—used as a trap by Brer Fox. In the retold folktale *Pepe and Papa,* Pepe tries to help out by taking the chiles grown by his family to market, but ends up getting the chiles, his father, and his burro all tangled up. "New readers will get lots of phonic practice in this very simple version" of a humorous tale, according to Hazel Rochman in *Booklist.*

The King's Chorus is an original tale that has the feel of a porquois tale. Kadoodle the rooster cannot understand why the other farm animals do not appreciate his crowing all through the night. When the sleepy farm animals can no longer stand Kadoodle's crowing, Honketta the goose tells the rooster a story that explains why roosters only crow to greet the sun. Won over by Honketta's tale, Kadoodle crows to greet the sun the very next morning. "Hayward's animated prose will be great for reading aloud," wrote Shelle Rosenfeld in *Booklist,* and a *Kirkus Reviews* contributor predicted that parents will appreciate Hayward's "ironic text and behavior-modification theme."

In addition to dictionaries and reading aides, Hayward has also written several other nonfiction works geared for young students. In *The First Thanksgiving* she tells the story of the first New England colonists as they battled against starvation and nature while surviving in their new home, and introduces such real-life characters as Native American Squanto. The book was praised by Roger Sutton, who wrote in the *Bulletin of the Center for Children's Books* that *The First Thanksgiving* is "welcome, particularly for its resistance to fictionalization." In her *Booklist* review, Hazel Rochman noted that Hayward's holiday offering should "appeal to both beginners and to reluctant readers" looking for information on colonial village life. Other nonfiction works include *My First Bible,* an edition designed especially for youngsters and published with illustrations by Maria Grazia Boldorini. Hayward has also adapted several other stories from the Bible, among them *Baby Moses,* a story of the infant's trip down the Nile in a basket made of bullrushes while escaping from Pharaoh's wrath. *School Library Journal* contributor Susan Kaminow commended *Baby Moses* as "unique" and "an interesting reading experience."

In *I Am a Book,* another of Hayward's nonfiction titles, a book explains to readers how it came to be made. From wood chips to pages in a binding, the book explains the typical life cycle of a book as well as vital parts of the final product, including the title and copyright pages. "The text maintains a light tone, keeping the information accessible to beginning readers," wrote Carolyn Phelan in *Booklist.*

On her home page, Hayward offered the following advice for young writers: "Try different kinds of writing. If you want something, write about why. If you disagree with someone, write down your arguments. If you

have an experience that makes you happy or angry or sad, write a poem. Use your imagination. When you write a story, imagine it is happening to you. Then try to make your reader imagine what you imagine."

Biographical and Critical Sources

PERIODICALS

Booklist, October 1, 1988, Phillis Wilson, review of *Hello, House!,* p. 330; December 1, 1990, Hazel Rochman, review of *The First Thanksgiving,* p. 754; November 1, 2001, review of *Pepe and Papa,* p. 486; January 1, 2006, Carolyn Phelan, review of *I Am a Book,* p. 105; February 15, 2007, Shelle Rosenfeld, review of *The King's Chorus,* p. 83.

Bulletin of the Center for Children's Books, March, 1981, review of *The Sesame Street Dictionary,* p. 135; September, 1985, review of *I Had a Bad Dream: A Book about Nightmares,* p. 10; June, 1987, review of *Noah's Ark: A Story from the Bible,* p. 182; June, 1989, review of *Baby Moses,* p. 251; July, 1990, review of *All Stuck Up,* p. 267; November, 1990, Roger Sutton, review of *The First Thanksgiving,* p. 61.

Instructor and Teacher, May, 1981, Allan Yeager, review of *A Phonic Dictionary,* p. 62.

Kirkus Reviews, October 15, 2006, review of *The King's Chorus,* p. 1072.

Publishers Weekly, June 25, 1973, review of *Letters, Sounds, and Words: A Phonic Dictionary,* p. 74; November 21, 1980, review of *Sesame Street Dictionary,* p. 59.

School Library Journal, December, 1980, Kenneth F. Kister, review of *The Sesame Street Dictionary,* p. 18; May, 1982, review of *The Sesame Street Dictionary,* p. 21; February, 1985, review of *A Phonic Dictionary,* p. 64; June-July, 1987, Nancy Palmer, review of *Noah's Ark,* p. 80; March, 1988, Patricia Pearl, review of *Bible Stories from the Old Testament,* p. 182; October, 1988, Gale W. Sherman, review of *Hello, House!,* pp. 117-118; December, 1989, Susan Kaminow, review of *Baby Moses,* p. 95; August, 1990, Sharon McElmeel, review of *All Stuck Up,* p. 130; June, 1994, Kathy Piehl, review of *My First Bible,* p. 122; February, 1999, Sharon R. Pearce, review of *Baker, Baker, Cookie Maker,* p. 84; November, 2002, Wendy S. Carroll, review of *What Homework?,* p. 124; October, 2005, Erlene Bishop Killeen, review of *I Am a Book,* p. 140; October, 2003, Pat Leach, review of *It Takes Three,* p. 125.

ONLINE

Linda Hayward Home Page, http://www.linda-hayward. com (December 2, 2007).

Reading Warehouse Web site, http://www.thereadingware house.com/ (December 2, 2007), "Linda Hayward."

Scholastic Web site, http://content.scholastic.com/ (December 2, 2007), "Linda Hayward."*

HO, Louise

Personal

Born in England. *Education:* University of Central Lancashire, B.A. 2003. *Hobbies and other interests:* Drawing, collecting fossils, learning to read Chinese and Japanese.

Addresses

Home—Northwest England.

Career

Illustrator.

Awards, Honors

Royal Mail Awards for Scottish Children's Books, for *The Sea Mice and the Stars.*

Illustrator

Claire Freedman, *One Magical Morning,* Good Books (Intercourse, PA), 2005.
Kenneth C. Steven, *The Sea Mice and the Stars,* Good Books (Intercourse, PA), 2005.
Gill Lewis, *The Most Precious Thing,* Good Books (Intercourse, PA), 2006.

Biographical and Critical Sources

PERIODICALS

Kirkus Reviews, September 15, 2006, review of *The Most Precious Thing,* p. 959.
Publishers Weekly, June 20, 2005, review of *One Magical Morning,* p. 75.
School Library Journal, May, 2005, Sheilah Kosco, review of *One Magical Morning,* p. 83; December, 2006, Daisy Porter, review of *The Most Precious Thing,* p 107.

ONLINE

Little Tiger Press Web site, http://www.littletigerpress.com/ (December 26, 2007), "Louise Ho."
University of Central Lancashire Web site, http://www. uclan.ac.uk/ (December 26, 2007), "Louise Ho."*

*   *   *

HURLEY, Jo
See DOWER, Laura

*   *   *

HURST, Carol Otis 1933-2007

Personal

Born October 13, 1933, in Springfield, MA; died of a heart attack, January 21 (one source says January 22), 2007, in Westfield, MA; daughter of Leo Derwood (a

Carol Otis Hurst (Reproduced by permission.)

science museum director) and Ruth (a homemaker) Otis; married John Hurst, 1954 (divorced, 1960); children: Rebecca Otis, Jill Hurst. *Education:* Westfield State College, B.S.Ed., M.Ed. *Politics:* Democrat.

Career

Author and educator. Taught school in Tennessee, Ohio, and Minnesota; school librarian in Westfield, MA; also served as an educational consultant, workshop conductor, and storyteller.

Writings

PICTURE BOOKS

Rocks in His Head, illustrated by James Stevenson, Greenwillow Books (New York, NY), 2001.
Terrible Storm, illustrated by S.D. Schindler, Greenwillow Books (New York, NY), 2007.

YOUNG ADULT NOVELS

Through the Lock, Houghton Mifflin (Boston, MA), 2001.
In Plain Sight, Houghton Mifflin (Boston, MA), 2002.

A Killing in Plymouth Colony, Houghton Mifflin (Boston, MA), 2003.

The Wrong One, Houghton Mifflin (Boston, MA), 2003.

You Come to Yokum, illustrated by Kay Life, Houghton Mifflin (Boston, MA), 2005.

Torchlight, Houghton Mifflin (Boston, MA), 2006.

FOR ADULTS

(With Margaret Sullivan Ahearn) *Long Ago and Far Away—: An Encyclopedia for Successfully Using Literature with Intermediate Readers,* DLM (Allen, TX), 1990.

Once upon a Time: An Encyclopedia for Successfully Using Literature with Young Children, DLM (Austin, TX), 1990.

(With daughter, Rebecca Otis) *Using Literature in the Middle-School Curriculum,* Linworth (Worthington, OH), 1998.

Open Books: Literature in the Curriculum, Kindergarten through Grade Two, Linworth (Worthington, OH), 1998.

Curriculum Connections: Picture Books in Grades Three and Up, Linworth (Worthington, OH), 1999.

(With Rebecca Otis) *Friends and Relations: Using Literature with Social Themes,* Northeast Foundation for Children (Greenfield, MA), 1999.

Contributor to professional magazines, including *Early Years* (now *Teaching K8*).

Sidelights

Carol Otis Hurst made children's literature the focus of her life, first as a classroom teacher and then as a school librarian, storyteller, and author of educational materials and juvenile literature. During her sixteen-year stint as a school librarian, Hurst built a library collection and taught courses in children's literature at local colleges. She also published material related to the curriculum, including articles for *Early Years* magazine (now *Teaching K8*) and books such as *Open Books: Literature in the Curriculum, Kindergarten through Grade Two, Curriculum Connections: Picture Books in Grades Three and Up,* and *Friends and Relations: Using Literature with Social Themes.*

In *Open Books* Hurst suggests classroom activities to accompany fourteen picture books and gave information on twenty-five authors. According to Hazel Rochman in *Booklist, Open Books* is "an excellent resource for bringing picture books into the lower-grade classroom." In *Curriculum Connections,* Hurst took a similar approach to using picture books for students in grade three and higher, providing activities for students of all learning styles. "I was most impressed by the variety and originality of the curriculum activities," wrote *Book Report* critic Pat Miller in appraising Hurst's work. In support of her classroom materials, Hurst conducted workshops nationwide, and in the process was encouraged to try her hand at fiction writing. As she once told

SATA: "At about the same time as the professional book writing career took off, so did the workshops. Soon I was on the road more than I was home and I had to tearfully bid goodbye to my library career."

Hurst continued: "Every so often someone would ask me why I hadn't written a children's book and I would say that that question was somewhat like asking an opera singer if she'd written any good operas. But I did have a lot of family stories rolling around in my head. I would tell people some of them and a couple of those stories began to take shape.

"One of the stories was about my Grandmother Clark. She was a wonderful woman and a great comfort and support to all my brothers and sisters. Her own early life had been a tragic one—orphaned at age eleven, the eldest of four. Her siblings had been split up and taken to different homes and she herself was tossed about from one foster home to another until being taken in by a wonderful family who loved her and sent her to school. Then there was my Grandfather Otis who had left his home at age nine. When we asked him, why he would only say that it was time to go.

"Then there was the Northampton New Haven Canal, a failed enterprise of the mid-1800s that had run practically through the backyard of the house in which I now live. I took the lives of those two grandparents, twisted them a bit, threw them back in time to have them establishing a home together on the banks of the canal and *Through the Lock* was born.

"*Rocks in His Head* came easier. It was my father's story and I wrote it first for my grandchildren. My father was an amazing man and my grandchildren will never know him. I wanted them to know how he had collected rocks and minerals from the time he was a child and made it his lifetime passion. He kept to that passion throughout his life and, because he did, wonderful things happened to him, but not until real hard times threatened to crush us all."

Hurst's middle-grade novel *Through the Lock* and her picture book *Rocks in His Head* marked the start of her career as a fiction writer. In *Rocks in His Head* she tells the story of a young man who has always been fascinated by rocks and retains that interest throughout his life, finding much success despite the hardships of the Depression. Reviewers found much to like in this picture book. *Booklist* contributor Shelle Rosenfeld described the work as "delightful," "charming," and "inspiring," while Kathleen Kelly MacMillan wrote in *School Library Journal* that Hurst "paints a touching picture of a man who quietly pursues his passion." "Readers will warm to Hurst's rock-solid tale of unwavering dedication and determination," punned a reviewer in *Horn Book.*

Through the Lock takes place at a lock on the Farmington Canal, a waterway that, in the nineteenth century, ran from New Haven, Connecticut, to Northampton,

Massachusetts. In the work, a young girl named Etta escapes the slavery of a foster home, to find herself sharing a small cabin near a canal lock with another fugitive from adversity, Walter. Together they each try to reunite their families. Although a *Publishers Weekly* critic noted some plausibility problems with elements of the novel, the reviewer praised the "likable" narrator and "atmospheric backdrop." "Hurst does an admirable job of presenting a topic" unfamiliar to most juvenile readers: the life along and importance of canals to America during the early years of the Industrial Revolution. "This story will grab readers from the first page," wrote Hazel Rochman in *Booklist.*

Another work of historical fiction, *In Plain Sight,* concerns Sarah Corbin, an eleven-year-old Massachusetts girl whose fun-loving but reckless father leaves his family behind to search for gold in California. When Sarah's mother takes a factory job to make ends meet, the youngster and her siblings are left to run the household and tend the family farm. The Corbins' problems are only beginning, however; they learn that their father has drowned at sea, and Sarah is burned while rescuing her brother from a disastrous barn fire. *In Plain Sight* received generally strong reviews. Writing in *School Library Journal,* Carol A. Edwards stated that the author "manages to keep sight of the child's perspective and longings while gradually uncovering the adult issues in the situation." Though some critics, such as Martha V. Parravano in *Booklist,* faulted the novel's "abrupt and extraneous" conclusion, they did not feel it diminished the work. "While enjoying the melodrama," noted a contributor in *Kirkus Reviews,* readers will "also learn a little American history."

Based on an episode from American history, *A Killing in Plymouth Colony* centers on John Bradford, the eleven-year-old son of William Bradford, the governor of Plymouth Colony. Although John's relationship with his father is strained, he finds comfort in his friends and the love of his stepmother. His peaceful world is shattered, however, when one of the colonists is murdered, and suspicion quickly falls on John Billington, an outcast with a fiery temper. According to *School Library Journal* reviewer Heather Dieffenbach, "The well-developed setting and picture of daily life in Colonial America provide an interesting backdrop" to the tale, and Carolyn Phelan, reviewing the work in *Booklist,* remarked, "The mystery element gives an added dimension to this historical novel."

Hurst explores the supernatural in *The Wrong One,* "an appealing family portrait animated by ample doses of intrigue," noted a critic in *Publishers Weekly.* After their father passes away, eleven-year-old Kate, her younger brother, Jesse, and her newly adopted Asian sister, Sookan, move with their mother from a comfortable Brooklyn brownstone to a dilapidated farmhouse in rural Massachusetts. Things immediately go from bad to worse: Sookan is inexplicably terrified by the doll-motif wallpaper in her bedroom, the television appears to turn

Cover of A Killing in Plymouth Colony, *a collaborative work of historical fiction by Hurst and her daughter Rebecca Otis.* (Illustration © 2003 by Carol Otis Hurst and Rebecca Otis. Reproduced by permission of Houghton Mifflin Company. All rights reserved.)

itself off and on, and a mysterious blue light appears. "Enough details are left untied to make this interesting, leaving the premise of ghosts a possibility," wrote a critic in *Kirkus Reviews.*

Set in the 1920s, *You Come to Yokum* follows the exploits of the Carlyle family. After Mrs. Carlyle, an ardent suffragist, is arrested for chaining herself to the White House gate, her husband, hoping to escape further embarrassment, agrees to run Yokum, a vacation lodge located in western Massachusetts. Twelve-year-old Frank and his brother, Jim, contribute their efforts to their father's dubious cause, which doesn't go exactly as planned. "Hurst has her historical details just right," observed a *Kirkus Reviews* contributor, and Julie Cummins, reviewing *You Come to Yokum* in *Booklist,* wrote that "the fight for the vote becomes more than just a dry history lesson."

Immigration is the subject of *Torchlight,* a work of fiction based on an actual event. Set in Westfield, Massachusetts, in 1854, *Torchlight* looks at the tensions between the Protestant "Yankees" who settled the town and the newly arrived Irish Catholics through the eyes of two young girls who form an unlikely friendship. The author's "fast-moving and interesting novel will spark discussions about prejudice and racism," commented Elizabeth M. Reardon in *School Library Journal.* *Terrible Storm,* a picture book inspired by Hurst's family history, also takes place in Westfield. The work concerns gregarious Grandpa Walt and shy Grandpa Fred, who were caught outdoors during the blizzard of 1888. While the lively Walt finds shelter in a lonely barn, the reclusive Fred is trapped for days at the bustling White Horse Inn. "Hurst's call-and-response narrative approach . . . captures the rhythms of a story told, back and forth, many times over," a *Publishers Weekly* critic remarked. According to Ilene Cooper in *Booklist,* Hurst's "lively, clever story . . . neatly captures both the oddities of nature and how differing natures view the same event."

Biographical and Critical Sources

PERIODICALS

Booklist, December 15, 1999, Hazel Rochman, review of *Open Books: Literature in the Curriculum, Kindergarten through Grade Two,* p. 792; April 1, 2001, Hazel Rochman, review of *Through the Lock,* p. 1482; June 1, 2001, Shelle Rosenfeld, review of *Rocks in His Head,* p. 1890; December 1, 2003, Carolyn Phelan, review of *A Killing in Plymouth Colony,* p. 666; September 1, 2005, Julie Cummins, review of *You Come to Yokum,* p. 133; November 15, 2006, Ilene Cooper, review of *Terrible Storm,* p. 44.

Book Report, May-June, 1999, Pat Miller, review of *Curriculum Connections: Picture Books in Grades Three and Up,* pp. 85-86.

California Kids!, February, 2003, Patricia M. Newman, "Who Wrote That? Featuring Carol Otis Hurst."

Bulletin of the Center for Children's Books, January, 2004, Elizabeth Bush, review of *A Killing in Plymouth Colony,* p. 194; February, 2007, Deborah Stevenson, review of *Terrible Storm,* p. 255.

Horn Book, March, 2001, Joanna Rudge Long, review of *Through the Lock,* p. 208; July, 2001, review of *Rocks in His Head,* p. 440; May-June, 2002, Martha V. Parravano, review of *In Plain Sight,* p. 331.

Kirkus Reviews, March 1, 2002, review of *In Plain Sight,* p. 337; May 1, 2003, review of *The Wrong One,* p. 678; September 1, 2003, review of *A Killing in Plymouth Colony,* p. 1124; October 15, 2005, review of *You Come to Yokum,* p. 1139; September 15, 2006, review of *Torchlight,* p. 955; December 15, 2006, review of *Terrible Storm,* p. 1269.

Publishers Weekly, April 30, 2001, review of *Rocks in His Head,* p. 78; April 30, 2001, review of *Through the Lock,* p. 79; May 12, 2003, review of *The Wrong One,* p. 67; January 15, 2007, review of *Terrible Storm,* p. 51.

Reference and Research Book News, November, 1999, review of *Using Literature in the Middle School Curriculum,* p. 151.

School Library Journal, March, 2001, Coney Tyrell Burns, review of *Through the Lock,* p. 250; June, 2001, Kathleen Kelly MacMillan, review of *Rocks in His Head,* p. 118; March, 2002, Carol A. Edwards, review of *In Plain Sight,* p. 232; May, 2003, Heather Dieffenbach, review of *The Wrong One,* p. 154; October, 2003, Heather Dieffenbach, review of *A Killing in Plymouth Colony,* p. 168; January, 2006, Kristen Oravec, review of *You Come to Yokum,* p. 134; January, 2007, Catherine Threadgill, review of *Terrible Storm,* p. 98, and Elizabeth M. Reardon, review of *Torchlight,* p. 129.

ONLINE

Carol Hurst's Children's Literature Web site, http://www.carolhurst.com/ (November 10, 2007).

OBITUARIES

PERIODICALS

Republican (Springfield, MA), January 30, 2007, Pat Cahill, "Author Wove a Lasting Legacy."

Teaching Pre K-8, March, 2007, Allen Raymond, "So Long, Carol."

ONLINE

School Library Journal Web site, http://www.schoollibraryjournal.com/ (February 5, 2007), "Author Carol Otis Hurst Dies at 73."*

I-J

ISAACS, Anne 1949-

Personal

Born March 2, 1949, in Buffalo, NY; daughter of Samuel (a materials handling engineer) and Hope (an anthropologist) Isaacs; married Samuel Koplowicz (a media producer), 1978; children: Jordan, Amy, Sarah. *Education:* University of Michigan, B.A., 1971, M.S., 1975; attended State University of New York at Buffalo, 1971-72. *Religion:* Jewish.

Addresses

Home—CA. *E-mail*—anne@anneisaacs.com.

Career

Author and storyteller. Held numerous positions in environmental education from 1975 to 1990.

Awards, Honors

Notable Books for Children selection, American Library Association (ALA), and Best Illustrated Books citation, *New York Times,* both 1994, and *Boston Globe/ Horn Book* Honor Book citation, Children's Book of the Year list, Child Study Children's Book Committee, and Notable Trade Book in Language Arts, National Council of Teachers of English, all 1995, all for *Swamp Angel;* 100 Titles for Reading and Sharing selection, New York Public Library, 1998, for *Cat up a Tree;* National Jewish Book Award finalist, Sydney Taylor Honor Book designation, Notable Book for a Global Society designation, International Reading Association, ALA Best Books for Young Adults selection, and 100 Titles for Reading and Sharing selection, New York Public Library, all 2000, all for *Torn Thread.*

Writings

Swamp Angel, illustrated by Paul O. Zelinsky, Dutton Children's Books (New York, NY), 1994.

Anne Isaacs (Reproduced by permission.)

Treehouse Tales, illustrated by Lloyd Bloom, Dutton Children's Books (New York, NY), 1997.

Cat up a Tree: A Story in Poems, illustrated by Stephen Mackey, Dutton Children's Books (New York, NY), 1998.

Torn Thread (young-adult novel), Scholastic Press (New York, NY), 2000.

Pancakes for Supper!, illustrated by Mark Teague, Scholastic Press (New York, NY), 2006.

Adaptations

Swamp Angel appeared on *Storytime,* PBS, 1995.

Sidelights

Anne Isaacs is an award-winning author of picture books for young readers, among them *Treehouse Tales* and *Pancakes for Supper!* She is perhaps best known for *Swamp Angel,* an imaginative historical tale spotlighting a young female heroine who sometimes appears larger than life. Isaacs is also the author of the fictional work *Torn Thread,* which is based on the true story of a young girl imprisoned in a Nazi labor camp during World War II.

Isaacs was born in Buffalo, New York, in 1949 and lived there until she left for college in 1967, when she began attending the University of Michigan. She was a voracious reader from a young age, though she did not begin writing seriously until she was an adult. The author once told *SATA:* "As a child, I did a limited amount of creative writing on my own. I had two poems published at the age of ten in a city-wide magazine of writing by school children. I read constantly, selecting books haphazardly from my parents' and the public library shelves. In fifth grade, for example, along with *The Wind in the Willows,* I read Shakespeare's *Romeo and Juliet* and *The Tempest,* plus *Lorna Doone* and *The Caine Mutiny.* As now, poetry affected me more profoundly than any other genre. At age ten, I memorized Coleridge's 'Kubla Khan' while reading it for the first time.

"Probably the greatest childhood influence on my writing was reading and re-reading, over a period of years, [Louisa May Alcott's] *Little Women.* I would finish the last page and immediately start over at the first. The story became a kind of life plan for me, although I didn't realize that until a few years ago. Like Alcott's semi-autobiographical heroine, Jo, I grew up to marry a kindly, professorial man with an unpronounceable name, to raise a passel of kids in the country, and to combine careers in educational program development and children's book writing. This experience has taught me to respect the long-term influence a children's book may have on its readers.

"I studied English literature in my undergraduate years at the University of Michigan, and in a year of graduate study at the State University of New York, Buffalo. I also studied French, Russian, Latin, and American literature during these years. I have always been especially interested in nineteenth-century novels and poetry. Only as an adult have I begun to read extensively in children's literature, often experiencing a book for the first time while reading it to my children.

"As a result of reading children's and adult literature interchangeably throughout my life, I have never recognized a clear distinction between them, nor do I apply different standards."

Isaacs's debut work, *Swamp Angel,* was described as "a brand-new backwoods legend, written mostly for girls, that has the feel of real frontier storytelling" by a contributor in *Time.* Written in a tongue-in-cheek style, *Swamp Angel* features Angelica Longrider, who, as an infant, is a bit taller than her mother, and who later accomplishes some amazing feats. In addition to building her first log cabin by the time she is two, Angelica rescues a wagon from Dejection Swamp and then defeats a bear, Thundering Tarnation, by throwing him up to the sky and creating a prairie from the bear's pelt. Commentators have compared Angelica to the legendary American hero Paul Bunyan, and *Swamp Angel* received stellar reviews. A Caldecott honor book, *Swamp Angel* was deemed "visually exciting, wonderful to read aloud, [and] . . . a picture book to remember" by Mary M. Burns in *Horn Book.* The author "tells her original story with the glorious exaggeration and uproarious farce of the traditional tall tale and with its typical laconic idiom," remarked *Booklist* contributor Hazel Rochman, and a critic in *Kirkus Reviews* exclaimed: "It is impossible to convey the sheer pleasure, the exaggerated loopiness, of newcomer Isaacs's wonderful story."

Set in rural Pennsylvania in the 1800s, *Treehouse Tales* collects three short stories that center on the members of the Barrett family. In the opening tale, Tom Barrett helps calm the fears of his brother, Natty, after the youngster spots a trail of smoke coming from their treehouse and becomes convinced that the dwelling is inhabited by a fire-breathing dragon. The second story concerns Emily, whose quick thinking saves the day after she awakens from a nap in the treehouse and spies a thief trying to rob the farm. The concluding story focuses on Natty who, inspired by the legend of George Washington and the cherry tree, attempts a similarly dramatic feat. "The tales are redolent of family affection and youthful ambitions," Ann A. Flowers stated in *Horn Book.* "Isaacs's lighthearted tales sparkle with warmth and humor," remarked *Booklist* contributor Kay Weisman.

Cat up a Tree: A Story in Poems was based on an event from Isaacs's life. While walking through San Francisco's Golden Gate Park in 1991, Isaacs and her children watched some firefighters rescue a cat that had climbed into a tall cedar tree. On her home page Isaacs recalled that she became "fascinated" by the people in the gathering crowd. "What kept them there, despite fog and cold and growing dark?" she asked. "What was going through their minds?" In *Cat up a Tree* the author presents, in verse, an account of the incident. According to a reviewer in *Publishers Weekly,* "cat lovers will go wild for this work, as will poets and dreamers."

A more serious work is presented in *Torn Thread,* which Isaacs once described to *SATA* as "a fictional account of the experiences of my mother-in-law, Eva Buchbinder Koplowicz, as a young woman in a Nazi labor camp in Czechoslovakia from 1943 to 1945. All of the incidents are either true or possible." To write this emotionally

Isaacs brings to life a joyous tale of the south in her picture book Swamp Angel, *featuring artwork by Paul O. Zelinsky.* (Illustration © 1994 by Paul O. Zelinsky. Reproduced by permission of Dutton Children's Books, a division of Penguin Putnam Books for Young Readers.)

painful story, Isaacs researched a number of Holocaust topics; read the testimony of Holocaust survivors; visited the site of concentration camps, death camps, and former ghettos in Europe; and also visited the labor camp and factory where Eva worked.

In *Torn Thread* Isaacs "turns her considerable literary gifts to a painful subject . . . and transforms it into a powerful work of fiction," observed a *Publishers Weekly* critic. The novel focuses on the relationship between Eva and Rachel, sisters who turn to each other for comfort and support in order to survive the brutal conditions in the camp. *School Library Journal* reviewer Virginia Golodetz called *Torn Thread* a "powerful testament to the human spirit," and Claire Rosser, writing in *Kliatt,* stated that in the book Isaacs shares "an important story of the Holocaust" as well as "a story of the extraordinary love of one sister for the other."

Six years after the publication of *Torn Thread,* Isaacs penned *Pancakes for Supper!,* "another winning, comical tall tale," according to *Booklist* contributor Gillian Engberg. Inspired by Helen Bannerman's *The Story of Little Black Sambo,* the work follows the adventures of Toby, a girl in a pioneering family who falls off the back of her parents' wagon and finds herself lost in the woods of New England, surrounded by wild animals.

Using only her wits and her brightly colored clothes, Toby manages to outsmart the ravenous creatures and earn herself a delicious meal. "Isaacs's clever, respectful take on an iconic tale is testament to its appeal," wrote Kathy Krasniewicz in *School Library Journal,* and a *Kirkus Reviews* critic deemed *Pancakes for Supper!* "totally delightful and a great new spin on an old story."

Biographical and Critical Sources

PERIODICALS

Booklist, October 15, 1994, Hazel Rochman, review of *Swamp Angel,* p. 424; September 15, 1997, Kay Weisman, review of *Treehouse Tales,* p. 235; March 1, 2000, Hazel Rochman, review of *Torn Thread,* p. 1236; October 15, 2006, Gillian Engberg, review of *Pancakes for Supper!,* p. 46.

Horn Book, March-April, 1995, Mary M. Burns, review of *Swamp Angel,* p. 184; September-October, 1997, Ann A. Flowers, review of *Treehouse Tales,* p. 572; November-December, 2006, Barbara Bader, review of *Pancakes for Supper!,* p. 699.

Kirkus Reviews, October 15, 1994, review of *Swamp Angels,* p. 1408; September 15, 2006, review of *Pancakes for Supper!,* p. 955.

Kliatt, March, 2000, Claire Rosser, review of *Torn Thread.*

Publishers Weekly, October 3, 1994, review of *Swamp Angel,* p. 69; August 24, 1998, review of *Cat up a Tree: A Story in Poems,* p. 57; May 26, 1997, review of *Treehouse Tales,* p. 86; May 22, 2000, review of *Torn Thread,* p. 94; September 4, 2006, review of *Pancakes for Supper!,* p. 65.

School Library Journal, April, 2000, Virginia Golodetz, review of *Torn Thread,* p. 136; October, 2006, Kathy Krasniewicz, review of *Pancakes for Supper!,* p. 113.

Time, December 19, 1994, "Imagine: A Cow in a Gown!," review of *Swamp Angel,* p. 70.

ONLINE

Anne Isaacs Home Page, http://www.anneisaacs.com (November 10, 2007).*

*   *   *

JAMES, Charlie 1961-

Personal

Born 1961, in Scotland.

Addresses

Home—Edinburgh, Scotland.

Career

Children's book author.

Writings

Billy the Fish (beginning reader), illustrated by Ned Jolliffe, Bloomsbury Children's Books (New York, NY), 2006.

Biographical and Critical Sources

PERIODICALS

Kirkus Reviews, September 15, 2006, review of *Billy the Fish,* p. 955.

School Library Journal, November, 2006, Elaine E. Knight, review of *Billy the Fish,* p. 96.

ONLINE

Bloomsbury Web site, http://www.bloomsbury.com/ (December 26, 2007), "Charlie James."*

JARROW, Gail 1952-

Personal

Born November 29, 1952, in Dallas, TX; married Robert Jarrow (a college professor), May, 1974; children: Kyle, Tate, Heather. *Education:* Duke University, B.A. (zoology), 1974; Dartmouth College, M.A., 1980. *Hobbies and other interests:* Gardening, cross-country skiing, reading, travel.

Addresses

Home—Ithaca, NY. *E-mail*—gailjarrow@gailjarrow.com.

Career

Children's book author and teacher. Taught elementary and middle-school math and science in Cambridge, MA, and Hanover, NH, 1974-79; freelance writer, beginning 1983; Institute of Children's Literature, Redding Ridge, CT, instructor, beginning 1991.

Member

Authors Guild, Society of Children's Book Writers and Illustrators.

Awards, Honors

American Booksellers Association Quick Picks for Reluctant Young-Adult Readers, and Public Library Association Top Title for New Adult Readers, both 1996, both for *Naked Mole-Rats;* National Science Teachers Association/Children's Book Council Outstanding Science Trade Book for Children, *Scientific American* Young Readers Book Award, and Society of School Librarians International Award in Science, all 1996, all for *The Naked Mole-Rat Mystery;* New York Public Library Books for the Teen Age designation, and *Natural History* Best Books for Young Readers designation, both 2006, both for *The Printer's Trial.*

Writings

MIDDLE-GRADE FICTION

That Special Someone, Berkley (New York, NY), 1985.
If Phyllis Were Here, Houghton (Boston, MA), 1987.
The Two-Ton Secret, Avon (New York, NY), 1989.
Beyond the Magic Sphere, Harcourt (New York, NY), 1994.

NONFICTION

(With Paul Sherman) *The Naked Mole-Rat Mystery: Scientific Sleuths at Work,* Lerner (New York, NY), 1996.
(With Paul Sherman) *Naked Mole-Rats,* Carolrhoda Books (Minneapolis, MN), 1996.

(With Paul Sherman) *Animal Baby Sitters,* Franklin Watts (New York, NY), 2001.

Bears ("Animals Attack!" series), Kidhaven Press (San Diego, CA), 2003.

Rhinos ("Animals Attack!" series), Kidhaven Press (San Diego, CA), 2003.

Chiggers, Kidhaven Press (San Diego, CA), 2004.

Hookworms, Kidhaven Press (San Diego, CA), 2004.

A Medieval Castle, Kidhaven Press (San Diego, CA), 2005.

The Printer's Trial: The Case of John Peter Zenger and the Fight for a Free Press, Calkins Creek (Honesdale, PA), 2006.

Robert H. Jackson: New Deal Lawyer, Supreme Court Justice, Calkins Creek (Honesdale, PA), 2008.

Contributor to periodicals, including *3-2-1 Contact, Highlights, Child Life, Spider, Muse, Cobblestone, Faces,* and *Pennywhistle Press.*

Sidelights

Gail Jarrow writes both fiction and nonfiction for younger readers. A former science teacher, she shares her interest in nature in books such as *Animal Baby Sitters, Rhinos,* and *The Naked Mole-Rat Mystery: Scientific Sleuths at Work.* Turning to more imaginative fare, her middle-grade novel *Beyond the Magic Sphere* mixes fantasy and the real-life problems of an eleven-year-old girl to produce what *Booklist* critic Mary Harris Veeder dubbed "an appealing coming-of-age story."

History provides the focus of *The Printer's Trial: The Case of John Peter Zenger and the Fight for a Free Press,* Jarrow's award-winning profile of the 1735 legal action aided by Andrew Hamilton that produced American colonists' right to a free press. Noting the book's "engaging narrative" in her *School Library Journal* review, Jayne Damron added that in *The Printer's Trial* the text reflects the author's "extensive research." In *Kliatt,* Patricia Moore praised Jarrow's book as "well written" and enhanced by a time line and notes that put the event into an historical context. Calling the Zenger trial "small but historically significant," Carolyn Phelan concluded her *Booklist* review of *The Printer's Trial* by predicting that Jarrow's "clear presentation may attract browsers as well as report writers."

Jarrow once told *SATA:* "I grew up in a small Pennsylvania town near Philadelphia, surrounded by extended family and by the same classmates from kindergarten through high school. Despite these close ties, as an only child I spent many hours alone, using my imagination to create triumphs and tragedies for my dolls and stuffed animals. When I learned to write down my thoughts, these pretend games were transformed into stories. I 'published' the first one, 'The King's Lesson,' at age seven. The same spark that inspired me then keeps my creative fires burning today.

"During my school years, I wrote stories and poetry and was the editor of the high school newspaper. A strong interest in animals and plants, however, led me to study biology at Duke University and later to teach elementary and middle-school science and math for five years in New England. But I didn't abandon the love of writing. And while working on my master's degree at Dartmouth College, I took a course in children's literature that fanned those creative fires again.

"Soon after finishing my graduate degree, I left full-time teaching to start my family and to begin my writing career. Combining my science background with my writing skills, I became a freelance writer of science articles for *3-2-1 Contact* magazine. Later I began writing short stories and novels for both middle-grade children and young adults.

"My strong childhood memories, my teaching experience, and my enjoyment of children's literature first led me to write for young people. I continue to create for them because I believe it is important for children to discover the joy and satisfaction of reading. I hope that my books will provide pleasure and entertainment, while broadening the young reader's view of the world.

"Ideas come from my past experiences, from my daily life, and from the activities of my children and their friends. For example, I developed the fantasy game in *Beyond the Magic Sphere* after observing my children as they created adventures in their secret land called 'The Green Realm.'

Gail Jarrow presents a little-known facet of history in her book **The Printer's Trial,** *which focuses on the legal case that established the rights of a free press.* (Calkins Creek Books, 2006. Reproduced by permission of Boyd's Mills Press.)

"I can usually pinpoint the day when I begin to think about a story idea. I witness an action that becomes the basis of the plot. I overhear a comment that suggests a conflict. Or I spot an interesting person in the grocery store, and I wonder about her life story. The details of the novel gradually come to me as a steady accumulation of characters, bits of dialogue, and scenes which are later seasoned and combined in my imagination.

"My themes are often influenced by my concern that today's over-programmed children lack the free time to develop *their* imaginations. The ability to think creatively comes from practice and nurturing. This skill plays an essential role in a child's success no matter what path his life takes. Creativity leads to better ideas whether one is a writer, artist, scientist, mechanic, teacher, or businessman. My books celebrate this power of imagination."

Biographical and Critical Sources

PERIODICALS

Booklist, October 15, 1987, review of *If Phyllis Were Here,* p. 396; October 15, 1994, Mary Harris Veeder, review of *Beyond the Magic Sphere,* p. 427; September 1, 1996, Leone McDermott, review of *The Naked Mole-Rat Mystery: Scientific Sleuths at Work,* p. 116; October 1, 2006, Carolyn Phelan, review of *The Printer's Trial: The Case of John Peter Zenger and the Fight for a Free Press,* p. 47.

Kirkus Reviews, August 15, 1987, review of *If Phyllis Were Here,* p. 1241; September 15, 2006, review of *The Printer's Trial,* p. 959.

Kliatt, March, 2007, Patricia Moore, review of *The Printer's Trial,* p. 39.

School Library Journal, September, 1987, review of *If Phyllis Were Here,* p. 180; November, 1994, review of *Beyond the Magic Sphere;* April, 2004, Cathie Bashaw Morton, review of *Bears* and *Rhinos,* p. 171; March, 2005, Kathleen Simonetta, review of *A Medieval Castle,* p. 23; November, 2006, Jayne Damron, review of *The Printer's Trial,* p. 162.

Voice of Youth Advocates, December, 2006, review of *The Printer's Trial.*

ONLINE

Gail Jarrow Home Page, http://www.gailjarrow.com (December 10, 2007).

*   *   *

JENNINGS, Richard W. 1945-

Personal

Born October 25, 1945, in Memphis, TN; married Linda Siggins (a nurse), 1987; children: five. *Education:* Rhodes College, B.A. (English). *Religion:* Methodist.

Addresses

Home—Overland Park, KS. *Agent*—George Nicholson, Sterling Lord Literistic, 65 Bleecker St., New York, NY 10012.

Career

Rainy Day Books, Kansas City, KS, cofounder, 1975—; *Kansas City* Magazine, Kansas City, editor, 1987-88; Bernstein-Rein Advertising, vice president and creative director, 1988-98. Cochairman, Kansas City Book Fair, 1984.

Member

Authors Guild.

Awards, Honors

First place award, Southern Literary Festival, Southwestern-at-Memphis, 1967; *Booklist* Editor's Choice, 2000, for *Orwell's Luck;* Pennsylvania School Librarians Association Top Ten Fiction Titles designation, 2001, for *The Great Whale of Kansas;* William Rockhill Nelson Fiction Award honorable mention, 2002, for *My Life of Crime.*

Writings

MIDDLE-GRADE NOVELS

The Tragic Tale of the Dog Who Killed Himself, Bantam (New York, NY), 1980.

Orwell's Luck, Houghton Mifflin (Boston, MA), 2000.

The Great Whale of Kansas, Houghton Mifflin (Boston, MA), 2001.

My Life of Crime, Houghton Mifflin (Boston, MA), 2002.

Mystery in Mt. Mole, Houghton Mifflin (Boston, MA), 2003.

Scribble, Houghton Mifflin (Boston, MA), 2004.

Ferret Island (originally serialized in the *Kansas City Star,* 2005), Houghton Mifflin (Boston, MA), 2007.

Stink City, Houghton Mifflin (Boston, MA), 2006.

Feature columnist for *Kansas City* magazine, 1990-2000.

Sidelights

Richard W. Jennings has added several unusual volumes to the array of books available to middle-grade readers. Praised by *Booklist* contributor Michael Cart as a "absolutely captivating tale . . . about everyday magic," Jennings' novel *Orwell's Luck* tells the story of a preteen girl who attempts to heal an injured wild rabbit, only to have the tables quickly turn when the rabbit, Orwell, starts communicating with her through coded messages published in the middle-school newspaper. "Quirky details and a warm, precocious twelve-year-old narrator add up to an engaging and imaginative novel," wrote a *Publishers Weekly* contributor, the critic adding that Jennings' story delves into both the philosophical and the practical. Noting that the novel's "Christian symbolism is sometimes obvious," a *Horn Book* contributor praised Jennings' narrator, writing that the girl's "always-searching mind poses lots of good questions." In *School Library Journal,* Judith Everitt dubbed *Orwell's Luck* "a challenging and thought-provoking" read and commented that "Jennings writes with natural grace and has a clear understanding" of the way a preteen views the world.

Jennings continues in the same unique vein in *The Great Whale of Kansas,* a novel in which his "refreshing style and distinctive voice are once again in evidence," according to *Horn Book* contributor Jonathan Hunt. In this novel, an imaginative and curious eleven year old living in Melville, Kansas, makes an incredible find while digging holes in his yard. He finds a set of mysterious bones that draws him into the field of paleontology, as well as fame, as he attempts to make sense of his find. Described by *Booklist* contributor Ilene Cooper as "odd yet engaging," *The Great Whale of Kansas*

Cover of Richard W. Jennings' humorous young-adult novel **Ferret Island**, *which features a cast of his characteristically quirky characters.*
(Photograph by Digital Vision/Getty Images. Reproduced by permission of Houghton Mifflin Company. All rights reserved.)

"will captivate children who naturally allow for mystery," the critic added. Noting that Jennings "doesn't talk down to readers," *School Library Journal* contributor Ellen Fader cited the book in particular for its "full cast of intriguing, supporting characters."

A mistreated classroom pet is the catalyst for Jennings' quirky comedy in *My Life of Crime.* When sixth-grade loner Fowler Young discovers that the third grade's class parrot is being ignored and mistreated, the boy steals the bird, then blames the theft on an unpopular fellow student. As he attempts to avoid detection, the young do-gooder is pushed into increasingly extreme—and increasingly absurd—measures. Although maintaining that Fowler's narration is sometimes overly mature in its irony, Gillian Engberg concluded in *Booklist* that "Jennings' humor is often irresistible, especially in the purely silly details" of his story. Fowler plays out as an "impulsive, appealingly bird-brained hero," according to a *Publishers Weekly* contributor, the reviewer calling *My Life of Crime* a "buoyant, briskly paced novel."

Dubbed "possibly the most outrageously imaginative" of Jennings' novels to date by *Booklist* contributor Stephanie Zvirin, *Mystery in Mt. Mole* follows twelve-year-old Andrew on his search for the missing assistant principal of Mt. Mole Middle School. The disappearance of Mr. Farley is not the only unusual occurrence; equally odd is how unconcerned the rest of the town is with regard to his absence. The oddly shaped mound of earth that has given the Kansas prairie town of Mt. Mole its name has also been issuing a strange rumbling sound. While more than distracted by his current love interest, the engaging Georgia Wayne, Andrew methodically pursues his sleuthing, uncovering more mysteries than he anticipated. In *Kirkus Reviews* a critic deemed *Mystery in Mt. Mole* "a wry, witty, and always intelligent work that's as individualistic as its hero," and *Kliatt* reviewer Claire Rosser praised the story's middle-school sleuth as "intelligent, articulate, and curious."

Jennings tells a characteristically unusual boy-and-dog story in *Scribble.* Lawson has been sad and lonely since the death of his best friend Jip after a long illness, and he finds consolation in the frisky terrier Jip gave him before she died. As months pass, and Lawson turns thirteen, he finds his memories of Jip fading, while he and Scribble become fast friends. When Lawson and his dog find themselves haunted by an odd assortment of important—but dead—people that no one else can see, the teen suspects that Jip may be trying to send him a message. Commenting on the "droll" tone used by the story's young narrator as the action moves between Jip's last days and Lawson's current haunting, Shelle Rosenfeld noted in *Booklist* that *Scribble* is an "inventive story of ghosts and loss and healing." "Lawson is a classic Jennings protagonist," asserted a *Kirkus Reviews* writer, the critic citing the young teen's mature perspective and "pure, unshakable faith" that things will work out for the best.

Animals of another sort entirely star in *Ferret Island,* a story that prompted *Horn Book* writer Betty Carter to write that Jennings "should win the Mel Brooks of the Middle Grade Novel Award any day now." Washed up on an island in the middle of the Mississippi River after falling overboard during a sightseeing cruise, fourteen-year-old Will Finn discovers that a reclusive local inhabitant is actually a terrorist. The looney islander plans to take on fast-food giant McDonald's by marshaling a trained force of giant ferrets, meat-eating creatures native to the island that have been conditioned to crave Big Macs. Befriended by a pacifist ferret named Jim, and by Julia, a girl who has flounder up on shore after falling from yet another riverboat, Will sets out to foil the terrorist plot. He hopes also to spare the lives of the region's gas station attendants, a species that the over-sized and carniverous attack ferrets seem to find particularly tasty. In a review for *Booklist,* John Peters praised the "goofball goings-on" in *Ferret Island,* adding that in his novel Jennings cooks up "a surreal happy meal for fans of tongue-in-cheek fiction."

Featuring the author's "trademark wit and offbeat characterization," according to a *Kirkus Reviews* writer, *Stink City* introduces a slightly older protagonist in fifteen-year-old Cade Carlsen. Actively involved in the family business—manufacturing catfish bait—Cade often smells rather fishy. This fact makes narrator Leigh Ann Moore the perfect best friend, because with her sinus condition she can rarely smell Cade's fishiness. When Cade is inspired by a fish-rights activist to denounce the family trade and help put an end to a major fishing tournament, chaos and a terrible odor are the result. In *Booklist,* Todd Morning wrote that readers will enjoy the "exaggerated humor" in *Stink City,* while a *Kirkus Reviews* writer dubbed Jennings "the master of Middle-American whimsy."

Hunt praised Jennings' approach to writing for children, comparing the author to noted writer Daniel Pinkwater and noting that "his novels are laced with droll tongue-in-cheek observations, philosophical musings, and slight hints of absurdity" designed to challenge and entertain middle-grade readers. Perhaps explaining the basis for Hunt's observations, Jennings quoted twentieth-century French playwright Eugene Ionesco: "I still feel surprised, sometimes, that I am no longer twelve years old."

Biographical and Critical Sources

PERIODICALS

Booklist, October 15, 2000, Michael Cart, review of *Orwell's Luck,* p. 435; June 1, 2001, Ilene Cooper, review of *The Great Whale of Kansas,* p. 1884; January 1, 2003, Gillian Engberg, p. 890; September 15, 2003, Stephanie Zvirin, review of *Mystery in Mt. Mole,* p. 238; November 1, 2004, Shelle Rosenfeld, review of *Scribble,* p. 475; October 15, 2006, Todd Morning, review of *Stink City,* p. 45; July 1, 2007, John Peters, review of *Ferret Island,* p. 59.

Bulletin of the Center for Children's Books, November, 2003, Deborah Stevenson, review of *Mystery in Mt. Mole,* p. 108.

Horn Book, September, 2000, review of *Orwell's Luck,* p. 571; September, 2001, Jonathan Hunt, review of *The Great Whale of Kansas,* p. 588; January-February, 2005, Christine M. Heppermann, review of *Scribble,* p. 93; November-December, 2006, Betty Carter, review of *Stink City,* p. 714; May-June, 2007, Betty Carter, review of *Ferret Island,* p. 284.

Journal of Adolescent and Adult Literacy, May, 2003, Katie Thomason, review of *My Life of Crime,* p. 700.

Kirkus Reviews, September 1, 2003, review of *Mystery in Mt. Mole,* p. 1125; October 1, 2004, review of *Scribble,* p. 962; September 15, 2006, review of *Stink City,* p. 956; October 15, 2002, review of *My Life of Crime,* p. 1532.

Kliatt, November, 2003, Claire Rosser, review of *Mystery in Mt. Mole,* p. 6.

Publishers Weekly, September 11, 2000, review of *Orwell's Luck,* p. 91; October 28, 2002, review of *My Life of Crime,* p. 71; October 13, 2003, review of *Mystery in Mt. Mole,* p. 80.

School Library Journal, October, 2000, Judith Everitt, review of *Orwell's Luck,* p. 161; August, 2001, Ellen Fader, review of *The Great Whale of Kansas,* p. 184; December, 2003, JoAnn Jonas, review of *Mystery in Mt. Mole,* p. 152; November, 2004, B. Allison Gray, review of *Scribble,* p. 146; May, 2007, Elizabeth Bird, review of *Ferret Island,* p. 134.

Voice of Youth Advocates, October, 2000, review of *Orwell's Luck,* p. 266.

ONLINE

Richard W. Jennings Home Page, http://www.richardwjennings.com (December 15, 2007).*

*   *   *

JONES, Sylvie
(Sylvie Michelle Jones)

Personal

Married; children: one son.

Addresses

Home—Seattle, WA.

Career

Author. Worked as a second-grade teacher.

Awards, Honors

Parents Choice Award, for *Go Back to Sleep,* 2006.

Writings

Go Back to Sleep, illustrated by Pascale Constantin, Blue Apple Books (Maplewood, NJ), 2006.

Who's in the Tub?, illustrated by Pascale Constantin, Blue Apple Books (Maplewood, NJ), 2007.

Biographical and Critical Sources

PERIODICALS

Kirkus Reviews, September 15, 2006, review of *Go Back to Sleep,* p. 956.

Resource Links, December, 2006, Adriane Pettit, review of *Go Back to Sleep,* p. 4.

ONLINE

Blue Apple Books Web site, http://www.blueapplebooks.com/ (December 27, 2007), "Sylvie Jones."*

* * *

JONES, Sylvie Michelle
See JONES, Sylvie

* * *

JUBERT, Hervé

Personal

Born in France.

Addresses

Home and office—France. *E-mail*—jubert.herve@neuf.fr.

Career

Writer.

Writings

Les aventures de Pierre Pèlerin 1: Sinedeis, Livre de Poche (Paris, France), 1999.

Les aventures de Pierre Pèlerin 2: In media res, Livre de Poche (Paris, France), 2000.

Les aventures de Pierre Pèlerin 3: Erat fatum, Livre de Poche (Paris, France), 2002.

Le quadrille des assassins, Broché, 2002, translated by Anthea Bell as *Dance of the Assassins,* Eos (New York, NY), 2004.

Un tango du diable, Broché, 2003, translated by Anthea Bell as *Devil's Tango,* Eos (New York, NY), 2006.

Sabbat Samba, Broché, 2004.

Blanche; ou la triple contrainte de l'enfer, Broché, 2005.

Alexandre le grande, Broché, 2006.

Blanche et l'oeil du grand Khan, Broché, 2006.

Blanche et le vampire de Paris, Broché, 2007.

Sidelights

French writer Hervé Jubert is the author of several series of novels featuring heroines triumphing against supernatural horrors. In one story line, an upper-class young woman, Blanche, finds herself at odds with the vampires of Paris in the 1870s. In another, Roberta, who lives in a futuristic world where the past serves the present as a theme park, is pitted against demons and servants of the devil. Jubert is also the author of a novel about the life of Alexander the Great of Macedonia: *Alexandre le grande.*

The character of Blanche was developed when Jubert and his wife were living in Paris. He placed her in the 1870s setting, during the Siege of Paris by the Prussians. As a young bourgeois woman, Blanche is proper in every way, but as she begins to discover the hidden world around her, she realizes that everything is not as she believed. "The separation between shadow and light is not as frank we may think," Jubert explained on the *ActuSF Web site.* "Blanche is someone who finally learns." Blanche's adventures, which begin in *Blanche; ou la triple contrainte de l'enfer,* have not yet been published in English.

The Dance of the Assassins—first published in the original French as *Le quadrille des assassins*—introduces readers to Roberta, a witch who graduated from the College of Sorcery and who lives in a world purposely fixed in the nineteenth century. Though the world outside may have moved on due to the advance in technology, London, Paris, and Venice are now historical stages for tourism, and crime is tracked through tracers—which work until the supernatural becomes involved. Luckily, Roberta needs no such tools, and when a modern-day Jack the Ripper begins committing murder, she is paired up with a novice investigator named Clement Martineau to solve the crime. Jack is not just making appearances to murder traditional targets, however; he joins together with three other assassins in hopes of summoning the devil himself.

"Jubert offers charismatic characters, a fascinating plot, descriptive imagery, and a unique blend of modern and mystic methods, with an unexpected ending," wrote J.A. Kaszuba Locke in an online review of *Dance of the Assassins* for *Book Loons.* Although noting that the dark subject material might not be suitable for younger teens, Douglas R. Cobb wrote for the Curled up with a Good Kid's Book Web site that Jubert's novel is "packed with action, adventure, murder, and mayhem." A *Kirkus Reviews* contributor found Roberta to be "an appealingly offbeat adult protagonist," and Lesley Farmer wrote in *Kliatt* that readers of *Dance of the Assassins* "will certainly root for the investigator pair."

Roberta and Martineau return in *Devil's Tango*, where they again solve a rash of murders. But their job gets more complicated when a corrupt official begins persecuting gypsies in order to boost support for his upcoming election. Between the suspicion that their murderer is the legendary Baron of Mists and that the would-be-mayor may be up to something much darker, Roberta and Martineau have their hands full. "Juvert takes well-worn conventions . . . and spins them into something fresh and new," wrote Donna Scanlon in *Kliatt.* A *Kirkus Reviews* contributor called the novel "a metaphysically creative and fantastical tale for fans of the offbeat."

When asked what writers served as his inspiration by an interviewer for the *ActuSF Web site,* Jubert responded: "[The books of J.R.R.] Tolkien when I was ten years old, Tim Powers when I was twelve, [Dashiell] Hammet later." Although Jubert admitted that he does not intentionally write for a young-adult audience, he is pleased that his books seem to fit well with that niche.

Biographical and Critical Sources

PERIODICALS

Booklist, October 1, 2006, Krista Hutley, review of *Devil's Tango,* p. 48.

Bulletin of the Center for Children's Books, September, 2005, Elizabeth Bush, review of *Dance of the Assassins,* p. 24; February, 2007, Elizabeth Bush, review of *Devil's Tango,* p. 256.

Kirkus Reviews, August 15, 2005, review of *Dance of the Assassins,* p. 916; September 15, 2006, review of *Devil's Tango,* p. 957.

Kliatt, September, 2005, Lesley Farmer, review of *Dance of the Assassins,* p. 9; November, 2006, Donna Scanlon, review of *Devil's Tango,* p. 12.

Publishers Weekly, November 7, 2005, review of *Dance of the Assassins,* p. 76.

School Library Journal, December, 2005, Sharon Rawlins, review of *Dance of the Assassins,* p. 148; February, 2007, Anthony C. Doyle, review of *Devil's Tango,* p. 120.

Voice of Youth Advocates, October, 2005, review of *Dance of the Assassins,* p. 324; December, 2006, Ann Welton, review of *Devil's Tango,* p. 443.

ONLINE

ActuSF Web site, http://www.actusf.com/ (November 21, 2007), interview with Jubert.

Book Loons Web site, http://www.bookloons.com/ (November 21, 2007), review of *Dance of the Assassins.*

Curled up with a Good Kid's Book Web site, http://www.curledupkids.com/ (November 21, 2007), review of *Dance of the Assassins.*

Hervé Jubert Home Page, http://www.blanche-paichain.net (November 16, 2007).*

K

KASLIK, Ibi 1973-

Personal
Born August 20, 1973, in Toronto, Ontario, Canada. *Education:* Concordia University, M.A. (creative writing and English literature).

Addresses
Home and office—Toronto, Ontario, Canada. *E-mail*—ibikas@hotmail.com.

Career
Author, teacher, and freelance journalist.

Awards, Honors
Best First Novel Award shortlist, Amazon.com/*Books in Canada,* 2004, Best Young-Adult Novel designation, Canadian Library Association, 2005, and Borders Original Voice award, 2006, all for *Skinny.*

Writings

Skinny, HarperCollins (Toronto, Ontario, Canada), 2004, Walker & Company (New York, NY), 2006.

Contributor to periodicals.

Sidelights
Ibi Kaslik has a flair for thought-provoking topics, as readers of her debut novel *Skinny* can attest. *Skinny* centers on a twenty-something medical student named Giselle, who suffers from anorexia. Kaslik noted in an interview with the *Danforth Review* online that the development of *Skinny* began in a creative-writing class during graduate school. She was inspired to write a book about anorexia because it was "a topic that I ex-perienced directly in my personal life and social group," as she explained in her interview. "I never saw eating disorders represented in the media discourse in the way it played itself out in life." According to Kaslik, her goal in writing the novel "was to demystify clichés about anorexia."

In *Skinny* Kaslik exposes the stereotypes surrounding the eating disorder by providing an intimate look into the anorexic protagonist's mindset, revealing the many contradictions within the young woman's thoughts and perceptions. Kaslik also weaves additional themes into her novel, including aspects of sibling rivalry and the struggles of identity experienced by children born to immigrant parents. A *Kirkus Reviews* critic noted that the author's prose is enriched by "intense and masterful poetic imagery" and added that the novelist tells her story "with clarity and truth." Kim Dane, in a review of Kaslik's debut novel for *School Library Journal,* commented that *Skinny* "hits the mark with characters with whom teens will empathize, and tackles a relevant and painful subject with grace."

Biographical and Critical Sources

PERIODICALS

Booklist, December 15, 2006, Gillian Engberg, review of *Skinny,* p. 43.
Bulletin of the Center for Children's Books, November, 2006, review of *Skinny,* p. 130.
Kirkus Reviews, September 15, 2006, review of *Skinny,* p. 957.
Library Media Connection, February, 2007, Luke Arnols, review of *Skinny,* p. 79.
Publishers Weekly, December 18, 2006, review of *Skinny,* p. 65.
School Library Journal, November, 2006, Kim Dare, review of *Skinny,* p. 138.
Voice of Youth Advocates, December, 2006, Kimberly Pa-one, review of *Skinny,* p. 425.

***Ibi Kaslik addresses a topic of concern to many teen girls in her young-adult novel* Skinny.** (Photograph © 2006 Jupiterimages/Brian Hagiwara. Reproduced by permission.)

ONLINE

AELAQ Web site, http://www.aelaq.org/ (November 17, 2007), Ian McGillis, "Food for Fiction: Ibi Kaslik Dissects a Misunderstood Disorder."

Danforth Review Online, http://www.danforthreview.com/ (November 17, 2007), interview with Kaslik.

Found in the Margins Web site, http://www.found inthemargins.com/ (March 20, 2007), Chris DePaul, "Ibi Kaslik."

Ibi Kaslik Home Page, http://www.ibikaslik.net (November 17, 2007).

*   *   *

KATZ, Alan
(I.B. Wrongo)

Personal

Married; wife's name Rose (a journalist); children: Simone, Andrew, Nathan, David.

Addresses

Home—CT.

Career

Children's writer and television writer. Has written for television programs including *Rosie O'Donnell Show,* Warner Brothers Animation's *Taz-Mania,* and Disney's *Raw Toonage,* as well as programs on Nickelodeon and ABC Television. XM Radio, host of *Dr. I.B. Wrongo* radio show.

Awards, Honors

Emmy Award nominations for work on *Rosie O'Donnell Show* and *Raw Toonage*; Cuffie Award, *Publishers Weekly,* for *Take Me out of the Bathtub, and Other Silly Dilly Songs.*

Writings

FOR CHILDREN

Take Me out of the Bathtub, and Other Silly Dilly Songs, Margaret K. McElderry (New York, NY), 2001.

I'm Still Here in the Bathtub: Brand New Silly Dilly Songs, Margaret K. McElderry (New York, NY), 2003.

Where Did They Hide My Presents?: Silly Dilly Christmas Songs, Margaret K. McElderry (New York, NY), 2005.

Stinky Thinking: The Big Book of Gross Games and Brain Teasers, illustrated by Laurie Keller, Aladdin (New York, NY), 2005.

(With Caissie St. Onge) *United Jokes of America,* illustrated by Mike Lester, Scholastic (New York, NY), 2005.

Stinky Thinking Number Two: Another Big Book of Gross Games and Brain Teasers, illustrated by Jennifer Kalis, Aladdin (New York, NY), 2005.

(With Pete Fornatale) *Elfis: A Christmas Tale,* illustrated by Dani Jones, Price Stern Sloan (New York, NY), 2006.

Are You Quite Polite?: Silly Dilly Manners Songs, illustrated by David Catrow, Margaret K. McElderry (New York, NY), 2006.

The Flim-Flam Fairies, Running Press (Philadelphia, PA), 2007.

Oops!, illustrated by Edward Koren, Margaret K. McElderry (New York, NY), 2007.

Don't Say That Word!, illustrated by David Catrow, Margaret K. McElderry (New York, NY), 2007.

On Top of the Potty, and Other Get-up-and-Go Songs, illustrated by David Catrow, Margaret K. McElderry (New York, NY), 2008.

Smelly Locker: Silly Dilly School Songs, illustrated by David Catrow, Margaret K. McElderry (New York, NY), 2008.

FOR ADULTS

(As told to Katz by Dr. Juice) *The Cat Not in the Hat!,* illustrated by Chris Wrinn, Dove (Beverly Hills, CA), 1996.

Wackronyms, Avon (New York, NY), 1996.

C'Mere, Kitty: A Cat Lover's Guide to Pestering Your Pet, Avon (New York, NY), 1998.

Maternity the Musical!: Funny Songs about Cravings, Sonograms, and Everything Else an Expectant Mom's Got or Gonna Get, Andrews McMeel (Kansas City, MO), 2004.

Contributor of humor essays to the *New York Times.*

Sidelights

Comedy writer Alan Katz has been successful at a career that draws on his ability to stay young at heart. "When a six-year old boy thinks like a grown man, they call him a child prodigy," Katz observed on his home page. "But what's the best way to describe a grown man who thinks like a six-year old boy? That's the problem my wife faces every time she has to introduce me." Whether writing his "Silly Dilly" song books or working on cartoons for Disney or Nickelodeon, Katz uses his ability to think like a child to make sure the silliness and jokes with which he fills his books appeal to young readers. Along with his books, Katz is also the creator of the trivia game "That's Right, That's Wrong!" which is hosted by his fictional alter ego Dr. I.B. Wrongo and airs regularly on XM Radio. He also visits schools and libraries to do readings, sing, and tell jokes.

Take Me out of the Bathtub, and Other Silly Dilly Songs was Katz's first book for young readers. Featuring a collection of new lyrics that are paired with familiar traditional old tunes, *Take Me out of the Bathtub, and Other Silly Dilly Songs* features lyrics "so clever that kids will want to burst into song immediately," according to Jane Marino in her review for *School Library Journal.* Ginny Gustin, also writing for *School Library Journal,* felt that in the collection, old songs "are given new life," and these new versions "will have kids giggling as they sing," predicted a *Publishers Weekly* contributor. The fun continues in *I'm Still Here in the Bathtub: Brand New Silly Dilly Songs.*

In *Where Did They Hide My Presents?: Silly Dilly Christmas Songs* Katz sets his humorous lyrics to familiar Christmas songs, focusing on holiday events ranging from shopping to decorating rooftops with lights. "The child's-perspective lyrics are often about the seemingly ridiculous lengths adults go to" during the holidays, noted Bridget T. McCaffrey in *Horn Book.* Although a *Kirkus Reviews* contributor found some of the rewrites "gross," the critic added that "most provide the sort of irreverent humor beloved by children."

Consistently silly, Katz's books frequently have an educational purpose as well. For example, the cunningly titled *On Top of the Potty, and Other Get-up-and-Go Songs* is geared toward helping young listeners with potty training. *Stinky Thinking: The Big Book of Gross Games and Brain Teasers* and *Stinky Thinking Number Two: Another Big Book of Gross Games and Brain Teas-* ers both use bathroom humor to ask real quiz questions, such as the number of Supreme Court justices in the United States. *Are You Quite Polite?: Silly Dilly Manners Songs* and *Don't Say That Word!,* both of which feature quirky illustrations by David Catrow, also double as off-beat guides to good manners. Noting the contrasting pairing of model behavior and bad habits in *Are You Quite Polite?* a *Kirkus Reviews* contributor wrote that Katz's examples "will induce hilarity." Hazel Rochman, writing in *Booklist,* concluded that "the gross humor" in *Don't Say That Word!* "is right-on for slapstick."

Biographical and Critical Sources

PERIODICALS

Booklist, August, 2003, Shelle Rosenfeld, review of *I'm Still Here in the Bathtub: Brand New Silly Dilly Songs,* p. 1985; November 15, 2006, Julie Cummins, review of *Are You Quite Polite?: Silly Dilly Manners Songs,* p. 50; July 1, 2007, Hazel Rochman, review of *Don't Say That Word!,* p. 64.

Bulletin of the Center for Children's Books, December, 2006, review of *Where Did They Hide My Presents?: Silly Dilly Christmas Songs,* p. 188.

Horn Book, November-December, 2005, Bridget T. McCafferty, review of *Where Did They Hide My Presents?,* p. 695.

Kirkus Reviews, March 1, 2003, review of *I'm Still Here in the Bathtub,* p. 389; November 1, 2005, review of *Where Did They Hide My Presents?,* p. 1194; September 15, 2006, review of *Are You Quite Polite?,* p. 957.

Publishers Weekly, April 16, 2001, review of *Take Me out of the Bathtub, and Other Silly Dilly Songs,* p. 63; March 24, 2003, review of *I'm Still Here in the Bathtub,* p. 78; June 25, 2007, review of *Don't Say That Word!,* p. 59.

School Library Journal, April, 2001, Jane Marino, review of *Take Me out of the Bathtub, and Other Silly Dilly Songs,* p. 132; July, 2003, Nina Lindsay, review of *I'm Still Here in the Bathtub,* p. 114; December, 2004, Ginny Gustin, review of *Take Me out of the Bathtub, and Other Silly Dilly Songs,* p. 59; June, 2005, Steven Engelfried, review of *Take Me out of the Bathtub, and Other Silly Dilly Songs,* p. 56; October, 2006, Grace Oliff, review of *Are You Quite Polite?,* p. 136; July, 2007, Mary Hazelton, review of *Don't Say That Word!,* p. 78.

ONLINE

Alan Katz Home Page, http://www.alankatzbooks.com (December 2, 2007).

Authors on the Web, http://www.authorsontheweb.com/ (December 2, 2007), "Alan Katz."

Book Report Web site, http://www.thebookreport.net/ (November 1, 2006), podcast interview with Katz.

Simon & Schuster Web site, http://www.simonsays.com/ (December 2, 2007), "Alan Katz."*

*   *   *

KELLEY, Ellen A.
(Ellen Chavez Kelley)

Personal

Born in Duluth, MN; married John Kelley (an architect); children. *Hobbies and other interests:* Visiting schools and meeting her readers, watching lizards in the garden, beach combing, baking cookies, growing sweet peas and wildflowers, traveling in the American southwest, singing and listening to all types of music.

Addresses

Home and office—Santa Barbara, CA. *E-mail*—ellen@ellenakelley.com.

Career

Writer and teacher. Formerly worked as an elementary-school teacher; California Poet in the Schools; instructor and lecturer in adult education and at University of California—Santa Barbara Writing Program.

Member

Society of Children's Book Writers and Illustrators.

Awards, Honors

Academy of American Poets Prize, 1998; Benjamin Saltman Poetry Award prize, 1999; National Poetry Competition award, Associated Writing Programs Intro Journal Project, 2000; Arizona State Literacy Project Award finalist, 2007, for *Buckamoo Girls.*

Writings

The Lucky Lizard, illustrated by Kevin O'Malley, Dutton (New York, NY), 2000.
Buckamoo Girls, illustrated by Tom Curry, Abrams (New York, NY), 2006.
My Life as a Chicken, illustrated by Michael Slack, Harcourt (Orlando, FL), 2007.

Author of poetry under name Ellen Chavez Kelley.

Sidelights

Children's writer and poet Ellen A. Kelley grew up reading, following the adventures of fictional sleuth Nancy Drew and the characters of *The Boxcar Children,* and sometimes just reading the backs of cereal boxes. She was also an author early on: her first story was published in the local newspaper when Kelley was seven years old. In addition to her work as a writer, which has produced books such as *The Lucky Lizard* and *Buckamoo Girls,* Kelley has also worked as a teacher, both in elementary schools and on the college level.

Kelley's first book for children, *The Lucky Lizard,* is a chapter book that is narrated by a pet lizard named Bima. The lizard helps its owner, Todd, by building the boy's confidence in activities ranging from riding his bike to confronting the class bully. "Bima has a wonderful sense of humor, true love for his owner, and determination to help out," wrote Wendy S. Carroll in a *School Library Journal* review of *The Lucky Lizard.* A *Publishers Weekly* critic noted of the same book that "Kelley pulls off her unusual premise with humor."

Buckamoo Girls, a picture book featuring illustrations by Tom Curry, was inspired by Kelley's childhood dream of becoming "The Lone Rangerette," as the writer admitted on her home page. In the story, this dream is flipped, as two cows decide to become cowgirls. Bovine beauties Joanna and Susanna ride the range, rope steers, munch clover chili, and dance by the light of the moooon while living out their cowgirl dreams. A *Kirkus Reviews* contributor dubbed *Buckamoo Girls* "an udderly hilarious parody," and a critic for *Publishers Weekly* predicted that Kelley's "bovine heroines will appeal to the dreamer in everyone."

In *My Life as a Chicken* Kelley tells the story of Pauline Poulet, a hen who escapes a hungry farmer only to find greater dangers beyond, from hungry foxes to pirate cats. Finally, the chicken makes her way to safety at a petting zoo. "Kelley's couplets sally forth unstoppably," quipped a *Publishers Weekly* reviewer in describing Kelley's rhyming text. Kathleen Kelly MacMillan, reviewing *My Life as a Chicken* for *School Library Journal,* wrote that "the tone and zany sensibilities . . . are a perfect match for the funny bones of an early elementary audience."

Discussing where her ideas come from, Kelley wrote on her home page that she "doesn't exactly think of stories, so much as hear the characters' voices and see pictures." Kelley continues her work as a teacher of poetry in workshops, conferences, and adult education, and visits schools an author fairs where she gives lively book presentations for young readers.

Biographical and Critical Sources

PERIODICALS

Booklist, October 1, 2000, John Peters, review of *The Lucky Lizard,* p. 340.
Children's Bookwatch, February, 2007, review of *Buckamoo Girls.*

Featuring artwork by Michael Slack, Ellen A. Kelley's picture book My Life as a Chicken *strays far beyond the farmyard in telling its quirky tale.*
(Illustration © 2007 by Michael Slack. Reproduced by permission of Harcourt, Inc. This material may not be reproduced in any form or by any means without the prior written permission of the publisher.)

Kirkus Reviews, September 15, 2006, review of *Buckamoo Girls,* p. 957.

Publishers Weekly, November 6, 2000, review of *The Lucky Lizard,* p. 91; November 6, 2006, review of *Buckamoo Girls,* p. 60; April 30, 2007, review of *My Life as a Chicken,* p. 159.

School Library Journal, October, 2000, Wendy S. Carroll, review of *The Lucky Lizard,* p. 128; January, 2007, Susan E. Murray, review of *Buckamoo Girls,* p. 98; June, 2007, Kathleen Kelly MacMillan, review of *My Life as a Chicken,* p. 110.

ONLINE

Ellen A. Kelley's Home Page, http://www.ellenakelley.com (November 16, 2007).

Santa Barbara Writers Conference Web site, http://www.sbwritersconference.com/ (November 22, 2007), "Ellen A. Kelley."

*   *   *

KELLEY, Ellen Chavez
See KELLEY, Ellen A.

*   *   *

KRECH, Bob 1956-
(Robert Krech)

Personal

Born July 27, 1956, in Trenton, NJ; son of Walter (a New Jersey state trooper) and Dorothy (a special education teacher's aide) Krech; married; wife's name Karen (an ESL teacher); children: Andrew, Faith. *Education:* Rutgers College, B.A. (art education), 1978, M.Ed., 1982.

Addresses

E-mail—bob@bobkrech.com.

Career

Author and elementary school teacher. Worked variously as a principal, curriculum specialist, consultant, and coach. New Jersey Mathematics Coalition, member of board of governors; member of New Jersey Department of Education Mathematics Task Force.

Awards, Honors

Presidential Award for Excellence in Mathematics Teaching, National Science Foundation, 1997; American Library Association Best Book designation, 2007, for *Rebound.*

Bob Krech (Courtesy of Bob Krech.)

Writings

Rebound (young-adult novel), Marshall Cavendish (New York, NY), 2006.

Contributor to various journals.

EDUCATIONAL BOOKS

Special Delivery: Putting Math to Work, ETA/Cuisenaire (Vernon Hills, IL), 1998.

Fresh and Fun Teaching with Kids' Names: Dozens of Instant and Irresistible Ideas from Creative Teachers across the Country, Scholastic (New York, NY), 2000.

Fresh and Fun December: Dozens of Instant and Irresistible Ideas from Creative Teachers across the Country, Scholastic (New York, NY), 2000.

Fresh and Fun September: Dozens of Instant and Irresistible Ideas from Creative Teachers across the Country, Scholastic (New York, NY), 2000.

More Special Delivery: Putting More Math to Work, ETA/Cuisenaire (Vernon Hills, IL), 2001.

Best-ever Activities for Grades 2-3: Listening and Speaking, Scholastic (New York, NY), 2002.

Best-ever Activities for Grades 2-3: Grammar, Scholastic (New York, NY), 2002.

Best-ever Activities for Grades 2-3: Measurement, Scholastic (New York, NY), 2002.

Best-ever Activities for Grades 2-3: Multiplication, Scholastic (New York, NY), 2002.

Best-ever Activities for Grades 2-3: Writing, Scholastic (New York, NY), 2002.

Meeting the Math Standards with Favorite Picture Books: Lessons, Activities, and Hands-on Reproducibles That Help You Teach Essential Math Skills and Concepts, Scholastic (New York, NY), 2002.

Best-ever Activities for Grades 2-3: Spelling, Scholastic (New York, NY), 2002.

Math Word Problems Made Easy: Grade 2, Scholastic (New York, NY), 2005.

Math Word Problems Made Easy: Grade 3, Scholastic (New York, NY), 2005.

Math Word Problems Made Easy: Grade 4, Scholastic (New York, NY), 2005.

50 Fill-in Math Word Problems: Grades 2-3: 50 Engaging Stories for Students to Read, Fill in, Solve, and Sharpen Their Math Skills, Scholastic (New York, NY), 2007.

50 Fill-in Math Word Problems: Grades 4-6: 50 Engaging Stories for Students to Read, Fill in, Solve, and Sharpen Their Math Skills, Scholastic (New York, NY), 2007.

Sidelights

With over two dozen years' experience teaching in schools, Bob Krech knows his young-adult audience well. In addition to writing instructional titles for Scholastic Teaching Resources, he also published the young-adult novel *Rebound. Rebound* reveals the harsh realities of racism by following protagonist Ray Wisniewski as he grapples with the prejudice he both experiences and witnesses. Seventeen-year-old Ray is a Polish-American teen who loves the game of basketball. He looks past the racial stereotypes in his high school—such as the assumption that only black kids play basketball—and tries out for the school basketball team. At first Ray is rejected from the team by a coach who only recruits black students, but he eventually gets the chance to play when a new, more-open-minded coach is hired. Once Ray joins the basketball team, however, the racism he has experienced heightens. As *Rebound* plays out, the teen must learn to overcome a variety of stereotypes. Reviewing the novel, *School Library Journal* reviewer Kristin Anderson called Krech's characters "compelling" and noted that his novel's storyline "is fast paced enough to hold the interest of reluctant readers." Keir Graff, assessing Krech's debut novel in *Booklist,* applauded *Rebound* for its raw honesty and remarked that the author "successfully shows the many shades of gray that keep racism from being a truly black-and-white issue."

Krech commented in an online interview for *Teens Read Too* that he knew he wanted to be a writer since the fourth grade. Noting that he finds inspiration in his interactions with teens, he advised would-be writers to Read everything they can get their hands on. And in writing, "'show, don't tell.' It really is the best guide to good writing."

Biographical and Critical Sources

PERIODICALS

Booklist, September 1, 2006, review of *Rebound,* p. 115.

Instructor, August, 2007, Hannah Trierweiler, review of *Rebound,* p. 75.

Kirkus Reviews, September 15, 2006, review of *Rebound,* p. 958.

Library Media Connection, February, 2007, Karen Scott, review of *Rebound,* p. 77.

School Library Journal, December, 2006, Kristin Anderson, review of *Rebound,* p. 148.

Voice of Youth Advocates, December, 2006, Jeff Mann, review of *Rebound,* p. 426.

ONLINE

Bob Krech Home Page, http://www.bobkrech.com/ (November 17, 2007).

Children's Bookwatch Web site, http://www.midwestbookreview.com/ (December 1, 2006), review of *Rebound.*

Staff Development Workshops Web site, http://www.sdworkshops.org/ (November 17, 2007), "Robert Krech."

Teen Reads Too Web site, http://www.teensreadtoo.com/ (November 17, 2007), interview with Krech.

*   *   *

KRECH, Robert
See KRECH, Bob

L

LEE, Carol Ann 1969-

Personal

Born 1969, in Yorkshire, England; children: River (son). *Education:* Manchester Polytechnic, earned degree (history of art, design).

Addresses

Home—Yorkshire, England.

Career

Author. Also worked for Manchester Jewish Museum and Anne Frank Trust.

Writings

NONFICTION

Roses from the Earth: The Biography of Anne Frank, foreword by Buddy Elias, Viking (London, England), 1999.
Anne Frank's Story: Her Life Retold for Children, Troll (Mahwah, NJ), 2002.
The Hidden Life of Otto Frank, Morrow (New York, NY), 2003.
(With Jacqueline van Maarsen) *A Friend Called Anne: One Girl's Story of War, Peace, and a Unique Friendship with Anne Frank,* Viking (New York, NY), 2005.
Anne Frank and Children of the Holocaust, foreword by Buddy Elias, Viking (New York, NY), 2006.

Contributor to periodicals.

Author's work has been translated into fifteen languages.

FICTION

The Winter of the World, HarperCollins (New York, NY), 2007.

Sidelights

British author Carol Ann Lee has published a number of critically acclaimed books focusing on Annelies Marie Frank, a Holocaust victim who died in the Bergen-Belsen concentration camp at age fifteen and whose writings have been read around the world as *The Diary of Anne Frank.* Among Lee's best-known works are *Roses from the Earth: The Biography of Anne Frank* and *The Hidden Life of Otto Frank,* a biography of Anne's father.

Lee developed a lifelong interest in Frank at the age of six, after reading an abridged version of her famous diary. The death of Lee's own father six years later increased the girl's appreciation of the work. "I started to see its deeper meaning and I became interested in Anne's ideals and how she managed to sustain her faith in mankind," the author related to Emma Brockes in the London *Guardian.* "I remember getting really upset on my sixteenth birthday because Anne's last birthday was fifteen and I had got past it. I read the diary over and over again and at every age it meant something different to me." By age seventeen, Lee had amassed a vast archive of Frank memorabilia, including newspaper clippings, photographs, and foreign editions of the diary. She also began writing a biography of Frank, although publishers showed little interest in the work. After graduating from Manchester Polytechnic with a degree in the history of art and design, Lee rekindled her interest in the manuscript. Her nonfiction debut, *Roses from the Earth,* appeared in 1999, the seventieth anniversary of Frank's birth.

Roses from the Earth, which includes a foreword by Buddy Elias, Frank's first cousin, is "a work of real sympathy and imagination," according to London *Mail on Sunday* contributor Julie Myerson. Lee's biography discusses Frank's childhood before her family went into hiding in Amsterdam and also describes the girl's tragic final months at a Dutch deportation camp and, later, at Auschwitz and Bergen-Belsen. "I wanted to set the diary in its context in a way that she [Frank] couldn't,"

Cover of A Friend Called Anne, *in which Carol Ann Lee retells Jacqueline van Maarsen's account of her childhood friendship with diarist* Anne Frank. (Photo of Anne Frank © Getty Images, Hulton Archive, 2005. Reproduced by permission of Puffin Books, a division of Penguin Putnam Books for Young Readers.)

Lee explained to Brocke. "It was like writing two books that would eventually come together: the rise of the Nazis and the story of this really ordinary family just trying to get along and enjoy themselves." Anne Karpf, writing in the London *Guardian,* described the biography as "copiously footnoted and thoroughly researched" and noted that Lee "doesn't shirk the horrors of the camps." The book's "final chapters which gather, from hearsay and fact, as much as we can possibly know of Anne's last days, make traumatic reading, containing as they do precise details of the mechanism of the camps," Myerson similarly noted.

In *The Hidden Life of Otto Frank* Lee profiles the only member of the Frank family to survive the horrors of the concentration camps. A World War I veteran and businessman, Otto Frank became the proprietor of his daughter's literary and financial legacy after World War II ended. The author also names Tony Ahlers, a Dutch Nazi, as the man who betrayed the Frank family. "Lee's portrayal of Frank's life's work preaching common humanity is well worth reading," remarked Julia Neuberger in the London *Times.*

In addition to her adult biographies, Lee has also published a number of works for young readers. *Anne Frank's Story: Her Life Retold for Children,* a reworking of *Roses from the Earth,* was praised for its "clear, engaging style" by *School Library Journal* contributor Martha Link. In *A Friend Called Anne: One Girl's Story of War, Peace, and a Unique Friendship with Anne Frank,* Lee looks at Anne's life through the eyes of childhood friend Jacqueline van Maarsen. "This absorbing book vividly portrays life in occupied Amsterdam and throws interesting sidelights on Anne Frank's story," noted *Booklist* critic Carolyn Phelan. Drawing on articles, interviews, and personal diaries, Lee examines the plight of young Holocaust victims and survivors in *Anne Frank and Children of the Holocaust.* The author "succeeds at illuminating the lives" of these individuals, observed Janet S. Thompson in a review of the work for *School Library Journal.*

Biographical and Critical Sources

PERIODICALS

Booklist, February 15, 2003, Brendan Driscoll, review of *The Hidden Life of Otto Frank,* p. 1036; April 1, 2005, Carolyn Phelan, review of *A Friend Called Anne: One Girl's Story of War, Peace, and a Unique Friendship with Anne Frank,* p. 1360; October 1, 2006, Hazel Rochman, review of *Anne Frank and the Children of the Holocaust,* p. 47.

Daily Telegraph (London, England), July 13, 2002, Linda Grant, review of *The Hidden Life of Otto Frank.*

Guardian (London, England), March 22, 1999, Emma Brockes, "After Anne," review of *Roses from the Earth: The Biography of Anne Frank;* April 3, 1999, Anne Karpf, review of *Roses from the Earth;* p. 10; July 13, 2002, Natasha Walter, review of *The Hidden Life of Otto Frank.*

Independent (London, England), July 11, 2002, Julia Pascal, review of *The Hidden Life of Otto Frank,* p. 14.

Kirkus Reviews, April 1, 2005, review of *A Friend Called Anne,* p. 427; September 15, 2006, review of *Anne Frank and the Children of the Holocaust,* p. 956; September 15, 2007, review of *The Winter of the World.*

Library Journal, February 15, 2003, Frederic Krome, review of *The Hidden Life of Otto Frank,* p. 151.

Mail on Sunday (London, England), March 21, 1999, Julie Myerson, review of *Roses from the Earth,* p. 20.

New Statesman, April 2, 1999, Martyn Bedford, review of *Roses from the Earth,* p. 47; August 5, 2002, Jennie Bristow, review of *The Hidden Life of Otto Frank,* p. 38.

Observer (London, England), July 14, 2002, Rachel Cooke, review of *The Hidden Life of Otto Frank.*

Publishers Weekly, May 23, 2005, review of *A Friend Called Anne,* p. 80; August 27, 2007, review of *The Winter of the World,* p. 61.

School Library Journal, November, 2002, Martha Link, review of *Anne Frank's Story: Her Life Retold for Children,* p. 189; April, 2005, Rita Soltan, review of *A*

Friend Called Anne, p. 158; December, 2006, Janet S. Thompson, review of *Anne Frank and the Children of the Holocaust,* p. 165.
Scotland on Sunday, July 14, 2002, Carol Ann Lee, "The Darkest Chapter," p. 9.
Times Literary Supplement, June 4, 1999, Adam Hochschild, review of *Roses from the Earth,* p. 10.
Times (London, England), July 10, 2002, Julia Neuberger, review of *The Hidden Life of Otto Frank,* p. 20.*

*   *   *

LEE, Tanith 1947-
(Esther Garber)

Personal

Born September 19, 1947; daughter of Bernard and Hylda Lee. *Education:* Studied art at college level. *Hobbies and other interests:* Study of past civilizations (Egyptian, Roman, Incan), psychic powers (their development, use, and misuse), music.

Addresses

Home and office—Kent, England.

Career

Writer. Formerly worked as a librarian.

Awards, Honors

August Derleth Award, 1980, for *Death's Master*; World Fantasy Convention Award, 1983, for "The Gorgon," and 1984, for "Elle est trois (la mort)"; Nebula nomination for "Red as Blood"; World Fantasy Award nomination for "Nunc Dimittis"; British Fantasy Society Award nominations for "Jedella Ghost" and "Where the Town Goes at Night."

Writings

FICTION; FOR YOUNG READERS

The Dragon Hoard, illustrated by Graham Oakley, Farrar, Straus (New York, NY), 1971.
Princess Hynchatti and Some Other Surprises, illustrated by Velma Ilsley, Macmillan (London, England), 1972, Farrar, Straus (New York, NY), 1973.
Animal Castle, illustrated by Helen Craig, Farrar, Straus (New York, NY), 1972.
Companions on the Road (also see below), Macmillan (London, England), 1975.
The Winter Players (also see below), Macmillan (London, England), 1975.
Companions on the Road, and The Winter Players, St. Martin's Press (New York, NY), 1977.

East of Midnight, St. Martin's Press (New York, NY), 1977.
The Castle of the Dark, Macmillan (London, England), 1978.
Shon the Taken, Macmillan (London, England), 1979.
Prince on a White Horse, Macmillan (London, England), 1982.
Madame Two Swords, illustrated by Thomas Canty, Donald M. Grant (New York, NY), 1988.
Black Unicorn, illustrated by Heather Cooper, Atheneum (New York, NY), 1991.
Gold Unicorn, Atheneum (New York, NY), 1994.
Red Unicorn, St. Martin's Press (New York, NY), 1997.
Islands in the Sky, Random House (New York, NY), 1999.
Piratica: Being a Daring Tale of a Singular Girl's Adventure upon the High Seas, Hodder (London, England), 2003, Dutton (New York, NY), 2004.
Piratica 2: Return to Parrot Island, Hodder (London, England), 2005.
Indigara, Firebird (New York, NY), 2007.

"CLAIDI JOURNALS" SERIES; FOR YOUNG ADULTS

Wolf Tower, Dutton (New York, NY), 2000.
Wolf Star, Dutton (New York, NY), 2001.
Wolk Queen, Dutton (New York, NY), 2002.
Wolf Wing, Hodder (London, England), 2002, Dutton (New York, NY), 2003.

NOVELS; FOR ADULTS

The Birthgrave, DAW (New York, NY), 1975.
Don't Bite the Sun, DAW (New York, NY), 1976.
The Storm Lord (also see below), DAW (New York, NY), 1976.
Drinking Sapphire Wine, DAW, 1977 (New York, NY), published with *Don't Bite the Sun,* Hamlyn, 1981.
Volkhavaar, DAW (New York, NY), 1977.
Vazkor, Son of Vaskor, DAW (New York, NY), 1978, published as *Shadowfire,* Futura (London, England), 1979.
Night's Master, DAW (New York, NY), 1978.
Quest for the White Witch, DAW (New York, NY), 1978.
Death's Master, DAW (New York, NY), 1979.
Electric Forest, DAW (New York, NY), 1979.
Kill the Dead (also see below), DAW (New York, NY), 1980.
Day by Night, DAW (New York, NY), 1980.
Lycanthia: or, The Children of Wolves, DAW (New York, NY), 1981.
Sometimes after Sunset (includes *Sabella* and *Kill the Dead*), Doubleday (New York, NY), 1981, portions published as *Sabella; or, The Blood Stone,* DAW (New York, NY), 1982.
Delusion's Master, DAW (New York, NY), 1981.
The Silver Metal Lover (also see below), DAW (New York, NY), 1982.
Sung in Shadow, DAW (New York, NY), 1983.
Anackire (also see below), DAW (New York, NY), 1983.
The Wars of Vis (includes *The Storm Lord* and *Anackire*), Doubleday (New York, NY), 1984.
Days of Grass, DAW (New York, NY), 1985.

Dark Castle, White Horse, DAW (New York, NY), 1986.

Delirium's Mistress, DAW (New York, NY), 1986.

The White Serpent, DAW (New York, NY), 1988.

The Book of the Beast, DAW (New York, NY), 1988.

A Heroine of the World, DAW (New York, NY), 1989.

The Blood of Roses, Legend (London, England), 1990.

Dark Dance, Dell (New York, NY), 1992.

Heart-Beast, Dell (New York, NY), 1993.

Personal Darkness, Dell (New York, NY), 1993.

The Book of the Mad, Overlook Press (Woodstock, NY), 1993.

Eva Fairdeath, Headline (London, England), 1994.

Darkness, I, Dell (New York, NY), 1994.

Reigning Cats and Dogs, Headline (London, England), 1995.

Elephantasm, Dell (New York, NY), 1996.

The Gods Are Thirsty, Overlook Press (Woodstock, NY), 1996.

Vivia, Little, Brown (Boston, MA), 1998.

Biting the Sun, Bantam Books (New York, NY), 1999.

White as Snow, Tor (New York, NY), 2000.

(With Susan Krinard and Evelyn Vaughn) *When Darkness Falls,* Silhouette (New York, NY), 2003.

(Under name Esther Garber) *Thirty-four,* Egerton (East Sussex, England), 2003.

(Under name Esther Garber; with Yolande Sorores) *Fatal Women,* Egerton (East Sussex, England), 2003.

Mortal Suns, Overlook Press (Woodstock, NY), 2003.

Metallic Love (sequel to *The Silver Metal Lover*), Bantam (New York, NY), 2005.

(With Mercedes Lackey and C.E. Murphy) *Winter Moon,* Luna (New York, NY), 2005.

"SECRET BOOKS OF VENUS" SERIES

Faces under Water, Overlook Press (Woodstock, NY), 1998.

Saint Fire, Overlook Press (Woodstock, NY), 2000.

A Bed of Earth: The Gravedigger's Tale, Overlook Press (Woodstock, NY), 2002.

Venus Preserved, Overlook Press (Woodstock, NY), 2003.

SHORT STORY COLLECTIONS

The Betrothed, Slughorn, 1968.

Unsilent Night, Nesfa Press, 1981.

Cyrion, DAW (New York, NY), 1982.

Red as Blood; or, Tales from the Sisters Grimmer, DAW (New York, NY), 1983.

The Beautiful Biting Machine, illustrated by Judy King-Rieniets, Cheap Street, 1984.

Tamastara; or, The Indian Nights, DAW (New York, NY), 1984.

The Gorgon and Other Beastly Tales, DAW (New York, NY), 1985.

Dreams of Dark and Light: The Great Short Fiction of Tanith Lee, foreword by Rosemary Hawley Johnson, illustrated by Douglas Smith, Arkham House (Sauk City, WI), 1986.

Night Sorceries, DAW (New York, NY), 1987.

Tales from the Flat Earth: Night's Daughter, Doubleday (Garden City, NY), 1987.

The Book of the Damned, Unwin (London, England), 1988, Overlook Press (Woodstock, NY), 1990.

Women as Demons: The Male Perception of Women through Space and Time, Women's Press, 1989.

Forests of the Night, Unwin (London, England), 1990.

Nightshades: Thirteen Journeys into Shadow, Headline (London, England), 1994.

RADIO AND TELEVISION PLAYS

Bitter Gate, BBC Radio, 1977.

Red Wine, BBC Radio, 1977.

Death Is King, BBC Radio, 1979.

The Silver Sky, BBC Radio, 1980.

Also author of "Sarcophagus" and "Sand," both for *Blake's Seven* (television series), 1980 and 1981, respectively.

OTHER

Lee's work has been translated into Swedish, Italian, French, and German. Contributor of short stories to collections, including *Vampire Sextette,* Ace Books (New York, NY), 2002.

Adaptations

The Silver Metal Lover was adapted for a graphic novel/comic-book format by Trina Robbins, Harmony Books (New York, NY), 1985; Lee's short story "Nunc Dimittis" was adapted to television by Hunger Productions.

Sidelights

Tanith Lee blends science fiction, fairy tale, and fantasy in her fictional explorations of good and evil, destiny versus free will, and the search for identity. Her stories and novels are known for their originality, their deeply textured language, and their evocative alternate realities. While primarily known for such adult novels as *The Birthgrave* and *Don't Bite the Sun,* as well as for her "Tales from the Flat Earth" and "Blood Opera" novel series, Lee has also written for children and young adults.

Born in London, England, Lee wrote her first story at age nine—"an embarrassingly trite thing to do," as she once told *SATA.* Bookish and introverted, she studied art for a time before becoming a librarian. Her first book of short stories appeared in 1968, and her first novel, *The Dragon Hoard,* was published in 1971. It is significant that this first book was written for young readers. "I intend my books for anyone who will enjoy them," Lee once told *SATA.* "My books are expressions of my private inner world. . . . So I can't say I aim my work at a particular audience. Even the children's books are not really specifically designed for children, which anyway seems a bit patronising. They contain ideas and fantasies and observations like all writing. I hope adults will read them as well as children, and children get a look at the adult stuff, too, if it's their kind of book."

A fairy-tale quest, *The Dragon Hoard* tells the story of Prince Jasleth, who receives an evil birthday gift from the witch Maligna, who feels slighted by the prince and his wife, Princess Goodness. Turned into a raven for an hour each day by the witch, Jasleth goes in search of the Dragon Hoard to end the spell. "I must admit to a certain element of wish fulfillment," Lee once noted in *SATA.* "I did so enjoy Jasleth's crazy voyage in *The Dragon Hoard,* for where can you find convenient dragons nowadays, when pure wonder is so thin on the ground?" Many of the Lee trademarks are present in this first book: fantasy and invention, refined language, and an element of humor bordering on zaniness that is much more subdued in her adult fiction. Virginia Haviland, writing in *Horn Book,* found the story to be "elaborate" and "entertaining."

Lee followed *The Dragon Hoard* with the children's picture book *Animal Castle.* In the book, a prince who lives in a land without animals goes on a collecting journey, returning with a handsome array to live in his castle with him. Pampered and spoiled, however, the animals soon displease the prince, who banishes them. In the end all is well, however: the animals realize in the nick of time how good they have it and promise to be proper animals if allowed to stay. A *Publishers Weekly* reviewer commented that *Animal Castle* is "an original and appealing story," while Barbara Joyce Duree described it in *Booklist* as "mildly amusing." Another early work, *Princess Hynchatti and Some Other Surprises,* stands traditional fairy tales on their heads by presenting stories in which royal heroes do no significant deeds and where a prince may even choose a witch over a beautiful princess. The work was characterized as containing "a dozen cheerfully silly tales" by a *Bulletin of the Center for Children's Books* critic. It would be some time before the adjective "cheerful" was again used to describe Lee's work.

With *Companions on the Road,* Lee moved into more serious themes and a more somber tone, producing the first of what Daphne J. Stroud referred to in *Junior Bookshelf* as her "dark" young-adult novels. These "are not cosy and comfortable books where we know everything will turn out all right in the end and that the good magic will prevail," Stroud noted. "There is a real aura of menace, which suggests that no one will be allowed to survive totally unscathed, supposing they survive at all!" In *Companions on the Road,* Havor the soldier, only eighteen and already a leader of a company of men, is sick of war and leaves the king's service after the fall and pillaging of Avilis. However, Havor engages in a bit of pillaging himself, taking a sorcerer's chalice to add to the few coins he had been entrusted with at the death of the youngest of his company. This dying soldier wanted Havor to deliver the coins to his

family, but the stolen chalice releases a mystical spell that shadows Havor and his two companions as they make their way from Avilis. Havor's two companions are killed by this spell and he is nearly done in as well, only to be saved by the young sister of the fallen soldier. A stark and haunting battle between good and evil, *Companions on the Road* "is an imaginative and impressive book," according to Graham Hammond in the *Times Literary Supplement.* Hammond also appreciated the "pared-down precision" of Lee's language.

The Winter Players is set bleakly next to the sea in a fishing village with an ancient shrine. Young Oaive was chosen at birth to guard the shrine, and guard it she does until the mysterious Grey comes to the village and transforms himself into a silver wolf to steal one of the relics. When Oaive pits her magic against the sorcerer who controls Grey, she succeeds in breaking the spell and restoring the wolf to the young man he once was. Magic spells also figure in *East of Midnight,* in which the slave Dekteon changes places and worlds with the mysterious Zaister. Dekteon, in his new world and as Zaister's stand-in, becomes the consort of Izvire, and learns he is to be sacrificed, as such consorts are every five years. Zaister, meanwhile, is faring poorly in the slave world into which he has fallen. To save himself, Dekteon must first save Zaister in the alternate world, and then somehow survive the ritual sacrifice. A complex story, *East of Midnight* has "moments of terror . . . that outdistance the average Dracula film," a reviewer for *Junior Bookshelf* commented, the critic adding that "Lee writes forcefully and with a sure grip on her tale." Writing in the *Times Literary Supplement,* Peter Hunt noted that while the exchange of minds is a typical fantasy device, the world of female kings and their five-year consorts "flashes with ideas," and the story ultimately "touches deeper themes of love, sex, and honor, and reaches a moving climax."

Set in a remote medieval age, *The Castle of the Dark* involves two protagonists, the harper Lir and the young maiden Lilune, guarded by two crones. Lilune is kept in a spell by a black power, a source of evil that surrounds her with darkness. Lir finally manages to find and destroy the evil power, thus saving Lilune. "The writing is beautiful, powerful, yet restrained," commented a *Junior Bookshelf* critic, who called *The Castle of the Dark* "a very fine book." Possession by evil powers is also at the center of *Shon the Taken,* in which the seventeen-year-old protagonist of the title becomes an outcast after being 'taken,' or possessed, by Crow, the symbol of death. Shon goes questing to the City of Crow, engages in deadly battle, finally vanquishes Crow, and, with the help of a beautiful young girl, reconciles his own people with Crow's subjects. "Lee is a fascinating writer of considerable force," Stroud asserted in *Junior Bookshelf.* The reviewer added that the story "reflects our vulnerable late twentieth century world with all its dangers and insecurities."

In a lighter vein, *Prince on a White Horse* is a mythical and humorous story of a prince who becomes a reluctant savior. As *Times Literary Supplement* contributor Cara Chanteau commented on the juxtaposition of language and content in *Prince on a White Horse,* "It is as though Le Morte d'Arthur had been written by the author of *Hitchhiker's Guide to the Galaxy.*"

Lee's ability to mix compelling humor and strong female characters are elements of her fantasy novels *Black Unicorn, Gold Unicorn,* and *Red Unicorn,* which she published in the 1990s. In *Black Unicorn* readers meet Tanaquil, whose mother is a sorceress. Although it does not seem that Tanaquil herself has inherited any of her mother's dark power, at age sixteen she becomes haunted by a black unicorn that appears magically from an object she has mended. Now she must find out why the beast has chosen her as a contact. Has it come to do good or evil? And does Tanaquil have magical powers after all? "Lee's language is wonderfully descriptive and lyrical," noted Mary Arnold in a *Voice of Youth Advocates* review of the novel, the critic going on to dub *Black Unicorn* "a coming of age story for fantasy lovers." A *Publishers Weekly* reviewer stated that Lee's "self-assured storytelling and the near-tangible evocation of a quirky world will have much appeal for fantasy devotees," while Ruth S. Vose concluded in *School Library Journal* that *Black Unicorn* is a "stylish, humorous fantasy."

Gold Unicorn continues the adventures of Tanaquil, as the teen is taken captive by the Empress Veriam who wants to conquer the world and make it perfect. Veriam turns out to be Tanaquil's half-sister, Lizra, whose major weapon in this war for perfection is a mechanical gold-plated unicorn that stubbornly refuses to work. Tanaquil is once again pressed into mending service—her one great skill, so it seems. Susan L. Rogers, writing in *School Library Journal,* found the sequel less successful than *Black Unicorn,* but also noted that in *Gold Unicorn* Lee "does introduce some new and interesting characters." In *Red Unicorn* Tanaquil returns home after several years of travel and adventure to find her sister, the empress Lizra, now engaged to Honj, the love of Tanaquil's own life. To make matters worse, her mother is romantically involved with another sorcerer and has no time for the girl. Tanaquil is magically transported into a parallel world, where she realizes that she not only has mending powers, but can also make herself invisible. She also meets her double, Tanakil, who is plotting to murder her sister, Sulkana Liliam. Tanaquil uses all her abilities to thwart the crime, and in the process both she and Tanakil are able to find true love.

Another series by Lee, "The Secret Books of Venus" features five titles, beginning with *Faces under Water* and *Saint Fire.* The stories are set in the fantasy world of Venus, an alternative version of medieval Venice. The first volume tells of Furian, a young man who has given up his family and now works for an alchemist in the city of Venice. As he searches through the Venetian canals for bodies, Furian discovers a mask of Apollo that belonged to a young musician who has been murdered. The find launches Furian into a series of adventures that lead him to various and strange places. The second volume in the series, *Saint Fire,* features a young, teenage slave named Volpa, who escapes a tyrannical master to begin a life of her own with the help of Cristiano, a soldier in the army of Major Danielus. A *Kirkus Reviews* critic described *Saint Fire* an "evocative" story written in "Lee's eerily crystalline prose." Commenting on the issues and themes Lee focuses on in this work, a critic for *Publishers Weekly* noted her use of "evocative imagery and memorable characters" and felt that the ideas Lee explores "about faith and hypocrisy, fear and justice, are deftly rendered and not easily answered." The final volume in the series, *Venus Preserved,* is as much a mystery novel as it is science fiction, as Picaro stumbles into his new home in Venus just as disaster strikes the city. "Lee builds to a totally unexpected climax, not to mention an interesting afterword," wrote Frieda Murray in her *Booklist* review of the novel.

In the "Claidi Chronicles," which include *Wolf Tower* and *Wolf Star,* Lee introduces a sixteen-year-old slave named Claidi, an orphan who serves as a lady's maid until she escapes from the Wolf Tower where she has been imprisoned. In the first book of the series, Claidi rescues Neiman, a dark-haired balloonist who lands into the grounds of her owner's house. When she and Neiman are finally able to escape, they encounter a group of bandits led by a young man named Argul. As Claidi is led back to Neiman's city and its ruling Wolf Tower, she realizes that she is really in love with Argul. The tower is now revealed to be a cruel and sad place run by Neiman's grandmother who had wanted Claidi as her successor. Reviewing this work for *School Library Journal,* Kathleen Isaacs praised Lee for her strong characterization of the protagonist, and anticipated that readers "will look forward to her continuing adventures." In *Wolf Wing,* the final entry in the series, Claidi and Argul discover that Argul's mother, thought dead, is actually alive, and has created a far away land. The trip to the utopia she has created leads Claidi to finally discover her own destiny. "Readers who have faithfully followed Claid's exploits . . . [will] want to see how everything ends," wrote Sally Estes in *Booklist.*

By Lee's own admission, her stories are not necessarily written for one audience or another. This may explain why younger readers have also become fans of some of her adult fiction, especially the short story collections *Cyrion, Red as Blood,* and *Tamastara.* Lee's adult novels also attract a young-adult readership, especially the "Tales from the Flat Earth" novels, which have been compared to *The Thousand and One Nights* because of their episodic nature and prose style that recalls old myths and fairy tales. In *Cyrion,* Lee creates a powerful male character whom she casts in short tales of mystery and violence. A sword and sorcery hero, Cyrion is not the typical "muscle-flexing macho," according to Rebecca Sue Taylor in *Voice of Youth Advocates.* Susan

Cover of Tanith Lee's young-adult novel White as Snow, *featuring artwork by Thomas Canty.* (Tom Doherty Associates, 2000. Illustration © by Thomas Canty. Reproduced by permission.)

L. Nickerson, writing in *Library Journal,* also noted the well-developed male protagonist and concluded that Lee's "continuing success with rich fantasy is remarkable."

In *Tamastara,* Lee tells seven stories set in India, some fantasy, some science fiction, and some a blending of both. Moments of self-discovery and understanding punctuate the seven, and Carolyn Caywood, writing in *Voice of Youth Advocates,* noted that "teenage readers who can appreciate these intricately structured tales will empathize with [the characters'] struggles for identity." As Lee explained in *Locus,* her fascination with India inspired the setting of both *Tamastara* and *Elephantism.* "In the mid-'80s, I just fell for India, and it was like a love affair," she explained. "I was obsessed with it," she recalled. "Later, I saw this person at a signing, and she said, 'Oh, you've obviously lived in India.' I said to her, 'Only mentally.'" Feeling part of a place she has never been is not a new experience for Lee. As she explained to an interviewer on the *Tabula Rasa Web site,* "My mind and heart go where they wish. America does influence my work, also France, Europe generally, the East and India."

Apart from setting, Lee's trademarks are her strong female characters, and in *Red as Blood* she plays with the fairy tales from the Brothers Grimm—telling them from the point of view of the Sisters Grimmer—giving the formerly passive female protagonists more than a little spunk and initiative. In *White as Snow,* she retells the tale of Snow White and the Seven Dwarves, peppering her version with various Greek myths, including those of Persephone and Demeter. Characterizing Lee's rendition of this popular children's classic as "chilling" due to the "frightening" nature of the issues she weaves into her story, *Locus* critic Dawn Castner added that readers of Lee's other short stories will be "in for a treat." Lee again draws on Greek myths for her epic *Mortal Suns,* a tale of a young, deformed girl raised in secret who rises to become the consort of a king. The author "excels at creating exotic worlds similar to our own but different enough to jar our perception and entice us," wrote Patricia Altner in a review of the title for *Library Journal.* Frieda Murray, reviewing *Mortal Suns* for *Booklist,* concluded that "Lee weaves style, subject, and characters into a seamless whole."

The heroine of Lee's YA novel *Piratica: Being a Daring Tale of a Singular Girl's Adventure upon the High Seas* is no less strong than the author's more mature heroines. A victim of amnesia, Artemesia begins to remember her past life as the daughter of famous pirate Molly Faith. When she seeks out her mother's pirate crew, however, Artemesia finds that her memory has more gaps than she thought: the fearsome pirates she remembers are in fact the adult members of an acting troupe rather than the real thing. That fact does not stop Artemesia from convincing the thespian crew to follow a treasure map, ultimately putting everyone in the center of a classic pirate adventure. "Lee cranks up the tension through shipwrecks, duels, tidal waves, cross and double-cross," wrote Jan Mark in the London *Guardian.* A *Kirkus Reviews* contributor noted of *Piratica* that Lee's "language is rip-roaring or glides like a seagull, as needed," and *School Library Journal* contributor Gerry Larson dubbed the novel a "refreshing, tongue-in-cheek, tangled tale."

Artemesia's adventures continue in *Piratica II: Return to Parrot Island,* in which Artemesia, bored with her pardoned life, becomes commander of a privateer. Gillian Engberg, reviewing the sequel for *Booklist,* recommended the title to readers of adventures, "particularly those in which young women steer the action." A *Kirkus Reviews* contributor noted that Artemesia's world, parallel to but different from historical Earth, creates humor: "Readers don't need to catch all the historical wordplay, though it's funnier if they do," the critic noted.

In *SATA* Lee once talked about inspiration and technique: "I don't know how I come to write my books," she admitted. "An idea, or group of ideas, appears suddenly in my mind. They worry and distract me until I begin to work on them, though the pre-writing stimula-

Cover of Lee's adventure novel Piratica, *featuring artwork by Glenn Harrington.* (Illustration © 2004 by Glenn Harrington. Used by permission of Penguin Group (USA), Inc.)

tion and excitement are often more enjoyable than the actual work of writing. Basically, I think my books are just a process of overspill from a particularly vivid and relentless imagination. When I write I reckon generally that about sixty percent of the story is an inspirational downhill slide, forty percent uphill slog, though there are exceptions. Mostly my children's books come easily. *The Dragon Hoard,* for example (about 160 pages long), I wrote in two weeks." A prolific writer, Lee's list of writings continues to grow. "As a writer who has been lucky enough to make writing her profession, I am most undisciplined and erratic," she once admitted. "One day I will commence work at four in the afternoon and persevere until four in the morning."

Biographical and Critical Sources

BOOKS

Contemporary Literary Criticism, Volume 46, Gale (Detroit, MI), 1987, pp. 230-234.

The Encyclopedia of Science Fiction, edited by John Clute and Peter Nicholls, St. Martin's Press (New York, NY), 1993, pp. 700-701.

Haut, Mavis, *The Hidden Library of Tanith Lee: Themes and Subtexts from Dionysos to the Immortal Gene,* McFarland & Co. (Jefferson, NC), 2001.

St. James Guide to Fantasy Writers, St. James Press (Detroit, MI), 1996.

St. James Guide to Science-Fiction Writers, 4th edition, St. James Press (Detroit, MI), 1996.

St. James Guide to Young-Adult Writers, 2nd edition, St. James Press (Detroit, MI), 1999.

PERIODICALS

Booklist, June 1, 1973, Barbara Joyce Duree, review of *Animal Castle,* p. 948; January 15, 1995, Sally Estes, review of *Gold Unicorn,* p. 912; June 1, 1997, Sally Estes, review of *Red Unicorn,* p. 1685; April 15, 2000, Sally Estes, review of *Wolf Tower,* p. 1543; April 15, 2001, Sally Estes, review of *Wolf Star,* p. 1558; April 15, 2002, Sally Estes, review of *Wolf Queen,* p. 1418; September 1, 2003, Frieda Murray, review of *Mortal Suns,* p. 75, Sally Estes, review of *Wolf Wing,* p. 119; October 15, 2003, Frieda Murray, review of *Venus Preserved,* p. 399; October 1, 2004, review of *Piratica: Being a Daring Tale of a Singular Girl's Adventure upon the High Seas,* p. 323; December 15, 2006, Gillian Engberg, review of *Piratica II: Return to Parrot Island,* p. 48.

Bulletin of the Center for Children's Books, January, 1974, review of *Princess Hynchatti and Some Other Stories,* p. 80.

Guardian (London, England), May 15, 2004, "The Saturday Review," p. 33.

Horn Book, February, 1972, Virginia Haviland, review of *The Dragon Hoard,* p. 49.

Junior Bookshelf, April, 1978, review of *East of Midnight,* p. 105; February, 1979, review of *The Castle Dark,* p. 54; April, 1990, Daphne J. Stroud, "Dark Quintet," p. 63.

Kirkus Reviews, September 15, 1999, review of *Saint Fire,* p. 1452; June 1, 2003, review of *Mortal Suns,* p. 783; September 1, 2004, review of *Piratica,* p. 869; September 15, 2006, *Piratica II,* p. 959; September 15, 2007, review of *Indigara,* p. 183.

Library Journal, September 15, 1982, Susan L. Nickerson, review of *Cyrion,* p. 1772; December, 1995, Patricia Altner, review of *Darkness, I,* p. 156; November 15, 1999, Jackie Cassada, review of *Saint Fire,* p. 101; December, 2000, Jeanne M. Leiboff, review of *White as Snow,* p. 197; July, 2003, Patricia Altner, review of *Mortal Suns,* p. 133; October 15, 2003, Michael Rogers, review of *Black Unicorn,* p. 103.

Locus, April, 1998, "Love, Death, and Publishers"; February, 2001, Dawn Castner, review of *White as Snow,* pp. 68-69.

New York Times Book Review, October 12, 2003, Gerald Jonas, review of *Mortal Suns,* p. 19.

Publishers Weekly, October 23, 1972, review of *Animal Castle,* p. 45; October 26, 1990, Sybil Steinberg, review of *The Book of the Damned,* p. 58; September

20, 1991, review of *Black Unicorn,* p. 136; January 1, 1992, review of *The Book of the Dead,* p. 50; October 26, 1992, review of *Dark Dance,* p. 61; May 10, 1993, review of *The Book of the Mad,* p. 56; June 13, 1994, review of *Personal Darkness,* p. 61; November 27, 1995, review of *Darkness, I,* p. 53; October 18, 1999, review of *Saint Fire,* p. 75; November 20, 2000, review of *White as Snow,* p. 51.

Review of Contemporary Fiction, fall, 1993, Laura Pedrick, review of *The Book of the Mad,* p. 238; October 15, 1996, Michele Leber, review of *The Gods Are Thirsty,* p. 405; May 19, 1997, review of *Red Unicorn,* p. 70; June 8, 1998, review of *Faces under Water,* p. 51.

School Library Journal, November, 1991, Ruth S. Vose, review of *Black Unicorn,* p. 134; February, 1995, Susan L. Rogers, review of *Gold Unicorn,* p. 112; December, 1995, p. 156; June, 2000, Kathleen Isaacs, review of *Wolf Tower,* p. 148; July, 2001, Patricia A. Dollisch, review of *Wolf Star,* p. 110; October, 2003, Beth L. Meister, review of *Wolf Wing,* p. 170; December, 2004, Gerry Larson, review of *Piratica,* p. 149; April, 2007, Nicki Clausen-Grace, review of *Piratica II,* p. 140.

Times Literary Supplement, December 3, 1971, p. 1511; November 3, 1972, p. 1332; April 2, 1976, Graham Hammond, review of *Companions on the Road,* p. 383;October, 25, 1977, Peter Hunt, review of *East of Midnight,* p. 1246; July 23, 1982, Cara Chanteau, review of *Prince on a White Horse,* p. 794.

Voice of Youth Advocates, April, 1983, Rebecca Sue Taylor, review of *Cyrion,* pp. 45-46; October, 1984, Carolyn Caywood, review of *Tamastara; or, The Indian Nights,* p. 206; December, 1991, Mary Arnold, review of *Black Unicorn,* p. 324; December, 1997, Gloria Grover, review of *Red Unicorn,* p. 326; April, 2003, review of *Wolf Queen,* p. 12; October, 2004, Michele Winship, review of *Piratica,* p. 316.

ONLINE

Tabula Rasa Web site, http://www.tabula-rasa.info/ (December 2, 2007), interview with Lee.

Tanith Lee Home Page, http://www.tanithlee.com (November 28, 2007).*

*   *   *

LLEWELLYN, Sam 1948-

Personal

Born August 2, 1948, in Tresco, England; son of William Somers (an Anglican bishop) and Innis Dorrien Smith Llewellyn; married Karen Margaret Wallace (a children's writer), 1975; children: William, Martin. *Education:* St. Catherine's College, Oxford, B.A., 1970, M.A., 1973. *Politics:* "Tory anarchist." *Hobbies and other interests:* Wine, sailing, gardening.

Addresses

Home—Herefordshire, England. *E-mail*—sam@sam-llewellyn.com.

Sam Llewellyn (Courtesy of Sam Llewellyn.)

Career

Writer, editor, and journalist. Arch Books, former director.

Member

League of Nightrunners, Baverstock Orpheans, Council for the Protection of Rural England.

Awards, Honors

Premio di Littratura per l'Infanzia, Cassa di Risparmio di Cento (Italy), for *Pig in the Middle.*

Writings

FOR CHILDREN

Pegleg, illustrations by Robert Bartelt, Dent (London, England), 1985.

Pig in the Middle, illustrations by Michael Trevithick, Walker (London, England), 1989.

The Rope School, Walker (London, England), 1994.

The Magic Boathouse, illustrated by Arthur Robins, Walker (London, England), 1995.

The Polecat Café, illustrated by Arthur Robbins, Walker (London, England), 1998.

Wonderdog, Walker (London, England), 1999.

Admiral Nelson: The Sailor Who Dared All to Win, Short (London, England), 2004.

Little Darlings, Razorbill (New York, NY), 2004.

Bad, Bad Darlings: Small but Deadly, illustrated by David Roberts, Puffin (New York, NY), 2005.

The Return of Death Eric, Puffin (London, England), 2005, Walker (New York, NY), 2006.

Desperado Darlings: Small but Deadly, Puffin (New York, NY), 2006.

The Haunting of Death Eric, Puffin (London, England), 2006.

Eye of the Cannon, Catnip (London, England), 2007.

THRILLERS

Dead Reckoning, Summit Books (New York, NY), 1987.

Blood Orange, Michael Joseph (London, England), 1988, Summit Books (New York, NY), 1989.

Death Roll, Summit Books (New York, NY), 1989.

Dead Eye, Michael Joseph (London, England), 1990, Summit Books (New York, NY), 1991.

Blood Knot, Michael Joseph (London, England), 1991, Pocket Books (New York, NY), 1992.

Riptide, Michael Joseph (London, England), 1992.

Clawhammer, Pocket Books (New York, NY), 1993.

Maelstrom, Pocket Books (New York, NY), 1994.

The Shadow in the Sands: Being an Account of the Cruise of the Yacht Gloria in the Frisian Islands in the April of 1903, and the Conclusion of the Events Described by Erskine Childers in His Narrative, The Riddle of the Sands, Headline (London, England), 1998, Sheridan House (Dobbs Ferry, NY), 1999.

The Sea Garden, Headline (London, England), 1999.

The Malpas Legacy, Headline (London, England), 2001.

OTHER

Gurney's Revenge, Arlington (London, England), 1977.

Gurney's Reward, Arlington (London, England), 1978.

Gurney's Release, Arlington (London, England), 1979.

Hell Bay, Arlington (London, England), 1980.

The Last Will and Testament of Robert Louis Stevenson, Arlington (London, England), 1981.

Yacky dar Mor Bewty!: A Phrasebook for the Regions of Britain (with Irish Supplement), illustrated by Nigel Paige, Elm Tree (London, England), 1985.

Small Parts in History (nonfiction), Sidgwick & Jackson (London, England), 1985.

The Worst Journey in the Midlands (nonfiction), illustrations by Chris Aggs, Heinemann (London, England), 1985, reprinted, Summersdale (Chichester, England), 2003.

Sea Story (novel), St. Martin's Press (New York, NY), 1987.

Great Circle, Weidenfeld & Nicholson (London, England), 1987.

Iron Hotel, Michael Joseph (London, England), 1996.

Storm Force from Navarone: The Sequel to Alistair MacLean's Force 10 from Navarone, HarperCollins (London, England), 1996.

Thunderbolt from Navarone, HarperCollins (London, England), 1997.

Emperor Smith, the Man Who Built Scilly, Dovecote Press (Dorset, England), 2005.

Contributor to periodicals, including the London *Times, Daily Telegraph, Independent, Practical Boat Owner, Yachting Monthly, Classic Boat*, and *Sailing*.

Sidelights

British journalist Sam Llewellyn, a frequent contributor to the London *Times,* is the author of several highly regarded books for children and teens, among them *Pig in the Middle* and *The Return of Death Eric*. Llewellyn also pens critically acclaimed suspense novels and works of nonfiction for adults.

Llewellyn is an avid sailor whose interest in the sea is reflected not only in his thrillers but also in his books for children. Born on the Isles of Scilly, a group of islands off the southwest tip of Cornwall, England, he once commented: "I have always lived on, by, in, or under the sea, and I have taken great pleasure in telling stories about it. It is always good to have an excuse to spend a lot of the year on a boat." One of Llewellyn's best-known works, *The Worst Journey in the Midlands,* chronicles his attempt to row from North Wales to London. Llewellyn's "journey encompassed canals filled with fridges, prams and supermarket trolleys," remarked Richard Williamson in the *Sunday Mercury.* "There were brusque, unfriendly fishermen, small boys throwing stones and bigger boys firing air rifles, racist graffiti around Kings Norton and slavering Alsatians attempting to board his vessel via the oars. All this he tells with wit and humour in one of the most entertaining and laid-back travel books around."

Pegleg, Llewellyn's first work for children, follows the adventures of young Gussie Smith, who tries not only to avoid the truant officer Snell, but also the secret Russian agent "Pegleg" Arthur Hopcraft. Set in the Scillies, the novel's action ranges from rescuing the spy's tin leg to Gussie's fight to keep his grandmother out of a retirement home. In a review of *Pegleg* for *School Librarian,* C.E.J. Smith wrote that Llewellyn's protagonists "balance neatly between caricature and character." A *Junior Bookshelf* critic expressed amazement at the "breakneck" tempo of the novel, going on to praise Llewellyn for his accurate description of the unique island setting.

Intended for younger readers, *Pig in the Middle* concerns a seal pup stranded in a lagoon. While a prosperous fisherman contends that his livelihood is threatened by the seal's presence, eleven-year-old Alec Whean, saddled with a constantly inebriated father and a mean-spirited mother, finds that his own troubled life is somehow enriched by the same creature. "The plot moves at a cracking pace," observed London *Times* contributor Brian Alderson, who also praised the author's "convincing treatment of locale." While admitting that the tale is "exciting enough for any reader looking for adventure," a reviewer in *Growing Point* suggested that *Pig in the Middle* also exposes children to environmentalism. Similarly, in a *Junior Bookshelf* review, Marcus Crouch wrote that, "as well as being a great yarn," Llewellyn's book is both "responsible and very thoughtful."

The Rope School and *The Magic Boathouse* both feature children who get their just deserts at the end. Running from an angry coachman whose horses she has lost, young Kate Griffiths takes momentary refuge in a British warship in *The Rope School*. Unable to jump ship before it sets sail and surrounded by sailors who do not realize she is a stowaway—or even worse, a female—Kate finds herself enrolled in the Rope School where she learns to become a sailor and even teams up with an attacking American privateer. In *The Magic Boathouse* Llewellyn introduces readers to Joe and Doris as they discover an old boathouse while on a seaside outing. When the man in the boathouse allows the two children to blow his foghorn, legions of Romans march from the sea, followed by conquering Normans, all of whom help the two children with their chores. Reviewing *The Rope School*, a *Junior Bookshelf* critic wrote that "the characters of both landlubber and seagoing personnel are briskly sketched," while another critic in the same publication claimed that in *The Magic Boathouse* Llewellyn "has written a lively and entertaining story."

Little Darlings, a work that was compared by several critics to Lemony Snicket's popular "A Series of Unfortunate Events" novels, centers on Cassian, Primrose, and Daisy Darling, a trio of children whose insanely wealthy father ignores their welfare, allowing them to be raised by host of tyrannical nannies. When the children discover that the latest group of nannies is really a burglar ring in disguise, they pool their talents to thwart the ring's criminal efforts. *School Library Journal* critic Melissa Christy Buron described *Little Darlings* as "a cleverly written satire on the ingenuity of children and the callous materialism of the" idle rich. Nicolette Jones, writing in the London *Sunday Times*, praised Llewellyn's narrative style as "sometimes arch but often witty, and in a knowing ellipsis that assumes intelligence in the reader." In a sequel, *Bad, Bad Darlings: Small but Deadly*, Daisy, Cassian, and Primrose find themselves on a remote island along with their father, who is determined to clear the way for development by paving over the isle's natural beauty. According to Jones, *Bad, Bad Darlings* "fulfils the eccentric promise of the first book, with its improbable premises, sophisticated wordplay and unconventional morality."

Aging rockers reunite in *The Return of Death Eric,* a work for middle-grade readers. Death Eric, once one of the world's most famous and outrageous rock-and-roll bands, suffered an abrupt end after lead singer Eric Thrashmettle convinced himself that the band was cursed by the appearance of a raven at the Chicken-

stock Festival. Now living in relative isolation in his estate, Eric is forced by financial concerns to the road after his unscrupulous manager runs off with the family fortune. With the help of his children, Lulubelle Flower Fairy and Living Buddha, the aging rocker attempts to convince his bandmates to give the music business another try in a novel that was dubbed "hilarious and wonderfully wacky" in a *Kirkus Reviews* appraisal.

In addition to writing children's fiction, Llewellyn has also written thrillers set at sea. One of his earliest books in this genre, *Dead Reckoning,* focuses on a yacht designer who discovers that his racing crafts are being sabotaged. Determined to prove the actual safety of his designs, the hero willingly risks his life by entering a key competition. In another thriller, *Blood Orange,* Llewellyn writes about a racing trio undone when their yacht founders and one of the crew, Alan, is believed drowned. The two surviving sailors, James and Ed, continue with their lives, though Ed himself is suspected of playing a part in Alan's drowning. James, however, suddenly discovers the missing Alan aboard another yacht. But before James can address him, Alan vanishes. Soon afterward, Alan is found truly dead. When another of James acquaintances suffers a boating mishap, he begins to suspect a conspiracy of foul play. Other thrillers include *Death Roll,* another tale of seaside sabotage, and *Blood Knot,* in which a former journalist is framed for the drowning of a Soviet sailor. In the latter story, the hero discovers a considerable plot in Estonia, and in unraveling the events, he finds himself uncovering the circumstances of his own father's mysterious demise.

The Shadow in the Sands: Being an Account of the Cruise of the Yacht Gloria in the Frisian Islands in the April of 1903, and the Conclusion of the Events Described by Erskine Childers in His Narrative, The Riddle of the Sands, is Llewellyn's sequel to Erskine Childers's 1903 novel *The Riddle of the Sands.* The book concerns Charles Webb, a yacht skipper who helps prevent a German invasion of England. According to *Booklist* reviewer Roland Green, the work contains "convincing characterization and seafaring milieu, not to mention nonstop action." In *The Malpas Legacy,* a novel set in Ireland, a man discovers that a crumbling mansion once belonging to his girlfriend's grandfather harbors some dark secrets. London *Times* critic Eve Peasnall called *The Malpas Legacy* "intelligent and macabre."

Llewellyn, who lives in a medieval farmhouse in Herefordshire, England, with his wife and children, often sails for several months during the year to research his books. Addressing aspiring writers, Llewellyn offered the following suggestion to an interviewer on the BBC News Web site, "Write two pages every day, rewrite the two pages you have written until you are completely happy with them—and be very lucky."

Biographical and Critical Sources

PERIODICALS

Birmingham Post (Birmingham, England), August 8, 2001, Alison Jones, "Digging Deep into Recesses of the Mind: Author Sam Llewellyn Tells Alison Jones about His Unusual Method of Research," p. 136.

Booklist, October 15, 1999, review of *The Shadow in the Sands: Being an Account of the Cruise of the Yacht Gloria in the Frisian Islands in the April of 1903, and the Conclusion of the Events Described by Erskine Childers in His Narrative, The Riddle of the Sands,* p. 420.

Growing Point, September, 1989, review of *Pig in the Middle,* p. 5206.

Independent on Sunday (London, England), April 5, 1998, Brandon Robshaw, review of *The Polecat Café,* p. 30.

Junior Bookshelf, October, 1985, review of *Pegleg,* p. 231; August, 1989, Marcus Crouch, review of *Pig in the Middle,* pp. 190-191; October, 1994, review of *The Rope School,* p. 182; February, 1995, review of *The Magic Boathouse,* p. 22.

Kirkus Reviews, September 15, 2006, review of *The Return of Death Eric,* p. 960.

Publishers Weekly, August 21, 2000, review of *The Sea Garden,* p. 52.

School Librarian, June, 1986, C.E.J. Smith, review of *Pegleg,* p. 170.

School Library Journal, August, 2005, Melissa Christy Buron, review of *Little Darlings,* p. 130; December, 2006, Michelle Roberts, review of *The Return of Death Eric,* p. 149.

Sun (London, England), July 22, 2005, Sam Wostear, review of *The Return of Death Eric,* p. 55.

Sunday Mercury (Birmingham, England), January 12, 2003, Richard Williamson, review of *The Worst Journey in the Midlands,* p. 42.

Sunday Times (London, England), March 28, 2004, Nicolette Jones, review of *Little Darlings,* p. 54; January 9, 2005, Nicolette Jones, review of *Bad, Bad Darlings: Small but Deadly,* p. 54.

Times (London, England), June 17, 1998, Brian Alderson, review of *Pig in the Middle,* p. 54; January 8, 2000, Gill Hornby, review of *The Sea Garden,* p. 22; September 15, 2001, Eve Peasnall, review of *The Malpas Legacy,* p. 19; May 15, 2004, Amanda Craig, review of *Little Darlings,* p. 17.

ONLINE

BBC News Web site, http://news.bbc.co.uk/ (August 3, 2005), "Sam Llewellyn: When I Was Twelve."

Penguin Books Web site, http://www.penguin.co.uk/ (November 10, 2007), "Sam Llewellyn."

Sam Llewellyn Home Page, http://www.samllewellyn.com (November 10, 2007).

LOIZEAUX, William

Personal

Married; wife's name Beth; children: Anna (deceased), Emma. *Education:* Colgate University, B.A.; University of Michigan, M.A.

Addresses

Home—Hyattsville, MD.

Career

Educator and author. Johns Hopkins University Writing Program, Baltimore, MD, lecturer.

Awards, Honors

New York Times Notable Book designation, 1993, for *Anna: A Daughter's Life;* Notable Essay designation, 2002; Henry Bergh Children's Award in Fiction, American Society for the Prevention of Cruelty to Animals, 100 Titles for Reading and Sharing designation, New York Public Library, *Christian Science Monitor* Notable Children's Book citation, and Golden Kite Award Honor Book for Fiction designation, all 2006, all for *Wings;* Maryland State Arts Council Work in Progress grant; Individual Artist Award.

Writings

Anna: A Daughter's Life (nonfiction), Arcade (New York, NY), 1993.

The Shooting of Rabbit Wells: An American Tragedy (nonfiction), Arcade (New York, NY), 1998.

Wings (young-adult novel), illustrated by Leslie Bowman, Farrar, Straus & Giroux (New York, NY), 2006.

Contributor of short fiction to anthologies and to periodicals, including *TriQuarterly* and *Massachusetts Review.* Contributor of essays to *American Scholar.*

Sidelights

William Loizeaux debuted as an author with a poignant look at his own daughter's brief life and death as the victim of VATER syndrome, an uncommon congenital condition. Loizeaux details his own feelings as well as the procedures undertaken to save the six-month-old baby in *Anna: A Daughter's Life.* A reviewer for *Publishers Weekly* found the work to be "written with luminous clarity and heartbreaking candor." Helen Epstein, writing in the *New York Times Book Review,* also had high praise for *Anna,* calling it an example of "honest writing that chooses to risk pathos and embarrassment rather than rewrite reality, that allows for humor, and that tracks the process of becoming a parent and the process of bereavement . . . with extraordinary precision."

Loizeaux examines another death in *The Shooting of Rabbit Wells: An American Tragedy.* Wells, who was twenty-one at the time of his death in 1973, was mistakenly shot by a police officer. Loizeaux had attended school with Wells, and in his book he attempts to trace his former schoolmate's life to discover how the young man's early promise led to his tragic death. A reviewer for *Publishers Weekly* faulted the author for inserting "slipshod" re-imaginings of some of the incidents and dialogue into his text, and *Library Journal* critic Faye Powell similarly considered such fictional additions "problematic." However, in *Booklist,* Brian McCombie asserted more positively that "Loizeaux creates surprising tension as his book drives to its bitter conclusion."

Loizeaux turns to juvenile fiction with *Wings,* a tale of a youth who cares for an injured bird and then must accept the day the animal will ultimately leave him. The story is told from the perspective of Nick, who looks back to the summer of 1960. Ten years old at the time, Nick rescues an injured mockingbird, names it Marcy, and nurses it back to health. The child of a widowed mother—his father died in the Korean War—Nick is a lonely boy, and through Marcy he learns the lessons of friendship he has missed—particularly about the importance of allowing others their freedom. *School Library Journal* contributor Susan Scheps, found *Wings* to be "both realistic and tender," while in *Horn Book* Joanna Rudge Long termed the novel "a touching, well-wrought tale." Long also observed that Loizeaux's writing is deft, [and] the bird lore authentic." A *Kirkus Reviews* critic had even higher praise for *Wings,* concluding: "Loss settles on the page with a longing that only time and reflection can heal, and that only a top-notch writer can create."

Biographical and Critical Sources

BOOKS

Loizeaux, William, *Anna: A Daughter's Life,* Arcade (New York, NY), 1993.

PERIODICALS

Booklist, January 1, 1998, Brian McCombie, review of *The Shooting of Rabbit Wells: An American Tragedy,* p. 768; September 1, 2006, Carolyn Phelan, review of *Wings,* p. 129.
Children's Bookwatch, November, 2006, review of *Wings.*
Critical Care Nursing Quarterly, May, 1996, Lisa Pilichi and Rae L. Schnuth, review of *Anna,* p. 88.
Horn Book, September-October, 2006, Joanna Rudge Long, review of *Wings,* p. 59.
Kirkus Reviews, August 15, 2006, review of *Wings,* p. 847.
Library Journal, December, 1997, Faye Powell, review of *The Shooting of Rabbit Wells,* p. 130.
New York Times Book Review, March 7, 1993, Helen Epstein, review of *Anna.*

Publishers Weekly, January 4, 1993, review of *Anna,* p. 64; November 3, 1997, review of *The Shooting of Rabbit Wells,* p. 71.
School Library Journal, September, 2006, Susan Scheps, review of *Wings,* p. 21.

ONLINE

Johns Hopkins University Web site, http://www.jhu.edu/ (March 12, 2007), brief biography of William Loizeaux.

*   *   *

LUBNER, Susan

Personal

Married; children: Hannah, Julia. *Hobbies and other interests:* Bike riding, reading, spending time with family and friends.

Addresses

Home and office—Southboro, MA. *E-mail*—slubner@charter.net.

Career

Author.

Member

Society of Children's Book Writers and Illustrators.

Awards, Honors

First place award, *Byline* magazine, for *Ruthie Bon Bair;* Mom's Choice Award, 2006, for both *Noises at Night* and *Ruthie Bon Bair.*

Writings

(With Beth Raisner Glass) *Noises at Night,* illustrated by Bruce Whatley, Harry N. Abrams (New York, NY), 2005.
Ruthie Bon Bair: Do Not Go to Bed with Wringing Wet Hair!, illustrated by Bruce Whatley, Harry N. Abrams (New York, NY), 2006.
A Horse's Tale, illustrated by Margie Moore, Harry N. Abrams (New York, NY), 2008.

Sidelights

Susan Lubner's first book for children, 2005's *Noises at Night,* was co-authored with Lubner's friend, Beth Raisner Glass. As she noted on her home page, Lubner's inspiration for writing comes from the things and the people around her. Her first solo picture book, *Ruthie Bon Bair: Do Not Go to Bed with Wringing Wet Hair!,* for instance, was inspired by her daughters.

Susan Lubner (Courtesy of Susan Lubner.)

A rhyming story, *Ruthie Bon Bair* tells the story of a young girl who always goes to bed with wet hair. One morning, Ruthie wakes to find that a garden of mushrooms, fern, and lilies has sprouted in her hair overnight. The story follows the girl as she tries to find a way to keep the garden from expanding into a jungle. Linda Ludke noted in *School Library Journal* that *Ruthie Bon Bair* is "propelled forward by jaunty, rhyming couplets," resulting in a "cautionary tale [that] makes a fun read-aloud."

With regard to her writing process, Lubner considers revision to be the most crucial aspect. As she wrote on her home page, "once I get a first version or first draft down on paper, I spend a lot of time reworking the story by moving things around, adding things to, or taking things out of the story."

Biographical and Critical Sources

PERIODICALS

Kirkus Reviews, October 1, 2005, review of *Noises at Night,* p. 1080; September 15, 2006, review of *Ruthie Bon Bair: Do Not Go to Bed with Wringing Wet Hair!,* p. 960.
Publishers Weekly, August 1, 2005, review of *Noises at Night,* p. 64.
School Library Journal, November, 2006, Linda Ludke, review of *Ruthie Bon Bair,* p. 105.

ONLINE

Children's Bookwatch Web site, http://www.midwest bookreview.com/ (September 1, 2005), review of *Noises at Night.*
Susan Lubner Home Page, http://www.susanlubner.com (November 17, 2007).

M

MALLORY, Kenneth 1945-

Personal

Born March 22, 1945, in Boston, MA; son of George Kenneth (a pathologist) and Carol (a homemaker) Mallory; married Margaret Thompson (a middle-school teacher), September, 19, 1978. *Education:* Harvard College, B.A. (English literature), 1967. *Politics:* "Independent."

Addresses

Home—Newton Highlands, MA. *E-mail*—ken.mallory@ comcast.net.

Career

MIT Press, Cambridge, MA, sales representative, 1971-74; Earthwatch, Belmont, MA, marketing director, 1975; New England Aquarium, Boston, MA, editor-in-chief of publishing programs, 1979-2004; freelance writer, editor, and photographer, 2004—.

Member

Authors Guild, Society of Children's Book Writers and Illustrators, New England Science Writers, Society for Environmental Journalists.

Awards, Honors

The Last Extinction selected among *Library Journal*'s One Hundred Most Important Books of 1986; Outstanding Nature Book for Children selection, John Burroughs Association, Outstanding Science Trade Book designation, Children's Book Council/National Science Teachers Association (CBC/NSTA), both 1989, and Choice designation, International Reading Association, 1991, all for *Rescue of the Stranded Whales; American Bookseller* Pick-of-the-Lists designation, 1995, for *Families of the Deep Blue Sea;* Notable Children's Books selec-

Kenneth Mallory (Photograph by Hirako Wada. Reproduced by permission of Harcourt.)

tion, 1998, *Smithsonian,* for *Home by the Sea;* Outstanding Science Trade Books for Students designation, CBC/NSTA, 2007, for *Diving to a Deep-Sea Volcano.*

Writings

(Editor with Les Kaufman) *The Last Extinction,* MIT Press (Cambridge, MA), 1986.
(With Andrea Conley) *Rescue of the Stranded Whales,* Crown (New York, NY), 1989.

Water Hole: Life in a Rescued Tropical Forest, Franklin Watts (New York, NY), 1991.

The Red Sea, Franklin Watts (New York, NY), 1991.

(With Scott Kraus) *The Search for the Right Whale: How Scientists Rediscovered the Most Endangered Whale in the Sea,* Crown (New York, NY), 1993.

Families of the Deep Blue Sea, illustrated by Marshall Peck III, Charlesbridge (Watertown, MA), 1995.

A Home by the Sea: Protecting Coastal Wildlife, Harcourt (San Diego, CA), 1998.

(With Mark Chandler) *Lake Victoria: Africa's Inland Sea,* New England Aquarium and Lowell Institute (Boston, MA), 2000.

(With Pamela Chanko and Susan Canzares) *Aquarium,* Scholastic (New York, NY), 2000.

(Editor) *Boston Harbor Islands National Park Area,* Down East Books (Camden, MA), 2003.

(With Scott Kraus) *Disappearing Giants: The North Atlantic Right Whale,* Bunker Hill Publishing (Charlestown, MA), 2003.

Also served as editor of *Aquasphere* magazine; editor for special issues of *Sea Frontiers* magazine.

"SCIENTISTS IN THE FIELD" SERIES

Swimming with Hammerhead Sharks, Houghton Mifflin (Boston, MA), 2001.

Diving to a Deep-Sea Volcano, Houghton Mifflin (Boston, MA), 2006.

Sidelights

Kenneth Mallory is a writer, editor, and photographer who specializes in science journalism. Mallory, a former editor-in-chief of publishing programs at Boston's New England Aquarium, is the author of such critically acclaimed books as *Rescue of the Stranded Whales,* coauthored with Andrea Conley, as well as *Swimming with Hammerhead Sharks* and *Diving to a Deep-Sea Volcano.*

Mallory's educational background in literature and biology led him to begin writing as a freelance journalist for magazines. He once commented that his interest in the natural ecology of Maine, where he grew up, inspired his interest in natural history, and that his experiences writing exhibit copy for the New England Aquarium helped develop a prose style that is suitable for children's books. He combined this writing ability with a developing interest in photography to produce nonfiction photo books that parallel themes highlighted by the aquarium, such as marine conservation and investigations and research into aquatic and natural life. Mallory noted that his position with the New England Aquarium also afforded him opportunities to travel to such destinations as New Zealand, the North Atlantic, and Costa Rica, resulting in books on the ecology and natural wildlife of these areas.

One of the first books Mallory issued, *The Red Sea,* focuses on the vast variety of species that inhabit this body of water. The work includes several maps, a glos-

sary, a list of further readings and index. A critic in *Kirkus Reviews* praised this book for its "vivid underwater photos" and "intriguing text." Similarly, Frances E. Millhouser praised Mallory's "fine full-color photographs" in a review for *School Library Journal,* and recommended the book as one that provides a good overview of the wildlife inhabiting the Red Sea.

Mallory's position with the New England Aquarium gave him the opportunity to be at close quarters when a herd of forty pilot whales beached themselves off the coast of Cape Cod in 1986. Due to exposure and the shock the whales were subjected to, scientists were able to only save three baby whales from the group. Mallory's book, *Rescue of the Stranded Whales,* tracks these efforts on behalf of the three babies, Baby, Notch, and Tag, from the initial encounter at the beach to their final release into the wild a few months later. A critic writing in *Kirkus Reviews* called the work an "appealing story of scientists and conservationists in action," and Phillis Wilson wrote in *Booklist* that *Rescue of the Stranded Whales* is "a prime example of an informative science narrative that works as a compelling story." Mallory and Conley were also lauded in *School Library Journal* by Millhouser, who called their text both informative and "fascinating," as well as "beautifully illustrated." Although *New York Times Book Review* contributor Faith McNulty contended that the narrative fails to bring the creatures fully to life, she added that the strengths of the work outweigh its weaknesses; "it is enough for now that such enlightened, and enlightening, things are being done. We can only be grateful that the good news is being conveyed to a new generation."

Whales are once again the focus of Mallory's *The Search for the Right Whale: How Scientists Rediscovered the Most Endangered Whale in the Sea.* Coauthored with Scott Kraus, the book contains a first-person narrative following the search for this species of whales. In her review of the work for *School Library Journal,* Valerie Lennox noted that the approach taken by Mallory and Kraus provides a good introduction to the events during a research expedition, and called *The Search for the Right Whale* a "top-notch resource for endangerment projects." Kay Weisman, writing in *Booklist,* praised the photographs and the descriptions of whale sightings in particular, labeling the work "an appealing and useful addition to the animal shelf."

Mallory went to Costa Rica on assignment from the New England Aquarium in the late 1980s, and this trip resulted in a book about the reclaimed tropical forest in the Guanacaste National Park area. Characteristically, he accompanies his text with colorful illustrations to produce *Water Hole: Life in a Rescued Tropical Forest.* Incorporating a glossary and a suggested list of other titles, and focusing primarily on a small band of tropical raccoon-like animals called coatis, Mallory tracks these and other creatures in the forest over a course of one year. Other geographical and aquatic regions are covered by Mallory in books such as *Families of the*

Deep Blue Sea, which focuses on fourteen different species of ocean dwellers, and *A Home by the Sea,* which focuses on efforts to protect coastal and marine animal life off the coast of New Zealand. Both these books have been praised for their clear text and photographs, as well as their focus on the scientists who work on these projects.

Scientist and marine biologist Pete Klimley and his IMAX film crew are the focus of Mallory's *Swimming with Hammerhead Sharks,* a work that tracks the film team as much as it does the sharks they are attempting to capture on camera. To research the book, Mallory traveled to the Cocos Island, some 330 miles off the Pacific coast of Costa Rica, where he met Klimley and filmmakers Howard and Michele Hall. According to *Horn Book* critic Danielle J. Ford, "Mallory's descriptions of the hammerheads he sees are filled with references to Klimley's work, emphasizing the importance of informed observation." Roger Leslie, writing in *Booklist,* praised *Swimming with Hammerhead Sharks* as an "engrossing, visually captivating" work, adding that "the text shares plenty that is worth knowing and remembering." Mallory's combined record of investiga-

tion and biology was also lauded by Patricia Manning in *School Library Journal* as an "exceptional" work that will prove to be a "useful tool for young report writers."

In *Diving to a Deep-Sea Volcano,* Mallory profiles Rich Lutz, a marine biologist who studies hydrothermal vents and their ecosystems. Using a submersible vessel, Lutz travels thousands of feet below the surface of the Pacific Ocean to document the rebirth of a biological community that had been destroyed by a volcanic eruption. "Mallory adeptly conveys the thrill of discovery and excitement in this field," Ford noted of the book, and Michael Santangelo, writing in *School Library Journal,* described *Diving to a Deep-Sea Volcano* as "a balanced mixture of biography and science that gives children a well-rounded exposure to intellectual pursuit."

Biographical and Critical Sources

PERIODICALS

Booklist, July, 1989, Phillis Watson, review of *Rescue of the Stranded Whales,* p. 1905; May, 1993, Janice Del

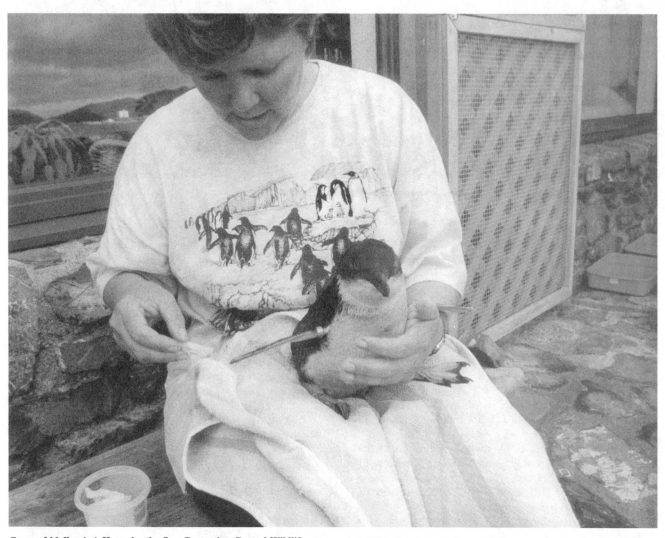

Cover of Mallory's **A Home by the Sea: Protecting Coastal Wildlife.** (Photograph © 1998 by New England Aquarium. Reproduced by permission of Kenneth Mallory.)

Cover of Mallory's **Diving to a Deep-Sea Volcano,** *featuring artwork by Diane Leyland.* (Art © 2006 by the Stephen Low Company. Reprinted by permission of Houghton Mifflin Company. All rights reserved.)

Negro, review of *Water Hole: Life in a Rescued Tropical Forest,* p. 1585; July, 1993, Kay Weisman, review of *The Search for the Right Whale: How Scientists Rediscovered the Most Endangered Whale in the Sea,* p. 1961; September 1, 1998, Chris Sherman, review of *A Home by the Sea: Protecting Coastal Wildlife,* p. 116; April 1, 2001, Roger Leslie, review of *Swimming with Hammerhead Sharks,* p. 1462; December 1, 2006, Jennifer Mattson, review of *Diving to a Deep-Sea Volcano,* p. 57.

Horn Book, July, 2001, Danielle J. Ford, review of *Swimming with Hammerhead Sharks,* p. 472; January-February, 2007, Danielle J. Ford, review of *Diving to a Deep-Sea Volcano,* p. 82.

Kirkus Reviews, June 1, 1989, review of *Rescue of the Stranded Whales,* p. 839; March 15, 1991, review of *The Red Sea,* p. 397; July 15, 1998, review of *A Home by the Sea,* p. 1038; September 15, 2006, review of *Diving to a Deep-Sea Volcano,* p. 961.

New York Times Book Review, May 21, 1989, Faith McNulty, review of *Rescue of the Stranded Whales.*

School Library Journal, June, 1989, Frances E. Millhouser, review of *Rescue of the Stranded Whales,* p. 119; August, 1991, Frances E. Millhouser, review of *The Red Sea,* p. 193; April, 1993, Eva Elisabeth Von Ancken, review of *Water Hole,* p. 137; August, 1993, Valerie Lenox, review of *The Search for the Right Whale,* p. 176; February, 1996, Lisa Wu Stowe, review of *Families of the Deep Blue Sea,* p. 96; September, 1998, Patricia Manning, review of *A Home by the Sea,* p. 222; July, 2001, Patricia Manning, review of *Swimming with Hammerhead Sharks,* p. 128; February, 2007, Michael Santangelo, review of *Diving to a Deep-Sea Volcano,* p. 143.

ONLINE

Agpix.com, http://www.agpix.com/ (December 1, 2007), Stock photos by Mallory.

Kenneth Mallory Home Page, http://kennethmallory.com (December 1, 2007).

MANNING, Jane K.

Personal
Female.

Addresses
Home—Deep River, CT.

Career
Author and illustrator.

Writings

SELF-ILLUSTRATED

This Little Piggy, HarperFestival (New York, NY), 1997.
My First Songs, HarperFestival (New York, NY), 1998.
Who Stole the Cookies from the Cookie Jar?, HarperFestival (New York, NY), 2001.
My First Baby Games, HarperFestival (New York, NY), 2001.
Cat Nights, Greenwillow Books (New York, NY), 2008.

ILLUSTRATOR

Susan Saunders, *The Ghost Who Ate Chocolate,* HarperCollins (New York, NY), 1996.
Susan Saunders, *The Haunted Skateboard,* HarperTrophy (New York, NY), 1996.
Alvin Granowsky, *Help Yourself, Little Red Hen!,* Steck-Vaughn (Austin, TX), 1996.
Susan Saunders, *The Revenge of the Pirate Ghost,* HarperCollins (New York, NY), 1997.
Susan Saunders, *The Phantom Pen Pal,* HarperCollins (New York, NY), 1997.
Susan Saunders, *The Ghost of Spirit Lake,* HarperTrophy (New York, NY), 1997.
Susan Saunders, *The Curse of the Cat Mummy,* HarperTrophy (New York, NY), 1997.
Susan Saunders, *The Chilling Tale of Crescent Pond,* HarperCollins (New York, NY), 1998.
Susan Saunders, *The Case of the Eyeball Surprise,* HarperTrophy (New York, NY), 1998.
Susan Saunders, *The Creature Double Feature,* HarperTrophy (New York, NY), 1998.
Susan Saunders, *The Creepy Camp-Out,* HarperTrophy (New York, NY), 1998.
Alice Low, *The Witch Who Was Afraid of Witches,* HarperCollins (New York, NY), 1999.
Sarah Weeks, *Drip, Drop,* HarperCollins (New York, NY), 2000.
Susan Lowell, *Cindy Ellen: A Wild Western Cinderella,* HarperCollins (New York, NY), 2000.
Shirley Climo, *Cobweb Christmas,* HarperCollins (New York, NY), 2001.
Melinda Luke, *The Green Dog,* Kane Press (New York, NY), 2002.

Linda Smith, *There Was an Old Woman Who Lived in a Boot,* HarperCollins (New York, NY), 2003.
Sarah Weeks, *Baa-choo!,* HarperCollins (New York, NY), 2004.
Pattie L. Schnetzler, *Fast 'n' Snappy,* Carolrhoda Books (Minneapolis, MN), 2004.
Megan McDonald, *Beetle McGrady Eats Bugs!,* Greenwillow Books (New York, NY), 2005.
Jane Kurtz, *Do Kangaroos Wear Seat Belts?,* Dutton Children's Books (New York, NY), 2005.
Gary L. Blackwood, *The Just-So Woman,* HarperCollins (New York, NY), 2006.
Sarah Weeks, *Pip Squeak,* Laura Geringer Books (New York, NY), 2007.
Lola M. Schaefer, *Look Behind!: Tales of Animal Ends,* Greenwillow Books (New York, NY), 2008.

Biographical and Critical Sources

PERIODICALS

Booklist, December 15, 1996, Denia Hester, review of *The Ghost Who Ate Chocolate,* p. 727; November 15, 1998, Kay Weisman, review of *That Toad Is Mine!,* p. 596; September 1, 1999, Kathy Broderick, review of *The Witch Who Was Afraid of Witches,* p. 146; September 15, 1999, Shelley Townsend-Hudson, review of *Lost Little Angel,* p. 269; July, 2000, Gillian Engberg, review of *Drip, Drop,* p. 2046; August, 2004, Hazel Rochman, review of *Baa-Choo!,* p. 1946; December 1, 2006, Hazel Rochman, review of *The Just-So Woman,* p. 51.

Horn Book, January-February, 2005, Martha V. Parravano, review of *Baa-Choo!,* p. 99; July-August, 2007, Betty Carter, review of *Pip Squeak,* p. 406.

Kirkus Reviews, February 15, 2003, review of *A Pet for Me: Poems,* p. 307; April 15, 2003, review of *There Was an Old Woman Who Lived in a Boot,* p. 1079; November 1, 2004, review of *Baa-Choo!,* p. 1047; January 1, 2005, review of *Do Kangaroos Wear Seat Belts?,* p. 53; April, 2005, review of *Beetle McGrady Eats Bugs!,* p. 421; October 15, 2006, review of *The Just-So Woman,* p. 1066.

Publishers Weekly, December 3, 2001, review of *A Wild Western Cinderella,* p. 63; August 4, 2003, review of *There Was an Old Woman Who Lived in a Boot,* p. 79; February 28, 2005, review of *Beetle McGrady Eats Bugs!,* p. 66; February 28, 2005, review of *Do Kangaroos Wear Seat Belts?,* p. 65.

School Library Journal, June, 2000, Starr LaTronica, review of *A Wild Western Cinderella,* p. 134; September, 2000, Martha Topol, review of *Drip, Drop,* p. 211; March, 2003, Jane Marino, review of *A Pet for Me,* p. 219; December, 2003, Blair Christolon, review of *There Was an Old Woman Who Lived in a Boot,* p. 128; April, 2004, Donna Cardon, review of *Fast 'n Snappy,* p. 124; January, 2005, Susan Lissim, review of *Baa-Choo!,* p. 98; April, 2005, Piper L. Nyman, review of *Do Kangaroos Wear Seat Belts?,* p. 105; May, 2005, Suzanne Meyers Harold, review of *Beetle McGrady Eats Bugs!,* p. 90; November, 2006, Melinda Piehler, review of *The Just-So Woman,* p. 84.

ONLINE

Houghton Mifflin Reading Web site, http://www.eduplace.com/ (December 27, 2007), "Meet Illustrator Jane Manning."*

*   *   *

MARCH, Carl
See FLEISCHMAN, Sid

*   *   *

MARKLE, Sandra L. 1946-
(Sandra Lee Markle)

Personal

Born November 10, 1946, in Fostoria, OH; daughter of Robert (a general foreman) and Dorothy (a secretary) Haldeman; immigrated to New Zealand; married William Markle (a programmer/analyst), August 10, 1968; children: Scott, Holly. *Education:* Bowling Green State University, B.S. (magna cum laude), 1968; graduate study at Ohio University, 1970-71, and University of North Carolina, 1973-74.

Addresses

Home—Amberley, New Zealand.

Career

Nonfiction author and curriculum designer. Teacher at elementary schools in Woodville, OH, 1968-69, Athens, OH, 1969-71, and Asheville, NC, 1971-79; Chapel Hill Middle School, Douglasville, GA, science teacher, 1979-80. CompuQuest, Inc., Bartlett, IL, founder, 1997, and director of Kit & Kaboodle curriculum pilot, 1997-99; freelance writer, beginning 1980. Developer of on-line learning programs, including *On-line Expedition: Antarctica* and *On-line Expedition: New Zealand.* Presenter at teacher workshops and science assembly programs; science consultant for publishers and educational television. Presenter and scriptwriter for television series, including *Science Shop,* WLOS-TV, 1978, and *Ms. Whiz,* WANX-TV, 1979-80; planner of television specials. Participant, Authors and Artist Program in Antarctica, National Science Foundation, 1996, 1998-99.

Member

Authors Guild, National Association of Science Writers.

Awards, Honors

Outstanding Book selection, National Science Teachers Association, for *Exploring Winter;* Pick of the List selection, American Booksellers Association, 1991, for

Sandra L. Markle (Photograph by Bob Byrd. Reproduced by permission.)

Outside and inside You, 1995, for *Outside and inside Snakes,* and 1997, for *Outside and inside Bats;* Best Books selection, National Council of Teachers of English, and Children's Book of the Year selection, Children's Book Committee at Bank Street College of Education, both 1993, both for *Outside and inside Trees;* Young Adults Choice designation, International Reading Association, 1994, and Society of School Librarians International Honor Book designation, 1998, both for *The Fledglings;* Outstanding Science Trade Books for Children designation, National Science Teachers Association/Children's Book Council, 1995, for *Outside and inside Spiders, Outside and inside Birds,* and *Science to the Rescue,* 1999, for *Outside and inside Kangaroos,* and 2003, for *Growing up Wild: Penguins;* Notable Books selection, American Library Association, 1995, for *Outside and inside Birds;* Best of Children's Nonfiction designation, Georgia Author of the Year Awards, 1997, for *Discovering Graph Secrets,* 1998, for *Outside and inside Bats,* 1999, for *Outside and inside Alligators,* and 2000, for *Outside and inside Kangaroos;* Women of the Year selection, Women in Technology International, 1999; Parents' Choice recommended book, 2000, for *Down, down, down in the Ocean;* Children's Book of the Year selection, Bank Street College of Education, 2002, for *Growing up Wild: Wolves; Boston Globe/Horn Book* Honor Book award, 2006, for *A Mother's Journey.*

Writings

NONFICTION

Kids' Computer Capers: Investigations for Beginners, illustrated by Stella Ormai, Lothrop (New York, NY), 1983.

The Programmer's Guide to the Galaxy, illustrated by Stella Ormai, Lothrop (New York, NY), 1984.

(And illustrator; with husband, William Markle) *In Search of Graphics: Adventures in Computer Art,* Lothrop (New York, NY), 1984.

(And illustrator) *Digging Deeper: Investigations into Rocks, Shocks, Quakes, and Other Earthy Matters,* Lothrop (New York, NY), 1987.

(And illustrator) *Science Mini-Mysteries,* Atheneum (New York, NY), 1988.

(And illustrator) *Power Up: Experiments, Puzzles, and Games Exploring Electricity,* Atheneum (New York, NY), 1989.

The Young Scientists' Guide to Successful Science Projects, Lothrop (New York, NY), 1990.

Earth Alive!, Lothrop (New York, NY), 1991.

(And illustrator) *The Kids' Earth Handbook,* Atheneum (New York, NY), 1991.

Discovering Science Secrets, Scholastic/Lucky (New York, NY), 1992.

Discovering More Science Secrets, Scholastic/Lucky (New York, NY), 1992.

Science in a Bag, Scholastic/Lucky (New York, NY), 1993.

(And illustrator) *Math Mini-Mysteries,* Atheneum (New York, NY), 1993.

A Rainy Day, illustrated by Cathy Johnson, Orchard Books (New York, NY), 1993.

Science: Just Add Salt, Scholastic (New York, NY), 1994.

Science to the Rescue, Atheneum (New York, NY), 1994.

Science in a Bottle, illustrated by June Otani, Scholastic/Lucky (New York, NY), 1995.

Measuring Up: Experiments, Puzzles, and Games Exploring Measurement, Atheneum (New York, NY), 1995.

What Happens Next?, Longstreet Press (Atlanta, GA), 1995.

What Happens Next? Two, Longstreet Press (Atlanta, GA), 1996.

Creepy, Crawly Baby Bugs, Walker (New York, NY), 1996.

Creepy, Spooky Science, illustrated by Cecile Schoberle, Hyperion (New York, NY), 1996.

Icky, Squishy Science, Hyperion (New York, NY), 1996.

Science Surprises, Scholastic/Lucky (New York, NY), 1996.

Still More What Happens Next?, Longstreet Press (Atlanta, GA), 1996.

A Hole in the Sky: Investigating the Ozone Problem, Sierra Club, 1997.

Discovering Graph Secrets: Experiments, Puzzles, and Games Exploring Graphs, Atheneum (New York, NY), 1997.

Super Science Secrets: Exploring Nature through Games, Puzzles, and Activities, Longstreet (Atlanta, GA), 1997.

Gone Forever! An Alphabet of Extinct Animals, illustrated by Felipe Dávalos, Simon & Schuster (New York, NY), 1998.

Windy Weather Science, Scholastic/Lucky (New York, NY), 1998.

Weird, Wacky Science, Hyperion (New York, NY), 1998.

Super Cool Science: South Pole Stations Past, Present, Future, Walker (New York, NY), 1998.

Down, down, down in the Ocean, illustrated by Bob Marstall, Walker (New York, NY), 1999.

After the Spill: The Exxon Valdez Disaster, Then and Now, Walker (New York, NY), 1999.

Super Science Magic, illustrated by Jamie Smith, Scholastic (New York, NY), 2001.

Really Wild Animals: Sea Babies, Scholastic (New York, NY), 2002.

Can You Believe?: Insects, illustrated by Jo-Ellen C. Bosson, Scholastic (New York, NY), 2002.

Can You Believe?: Hurricanes, illustrated by Jo-Ellen C. Bosson, Scholastic (New York, NY), 2002.

Can You Believe?: Volcanoes, illustrated by Jo-Ellen C. Bosson, Scholastic (New York, NY), 2002.

Amazing Human Body, illustrated by Jo-Ellen C. Bosson, Scholastic (New York, NY), 2002.

Amazing Earth: Earthquakes, illustrated by Jo-Ellen C. Bosson, Scholastic (New York, NY), 2002.

Predators, illustrated by Jo-Ellen C. Bosson, Scholastic (New York, NY), 2003.

Grow a Giant Beanstalk, and Fifteen More Amazing Plant Projects, illustrated by Eric Brace, Scholastic (New York, NY), 2003.

Build a Room Alarm, and Sixteen More Electrifying Projects, illustrated by Eric Brace, Scholastic (New York, NY), 2003.

Build a Rocket Boat, and Eighteen More Wild Wind Projects, illustrated by Eric Brace, Scholastic (New York, NY), 2003.

Make Fake Blood, and Eighteen More Spooky Special Effects, illustrated by Eric Brace, Scholastic (New York, NY), 2004.

Spiders: Biggest! Littlest!, photographs by Simon Polard, Boyds Mills Press (Honesdale, PA), 2004.

Snakes: Biggest! Littlest!, photographs by Simon Polard, Boyds Mills Press (Honesdale, PA), 2004.

Rescues, Lerner (Minneapolis, MN), 2005.

Chocolate: A Sweet History, illustrated by Charise Mericle Harper, Grosset & Dunlap (New York, NY), 2005.

Family Science, J. Wiley (Hoboken, NJ), 2005.

A Mother's Journey, illustrated by Alan Marks, Charlesbridge (Watertown, MA), 2005.

Little Lost Bat, illustrated by Alan Marks, Charlesbridge (Watertown, MA), 2006.

Slippery, Slimy Baby Frogs, Walker (New York, NY), 2006.

Tough, Toothy Baby Sharks, Walker (New York, NY), 2007.

Animals Christopher Columbus Saw, Chronicle Books (San Francisco, CA), 2008.

Animals Robert Scott Saw: An Adventure in Anarctica, illustrated by Phil, Chronicle Books (San Francisco, CA), 2008.

Finding Home, illustrated by Alan Marks, Charlesbridge (Watertown, MA), 2008.

"SEASON OF SCIENCE" SERIES; SELF-ILLUSTRATED

Exploring Winter, Atheneum (New York, NY), 1984.
Exploring Summer, Atheneum (New York, NY), 1987.
Exploring Spring, Atheneum (New York, NY), 1990.
Exploring Autumn, Atheneum (New York, NY), 1991.

"OUTSIDE AND INSIDE" SERIES

Outside and inside You, Simon & Schuster (New York, NY), 1991.
Outside and inside Trees, Simon & Schuster (New York, NY), 1993.
Outside and inside Spiders, Simon & Schuster (New York, NY), 1994.
Outside and inside Birds, Simon & Schuster (New York, NY), 1994.
Outside and inside Snakes, Simon & Schuster (New York, NY), 1995.
Outside and inside Sharks, Atheneum (New York, NY), 1996.
Outside and inside Bats, Atheneum (New York, NY), 1997.
Outside and inside Alligators, Atheneum (New York, NY), 1998.
Outside and inside Kangaroos, Atheneum (New York, NY), 1999.
Outside and inside Dinosaurs, Atheneum (New York, NY), 2000.
Outside and inside Rats and Mice, Atheneum (New York, NY), 2001.
Outside and inside Big Cats, Atheneum (New York, NY), 2002.
Outside and inside Giant Squids, Atheneum (New York, NY), 2003.
Outside and inside Killer Bees, Walker (New York, NY), 2004.
Outside and inside Mummies, Walker (New York, NY), 2005.
Outside and inside Woolly Mammoths, Walker (New York, NY), 2007.

"PIONEERING" SERIES

Pioneering Space, Atheneum (New York, NY), 1992.
Pioneering Ocean Depths, Atheneum (New York, NY), 1995.
Pioneering Frozen Worlds: Polar Region Exploration, Atheneum (New York, NY), 1996.

"GROWING UP WILD" SERIES

Growing up Wild: Bears, Atheneum (New York, NY), 2000.

Growing up Wild: Wolves, Atheneum (New York, NY), 2001.
Growing up Wild: Penguins, Atheneum (New York, NY), 2002.

"ANIMAL PREDATORS" SERIES

Polar Bears, Carolrhoda Books (Minneapolis, MN), 2004.
Owls, Carolrhoda Books (Minneapolis, MN), 2004.
Lions, Carolrhoda Books (Minneapolis, MN), 2004.
Killer Whales, Carolrhoda Books (Minneapolis, MN), 2004.
Great White Sharks, Carolrhoda Books (Minneapolis, MN), 2004.
Crocodiles, Carolrhoda Books (Minneapolis, MN), 2004.
Wolves, Carolrhoda Books (Minneapolis, MN), 2004.

"ANIMAL SCAVENGERS" SERIES

Army Ants, Lerner (Minneapolis, MN), 2005.
Hyenas, Lerner (Minneapolis, MN), 2005.
Jackals, Lerner (Minneapolis, MN), 2005.
Tasmanian Devils, Lerner (Minneapolis, MN), 2005.
Vultures, Lerner (Minneapolis, MN), 2005.
Wolverines, Lerner (Minneapolis, MN), 2005.

"ANIMAL PREY" SERIES

Skunks, Lerner (Minneapolis, MN), 2007.
Zebras, Lerner (Minneapolis, MN), 2007.
Musk Oxen, Lerner (Minneapolis, MN), 2007.
Octopuses, Lerner (Minneapolis, MN), 2007.
Porcupines, Lerner (Minneapolis, MN), 2007.
Prairie Dogs, Lerner (Minneapolis, MN), 2007.

"INSECT WORLD" SERIES

Diving Beetles: Underwater Insect Predators, Lerner (Minneapolis, MN), 2008.
Hornets: Incredible Insect Architects, Lerner (Minneapolis, MN), 2008.
Locusts: Insects on the Move, Lerner (Minneapolis, MN), 2008.
Luna Moths: Masters of Change, Lerner (Minneapolis, MN), 2008.
Mosquitoes: Tiny Insect Troublemakers, Lerner (Minneapolis, MN), 2008.
Praying Mantises: Hungry Insect Heroes, Lerner (Minneapolis, MN), 2008.
Stick Insects: Masters of Defense, Lerner (Minneapolis, MN), 2008.
Termites: Hard-working Insect Families, Lerner (Minneapolis, MN), 2008.

OTHER

Primary Science Sampler, Learning Works, 1980.
Science Sampler, Learning Works, 1980.

Computer Tutor: An Introduction to Computers, illustrated by Bev Armstrong, Learning Works, 1981.

Computer Tutor Junior, illustrated by Bev Armstrong, Learning Works, 1982.

Weather/Electricity/Environmental Investigations, Learning Works, 1982.

The Fledglings (young adult novel), Bantam (New York, NY), 1992.

Author of books for instructors, including *Instructor's Big Book of Health and Safety,* 1985; *Hands-on Science,* 1988; and *Creative Science Classrooms,* 1991. Also author of monthly columns "Natural Wonder Notebook," in *Instructor,* and "The Learning Center," in *Teaching and Computers.* Contributing editor, *Teaching and Computers,* 1983—. Contributor to magazines, including *Cricket, Highlights for Children, Jack and Jill, Ranger Rick, 3-2-1 Contact, Woman's Day, Macintosh Buyer's Guide, PC World, Early Childhood Teacher, Classworks, Big, Parenting, Family Fun, Instructor, National Geographic for Kids, Time for Kids,* and *Learning.*

Sidelights

Sandra L. Markle, who once worked as a science teacher in the United States, now devotes much of her time to creating science books for children from her new home in New Zealand. With books on animals, science experiments, computers, exploration, geology, and other specific topics to her credit, Markle has also become a sought-after science education consultant through her company CompuQuest, Inc. "Few writers have quite the handle Markle does on how kids think about science," wrote a *Kirkus Reviews* critic in a review of *Icky, Squishy Science.* In *Outside and inside Woolly Mammoths,* an installment of one of the many book series she has created, "Markle works her magic on the topic," according to *Horn Book* contributor Danielle J. Ford. The author "is perfectly attuned to her elementary-age audience," the impressed critic continued, "employing a friendly tone and style, asking interesting questions to prompt further discussion, and making helpful references" that connect her prehistoric subject to the far-more-familiar elephant.

Critics have identified more than one reason for Markle's success as a science writer for children. Foremost, she carefully pairs science with fiction. In *Little Lost Bat,* for example, her profile of one of the world's largest bat colonies—in this case a colony of Mexican free-tail bats living in a Texas cave—is couched within the simple story of a bat's daily life during the first few months after birth. Noting that Markle's focus on the "motherly connection" is something even young children can relate to, *Horn Book* contributor Caitlin J. Berry cited the picture book for providing "a fascinating glimpse of a truly exquisite creature of the night." Praised as a "sparkling introduction to . . . our planet's most challenging environment" by *Horn Book* critic Mary Beth Dunhouse, Markle's award-winning *A Moth-*

er's Journey introduces a female Antarctic emperor penguin as she gathers food for her young. Turning to technology, *The Programmer's Guide to the Galaxy* frames instruction about computer BASIC programming within an adventure story, an effort that R. Scott Grabinger lauded in *Voice of Youth Advocates* as "fun," "instructional," and an "excellent book for beginning and intermediate BASIC programmers."

Second, Markle writes about science in a lucid, straightforward manner. Reviewing *Digging Deeper: Investigations into Rocks, Shocks, Quakes, and Other Earthy Matters,* which educates children about geography while showing them how to construct volcanoes and conduct other projects, Beth Ames Herbert commented in *Booklist* that "Markle's lighthanded touch makes even technical jargon unintimidating." In *A Rainy Day* she explains such question-prompting things as how a cloud forms and why umbrellas are shaped the way they are. Janice Del Negro remarked in *Booklist* that *A Rainy Day* uses "a picture book format with strong visual narrative." Finally, in books like *Icky Squishy Science* and *Creepy, Spooky Science,* Markle encourages children to learn about science as they do something they love: get their hands dirty.

Markle's love of science is infectious, and it is this fact that makes her books so effective. She once told *SATA,* "I can't believe the opportunities writing provides me! . . . I was able to travel to the South Pole—something I'd always dreamed of doing—and was transported by helicopter to spend a few hours as the only human in the midst of a penguin rookery. I've also spent a few days behind the scenes with the Ringling Brothers Barnum & Bailey Circus, been up in the Good Year Blimp, and lots more. Each new project brings new adventures. I always think of myself as the eyes and ears and fingers of all the young readers that will eventually be sharing my experiences through my books and magazine articles."

Many of Markle's books are published in series or thematically related groups. The "Outside and inside" series provides children with a scientific understanding of some of their favorite plants and creatures, and incorporates color photos as well as glossaries, indexes, and pronunciation guides. *Outside and inside Sharks,* for example, explains how a shark's body works to make it a good hunter. *Outside and inside Snakes,* which, according to *School Library Journal* critic Karey Wehner, is a "remarkably perceptive introduction to the ever-fascinating slitherer," discusses the anatomy, bodily functions, habits, and life cycle of the snake. "Succinctly written," as Wehner explained in *School Library Journal, Outside and inside Spiders* "offers more detail on body functions than is currently available in other books." *Booklist* critic Chris Sherman described *Outside and inside Birds* as an "introduction to avian anatomy" that "will fascinate browsers," while a *Kirkus Reviews* critic asserted that young readers will "be captivated by [Markle's] . . . clear and detailed discus-

Science writer Markle's award-winning picture book **A Mother's Journey** *features evocative paintings by Alan Marks.* (Illustration © 2005 by Alan Marks. Reproduced by permission of Charlesbridge Publishing, Inc.)

sion" of everything to do with rodents in *Outside and inside Rats and Mice*. Citing *Outside and inside Kangaroos* for particular praise, an *Appraisal* contributor noted that this book, like others in the series, "is full of intriguing science details and questions which encourage the reader to predict the reasons for adaptations and habits."

One of the "Outside and inside" books takes a look at a familiar creature: the healthy human child. *Outside and inside You* includes questions, suggestions, answers, and comparisons illustrated with close-up photos, X-rays, and computer-generated images that provide young readers with the opportunity to understand their bodies, right down to the skin, muscles, bones, and major organs. Stephanie Zvirin, writing in *Booklist*, described Markle's text as "accessible," commenting that the author's "clear explanations are rooted in children's everyday experience." In a twist on the subject that most children will find intriguing, *Outside and inside Mummies* also focuses on the human body, but in this case the bodies in question are ancient ones that have endured ritualistic burial for thousands of years. Featuring information about X-rays, carbon dating, and the forensic techniques used in studying mummies, Markle also "effectively supports scientific thinking by applying children's curiosity about mummies to their own lives," observed Ford in *Horn Book*. The book concludes with

a home-mummification project, fortunately involving a piece of fruit rather than a creature of skin and bone!

Another group of books by Markle that focuses on animals is the "Growing up Wild" series, which includes *Growing up Wild: Bears*. In this series, which is designed for readers in grades two to four, full-color photographs accompany a clearly written text that describes the life of several species. In *Growing up Wild: Bears,* readers meet a day-old black bear cub, two young polar bears, and young grizzlies fishing for salmon. The volume on wolves describes the challenges a young wolf must overcome to reach its first birthday and also explains life in a wolf pack, where play and sleep are balanced with hunting and learning to identify predators. Markle presents *Growing up Wild: Wolves* through the eyes of the young animals, "an appealing angle that makes use of the experiences of young readers," according to a *Horn Book* contributor. Praising the same volume in *Kirkus Reviews,* a critic noted that Markle's selection of facts is "perfectly designed to interest young readers," going on to remark that the author adds "intimate details" aimed to "astonish and intrigue" young imaginations.

In *Growing up Wild: Penguins,* as in *Growing up Wild: Wolves,* Markle does not hide the fact that life in the wild is harsh and survival is not guaranteed, a fact that *Horn Book* contributor Danielle J. Ford claimed make the books noteworthy. Ford found "an element of tension" runs through *Growing up Wild: Penguins* due to the fact that the Adelie penguin chicks are constantly hunted by shore birds. *Booklist* contributor Kay Weisman commended Markle for her "clearly written, succinct text" and her "especially detailed picture of the [penguin's] infancy period."

Markle's "Pioneering" books allow children to witness the scientific exploration of far away worlds and encourage them to use their own scientific skills. In *Pioneering Frozen Worlds: Polar Region Exploration,* she follows scientists working in the North and South Poles and explains how they live and work. She describes the experiments the scientists are conducting and includes notes and suggestions for minor experiments that can help children better understand the rugged climate. *Pioneering Space* tells about space travel, space equipment, and future space colonization. It provides instructions for two experiments (one on rocket power and another on hydroponics systems). "This timely, attractively illustrated treatment of space exploration will excite young readers," Margaret M. Hagel commented in *School Library Journal.*

The "Season of Science" series, which is illustrated with Markle's own line drawings, explains seasonal changes as well as traditional seasonal activities. The books provide a variety of lessons, science experiments, crafts, and games for children. A number of historical facts, mythical stories, riddles, and jokes are also included. *Exploring Spring,* for example, shows readers how to identify flowers and teaches them about egg development. Gayle Berge explained in *School Library Journal* that *Exploring Summer* could "provide an entire summer of . . . growing in scientific knowledge." "The number of winter tidbits assembled here is amazing," *School Library Journal* contributor Jeffrey A. French wrote in a review of *Exploring Winter.* These seasonal books are designed to make learning fun, and Markle's style reflects this. As Hazel Rochman pointed out in her *Booklist* review of *Exploring Autumn,* "Markle isn't afraid to be lyrical . . . or silly."

Other series by Markle include her "Animal Predator," "Animal Prey," and "Animal Scavenger" series, as well as her "Insect World" titles, such as *Diving Beetles: Underwater Insect Predators, Hornets: Incredible Insect Architects, Luna Moths: Masters of Change,* and *Praying Mantises: Hungry Insect Heroes.* The "Animal Prey" books are particularly unique; in volumes that include *Musk Oxen, Porcupines,* and *Octopuses,* the author focuses on the creature's behavior as both predator and prey and how nature has provided the means to ward off or otherwise discourage creatures that pose a significant and frequent threat. Praising the "Animal Scavenger" books, which include *Vultures, Hyenas, Army Ants,* and *Tasmanian Devils,* Rochman commented in *Booklist* that each book's "astonishing color photos of action in the wild share space with [the] clear, dramatic zoological facts and connections" set forth in Markle's text.

In 1989, an oil tanker named the *Exxon Valdez* crashed near Prince William Sound, Alaska, spilling thousands of gallons of oil into the water and creating an ecological disaster for the region's wildlife. In *After the Spill: The Exxon Valdez Disaster, Then and Now,* Markle returns readers to the scene of the accident ten years later and studies the aftereffects. Dividing the book into several sections, she explains how local birds, fish, and otters fared, examines the economic impact to the area, and lists new regulations that have been implemented to prevent such a catastrophe from occurring again. An *Appraisal* reviewer commended the "wealth of practical experience" Markle brings to her task and praised the author for being able "to anticipate the questions and interests of her readers." Citing its "child-friendly format, and attractive photos," *School Library Journal* reviewer Dawn Amsberry commended the "clear, journalistic style" of *After the Spill,* while Deborah Stevenson maintained in the *Bulletin of the Center for Children's Books* that the photo-filled volume will give readers an enhanced "understanding of the different kinds of impact such an event can have."

Although most of Markle's books are nonfiction, she is also the author of an award-winning novel titled *The Fledglings.* In this story, Kate's mother is killed by a drunk driver, leaving the fourteen-year-old protagonist an orphan. Facing the prospect of living with the family of her disagreeable uncle and aunt, she then learns that her paternal grandfather is still alive. Although this grandfather has refused to care for her, Kate runs away to Cherokee, North Carolina, to find him. At first, her grandfather does not welcome her. Gradually, however, Kate earns his trust and comes to learn about her Cherokee heritage and life in the forest. In addition, she helps fight illegal poaching and cares for a fledgling eagle. Kate's resilience prompted a *Publishers Weekly* reviewer to praise her "pluck and resourcefulness in daunting surroundings," the critic going on to dub *The Fledglings* "fun to read."

Markle has not focused her talents solely on written text. She has also worked on television programs for many years and has also moved into cyberspace through an online science curriculum she has developed. "I've been communicating via the Internet and my special project called Online Expeditions," she once told *SATA.* "The Internet is perfect for me because now I'm able to share what's happening in real time—including digitized pictures—even from places as remote as an icebreaker in the middle of the Ross Sea off the coast of Antarctica."

Biographical and Critical Sources

PERIODICALS

American Scientist, November-December, 1997, Cynthia Harris, review of *Icky, Squishy Science,* p. 557.

Appraisal, spring-summer-fall, 2000, review of *After the Spill: The Exxon Valdez Disaster, Then and Now,* pp. 68-69, and *Outside and inside Kangaroos,* pp. 69-70.

Booklist, December 15, 1987, Beth Ames Herbert, review of *Digging Deeper: Investigations into Rocks, Shocks, Quakes, and Other Earthy Matters,* pp. 710-711; March 15, 1991, Stephanie Zvirin, review of *Outside and inside You,* p. 1494; November 1, 1991, Hazel Rochman, review of *Exploring Autumn,* p. 514; March 1, 1993, Janice Del Negro, review of *A Rainy Day,* p. 1233; November 1, 1994, Chris Sherman, review of *Outside and inside Birds,* p. 504; October 1, 1997, Sally Estes, review of *Outside and inside Bats,* p. 320; March 15, 1998, Carolyn Phelan, review of *Super Cool Science,* p. 1238; June 1, 1998, Kathleen Squires, review of *Gone Forever!,* p. 1722; December 1, 1998, Helen Rosenberg, review of *Outside and inside Alligators,* p. 681; August, 1999, Carolyn Phelan, review of *After the Spill,* p. 2054; January 1, 2000, Shelle Rosenfeld, review of *Outside and inside Kangaroos,* p. 914; May 15, 2000, Ellen Mandel, review of *Growing up Wild: Bears,* p. 1746; December 1, 2000, Carolyn Phelan, review of *Outside and inside Dinosaurs,* p. 702; April 1, 2001, Carolyn Phelan, review of *Growing up Wild: Wolves,* p. 1462; September 15, 2001, Shelle Townsend-Hudson, review of *Outside and inside Rats and Mice,* p. 220; December 15, 2001, Kay Weisman, review of *Growing up Wild: Penguins,* p. 728; September 15, 2003, Terry Glover, review of *Outside and inside Giant Squids,* p. 233;

October 1, 2003, Lauren Peterson, review of *Outside and inside Big Cats,* p. 314; September 1, 2005, Julie Cummins, review of *A Mother's Journey,* p. 138; September 15, 2005, Ilene Cooper, review of *Outside and Inside Mummies,* p. 60; December 1, 2005, Hazel Rochman, review of *Vultures,* p. 61; May 1, 2006, Hazel Rochman, review of *Slippery, Slimy Baby Frogs,* p. 83; June 1, 2006, Hazel Rochman, review of *Little Lost Bat,* p. 74; April 1, 2006, Hazel Rochman, review of *Rescues!,* p. 43.

Bulletin of the Center for Children's Books, April, 1998, Deborah Stevenson, review of *Super Cool Science,* p. 288; July, 1999, Deborah Stevenson, review of *After the Spill,* pp. 395-396; June, 2006, Elizabeth Bush, review of *Rescues!,* p. 462.

Horn Book, January-February, 1998, Elizabeth S. Watson, review of *Outside and inside Bats,* p. 93; November, 1999, Marilyn Bousquin, review of *Outside and inside Kangaroos,* p. 759; September, 2000, review of *Outside and inside Dinosaurs,* p. 597; March, 2001, review of *Growing up Wild: Wolves,* p. 231; September, 2001, review of *Outside and inside Rats and Mice,* p. 612; May-June, 2002, Danielle J. Ford, review of *Growing up Wild: Penguins,* p. 347; July-August, 2003, Danielle J. Ford, review of *Outside and inside Big Cats,* p. 482; July-August, 2005, Margaret A. Bush, review of *A Mother's Journey,* p. 487; September-October, 2005, Danielle J. Ford, review of *Outside and inside Mummies,* p. 604; July-August, 2006, Caitlin J. Berry, review of *Little Lost Bat,* p. 465; January-February, 2007, Mary Beth Dunhouse, review of *A Mother's Journey,* p. 24; July-August, 2007, Danielle J. Ford, review of *Outside and inside Woolly Mammoths,* p. 414.

Kirkus Reviews, March 15, 1994, review of *Outside and inside Spiders,* p. 399; April 18, 1996, review of *Icky Squishy Science,* p. 230; January, 1998, review of *Gone Forever!,* p. 115; February 15, 2001, review of *Growing up Wild: Wolves,* p. 262; August 1, 2001, review of *Outside and inside Rats and Mice,* p. 1128; November 15, 2001, review of *Growing up Wild: Penguins,* p. 1613; June 1, 2003, review of *Outside and inside Big Cats,* p. 807; August 1, 2005, review of *Outside and inside Mummies,* p. 854; April 1, 2006, review of *Slippery, Slimy Baby Frogs,* p. 351.

Publishers Weekly, June 8, 1992, review of *The Fledglings,* p. 64; August 7, 2006, review of *Little Lost Bat,* p. 58.

Reading Teacher, May, 2002, review of *Outside and inside Dinosaurs,* p. 782.

School Library Journal, November, 1984, Jeffrey A. French, review of *Exploring Winter,* p. 126; April, 1987, Gayle Berge, review of *Exploring Summer,* p. 100; February, 1993, Margaret M. Hagel, review of *Pioneering Space,* p. 101; June, 1994, Karey Wehner, review of *Outside and inside Spiders,* p. 141; June, 1995, Karey Wehner, review of *Outside and inside Snakes,* p. 122; March, 1996, Melissa Hudak, review of *Outside and inside Sharks,* p. 212; April, 1997, Karey Wehner, review of *Creepy, Crawly Baby Bugs,* p. 128; July, 1997, Kathryn Kosiorek, review of *Science Surprises,* p. 85; September, 1997, Cynthia M.

Sturgis, review of *Super Science Secrets,* p. 206; November, 1997, Margaret Bush, review of *Outside and inside Bats,* pp. 130, 132; March, 1998, Jody McCoy, review of *Discovering Graph Secrets,* p. 236; April, 1998, John Peters, review of *Super Cool Science,* p. 120; May, 1998, Marilyn Payne Phillips, review of *Gone Forever!,* p. 134; November, 1998, Anne Chapman Callaghan, review of *Outside and inside Alligators,* pp. 107-108; September, 1999, Dawn Amsberry, review of *After the Spill,* p. 238; November, 1999, Patricia Manning, review of *Down, down, down in the Ocean,* p. 146; December, 1999, Sally Bates Goodroe, review of *Outside and inside Kangaroos,* pp. 154-155; May, 2000, Randi Hacker, review of *Growing up Wild: Bears,* p. 163; November, 2000, Patricia Manning, review of *Outside and inside Dinosaurs,* p. 173; September, 2001, Susan Scheps, review of *Growing up Wild: Wolves,* p. 218; November, 2001, Cynthia M. Sturgis, review of *Outside and inside Rats and Mice,* p. 147; March, 2002, Margaret Bush, review of *Growing up Wild: Penguins,* p. 218; August, 2003, Patricia Manning, review of *Outside and inside Big Cats,* p. 182; December, 2003, Doris Losey, review of *Outside and inside Giant Squids,* p. 172; August, 2005, Patricia Manning, review of *Outside and inside Mummies,* p. 146; September, 2005, Pantricia Manning, review of *A Mother's Journey,* p. 194; February, 2006, Nancy Call, review of *Jackals,* p. 122; May, 2006, Christine Markley, review of *Slippery, Slimy Baby Frogs,* p. 152; August, 2006, Susan E. Murray, review of *Little Lost Bat,* p. 107, and Eldon Younce, review of *Rescues!,* p. 140; April, 2007, Debbie Whitbeck, review of *Musk Oxen,* p. 124; June, 2007, Patricia Manning, review of *Outside and inside Wooly Mammoths,* p. 174.

Voice of Youth Advocates, April, 1985, R. Scott Grabinger, review of *The Programmer's Guide to the Galaxy,* p. 66.

ONLINE

Christchurch City Libraries Web site, http://library. christchurch.org.nz/ (December 26, 2007), interview with Markle."

Women in Science and Technology Web site, http://www. witi.com/ (June 8, 1999), "Sandra L. Markle."*

*　　　*　　　*

MARKLE, Sandra Lee
See MARKLE, Sandra L.

*　　　*　　　*

MATHIEU, Joe 1949-
(Joseph P. Mathieu)

Personal

Born January 23, 1949, in Springfield, VT; son of Joseph A. (a car dealer) and Patricia Mathieu; married

Joe Mathieu (Photograph by Melanie Mathieu. Courtesy of Joe Mathieu.)

Melanie Gerardi, September 7, 1970; children: Kristen, Joseph Michael. *Education:* Rhode Island School of Design, B.F.A., 1971. *Hobbies and other interests:* Bicycling (especially touring the New England states), jazz and ragtime.

Addresses

Home and office—Hudson, MA. *E-mail*—joe@joe-mathieu.com.

Career

Author and illustrator of books for children. Designer of covers for books and recordings, including album covers for Stomp Off records.

Awards, Honors

Best Books selection, American Institute of Graphic Arts, 1973, for *The Magic Word Book, Starring Marko the Magician!;* Children's Choice selection, International Reading Association, 1982, for *Ernie's Big Mess*; Ten Best Children's Books designation, *Time* magazine, 2005, for *Don't Be Silly, Mrs. Millie!*

Writings

SELF-ILLUSTRATED

The Amazing Adventures of Silent "E" Man, Random House (New York, NY), 1973.

The Magic Word Book, Starring Marko the Magician! Random House (New York, NY), 1973.

Big Joe's Trailer Truck, Random House (New York, NY), 1974.

I Am a Monster ("Sesame Street" series), Golden Press (New York, NY), 1976.

The Grover Sticker Book, Western Publishing (Racine, WI), 1976.

The Count's Coloring Book, Western Publishing (Racine, WI), 1976.

The Sesame Street Mix or Match Storybook: Over Two Hundred Thousand Funny Combinations, Random House (New York, NY), 1977.

Who's Who on Sesame Street, Western Publishing (Racine, WI), 1977.

Busy City (nonfiction), Random House (New York, NY), 1978.

The Olden Days (nonfiction), Random House (New York, NY), 1981.

Bathtime on Sesame Street, edited by Jane Schulman, Random House (New York, NY), 1983.

Big Bird Visits the Dodos, Random House (New York, NY), 1985.

Fire Trucks, Random House (New York, NY), 1988.

Trucks in Your Neighborhood, Random House (New York, NY), 1988.

Sesame Street 123: A Counting Book from 1 to 100 (also see below), Random House (New York, NY), 1991.

Sounds ("Sesame Street" series), Publications International (Lincolnwood, IL), 1997.

On the Go ("Sesame Street" series), Publications International (Lincolnwood, IL), 1997.

Counting ("Sesame Street" series), Publications International (Lincolnwood, IL), 1997.

Colors ("Sesame Street" series), Publications International (Lincolnwood, IL), 1997.

Sesame Street Lift-and-Peek Party!, Children's Television Workshop (New York, NY), 1998.

Learn about Numbers: With Flips, Flaps, Slides, Tabs, and Pop-up Surprises! ("Sesame Street" series), Children's Television Workshop (New York, NY), 1998.

ABC and 123: A Sesame Street Treasury of Words and Numbers (includes *Sesame Street 123: A Counting Book from 1 to 100*), Children's Television Workshop (New York, NY), 1998.

Fun with Opposites ("Sesame Street" series), Children's Television Workshop (New York, NY), 2000.

ILLUSTRATOR

Ossie Davis, *Purlie Victorious,* Houghton (Boston, MA), 1973.

Scott Corbett, *Dr. Merlin's Magic Shop,* Little, Brown (Boston, MA), 1973.

Genevieve Gray, *Casey's Camper,* McGraw, 1973.

Byron Preiss, *The Electric Company: The Silent "E's" from Outer Space,* Western Publishing (Racine, WI), 1973.

Scott Corbett, *The Great Custard Pie Panic,* Little, Brown (Boston, MA), 1974.

Suzanne W. Bladow, *The Midnight Flight of Moose, Mops, and Marvin,* McGraw, 1975.

Howard Liss, *The Giant Book of Strange but True Sports Stories,* Random House (New York, NY), 1976.

Hedda Nussbaum, *Plants Do Amazing Things* (nonfiction), Random House (New York, NY), 1977.

Katy Hall and Lisa Eisenberg, *A Gallery of Monsters,* Random House (New York, NY), 1981.

Cindy West, *The Superkids and the Singing Dog,* Random House (New York, NY), 1982.

Harold Woods and Geraldine Woods, *The Book of the Unknown* (nonfiction), Random House (New York, NY), 1982.

Howard Liss, *The Giant Book of More Strange but True Sports Stories,* Random House (New York, NY), 1983.

Deborah Kovacs, *Brewster's Courage,* Simon & Schuster (New York, NY), 1992.

Leslie McGuire, *Big Dan's Moving Van,* Random House (New York, NY), 1993.

Laura Joffe Numeroff, *Dogs Don't Wear Sneakers,* Simon & Schuster (New York, NY), 1993.

Laura Joffe Numeroff, *Chimps Don't Wear Glasses,* Simon & Schuster (New York, NY), 1995.

Leslie McGuire, *Big Frank's Fire Truck,* Random House (New York, NY), 1995.

Lori Haskins, *Too Many Dogs!,* Random House (New York, NY), 1998.

Theo LeSieg, *The Eye Book,* Random House (New York, NY), 1999.

Theo LeSieg, *The Tooth Book,* Random House (New York, NY), 2000.

Louise Gikow, *Red Hat, Green Hat,* Golden Books (New York, NY), 2000.

Tennant Redbank, *Walk, Don't Walk,* Golden Books (New York, NY), 2001.

Stephen Krensky, *What a Mess!,* Random House (New York, NY), 2001.

Anna Jane Hays, *Happy Alphabet!: A Phonics Reader,* Random House (New York, NY), 2001.

Robert Skutch, *Albie's Trip to the Jumble Jungle,* Tricycle Press (Berkeley, CA), 2002.

Al Perkins, *The Nose Book,* Random House (New York, NY), 2002.

Leslie McGuire, *Big Mike's Police Car,* Random House (New York, NY), 2003.

Bonnie Worth, *Hurray for Today!,* Random House (New York, NY), 2004.

Lisa and Cindy Moran, *Big Cindy's School Bus,* Random House (New York, NY), 2004.

Kara McMahon, *Just the Way You Are,* Random House (New York, NY), 2004.

(With Aristides Ruiz) Tish Rabe, *Clam-I-Am,* Random House (New York, NY), 2005.

Laura Joffe Numeroff, *Dogs Don't Wear Sneakers,* Aladdin (New York, NY), 2005.

Stephanie Greene, *Moose's Big Idea,* Marshall Cavendish (New York, NY), 2005.

Stephanie Greene, *Moose Crossing,* Marshall Cavendish (New York, NY), 2005.

Judy Cox, *Don't Be Silly, Mrs. Millie!,* Marshall Cavendish (New York, NY), 2005.

(With Aristides Ruiz) Bonnie Worth, *A Whale of a Tale!: All about Porpoises, Dolphins, and Whales,* Random House (New York, NY), 2006.

(With Aristides Ruiz) Bonnie Worth, *I Can Name Fifty Trees Today!,* Random House (New York, NY), 2006.

Stephanie Greene, *Pig Pickin',* Marshall Cavendish (Tarrytown, NY), 2006.

Tish Rabe, *My, Oh My—A Butterfly!,* Random House (New York, NY), 2007.

Stephanie Greene, *The Show-Off,* Marshall Cavendish (New York, NY), 2007.

Sarah Albee, *Field Trip!,* Reader's Digest (Pleasantville, NY), 2007.

Bonnie Worth, *One Cent, Two Cent, Old Cent, New Cent: All about Money,* Random House (New York, NY), 2008.

Judy Cox, *Mrs. Millie Goes to Philly!,* Marshall Cavendish (New York, NY), 2008.

ILLUSTRATOR; "SESAME STREET" SERIES

Matt Robinson, *Matt Robinson's Gordon of Sesame Street Storybook,* Random House (New York, NY), 1972.

Emily Perl Kingsley and others, *The Sesame Street 1,2,3 Storybook,* Random House (New York, NY), 1973.

Norman Stiles and Daniel Wilcox, *Grover and the Everything in the Whole Wide World Museum: Featuring Lovable, Furry Old Grover,* Random House (New York, NY), 1974.

Jeffrey Moss, Norman Stiles, and Daniel Wilcox, *The Sesame Street ABC Storybook,* Random House (New York, NY), 1974.

Anna Jane Hays, *See No Evil, Hear No Evil, Smell No Evil,* Western Publishing (Racine, WI), 1975.

E.P. Kingsley, David Korr, and Jeffrey Moss, *The Sesame Street Book of Fairy Tales,* Random House (New York, NY), 1975.

Norman Stiles, *Grover's Little Red Riding Hood,* Western Publishing (Racine, WI), 1976.

Norman Stiles, *The Ernie and Bert Book,* Western Publishing (Racine, WI), 1977.

Patricia Thackray, *What Ernie and Bert Did on Their Summer Vacation,* Western Publishing (Racine, WI), 1977.

E.P. Kingsley, *The Exciting Adventures of Super-Grover,* Golden Press (New York, NY), 1978.

Sharon Lerner, *Big Bird's Look and Listen Book,* Random House (New York, NY), 1978.

Patricia Thackray, *Grover Visits His Granny,* Random House (New York, NY), 1978.

Daniel Korr, *Cookie Monster and the Cookie Tree,* Western Publishing (Racine, WI), 1979.

Valjean McLenigham, *Ernie's Work of Art,* Western Publishing (Racine, WI), 1979.

Linda Hayward, *The Sesame Street Dictionary,* Random House (New York, NY), 1980, reprinted, 2004.

Sarah Roberts, *Ernie's Big Mess,* Random House (New York, NY), 1981.

Jon Stone and Joe Bailey, *Christmas Eve on Sesame Street* (based on the television special "Christmas Eve on Sesame Street"), Random House (New York, NY), 1981.

Sarah Roberts, *Nobody Cares about Me!,* Random House (New York, NY), 1982.

Dan Elliott, *Ernie's Little Lie,* Random House (New York, NY), 1983.

Dan Elliott, *A Visit to the Sesame Street Firehouse,* Random House (New York, NY), 1983.

Sarah Roberts, *Bert and the Missing Mop Mix-Up,* Random House (New York, NY), 1983.

Norman Stiles, *I'll Miss You, Mr. Hooper,* Random House (New York, NY), 1984.

Dan Elliott, *Two Wheels for Grover,* Random House (New York, NY), 1984.

Sharon Lerner, *Big Bird's Copycat Day,* Random House (New York, NY), 1984.

Dan Elliott, *My Doll Is Lost,* Random House (New York, NY), 1984.

Sarah Roberts, *The Adventures of Big Bird in Dinosaur Days,* Random House (New York, NY), 1984.

Sarah Roberts, *I Want to Go Home,* Random House (New York, NY), 1985.

Deborah Hautzig, *A Visit to the Sesame Street Hospital,* Random House (New York, NY), 1985.

Sharon Lerner, *Big Bird Says,* Random House (New York, NY), 1985.

Deborah Hautzig, *A Visit to the Sesame Street Library,* 1986.

Judy Freudberg and Tony Geiss, *Susan and Gordon Adopt a Baby,* Random House (New York, NY), 1986.

Liza Alexander, *A Visit to the Sesame Street Museum,* Random House (New York, NY), 1987.

Molly Cross, *Wait for Me,* Random House (New York, NY), 1987, published as *Wait for Elmo,* Random House (New York, NY), 1998.

Deborah Hautzig, *It's Easy,* Random House (New York, NY), 1988.

Virginia Holt, *A My Name Is Alice,* Random House (New York, NY), 1989.

Deborah Hautzig, *Get Well, Granny Bird,* Random House (New York, NY), 1989.

Deborah Hautzig, *Grover's Bad Dream,* Random House (New York, NY), 1990.

Lisa Alexander, *How to Get to Sesame Street,* Western Publishing (Racine, WI), 1990.

Deborah Hautzig, *Ernie and Bert's New Kitten,* Random House (New York, NY), 1990.

Deborah Hautzig, *Big Bird Plays the Violin,* Random House (New York, NY), 1991.

Liza Alexander, *Bird Watching with Bert,* Western Publishing (Racine, WI), 1991.

Bobbi Jane Kates, *We're Different, We're the Same,* Random House (New York, NY), 1992.

Elizabeth Rivlin, *Elmo's Little Glowworm,* Random House (New York, NY), 1994.

Anna Ross, *Elmo's Big Lift-and-Look Book,* Random House (New York, NY), 1994.

Norman Stiles, *Around the Corner on Sesame Street,* Random House (New York, NY), 1994.

Lou Berger, *Sesame Street Stays up Late,* Random House (New York, NY), 1995.

Annie Cobb, *B Is for Books,* Random House (New York, NY), 1996.

Anna Ross, *Elmo's Lift-and-Peek around the Corner Book,* Random House (New York, NY), 1996.

Tish Rabe, *The King's Beard,* Random House (New York, NY), 1997.

Eleanor Hudson, *Can You Tell Me How to Get to Sesame Street?,* Beginner Books (New York, NY), 1997.

Stephanie St. Pierre, *Ernie's Wishes,* Random House (New York, NY), 1998.

Stephanie St. Pierre, *Elmo's Wishes,* Random House (New York, NY), 1998.

Stephanie St. Pierre, *Elmo's Busy Baby Book: With Great Big Flaps!,* Children's Television Workshop (New York, NY), 1999.

Sarah Albee, *If You're Happy and You Know It—Clap Your Paws!,* Random House (New York, NY), 2001.

Sarah Albee, *Ernie's Joke Book,* Random House (New York, NY), 2001.

Sharon Lerner, *Big Bird's Copycat Day,* Random House (New York, NY), 2003.

Sharon Lerner, *Big Bird Says—: A Game to Read and Play,* Random House (New York, NY), 2003.

Kara McMahon, *Brought to you by—Sesame Street!,* Random House (New York, NY), 2004.

Abigail Tabby, *The City Sings a Song!: A Story for Two to Share,* Random House (New York, NY), 2005.

Kama Einhorn, *My First Book about Dogs,* Random House (New York, NY), 2006.

Sidelights

Joe Mathieu has made a career illustrating many of the children's books featuring Jim Henson's Muppets from the award-winning *Sesame Street* program, which airs on public television. Although Mathieu began his career in children's publishing illustrating his own texts in books such as *The Magic Word Book, Starring Marko the Magician!* and *The Amazing Adventures of Silent "E" Man,* the bulk of his work as an artist has been paired with stories by other writers. Among these are *Elmo's Lift-and-Peek around the Corner Book,* in which author Anna Ross introduces numbers, opposites, and matching concepts with the aid of Mathieu's "loudly colored, chaotic-looking pages," in the estimation of a *Publishers Weekly* reviewer.

Other *Sesame Street* tie-in books illustrated by Mathieu include *We're Different, We're the Same,* featuring a story by Bobbi Jane Kates in which Mathieu's Muppet characters "cavort cheerfully with people of all sizes, shapes and ethnicities," according to a *Publishers Weekly* critic. In *A Visit to the Sesame Street Hospital,* by Deborah Hautzig, Grover is given a tour of the hospital where he will stay during a tonsillectomy operation, and Hautzig's *Get Well, Granny Bird* finds Big Bird visiting his grandmother when she gets a cold. Mathieu's illustrations for both these books "are typical" of the *Sesame Street* books; they are "realistically drawn and in full color," as Sharron McElmeel observed in her *School Library Journal* review of those titles.

Mathieu has also illustrated a number of books that range outside the *Sesame Street* world. A *Publishers Weekly* critic praised the "exuberant art" he contributes to Laura Numeroff's *Dogs Don't Wear Sneakers,* in which his pictures of animals in implausible situations accompany Numeroff's nonsensical rhymes. In fact, according to *School Library Journal* contributor Lori A. Janick, "Mathieu's wacky and inventive illustrations . . . really carry the show" in this title. The book's sequel, *Chimps Don't Wear Glasses,* was deemed less successful by a *Kirkus Reviews* critic, although the reviewer nonetheless praised Mathieu's "busy, literal cartoons." Carolyn Phelan, writing in *Booklist,* predicted that young readers "will enjoy the humorous interpretation of the rhyming words in the colorful pictures."

Mathieu portrays a teacher every young student would love to have in **Don't Be Silly, Mrs. Millie!,** *a story by Judy Cox.* (Illustration © 2005 by Joe Mathieu. Reproduced by permission.)

Deborah Kovacs's picture book *Brewster's Courage* features a ferret who travels to Louisiana to enjoy the region's zydeco music and learns how to make friends in a new situation. In this work, Mathieu's "amusing drawings" accompany "a story with appeal for anyone who has ever felt like an outsider," according to a *Kirkus Reviews* commentator. Robert Skutch's *Albie's Trip to the Jumble Jungle* features a number of hybrid animals, such as a lion with wings. "The playful cartoons are colorful and appealing," wrote Be Astengo, discussing Mathieu's imaginative contribution in *School Library Journal.*

Mathieu has also illustrated three chapter-book adventures featuring Moose and his pig friend, Hildy, that are written by Stephanie Green. In *Moose Crossing* Moose and Hildy believe that Moose has become famous when a bright yellow sign with Moose's silhouette on it is posted alongside a local road. A *Kirkus Reviews* contributor called Mathieu's pencil sketches for the story "humorous." In *Moose's Big Idea,* Moose decides to sell coffee and doughnuts to the local hunters, hoping they will not recognize him without his antlers. "Mathieu's frequent black-and-white illustrations expand on the fun," wrote Laura Scott in *School Library Journal. Pig Pickin',* another story by Green, gives Hildy a chance to shine as the pig asks Moose to accompany her to what she thinks is a beauty contest. In

reality, Hildy is being fattened up for a barbecue, and Moose has to save her. "Readers will enjoy the . . . playful . . . pencil and gray-wash drawings," wrote Marilyn Ackerman in a *School Library Journal* review of the book. The illustrations "feature largely throughout the tale," noted a *Kirkus Reviews* contributor who added that Mathieu's numerous illustrations for the book will encourage beginning readers.

Judy Cox's *Don't Be Silly, Mrs. Millie!,* which features Mathieu's art, was selected by *Time* magazine as one of the best children's books of 2005. In Cox's text, kindergarten teacher Mrs. Millie uses the wrong words to describe activities she wants the children to perform (such as hanging up their "goats"), and Mathieu's humorous illustrations bring the teacher's misstatements to literal life. Stephanie Zvirin, writing in *Booklist,* praised the book's "rainbow-bright, color-saturated art," and Erin Senig noted in *School Library Journal* that "the artist's lively and imaginative cartoons aid in understanding" Cox's wordplay.

Mathieu once told *SATA:* "I became addicted to drawing pictures at about three years old. I was never interested in drawing completely straight. It's almost impossible for me to avoid humor, caricature and lots of action.

"I don't feel that an artist has to be particularly encouraged to draw. I think he'll draw no matter what. The same with a writer or a musician for that matter. As a youngster, I became enamored of Jim Henson and the Muppets long before they were really famous. I would beg permission to miss the bus if they were going to appear on the *Dave Garroway Show* or I'd get special permission to stay up late if they were scheduled for Jack Parr.

"When Random House and the Children's Television Workshop started looking for illustrators to interpret the Muppet characters from *Sesame Street,* I just fell into it and I love drawing them. The *Sesame Street* characters are my favorites of all the many Muppet characters."

Along with his work for children's books, Mathieu's illustrations have appeared on numerous *Sesame Street* products, ranging from toys to clothing. He has also illustrated album and CD covers for musical groups, giving him a chance to express his love of ragtime piano and jazz.

Biographical and Critical Sources

PERIODICALS

Booklist, September 1, 1995, Carolyn Phelan, review of *Chimps Don't Wear Glasses,* p. 89; August, 2005, Stephanie Zvirin, review of *Don't Be Silly, Mrs. Millie!* p. 2038; May 1, 2006, Edie Ching, review of *Don't Be Silly, Mrs. Millie!* p. 96.

Kirkus Reviews, June 15, 1992, review of *Brewster's Courage,* p. 780; August 1, 1995, review of *Chimps Don't Wear Glasses,* p. 1115; June 15, 2005, review of *Don't Be Silly, Mrs. Millie!,* p. 680; September 15, 2005, review of *Moose Crossing,* p. 1026; September 15, 2006, review of *Pig Pickin',* p. 954.

Publishers Weekly, November 23, 1992, review of *We're Different, We're the Same,* p. 61; January 29, 1996, review of *Elmo's Lift-and-Peek around the Corner Book,* p. 99; August 19, 1996, review of *Dogs Don't Wear Sneakers,* p. 69; November 9, 1998, review of *Chimps Don't Wear Glasses,* p. 79.

School Library Journal, August, 1989, Sharron McElmeel, review of *Get Well, Granny Bird,* p. 122; September, 1992, p. 254; January, 1994, Lori A. Janick, review of *Dogs Don't Wear Sneakers,* p. 96; February, 2003, Be Astengo, review of *Albie's Trip to Jumble Jungle,* p. 122; October 2005, Laura Scott, review of *Moose's Big Idea,* p. 114; February, 2006, Barbara Auerbach, review of *Don't Be Silly, Mrs. Millie!,* p. 67; March, 2006, Kristine M. Casper, review of *Moose Crossing,* p. 190; October, 2006, Marilyn Ackerman, review of *Pig Pickin',* p. 112.

ONLINE

Joe Mathieu Home Page, http://www.joemathieu.com (November 28, 2007).

Ten Speed Press Web site, http://www.tenspeed.com/authors/ (December 2, 2007), profile of Mathieu.

MATHIEU, Joseph P.
See MATHIEU, Joe

*   *   *

MILLER, Kirsten 1973-

Personal

Born 1973; married; husband a writer.

Addresses

Home—New York, NY.

Career

Writer. Works in advertising in New York, NY.

Writings

Kiki Strike: Inside the Shadow City, Bloomsbury Children's Books (New York, NY), 2006.

Sidelights

In her first book in a projected new series, *Kiki Strike: Inside the Shadow City,* author Kirsten Miller introduces readers to fourteen-year-old Kiki Strike, an adventurous and heroic orphan whose goal is to be "dangerous." The story is narrated by Kiki's newfound friend, the meek Ananka Fishbein. When Ananka discovers a secret entrance to forgotten catacombs located below New York City, Kiki sees an opportunity for adventure and a way to have quick access to all parts of the city. Along with four other Girl Scouts who have a variety of skills, such as forgery and computer hacking, Kiki and Ananka begin exploring the Shadow City, finding gold and other riches, as well as cadavers.

In a review of *Kiki Strike* in *Publishers Weekly,* a contributor wrote that "the author's love for New York's nooks and crannies shines from every page, making this a rare adventure story." Frances Bradburn, writing in *Booklist,* noted that "first-time author Miller has created a fascinating, convoluted mystery-adventure." Sue Giffard commented in the *School Library Journal* that the novel "celebrates the courage and daring of seemingly ordinary girls, and it will thrill those who long for adventure and excitement." Also enthusiastic, a *Kirkus Reviews* contributor dubbed *Kiki Strike* "an absurdly satisfying romp for a disaffected smart girl."

Biographical and Critical Sources

PERIODICALS

Booklist, July 1, 2006, Frances Bradburn, review of *Kiki Strike: Inside the Shadow City,* p. 56.

Kirkus Reviews, May 15, 2006, review of *Kiki Strike,* p. 521.

Publishers Weekly, March 6, 2006, review of *Kiki Strike,* p. 37; June 12, 2006, review of *Kiki Strike,* p. 53.

School Library Journal, June, 2006, Sue Giffard, review of *Kiki Strike,* p. 162.

Vanity Fair, June, 2006, Elissa Schappell, review of *Kiki Strike,* p. 62.

ONLINE

Kiki Strike Web site, http://www.kikistrike.com (January 1, 2008).

TeenReads.com, http://www.teenreads.com/ (June 1, 2006), interview with Miller; (January 1, 2007) Chris Shanley-Dillman, review of *Kiki Strike.**

*   *   *

MILLER, Mary Beth 1964-

Personal

Born 1964; married; children: four. *Education:* Attended Fairfield University (Fairfield, CT). *Hobbies and other interests:* Quilting, horseback riding.

Career

Writer. Previously worked for a medical and nursing publishing house.

Writings

Aimee (novel), Dutton Books (New York, NY), 2002.
On the Head of a Pin (novel), Dutton Books (New York, NY), 2006.

Sidelights

In her first young-adult novel, *Aimee,* Mary Beth Miller tackles the subject of a teen suicide. The novel's narrator is a young girl named Zoe whose best friend, Aimee, is dead. As Zoe tells the story in a journal she is keeping as part of her therapy treatment, she drifts back and forth from the past to present, revealing that she has been accused of murdering Aimee. Living in a new town with her parents, Zoe must deal with anorexia and her parents' eventual breakup, which comes not only as a result of the ordeal over Aimee but also due to their own faults as people and parents. As the novel progresses, readers learn what drove Aimee to kill herself.

Aimee was described as "a fascinating character study that will intrigue readers wanting to go beyond sensationalistic headlines," by a Kirkus Reviews contributor, while in *Kliatt* CLaire Rosser found there to be "a tale

of woe almost on every page." In the *Pittsburgh Post-Gazette,* Karen MacPherson noted that Miller "masterfully controls the book's narrative so that the reader isn't quite certain until the very end of the book exactly what happened the night Aimee died." A *Publishers Weekly* reviewer predicted that "readers will readily recognize the feelings and conflicts that fuel this engrossing novel," and Debbie Carton, writing in *Booklist,* called *Aimee* an "edgy" work in which "the portrayal of therapy is especially good."

Miller's next novel, *On the Head of a Pin,* tells a story death and lies. High school student Andy accidentally shoots and kills Helen, the high school's homecoming queen, while fooling around with a gun at his father's cabin. Panicking, Andy and his friends Josh and Victor drug Helen's boyfriend, an artist named Michael, and then go out and bury the dead teen. Josh, a devout Catholic, is impelled by his faith to tell the truth, but he is threatened by Andy and Victor to keep silent. As a result of the boys' deception, Helen's boyfriend Michael, who comes from a poor family, becomes the prime suspect in Helen's murder. Ultimately, the story's catastrophic denouement changes the boys and their parents' lives forever. "Alternating between Josh's and Michael's perspectives, the author delves deep into the psyches of these two sensitive and vulnerable boys," wrote a *Publishers Weekly* contributor. *On the Head of a Pin* "is a book that asks big questions," stated Myrna Marler in *Kliatt,* the critic noting that the novel "also brings up religious themes." Frances Bradburn commented in *Booklist* that Miller "skillfully weaves together numerous strands to create a horrifying yet thought-provoking and disturbingly real scenario." In *School Library Journal,* Johanna Lewis concluded of the work that the author's "beautifully rendered [teen] narrators manage to compel readers on to the last page."

Biographical and Critical Sources

PERIODICALS

Booklist, May 1, 2002, Debbie Carton, review of *Aimee,* p. 1518; February 15, 2006, Frances Bradburn, review of *On the Head of a Pin,* p. 95.

Kirkus Reviews, May 1, 2002, review of *Aimee,* p. 661; January 15, 2006, review of *On the Head of a Pin,* p. 87.

Kliatt, May, 2002, Claire Rosser, review of *Aimee,* p. 11; March, 2006, Myrna Marler, review of *On the Head of a Pin,* p. 15.

Pittsburgh Post-Gazette, October 1, 2002, Karen MacPherson "Deft Whodunit Gracefully Handles Teen Suicide Topic" (interview).

Publishers Weekly, May 20, 2002, review of *Aimee,* p. 68; February 27, 2006, review of *On the Head of a Pin,* p. 63.

School Library Journal, April, 2006, Johanna Lewis, review of *On the Head of a Pin,* p. 144.

Mary Beth Miller Home Page, http://www.marybethmiller. net (January 1, 2007).*

*   *   *

MILLER, Ron 1947-

Personal

Born May 8, 1947, in Minneapolis, MN; son of Robert (an engineer) and Marilynn (an office manager) Miller; married Judith Toth (a model maker), July 3, 1972. *Education:* Columbus College of Art and Design, B.F. A., 1970.

Addresses

Home and office—906 Caroline St., Fredericksburg, VA 22401. *E-mail*—spaceart@embarqmail.com.

Career

Artist, author, and editor. National Air and Space Museum, Washington, DC, art director for Albert Einstein Spacearium, 1972-77; Black Cat Studios, Fredericksburg, VA, owner, 1977—. Space art consultant to *Starlog;* co-administrator of Bonestell Space Art; created commemorative stamps for U.S. Postal Service. Film works includes production illustrator for *Dune* and *Total Recall;* conceptual artist and consultant for films, including *Contact;* designer and co-creator of *Comet Impact!* (computer-generated film); conceptual artist on documentaries and short films. International Space University, member of faculty; Presenter at numerous international space art workshops and exhibitions; lecturer on space art throughout the world. *Exhibitions:* Works included in numerous public and private collections, including Smithsonian Institution and Pushkin Museum (Moscow, Russia).

Member

International Academy of Astronautics, International Association for the Astronomical Arts (former trustee), North American Jules Verne Society, British Interplanetary Society (fellow).

Awards, Honors

Hugo Award nominations, 1981, for *The Grand Tour,* 1987, for *Cycles of Fire,* 1990, for *In the Stream of Stars,* 1992, for *The History of Earth;* American Institute of Physics Award of Excellence, for "Worlds Beyond" series; Hugo Award in nonfiction category (with Frederick C. Durant III and Melvin H. Schuetz), 2002, for *The Art of Chesley Bonnestell; ForeWord* Silver Award, for *Palaces and Prisons;* IAF Manuscript Award nomination, for *The Dream Machines;* Violet Crown Award, Writer's League of Texas, for *Bradamant;* honorary member of Société Jules Verne.

Writings

NONFICTION

(Editor and contributor) *Space Art,* Starlog, 1978.

(Editor and contributor) *Space Art Poster Book,* Stackpole, 1979.

(With William K. Hartmann) *The Grand Tour: A Traveler's Guide to the Solar System,* Workman Publishing (New York, NY), 1981, third revised edition, 2005.

(With F.C. Durant III) *Worlds Beyond: The Art of Chesley Bonnestell,* Donning, 1983.

(With William K. Hartmann and Pam Lee) *Out of the Cradle: Exploring Frontiers beyond Earth,* Workman Publishing (New York, NY), 1984.

(Editor with Jim Kenney) *Fireball and the Lotus: Emerging Spirituality from Ancient Roots,* Bear & Company (Sante Fe, NM), 1987.

Decalomania: A Tourist's Handbook and Guide, Black Cat Press (Fredericksburg, VA), 1987.

Mathematics, Doubleday (New York, NY), 1989.

(With Andrei Sokolov and Vitaly Myagkov) *In the Stream of Stars: The Soviet-American Space Art Book,* Workman Publishing (New York, NY), 1990.

The History of Earth, Workman Publishing (New York, NY), 1992.

The Dream Machines: An Illustrated History of the Spaceship in Art, Science, and Literature, Krieger (Malabar, FL), 1993.

Extraordinary Voyages, Black Cat Press (Fredericksburg, VA), 1994.

Brainquest, Workman Publishing (New York, NY), 1994.

The History of Rockets, Grolier (Danbury, CT), 1999.

The History of Science Fiction, Franklin Watts (New York, NY), 2000.

(With Frederick C. Durant III and Melvin H. Schuetz) *The Art of Chesley Bonnestell,* Sterling, 2001.

Extrasolar Planets, Twenty-first Century Books (Brookfield, CT), 2002.

Special Effects: An Introduction to Movie Magic, Twenty-first Century Books (Minneapolis, MN), 2006.

The Elements: What You Really Want to Know, Twenty-first Century Books (Minneapolis, MN), 2006.

Extreme Aircraft, Collins (New York, NY), 2007.

Ellen Jackson, *Worlds around Us: A Space Voyage,* Millbrook Press (Minneapolis, MN), 2007.

Digital Art: Painting with Pixels, Twenty-first Century Books (Minneapolis, MN), 2008.

Contributing editor, *Air & Space/Smithsonian* magazine.

"WORLDS BEYOND" SERIES; CHILDREN'S NONFICTION

The Sun, Twenty-first Century Books (Brookfield, CT), 2002.

Jupiter, Twenty-first Century Books (Brookfield, CT), 2002.

Earth and the Moon, Twenty-first Century Books (Brookfield, CT), 2003.

Mercury and Pluto, Twenty-first Century Books (Brookfield, CT), 2003.

Saturn, Twenty-first Century Books (Brookfield, CT), 2003.

Venus, Twenty-first Century Books (Brookfield, CT), 2003.

Uranus and Neptune, Twenty-first Century Books (Brookfield, CT), 2003.

Asteroids, Comets, and Meteors, Twenty-first Century Books (Brookfield, CT), 2005.

Stars and Galaxies, Twenty-first Century Books (Brookfield, CT), 2006.

Mars, Twenty-first Century Books (Brookfield, CT), 2006.

"SPACE INNOVATIONS" SERIES; CHILDREN'S NONFICTION

Robot Explorers, Twenty-first Century Books (Minneapolis, MN), 2007.

Satellites, Twenty-first Century Books (Minneapolis, MN), 2007.

Space Exploration, Twenty-first Century Books (Minneapolis, MN), 2007.

Rockets, Lerner (Minneapolis, MN), 2008.

FICTION

Palaces and Prisons ("Bronwyn Trilogy"), Ace (New York, NY), 1991.

Silk and Steel ("Bronwyn Trilogy"), Ace (New York, NY), 1991.

Hearts and Armor ("Bronwyn Trilogy"), Ace (New York, NY), 1992.

Bradamant, Timberwolf Press, 2000.

Mermaids and Meteors, Timberwolf Press, 2002.

Velda (detective novel), Timberwolf Press, 2003.

13 Steps to Velda (short stories), Black Cat Press (Fredericksburg, VA), 2005.

Captain Judikah, Black Cat Press (Fredericksburg, VA), 2005.

Pathetic Sections, Black Cat Press (Fredericksburg, VA), 2005.

ILLUSTRATOR

Roy A. Gallant, *The Macmillan Book of Astronomy,* Macmillan (New York, NY), 1986.

William K. Hartmann, *Cycles of Fire: Stars, Galaxies, and the Wonder of Deep Space,* Workman (New York, NY), 1987.

Christopher Lampton, *Stars and Planets,* Doubleday (Garden City, NY), 1988.

Mark R. Chartrand, *Planets: A Guide to the Solar System,* Golden Press (New York, NY), 1990.

Barbara Brenner, *Planetarium,* Bantam Books (New York, NY), 1993.

(And translator) Jules Verne, *20,000 Leagues under the Sea,* DK (New York, NY), 1998.

Pamela Sargent, *Firebrands: Heroines of Science Fiction and Fantasy,* Paper Tiger, 1998.

Alain Dupas, *Destination Mars,* Firefly Books, 2000.

(And translator) Jules Verne, *Journey to the Center of the Earth,* Black Cat Press (Fredericksburg, VA), 2005.

Ellen Jackson, *Worlds around Us: A Space Voyage,* Millbrook Press (Minneapolis, MN), 2007.

Contributor of illustrations to magazines, including *National Geographic, Reader's Digest, Discover, Geo, Future, Natural History, Newsweek, Scientific American, Smithsonian, Air & Space, Sky & Telescope, Passages, Starlog, L5 News, Future,* and *Science Digest.*

Sidelights

Ron Miller worked as a commercial advertising illustrator before concentrating his art on his primary area of interest: space science. A job as art director of the National Air & Space Museum's Albert Einstein Planetarium in the early 1970s led Miller to a successful career as a freelance artist and writer, and his expertise on space art, as well as on the writings of Jules Verne, have resulted in numerous other opportunities within his chosen field. In addition to his illustration work, Miller is the author or editor of astronomy-and science-based nonfiction as well as fiction. In addition to his work as an author and artist, he has also worked as production illustrator and designer on motion pictures, among them *Dune* and *Total Recall.*

The books in Miller's "Worlds Beyond" and "Space Innovations" series are designed to inspire younger readers with the same fascination with science that has fueled his own career. Comprised of eleven volumes, including *The Sun, Extrasolar Planets,* and *Asteroids, Comets, and Meteors,* the award-winning "Worlds Beyond" books pair dozens of Miller's illustrations with a detailed, fact-centered text. Other books for teen readers include *The Elements: What You Really Want to Know* and *The Dream Machines: An Illustrated History of the Spaceship in Art, Science, and Literature,* the latter a 750-page illustrated history of the space ship, beginning with conceptual vehicles devised by the ancient Greeks through those actually in use by the twenty-first century.

One of Miller's best-known books for general readers, *The Grand Tour: A Traveler's Guide to the Solar System,* was coauthored by William K. Hartmann and first published in 1981. Revised and updated in 1993 and again in 2005, *The Grand Tour* is considered a classic in its field. The new edition draws on discoveries made by Voyager I and II, Magellan, Galileo, the Hubble Space Telescope, the Mars Global Surveyor Mission and other space initiatives, providing budding astronomers with timely information on subjects about which much is still to be discovered. *The Grand Tour* is enhanced by over a hundred paintings by the author.

As Miller once noted of his work: "My main interest is in making astronomy understandable to the public, especially in making the planets in our solar system seem to be real places. I particularly enjoy playing 'Mr. Wizard' and making science fun for kids."

Biographical and Critical Sources

PERIODICALS

Booklist, March 15, 2006, Gillian Engberg, review of *Special Effects: An Introduction to Movie Magic,* p. 43.
Future, November, 1978, review of *Space Art.*
School Library Journal, March, 2006, Maren Ostergard, review of *The Elements: What You Really Want to Know,* p. 244; June, 2006, Tim Wadham, review of *Special Effects,* p. 182.
Science Teacher, November, 2003, John Cirucci, review of *Venus,* pp. 88-89.

ONLINE

Ron Miller Home Page, http://www.black-cat-studios.com (December 5, 2007).*

*   *   *

MORRISON, Frank 1971-

Personal

Born 1971, in MA; married; wife's name Connie; children: three sons, one daughter.

Addresses

Home—Morrison Arts, 659 Auburn Ave., Ste. G17, Atlanta, GA 30312.

Career

Illustrator. Gallery of Morrison Arts, Atlanta, OH, owner. Clothing designer for Phat Pharm label. Former break dancer and member of traveling dance troupe Sugar Hill Gang. *Exhibitions:* Solo exhibit at Savacaou Gallery, New York, NY, and Schomberg Center for Research in Black Culture.

Awards, Honors

Coretta Scott King/ John Steptoe New Talent Award for Illustration, 2005, for *Jazzy Miz Mozetta* by Brenda C. Roberts.

Illustrator

Brenda C. Roberts, *Jazzy Miz Mozetta,* Farrar, Straus (New York, NY), 2004.
Debbie A. Taylor, *Sweet Music in Harlem,* Lee & Low (New York, NY), 2004.
Queen Latifah, *Queen of the Scene,* Laura Geringer Books (New York, NY), 2006.
Lissette Noman, *My Feet Are Laughing,* Farrar, Straus (New York, NY), 2006.
Gaylia Taylor, *George Crum and the Saratoga Chip,* Lee & Low (New York, NY), 2006.

Alex Rodriguez, *Out of the Ballpark,* HarperCollins (New York, NY), 2007.
Melanie Turner-Denstaedt, *Grandma's Good Hat,* Farrar, Straus (New York, NY), 2008.

Sidelights

Winner of the 2005 Coretta Scott King/John Steptoe Award for New Talent in Illustration, painter Frank Morrison creates art that reflects the rich culture of inner-city life. The Georgia-based artist's first book illustration project, Debbie A. Taylor's *Sweet Music in Harlem,* was dubbed "a confident debut" by a *Publishers Weekly* contributor while a *Kirkus Reviews* writer noted that Morrison's "elongated" characters move "against backgrounds that curve, slant, and boogie-woogie—but almost never stay still." Reviewing the book that won Morrison the 2005 award, Brenda C. Roberts' *Jazzy Miz Mozetta,* a *Kirkus Reviews* writer noted that the story about a woman who loves to dance is paired with a "colorful jumble of exaggeratedly long, skinny limbs in dynamic illustrations that dance to the beat of a fresh, rhythmic story." "Morrison captures the linear angles and smooth curves of jazz swing" concluded Mary Elam in a review of the same book for *School Library Journal,*

Out of the Ballpark, a picture book by New York Yankees third baseman Alex Rodriguez, focuses on a boy dreaming of becoming a sports star and was considered by many to be a perfect match for Morrison's art. The illustrator's "stylized paintings capture the story's energy and his playfully skewed perspectives keep things light," wrote a *Publishers Weekly* contributor, while in *School Library Journal* Marilyn Taniguchi noted that the artist's "action-packed illustrations, in vivid hues, help keep the story moving at a brisk pace." In Lissette Norman's *My Feet Are Laughing,* his artwork, which *Booklist* contributor Hazel Rochman described as "full of swirling curves and angles," exhibits versatility, exuding Morrison's characteristic energy as well as capturing the story's more subdued moments," in Rochman's view.

Discussing Morrison's work for Queen Latifah's *Queen of the Scene,* about a young African-American girl who excels at all playground activities, *School Library Journal* contributor Mary Hazelton wrote that the illustrator's "elastic-bodied figures are graceful and brazen," making each page of the picture book "spin with movement and action." A *Kirkus Reviews* writer had a similar assessment of the work, writing that "Morrison's illustrations burst with originality, vibrancy and humor." The illustrator's "bold signature acrylics" for the book "capture the rhythm of the text and the energy" of Latifah's text, the critic added, and capture the upbeat attitude reflected by the story's urban neighborhood setting."

Biographical and Critical Sources

PERIODICALS

Booklist, May 1, 2004, Terry Glover, review of *Sweet Music in Harlem,* p. 1564; April 1, 2006, Linda Perkins, review of *George Crum and the Saratoga Chip,* p. 46, and Hazel Rochman, review of *My Feet Are Laughing,* p. 49.

Kirkus Reviews, April 15, 2004, review of *Sweet Music in Harlem,* p. 402; October 1, 2004, Brenda C. Roberts, review of *Jazzy Miz Mozetta,* p. 967; March 15, 2006, Gaylia Taylor, review of *George Crum and the Saratoga Chip,* p. 301; October 1, 2006, review of *Queen of the Scene,* p. 1022; February 1, 2007, review of *Out of the Ballpark,* p. 128.

Publishers Weekly, May 24, 2004, review of *Sweet Music in Harlem,* p. 61; January 3, 2005, review of *Jazzy Miz Mozetta,* p. 54; October 2, 2006, review of *Queen of the Scene,* p. 61; February 5, 2007, review of *Out of the Ballpark,* p. 58.

School Library Journal, July, 2004, Jane Marino, review of *Sweet Music in Harlem,* p. 89; December, 2004, Mary Elam, review of *Jazzy Miz Mozetta,* p. 118; December, 2006, Mary Hazelton, review of *Queen of the Scene,* p. 101; May, 2007, Marilyn Taniguchi, review of *Out of the Ballpark,* p. 107.

Toldedo Blade, February 1, 2007, Tahree Lane, "Atlanta Artist Plays with the Human Form."

ONLINE

Frank Morrison Home Page, http://www.morrisongraphics.com (December 20, 2007).*

*   *   *

MOSER, Barry 1940-

Personal

Born October 15, 1940, in Chattanooga, TN; son of Arthur Boyd (a professional gambler) and Wilhemina Elizabeth (a homemaker) Moser; married Kay Richmond (an artist), 1962 (divorced, April, 1978); children: Cara, Ramona, Madeline. *Ethnicity:* "Austrian extraction, pig thieves." *Education:* Attended Baylor Military Academy, 1951-57, and Auburn University, 1958-60; University of Chattanooga, B.S., 1962; graduate study at University of Massachusetts, 1968-70; studied with Leonard Baskin, Fred Becker, Jack Coughlin, George Cross, Harold McGrath, and Wang Hui-Ming. *Politics:* "Liberal." *Hobbies and other interests:* Aviation, film, culinary arts.

Addresses

Home and office—North Hatfield, MA. *Agent*—R. Michelson Galleries, 132 Main St., Northampton, MA 01060.

Barry Moser (Reproduced by permission.)

Career

Author, illustrator, fine artist, and educator. Hixson Methodist Church, Hixson, TN, youth director and assistant minister, 1960; McCallie School, Chattanooga, TN, teacher, 1962-63; Williston Academy (now Williston-Northampton School), Easthampton, MA, teacher, 1967-c. 73. Pennyroyal Press, Northampton, MA, founder and major domo, 1968. Member of faculty at Rhode Island School of Design, Providence, and Smith College, Northampton; Queens College, Kingston, TN, Geneva lecturer, 2001; also taught at Princeton University and Vassar College. Visiting artist at University of Tennessee, 1972, 1975; Rhode Island College, 1976; University of Nebraska at Omaha, 1976; College of Arts and Crafts, Oakland, 1977, 1982, 1983; University of Washington, Seattle, 1981; Carnegie-Mellon University, 1986; and Ringling School of Art and Design, 1986; Allen R. Hite Art Institute, University of Louisville, distinguished visiting scholar, 2001. Juror, Fifty Books of the Year, American Institute of Graphic Arts, 1981. *Exhibitions:* Art work exhibited in solo and group shows; works included in numerous public and private collections, including Library of Congress, British Museum, National Library of Australia, Metropolitan Museum of Art, National Gallery of Art, Houghton Library at Harvard University, Beinecke Library at Yale University, Princeton University, University of British Columbia, University of Iowa Libraries and Center for the Book, and London College of Printing.

Member

National Academy of Design, American Printing History Association (charter member).

Awards, Honors

Purchase Prize and Faculty Purchase Prize, Westfield State Annual, 1970; Second Prize, Cape Cod Annual, 1971; Award of Merit, New Hampshire International, 1974; Award of Merit, American Institute of Graphic Arts, 1982-86; American Book Award for pictorial design and illustration, 1983, for *Alice's Adventures in Wonderland;* Award of Merit, Bookbuilders West, 1983-86; Award of Merit, *Communication Arts* magazine, 1984-86; Best Books for Young Adults designation, *School Library Journal,* and Children's Book of the Year designation, Child Study Association, both 1987, both for *Jump!;* American Library Association (ALA) Notable Book designation, and *New York Times* Best Illustration Book of the Year designation, both 1987, both for *Jump Again!;* Boston Globe/Horn Book Award, 1991, for *Appalachia;* International Board of Books for Young People (IBBY) Best Book designation, 1991, for *Little Trickster the Squirrel Meets Big Double the Bear;* Parents Choice Award, 1992, for *Through the Mickle Woods;* ALA Notable Book designation, 1995, for *Whistling Dixie;* Pick of the Lists selection, American Booksellers Association, 1995, for *What You Know First;* ALA Notable Book designation, 1997, for *When Birds Could Talk and Bats Could Sing;* Toronto Book Award shortlist, 1998, for *Dippers;* honorary Doctor of Fine Arts, Westfield State College, 2000; honorary Doctor of Humanity, Anna Maria College, 2001; Carl Herzog Award for Excellence in Book Design, University of Texas at El Paso/Friends of the University Library, 2002, for *No Shortcuts: An Essay in Wood Engraving.*

Writings

SELF-ILLUSTRATED; FOR CHILDREN

(Reteller) *The Tinderbox,* Little, Brown (Boston, MA), 1990.

(Reteller) *Polly Vaughan: A Traditional British Ballad,* Little, Brown (Boston, MA), 1992.

Fly! A Brief History of Flight (nonfiction), HarperCollins (New York, NY), 1993.

(Reteller) *Tucker Pfeffercorn: An Old Story Retold,* Little, Brown (Boston, MA), 1993.

(Reteller) *Good and Perfect Gifts: An Illustrated Retelling of O. Henry's "The Gift of the Magi,"* Little, Brown (Boston, MA), 1997.

(Editor) *Great Ghost Stories,* Morrow (New York, NY), 1998.

(Reteller) *The Three Little Pigs,* Little, Brown (Boston, MA), 2001.

(Editor) *Scary Stories,* Chronicle Books (San Francisco, CA), 2006.

(Editor) *Cowboy Stories,* Chronicle Books (San Francisco, CA), 2007.

SELF-ILLUSTRATED; FOR ADULTS

(With Parrot) *Cirsia and Other Thistles,* Pennyroyal Press (Northampton, MA), 1978.

Fifty Wood Engravings, Pennyroyal Press (Northampton, MA), 1978.

Notes of the Craft of Wood Engraving, Pennyroyal Press (Northampton, MA), 1980.

A Family Letter, Pennyroyal Press (Northampton, MA), 1980.

Pan, Pennyroyal Press (Northampton, MA), 1980.

In the Face of Presumptions: Essays, Speeches, and Incidental Writings, edited by Jessica Renaud, David R. Godine (Boston, MA), 2000.

No Shortcuts: An Essay in Wood Engraving, Center for the Book, University of Iowa Press (Iowa City, IA), 2001.

Wood Engraving: The Art of Wood Engraving and Relief Engraving, photographs by daughter, Cara Moser, foreword by Martin Antonetti, David R. Godine (Boston, MA), 2006.

ILLUSTRATOR

Ely Green, *Ely: Too Black, Too White,* University of Massachusetts Press (Amherst, MA), 1969.

James Abbott McNeil Whistler, *The Red Rag,* Castalia Press (Northampton, MA), 1970.

E.M. Beekman, *Homage to Mondrian,* Pennyroyal Press (Northampton, MA), 1973.

E.M. Beekman, *The Oyster and the Eagle,* University of Massachusetts Press (Amherst, MA), 1973.

Twelve American Writers, Pennyroyal Press (Northampton, MA), 1974.

John V. Brindle, *Thirteen Botanical Woodengravings,* Pennyroyal Press (Northampton, MA), 1974.

Gerald W. McFarland, *Mugwumps, Morals, and Politics,* University of Massachusetts Press (Amherst, MA), 1975.

Alan W. Friedman, *Forms of Modern British Fiction,* University of Texas Press (Austin, TX), 1975.

Reginald Cook, *Robert Frost: A Living Voice,* University of Massachusetts Press (Amherst, MA), 1975.

Sheila Steinberg and Cathleen McGuigan, *Rhode Island: An Historical Guide,* Rhode Island Bicentennial Commission, 1975.

E.M. Beekman, *Carnal Lent,* Pennyroyal Press (Northampton, MA), 1976.

J. Walsdorf, *Men of Printing,* Pennyroyal Press (Northampton, MA), 1976.

Octavio Paz, *The Poetry of Octavio Paz,* University of Texas Press (Austin, TX), 1976.

Paul Smyth, *Thistles and Thorns,* University of Nebraska (Lincoln, NE), 1976.

Paul Ramsey, *Eve Singing,* Pennyroyal Press (Northampton, MA), 1977.

Marcia Falk, *Song of Songs,* Harcourt (New York, NY), 1977.

J. Chametzky, _From the Ghetto,_ University of Massachusetts Press (Amherst, MA), 1977.

Leland J. Bellot, _William Knox: The Life and Thought of an Eighteenth-Century Imperialist,_ University of Texas Press (Austin, TX), 1977.

Roger Manvell, _Chaplin,_ Little, Brown (Boston, MA), 1977.

David Smith, _Elizabeth Taylor: Portrait of a Queen,_ Little, Brown (Boston, MA), 1977.

Morris Bishop, _St. Francis of Assisi,_ Little, Brown (Boston, MA), 1977.

E.M. Beekman, _The Killing Jar,_ Houghton Mifflin (Boston, MA), 1977.

Arthur MacAlpine, _Man in a Metal Cage,_ Pennyroyal Press (Northampton, MA), 1977.

Robert Sprich and Richard W. Noland, _The Whispered Meanings,_ University of Massachusetts Press (Amherst, MA), 1977.

Allen Mandelbaum, _Chelmaxims,_ David R. Godine (Boston, MA), 1977.

Paul Mariani, _Timing Devices,_ Pennyroyal Press (Northampton, MA), 1977.

Jane Yolen, _The Lady and the Merman,_ Pennyroyal Press (Northampton, MA), 1977.

Lawrence Ferlinghetti, _Director of Alienation,_ Main Street Press (Lawrenceville, NJ), 1977.

William Stafford, _Late Passing Prairie Farm,_ Main Street Press (Lawrenceville, NJ), 1977.

Louis Simpson, _The Invasion of Italy,_ Main Street Press (Lawrenceville, NJ), 1977.

Nancy Bubel, _The Adventurous Gardner,_ David R. Godine (Boston, MA), 1977.

Stephen Brook, _Bibliography of the Gehenna Press,_ J.P. Dwyer, 1977.

Mark Twain, _1601,_ Taurus Books, 1978.

David Smith, _Goshawk and Antelope,_ University of Illinois Press (Champaign, IL), 1978.

Lydia Crowson, _The Esthetic of Jean Cocteau,_ University Press of New England (Lebanon, NH), 1978.

Walter Chamberlain, _Woodengraving,_ Thames & Hudson (New York, NY), 1979.

M.W. Ryan, editor, _Irish Historical Broadsides,_ J.P. Dwyer, 1979.

Vernon Ahmadjian, _The Flowering Plant of Massachusetts,_ University of Massachusetts Press (Amherst, MA), 1979.

Herman Melville, _Moby-Dick; or, The Whale,_ Arion Press (San Francisco, CA), 1979.

Stephen Vincent Benét, _John Brown's Body,_ Doubleday (New York, NY), 1979.

Herbert W. Warden, _In Praise of Sailors,_ H. Abrams (New York, NY), 1979.

A Family Letter Written in Nineteen Thirty-two by Georga Moser to His Nephew Arthur Moser . . . , Pennyroyal Press (Northhampton, MA), 1979.

Allen Mandelbaum, _A Lied of Letterpress,_ Pennyroyal Press (Northampton, MA), 1980.

Dante, _Volume One: The Inferno, the Divine Comedy of Dante Alighieri,_ translated by Allen Mandelbaum, University of California Press (Berkeley, CA), 1980.

Virgil, _Aeneid,_ translated by Allen Mandelbaum, University of California Press (Berkeley, CA), 1980.

Paul Smyth, _The Cardinal Sins: A Bestiary,_ Pennyroyal Press (Northampton, MA), 1980.

Galway Kinnell, _The Last Hiding Place of Snow,_ Red Ozier Press (Madison, WI), 1980.

Homer, _Odyssey,_ translated by T.E. Shaw, Limited Editions Press (Lubbock, TX), 1980.

David Smith, _Blue Spruce,_ Tamarack Editions (Syracuse, NY), 1981.

Galway Kinnell and Diane Wakowski, _Two Poems,_ Red Ozier Press (Madison, WI), 1981.

Gene Bell-Villada, _Borges and His Fiction,_ University of North Carolina Press (Chapel Hill, NC), 1981.

Dante, _Purgatorio,_ translated by Allen Mandelbaum, University of California Press (Berkeley, CA), 1982.

Lewis Carroll, _Alice's Adventures in Wonderland,_ University of California Press (Berkeley, CA), 1982.

Lewis Carroll, _Through the Looking Glass, and What Alice Found There,_ University of California Press (Berkeley, CA), 1982.

Robert Bly, _The Traveler Who Repeats His Cry,_ Red Ozier Press (Madison, WI), 1982.

Mary Shelley, _Frankenstein; or, The Modern Prometheus,_ University of California Press (Berkeley, CA), 1983.

David Smith, _Gray Soldiers,_ Stuart, 1983.

Robert Bly, _The Whole Misty Night,_ Red Ozier Press (Madison, WI), 1983.

Lewis Carroll, _The Hunting of the Snark,_ Pennyroyal Press (Northampton, MA), 1983.

Carl Rapp, _William Carlos Williams and Romantic Idealism,_ University Press of New England (Lebanon, NH), 1984.

Dante, _Paradiso,_ translated by Allen Mandelbaum, University of California Press (Berkeley, CA), 1984.

Paul Mariani, _A Usable Past,_ University of Massachusetts Press (Amherst, MA), 1984.

E.M. Beekman, _Totem and Other Poems,_ Pennyroyal Press (Northampton, MA), 1984.

Robert Francis, _The Trouble with God,_ Pennyroyal Press (Northampton, MA), 1984.

Mark Taylor, _Erring,_ University of Chicago Press (Chicago, IL), 1984.

Robert Penn Warren, _Fifty Years of American Poetry,_ Abrams (New York, NY), 1984.

Stephen Crane, _The Red Badge of Courage,_ Pennyroyal Press (Northampton, MA), 1984.

Nathaniel Hawthorne, _The Scarlet Letter,_ Pennyroyal Press (Northampton, MA), 1984.

Mark Twain, _The Adventures of Huckleberry Finn,_ University of California Press (Berkeley, CA), 1985.

Anne Frank, _Anne Frank: Diary of a Young Girl,_ Pennyroyal Press/Jewish Heritage (Northampton, MA), 1985.

Richard de Fournival, _Master Richard's Bestiary of Love and Response,_ translated by Jeanette Beer, University of California Press (Berkeley, CA), 1985.

L. Frank Baum, _The Wonderful Wizard of Oz,_ University of California Press (Berkeley, CA), 1985.

Giants and Ogres ("Enchanted World" series), Time-Life Books (Alexandria, VA), 1985.

Sylvia Plath, _Above the Oxbow,_ Catawba Press (Catawba, SC), 1985.

Richard Michelson, *Tap Dancing for the Relatives,* University Press of Florida (Gainesville, FL), 1985.

Marcia Falk, *It Is July in Virginia,* Scripps College Press (Claremont, CA), 1985.

Joel Chandler Harris, *Jump! The Adventures of Brer Rabbit,* adapted by Van Dyke Parks and Malcolm Jones, Harcourt (San Diego, CA), 1986.

Emily Dickinson, *Broadside,* Pennyroyal Press, 1986.

Washington Irving, *Two Tales: Rip Van Winkle [and] The Legend of Sleepy Hollow,* Harcourt (New York, NY), 1986.

Barbara Stoler Miller, translator, *The Bhagavad-Ghita,* Columbia University Press (New York, NY), 1986.

The Fall of Camelot ("Enchanted World" series), Time-Life Books (Alexandria, VA), 1986.

American Heritage Dictionary editors, *Word Mysteries and Histories: From Quiches to Humble Pie,* Houghton (Boston, MA), 1986.

Robert Louis Stevenson, *The Strange Case of Dr. Jekyll and Mr. Hyde,* Pennyroyal Press (Northampton, MA), 1986.

Robert D. Richardson, Jr., *Henry David Thoreau: A Life of the Mind,* University of California Press (Berkeley, CA), 1986.

Joel Chandler Harris, *Jump Again! More Adventures of Brer Rabbit,* adapted by Van Dyke Parks, Harcourt (San Diego, CA), 1987.

Eudora Welty, *The Robber Bridegroom,* Pennyroyal Press (Northampton, MA), 1987.

Truman Capote, *I Remember Grandpa,* Peachtree (Atlanta, GA), 1987.

Virginia Hamilton, reteller, *In the Beginning: Creation Stories from around the World,* Harcourt (San Diego, CA), 1988.

Jules Verne, *Around the World in Eighty Days,* Morrow (New York, NY), 1988.

Ernest L. Thayer, *Casey at the Bat: A Centennial Edition,* David R. Godine (Boston, MA), 1988.

Mark Twain, *The Adventures of Tom Sawyer,* Morrow (New York, NY), 1989.

Nancy Willard, *The Ballad of Buddy Early,* Knopf (New York, NY), 1989.

Nancy Willard, *East of the Sun and West of the Moon: A Play,* Harcourt, (San Diego, CA) 1989.

Norman Maclean, *A River Runs through It,* University of Chicago Press (Chicago, IL), 1989.

Marie Rudisill, *Sook's Cookbook: Memories and Traditional Recipes from the Deep South,* Longstreet Press (Atlanta, GA), 1989.

Joel Chandler Harris, *Jump on Over! The Adventures of Brer Rabbit and His Family,* adapted by Van Dyke Parks, Harcourt (San Diego, CA), 1989.

William Shakespeare, *The Guild Shakespeare,* Doubleday Book Club (New York, NY), 1990.

Ken Kesey, *Little Tricker the Squirrel Meets Big Double the Bear,* Viking (New York, NY), 1990.

Jane Yolen, *Sky Dogs,* Harcourt (San Diego, CA), 1990.

Sheila MacGill-Callahan, *And Still the Turtle Watched,* Dial (New York, NY), 1991.

Cynthia Rylant, *Appalachia: The Voices of Sleeping Birds,* Harcourt (San Diego, CA), 1991.

Sean O'Huigin, *The Ghost Horse of the Mounties,* David R. Godine (Boston, MA), 1991.

The Holy Bible, Oxford University Press/Doubleday (New York, NY), 1991.

Margaret Hodges, *St. Jerome and the Lion,* Orchard (New York, NY), 1991.

Anton Chekhov, *Kastanka,* Putnam (New York, NY), 1991.

Edgar Allan Poe, *Tales of Edgar Allan Poe,* Morrow (New York, NY), 1991.

Carmen Bernos de Gasztold, *Prayers from the Ark: Selected Poems,* translated by Rumer Godden, Viking (New York, NY), 1992.

Arielle N. Olson, *Noah's Cats and the Devil's Fire,* Orchard (New York, NY), 1992.

Henry Treece, *The Magic Wood,* HarperCollins (New York, NY), 1992.

Donald Barthelme, *The King,* Viking (New York, NY), 1992.

Arthur Conan Doyle, *The Adventures of Sherlock Holmes,* Morrow (New York, NY), 1992.

George Frederich Handel, *Messiah: The Wordbook for the Oratorio,* HarperCollins (New York, NY), 1992.

Marcia Falk, *The Song of Songs: A New Translation and Interpretation,* Harper (New York, NY), 1993.

Lynne Reid Banks, *The Magic Hare,* Morrow (New York, NY), 1993.

Ann Turner, *Grass Songs: Poems,* Harcourt (San Diego, CA), 1993.

Cynthia Rylant, *The Dreamer,* Scholastic (New York, NY), 1993.

Ethel Pochocki, *The Mushroom Man,* Green Tiger Press (San Diego, CA), 1993.

Donald Hall, *The Farm Summer,* Dial (New York, NY), 1994.

Donald Hall, *I Am the Dog, I Am the Cat,* Dial (New York, NY), 1994.

Kathryn Lasky, *Cloud Eyes,* Harcourt (San Diego, CA), 1994.

Jack London, *Call of the Wild,* Macmillan (New York, NY), 1994.

Doris Orgel, *Ariadne, Awake!* Viking (New York, NY), 1994.

Richard Wilbur, *A Game of Catch,* Harcourt (San Diego, CA), 1994.

(With Cara Moser) Gerald Hausman, *Turtle Island ABC: A Gathering of Native American Symbols,* HarperCollins (New York, NY), 1994.

John Bunyan, *Pilgrim's Progress,* retold by Gary D. Schmidt, Eerdmans (Grand Rapids, MI), 1994.

Isabelle Harper, *My Dog Rosie,* Blue Sky Press (New York, NY), 1994.

Karen Ackerman, *Bingleman's Midway,* Boyds Mills Press (Honesdale, PA), 1995.

Willie Morris, *A Prayer for the Opening of the Little League Season,* Harcourt (San Diego, CA), 1995.

Isabelle Harper, *My Cats Nick and Nora,* Blue Sky Press (New York, NY), 1995.

Ted Hughes, *The Iron Woman,* Dial (New York, NY), 1995.

Patricia MacLachlan, *What You Know First,* HarperCollins (New York, NY), 1995.

Marcia Vaughan, *Whistling Dixie,* HarperCollins (New York, NY), 1995.

Weldon Kees, *Five Lost Poems,* Center for the Book, University of Iowa Press (Iowa City, IA), 1995.

Donald Hall, *When Willard Met Babe Ruth,* Browndeer Press (San Diego, CA), 1996.

Isabelle Harper, *Our New Puppy,* Blue Sky Press/Scholastic (New York, NY), 1996.

Virginia Hamilton, reteller, *When Birds Could Talk and Bats Could Sing: The Adventures of Bruh Sparrow, Sis Wren, and Their Friends,* Blue Sky Press (New York, NY), 1996.

(With Cara Moser) Gerald Hausman, reteller, *Eagle Boy: A Traditional Navajo Legend,* HarperCollins (New York, NY), 1996.

Rudyard Kipling, *Just So Stories,* Morrow (New York, NY), 1996.

Rafe Martin, reteller, *Mysterious Tales of Japan,* Putnam (New York, NY), 1996.

Madeline Moser, compiler, *Ever Heard of an Aardwulf? A Miscellany of Uncommon Animals,* Harcourt (San Diego, CA), 1996.

Eve Bunting, *On Call Back Mountain,* Blue Sky Press (New York, NY), 1997.

Padraic Colum, reteller, *The Trojan War and the Adventures of Odysseus,* Morrow (New York, NY), 1997.

Virginia Hamilton, reteller, *A Ring of Tricksters: Animal Tales from America, the West Indies, and Africa,* Blue Sky Press (New York, NY), 1997.

Barbara Nichol, *Dippers,* Tundra Books of Northern New York (Pittsburgh, NY), 1997.

(With Cara Moser) Dan Harper, *Telling Time with Big Mama Cat,* Harcourt (San Diego, CA), 1998.

Tony Johnston, *Trail of Tears,* Blue Sky Press (New York, NY), 1998.

Cynthia Rylant, *The Bird House,* Scholastic/Blue Sky Press (New York, NY), 1998.

Richard Michelson, *Grandpa's Gamble,* Marshall Cavendish (Tarrytown, NY), 1999.

The Holy Bible: Containing All the Books of the Old and New Testaments: King James Version, Pennyroyal Caxton Press (Northampton, MA)/Viking Studio (New York, NY), 1999, published as *The Family Bible with Apocrypha, New Revised Standard Version (NRSV),* Oxford University Press (New York, NY), 2000.

Kathyrn Lasky, *A Brilliant Streak: The Making of Mark Twain,* Harcourt (San Diego, CA), 1999.

Milton Meltzer, *Witches and Witch-Hunts: A History of Persecution,* Scholastic (New York, NY), 1999.

Gerald Hausman and Loretta Hausman, retellers, *Dogs of Myth: Tales from around the World,* Simon & Schuster (New York, NY), 1999.

Bram Stoker, *Dracula,* Morrow (New York, NY), 2000.

Virginia Hamilton, *Wee Winnie Witch's Skinny: An Original Scare Tale for Halloween,* Blue Sky Press (New York, NY), 2001.

(With Cara Moser) Dan Harper, *Sit, Truman!,* Harcourt (San Diego, CA), 2001.

Isabelle Harper, *Our New Puppy,* Scholastic (New York, NY), 2001.

Angela Johnson, *Those Building Men,* Blue Sky Press (New York, NY), 2001.

Robert D. San Souci, reteller, *Sister Tricksters,* Simon & Schuster (New York, NY), 2001.

Barbara Nichol, *One Small Garden,* Tundra Books (Pittsburgh, NY), 2001.

Elizabeth George Speare, *The Witch of Blackbird Pond,* Houghton (Boston, MA), 2001.

Tony Johnston, *That Summer,* Harcourt (San Diego, CA), 2002.

Margie Palatini, *Earthquack!,* Simon & Schuster (New York, NY), 2002.

Gary Schmidt and Susan M. Fetch, editors, *Winter: A Spiritual Biography of the Season* (anthology), SkyLight Paths Publications, 2002.

Kay Winters, *Voices of Ancient Egypt,* National Geographic Society (Washington, DC), 2003.

Kristine O'Connell George, *Hummingbird Nest: A Journal of Poems,* Harcourt (Orlando, FL), 2004.

Gary Schmidt and Susan M. Felch, editors, *Summer: A Spiritual Biography of the Season,* Skylight Paths, 2005.

Margie Palatini, *The Three Silly Billies,* Simon & Schuster (New York, NY), 2005.

Ethel Polchocki, *The Mushroom Man,* Tilbury House (Gardiner, ME), 2006.

Psalm 23, Zonderkids (Grand Rapids, MI), 2006.

The Funny Cide Team, *A Horse Named Funny Cide,* Putnam's (New York, NY), 2006.

Ethel Polchocki, *The Blessing of the Beasts,* Paraclete Press (Brewster, MA), 2007.

Pliny the Younger, *Ashen Sky: The Letters of Pliny the Younger on the Eruption of Vesuvius,* J. Paul Getty Museum (Los Angeles, CA), 2007.

Margaret Hodges, *Moses,* Harcourt (Orlando, FL), 2007.

Joseph Epstein, editor, *Literary Genius: Twenty-five Classic Writers Who Define English and American Literature,* Paul Dry Books (Philadelphia, PA), 2007.

Howard Mansfield, *Hogwood Steps Out,* Roaring Book Press (New York, NY), 2008.

Margie Palatini, *Lousy Rotten Stinkin' Grapes,* Simon & Schuster (New York, NY), expected 2009.

OTHER

The Death of the Narcissus, Castalia Press (Northampton, MA), 1970.

Bacchanalia, Pennyroyal Press (Northampton, MA), 1970.

Cautantowitt's House, Brown University Press (Providence, RI), 1970.

Gaudy Greek, Pennyroyal Press (Northampton, MA), 1976.

Osip Mandelstaum, University of Texas Press (Austin, TX), 1977.

The Pilot, Pennyroyal Press (Northampton, MA), 1978.

Une Encraseuse, 1978.

Bestiare D'Amour: Portfolio, Pennyroyal Press (West Hatfield, MA), 1985.

Also illustrator of *An Alphabet,* and *Liber Occasionum.* Contributor of illustrations to books, including *Visages d'Alice: ou, les illustrateurs d' Alice,* Gallimard (Montreal, Quebec, Canada), 1983; *For Our Children: A Book to Benefit the Pediatric AIDS Foundation,* Disney Press (Burbank, CA), 1991; *Emerson: The Mind on Fire* by Robert D. Richardson, University of California Press,

1995; *Selected Poems* by Herman Melville, Arion Press, 1995; *Once upon a Fairy Tale: Four Favorite Stories Retold by the Stars* (anthology), Penguin Putnam (New York, NY), 2001; and *Tikvah: Children's Book Creators Reflect on Human Rights* (anthology), North-South Books (New York, NY), 2001. Contributor of illustrations to periodicals, including *Audubon, New York Review of Books, New York Times Book Review, Parabola, Publishers Weekly,* and *Yankee.*

Moser's papers are housed at the Thomas J. Dodd Research Center, University of Connecticut, Storrs.

Adaptations

Books of Wonder, an imprint of Morrow, released several of Moser's titles in an e-book format.

Sidelights

Barry Moser, an American artist, writer, and publisher, is acclaimed for his dramatic wood engravings and luminous watercolors, as well as for his unique retellings of classic folk and fairy tales. A prolific illustrator, his artwork has appeared in novels, retellings, professional literature, historical documents, literary criticism, biographies, poetry, and alphabet books, paired with text by well-known writers ranging from Homer and Pliny to Margie Palatini and Cynthia Rylant. Sometimes Moser's book projects stay in the family: he has illustrated texts by daughters Madeline and Cara Moser, and has also created art for picture-books by granddaughter Isabelle Harper and son-in-law Dan Harper. Literary classics also have a great appeal for the illustrator, and his versions of such titles as *Alice's Adventures in Wonderland* and *Through the Looking Glass* by Lewis Carroll; *Frankenstein* by Mary Shelley; *The Wonderful Wizard of Oz* by L. Frank Baum; and the Holy Bible have been credited with breaking free of the influence of each work's original illustrator and reconfirming his own singular style.

Assessing his own career, Moser often describes himself as a "booksmith" who pays careful attention to all aspects of design and production. Viewing each book as a total work of art, he designs the entire volume: cover, typeface, page layout, and illustrations. In some cases he has also assumed the role of author, penning a self-illustrated history of flight, editing collections of short stories for children and young adults, and written several volumes on the art of wood engraving. As a literary stylist, he is noted for his clear, straightforward prose. As an artist, he often creates wood engravings, a method of printmaking where images are carved into wood, to create his works. His watercolors reflect his preference for a dark palette, and his high-contrast pictures, which range from witty and lighthearted to frightening and grotesque, are noted for their realism and their polished, formal style. Writing in *Newsweek,* John Ashbery called Moser's art "never less than dazzling."

Born in Chattanooga, Tennessee, Moser is the son of a professional gambler who died when his son was ten months old and a homemaker who remarried when Moser was two years old. The only books that his family owned were the Bible, the *World Book Encyclopedia,* and the first two volumes of the *Standard American Encyclopedia.* In *Horn Book,* the artist recalled of his childhood: "I . . . had no books to speak of, was not read to insofar as I remember, and did not begin to read *seriously* until, as an adult, I learned how to engrave wood, how to set type, and how to print books." On Saturday afternoons, when he was not at the movies, Moser listened to the Metropolitan Opera on the radio while he built model airplanes. As he later noted, "It is little wonder that words like timbre, rhythm, cadence, pocoissimo, fortissimo, and so forth are frequent terms in my critical vocabulary."

Moser was no fan of school, and as an adult he would learn that he had dyslexia, a condition in which the brain mixes up letters and numbers, thus affecting the ability to read. Turning to drawing rather than reading, he drew cowboys and Indians, ships, Mounties, animals, and airplanes, and also drew and traced photographs and characters from comic books and magazines. He also drew at school, preferring pictures to school work, and quickly earned a reputation as class artist. "As I see it now," he once commented, "I really didn't draw better than the other kids, it was just that they and our teachers thought I could because my subjects were drawn 'realistically.' . . . For me, those praises, erroneous as they may have been, initiated a myth which set the course of my life."

Moser was eventually sent to Baylor Military Academy, on the banks of the Tennessee River, where he spent six years. Still unenthusiastic about reading, he gravitated to biology, a class in which his drawings skills could be utilized. When not in the classroom, Moser played football and was captain of the junior varsity team; he also wrestled and was a shot-putter. Moser reflected of this time that "six years of close order drill instilled in me a need (or love) for discipline, alignment, right angles, symmetry, orderliness, rhythm, and tradition—identifiable and palpable in my work today. The Baylor legacy does not, however, extend to my perception or respect for authority. I am instinctively distrustful of authority of all kinds—religious, political, economic, journalistic, critical, academic, and military."

After graduating from Baylor in 1957, Moser planned to skip college and go to California where he hoped to become an animator for Walt Disney or Warner Brothers. His parents did not share his enthusiasm for a career as a cartoon animator, however, and ultimately Moser enrolled at Atlanta's Auburn University as a student of industrial design. He spent two years at Auburn, taking courses in drawing, perspective, and design. He also learned how to use a printing press.

In 1960, Moser transferred to the University of Chattanooga, where he studied painting under George Cross until a woodcut illustration by artist Leonard Baskin inspired him to turn to engraving. He also attempted two minors, one in biology and the other in pre-ministerial studies. However, his difficulty with the required Latin and Greek, which he took simultaneously, convinced him to switch to a major that had no language requirement: art education. "Little did I know," he once wrote, "that teaching would become one of the loves of my life."

Despite his dyslexia and his struggles with ancient languages, Moser became interested in words and letters. His reading included religious materials like the Bible and this led to literature by writers such as William Faulkner and Albert Camus. At Chattanooga he met Kay Richmond, an artist and fellow student; the couple married in 1962 and had three children, Cara, Ramona, and Madeline, before their divorce in 1977. In 1962, Moser began teaching at another military school, the McCallie School in Chattanooga, to support his family. He taught art, mechanical drawing, and typing, and coached weightlifting and eighth-grade football. In 1967, disenchanted with what he perceived as the region's narrow-mindedness, Moser left the South. He once commented, "Like a latter-day Huck Finn, I lit out for New England with my little family."

The Mosers settled in Easthampton, Massachusetts, where Barry became art instructor at the Williston Academy (now Wiliston-Northampton School). A meeting with Baskin, who also lived in western Massachusetts, led to an introduction to the process of publishing handmade books when he toured Baskin's small publisher, Gehenna Press. When the Academy bought printing and printmaking equipment for his department, Moser taught himself and his students how to set type, run a printing press, and make etchings and wood engravings. He also began graduate work at the University of Massachusetts, although he left after a year because "that I was doing as much teaching as learning." In 1968 Moser co-founded Pennyroyal Press, a publishing company that specializes in producing finely designed and limited edition books; his cofounders were Harold McGrath, a master printer, and Jeff Dwyer. In 1969 the University of Massachusetts Press gave Moser an assignment to illustrate an adult title, *Ely: Too Black, Too White.* The next year, he designed, illustrated, and printed his first book, a new edition of James Abbott McNeil Whistler's essay *The Red Rag,* under the Castalia Press imprint. Although Moser's first books were created for fun, when the Arion Press of San Francisco invited him to illustrate Herman Melville's novel *Moby-Dick; or, The Whale* in 1978, it was an offer Moser considered "the real beginning of my present life in books."

When the University of California Press began reprinting Pennyroyal Press editions of classic works, Moser's accompanying art attained wide critical acclaim. In his rustic woodcut art for *Alice's Adventures in Wonderland* and *Through the Looking Glass, and What Alice Found*

Moser's artwork for **Jump Again!** *brings to life Joel Chandler Harris's stories featuring the wily Brer Rabbit.* (Illustration © 1987 by Barry Moser. Reproduced by permission of Harcourt, Inc. This material may not be reproduced in any form or by any means without the prior written permission of the publisher.)

There Moser views Lewis Carroll's topsy-turvy world directly through the eyes of Alice, a dark-haired girl modeled on Moser's own daughter. Done in a tactile, somewhat rough style, Moser's woodcut illustrations portray Wonderland as a bizarre and even sinister place and depict Alice's world through her own eyes. Writing in *Newsweek* about *Alice's Adventures in Wonderland,* John Ashbery noted that "there have been some far-out visual interpretations of Alice before, but none so convincingly elaborated into a world view where innocence and malignancy are inextricably intertwined." Calling Moser's version "extraordinary," Edward Guiliano predicted in *Fine Print* that the author's "complex vision . . . will speak sharply and eloquently to readers." Assessing Moser's illustrations for both *Through the Looking Glass, and What Alice Found There* and a new edition of Carroll's *The Hunting of the Snark,* a *New York Times Book Review* critic wrote that the books "should delight anyone who loves Carroll, and he could hardly be introduced more elegantly to anyone who does not know him."

As a small boy, Moser enjoyed Walt Disney's animated film *Song of the South.* The film was based on the books of Joel Chandler Harris, a white Southerner who wrote his tales and poems under the guise of African-American slave Uncle Remus. The books and movie feature Brer Rabbit, an irrepressible trickster who always outsmarts those who seek to capture him, such as rascally Brer Fox and Brer Bear. In 1985 he was invited to illustrate an adaptation titled *Jump! The Adventures of Brer Rabbit,* retold by Van Dyke Parks and Malcolm Jones, Jr. After the success of *Jump!,* he illustrated two additional volumes of tales featuring Brer Rabbit: *Jump Again! More Adventures of Brer Rabbit* and *Jump on Over! The Adventures of Brer Rabbit and His Family.* In a review of the latter, *Horn Book* critic Ethel L. Twichell wrote that "the strong characterizations of the animals seems to leap out of the pictures, adding rich drama and playful humor to the endless struggle of Brer Rabbit's wits against the greater strength and size of Brer Fox, Brer Bear, and Brer Wolf." Betsy Hearne, commenting in the *Bulletin of the Center for Children's Books* concluded that "no child can resist such a trickster [as Brer Rabbit], and no adult can resist Moser's sly portraits, with their varied perspectives, uncanny draftsmanship, and sparely detailed southern settings." Moser serves as author and illustrator of three other retellings set in the American South: *Polly Vaughn,* a refashioning of an old English ballad; *Tucker Pfeffercorn: An Old Story Retold,* which refigures the well-known fairy tale of Rumplestiltskin; and *Good and Perfect Gifts: An Illustrated Retelling of O. Henry's "The Gift of the Magi."*

Moser's illustrated retelling *The Three Little Pigs* is based on the classic folktale but includes a new dimension as well. The story is set in the present day, and finds the hungry wolf efficiently disposing of the first two plump pigs before meeting his match when he tries to make a meal of the third. The wolf invites the third little pig on three outings, but gets outsmarted each time; finally, he ends up as the main course of the victorious pig's dinner. Moser's humorous, detailed watercolor illustrations amplify the events of the text while providing examples of the artist's sly wit, such as the third pig using "Wolfe Pruf" cement on the bricks of his house and wearing slippers made of wolf fur after his nemesis gets his comeuppance. In her review of *The Three Little Pigs* for *Horn Book,* Mary M. Burns commented that "Moser has a gift for endowing the commonplace with elegance, the familiar with new perspectives, as he demonstrates in this retelling of a storyteller's staple." Writing in *School Library Journal,* Jody McCoy stated that, "with all the amusing alternatives to the traditional 'Three Little Pigs,' it is somehow satisfying to have a retelling that embraces the best of the classic." Gillian Engberg, writing in *Booklist,* also noted that "the words are satisfying and perfectly paced for reading aloud. But it's the watercolor-and-graphite illustrations that add freshness."

With *Fly! A Brief History of Flight* Moser made his first foray into nonfiction. In this work, which is directed at young adults, the author outlines sixteen pivotal moments in the history of aviation, from the invention of the hot-air balloon to the launching of the space shuttle. The first half of the book follows a traditional picture-book format of brief text and expansive water-color illustrations, while the second half includes expanded notes and a timeline recording concurrent historical and cultural events. Writing in *School Library Journal,* Dorcas Hand noted that "Moser's love of aviation shines through" in the book, and *Booklist* critic Stephanie Zvirin commented that the artist's "impressive paintings . . . show the beauty and variety of the aircraft." As Zvirin added, "Moser's text, though brief, contains enough to pique curiosity, and his pictures are certain to attract browsers."

Working as an editor, Moser compiled and illustrated *Great Ghost Stories,* a collection of thirteen tales directed to young people. Here he includes classic horror stories by authors such as H.P. Lovecraft, Bram Stoker, and Sir Arthur Conan Doyle, as well as some eerie modern tales by writers such as Madeleine L'Engle, James Haskins, and Joyce Carol Oates. Each story in *Great Ghost Stories* is accompanied by a spooky color illustration. He pairs his unique art with short tales in several other collections geared for older, teen readers in *Scary Stories* and *Cowboy Stories.* Featuring twenty tales set in the American West, *Cowboy Stories* was a fun work for Moser as it tapped into childhood memories. As he noted in an interview for the Chronicle Books Web site, "I have always been a fan of Western movies—ever since my childhood days with Hopalong Cassidy, Gene Autry, and Roy Rogers—but had read little Western literature until I undertook this collection. And I have to say that I was quite taken with it. There was a lot more really good writing than I had supposed. And went it came time to do the engravings, I went back to my collection of books on the Western films as my basic source, resulting in what I think of as a personal paean to the genre." Reviewing *Cowboy Stories,* which includes tales by Louis L'Amour, Elmore Leonard, and O. Henry, Ian Chipman wrote in *Booklist* that Moser's "moody, weathered" woodcut illustrations bring to life the stories' "grim-faced" protagonists, "whose cold steel is never far [away and] . . . action coils around every corner." The book's art reflects "the true grit" of the stories' "cowboy subjects and galvanize[s] readers," concluded Patricia Ann Owens in *School Library Journal.*

Throughout his career, Moser has contributed detailed watercolor illustrations as well as textured engraved images to a variety of books by other writers, from humorous, lighthearted picture-book texts to prominent works of literature, some of which feature religious themes. His best-known work in the latter vein, the Pennyroyal Caxton Bible, was published in 1999 and contains over two hundred engravings along with the King James Version of both the Old and New Testaments. Considered a publishing event, the Pennyroyal Caxton Bible was the only Bible issued in the twentieth century that was illustrated by a single artist. Moser spent four years working on the project, designing the volume and creating wood engravings—both decorations and full-page illustrations—for every book of both Testaments. Characteristic of Moser's approach, his

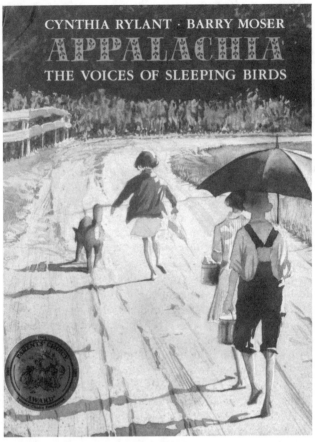

Cover of Cynthia Rylant's evocative picture book **Appalachia: The Voices of Sleeping Birds,** *featuring artwork by Moser.* (Illustration © 1991 by Pennyroyal Press. Reproduced by permission of Harcourt, Inc. This material may not be reproduced in any form or by any means without the prior written permission of the publisher.)

work for the Bible reflect a nontraditional interpretation. For example, he depicts many biblical personages, including Jesus, as looking as if they came from the Middle East rather than from Europe, and his pictures allude to contemporary history such as the suffering of the Jews during the Holocaust. Moser's Bible was first published in a limited edition by Pennyroyal Press; fifty copies of a deluxe edition were priced at fifty thousand dollars, while the 400 copies of the standard edition sold for ten thousand dollars each. The book was also issued in a trade edition by Viking Studio and has since been published in the New Revised Standard Version.

In addition to his work as an author, illustrator, and fine artist, Moser has served on the faculty at the Rhode Island School of Design and at Smith College; he has also been a visiting scholar and a visiting artist at several schools. A strong advocate for quality children's literature, he believes that children's books should hold to high artistic standards. Moser told a *BookPage* online interviewer that he hopes children come away from his books feeling that "they've had a full meal, not just icing and ice cream from a birthday party. When kids sit down at my books, they're sitting down at Thanksgiving dinner." "If there's one thing I have learned from these books and the years it has taken me to do

them, it is that illustrations by themselves do not make handsome books," he wrote in *Children's Books and Their Creators.* "Handsome books are the result of harmony—the arranging and combining of all the various graphic elements in pleasant and interesting ways that ultimately form a whole. The books I make for children, like the books I make for adults, are all done for the same purpose—to make a beautiful book."

Biographical and Critical Sources

BOOKS

Children's Literature Review, Volume 49, Gale (Detroit, MI), 1998, pp. 159-193.

Cummins, Julie, editor, *Children's Book Illustration and Design,* PBC International, 1992.

Silvey, Anita, editor, *Children's Books and Their Creators,* Houghton (Boston, MA), 1995, pp. 469-471.

Something about the Author Autobiography Series, Volume 15, Gale (Detroit, MI), 1993, pp. 235-247.

PERIODICALS

America, October 30, 1999, James Martin, "The Good Book," p. 12.

Booklist, January 1, 1984, Joseph Parisi, review of *Through the Looking-Glass, and What Alice Found There,* p. 666; October, 1991, Carolyn Phelan, review of *The Tinderbox,* p. 438; October 15, 1993, Stephanie Zvirin, review of *Fly! A Brief History of Flight,* p. 438; June 1, 2001, Gillian Engberg, review of *The Three Little Pigs,* p. 1886; February 1, 2004, Hazel Rochman, review of *Hummingbird Nest: A Journal of Poems,* p. 974; March 1, 2005, Hazel Rochman, review of *The Three Silly Billies,* p. 1205; October 1, 2006, Ilene Cooper, review of *Moses,* p. 62; December 1, 2006, John Peters, review of *Scary Stories,* p. 38; September 15, 2007, Ian Chipman, review of *Cowboy Stories,* p. 59; October 1, 2007, Ilene Cooper, review of *The Blessing of the Beasts,* p. 72.

Bulletin of the Center for Children's Books, October, 1989, Betsy Hearne, review of *Jump on Over! The Adventures of Brer Rabbit and His Family,* p. 33; July, 2002, review of *Earthquack!,* p. 414; December, 2003, Elizabeth Bush, review of *Voices of Ancient Egypt,* p. 169; September, 2004, Janice Del Negro, review of *Wee Winnie Witch's Skinny: An Original African-American Scare Tale,* p. 18.

Communication Arts, September-October, 1985, "Barry Moser, Designer, Illustrator, and Publisher."

Cross Currents, spring/summer, 2000, Catherine Madsen, "A Terrible Beauty: Moser's Bible," p. 136.

Fine Print, July, 1982, Edward Guiliano, review of *Alice's Adventures in Wonderland,* pp. 103-106.

Horn Book, March-April, 1990, Ethel L. Twichell, review of *Jump on Over!,* p. 213; January-February, 1992, Barry Moser, "Appalachia: The Front Porch," pp. 28-30; May, 2001, Mary M. Burns, review of *The Three Little Pigs,* p. 340; September-October, 2004, Betsy Hearne, review of *Wee Winnie Witch's Skinny,* p. 567.

Kirkus Reviews, May 1, 2002, review of *Earthquack!,* p. 664; March 1, 2004, review of *Hummingbird Nest,* p. 222; June 1, 2005, review of *The Three Silly Billies,* p. 642; September 1, 2007, review of *Cowboy Stories.*

Newsweek, March 1, 1982, John Ashbery, "A Brilliant New 'Alice,'" pp. 74-75; October 12, 1998, Malcolm Jones, Jr., "Illustrating the Word," p. 62.

New York Times Book Review, November 13, 1983, "Woodcuts from Wonderland," p. 13.

Publishers Weekly, May 6, 2002, review of *Earthquack!,* p. 57; April 5, 1004, review of *Hummingbird Nest,* p. 61; August 9, 2004, review of *Wee Winnie Witch's Skinny,* p. 248.

School Library Journal, October, 1990, Patricia Dooley, review of *The Tinderbox,* p. 113; October, 1993, Dorcas Hand, review of *Fly!,* p. 145; May, 2001, Jody McCoy, review of *The Three Little Pigs,* p. 145; September, 2003, Eve Ortega, review of *Voices of Ancient Egypt,* p. 239; April, 2004, Susan Scheps, review of *Hummingbird Nest,* p. 111; August, 2004, Marianne Saccardi, review of *Wee Winnie Witch's Skinny,* p. 88; December, 2006, Susan Scheps, review of *Moses,* p. 124; January, 2007, Michele Capozzella, review of *Scary Stories,* p. 138; September, 2007, Patricia Ann Owens, review of *Cowboy Stories,* p. 194.

Sojourners, July-August, 2000, Julie Polter, "A Revelation in Black and White," p. 34.

ONLINE

AppLit, http://www.ferrum.edu/ (February 7, 2002), Tina L. Hanlon, "Transplanted in Appalachia: Illustrated Folk Tales by Barry Moser."

Barry Moser Home Page, http://www.moser-pennyroyal.com (December 22, 2007).

Chronicle Books Web site, http://www.chroniclebooks.com (December 17, 2007), "*Cowboy Stories:* A Conversation with Barry Moser."

Cross Currents Web site, http://www.crosscurrents.org/ (summer, 2002), Barry Moser, "Uncomfortable, Uncertain, and Unarmed: When Artists Pray."

Purple Crayon Web site, http://www.underdown.org/ (June 13, 2000), Anna Olswanger, "The Object Is That Bloody Book: A Conversation with Barry Moser."

OTHER

A Thief among the Angels: Barry Moser and the Making of the Pennyroyal Caxton Bible (short film), 2000.

Wood Engraving Workshop (short film), Ritchie Video, 1982.*

MURDOCK, Catherine Gilbert (Catherine Gilbert)

Personal

Married James Murdock; children: two. *Education:* Bryn Mawr College, graduated 1988; University of Pennsylvania, Ph.D.

Addresses

Home—PA. *Agent*—Anderson Grinberg Literary Management, 244 5th Ave., 11th Fl., New York, NY 10001. *E-mail*—catherine_murdock@earthlink.net.

Career

Writer.

Writings

Domesticating Drink: Women, Men, and Alcohol in America, 1870-1940, Johns Hopkins University Press (Baltimore, MD), 1998.

Dairy Queen (young-adult novel), Houghton Mifflin (Boston, MA), 2006.

The Off Season (young-adult novel; sequel to *Dairy Queen*), Houghton Mifflin (Boston, MA), 2007.

Adaptations

Dairy Queen was adapted for audio, read by Natalie Moore, Listening Library, 2006.

Sidelights

Catherine Gilbert Murdock's first foray into fiction was a young-adult novel set in rural Wisconsin. *Dairy Queen* is narrated by fifteen-year-old D.J. Schwenk, the only girl in a household full of boys. Her two older brothers play college football, and her younger brother plays at the local school. The members of D.J.'s family do not convey their feelings easily, and there is an emotional chasm between her father and older brothers, while her younger brother, Curtis, barely speaks to anyone. When her father is injured, D.J. picks up the slack on their farm by milking the cows, baling hay, and shoveling manure. All of these extra chores cut into her basketball-playing and studying time, resulting in lowered grades. D.J. also tutors quarterback Brian Nelson, the privileged and self-centered star of the rival high school football team, at the request of his coach, a family friend. She falls for him, and then decides that she wants to try out for her own team.

Anita L. Burkam wrote in *Horn Book* that D.J. "invites readers into her confidence and then rewards them with an engrossing tale of love, family, and football." A *Publishers Weekly* contributor also enjoyed Murdoch's fiction debut, calling *Dairy Queen* "a football book a girl can love." Murdock continues to explore the lives of D.J. and her peers in the sequel, *The Off Season.*

Biographical and Critical Sources

PERIODICALS

Booklist, April 1, 2006, Jennifer Hubert, review of *Dairy Queen,* p. 150.

Historian, spring, 2001, W.J. Rorabaugh, review of *Domesticating Drink: Women, Men, and Alcohol in America, 1870-1940,* p. 651.

Horn Book, May-June, 2006, Anita L. Burkam, review of *Dairy Queen,* p. 323.

Journal of Social History, summer, 2001, James Kirby Martin, review of *Domesticating Drink,* p. 1006.

Kirkus Reviews, April 15, 2006, review of *Dairy Queen,* p. 412.

Kliatt, May, 2006, Myrna Marler, review of *Dairy Queen,* p. 12.

Publishers Weekly, May 15, 2006, review of *Dairy Queen,* p. 73.

School Library Journal, April, 2006, Amy Pickett, review of *Dairy Queen,* p. 145; June, 2006, Rick Margolis, "Punt, Pass, Moo: In Catherine Gilbert Murdock's *Dairy Queen,* a Farm Gal Tackles a Guys's Game" (interview).

ONLINE

Catherine Gilbert Murdock Home Page, http://www.catherinemurdock.com (December 19, 2006).

Houghton Mifflin Web site, http://www.houghtonmifflinbooks.com/ (December 19, 2006), "About the Author" (profile and interview).

Teenreads.com, http://www.teenreads.com/ (December 19, 2006), Kristi Olson, review of *Dairy Queen,* and interview with Murdock.*

*   *   *

MURPHY, Jim 1947-
(Tim Murphy)

Personal

Born James John Murphy, September 25, 1947, in Newark, NJ; son of James K. (a certified public accountant) and Helen Irene (a bookkeeper and artist) Murphy; married Elaine A. Kelso (a company president), December 12, 1970 (marriage ended); married Allison Blank (a television producer, writer, and editor); children (second marriage): Michael, Benjamin. *Education:* Rutgers University, B.A., 1970; graduate study at Radcliffe College, 1970. *Hobbies and other interests:* Cooking, reading, gardening, collecting old postcards of ships and trains.

Addresses

Home—Upper Montclair, NJ. *E-mail*—jim@jimmurphybooks.com.

Jim Murphy (Reproduced by permission.)

Career

Children's book author. Seabury Press, Inc. (now Clarion Books), New York, NY, 1970-77, began as editorial secretary in juvenile department, became managing editor; freelance writer and editor, 1977—. Worked as a freelance editor for publishers such as Crowell, Crown, Farrar, Straus & Giroux, and Macmillan. Formerly worked in construction in New York and New Jersey.

Member

Asian Night Six Club (founding member).

Awards, Honors

Children's Choice designation, International Reading Association (IRA), and Best Book of the Year designation, *School Library Journal,* both 1979, both for *Weird and Wacky Inventions;* Children's Choice designation, IRA, and Children's Book of the Year designation, Child Study Association, both 1980, both for *Harold Thinks Big;* Best Book for Young Adults designation, American Library Association (ALA), 1982, for *Death Run;* Outstanding Science Trade Book for Children designation, National Science Teachers Association (NSTA)/ Children's Book Council (CBC), 1984, for *Tractors;* Children's Choice designation, IRA, 1988, for *The Last Dinosaur;* Recommended Book for Reluctant Readers, ALA, and International Best Book designation, Society of School Librarians, both 1990, both for *Custom Car;*

Golden Kite Award for nonfiction, Society of Children's Book Writers and Illustrators (SCBWI), 1990, Dorothy Canfield Fisher Book Award nomination, 1991-92, William Allen White Children's Book Award nomination, 1992-93, Children's Book of the Year designation, Bank Street College of Education, and Best Book of the Year designation, *School Library Journal,* all for *The Boys' War;* Nevada Young Readers Award, and Outstanding Science Trade Book for Children, NSTA/CBC, both 1992, both for *The Call of the Wolves;* Pick of the Lists designation, *American Bookseller,* 1992, for *Backyard Bear;* Golden Kite Award for nonfiction, 1992, Editors' Choice designation, *Booklist,* and Best Books of the Year designation, *School Library Journal,* all 1992, all for *The Long Road to Gettysburg;* Orbis Pictus Award, National Council of Teachers of English (NCTE), Jefferson Cup, Virginia Librarians, and Best Books of the Year designation, *School Library Journal,* all 1994, all for *Across America on an Emigrant Train; Boston Globe/Horn Book* Award for nonfiction, 1995, Orbis Pictus Award, Jefferson Cup, and Newbery Medal Honor Book designation, ALA, all 1996, all for *The Great Fire;* Robert F. Sibert Informational Book Award, Association of Library Services to Children, Jefferson Cup Award, and ALA Notable Book and Best Books for Young People designations, all 2000, all for *Blizzard!;* National Book Award finalist, Robert F. Sibert Informational Book Award, ALA Notable Children's Book designation, YALSA Best Book for Young Adults designation, NCTE Orbis Pictus Award, and Newbery Honor designation, all 2004, all for *An American Plague;* ALA Best Book for Young Adults designation, 2004, for *Inside the Alamo;* nominations for several regional awards.

Writings

NONFICTION; FOR CHILDREN AND YOUNG ADULTS

Weird and Wacky Inventions, Crown (New York, NY), 1978.
Two Hundred Years of Bicycles, Harper (New York, NY), 1983.
The Indy 500, Clarion (New York, NY), 1983.
Baseball's All-Time All-Stars, Clarion (New York, NY), 1984.
Tractors: From Yesterday's Steam Wagons to Today's Turbo-charged Giants, Lippincott (Philadelphia, PA), 1984.
The Custom Car Book, Clarion (New York, NY), 1985.
Guess Again: More Weird and Wacky Inventions (sequel to *Weird and Wacky Inventions*), Four Winds Press (New York, NY), 1985.
Napoleon Lajoie: Modern Baseball's First Superstar, Four Winds Press (New York, NY), 1985.
Custom Car: A Nuts-and-Bolts Guide to Creating One, Clarion (New York, NY), 1989.
The Boys' War: Confederate and Union Soldiers Talk about the Civil War, Clarion (New York, NY), 1990.

The Long Road to Gettysburg, Clarion (New York, NY), 1992.
Across America on an Emigrant Train, Clarion (New York, NY), 1993.
Into the Deep Forest with Henry David Thoreau, illustrated by Kate Kiesler, Clarion (New York, NY), 1995.
The Great Fire, Scholastic (New York, NY), 1995.
A Young Patriot: The American Revolution as Experienced by One Boy, Clarion (New York, NY), 1995.
Gone A-Whaling: The Lure of the Sea and the Hunt for the Great Whale, Clarion (New York, NY), 1998.
Pick and Shovel Poet: The Journeys of Pascal D'Angelo, Clarion (New York, NY), 2000.
Blizzard!: The Storm That Changed America, Scholastic (New York, NY), 2000.
An American Plague: The True and Terrifying Story of the Yellow Fever Epidemic of 1793, Clarion (New York, NY), 2003.
Inside the Alamo, Delacorte Press (New York, NY), 2003.
The Real Benedict Arnold, Clarion (New York, NY), 2007.

Contributor of articles to *Cricket* magazine. Some of author's work appears under the name Tim Murphy.

PICTURE BOOKS

Rat's Christmas Party, illustrated by Dick Gackenbach, Prentice-Hall (Englewood Cliffs, NJ), 1979.
Harold Thinks Big, illustrated by Susanna Natti, Crown (New York, NY), 1980.
The Last Dinosaur, illustrated by Mark Alan Weatherby, Scholastic (New York, NY), 1988.
The Call of the Wolves, illustrated by Mark Alan Weatherby, Scholastic (New York, NY), 1989.
Backyard Bear, illustrated by Jeffrey Greene, Scholastic (New York, NY), 1992.
Dinosaur for a Day, illustrated by Mark Alan Weatherby, Scholastic (New York, NY), 1992.
Fergus and the Night-Demon: An Irish Ghost Story, illustrated by John Manders, Clarion Books (New York, NY), 2006.

FICTION; FOR YOUNG ADULTS

Death Run (novel), Clarion (New York, NY), 1982.
Night Terrors (short stories), Scholastic (New York, NY), 1993.
West to a Land of Plenty: The Diary of Teresa Angelino Viscardi, New York to Idaho Territory, 1883 (novel), Scholastic (New York, NY), 1998.
The Journal of James Edmond Pease: A Civil War Union Soldier, Virginia, 1863 (novel), Scholastic (New York, NY), 1998.
My Face to the Wind: The Diary of Sarah Jane Price, a Prairie Teacher (novel), Scholastic (New York, NY), 2001.
The Journal of Brian Doyle: A Greenhorn on an Alaskan Whaling Ship (novel), Scholastic (New York, NY), 2004.
Desperate Journey (novel), Scholastic Press (New York, NY), 2006.

Adaptations

The Great Fire and _The Boys' War_ were released on audio cassette by Recorded Books in 1998 and 1999, respectively.

Sidelights

Called "one of the best writers of nonfiction for young people today" by a reviewer in _Voice of Youth Advocates,_ Jim Murphy writes on a variety of topics, among them sports, transportation, inventions, dinosaurs, animal life, mechanical devices, and historical figures. In addition, he has created picture books such as _Fergus and the Night-Demon: An Irish Ghost Story,_ that appeal to younger children, as well as historical fiction, contemporary realistic fiction, and a collection of horror stories for teen readers. A prolific writer, Murphy is perhaps best known for his books on American military history and natural disasters, including well-received works focusing on the U.S. Civil War, Chicago's Great Fire of 1871, and the blizzard that paralyzed the northeastern United States in 1888.

Murphy has also written several works that draw on autobiographies or journals to create larger perspectives on such topics as the American Revolution, the American West, the immigrant experience, and the impact of industrialization on the environment. These books feature the writings of famous authors such as Robert Louis Stevenson and Henry David Thoreau as well as lesser-known writers such as poet Pascal D'Angelo and teenage soldier Joseph Plumb Martin. Characteristically, Murphy begins by drawing on the diaries, memoirs, journals, and letters of such people, positioning the writer in the events he describes. He embroiders his narrative with fictional details such as thoughts and emotions, descriptions of the physical surroundings, and discussions of the social conditions and prejudices of the time. Pairing these things with Murphy's insightful analyses insights, each work brings to life a particular moment in history wherein ordinary people were involved in dramatic events. Murphy also frequently includes eyewitness accounts by young people, demonstrating that children have made valuable contributions to history. Photographs, lithographs, engravings, and other archival materials as well as original art illustrate these titles. As a _St. James Guide to Children's Writers_ essayist noted, in his book for young readers Murphy "has consistently made fact more interesting than any fiction."

Born in Newark, New Jersey, Murphy was raised in the nearby suburb of Kearny, where "my friends and I did all the normal things—played baseball and football endlessly, explored abandoned factories, walked the railroad tracks to the vast Jersey Meadowlands, and, in general, cooked up as much mischief as we could." Murphy and his friends also enjoyed exploring Newark and New York City, both of which were close by, and playing games of "let's pretend."

Murphy was an indifferent reader as a boy, partially because he had an eye condition that went undiagnosed until he was nine or ten. He once commented, "I hardly cracked open a book willingly until a high school teacher announced that we could 'absolutely, positively _not_ read' Hemingway's _A Farewell to Arms._ I promptly read it, and every other book I could get ahold of that I felt would shock my teacher. I also began writing, mostly poetry, but with an occasional story or play tossed in there." Murphy became a voracious reader, moving from historical fiction and mysteries to poetry to books about medicine or history as his interests shifted during middle school.

In college, Murphy's interests centered on history, English, geology, art history, and track. After graduating from Rutgers, he briefly attended graduate school, then returned home and worked at a variety of construction jobs. At the same time, he was looking for a job in publishing, especially in the area of children's books. After thirty or forty interviews, he was hired as a secretarial assistant by the Seabury Press (now Clarion Books), where he learned about all stages of book writing and production. After rising to the position of managing editor at Clarion, Murphy realized that he wanted to write his own books. In 1977, he left Clarion to become a freelance writer.

In Murphy's first published book, 1978's _Weird and Wacky Inventions,_ he mined the files of the U.S. Patent Office to present young readers with a selection of the often-bizarre gadgets and contraptions that have been registered since the 1700s. The inventions include such creations as a dimple-maker, a bird diaper, an automatic hat-tipper, a portable fire escape, a portable bathtub, jumping shoes, and the safety pin. Together with a reproduction of the picture that originally accompanied each invention, Murphy asks readers to guess its use; the answer and a further explanation are given on the following page. Final chapters discuss how one invention leads to another and detail the process of getting a patent. A reviewer in _Publishers Weekly_ wrote that "the reaction of kids to an aptly named book will range from smiles to giggles to guffaws," and Barbara Elleman, writing in _Booklist,_ called _Weird and Wacky Inventions_ "a browser's delight." Continuing the theme, _Guess Again: More Weird and Wacky Inventions_ uses a similar format to introduce readers to a coffin with an escape hatch, a trap for tapeworms, and training pants for dogs. A critic for _Publishers Weekly_ dubbed _Guess Again_ "just as wacky as its predecessor," and in _Appraisal_ Arrolyn H. Vernon concluded that Murphy's book "should be fun for those who enjoy the cryptic, especially when imaginative visualization is exercised."

On of Murphy's first books geared for young children, _The Last Dinosaur_ is a fact-based fictional speculation on the passing of the age of dinosaurs. Set sixty-five million years ago, the book features paintings by Mark Alan Weatherby. In the book, a female Triceratops is left alone when the only males in her herd are killed in a fight with a T-Rex. After she abandons her nest to escape a forest fire, her eggs are eaten by some small shrewlike mammals. On the last page, the triceratops pads away, in search of food and perhaps another herd. Another collaboration with Weatherby, *Dinosaur for a Day,* follows a mother hypsilophodon and her eight children on their search for food. When the family encounters a deinonychus pack that charges their clearing, the mother must outrun the carnivores and divert them from her babies. Janet Hickman, writing in *Language Arts,* called *The Last Dinosaur* "surprisingly poignant," adding that "it's quite an accomplishment to make a sixty-five-million-year-old setting seem immediate." Hickman deemed Murphy's book "a welcome companion for . . . informational books that examine possible reasons for the dinosaurs' extinction," and *Bulletin of the Center for Children's Books* contributor Betsy Hearne concluded that "the scenario certainly renders the end of the Age of Dinosaurs more immediate than many nonfiction accounts." *Dinosaur for a Day* prompted Nicholas Hotton III to write in *Science Books & Films* that "this very attractive book is simple in concept, well executed, and gorgeously illustrated."

Weatherby also provided the illustrations for *The Call of the Wolves.* Here Murphy's story follows a young wolf that becomes separated from its pack while hunting for caribou in the Arctic. Trapped by illegal hunters who shoot at it from a plane, the wolf plunges over a cliff, injuring its leg. A painful and dangerous journey through a snowstorm through another pack's territory follows as the injured creature makes its way home. Hearne noted of *The Call of the Wolves* that, "with an involving text and arresting art, this is a nature narrative that commands attention without ever becoming sentimental or anthropomorphic." A critic in *Kirkus Reviews* dubbed Murphy's book an "effective plea for respect for and conservation of an often misunderstood fellow creature."

Nineteenth-century history and the U.S. Civil War have yielded a wealth of book ideas for Murphy. One of his most highly praised works, *The Boys' War: Confederate and Union Soldiers Talk about the Civil War,* incorporates eyewitness accounts by soldiers aged twelve to sixteen, a group that made up as much as twenty percent of the total number of enlisted men, to present a unique view of the War between the States. Inspiration for the book came from the journal of a fifteen-year-old Union soldier that Murphy found in a library. The book covers battles, living conditions, imprisonment, suffering and death, the mixed emotions brought on by returning home following war, and the psychological effects of war on these young people. Writing in *Voice of Youth Advocates,* Joanne Johnson stated that "the excerpts from the diaries and letters written home by this group of young men" make the Civil War "come alive in a way that the diaries and letters of adults may not." Margaret A. Bush, writing in *Horn Book,* noted that "it is startling to learn of the large numbers of very young soldiers whose lives were given to the war, and this

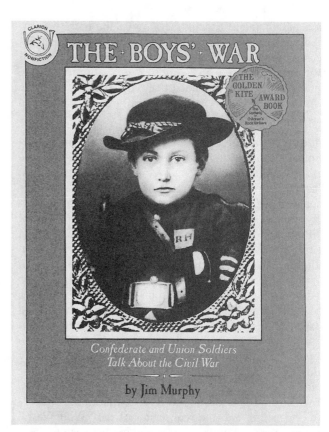

Cover of Murphy's Civil War history The Boys' War, *which profiles the young Americans from both North and South who joined the military in defense of their homeland.* (Illustration © 1990 by Jim Murphy. Reprinted by permission of Clarion Books, an imprint of Houghton Mifflin Company. All rights reserved.)

well-researched and readable account provides fresh insight into the human cost of a pivotal event in United States history." A *St. James Guide to Children's Literature* essayist observed that, with *The Boys' War,* the author's mix of primary sources and a compelling, informative text has become characteristic of the author, marking "Murphy's most important contribution to children's and young adult literature."

Murphy also focuses on the U.S. Civil War in *The Long Road to Gettysburg,* which features excerpts from the journals of nineteen-year-old Confederate lieutenant John Dooley and seventeen-year-old Union corporal Thomas Galway, who were involved in one of the war's most pivotal battles. Beginning and ending with the dedication ceremony at which President Abraham Lincoln delivered his famous address at Gettysburg, Pennsylvania, Murphy recounts the battle from the point of view of both young men. The book's text does not spare readers the grim details of the battle; in his epilogue, the author outlines the postwar lives of Dooley and Galway. Writing in *Horn Book,* Anita Silvey commented that *The Long Road to Gettysburg* draws on Murphy's "fine skills as an information writer—clarity of detail, conciseness, understanding of his age group, and ability to find the drama appealing to readers—to frame a well-crafted account of a single battle in the war." Carolyn Phelan, writing in *Booklist,* maintained that the inclusion of "firsthand accounts . . . give the narrative immediacy and personalize the horrors of battle," and described the book as "an important addition to the Civil War shelf." Writing in *School Library Journal,* Elizabeth M. Reardon concluded that, "by focusing on these two ordinary soldiers, readers get a new perspective on this decisive and bloody battle."

Murphy turns to an interesting facet of nineteenth-century history in *Across America on an Emigrant Train,* an informational books directed to young adults. The1879 journey of twenty-nine-year-old Scottish author Robert Louis Stevenson is the basis by which Murphy explores the development of the transcontinental railroad and the growth of the westward movement in the 1800s. Stevenson traveled by boat and train from Edinburgh, Scotland, to Monterey, California, to visit his friend Fanny Osbourne, an American woman who had become gravely ill with brain fever. On his journey, the writer traveled with other newcomers to the United States, immigrants who faced cramped, unsanitary conditions on the train but were nonetheless filled with hope. While quoting Stevenson's point of view, Murphy adds historical context and discusses topics such as the roles of various ethnic groups in building the railroads, how the railroads destroyed forever traditional Native-American life, and the real nature of the "Wild West." He ends the book with a joyful reunion between Stevenson and Osbourne, who recovered from her illness and eventually became his wife; an epilogue summarizes Stevenson's subsequent rise to fame and brief last years. Noting Murphy's "delightfully effective narrative device," a *Kirkus Reviews* critic called *Across America on an Emigrant Train* a "fascinating, imaginatively structured account that brings the experience vividly to life in all its details; history at its best." In *School Library Journal,* Diane S. Marton called the book "a readable and valuable contribution to literature concerning expansion into the American West." *Booklist* contributor Hazel Rochman stated that the facts and feelings Murphy represents "tell a compelling story of adventure and failure, courage and cruelty, enrichment and oppression" and "revitalizes the myths of the West."

In 1871, the city of Chicago was devastated by a conflagration that killed 300 people and destroyed 17,500 buildings. In *The Great Fire* Murphy explores the causes and effects of this disaster, one of the most extensive in American history. Combining details of the fire and its damage with personal anecdotes from newspaper accounts and quotes from historians and commentators, Murphy suggests that the fire could have been contained. He also argues that factors such as architectural and human errors, the dry weather, the high winds, and the city fire brigade's lack of organization contributed to the ultimate tragedy. The author also notes the discrimination that surfaced as a result of the blaze. Rich residents, many of whom lost their homes, were quick to blame the city's poor immigrant population for the fire; as a result, the poor were forced into slums or out of Chicago permanently. Writing in the *Bulletin of the*

Center for Children's Books, Elizabeth Bush noted that Murphy's account "offers not only the luridly enticing details disaster junkies crave, but also a more complex analysis . . . than is usually offered in children's history books." Frances Bradburn also praised the work in *Booklist,* calling Murphy's text "dramatic" and "riveting" before concluding that *The Great Fire* "will automatically draw readers with its fiery cover and illustrations of disasters." Writing in *School Library Journal,* Susannah Price added that the book "reads like an adventure/survival novel and is just as hard to put down"; in fact, according to Price, *The Great Fire* is "history writing as its best."

With *Blizzard!: The Storm That Changed America* Murphy gives an account of the snowstorm that hit the northeastern United States in March of 1888. Drawing on newspaper articles, letters, journals, and histories of the period, he describes the freak blizzard from the perspectives of people of various ages and social positions, some of whom survived the storm and others who did not. He also discusses the political and social conditions of the time and outlines how life in the United States was changed following the storm: for example, the effects of the blizzard led to the founding of the U.S. Weather Bureau and to the development of subways in New York City. Writing in *Booklist,* Jean Franklin called *Blizzard!* "an example of stellar nonfiction," and in *Children's Literature Review* a critic wrote that

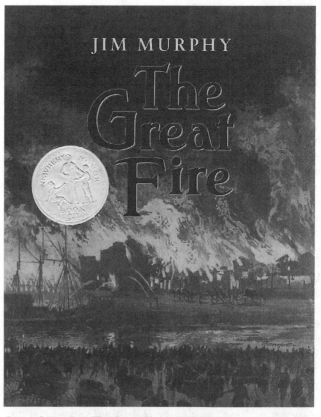

Cover of Murphy's **The Great Fire,** *which features a painting of the San Francisco Fire by John Thompson,* (Illustration © 1995 by John Thompson. Reproduced by permission of Scholastic, Inc.)

Murphy's "clear and even-handed approach to describing the details makes this a page-turner." Writing in *School Library Journal,* Andrew Medlar concluded by calling *Blizzard!* "a superb piece of writing and history."

Moving half a century back in time, to February of 1836, *Inside the Alamo* benefits from the "thorough research and solid narrative style" that *Booklist* reviewer Kay Weisman cited as characteristic of Murphy. Here readers are transported to the rustic mission at San Antonio de Bexar, where a group of less than 200 Texans led by Lieutenant Colonel William Travis and including Jim Bowie and Davie Crockett held off a Mexican military force led by General Antonio Lopez de Santa Ana for thirteen days before being overrun. Murphy discusses the complex political changes that precipitated this stand-off, an event that took place on Mexican soil as part of the Texas War for Independence. Noting the myths and legends that have grown up around this historic event, Weisman noted that Murphy takes care to address such elements, "allowing readers to judge where the truth may lie and giving them insight into how historical research works." A *Publishers Weekly* contributor commended Murphy for "ably captur[ing] . . . the mood of suspense" that existed up to the Mexican Army's attack, and providing "a compelling behind-the-scenes look at the defeat that, ironically, helped create the state of Texas." "This is history writing at its finest," proclaimed a *Kirkus Reviews* writer of *Inside the Alamo,* the critic citing the book's "lively prose, sidebars, profiles of key players," and "abundance" of photographs, paintings, and other visual images.

Murphy moves still earlier in history in *A Young Patriot: The American Revolution as Experienced by One Boy* and *An American Plague: The True and Terrifying Story of the Yellow Fever Epidemic of 1793.* When yellow fever overran Philadelphia in 1793, the disease killed thousands and caused a mass exodus from that city. With little knowledge of the disease—which is in fact carried by mosquitoes—and fearing its spread, the governments of surrounding states ordered their militias to prevent the city's frightened residents to enter their own borders. In *An American Plague* Murphy places the Philadelphia crisis within the context of its age, and discusses the sometimes humorous ways people attempted to guard against the disease as well as the way both people and governments responded to the catastrophic illness and resulting hysteria. Calling the book "a mesmerizing, macabre account that will make readers happy they live in the 21st century," a *Kirkus Reviews* writer added that Murphy also introduces many of the individuals who played an important part in dealing with the tragedy, and his assessment of the contemporary accounts upon which he draws present readers with "a valuable lesson in reading and writing history."

Murphy's first novel for young adults, *Death Run,* was published in 1982. The story, which has a contemporary setting and is told from different points of view, out-

Murphy includes a wealth of original accounts and illustrations in A Young Patriot, *among them an engraving of General George Washington by noted American illustrator Howard Pyle.* (George Washington, mounted on white horse, July 9, 1776. Illustration from *Harper's* magazine.)

lines how sophomore Brian Halihan, hanging out in the park with three older schoolmates, is involved in the death of star basketball player Bill Jankowski. When the boys see Bill coming through the park with his basketball, they tease and taunt him; gang leader Roger then slams Bill's basketball against his face, knocking him down. Bill has an epileptic seizure, then a burst aneurysm. Brian wants to report the incident, but is talked out of doing so by Roger. Brian becomes obsessed with Bill's death and begins hanging around the dead boy's home. Meanwhile, a detective suspects that Bill's death was not an accident. Writing in the *ALAN Review,* Tony Manna noted that "the psychology of detection and the anatomy of fear . . . makes Murphy's first novel such an enticing read. Despite his inclination to tell more than he shows, Murphy is a master at creating tension and sustaining the complex emotions of the hunter and the hunted." Stephanie Zvirin, reviewing *Death Run* for *Booklist,* concluded that "few stories of this genre are written specifically for a teenage audience, and Murphy handles his competently, keeping a firm hold on tough talk, including plenty of fast-action sequences, and providing just enough character motivation to fill out the plot."

Moving to historical fiction, Murphy often draws on the same themes that he deals with in his nonfiction writing. Set in the late 1840s, *Desperate Journey* focuses on a family who works a boat along the Erie Canal in upstate New York. Taking place later in the century, *West to a Land of Plenty: The Diary of Teresa Angelino Viscardi, New York to Idaho Territory, 1883* is one of several books Murphy has contributed to the "My Name Is America" series. *West to a Land of Plenty* describes how a family of Italian immigrants journeys to the northwest territory by train and covered wagon. Written in the form of diary entries by fourteen-year-old Teresa and her younger sister Netta, the novel outlines the family's experiences as they go west to settle in an Idaho town optimistically called Opportunity. Teresa, the main narrator, describes how her family survived the arduous journey, which includes sickness, danger, and, for Netta, even death. Throughout her narrative, Teresa grows: she has her first romance and also shows courage and presence of mind when she saves her grandmother from thieves. In an epilogue dated 1952, Teresa speaks of her happiness with her life, addressing herself to her late sister. Janet Gillen, writing in *School Library Journal,* noted of Teresa that, "reminiscent of a Willa Cather heroine," Murphy's protagonist "is resourceful, strong-minded, and intelligent." For Bush, reviewing *West to a Land of Plenty* for the *Bulletin of the Center for Children's Books,* "what could have been merely another overland trail story is considerably enriched by Murphy's attention to the rapid and profound Americanization of these fictional Italian immigrants."

Murphy continues his diary approach in *The Journal of James Edward Pease: A Civil War Union Soldier, Virginia, 1863,* which finds a sixteen-year-old private serving in the New York Volunteers considered to be the "Jonah," or bad-luck charm, of his outfit. Assigned, nonetheless, to be the historian of his company, James describes infantry life, the horrors of battle and of the medical practices of the period, and his own thoughts and emotions. He loses several friends to death and desertion. When he is lost behind enemy lines, James is hidden from Confederate soldiers by a slave family whom he has befriended. Throughout the course of the novel, the young man matures, learns the meaning of friendship, and receives a promotion for doing a good job. Writing in *Catholic Library World,* Carol L. Kennedy called *The Journal of James Edmond Pease* an "excellent piece of historical fiction." In *Booklist,* Roger Leslie concluded that, despite ambiguities, the diary-like text "is very well written, and Pease's unassuming personality keeps him a vivid, accessible narrator throughout." Other contributions to the "My Name Is America" series include *My Face to the Wind: The Diary of Sarah Jane Price, a Prairie Teacher* and *The Journal of Brian Doyle: A Greenhorn on an Alaskan Whaling Ship.*

In assessing his career, Murphy once wrote, "The nonfiction projects let me research subjects that I'm really interested in; they provide an opportunity to tell kids some unusual bits of information. The fiction lets me get out some of the thoughts and opinions that rattle around in my head." "I view research as a kind of detective work where I try to discover all of the secrets about any subject," he commented on the Scholastic Web site." "I really enjoy taking topics that might seem commonplace or like they've been done before and finding new ways to tell the story of the event," he added. "I do it specifically for young readers because I hope that in some way my enthusiasm will get them to read more about the subject." "Life is made up of many kinds of journeys," he concluded in his online commentary. "Some are physical, like moving from one home to another, but most are interior journeys of the heart or soul. The important thing is to face each with a positive attitude. And to try and learn as much about yourself and other as you can along the way. Oh, yes—and to have fun while you are experiencing all of these things."

Biographical and Critical Sources

BOOKS

Beacham's Guide to Literature for Young Adults, Volume 10, Gale (Detroit, MI), 2000.
Children's Literature Review, Volume 53, Gale (Detroit, MI), 1999.
Roberts, Patricia, *Taking Humor Seriously in Children's Literature,* Scarecrow Press (Metuchen, NJ), 1997.
St. James Guide to Children's Writers, 5th edition, St. James Press (Detroit, MI), 1999.

PERIODICALS

ALAN Review, fall, 1982, Tony Manna, review of *Death Run,* p. 21.
Appraisal, winter, 1987, Arrolyn H. Vernon, review of *Guess Again: More Weird and Wacky Inventions,* pp. 48-49.
Booklist, September 1, 1978, Barbara Elleman, review of *Weird and Wacky Inventions,* p. 52; May 1, 1982, Stephanie Zvirin, review of *Death Run,* p. 1153; May 15, 1992, Carolyn Phelan, review of *The Long Road to Gettysburg,* p. 1677; Hazel Rochman, review of *Across America on an Emigrant Train;* June 1, 1995, Frances Bradburn, review of *The Great Fire,* p. 1757; November 15, 1998, Roger Leslie, review of *The Journal of James Edmond Pease: A Civil War Union Soldier,* p. 581; February 15, 2001, Jean Franklin, review of *Blizzard!: The Storm That Changed America,* p. 1135; March 14, 2003, Kay Weisman, review of *Inside the Alamo,* p. 1323; September 1, 2006, Abby Nolan, review of *Fergus and the Night-Demon: An Irish Ghost Story,* p. 138.
Bulletin of the Center for Children's Books, June, 1988, Betsy Hearne, review of *The Last Dinosaur,* p. 213; September, 1989, Betsy Hearne, review of *The Call of the Wolves,* p. 13; May, 1995, Elizabeth Bush, review of *The Great Fire,* pp. 297-298; March, 1998, Elizabeth Bush, review of *West to a Land of Plenty: The*

Diary of Teresa Angelino Viscardi, p. 253; December, 2000, review of *Pick and Shovel Poet: The Journeys of Pascal D'Angelo,* p. 156; January, 2001, review of *Blizzard!,* p. 190; September, 2003, Elizabeth Bush, review of *Inside the Alamo,* p. 25.

Catholic Library World, June, 1999, Carol L. Kennedy, review of *The Journal of James Edmond Pease,* p. 64.

Horn Book, January-February, 1991, Margaret A. Bush, review of *The Boys' War: Confederate and Union Soldiers Talk about the Civil War,* pp. 86-87; July-August, 1992, Anita Silvey, review of *The Long Road to Gettysburg,* pp. 469-470; November, 1998, Kristi Beavin, review of *The Great Fire,* p. 768; January, 2001, reviews of *Blizzard!,* p. 113, and *Pick and Shovel Poet,* p. 114; July-August, 2003, Betty Carter, review of *Inside the Alamo,* p. 484.

Kirkus Reviews, November 15, 1989, review of *The Call of the Wolves,* p. 1674; November 15, 1993, review of *Across America on an Emigrant Train,* p. 1465; October 15, 2001, review of *My Face to the Wind: The Diary of Sarah Jane Price, a Prairie Teacher,* p. 1489; March 1, 2003, review of *Inside the Alamo,* p. 393; April 1, 2003, review of *An American Plague: The True and Terrifying Story of the Yellow Fever Epidemic of 1793,* p. 538; September 1, 2006, reviews of *Fergus and the Night-Demon,* p. 909, and *Desperate Journey,* p. 910; September 1, 2007, review of *The Real Benedict Arnold.*

Language Arts, September, 1988, Janet Hickman, review of *The Last Dinosaur,* p. 500.

Publishers Weekly, July 17, 1978, review of *Weird and Wacky Inventions,* p. 168; June 27, 1986, review of *Guess Again,* p. 97; January 25, 1993, review of *Backyard Bear,* p. 87; March 13, 1995, review of *Into the Deep Forest with Henry David Thoreau,* p. 69; May 8, 1995, review of *The Great Fire,* p. 297; December 9, 1996, review of *My Dinosaur,* p. 67; March 10, 2003, review of *Inside the Alamo,* p. 73; October 9, 2006, review of *Fergus and the Night-Demon,* p. 56; November 5, 2007, review of *The Real Benedict Arnold,* p. 66.

School Library Journal, November, 1978, Robert Unsworth, review of *Weird and Wacky Inventions,* p. 66; June, 1992, Elizabeth M. Reardon, review of *The Long Road to Gettysburg,* p. 146; December, 1993, Diane S. Marton, review of *Across America on an Emigrant Train,* pp. 129-130; July, 1995, Susannah Price, review of *The Great Fire,* pp. 89-90; Janet Gillen, review of *West to a Land of Plenty;* December, 2000, Andrew Medlar, review of *Blizzard!,* p. 164; December, 2001, Lana Miles, review of *My Face to the Wind,* p. 139; April, 2003, Diane S. Marton, review of *Pick and Shovel Poet,* p. 105; May, 2004, Shelley B. Sutherland, review of *The Journey of Brian Doyle: A Greenhorn on an Alaskan Whaling Ship,* p. 154; September, 2004, David Bilmes, review of *An American Plague,* p. 82; August, 2005, Blair Christolon, review of *Inside the Alamo,* p. 49; August, 2006, Kirsten Cutler, review of *Fergus and the Night-Demon,* p. 94; November, 2006, Adrienne Furness, review of *Desperate Journey,* p. 142.

Science Books & Films, August-September, 1993, Nicholas Hotton III, review of *Dinosaur for a Day,* p. 180.

Voice of Youth Advocates, April, 1991, Joanne Johnson, review of *The Boys' War,* p. 60; June, 1996, review of *The Great Fire,* p. 88.

ONLINE

Jim Murphy Home Page, http://www.jimmurphybooks.com (December 15, 2007).

Scholastic Web site, http://teacher.scholastic.com/ (April 20, 2001), interview with Murphy.*

* * *

MURPHY, Tim
See MURPHY, Jim

O-P

OWEN, James A.

Personal

Born November 11; married; wife's name Cindy; children: Sophie, Nathaniel.

Addresses

Home—Silvertown, AZ. *Office*—Coppervale International, 313 E. Center St., P.O. Box 1459, Taylor, AZ 85939; fax: 928-536-4293. *E-mail*—coppervale@frontiernet.net.

Career

Author, illustrator, storyteller, designer, and publisher. Founder of comic book mail order company, 1984; founder of publishing company specializing in limited-edition prints, 1985; freelance designer and commercial illustrator, until 1992; Taliesin Press, Taylor, AZ, founder and executive director, 1992, renamed Coppervale International (art and design studio), 1995—, publisher of *International Studio*, 1999—, and *Argosy Quarterly;* Coppervale Filmworks, founder, beginning 2001.

Awards, Honors

Named among one hundred most influential people in the comic-book industry, *Hero Illustrated*, 1994, 1995; Chesley Award nomination for best monochrome work, Association of Science Fiction & Fantasy Artists, 2003, for *Old Tom's Study;* AI award for Best Novel, 2003, and Phantastik Preis nomination for Best International Novel, both for first book in "Mythworld" series; Chesley Award nominations for best hardcover illustration and for best interior illustration, Association of Science Fiction & Fantasy Artists, 2007, and Best Books for Young Adults selection, American Library Association, all for *Here, There Be Dragons.*

Writings

"CHRONICLES OF THE IMAGINARIUM GEOGRAPHICA" SERIES

(Self-illustrated) *Here, There Be Dragons,* Simon & Schuster Books for Young Readers (New York, NY), 2006.
(Self-illustrated) *The Search for the Red Dragon,* Simon & Schuster Books for Young Readers (New York, NY), 2007.

OTHER

(With Jeremy Owen, Lon Saline, and Mary McCray; and illustrator) *Lost Treasures of the Pirates of the Caribbean,* Simon & Schuster Books for Young Readers (New York, NY), 2007.

Author and illustrator of "Starchild" and "Obscuro" comic-book series. Also author of "Mythworld" novel series, published in Germany and France. Author of *James A. Owen's Sketchbook & Journal,* located at http://coppervale.livejournal.com.

Sidelights

James A. Owen, an acclaimed illustrator and storyteller, is the founder and executive director of Coppervale International, an art and design studio housed in a century-old restored church in Arizona. As an author, Owen has written and illustrated more than twenty installments in the "Starchild" comic-book series and has penned the seven-volume "Mythworld" novel series. Other works include the novel *Here, There Be Dragons,* one of several volumes in his "Chronicles of the Imaginarium Geographica" series of fantasy novels for young adults.

Owen developed an early interest in literature and began writing and drawing comics at age six. "My mother painted, and also taught first grade," he told *One Ring* online interviewer Jonathan Watson. "Her brothers and sister were a painter, printer, and graphic designer, respectively. And their father was an English teacher (among many other things). So I have it in the blood to love art, and books." Owen, an avid reader, was particularly influenced by the work of one particular writer, as he recalled to a contributor in *Pink Raygun.* "I loved Ray Bradbury and the way he wrote about evoking the magic of childhood." "These things that I loved when I was a kid," he added, "I surround myself with in my studio, and fantasy was a big part of it."

Owen started his first business venture, a comic-book mail-order company, in 1984, and founded Taliesin Press, the forerunner to Coppervale International, founded eight years later. His first work, the comic-book series "Starchild," sold sporadically; remarkably, after Owen broke his hand in a devastating car accident and was forced to turn to more established artists for help, the comic established a foothold in the marketplace. Owen later secured the rights to *International Studio,* an arts periodical, and also began publishing *Argosy Quarterly,* a magazine of literary fiction. He later completed the seven-volume "Mythworld" series, which has been published in Europe.

In 2006 Owen published *Here, There Be Dragons,* the first novel in his "Chronicles of the Imaginarium Geographica." "The core inspiration for all of my work is the question 'What If?'" he told Watson. "I like to find those gaps in history, where what-ifs could have occurred. That's where great stories can be found. And my what-if here had to do with lost books—specifically lost atlases. What if early on in cartography, someone mapped an undiscovered land, then lost the atlas, then never went back? And what if someone FOUND that atlas, which detailed a map to a place that no other evidence on earth could prove to exist? Thus was born the Imaginarium Geographica."

Set in 1917, the self-illustrated work concerns three strangers—John, Jack, and Charles—who are given possession of the Imaginarium Geographica, an atlas of the imaginary lands from legend, myth, and fable. The trio journeys to the Archipelago of Dreams, where the forces of the Winter King threaten Arthur Pendragon's throne. The caretakers of the atlas are later revealed to be authors J.R.R. Tolkien, C.S. Lewis, and Charles Williams; according to *School Library Journal* contributor Kathleen Isaacs, readers "with extensive reading background in both fantasies and mythology may be keen to identify the allusions" in the novel. Krista Hutley, writing in *Booklist,* offered praise for Owen's artwork, stating that his "amazingly detailed pen-and-ink illustrations, dark and atmospheric, lend a real storybook flavor."

The Search for the Red Dragon, the sequel to *Here, There Be Dragons,* takes place nine years after its predecessor. John, Jack, and Charles learn that someone is kidnaping children from the Archipelago of Dreams, and their investigation leads them to the Red Dragon, the last of the fabled Dragonships.

Though Owen strives to create entertaining comics and novels, he believes his works should serve a greater purpose. As he remarked to Watson, "I make the point that our stories are what define us as families, and communities, and cultures. And it is in sharing those stories that we come to understand other families, and communities, and cultures. And how can we do that, truly, if the stories we share do not contain at some level, the values that we hold and hope to preserve?"

Biographical and Critical Sources

PERIODICALS

Booklist, December 15, 2006, Krista Hutley, review of *Here, There Be Dragons,* p. 43.
Kliatt, September, 2006, Deirdre Root, review of *Here, There Be Dragons,* p. 16.
Publishers Weekly, October 16, 2006, review of *Here, There Be Dragons,* p. 54.
School Library Journal, November, 2006, Kathleen Isaacs, review of *Here, There Be Dragons,* p. 144.
Voice of Youth Advocates, December, 2006, Rachelle Bilz, review of *Here, There Be Dragons,* p. 448.

ONLINE

Coppervale International Web site, http://www.coppervaleinternational.com/ (November 20, 2007), "James A. Owen."
Here, There Be Dragons Web site, http://www.heretherebedragons.net/ (November 20, 2007), "James A. Owen."
One Ring Web site, http://www.theonering.com/ (October 25, 2006), Jonathan Watson, interview with Owen.
Pink Raygun Web site, http://www.pinkraygun.com/ (June 27, 2007), two-part interview with Owen.
Simon & Schuster Web site, http://www.simonsays.com/ (November 20, 2007), "James A. Owen."

*   *   *

OWENS, Dana Elaine
See QUEEN LATIFAH

*   *   *

PAPARONE, Pam
(Pamela Paparone)

Personal
Female.

Addresses
Home—Philadelphia, PA.

Career

Illustrator and graphic artist.

Writings

SELF-ILLUSTRATED

Who Built the Ark?: Based on an African-American Spiritual, Simon & Schuster Books for Young Readers (New York, NY), 1994.

(Under name Pamela Paparone) *Five Little Ducks: An Old Rhyme,* North-South Books (New York, NY), 1995.

Down by the Station, HarperFestival (New York, NY), 2002.

ILLUSTRATOR

(Under name Pamela Paparone) Patrick J. Lewis, *Two-Legged, Four-Legged, No-Legged Rhymes,* Knopf (New York, NY), 1991.

Norma Simon, *Fire Fighters,* Simon & Schuster Books for Young Readers (New York, NY), 1995.

(Under name Pamela Paparone) Reeve Lindbergh, *Nobody Owns the Sky: The Story of "Brave Bessie" Coleman,* Candlewick Press (Cambridge, MA), 1996.

(Under name Pamela Paparone) Claire Masurel, *Ten Dogs in the Window: A Countdown Book,* North-South Books (New York, NY), 1997.

(Under name Pamela Paparone) Nola Buck, *How a Baby Grows,* HarperFestival (New York, NY), 1998.

(Under name Pamela Paparone) Charlotte Zolotow, *Wake up and Goodnight,* HarperCollins (New York, NY), 1998.

(Under name Pamela Paparone) Carol Roth, *Ten Dirty Pigs: Ten Clean Pigs,* North-South Books (New York, NY), 1999.

Barbara Shook Hazen, *City Cats, Country Cats,* Golden Books (New York, NY), 1999.

Mary Louise Cuneo, *Mail for Husher Town,* Greenwillow Books (New York, NY), 2000.

Eve Merriam, *Low Song,* Margaret K. McElderry Books (New York, NY), 2001.

(Under name Pamela Paparone) Carol Roth, *The Little School Bus,* North-South Books (New York, NY), 2002.

(Under name Pamela Paparone) Shana Corey, *Ballerina Bear,* Random House (New York, NY), 2002.

(Under name Pamela Paparone) Patricia Hubbell, *I Like Cats,* North-South Books (New York, NY), 2003.

Wendy Cheyette Lewison, *Raindrop, Plop!,* Viking (New York, NY), 2004.

(Under name Pamela Paparone) Kristi T. Butler, *A Big Surprise,* Harcourt (Orlando, FL), 2005.

Amy E. Sklansky, *Where Do Chicks Come From?,* HarperCollins (New York, NY), 2005.

Lynn Downey, *The Tattletale,* Henry Holt (New York, NY), 2006.

Gary Soto, *My Little Car = Mi Carrito,* G.P. Putnam's (New York, NY), 2006.

D. Anne Love, *Of Numbers and Stars: The Story of Hypatia,* Holiday House (New York, NY), 2006.

Christine Loomis, *The Best Father's Day Present Ever,* G.P. Putnam's (New York, NY), 2007.

(Under name Pamela Paparone) Nancy Polette, *The Greatest Invention: The Story of Walter Hunt,* Harcourt (Orlando, FL), 2008.

JoaAnn Early Macken, *Flip, Float, Fly: Seeds on the Move,* Holiday House (New York, NY), 2008.

Also contributor of art to magazines, including *New Yorker,* under name Pamela Paparone.

Biographical and Critical Sources

PERIODICALS

Booklist, July, 1994, Carolyn Phelan, review of *Who Built the Ark?: Based on an African-American Spiritual,* p. 1951; September 15, 1995, Ilene Cooper, review of *Fire Fighters,* p. 166; December 1, 1999, John Peters, review of *Ten Dirty Pigs, Ten Clean Pigs: An Upside-Down, Turn-around Bathtime Counting Book,* p. 714; July, 2000, John Peter, review of *Mail for Husher Town,* p. 2038; January 1, 2001, Ilene Cooper, review of *Low Song,* p. 970; March 15, 2004, Terry Glover, review of *Raindrop, Plop!,* p. 1309; February 1, 2005, Carolyn Phelan, review of *Where Do Chicks Come From?,* p. 964; April 15, 2006, Carolyn Phelan, review of *Of Numbers and Stars: The Story of Hypatia,* p. 49; November 1, 2006, Ilene Cooper, review of *The Tattletale,* p. 60.

Horn Book, July-August, 1994, Martha V. Parravano, review of *Who Build the Ark?,* p. 468.

Kirkus Reviews, March 1, 2004, review of *Raindrop, Plop!,* p. 225; December 15, 2004, review of *Where Do Chicks Come From?,* p. 1207; March 1, 2006, review of *Of Numbers and Stars,* p. 235; September 15, 2006, review of *The Tattletale,* p. 951.

Publishers Weekly, April 4, 1994, review of *Who Built the Ark?,* p. 77; September 25, 1995, review of *Fire Fighters,* p. 55; January 15, 2001, review of *Low Song,* p. 74.

School Library Journal, June, 2000, Tina Hudak, review of *Mail for Husher Town,* p. 111; March, 2001, Lisa Dennis, review of *Low Song,* p. 215; February, 2005, Carolyn Janssen, review of *Where Do Chicks Come From?,* p. 128; May, 2006, Julie R. Ranelli, review of *Of Numbers and Stars,* p. 114; November, 2006, Lucinda Snyder Whitehurst, review of *The Tattletale,* p. 90; April, 2007, Barbara Katz, review of *The Best Father's Day Present Ever,* p. 111.*

* * *

PAPARONE, Pamela
See PAPARONE, Pam

PARKER, Daniel
See EHRENHAFT, Daniel

*   *   *

PAYE, Won-Ldy

Personal

Born in Tapita, Liberia; immigrated to United States, 1990. *Education:* Completed college.

Addresses

Home and office—396 W. Preston St., Hartford, CT 06114. *E-mail*—wonldy@wonldypaye.com.

Career

Artist, drummer, performer, and writer. Tlo-Tlo Artists Workshop, Liberia, founder, c. 1980s; University of Washington, Seattle, instructor in storytelling and African dance, c. 1990s. *Exhibitions:* Paintings exhibited in galleries in CT, CA, and elsewhere in the United States.

Awards, Honors

Charlotte Zolotow Award, 2004, for *Mrs. Chicken and the Hungry Crocodile.*

Writings

(Reteller, with Margaret H. Lippert) *Why Leopard Has Spots: Dan Stories from Liberia,* illustrated by Ashley Bryan, Fulcrum (Golden, CO), 1998.

(Reteller, with Margaret H. Lippert) *Head, Body, Legs: A Story from Liberia,* illustrated by Julie Paschkis, Henry Holt (New York, NY), 2002.

(Reteller, with Margaret H. Lippert) *Mrs. Chicken and the Hungry Crocodile,* illustrated by Julie Paschkis, Henry Holt (New York, NY), 2003.

(Reteller, with Margaret H. Lippert) *The Talking Vegetables,* illustrated by Julie Paschkis, Henry Holt (New York, NY), 2006.

Sidelights

Won-Ldy Paye is a Liberian-born artist and performer who works to bring the stories and traditions of his native Africa to an English-speaking audience. Along with performing drumming and storytelling, Paye retells Liberian folk tales in children's picture books such as *Mrs. Chicken and the Hungry Crocodile* and *The Talking Vegetables.* He is also a painter, and many of his works hang in private collections in California and throughout the East Coast. The costumes Paye wears when performing his stories incorporate garments he has stitched and dyed himself utilizing the Dan, or traditional Liberian, style.

Paye grew up in Tapita, Liberia in a family of traditional storytellers, called *tlo ker mehn,* or "people who play story" in the Dan language. Though he worked alongside his family in their rice fields and vegetable gardens, he was also trained in the art of storytelling by his grandmother, who taught him traditional Dan music, wood carving, mask making, instrument making, fabric dyeing, mural painting, and dancing. As an adult, Paye worked in Liberian theater, and founded the Tlo-Tlo Artists Workshop, which became the fourth-largest theater company in Liberia, to train young storytellers. In 1990, Paye moved to the United States, working as a storyteller and teaching African drumming and dance at the University of Washington in Seattle.

It was in Seattle that Paye first collaborated with Margaret H. Lippert on the children's collection *Why Leopard Has Spots: Dan Stories from Liberia.* The book features several tales that find a lazy spider scheming to make situations turn out the best for him. Other tales focus on how the world came to be the way it is, and still others include morals to be learned. Denia Hester, writing in *Booklist,* noted that readers familiar with African folklore may be familiar with many of the themes, and that the collection includes "rousing tales for new readers and the initiated."

Lippert and Paye collaborated on the picture book *Head, Body, Legs: A Story from Liberia,* a creation story about how humans came to be. The tale begins with head, body, and legs all existing on their own; eventually all the parts of the body get together to make a single person. "The graceful, spare text pauses in just the right places for comic effect," wrote Gillian Engberg in *Booklist.* Noting the theme of cooperation in the story, a *Publishers Weekly* critic wrote that Paye's "attractive volume delivers its upbeat message with intelligence and humor." Lauren Adams, in a *Horn Book* review, noted that the coauthors' "message is clear but takes second place to the[ir] strange and silly tale." Susan Hepler recommended *Head, Body, Legs* as "a good tale to add to the storytelling repertoire" in her *School Library Journal* review.

In *Mrs. Chicken and the Hungry Crocodile* Mrs. Chicken is captured by a hungry crocodile and must escape by using her wits. The crocodile, none too savvy, is taken in by the hen's clever plans, and Mrs. Chicken manages to escape. "Story-hour audiences will enjoy being in on Mrs. Chicken's egg-swapping trick," wrote Kitty Flynn in a review for *Horn Book.* "Readers young and old will cluck with delight," a *Publishers Weekly* critic added of the tale. Susan Oliver, noting that Paye also includes the same story in his book *Why Leopard Has Spots,* felt that "this newly illustrated version is perfect for a younger audience."

Like *Mrs. Chicken and the Hungry Crocodile, The Talking Vegetables* also appeared in *Why Leopard Has Spots.* In the tale, coauthored with Lippert, Spider wants to have nothing to do with the work required at harvest time. When the lazy arachnid expects to be given a share equal to those who worked to bring in the harvest, the other animals drive him away, and as a result Spider must eat his rice without any flavoring. "There's no explicit moral, but the point's not going to escape many readers," wrote a *Kirkus Reviews* contributor, who suggested pairing Paye's tale with a retelling of "The Little Red Hen" for a story-hour treat. Susan Scheps, writing in *School Library Journal,* also recommended *The Talking Vegetables* as a read aloud, writing that Paye and Lippert's "simple but solid moralistic tale will delight youngsters."

In 2004, Paye moved from the west coast to Connecticut, where he continues to promote Liberian culture. "In our villages, music, dance, and storytelling are all integral parts of our daily lives," he wrote on his home page. "It is our hope that through these unique and exciting performances, our audiences will satisfy the universal need for laughter and spirituality."

Biographical and Critical Sources

PERIODICALS

Booklist, September 1, 1998, Denia Hester, review of *Why Leopard Has Spots: Dan Stories from Liberia,* p. 117; August, 2002, Gillian Engberg, review of *Head, Body, Legs: A Story from Liberia,* p. 1968.
Horn Book, May-June, 2002, Lauren Adams, review of *Head, Body, Legs,* p. 340; May-June, 2003, Kitty Flynn, review of *Mrs. Chicken and the Hungry Crocodile,* p. 361.
Instructor, April, 2003, Judy Freeman, review of *Head, Body, Legs,* p. 55.
Kirkus Reviews, September 15, 2006, review of *The Talking Vegetables,* p. 963.
New York Times Book Review, September 29, 2002, review of *Head, Body, Legs,* p. 26.
Publishers Weekly, April 1, 2002, review of *Head, Body, Legs,* p. 82; April 14, 2003, review of *Mrs. Chicken and the Hungry Crocodile,* p. 69.
School Library Journal, April, 2002, Susan Helper, review of *Head, Body, Legs,* p. 140; July, 2003, Susan Oliver, review of *Mrs. Chicken and the Hungry Crocodile,* p. 116; June, 2005, Steven Engelfried, review of *Head, Body, Legs,* p. 56; November, 2006, Susan Scheps, review of *The Talking Vegetables,* p. 122.

ONLINE

Seattle Art Museum Web site, http://www.seattleartmuseum.org/ (November 22, 2007), profile of Paye.
State of Connecticut Heritage Arts Web site, http://www.ct.gov/cct/cwp/ (November 22, 2007), profile of Paye.
Story Power Web site, http://www.storypower.net/ (November 22, 2007), profile of Paye.
Won-Ldy Paye Home Page, http://www.wonldypaye.com (November 16, 2007).*

PLATT, Chris 1959-

Personal

Born 1959; married. *Education:* University of Nevada-Reno, B.A. (journalism).

Addresses

Home—NV.

Career

Author and jockey. Earned gallop license Salem, OR, c. 1975; earned jockey license in OR; jockey at racecourses in Salem and Portland, OR; has also worked as a groom and a trainer's assistant, and as a driver of draft horses.

Member

Romance Writers of America, TeenLitAuthors.com.

Awards, Honors

Gold Heart Award, Romance Writers of America, for *Willow King.*

Writings

Willow King, Random House (New York, NY), 1998.
Race the Wind! (sequel to *Willow King*), Random House (New York, NY), 2000.
Moon Shadow, Peachtree Publications (Atlanta, GA), 2006.

"ASHLEIGH" SERIES

Holiday Homecoming, HarperEntertainment (New York, NY), 2000.
The Lost Foal, HarperEntertainment (New York, NY), 2000.
Ashleigh's Promise, HarperEntertainment (New York, NY), 2000.
Derby Dreams, HarperEntertainment (New York, NY), 2001.
Ashleigh's Western Challenge, HarperEntertainment (New York, NY), 2002.
The Prize, HarperEntertainment (New York, NY), 2002.
Winter Race Camp, HarperEntertainment (New York, NY), 2002.
Stardust's Foal, HarperEntertainment (New York, NY), 2003.

Sidelights

Chris Platt is the author of *Willow King,* winner of the Romance Writers of America's Golden Heart Award, as well as other books for middle-grade readers. Platt, whose books are based on her experiences as a jockey, groom, and horse trainer, earned her gallop license when she was just sixteen years old. A few years later she became one of the first female jockeys in Oregon, and she raced at tracks throughout that state. After earning a degree in journalism from the University of Nevada-Reno, Platt combined her two loves—writing and horses—in a new career as a children's author. Among her novels are several books in the "Ashleigh" series, including *Derby Dreams* and *Stardust's Foal.* Created by Joanna Campbell, the series focuses on Ashleigh Griffin and the horses she trains at her family's Edgardale farm. Platt counts Marguerite Henry, author of *Misty of Chincoteague,* and Walter Farley, author of *The Black Stallion,* among her literary idols.

Platt's first book, *Willow King,* centers on the relationship between a handicapped horse and the handicapped girl who nurses him back to health. When Katie Durham, who was born with one leg shorter than the other, discovers that Willow King, a colt born with crooked legs, is about to be destroyed, she convinces his owner to let her raise the horse. With the help of Jason, her handsome neighbor, Katie turns Willow King into a champion, despite the machinations of Cindy, her nemesis, and Orlin Caldwell, an unscrupulous trainer who attempts to drug the challenged race horse. A critic in *Publishers Weekly* noted that the author salts her novel with "credible moments of suspense," and Lauren Peterson, writing in *Booklist,* called *Willow King* a "heartwarming story" that "demonstrates the amazing capacity that humans and animals have to overcome disabilities."

In *Race the Wind!,* the sequel to *Willow King,* Katie prepares her horse for the first jewel in the Triple Crown: the Kentucky Derby. Despite her inexperience, she hopes to earn her jockey's license in time to ride Willow King in the Run for the Roses, although she faces competition from Mark, a confident new jockey who also plans to be in saddle. According to *School Library Journal* contributor Carol Schene, "Katie is still a likable and intelligent character." Kim D. Headlee, writing for *Crescent Blues* online, remarked that "solid storytelling, a clean prose style and well-rounded characters make *Race the Wind!* enjoyable for adults and youths alike."

Moon Shadow concerns Nevada farm girl Callie, an exuberant, horse-loving thirteen year old who is devastated after officials from the Bureau of Land Management round up the herd of wild mustangs that live near her family's ranch. When Callie learns that her favorite horse, Moonbeam, died while giving birth, she determines to adopt Moonbeam's newborn foal, and raise it with the assistance of a friendly cowboy and a helpful veterinarian. Though some critics believed that the plot of *Moon Shadow* relies too heavily on stock situations, Platt's work received generally strong reviews. A contributor in the *Midwest Book Review* described *Moon Shadow* as "a gentle novel of compassion and forming connections," while Carolyn Phelan stated in *Booklist* that "readers will quickly come to care about the life-

or-death issue at the heart of the story." "Combining a hardworking heroine, supportive and loving secondary characters, and a few coincidences, Platt creates a heartwarming, wish-come-true story," Nancy Call concluded in her *School Library Journal* review of *Moon Shadow.*

Biographical and Critical Sources

PERIODICALS

Booklist, April 15, 1998, Lauren Peterson, review of *Willow King,* p. 1446; November 1, 2006, Carolyn Phelan, review of *Moon Shadow,* p. 55.
Kirkus Reviews, September 15, 2006, review of *Moon Shadow,* p. 964.
Midwest Book Review, April, 2007, review of *Moon Shadow.*
Publishers Weekly, March 23, 1998, review of *Willow King,* p. 100.
School Library Journal, July, 1998, Carol Schene, review of *Willow King,* p. 98; September, 2000, review of *Race the Wind!,* p. 236; January, 2007, Nancy Call, review of *Moon Shadow,* p. 136.

ONLINE

Crescent Blues Online, http://www.crescentblues.com/ (November 20, 2007), Kim D. Headlee, review of *Race the Wind!**

*   *   *

PRATCHETT, Terence David John
See PRATCHETT, Terry

*   *   *

PRATCHETT, Terry 1948-
(Terence David John Pratchett)

Personal

Born Terence David John Pratchett, April 28, 1948, in Beaconsfield, England; son of David (an engineer) and Eileen (a secretary) Pratchett; married, 1968; wife's name Lyn; children: Rhianna. *Education:* Attended Wycombe Technical High School. *Hobbies and other interests:* Growing carnivorous plants.

Addresses

Home—Somerset, England. *Agent*—Colin Smythe, Ltd., P.O. Box 6, Gerrards Cross, Buckinghamshire SL9 8XA, England.

Career

Author. Journalist in Buckinghamshire, Bristol, and Bath, England, 1965-80; Central Electricity Board, Western Region, press officer, 1980-87; novelist. Co-host of wildlife documentary on Borneo orangutans.

Terry Pratchett (Photograph © by Rune Hellestad/Corbis.)

Member

British Society of Authors (past chairman).

Awards, Honors

British Science Fiction Awards, 1989, for "Discworld" series, and 1990 (with Neil Gaiman), for *Good Omens;* Best Children's Book award, Writers' Guild of Great Britain, 1993, for *Johnny and the Dead;* British Book Award for Fantasy and Science Fiction of the Year, 1993; named member, Order of the British Empire, 1998; honorary LL.D., University of Warwick, 1999; Carnegie Medal, British Library Association, 2002, for *The Amazing Maurice and His Educated Rodents.*

Writings

"DISCWORLD" SERIES

The Colour of Magic, Smythe (Gerrards Cross, England), 1983, published as *The Color of Magic,* St. Martin's (New York, NY), 1983, new edition with foreword by Pratchett, Smythe (Buckinghamshire, England), 1988, reprinted, HarperCollins (New York, NY), 2005.

The Light Fantastic, St. Martin's (New York, NY), 1986, reprinted, HarperCollins (New York, NY), 2005.

Equal Rites, Gollancz (London, England), 1986, New American Library (New York, NY), 1987, reprinted, HarperCollins (New York, NY), 2005.

Mort, Gollancz (London, England), New American Library (New York, NY), 1987.

Sourcery, Gollancz (London, England), 1988, New American Library (New York, NY), 1989.

Wyrd Sisters, Gollancz (London, England), 1988, Roc (New York, NY), 1990.

Pyramids, Penguin (New York, NY), 1989.

Eric, Gollancz (London, England), 1989, published without illustrations, 1990.

Guards! Guards!, Gollancz (London, England), 1989, Roc (New York, NY), 1991.

Moving Pictures, Gollancz (London, England), 1990, Roc (New York, NY), 1992.

Reaper Man, Gollancz (London, England), 1991, Roc (New York, NY), 1992.

Witches Abroad, Gollancz (London, England), 1991, New American Library (New York, NY), 1993.

Small Gods, Gollancz (London, England), 1992, Harper-Collins (New York, NY), 1994.

(With Stephen Briggs) *The Streets of Ankh Morpork,* Corgi (London, England), 1993, Bantam (New York, NY), 1994.

Lords and Ladies, Gollancz (London, England), 1993, HarperCollins (New York, NY), 1995.

Men at Arms, Gollancz (London, England), 1993, Harper-Collins (New York, NY), 1996.

(With Stephen Briggs) *The Discworld Companion,* Gollancz (London, England), 1994.

Interesting Times, HarperPrism (New York, NY), 1994.

Soul Music, Gollancz (London, England), 1994, Harper-Prism (New York, NY), 1995.

(With Stephen Briggs) *The Discworld Mapp,* Corgi (London, England), 1995.

Maskerade, Gollancz (London, England), 1995, Harper-Prism (New York, NY), 1997.

Terry Pratchett's Discworld Quizbook: The Unseen University Challenge, Vista (London, England), 1996.

Feet of Clay, HarperPrism (New York, NY), 1996.

The Pratchett Portfolio, illustrated by Paul Kidby, Gollancz (London, England), 1996.

Hogfather, Gollancz (London, England), 1996, Harper-Prism (New York, NY), 1998.

Jingo, Gollancz (London, England), 1997, HarperPrism (New York, NY), 1998.

The Last Continent, Doubleday (London, England), 1998, HarperPrism (New York, NY), 1999.

Carpe Jugulum, Doubleday (London, England), 1998, HarperPrism (New York, NY), 1999.

(With Tina Hannan and Stephen Briggs) *Nanny Ogg's Cookbook,* illustrated by Paul Kidby, Doubleday (London, England), 1999.

(With Paul Kidry) *Death's Domain: A Discworld Mapp,* Corgi (London, England), 1999.

The Fifth Elephant, Doubleday (London, England), 1999, HarperCollins (New York, NY), 2000.

The Truth, Corgi (London, England), 2001.

Thief of Time, HarperCollins (New York, NY), 2001.

The Last Hero: A Discworld Fable, illustrated by Paul Kidby, HarperCollins (New York, NY), 2001.

The Amazing Maurice and His Educated Rodents (children's novel), HarperCollins (New York, NY), 2001.

Night Watch, HarperCollins (New York, NY), 2002.

Discworld Roleplaying Game, illustrated by Paul Kidby, Steve Jackson Games (Austin, TX), 2002.

Monstrous Regiment, HarperCollins (New York, NY), 2003.

The Wee Free Men (children's novel), HarperCollins (New York, NY), 2003, published with illustrations by Stephen Player, edited by Anne Hoppe, 2007.

Going, HarperCollins (New York, NY), 2004.

A Hat Full of Sky (children's novel), HarperCollins (New York, NY), 2004.

Where's My Cow? (for children), illustrated by Melvyn Grant, HarperCollins (New York, NY), 2005.

Thud!, HarperCollins (New York, NY), 2005.

Wintersmith (children's novel), HarperTempest (New York, NY), 2006.

Making Money HarperCollins (New York, NY), 2007.

The Wit and Wisdom of Discworld, compiled by Stephen Briggs, HarperCollins (New York, NY), 2007.

"BROMELIAD" TRILOGY; JUVENILE FANTASY

Truckers (also see below), Doubleday (New York, NY), 1989, reprinted, Harper Collins), 2004.

Diggers (also see below), Doubleday (New York, NY), 1990, reprinted, Harper Collins), 2004.

Wings (also see below), Doubleday (New York, NY), 1990.

The Bromeliad Trilogy (contains *Truckers, Diggers,* and *Wings*), HarperCollins (New York, NY), 2003.

"JOHNNY MAXWELL" TRILOGY; JUVENILE FANTASY

Only You Can Save Mankind (also see below), Doubleday (London, England), 1992, HarperCollins (New York, NY), 2005.

Johnny and the Dead (also see below), Doubleday (London, England), 1993, HarperCollins (New York, NY), 2007.

Johnny and the Bomb (also see below), Doubleday (London, England), 1996, HarperCollins (New York, NY), 2007.

The Johnny Maxwell Trilogy (contains *Only You Can Save Mankind, Johnny and the Dead,* and *Johnny and the Bomb*), Doubleday (London, England), 1999.

OTHER

The Carpet People (children's fantasy), Smythe (Gerrards Cross, England), 1971, revised edition, Doubleday (New York, NY), 1992.

The Dark Side of the Sun (science fiction), St. Martin's (New York, NY), 1976.

Strata (science fiction), St. Martin's (New York, NY), 1981.

The Unadulterated Cat, illustrated by Gray Jolliffe, Gollancz (London, England), 1989.

(With Neil Gaiman) *Good Omens: The Nice and Accurate Predictions of Agnes Nutter, Witch,* Workman (New York, NY), 1990.

Contributor to *Legends,* edited by Robert Silverberg, Voyager (London, England), 1998.

Pratchett's novels have been published in eighteen languages.

Adaptations

The Colour of Magic was adapted as a four-part work by Scott Rockwell with illustrations by Steven Ross, Innovation Corporation, 1991, and published as a graphic novel, Corgi, 1992. *The Light Fantastic* was adapted as a four-part work by Scott Rockwell with illustrations by Steven Ross, Innovation Corporation, 1992, and published as a graphic novel, Corgi, 1993. *Mort* was adapted as a graphic novel, illustrated by Graham Higgins, Gollancz (London, England), 1994. The "Bromeliad" trilogy and the first six books of the "Discworld" series were released on audio-cassette by Corgi. An album, *Music from the Discworld* by Dave Greenslade, was released by Virgin Records, 1994. Two video games, *Discworld* and *Discworld Two,* were released by Sony/Psygnosis. A stage adaptation of *Truckers* toured England, 2002. *Wyrd Sisters* and *Soul Music* became animated cartoons, created by Cosgrove Hall Films and released by Acorn Media. Stephen Briggs has adapted *Johnny and the Dead* and several books in the "Discworld" series to plays, including *Mort,* Corgi, 1996; *Wyrd Sisters,* Corgi, 1996; *Men at Arms,* Corgi, 1997; *Maskerade,* Samuel French, 1998; *Carpe Jugulum,* Samuel French, 1999; *Guards! Guards!,* illustrated by Graham Higgins, Gollancz, 2000; *The Fifth Elephant,* Methuen Drama, 2002; *The Truth,* Methuen Drama, 2002; *Interesting Times,* Methuen Drama, 2002; and *Going Postal,* Methuen Drama, 2005.

Sidelights

Called the "master of humorous fantasy" by a critic for *Publishers Weekly,* British author Terry Pratchett won the prestigious Carnegie Medal in 2002 for his novel *The Amazing Maurice and His Educated Rodents.* The author of numerous science fiction and fantasy novels, Pratchett is known primarily for his "Discworld" series and his "Bromeliad" trilogy for children. As David V. Barrett stated in *New Statesman & Society,* Pratchett's "Discworld" novels feature "marvelous composition and rattling good stories." "Pratchett is an acquired taste," wrote a critic for *Publishers Weekly* in a review of "Discworld" installment *Interesting Times,* "but the acquisition seems easy, judging from the robust popularity of Discworld." "Discworld"—as well as most of Pratchett's other works—also offers humorous parodies of other famous science-fiction and fantasy writers, such as J.R.R. Tolkien and Larry Niven. In his solo works he frequently spoofs such modern trends as New Age philosophy and universal concerns, and does the same in *Good Omens: The Nice and Accurate Predic-*

"A DIRECT DESCENDANT OF THE HITCHHIKER'S GUIDE TO THE GALAXY."
—New York Times

"IT'S A WOW!"
—Washington Post

GOOD OMENS

A NOVEL BY

NEIL GAIMAN AND TERRY PRATCHETT

Cover of **Good Omens,** *a novel coauthored by Pratchett and Neil Gaiman.* (Berkley Books, 1992. Used by permission of Penguin Group (USA), Inc.)

tions of Agnes Nutter, Witch, his humorous collaboration with acclaimed writer Neil Gaiman. Nevertheless, "in among the slapstick and clever word-play are serious concepts," as Barrett pointed out. In "genres assailed by shoddiness, mediocrity, and . . . the endless series," asserted *Locus* critic Faren Miller, "Pratchett is never shoddy, and under the laughter there's a far from mediocre mind at work."

Pratchett was born in 1948, and grew up in Buckinghamshire, England. During his youth, he developed a love of reading science fiction and fantasy, and considered Kenneth Grahame's *The Wind in the Willows* his favorite book. From fantasy he went to myth, and from myth to reading ancient history. Pratchett published his first story in his school magazine, and years later, in 1963, sold his first story to *Science Fantasy.* At age seventeen, while working as a journalist, he wrote his first novel, a children's fantasy titled *The Carpet People,* and in 1971 the book found a publisher. Pratchett continued working as a journalist until 1980, by which time he was a press officer for a nuclear power plant. Seven years later, in 1987, he made the move to full-time writer, confident of success due to the novels he had already published.

The Carpet People introduces readers to the world of creatures living in a carpet: deftmenes, mouls, and wights. The novel's protagonist, Snibril the Munrung, travels with his brother Glurk through the many Carpet regions—areas distinguished by different colors—to do battle with the evil concept of Fray. A *Times Literary Supplement* reviewer recommended *The Carpet People,* predicting that "the Tolkienian echoes" in Pratchett's tale "may draw in some older readers."

Pratchett used the concept of a flat world when he embarked upon his first "Discworld" novel, *The Color of Magic.* Discworld sits on the shoulders of four giant elephants, which in turn rest on the back of a giant turtle that swims through space. As W.D. Stevens reported in *Science Fiction and Fantasy Review,* Discworld is "populated with wizards, warriors, demons, dragons," and other fantastic attributes. The protagonist of *The Color of Magic* is a hapless wizard named Rincewind. The wizard teams up with Discworld's first tourist, Twoflower, who is visiting from a remote portion of the disc, along with Twoflower's sapient suitcase, known as the Luggage. The result, according to Stevens, is "one of the funniest, and cleverest, satires to be written."

Rincewind returns in *The Light Fantastic.* This time he and Twoflower must try to prevent Discworld from colliding with a red star that has recently appeared in its sky. This episode introduces toothless octogenarian Cohen the Barbarian. The next book in the series, *Equal Rites,* puts the emphasis on the character of Granny Weatherwax, and the fourth novel in the series, *Mort,* stars the recurring character, Death. Granny Weatherwax also appears in *Wyrd Sisters,* this time accompanied by two fellow witches. In the novel Granny and her companions form a trio of witches (reminiscent of those in William Shakespeare's play *Macbeth*) to foil the plot of the evil Lord Felmet and his wife, who have usurped the rightful king. *Wyrd Sisters* prompted Miller to declare that "Pratchett continues to defy the odds. An open-ended series that just keeps getting better? Humorous fantasy with resources beyond puns, buffoonery, and generations of cardboard characters? Unheard of—until Pratchett."

Continuing with the "Discworld" books, *Lords and Ladies* examines the darker nature of elves. Jackie Cassada, writing in *Library Journal,* remarked that this book shows why Pratchett "may be one of the genre's . . . most inventive humorists." In *Men at Arms* the author blends fantasy and mystery in an "average installment in this always entertaining, sometimes hysterically funny series," according to a critic for *Kirkus Reviews.* In *Interesting Times* Rincewind is sent thousands of miles away to intercede in a squabble on the Counterweight Continent. Twoflower and Cohen the Barbarian also make returns in this installment of the "Discworld" saga. Granny Weatherwax returns in *Maskerade,* called "an enjoyable jaunt into the fantasy world" by Meg Wilson in *Voice of Youth Advocates.*

An exploration of discrimination informs *Jingo,* in which war is averted with a land neighboring the city-state Ankh-Morpork, with its mixed population of humans, trolls, and dwarves. Nancy K. Wallace praised the novel in *Voice of Youth Advocates,* remarking that Pratchett's story, with its "dizzying array of favorite characters and rowdy Pythonesque humor," offers a "capricious, lighthearted look at the inanity of war and the warped ethics of diplomatic procedure." *Hogfather* features that eponymous Santa Claus of Discworld, but when Hogfather is kidnapped it falls to Death and his daughter, Susan, to figure out who is behind this dastardly deed. With this novel, declared a reviewer for *Publishers Weekly,* Pratchett has "moved beyond the limits of humorous fantasy, and should be recognized as one of the more significant contemporary English-language satirists." Tom Pearson, reviewing *Hogfather* for *Voice of Youth Advocates,* concluded that "Pratchett has once again brought Discworld to life in all its off-kilter glory."

Once again set in the "Discworld" universe, *The Last Continent* spoofs things Australian, while in the twenty-third "Discworld" outing, *Carpe Jugulum,* vampires attempt to overthrow the kingdom of Lancre. "Pratchett lampoons everything from Christian superstition to Swiss Army knives here," wrote a *Publishers Weekly* reviewer of the novel. Susan Salpini, writing in *School Library Journal,* dubbed *Carpe Jugulum* a "marvelous sendup of old horror movies."

The Fifth Elephant deals with the legend of the fifth pachyderm that once stood on the back of the giant tortoise. When it fell off the tortoise, its impact on Discworld left rich mineral and fat deposits in what is now Uberwald. Chief Constable Sam Vimes and his wife from Ankh-Morpork are on hand in this episode to help in a succession crisis on Uberwald. "Pratchett is now inviting comparison with Kurt Vonnegut," declared Roland Green in a *Booklist* review of *The Fifth Elephant.* A critic for *Publishers Weekly* had similar praise, calling the novel a "first-rate addition to [Pratchett's] . . . long-running Discworld fantasy series." In *The Truth,* a newspaper is established in Ankh-Morpork. Pratchett takes advantage of this opportunity to skewer the press and investigative journalism in this "hilarious romp," as Jackie Cassada described the tale in a *Library Journal* review. A contributor for *Publishers Weekly* concluded that readers new to the "Discworld" series "may find themselves laughing out loud . . . while longtime fans are sure to call [*The Fifth Elephant*] . . . Pratchett's best one yet."

Time, religion, and history serve as the philosophical compass in *Thief of Time,* in which a perfect timepiece will stop time unless a member of the History Monks can do something about it. "How can readers resist a book in which the world is saved by the awesome power of chocolate?" wondered Susan Salpini in a *School Library Journal* review. Cohen the Barbarian shows up

again in *The Last Hero: A Discworld Fable,* and decides that he and his elderly buddies will go out in a blaze of glory, taking Ankh-Morpork along with them. Rincewind, Captain Carrot, and the inventor/artist Leonard of Quirm must stop Cohen and company before it is too late. In *Booklist,* Ray Olson dubbed *Thief of Time* "another Discworld delight," while a reviewer for *Publishers Weekly* lauded Pratchett's "far-out farce."

City Watch leader Sam Vimes returns in *Night Watch* and is joined by the villainous Carcer in a story that is "bubbling with wit and wisdom" and designed as a "tribute to beat cops everywhere," according to a critic for *Kirkus Reviews.* Vimes reprises his commander watchman role in *Thud!,* which finds the Ankh-Morpork City Watch commander determined to halt the disruption caused by the murder of a rabble-rousing dwarf named Grag Hamcrusher. "As always," concluded Regina Schroeder in *Booklist, Thud!* "is funny, fast-paced, [and] the kind of satire that explores serious issues" while also captivating readers. Calling the city of Ankh-Morpork "the most rewarding part of Discworld," a contributor to *Kirkus Reviews* noted that in *Thud!* Pratchett skewers everything from Blackberries to the novel *The DaVinci Code,* allowing the stalwart Vimes

In **Wyrd Sisters** *Pratchett's creepy cast is brought to life in illustrations by Tom Kidd.* (ROC, 1988. Used by permission of Penguin Group (USA), Inc.)

to cope with the resulting "chaos and idiocy as the exasperated, excruciatingly decent British voice of reason."

Sam Vines has earned a dukedom by the time readers meet up with him in *Monstrous Regiment,* but his battle to keep the peace continues to keep him busy. In fact, war has broken out, and the army of the Borogravians is winning adherents from among the citizens of Ankh-Morpork. Polly Oliver is so hawkish, in fact, that she has joined one of the Borogravian regiments by disguising herself as a boy. In *Booklist,* Regina Schroeder dubbed *Monstrous Regiment* "thoroughly funny and surprisingly insightful," and a *Kirkus Reviews* contributor expressed relief that "Pratchett's droll satire . . . isn't afraid to stoop to things like cross-dressing to get a giggle."

The "Discworld" saga continues to spin in *Going Postal,* as con man Moist von Lipwig is forced by law to endure the ultimate punishment for his crimes: a government job. Charged with turning his criminal mind to improving the British postal system, Moist rises to the occasion, battling a complex communications system, a sea of unsent mail, and a hidden guiding bureaucracy seeking profits above all else. To accomplish the impossible, Moist turns to golem friend and eventual love interest Adora Belle Darkheart as well as Oscar the vampire and a secret society of former postal workers. His exploits continue in *Making Money,* as Moist begins to look beyond his successes at the postal system but finds his steady climb to the top less than exciting. In *Going Postal* Pratchett's "inventiveness seems to know no end," according to Carolyn Lehman in *School Library Journal,* and "his playful and irreverent use of language is a delight." In the opinion of a *Kirkus Reviews* writer, it is "almost shamefully enjoyable to watch [Moist] . . . restore the mail routes, invent the idea of stamps, and go toe-to-toe with everything from rapacious businessmen to bloodthirsty banshees." Chock full of "beautifully crafted, wickedly cutting satire on the underpinnings of modern human society," in the opinion of Schroeder, *Making Money* was described as a "smart, funny, and . . . thoroughly entertaining."

Pratchett won both critical acclaim and a Carnegie Medal for *The Amazing Maurice and His Educated Rodents.* The first of his "Discworld" books specifically geared for younger readers, the novel was described by *School Library Journal* contributor Miranda Doyle as a "laugh-out-loud fantasy" that turns the pied-piper tale on its head. Maurice is a rather ill-tempered cat who comes up with a clever scheme: send a horde of unpleasant rats into various towns so that the inhabitants will have to summon a piper to get rid of them. The said piper will be Keith, a young musician who is in cahoots with the cat. Their scheme: After Keith performs his piper schtick, he will meet up with Maurice and the rats, and the three parties will split the fee earned for ridding the town of rodents. This scheme works fine until they arrive at the town of Blintz where

there are no resident rodents to create the needed infestation. Instead, Maurice and his team are called into service when some evil rat catchers capture all the local humans. A critic for *Publishers Weekly* called the novel an "outrageously cheeky tale," and in *Horn Book* Anita L. Burkam wrote that Pratchett's "absorbing, suspenseful adventure is speeded along by the characters' wisecracking patter." Similarly, a contributor to *Kirkus Reviews* noted that *The Amazing Maurice* "is at heart a story about stories" and both "excruciatingly funny" and "ferociously intelligent."

With *The Wee Free Men* Pratchett introduces a trilogy of novels for younger readers that, like *The Amazing Maurice and His Educated Rodents,* is part of the "Discworld" saga. The series follows a nine-year-old dairymaid named Tiffany Aching, who finds that her annoying baby brother has been kidnaped from his home in the rural Chalk by the Elf Queen. Although Tiffany has a few special abilities, such as second sight, she draws on the help of both a talking toad and the Nac Mac Feegle, a band of fearless, rabble-rousing, drunken, blue miniature gnomes no more than six inches in height and fearless. The group bravely infiltrates Fairyland to rescue the tot, and there Tiffany confronts a headless horseman who turns her dreams against her. Her strength—her magic—is "quiet, inconspicuous . . . , grounded in the earth and tempered with compassion, wisdom, and justice for common folk," explained Sue Giffard in a review of *The Wee Free Men* for *School Library Journal.* Described as an "ingenious melánge of fantasy, action, humor, and sly bits of social commentary" by a *Kirkus Reviews* writer, *The Wee Free Men* also addresses weighty issues such as "the nature of love, reality, and dreams," the critic added.

In *A Hat Full of Sky* Pratchett's "humor . . . races from cerebral to burlesque without dropping a stitch," according to *Booklist* contributor Roger Sutton. Now age eleven, Tiffany becomes a witch in training to Miss Level, but her lessons are derailed when the teen is taken over by a parasitic hiver who intends to steal her very soul. Granny Aching draws on the power of the Chalk, and the small but feisty Nac Mac Feegle lend their efforts to driving the deadly hiver away. *A Hat Full of Sky* is, "by turns hilarious and achingly beautiful," noted a *Kirkus Reviews* writer, the critic noting that Pratchett ranges from "biting satire" to a serious examination of "the critical question of identity" and the importance of reconciling all aspects of one's true nature.

The third "Discworld" story geared for younger readers is *Wintersmith,* which finds thirteen-year-old Tiffany dancing into the Dark Morris and thereby attracting the romantic ardor of the chilly god of Winter. To show his love, the Wintersmith powders the world with snowflakes in the shape of his beloved. Because Tiffany has accidentally disrupted the change of the seasons, she must call upon Granny Weatherwax, as well as a clutch of other witches, to help put an end to the blizzard of

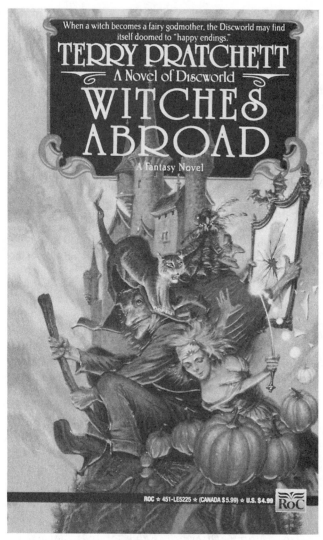

Cover of Pratchett's Witches Abroad, *a "Discworld" novel that features artwork by Darrel K. Sweet.* (New American Library. Reproduced by permission of Darrell K. Sweet.)

love that threatens to bury the world. In *Booklist,* Holly Koelling described *Wintersmith* as a "rollicking, clever, and quite charming adventure" that is fuelled by Pratchett's "exuberant storytelling." In praise of the book's heroine, *Horn Book* contributor Deirdre F. Baker wrote that Tiffany's "tenacity, fierce intelligence, and common sense lift her to almost mythic stature." *Wintersmith* is "full of rich humor, wisdom, and eventfulness," Baker concluded, and a *Kirkus Reviews* writer noted that the book's "sidesplittingly funny adventure . . . overlays a deeply thoughtful inquiry into . . . how the stories we tell shape our understanding of ourselves and of the world we inhabit."

Pratchett has addressed younger readers in several other series of books throughout his writing career. His "Bromeliad" fantasy series begins with *Truckers,* which introduces young readers to the nomes. Four-inch-tall people from another planet, the nomes have crashed on Earth and made a new world for themselves under the floorboards of a department store. Some of the nomes,

however, have lived on the outside; the fun begins when one of these, Masklin, meets with the nomes of the store. When they learn that their store is going out of business and will be torn down, they must cooperate with the outside nomes to find a new home and escape their old one. "A wild and hilarious chase sequence follows, with the baffled police doubting their sanity," observed a *Horn Book* reviewer. Elizabeth Ward summed up *Truckers* in the *Washington Post Book World,* calling it "a delightful surprise" and a "benevolent little satire."

Diggers takes Masklin and his fellow nomes to their new home in an abandoned quarry. Problems ensue, however, when humans attempt to reactivate the quarry. "In the book's funniest scene," according to Patrick Jones in *Voice of Youth Advocates,* "a group of nomes 'attacks' one of the humans, ties him to his desk chair, and stuffs a note in his hand proclaiming: 'leave us alone.'" "Satire and allegory abound," a *Horn Book* reviewer concluded of *Diggers,* although the critic also noted that the nomes' "trials and emotions are both moving and amusing." In *Wings,* the third "Bromeliad" novel, Masklin and his friends attempt to return to their home planet by placing the Thing—the "magic" box that in *Truckers* had warned them of the store's demise—aboard a communications satellite so that it can summon their old mother ship, which has been waiting for them throughout their earthly exile. Margaret A. Chang lauded *Wings* in *School Library Journal* as a "cheerful, unpretentious tale."

Pyramids, which appeared in 1989, spoofs ancient Egypt. In *Pyramids* loyal Discworld fans meet Teppic, a teenager who is studying to become an assassin until a relative's death makes him Pharaoh. Other well-received Discworld books include *Witches Abroad,* which again features Granny Weatherwax and her witch companions. This time their mission is to stop the inevitable happy ending of a fairy tale because of the deeper disaster it will cause. A later Discworld novel is *Small Gods,* which Miller described in his *Locus* review of the work as "a book about tortoises, eagles, belief systems, conspiracies, religious bigotry, man's need for gods, and gods' even greater need for man." Reviewing the same novel in the *Spectator,* Tom Shone noted that Pratchett's "parodies of sword and sorcery novels are a permanent fixture on the bestseller lists throughout most of the year." Shone further commented that "Pratchett is the lucky person on whom the general public's desire for self-parodic fantasy has come to rest and it would now take a very bad book indeed to dislodge it."

Another trio of books set outside his "Discworld" series, Pratchett's "Johnny Maxwell" books, were written in the early 1990s but remain in print due to their popularity. The series begins with *Only You Can Save Mankind,* a novel that spoofs, among other things, the 1991 Persian Gulf War. In this fantasy tale, the computer game-playing protagonist is faced with a strange dilemma when the commander of the alien force he is about to destroy on-screen asks to surrender. Accepting his role as the Chosen One, the protector of the Scree Wee Empire, Johnny must rescue the aliens from the rest of the world's computer game players. *Only You Can Save Mankind* garnered strong reviews from critics for its blend of humor and suspense. A *Junior Bookshelf* contributor remarked that teen readers "should thoroughly enjoy the teasing competence of Mr. Pratchett's high-tech conundrum, by turns comical, whimsical, and downright terrifying." Miller, in an *Locus* review, stated that the "serious message of this novel shows clearly, but it's delightfully packaged, with the typical Pratchett combination of wit and level-headed humanity."

Johnny Maxwell returns in *Johnny and the Dead,* which finds the hero mixed up in another creepy yet humorous adventure. The residents of an old graveyard—the dead and buried residents, that is—take offense at the city council's plans to sell the cemetery to a corporation intent on replacing the gravesites with a new housing development. Enlisting the aid of Johnny as their spokesperson, the deceased try to sway public opinion against demolition of their "home." Marcus Crouch, reviewing *Johnny and the Dead* in *Junior Bookshelf,* remarked that the "story surprised with its depth and seriousness" and called it "a lovely, funny, witty, sometimes wise book, exciting and entertaining and always highly readable."

Johnny Maxwell makes a final appearance in *Johnny and the Bomb.* In this episode, he and his friends assist an old bag lady only to discover that her bags are full of time. The teens find themselves traveling back in time to 1941, just as an air raid is scheduled to hit their town during World War II. Having studied the event in school, they know what to expect but are unsure what to do now that they are in the middle of the action. Michael Gregg, reviewing *Johnny and the Bomb* in *Magpies,* concluded that "there's a giggle on every page and enough to keep the mind mulling over long after the book is put down." A reviewer for *Junior Bookshelf* also had praise for *Johnny and the Bomb,* writing that "no summary can give a fair picture of the intriguing events and lively crosstalk that make up this fascinating story."

Pratchett once told *SATA* "I've been a journalist of some sort all my working life, and I suppose I tend to think of the books as a kind of journalism—although writing them is as much fun as anyone can have by themselves sitting down with all their clothes on."

"I can't speak for the United States—3,000 miles is a great barrier to casual feedback—but what does gratify me in the United Kingdom is that the 'Discworld' books, which are not intended for children, have a big following among kids who, in the words of one librarian, 'don't normally read.'

"I got my education from books. The official schooling system merely prevented me from reading as many books as I would have liked. So from personal experience I know that getting children to read is important. Civilization depends on it."

Biographical and Critical Sources

BOOKS

Contemporary Novelists, 6th edition, St. James Press (Detroit, MI), 1996.

Marcus, Leonard S., *The Wand in the Word: Conversations with Writers of Fantasy,* Candlewick Press (New York, NY), 2006.

St. James Guide to Fantasy Writers, St. James Press (Detroit, MI), 1996.

Twentieth-Century Children's Writers, 4th edition, St. James Press (Detroit, MI), 1995.

Twentieth-Century Science-Fiction Writers, St. James Press (Chicago, IL), 1991.

PERIODICALS

Booklist, December 15, 1994, Carl Hays, review of *Soul Music,* p. 740; September 1, 1995, Roland Green, review of *Eric,* p. 48; September 15, 1995, Roland Green, review of *Lords and Ladies,* p. 145; March 15, 1996, Roland Green, review of *Men at Arms,* p. 1245; October 1, 1996, Roland Green, review of *Feet of Clay,* p. 326; June 1, 1998, Roland Green, review of *Jingo,* p. 1736; January 1, 2000, Roland Green, review of *The Fifth Elephant,* p. 834; August, 2000, Ray Olson, review of *The Truth,* p. 2075; April 15, 2001, Ray Olson, review of *The Thief of Time,* p. 1510; September 15, 2001, Ray Olson, review of *The Last Hero: A Discworld Fable,* p. 164; January 1, 2002, Sally Estes, review of *The Amazing Maurice and His Educated Rodents,* pp. 842-843; September 1, 2002, Regina Schroeder, review of *Night Watch,* p. 7; April 15, 2003, Sally Estes, review of *The Wee Free Men,* p. 1465; August, 2003, Regina Schroeder, review of *Monstrous Regiment,* p. 1927; April 15, 2004, Sally Estes, review of *A Hat Full of Sky,* p. 145; September 1, 2004, Regina Schroeder, review of *Going Postal,* p. 6; September 1, 2005, Regina Schroeder, review of *Thud!,* p. 7; September 1, 2006, Holly Koelling, review of *Wintersmith,* p. 127; August, 2007, Regina Schroeder, review of *Making Money,* p. 9.

Bulletin of the Center for Children's Books, February, 2002, review of *The Amazing Maurice and His Educated Rodents,* p. 217; July, 2003, review of *The Wee Free Men,* p. 458.

Horn Book, March-April, 1990, review of *Truckers,* p. 202; May-June, 1991, review of *Diggers,* p. 332; March-April, 2002, Anita L. Burkam, review of *The Amazing Maurice and His Educated Rodents,* p. 217; May-June, 2003, Anita L. Burkam, review of *The Wee Free Men,* p. 355; July-August, 2004, Roger Sutton, review of *A Hat Full of Sky,* p. 460; January-February, 2006, Claire E. Gross, review of *Johnny and the Dead,* p. 87; September-October, 2006, Deirdre F. Baker, review of *Wintersmith,* p. 289.

Junior Bookshelf, February, 1993, review of *Only You Can Save Mankind,* p. 33; August, 1993, Marcus Crouch, review of *Johnny and the Dead,* p. 157; June, 1996, review of *Johnny and the Bomb,* p. 124.

Kirkus Reviews, January 1, 1996, review of *Men at Arms,* p. 32; March 1, 1997, review of *Interesting Times,* p. 342; October 1, 1999, review or *Carpe Jugulum,* p. 1531; September 1, 2001, review of *The Last Hero,* p. 1254; October 15, 2001, review of *The Amazing Maurice and His Educated Rodents,* p. 1490; August 15, 2002, review of *Night Watch,* p. 1183; April 15, 2003, review of *The Wee Free Men,* p. 610; August 15, 2003, review of *Monstrous Regiment,* p. 105; May 1, 2004, review of *A Hat Full of Sky,* p. 446; September 1, 2004, review of *Going Postal,* p. 830; June 15, 2005, review of *Only You Can Save Mankind,* p. 689; August 1, 2005, review of *Thud!,* p. 810; September 15, 2006, review of *Wintersmith,* p. 964; March 1, 2007, review of *Johnny and the Bomb,* p. 230; August 1, 2007, review of *Making Money,* p. 265.

Kliatt, May, 2004, Paula Rohrlick, review of *A Hat Full of Sky,* p. 12; September, 2005, Paula Rohrlick, review of *Only You Can Save Mankind,* p. 12; May, 2007, Paula Rohrlick, review of *Johnny and the Dead,* p. 31; November, 2007, Paula Rohrlick, review of *Wintersmith,* p. 26.

Library Journal, September 15, 1995, Jackie Cassada, review of *Lords and Ladies,* p. 97; April 15, 1997, Susan Hamburger, review of *Interesting Times,* p. 124; March 15, 2000, Jackie Cassada, review of *The Fifth Elephant,* p. 132; October 1, 2000, Douglas C. Lord, review of *Guards! Guards!,* p. 165; October 15, 2000, Jackie Cassada, review of *The Truth,* p. 108; March 15, 2001, Ann Burns, review of *Jingo,* p. 126; May 15, 2001, Jackie Cassada, review of *The Thief of Time,* p. 166; November 15, 2001, Jackie Cassada, review of *The Last Hero,* p. 100, November 15, 2002, Jackie Cassada, review of *Night Watch,* p. 106.

Locus, January, 1989, Faren Miller, review of *Wyrd Sisters,* p. 17; October, 1991, Faren Miller, review of *Witches Abroad,* pp. 15, 17; June, 1992, Faren Miller, review of *Small Gods,* p. 17; September, 1992, Faren Miller, review of *Only You Can Save Mankind,* p. 66.

Magazine of Fantasy and Science Fiction, April, 1999, Michelle West, review of *Hogfather,* p. 36; October, 2000, Michelle West, review of *The Fifth Elephant,* p. 44; March, 2002, Michelle West, review of *The Last Hero,* pp. 34-39.

Magpies, September, 1996, Michael Gregg, review of *Johnny and the Bomb,* p. 34.

New Scientist, July 10, 1999, "The World of If," pp. 46-48; May 18, 2002, Roger Bridgman, "Narrative Drive: What Makes Us Human?," p. 56.

New Statesman & Society, January 3, 1992, David V. Barrett, "Serious Fun," p. 33.

Publishers Weekly, March 31, 1997, review of *Interesting Times,* p. 67; October 26, 1998, review of *Hogfather,* p. 47; September 27, 1999, review of *Carpe Jugulum,* p. 77; March 6, 2000, review of *The Fifth Elephant,* p. 87; October 30, 2000, review of *The Truth,* p. 52; April 9, 2001, review of *Thief of Time,* p. 55; October 15, 2001, review of *The Last Hero,* p. 51; November

5, 2001, review of *The Amazing Maurice and His Educated Rodents,* p. 70; September 30, 2002, review of *Night Watch,* p. 54.

School Library Journal, September, 1991, Margaret A. Chang, review of *Wings,* pp. 258-259; August, 1998, Susan Salpini, review of *Jingo,* p. 197; April, 2000, Susan Salpini, review of *Carpe Jugulum,* p. 162; July, 2000, review of *The Fifth Elephant,* p. 130; August, 2001, Susan Salpini, review of *Thief of Time,* p. 211; December, 2001, Miranda Doyle, review of *The Amazing Maurice and His Educated Rodents,* pp. 142-143; May 20, 2003, Sue Giffard, review of *The Wee Free Men,* p. 158; July, 2004, Sharon Rawlins, review of *A Hat Full of Sky,* p. 111; February, 2005, Carolyn Lehman, review of *Going Postal,* p. 157; November, 2006, Heather M. Campbell, review of *Wintersmith,* p. 148.

Spectator, August 22, 1992, Tom Shone, "A View from the Back of a Giant Tortoise," p. 23.

Times Literary Supplement, April 28, 1972, review of *The Carpet People,* p. 475.

Voice of Youth Advocates, February, 1991, Patrick Jones, review of *Diggers,* p. 366; April, 1998, Meg Wilson, review of *Maskerade,* p. 60; December, 1998, Nancy K. Wallace, review of *Jingo,* p. 370; April, 1999, Tom Pearson, review of *Hogfather,* p. 50.

Washington Post Book World, February 11, 1990, Elizabeth Ward, review of *Truckers,* p. 6.

ONLINE

Colin-Smyth Web Site, http://www.colin-smythe.com (March 14, 2003), "About the Author: Terry Pratchett."

Midweek (BBC Radio 4), April 26, 1995, Christina Hardimant, interview with Pratchett.*

*   *   *

PRIMAVERA, Elise 1954-

Personal

Born May 19, 1954, in West Long Branch, NJ; daughter of Jerry (a builder) and Corrine (a homemaker) Primavera. *Education:* Moore College of Art, B.F.A., 1976; attended Arts Students League, 1980-84.

Addresses

Home—Red Bank, NJ. *E-mail*—eprimavera@earthlink.net.

Career

Freelance fashion illustrator, 1976-79; freelance children's book illustrator, 1979—.

Awards, Honors

New Jersey Institute of Technology Award, 1983, for *The Bollo Caper* by Art Buchwald, and 1988, for *Christina Katerina and the Time She Quit the Family* by Patricia Lee Gauch; Christopher Award, 1998, Oppenheim Toy Portfolio Platinum Award, 1999, and Irma S. and James H. Black Book Award, all for *Raising Dragons*.

Writings

SELF-ILLUSTRATED

Basil and Maggie, J.B. Lippincott (Philadephia, PA), 1983.
Ralph's Frozen Tale, Putnam (New York, NY), 1991.
The Three Dots, Putnam (New York, NY), 1993.
Plantpet, Putnam (New York, NY), 1994.
Auntie Claus, Harcourt (New York, NY), 1999.
Auntie Claus and the Key to Christmas, Harcourt (New York, NY), 2002.
The Secret Order of the Gumm Street Girls (juvenile novel), 2006.
Ghosts, Monsters, Blood, and Guts: Fred and Anthony's Awesome Guide to the Netherworld (graphic novel), Hyperion (New York, NY), 2007.
Fred and Anthony Meet the Super-Degermo Zombie, Hyperion (New York, NY), 2007.
Fred and Anthony Meet the Heine Goblins from the Black Lagoon, Hyperion (New York, NY), 2007.

ILLUSTRATOR

Joyce St. Peter, *Always Abigail,* J.B. Lippincott (Philadelphia, PA), 1981.
Dorothy Crayder, *The Joker and the Swan,* Harper (New York, NY), 1981.
Margaret K. Wetterer, *The Mermaid's Cape,* Atheneum (New York, NY), 1981.
Eila Moorhouse Lewis, *The Snug Little House,* Atheneum (New York, NY), 1981.
Margaret K. Wetterer, *The Giant's Apprentice,* Atheneum (New York, NY), 1982.
Art Buchwald, *The Bollo Caper: A Furry Tale for All Ages,* Putnam (New York, NY), 1983.
Natalie Savage Carlson, *The Surprise in the Mountains,* Harper (New York, NY), 1983.
Delia Ephron, *Santa and Alex,* Little, Brown (Boston, MA), 1983.
Miriam Anne Bourne, *Uncle George Washington and Harriot's Guitar,* Putnam (New York, NY), 1983.
Elaine Moore, *Grandma's House,* Lothrop (New York, NY), 1985.
Margaret Poynter, *What's One More?,* Atheneum (New York, NY), 1985.
Jean Fritz, *Make Way for Sam Houston,* Putnam (New York, NY), 1986.
Jamie Gilson, *Hobie Hanson, You're Weird,* Lothrop (New York, NY), 1987.
Patricia Lee Gauch, *Christina Katerina and the Time She Quit the Family,* Putnam (New York, NY), 1987.
Jamie Gilson, *Double Dog Dare,* Lothrop (New York, NY), 1988.
Elaine Moore, *Grandma's Promise,* Lothrop (New York, NY), 1988.

Jane Yolen, *Best Witches: Poems for Halloween,* Putnam (New York, NY), 1989.
Patricia Lee Gauch, *Christina Katerina and the Great Bear Train,* Putnam (New York, NY),1990.
Diane Stanley, *Moe the Dog in Tropical Paradise,* Putnam (New York, NY), 1992.
Diane Stanley, *Woe Is Moe,* Putnam (New York, NY), 1995.
Mary-Claire Helldorfer, *Jack, Skinny Bones, and the Golden Pancakes,* Viking (New York, NY), 1996.
Helen Elizabeth Buckley, *Moonlight Kite,* Lothrop (New York, NY), 1997.
Jerdine Nolen, *Raising Dragons,* Silver Whistle (San Diego, CA), 1998.

Sidelights

Elise Primavera has contributed her artwork to numerous picture books, some self-penned and others written by such noted authors as Jane Yolen, Natalie Savage Carlson, and Jerdine Nolen. Combining soft-edged, brightly colored pastels and subtle charcoal with more-opaque media such as gouache and acrylics, Primavera's illustrations have been praised for their liveliness and imagination, and compared to the work of fellow illustrator Lane Smith. "Primavera's . . . illustrations . . . fairly burst forth from the pages, adding to the exaggerated humor" of Mary-Claire Helldorfer's *Jack, Skinny Bones, and the Golden Pancakes,* in the opinion of *Booklist* contributor Kay Weisman, while a *Publishers Weekly* reviewer noted that the artist's "rip-roaring" and "dynamic spreads heighten the suspense" of the story.

Primavera began her career by producing fashion illustrations, but after several years began to feel that her creativity was not being challenged. In 1979, she decided to make a change and delve into children's book illustration. As part of her career transition she attended an illustrator's workshop, which gave her the confidence she needed. "I felt very encouraged after three weeks," Primavera recalled to Jim Roginski in an interview for *Behind the Covers: Interviews with Authors and Illustrators of Books for Children and Young Adults.* While she had an agent market her fashion illustration skills, Primavera decided to represent herself as a children's illustrator. Walking the streets of New York City with her portfolio, "I saw everybody and anybody who would give me an appointment," the author-illustrator recalled of her first year, "and once I got in the door I'd always ask if there was anyone else that could see me while I was there."

Primavera's first break came when she was hired to create a book jacket for Harper & Row. A picture-book assignment followed a few months later. By 1981, Primavera had two illustrated picture books to her credit: Dorothy Crayder's *The Joker and the Swan* and Joyce St. Peter's *Always Abigail.* Two years later, she could add "author" to her credits with the publication of *Basil and Maggie,* the story of a young girl who receives an unusual gift of a pony named Basil. Visions of walking away with a blue ribbon at the local horse show vanish into smoke after Basil proves himself less than sure-footed next to his sleek thoroughbred competitors, but Maggie falls in love with him anyway in a story that a *Publishers Weekly* contributor called "just the antidote to have on hand when everything goes wrong." Primavera's illustrations were the object of praise as well; *School Library Journal* contributor Roberta Magid commented that the book's "charcoal drawings accentuate the humorous situation."

Other books by Primavera include *The Three Dots,* a story of a trio of animals—Sal the moose, Henry the frog, and Margaret the duck—whose odd polka-dotted markings inspire them to form a musical group and take Manhattan by storm. Citing Primavera's "off-the-wall volume" for its "kicky watercolors" and "hilarious scenes," a *Publishers Weekly* contributor concluded that *The Three Dots* "should get lots of play." While less than enthusiastic about the text, Dot Minzer appreciated the book's "colorful, oversized" pictures. In her *School Library Journal* appraisal of *The Three Dots,* she observed that Primavera's "spirited and amusing . . . pictures will grab a young audience and bring smiles to their faces." An animal protagonist is also featured in *Ralph's Frozen Tale,* a picture book that finds Arctic explorer Ralph stuck without a dogsled until he is helped by a polar bear that can speak. "Primavera's swirling blues, greens, purples and whites give depth and beauty to the trackless, snowy wastes traversed by her heros," noted *School Library Journal* contributor Lisa Dennis in regard to the volume's humorous and highly detailed illustrations. In the intriguingly titled *Plantpet,* the story of a lonely junk collector who discovers a caged plant which, when given suitable care, grows into a leaf-covered gardener, she creates what a *Publishers Weekly* critic characterized as "another quirky tale that celebrates buddydom."

A disciplined artist, Primavera's workday begins at 7:00 a.m. "I work straight through until three o'clock or so," she told Roginski. "As far as my work time goes I spend much of it working out the sketches and dummy and the 'look' of the book. I try to capture its mood through an appropriate style. This takes a good deal of time because I'm not always comfortable or facile in a particular style. So I spend a lot of time not only on sketches, composition, and characterization (and the dummy in general), but also on the finishes because I'm working in an unfamiliar medium."

In all her illustration projects, whether for her own books or for texts by other authors, Primavera makes it a point to "make the most bizarre thing seem possible and real to the reader. It's sort of like watching a good magician perform: you know he really can't be pulling that rabbit out of the hat, but it all looks so real that for a moment something magical really is happening. This is the response that I try to work for through my illustrations."

Primavera counts among her inspirations the artist-illustrators associated with Howard Pyle and the Brandywine School that developed in and around Chadd's Ford, Pennsylvania, in the early 1900s. "I especially like N.C. Wyeth, Jessie Willcox Smith, and Charlotte Harding," she commented. Of her own artwork, one of the most memorable projects was creating the illustrations for Jane Yolen's *Best Witches: Poems for Halloween.* "For research, I spent a lot of time in the local costume store," Primavera recalled. "When I actually finished *Best Witches* (nine months later), my studio was crammed with witches' hats, rubber skeletons, fright wigs, plastic frogs, and black hairy spiders. At the time I was selling my house, and I used to love to watch my real estate agent show prospective buyers the studio—I don't think they knew whether to laugh or report me to the local authorities!"

Biographical and Critical Sources

BOOKS

Behind the Covers: Interviews with Authors and Illustrators of Books for Children and Young Adults, Libraries Unlimited (Littleton, CO), 1985, pp. 161-166.

PERIODICALS

Booklist, March 15, 1995, Stephanie Zvirin, review of *Woe Is Moe,* p. 1338; October 15, 1996, Kay Weisman, review of *Jack, Skinny Bones, and the Golden Pancakes,* p. 426; April, 1998, Stephanie Zvirin, review of *Raising Dragons,* p. 1334.

Bulletin of the Center for Children's Books, September, 1994, review of *Plantpet,* p. 24.

Horn Book, March-April, 1998, Susan P. Bloom, review of *Raising Dragons,* p. 217.

Kirkus Reviews, November 15, 1991, review of *Ralph's Frozen Tale,* p. 1474.

Publishers Weekly, April 29, 1983, review of *Basil and Maggie,* p. 52; October 11, 1991, review of *Ralph's Frozen Tale,* p. 63; October 4, 1993, review of *The Three Dots,* p. 78; August 8, 1994, review of *Plantpet,* p. 434; March 13, 1995, review of *Woe Is Moe,* p. 69; November 11, 1996, review of *Jack, Skinny Bones, and the Golden Pancakes,* p. 73.

Quill and Quire, November, 1993, review of *The Three Dots,* p. 40.

School Library Journal, May, 1983, Roberta Magid, review of *Basil and Maggie,* p. 65; February, 1992, Lisa Dennis, review of *Ralph's Frozen Tale,* pp. 76-77; January, 1994, Dot Minzer, review of *The Three Dots,* p. 97; November, 1994, Lynn Cockett, review of *Plantpet,* p. 88; June, 1995, Karen James, review of *Woe Is Moe,* p. 96; October, 1996, Lauralyn Persson, review of *Jack, Skinny Bones, and the Golden Pancakes,* p. 96.

Q-R

QUATTLEBAUM, Mary 1958-

Personal
Born May 2, 1958, in Bryan, TX; daughter of Con (an operations analyst) and Helen (a school nurse) Quattlebaum; married Christopher David (a chief technical officer and director of information systems), September 24, 1988; children: Christy. *Education:* College of William and Mary, B.A. (high honors), 1980; Georgetown University, M.A., 1986. *Politics:* "Independent." *Religion:* Roman Catholic. *Hobbies and other interests:* Travel, juggling, Greyhound buses, local history, cartooning, gardening.

Addresses
Home—Washington, DC. *E-mail*—mary@maryquattlebaum.com.

Career
Writer, editor, and teacher. Children's National Medical Center, Washington, DC, medical writer/editor, 1986-88; Arts Project Renaissance, Washington, DC, part-time director of creative-writing program for older adults, 1986-98; Georgetown University School for Summer and Continuing Education, Washington, DC, writing instructor, 1986—; freelance writer and editor, 1989—. Also teaches at Writer's Center, Bethesda, MD.

Member
Society of Children's Book Writers and Illustrators, Women's National Book Association, Authors Guild.

Awards, Honors
Marguerite de Angeli Prize, and Best Book award, *Parenting* magazine, both 1994, both for *Jackson Jones and the Puddle of Thorns;* Judy Blume novel-in-progress grant, Society of Children's Book Writers and Illustrators, 1991; creative-writing fellowships, District

Mary Quattlebaum (Photograph by Mark Darling. Reproduced by permission.)

of Columbia Commission on the Arts and Humanities, 1994, 1999, 2001; Sugarman Award for Children's Literature, 1998, for *The Magic Squad and the Dog of Great Potential;* American Bookseller Association Kids' Pick of the List choice, for *Aunt CeeCee, Aunt Belle, and Mama's Surprise;* Best Picture Book Award finalist, Texas Institute of Letters, for *Family Reunion* illus-

siblings and would make up stories and plays
to perform. It was not until she began working
dical writer for Children's National Medical
owever, that Quattlebaum seriously considered
er stories down. "While there," she recalled in
view on the Eerdmans Books for Young Read-
site, "my husband (who had been a profes-
magician as a kid) and I started a volunteer
called Magic Words. Once a week we would
e or two of the hospitalized kids and, through
and poetry, encourage them to write their own
and poems. What a range of emotions their work
sed—courage, curiosity, anger, fear, boredom,
ess, love! Their example was truly inspiring and
aged me to try writing for an audience of chil-

w up with three brothers, three sisters, and lots of
and often draw upon my childhood adventures
nisadventures) in my writing," the author once re-
l. "For example, the warm and wacky family in
CeeCee, Aunt Belle, and Mama's Surprise is a lot
my own family. The hamster in *Jazz, Pizzazz, and
ilver Threads* and the big, goofy dog in *The Magic
d and the Dog of Great Potential* are based on
life pets."

strong sense of place is also very important to my
k," Quattlebaum also noted. "The poems in *A Year
My Street* focus on images and sounds from my
ghborhood in Washington, DC. There's a sax-playing
n, a jump-roping girl, and an old cat who likes to be
atched. The setting for my first book, *Jackson Jones
d the Puddle of Thorns*, is a plot in a city community
rden, similar to my own, which started fifty years ago
a Victory Garden to grow food during World War II.
ke my main character Jackson, I often feel my most
undant crop is weeds! And the country setting and
veet gum trees of *Grover G. Graham and Me* were in-
ired by my childhood in rural Virginia, whereas
arks Fly High: The Legend of Dancing Point* drew
pon my college years and time spent working in Colo-
ial Williamsburg, Virginia."

Jackson Jones and the Puddle of Thorns is a humorous
story about a ten-year-old boy who wants a basketball
for his birthday but gets instead a plot in the community garden. The resourceful lad decides to grow flowers in his garden, sell them, and in this way raise the
money he will need to buy himself a basketball. Unfortunately, Jackson does not find flower-growing as easy
as it appears, and the teasing he gets from "Blood"
Green, the neighborhood bully, a fight with his best
friend, Reuben, over a rosebush, and the unexpected
pleasure he gets from gardening further complicate
Jackson's money-making scheme. "A host of colorful
characters and their lively banter keep the bloom on
these pages," remarked a *Publishers Weekly* contributor
in a favorable review of *Jackson Jones and the Puddle
of Thorns.*

Cover of Quattlebaum's middle-grade mystery Jackson Jones and the
Curse of the Outlaw Rose, *featuring artwork by Patrick Faricy.* (Illustration © 2006 by Patrick Faricy. Used by permission of Random House Children's Books, a
division of Random House, Inc.)

Several reviewers of *Jackson Jones and the Puddle of
Thorns* singled out Quattlebaum's array of secondary
characters, noting her realistic rendering of their speech
patterns. The novel's cast was described as one comprised of "distinctive and dignified individuals" by a reviewer for *Bulletin of the Center for Children's Books.*
The young narrator's "humorous, street-smart style"
draws in readers immediately, according to a *Publishers
Weekly* critic, and "the cozy, apparently multi-ethnic
apartment building makes for a lively urban milieu,"
according to a reviewer for the *Bulletin of the Center
for Children's Books,* the critic dubbing the book "fresh,
sweet, and vigorous—a real daisy."

In a sequel, *Jackson Jones and Mission Greentop,* the
enthusiastic ten year old learns that a land developer
plans to build an apartment complex at Rooter's, the
community garden where he grows roses and zucchini
amid the weeds. Undaunted, Jackson uses his wits to
prevent a corporate takeover and meet another challenge from nemesis "Blood" Green. "Jackson's way of
looking at life is original and appealing," observed
School Library Journal contributor Edith Ching. According to *Horn Book* contributor Susan Dove Lempke,

trated by Andrea Shine; Notable Social Studies Trade Book designation, Children's Book Council/National Council for the Social Studies, 2004, for *Jackson Jones and Mission Greentop;* Bank Street School of Education Best Book selection, 2006, for *Sparks Fly High;* gold and bronze medals for children's book reviews, from Parenting Publications of America; books included on many state children's choice lists.

Writings

MIDDLE-GRADE NOVELS

Jackson Jones and the Puddle of Thorns, illustrated by Melodye Rosales, Delacorte (New York, NY), 1994.

Jazz, Pizzazz, and the Silver Threads, illustrated by Robin Oz, Delacorte (New York, NY), 1996.

The Magic Squad and the Dog of Great Potential, illustrated by Frank Remkiewicz, Delacorte (New York, NY), 1997.

Grover G. Graham and Me, Delacorte (New York, NY), 2001.

Jackson Jones and Mission Greentop, Delacorte (New York, NY), 2004.

Jackson Jones and the Curse of the Outlaw Rose, Delacorte (New York, NY), 2006.

PICTURE BOOKS

In the Beginning, illustrated by Bryn Barnard, Time-Life Books (New York, NY), 1995.

Jesus and the Children, illustrated by Bill Farnsworth, Time-Life Books (New York, NY), 1995.

A Year on My Street, illustrated by Cat Bowman Smith, Delacorte (New York, NY), 1996.

Underground Train, illustrated by Cat Bowman Smith, Doubleday (New York, NY), 1997.

Aunt CeeCee, Aunt Belle, and Mama's Surprise, illustrated by Michael Chesworth, Doubleday (New York, NY), 1999.

The Shine Man, illustrated by Tim Ladwig, Eerdmans Books for Young Readers (Grand Rapids, MI), 2001.

Family Reunion, illustrated by Andrea Shine, Eerdmans Books for Young Readers (Grand Rapids, MI), 2004.

Winter Friends, illustrated by Hiroe Nakata, Doubleday (New York, NY), 2005.

(Reteller) *Sparks Fly High: The Legend of Dancing Point,* illustrated by Leonid Gore, Farrar, Straus & Giroux (New York, NY), 2006.

OTHER

Contributor of numerous stories and poems to children's magazines, including *Cricket, Ladybug, Spider, Babybug, Boys' Life,* and *Children's Digest,* and to literary magazines for adults, including *Poet Lore, Formalist,* and *Gettysburg Review.* Contributor of articles and reviews to *Washington Post,* 1995—. Reviewer of children's books, 1986—, and columnist, 1997—, for *Washington Parent.*

Sidelights

Mary Quattlebaum is the auth regarded picture books for c middle-grade readers. A frequ *Washington Post* and *Washingto* also teaches courses in writing Georgetown University and th Maryland. She writes children's ety of topics, from a young girl's the subway in Washington, DC, i to a story about a long-time foste attached to a foster baby living wit *Grover Graham and Me.* "Ideas a mented the author on her home p come from a hodge-podge of experi

"My first memory is of my dad recit right before bedtime," Quattlebaum Children's Book Guild Web site. Sin added, "I've been fascinated with s bring a sense of different rhythms and ems and books for children." The olde ily of seven children, she often rea

younger for them as a m Center, writing an inter ers We sional projec visit c magic stories expre tende encou dren.

"I gr pets, (and calle Aun like the Squ rea

"A wo on ne ma sc ar g as L

Cover of Quattlebaum's middle-grade novel Jazz, Pizzazz, and the ver Threads, *featuring an illustration by Robin Oz.* (Illustration © 1996 Robin Oz. Used by permission of Random House Children's Books, a division of Rand House, Inc.)

"Quattlebaum's talent for depicting a lively, diverse neighborhood and funny interchanges between kids remains strong," and a *Kirkus Reviews* critic wrote that the author "has created a warm neighborhood with a good-hearted boy at its center."

Bad luck follows Jackson and Reuben after they steal a rose clipping from an abandoned cemetery in *Jackson Jones and the Curse of the Outlaw Rose,* "a well-written, fast-paced adventure," according to Jennifer Cogan in *School Library Journal.* "With *Outlaw Rose,* I wanted to play with the conventions of the ghost story," Quattlebaum explained on her home page. "Rather than an old house, this ghost haunts an antique rosebush. Because this ghost doesn't moan and rattle chains in stereotypical fashion, Jackson is slow to realize that he is, indeed, dealing with a ghost, which hopefully makes for some funny moments in the book."

The Shine Man: A Christmas Story is based on Quattlebaum family lore and takes place in 1932, just three years after the start of the Great Depression. Times are hard, but a poor shoeshine man still finds it in his heart to give a child his cap, gloves, and a toy angel made from empty wooden spools. In the process of shining the child's shoes, the man discovers the child's true identity and becomes an angel himself. "With a light touch, Quattlebaum leaves the deeper meaning of the story to the reader's imagination," wrote a contributor to *School Library Journal.* A *Publishers Weekly* reviewer called *The Shine Man* a "lyrical, mystical tale."

A novel for middle graders, *Grover G. Graham and Me* centers on Ben Watson, a young boy who has lived in several foster homes. Over the years, Ben has hardened himself to leaving his various foster parents behind. At age eleven, he lands in a foster home where he finds himself becoming attached to the family, especially to Grover G. Graham, an infant whose real mother is trying to regain custody of him. Fearing for Grover's well being and convinced he can care for the infant better than his teenaged mom can, Ben makes a rash decision and takes Grover along for the ride. Reviewing *Grover G. Graham and Me* in *Horn Book,* Kitty Flynn remarked that "Quattlebaum pulls off this unlikely pairing with restraint and without resorting to sentimentality," ultimately "build[ing] . . . naturally to a heartbreaking climax." A *Kirkus Reviews* contributor commented that, "as the tension skillfully builds, Quattlebaum ratchets up the stakes, thrusting her sympathetic but wrong-headed protagonist in a position where he could lose everything, finally delivering a credible, emotionally satisfying ending that will have readers reaching for their hankies."

In *Why Sparks Fly High* Quattlebaum retells a Virginia folktale about Colonel Lightfoot, a skillful but vain dancer, and the devil who challenges him to a contest for his stretch of land along the James River. "I discovered the tale . . . in a book of Williamsburg ghost stories and loved the idea of opponents fighting not with fists but with fancy footwork," Quattlebaum recalled in an interview on the Farrar, Straus & Giroux Web site. *Horn Book* reviewer Joanna Rudge Long called the work "witty and nimbly paced," and in *Booklist* Gillian Engberg praised the author's "folksy words, which have all the infectious rhythm of a country dance."

Several of Quattlebaum's books for young readers feature verses accompanied by engaging illustrations. "Poems are these amazing little word packages," she told *Washington Post Book World* contributor Ron Charles. "In just a few lines you can play around with form, rhythm, rhyme, image and sound." In *Family Reunion,* a collection of fifteen poems, she looks at a family gathering through the eyes of ten-year-old Jodie. "The rhythms and rhymes in many of the selections lend an easy tone to the text," remarked *School Library Journal* contributor Shawn Brommer. Another book comprised of verse, *Winter Friends,* focuses on a young girl spending a snowy day playing outdoors. Here Quattlebaum "uses a variety of forms to good effect, including haiku and concrete poems," noted a *Kirkus Reviews* contributor of the book.

"Writing for young readers continues to be a wonderful challenge," Quattlebaum noted on her home page. "I try to listen carefully to the world (to others this might look like daydreaming) and bring a sense of different voices and rhythms to the page."

Biographical and Critical Sources

PERIODICALS

Booklist, February 15, 1996; February 1, 1997, Kay Weisman, review of *The Magic Squad and the Dog of Great Potential,* p. 942; December 1, 1997, review of *Underground Train,* p. 643; September 1, 2001, Ilene Cooper, review of *The Shine Man: A Christmas Story,* p. 121; April 1, 2004, Ilene Cooper, review of *Family Reunion,* p. 1367; November 1, 2005, Ilene Cooper, review of *Winter Friends,* p. 41; October 15, 2006, Gillian Engberg, review of *Sparks Fly High: The Legend of Dancing Point,* p. 52; January 1, 2007, Hazel Rochman, review of *Jackson Jones and the Curse of the Outlaw Rose,* p. 81.

Bulletin of the Center for Children's Books, March, 1994, review of *Jackson Jones and the Puddle of Thorns,* pp. 230-31; February, 1997, review of *The Magic Squad and the Dog of Great Potential,* p. 220; December, 1997, review of *Underground Train,* p. 137.

Children's Book Review Service, March, 1998, review of *Underground Train,* p. 87; August, 1999, review of *Aunt Ceecee, Aunt Belle, and Mama's Surprise,* p. 165.

Horn Book, May-June, 1997, Elizabeth S. Watson, review of *The Magic Squad and the Dog of Great Potential,* p. 327; fall, 1999, review of *Aunt Ceecee, Aunt Belle, and Mama's Surprise,* p. 624; January-February, 2002,

Kitty Flynn, review of *Grover G. Graham and Me*, p. 83; September-October, 2004, Susan Dove Lempke, review of *Jackson Jones and Mission Greentop*, p. 595; September-October, 2006, Joanna Rudge Long, review of *Sparks Fly High*, p. 601.

Kirkus Reviews, November 1, 1997, review of *Underground Train*, p. 1648; May 1, 1999, review of *Aunt Ceecee, Aunt Belle, and Mama's Surprise*, p. 726; October 15, 2001, review of *Grover G. Graham and Me*, p. 1490; July 1, 2004, review of *Jackson Jones and Mission Greentop*, p. 636; September 15, 2005, review of *Winter Friends*, p. 1032; September 15, 2006, review of *Sparks Fly High*, p. 964.

Publishers Weekly, November 29, 1993, review of *Jackson Jones and the Puddle of Thorns*, p. 66; November 24, 1997, review of *Underground Train*, p. 73; April 19, 1999, review of *Underground Train*, p. 75; June 7, 1999, review of *Aunt Ceecee, Aunt Belle, and Mama's Surprise*, p. 82; September 24, 2001, review of *The Shine Man*, p. 53; February 23, 2004, review of *Family Reunion*, p. 74; November 28, 2005, review of *Winter Friends*, p. 50.

School Library Journal, March, 1996; May, 1997, review of *The Magic Squad and the Dog of Great Potential*, p. 111; November, 1997, review of *Underground Train*, p. 97; July, 1999, review of *Aunt Ceecee, Aunt Belle, and Mama's Surprise*, p. 78; October, 2001, review of *The Shine Man*, p. 68; June, 2004, Shawn Brommer, review of *Family Reunion*, p. 132; November, 2004, Edith Ching, review of *Jackson Jones and Mission Greentop*, p. 116; October, 2005, Kara Schaff Dean, review of *Winter Friends*, p. 144; November, 2006, Jennifer Cogan, review of *Jackson Jones and the Curse of the Outlaw Rose*, p. 108; December, 2006, Lucinda Snyder Whitehurst, review of *Sparks Fly High*, p. 127.

Washington Post Book World, April 29, 2007, Ron Charles, interview with Quattlebaum, p. 9.

ONLINE

Childrens Book Guild Web site, http://www.childrensbookguild.org/ (December 1, 2007), "Mary Quattlebaum."

Eerdmans Books for Young Readers Web site, http://www.eerdmans.com/ (June 1, 2004), interview with Quattlebaum.

Farrar, Straus & Giroux Web site, http://www.fsgkidsbooks.com/ (December 1, 2007), "Q&A with Mary Quattlebaum."

Mary Quattlebaum Home Page, http://www.maryquattlebaum.com (December 1, 2007).

*   *   *

QUEEN LATIFAH 1970-
(Dana Elaine Owens)

Personal

Born Dana Elaine Owens, March 18, 1970, in East Orange, NJ; daughter of Lancelot (a police officer) and Rita (a teacher) Owens.

Addresses

Home—NJ. *Agent*—William Morris Agency, 1325 Avenue of the Americas, New York, NY 10019.

Career

Musician, actor, film producer, and author. Performer with Ladies Fresh, c. 1988; recording artist; recordings include *All Hail the Queen*, 1989; *Nature of a Sista'*, 1991; *Latifah's Had It up 2 Here*, 1991; *How Do I Love Thee*, 1991; *She's a Queen: A Collection of Hits*, 2002; and *Order in the Court2; Black Reign; New Jersey Drive; Trav'lin' Light*, 2007. Actor in films, including: (as Lashawn) *Jungle Fever*, 1991; (as Zora) *House Party 2*, 1991; (as Ruffhouse M.C.) *Juice*, 1992; (as Theresa) *My Life*, 1993; (as Cleo Sims) *Set It Off*, 1996; (as Sulie) *Hoodlum*, 1997; (as Teeny Fletcher) *Sphere*, 1998; (as Liz Bailey) *Living Out Loud*, 1998; (as Thelma) *The Bone Collector*, 1999; (as voice of Dispatcher Love) *Bringing out the Dead*, 1999; (as Cha-Cha) *The Country Bears*, 2002; (as Francine) *Brown Sugar*, 2002; (as voice of Dove) *Pinocchio*, 2002; (as Matron Mama Morton) *Chicago*, 2002; (as Charlene Morton) *Bringing down the House*, 2003; (as Aunt Shaneequa) *Scary Movie 3*, 2003; (as Gina) *Barbershop 2: Back in Business*, 2004; (as security guard) *The Cookout*, 2004; (as Belle Williams) *Taxi*, 2004; (as Gina Norris) *Beauty Shop*, 2005; (as Georgia Byrd) *Last Holiday*, 2006; (as voice of Ellie) *Ice Age: The Meltdown*, 2006; (as Penny Escher) *Stranger than Fiction*, 2006; (as Ana) *Life Support*, 2007; (as Motormouth Maybelle) *Hairspray*, 2007; (as Mrs. Christmas) *The Perfect Holiday*, 2007; and (as Nina Brewster) *Mad Money*, 2008. Actor in television movies and television series, including *The Fresh Prince of Bel-Air*, 1991; *Living Single*, 1997-98; and *Spin City*, 2001.

Awards, Honors

Grammy Award for Best Solo Rap Performance, 1994, for "U.N.I.T.Y."; Acapulco Black Film Festival Award for Best Actress, 1997, for *Set It Off*; Academy Award nomination for Best Supporting Actress, and British Academy of Film and Television Arts Award for Best Supporting Actress, Broadcast Film Critics Association Critics Choice Award for Best Acting Ensemble (with others), Screen Actors Guild Award for Outstanding Cast in a Motion Picture (with others), Golden Globe Award nomination for Best Supporting Actress, and Black Reel Award for Best Actress, all 2003, all for *Chicago*; BET Award for Favorite Actress, 2003; Teen Choice Award for Best Movie Actress—Comedy, 2003, and Image Award for Outstanding Actress in a Motion Picture, 2004, both for *Bringing Down the House*; BET Comedy Award for Outstanding Supporting Actress, 2004, for *Barbershop 2*; Black Movie Awards nomination for Outstanding Performance by an Actress, 2005, for *Beauty Shop*, 2006, for *Last Holiday*; honored with a star on the Hollywood Walk of Fame, 2006; Hollywood Film Festival Film Award for Ensemble of the Year (with others), 2007, for *Hairspray*; Emmy Award nomination for Outstanding Lead Actress in a Miniseries or Movie, 2007, and Golden Globe Award nomination for Best Performance by an Actress in a Miniseries or Motion Picture Made for Television, 2008, both for *Life Support;* named among VH1's 100 Greatest Women of Rock 'n' Roll.

Writings

(With Karen Hunter) *Ladies First: Revelations of a Strong Woman,* foreword by Rita Owens, William Morrow (New York, NY), 1999.

(Author of story, with Shakim Compere) *The Cookout* (screenplay), Lions Gate Films, 2004.

Queen of the Scene (for children), illustrated by Frank Morrison, Laura Geringer Books (New York, NY), 2006.

Sidelights

Queen Latifah—her stage name is Arabic for "fragile and sensitive"—is an American rap and hip-hop artist who has also gained acclaim as the first woman rapper to be nominated for an Academy award. Harnessing her talent, her natural charisma, and her commanding, energetic presence, Queen Latifah has expanded her audience through her work in films such as *Bringing Down the House, Chicago, Last Holiday,* and *Hairspray.* In her many public appearances, as well as in books such as her inspiring memoir *Ladies First: Revelations of a Strong Woman* and the picture book *Queen of the Scene,* she also works to inspires others to learn from her success.

Queen Latifah was born Dana Owens, in 1970 and grew up in New Jersey, where her father worked as a police officer. In high school, she was a key member of her school's basketball team, and her first job was at Burger King. Fortunately for Queen Latifah, her musical talent allowed her to find a more lucrative career, however, and by age eighteen she was rapping as part of Ladies Fresh. In 1988 she made her solo recording debut with the single "Wrath of My Madness," followed by her album *All Hail the Queen.* Combining jazz, rap, and rock, Queen Latifah brings a strong woman-centered viewpoint to her music. This view also runs through *Ladies First,* which reveals Queen Latifah's unique take on her sometimes difficult, sometimes controversial, and ultimately inspiring life.

With *Queen of the Scene* Queen Latifah turns to a younger audience, gearing her story to early elementary-grade readers. Illustrated by award-winning artist Frank Morrison and accompanied by a CD, *Queen of the Scene* introduces readers to a confident young girl whose belief in her own abilities allows her to work toward success in everything she tries, and have fun at the same time. Basketball, stickball, and hula-hooping are sports she excels at, and the girl has no qualms about stating

the obvious: She's good! *Queen of the Scene* is "delivered with lots of sass," according to *School Library Journal* contributor Mary Hazelton, and "is sure to appeal to those who can celebrate their own special gifts." In praise of Queen Latifah's "rollicking" rhyming text, an *Ebony* critic cited the author for illustrating "the elements of self-respect," while in *Publishers Weekly* a critic dubbed the picture book a "sassy debut."

Biographical and Critical Sources

PERIODICALS

Ebony, November, 2006, review of *Queen of the Scene,* p. 43.

Kirkus Reviews, October 1, 2006, review of *Queen of the Scene,* p. 1022.

Publishers Weekly, October 2, 2006, review of *Queen of the Scene,* p. 61.

School Library Journal, December, 2006, Mary Hazelton, review of *Queen of the Scene,* p. 101.

ONLINE

Queen Latifah Home Page, http://www.queenlatifah.com (December 15, 2007).*

*   *   *

QUENTIN
See SHELDON, David

*   *   *

RIES, Lori

Personal

Married; husband's name David; children: three.

Addresses

Home and office—Tigard, OR. *E-mail*—readermail@ LoriRies.net.

Career

Children's writer.

Writings

Super Sam!, illustrated by Sue Ramá, Charlesbridge (Watertown, MA), 2004.

Mrs. Fickle's Pickles, illustrated by Nancy Cote, Boyds Mills (Honesdale, PA), 2006.

Aggie and Ben: Three Stories, illustrated by Frank W. Dormer, Charlesbridge (Watertown, MA), 2006.

Fix It, Sam, illustrated by Sue Ramá, Charlesbridge (Watertown, MA), 2007.

Punk Wig, illustrated by Erin Eitter-Kono, Boyds Mills (Honesdale, PA), 2008.

Sidelights

While growing up, children's author and literacy advocate Lori Ries loved to read. She wrote her first tale, "Jo-Jo the Raccoon," at the age of ten, and continued making up stories with her mother's encouragement. In high school, after a short-story writing assignment, Ries was taken aside by her English teacher and told: "Lori, this isn't a short story, this is a preface to a novel, and if you work hard enough you could become a great writer." Ries always enjoyed keeping a personal journal, but it was not until she had children of her own that she began to consider writing as a career. She enrolled with the Institute of Children's Literature, and started attending workshops provided by the Highlights Foundation. "I think that having kids, being around kids, being a stay-at-home mom let me know kids," she explained in an interview in Oregon's *Tigard Times.*

It was being around children that sparked the idea for Ries's first book, *Super Sam!* While attending the Highlights Chautauqua Writer's Workshop, she spotted a little boy playing very earnestly, and she watched him

Cover of Lori Ries' picture book **Super Sam!,** *featuring colorful cartoon illustrations by Sue Ramá.* (Illustration © 2004 by Sue Ramá. Reproduced by permission of Charlesbridge Publishing, Inc.)

for awhile, appreciating how he was in his own world. When she identified his mother, the two women chatted, and soon Ries met Sam, who, his mother told her, posed as a super hero at home. That tale turned into a picture book, introducing young readers to *Super Sam!*

Home from preschool, the fictional Sam borrows baby brother Petey's blanket for use as the cape that transforms him into a super hero. The boy piles up pillows to prepare for leaping over tall buildings, hefts toys over his head to show his strength, and performs other feats of daring. When Sam accidentally steps on Petey's finger, however, he realizes that his super powers cannot solve the problem—but his cape can. Given back the baby blanket, Petey's tears soon end. "Ries tells the story in short sentences, using only fifty-three words," noted a *Kirkus Reviews* contributor, and a *Publishers Weekly* critic maintained that in this brief text "Ries expresses everything there is to say" about the relationship between young siblings. Gay Lynn Van Vleck, writing in *School Library Journal,* dubbed *Super Sam!* "a cozy tale of brotherly affection."

Sam and Petey return in *Fix It, Sam.* When the siblings attempt to build a tent from a blanket and chairs, it keeps sagging in the middle. Although Petey has absolute faith that Sam will come up with a solution, it is Petey who solves the problem: when he sits in the middle of the tent, his head holds up the blanket. "Little sibs will easily grasp the story," wrote Shelle Rosenfeld in *Booklist.*

In *Aggie and Ben: Three Stories,* Ries introduces readers to narrator Ben and his new puppy, Aggie. In the first story, Ben brings Aggie home from the pet shop. The second tale shows Ben trying to act like a puppy, but his experiment stops short of drinking from the toilet bowl. In the third tale, Ben and Aggie keep each other safe from fears in the dark. "This unassuming tale will prove a welcome addition to any collection for emerging readers," wrote Jill Heritage Maza in *School Library Journal,* and a *Publishers Weekly* critic called *Aggie and Ben* "an impressive and original effort" that "bodes well for a sequel." Betty Carter, writing in *Horn Book,* explained that, while "kids can't be dogs, . . . Ben and Aggie let them know they can be readers."

Mrs. Fickle's Pickles is a simple verse story that shows Mrs. Fickle making pickles by growing them from seed to cucumber and then pickling them in jars where they eventually win the blue ribbon at the county fair. "The simplicity of this breezy rural story will invite repeat readings," wrote a *Kirkus Reviews* contributor of Ries' picture book.

Ries wrote *Punk Wig* in response to her concern over a friend's journey with bone cancer. The woman's worries over how to tell her child that she will lose all her hair was heart-wrenching, Ries explained to *SATA.* "*Punk Wig* is a humorous story with serious undertones that opens communications for kids whose lives are turned upside down by cancer," explained the author. "In the story, a boy is a support to his mother throughout her chemo treatments. When she loses her hair, they both go to Harriet's hair for some serious wig play. In the book, the seasons pass, and the ending holds a celebration when all the 'alien blobs' (cancer) have gone away."

"I don't know why a lot of people write, but I write because I really love it," Ries told the *Tigard Times* interviewer. "Books embrace children," she added, "and I like that."

Biographical and Critical Sources

PERIODICALS

Booklist, January 1, 2007, Shelle Rosenfeld, review of *Fix It, Sam,* p. 116.
Bulletin of the Center for Children's Books, May, 2007, Karen Coats, review of *Fix It, Sam,* p. 382.
Horn Book, September-October, 2006, Betty Carter, review of *Aggie and Ben: Three Stories,* p. 595; January-February, 2007, review of *Aggie and Ben,* p. 13.
Kirkus Reviews, June 1, 2004, review of *Super Sam!,* p. 540; October 15, 2006, review of *Mrs. Fickle's Pickles,* p. 1078.
Publishers Weekly, July 5, 2004, review of *Super Sam!,* p. 54; July 31, 2006, review of *Aggie and Ben,* p. 74.
School Library Journal, September, 2004, Gay Lynn Van Vleck, review of *Super Sam!,* p. 177; July, 2006, Jill Heritage Maza, review of *Aggie and Ben,* p. 86; February, 2007, Catherine Callegari, review of *Fix It, Sam,* p. 94.

ONLINE

Lori Ries Home Page, http://loriries.net (November 16, 2007).
Tigard Times Online, http://www.tigardtimes.com/ (January 18, 2007), interview with Ries.

* * *

ROCKWELL, Lizzy 1961-

Personal

Born 1961; daughter of Harlow (a painter and illustrator) and Anne F. (an author and artist) Rockwell; married Kenneth Alcorn; children: Nicholas, Nigel. *Education:* Attended Connecticut College and School of Visual Arts.

Addresses

Home and office—14 Nolan St., Norwalk, CT 06850. *E-mail*—lizzyrocwell@mac.com.

Lizzy Rockwell (Photograph by Kenneth Alcorn. Courtesy of Lizzy Rockwell.)

Career

Writer and illustrator. Illustrator, beginning 1984

Awards, Honors

The Busy Body Book named among top-ten science and technology books for youth, *Booklist,* 2004.

Writings

SELF-ILLUSTRATED

Hello Baby!, Crown (New York, NY), 1999.
Good Enough to Eat: A Kid's Guide to Food and Nutrition, HarperCollins (New York, NY), 1999.
The Busy Body Book: A Kid's Guide to Fitness, Crown (New York, NY), 2004.

ILLUSTRATOR

Anne F. Rockwell, *Apples and Pumpkins,* Macmillan (New York, NY), 1989, reprinted, Aladdin (New York, NY), 2005.
(With father, Harlow Rockwell) Anne F. Rockwell, *My Spring Robin,* Macmillan (New York, NY), 1989.
Amy Hest, *A Sort-of Sailor,* Four Winds (New York, NY), 1990.
(With Pam Braun and Rina Horiuchi) Pyke Johnson, *Pyke's Poems: Verse for Kids,* Shorelands (Old Greenwich, CT), 1992.

Anne F. Rockwell, *Our Yard Is Full of Birds,* Collier (New York, NY), 1992.
Anne F. Rockwell, *Pots and Pans,* Macmillan (New York, NY), 1993.
Anne F. Rockwell, *Ducklings and Pollywogs,* Macmillan (New York, NY), 1994.
Anne F. Rockwell, *Apples and Pumpkins,* Aladdin (New York, NY), 1994.
Priscilla Belz Jenkins, *A Nest Full of Eggs,* HarperCollins (New York, NY), 1995.
Deborah Heiligman, *On the Move,* HarperCollins (New York, NY), 1996.
Anne F. Rockwell, *Halloween Day,* HarperCollins (New York, NY), 1997.
Anne F. Rockwell, *Show and Tell Day,* HarperCollins (New York, NY), 1997.
I.K. Swobud, *Don't Go up Haunted Hill—or Else!,* Golden Books (New York, NY), 1999.
Anne F. Rockwell, *Thanksgiving Day,* HarperCollins (New York, NY), 1999.
Anne F. Rockwell, *Career Day,* HarperCollins (New York, NY), 2000.
Anne F. Rockwell, *Valentine's Day,* HarperCollins (New York, NY), 2001.
Anne F. Rockwell, *One Hundred School Days,* HarperCollins (New York, NY), 2002.
Gloria Rothstein, *Sheep Asleep,* HarperCollins (New York, NY), 2003.
Maya Angelou, *Izak of Lapland,* Random House (New York, NY), 2004.
Maya Angelou, *Renée Marie of France,* Random House (New York, NY), 2004.
Maya Angelou, *Mikale of Hawaii,* Random House (New York, NY), 2004.
Maya Angelou, *Angelina of Italy,* Random House (New York, NY), 2004.
Anne F. Rockwell, *Mother's Day,* HarperCollins (New York, NY), 2004.
Anne F. Rockwell, *Father's Day,* HarperCollins (New York, NY), 2005.
Anne F. Rockwell, *Who Lives in an Alligator Hole?,* Collins (New York, NY), 2006.
Joy N. Hulme, *Mary Clare Likes to Share: A Math Reader,* Random House (New York, NY), 2006.
Anne F. Rockwell, *Presidents' Day,* HarperCollins (New York, NY), 2007.

Sidelights

Lizzy Rockwell is an illustrator whose work has appeared in picture books and magazines, as well as in games and other products for children. A prolific artist, she has illustrated more than twenty books, many of them written by her mother, children's author Anne F. Rockwell. In addition to her work as an artist, Rockwell has also created art for her original texts, which include *Hello Baby!, Good Enough to Eat: A Kid's Guide to Food and Nutrition,* and *The Busy Body Book: A Kid's Guide to Fitness.*

As the daughter of two creative parents—her father, Harlow Rockwell, is an illustrator and author—Rockwell grew up around art and storytelling, and saw her

Lizzy Rockwell's illustration projects include the original holiday illustration "Let There Be Peace." (Courtesy of Lizzy Rockwell.)

parents collaborate on books together. "There were plenty of art materials around the house and my brother, sister, and I were always encouraged to be creative and to express our ideas," she recalled on her home page. After attending college and art school, Rockwell started her career in 1984, illustrating magazines and book jackets. Her first picture-book project, illustrating her mother's text for *Apples and Pumpkins,* was published in 1989.

As an illustrator, Rockwell is noted for her use of color. Her "realistically rendered illustrations are drenched in color," wrote Lisa Gangemi in a *School Library Journal* review of the artist's contribution to *One Hundred School Days,* a mother-daughter collaboration. In a review of another book by Anne F. Rockwell, *Pots and Pans,* a *Publishers Weekly* wrote that the "bright watercolors capture an impressive variety of textures." Another *Publishers Weekly* critic, reviewing *Halloween Day,* noted that author and artist collaborate to "create believable multiethnic characters." Wendy S. Carroll, writing in *School Library Journal,* complimented the easy-to-read text in *Career Day,* adding that Lizzy Rockwell's "colorful pictures are [as] . . . appealing"

as her mother's text. In a review of *Angelina of Italy,* Hazel Rochman wrote in *Booklist* that the illustrator's "clear, cheerful pictures will appeal to kids." Of her work on *Who Lives in an Alligator Hole?,* a *Kirkus Reviews* contributor wrote that "a non-reading child would be able to get much of the text's information from Lizzy Rockwell's pictures alone."

In her self-illustrated work, Rockwell explains good nutrition to a young audience in *Good Enough to Eat.* Designed for the preschool set, the book addresses such topics as fighting germs, vitamins, and how good foods help improve movement, respiration, warmth, and growing. "This could be a valuable classroom tool for teaching about health and nutrition," Rochman concluded in a *Booklist* review. Regarding the illustrations, a *Publishers Weekly* critic wrote that Rockwell's "compositions are cheerful and sometimes playful."

Another original self-illustrated picture book, *Hello Baby!,* is again geared for very young readers and was created by Rockwell to help soon-to-be-older-siblings prepare for an infant's arrival. The picture book depicts parents including their child in the entire process of pregnancy, including doctor visits, and describes the biology behind a growing baby. Noting that some of the concepts might be beyond the scope of the youngest readers, Rochman nonetheless noted that parents may "welcome the chance to include the fascinating biology as well as the usual reassuring message." The narrator's voice and explanations "accurately reflect a happy child's point of view," wrote a *Publishers Weekly* contributor.

The Busy Body Book uses some of the same techniques as *Good Enough to Eat*, presenting factual material in a way that makes it easy for preschoolers to understand. "The design is clear and inviting," wrote Rochman of the title in her *Booklist* review. Shauna Yusko, writing in *School Library Journal*, felt that Rockwell's "text is purposely motivating, yet easy to understand and informative."

On her home page, Rockwell explained that she enjoys both writing and illustrating. "It is such a great challenge to tell a story or explain something complicated using as few words as possible," she explained. "It's fun to write picture books, because you know that the pictures will do a lot of the work for you. Even when I am writing nonfiction, I want the words to sound as beautiful as a poem, flow from the mouth as easily as a song, and have meaning as compelling as a novel." "In my pictures, I want all children to recognize themselves, and feel proud and included," Rockwell told *SATA*. "I strive to model good citizenship, high self-esteem, and positive interpersonal relationships in ways that are realistic and natural, but never sentimental or preachy." Of being an author and illustrator as a career, she wrote: "My job is one of the most creative and expressive things I can imagine doing. I love carrying on my parent's tradition in children's books."

Biographical and Critical Sources

BOOKS

Marcus, Leonard S., *Pass It Down: Five Picture Book Families Make Their Mark*, Walker (New York, NY), 2006.

PERIODICALS

Booklist, December 15, 1994, Mary Harris Veeder, review of *Ducklings and Pollywogs*, p. 760; June 1, 1995, Hazel Rochman, review of *A Nest Full of Eggs*, p. 1778; May 1, 1996, Hazel Rochman, review of *On the Move*, p. 1510; April 1, 1997, Hazel Rochman, review of *Show and Tell Day*, p. 1339; January 1, 1999, Hazel Rochman, review of *Good Enough to Eat: A Kid's Guide to Food and Nutrition*, p. 883; March 15, 1999, review of *Hello Baby!*, p. 1334; September 1, 1999, Shelley Townsend-Hudson, review of *Thanksgiving Day*, p. 150; May 1, 2000, review of *Career Day*, p. 1679; December 1, 2003, review of *The Busy Body Book: A Kid's Guide to Fitness*, p. 681; November 15, 2004, Hazel Rochman, review of *Angelina of Italy*, p. 589; January 1, 2005, review of *The Busy Body Book*, p. 776; May 15, 2005, Ilene Cooper, review of *Father's Day*, p. 1666; December 1, 2006, Carolyn Phelan, review of *Who Lives in an Alligator Hole?*, p. 62.

Horn Book, May-June, 1993, Martha V. Parravano, review of *Pots and Pans*, p. 350; March, 2001, Martha V. Parravano, review of *Valentine's Day*, p. 202.

Kirkus Reviews, January 15, 2004, review of *The Busy Body Book*, p. 88; October 15, 2006, review of *Mary Clare Likes to Share*, p. 1073; November 1, 2006, review of *Who Lives in an Alligator Hole?*, p. 1124.

Publishers Weekly, April 5, 1993, review of *Pots and Pans*, p. 75; October 6, 1997, review of *Halloween Day*, p. 48; January 18, 1999, review of *Good Enough to Eat*, p. 338; May 10, 1999, review of *Hello Baby!*, p. 67.

School Library Journal, July, 2000, Wendy S. Carroll, review of *Career Day*, p. 86; September, 2002, Lisa Gangemi, review of *One Hundred School Days*, p. 205; January, 2004, Shauna Yusko, review of *The Busy Body Book*, p. 121; July, 2004, Lisa G. Kropp, review of *One Hundred School Days*, p. 44; May, 2005, Mary Hazelton, review of *Father's Day*, p. 95; November, 2006, Christine Markley, review of *Who Lives in an Alligator Hole?*, p. 123.

ONLINE

Kids at Random Web site, http://www.randomhouse.com/kids/ (November 21, 2007), profile of Rockwell.

Lizzy Rockwell Home Page, http://www.lizzyrockwell.com (November 16, 2007).

*   *   *

RODMAN, Mary Ann

Personal

Born March 26, in Washington, DC; married; husband's name Craig; children: Lily. *Education:* Lenoir-Rhyne College, B.A. (theater arts); University of Tennessee-Knoxville, M.L.S.; Vermont College, M.F.A. (writing). *Hobbies and other interests:* Antiques, listening to music, cycling, photography.

Addresses

Home—Alpharetta, GA. *E-mail*—maryannrodman@maryannrodman.com.

Career

Author and writing instructor. Has also worked as a school media specialist and university librarian.

Awards, Honors

Choice selection, Cooperative Children's Book Center (CCBC), Notable Book for Children selection, American Library Association, and Notable Trade Book in

Mary Ann Rodman (Photograph by Lily Neil Downing. Courtesy of Mary Ann Rodman.)

Social Studies, National Council for the Social Studies/ Children's Book Council, all for *Yankee Girl;* CCBC Choice selection, Charlotte Zolotow Award, Bank Street College of Education Best Book designation, and Ezra Jack Keats Award, New York Public Library/Ezra Jack Keats Foundation, all 2006, all for *My Best Friend.*

Writings

JUVENILE FICTION

Yankee Girl, Farrar, Straus & Giroux (New York, NY), 2004.
My Best Friend, illustrated by E.B. Lewis, Viking (New York, NY), 2005.
First Grade Stinks!, illustrated by Beth Spiegel, Peachtree Publishers (Atlanta, GA), 2006.
Jimmy's Stars, Farrar, Straus & Giroux (New York, NY), 2008.

Short fiction anthologized in *Such a Pretty Face: Short Stories about Beauty,* Amulet (New York, NY), 2007.

Sidelights

Mary Ann Rodman, a former school librarian, is the author of *My Best Friend,* a 2005 picture book that garnered both the Charlotte Zolotow Award and the Ezra Jack Keats Award. Rodman has also published *First Grade Stinks!,* another work for young readers, as well as the critically acclaimed middle-grade novel *Yankee Girl.*

Rodman developed an early interest in the written word. "I don't remember a time when I didn't want to be a writer," she remarked on her Web site. "I also don't remember when I didn't know how to read. My mom says I taught myself to read at age three, from TV commercials (back in the days when TV commercials had writing on the screen.)" Rodman recalled that she penned her first story at the age of seven, using a clothes hamper in the family bathroom as her desk. In high school, she became a reporter for her local paper and completed a number of award-winning short stories. Rodman stopped writing seriously, however, after beginning her career as a librarian. When her husband was transferred to Bangkok, Thailand, in 1997, she started her first book, *Yankee Girl,* and enrolled in a low-residency master's degree program at Vermont College. "It was the making of me as a writer," Rodman told *Publishers Weekly* interviewer Lynda Brill Comerford. "I can't stress enough the importance of having a

Rodman explores the challenges of young friendships in her picture book My Best Friend, *featuring E.B. Lewis's light-filled paintings.* (Illustration © by E.B. Lewis, 2005. Reproduced by permission of Viking, a division of Penguin Putnam Books for Young Readers.)

support group. The people I met in Vermont continue to be my best friends and critiquers."

Set in 1964, the semi-autobiographical *Yankee Girl* concerns sixth-grader Alice Ann Moxley, the daughter of an FBI agent who moves with her family from Chicago to Mississippi, just as her new school is about to be integrated. Dubbed "Yankee Girl" by the other students, Alice Ann witnesses the cruel treatment her African-American classmate, Valerie, receives at their hands. As the school year progresses, Alice Ann is torn between her desire to be accepted by the popular crowd and her friendship with Valerie. A *Kirkus Reviews* critic observed that Rodman's "novel is rich in detail and lively writing," and Susan Oliver remarked in *School Library Journal* that "the dialogue and narrative flow naturally." According to a *Publishers Weekly* reviewer, "Rodman shows characters grappling with hard choices, sometimes courageously, sometimes willfully, sometimes inconsistently, but invariably believably."

My Best Friend, which centers on six-year-old Lily's attempts to impress an older girl, is based on Rodman's experiences as a parent. As the author told *Cooperative Children's Book Center* online interviewer Andrea Schmitz, "my daughter was in a playgroup in Bangkok that met every week, and she had her best friend all picked out, just like the Lily in the story. Unfortunately, this little girl, who was a year older, wanted nothing to do with her . . . unless her own friends happened to be away." *My Best Friend* received strong reviews. "Rodman is attuned to the feelings of young children," stated a contributor in *Kirkus Reviews,* and *School Library Journal* critic Catherine Threadgill described the work as "simple but powerful," adding that it "speaks to the yearning outsider in every child."

In *First Grade Stinks!,* Haley discovers, much to her dismay, that she must leave the joys of kindergarten behind and adjust to a new teacher and new routines. When the young girl suffers a meltdown in the classroom, Ms. Gray helps the youngster overcome her fears. "Rodman's humorous tale serves as a gentle reminder to search for the silver lining," noted a contributor in *Kirkus Reviews.* Stephanie Zvirin, writing in *Booklist,* called *First Grade Stinks!* "an important book for kids making a pretty tough transition."

Biographical and Critical Sources

PERIODICALS

Booklist, March 1, 2004, Hazel Rochman, review of *Yankee Girl,* p. 1204; March 15, 2005, Hazel Rochman, review of *My Best Friend,* p. 1299; August 1, 2006, Stephanie Zvirin, review of *First Grade Stinks!,* p. 96.

Bulletin of the Center for Children's Books, June, 2004, Karen Coats, review of *Yankee Girl,* p. 435; July-August, 2005, review of *My Best Friend,* p. 509; September, 2006, Deborah Stevenson, review of *First Grade Stinks!,* p. 31.

Cover of Rodman's novel Yankee Girl, *which features artwork by Douglas B. Jones.* (Illustration ©2004 by Douglas B. Jones. Reproduced by permission of Farrar Straus & Giroux, a division of Farrar, Straus & Giroux, LLC.)

Horn Book, July-August, 2005, Michelle Martin, review of *My Best Friend,* p. 456.

Kirkus Reviews, March 15, 2004, review of *Yankee Girl,* p. 276; May 1, 2005, review of *My Best Friend,* p. 545; September 1, 2006, review of *First Grade Stinks!,* p. 912.

Publishers Weekly, April 12, 2004, review of *Yankee Girl,* p. 66; June 28, 2004, Lynda Brill Comerford, "Flying Starts," p. 19.

School Library Journal, April, 2004, Susan Oliver, review of *Yankee Girl,* p. 161; May, 2005, Catherine Threadgill, review of *My Best Friend,* p. 95; August, 2006, Marge Loch-Wouters, review of *First Grade Stinks!,* p. 96.

Voice of Youth Advocates, February, 2005, review of *Yankee Girl,* p. 443.

ONLINE

Cooperative Children's Book Center Web site, http://www.education.wisc.edu/ccbc/ (June 1, 2006), Andrea Schmitz, "Stories from Real Life: An Interview with Mary Ann Rodman."

Mary Ann Rodman Home Page, http://www.maryannrodman.com (November 10, 2007).

ROSE, Deborah Lee 1955-

Personal

Born October 24, 1955, in Philadelphia, PA; daughter of Bernard and Helen Rose; married; children: one daughter, one son. *Education:* Cornell University, B.A., 1977.

Addresses

Home—San Francisco Bay area, CA. *Agent*—c/o Jason Wells, jwellshnabooks.com.

Career

Time-Life Books, Alexandria, VA, editorial researcher, 1977-82; University of California at Berkeley, Berkeley, CA, science writer and speech writer, 1984-91; Lawrence Hall of Science, Berkeley, CA, development, marketing, and exhibit writer, 1998—; freelance writer.

Member

Society of Children's Book Writers and Illustrators, Northern California Science-Writers Association.

Awards, Honors

Council for the Advancement of Science Writing, national science writing fellow, 1983-84; Jane Addams Children's Peace Book Award recommended list, 1990, for *The People Who Hugged the Trees;* First Prize for juvenile trade books, Chicago Women in Publishing, 1991, for *Meredith's Mother Takes the Train;* Pick of the Lists selection, American Library Association, and 100 Children's Books to Read and Share selection, New York Public Library, both for *Into the A, B, Sea: An Ocean Alphabet;* Gold Award, National Parenting Publications, for *The Twelve Days of Kindergarten;* Gold Award, National Parenting Publications, for *The Twelve Days of Winter.*

Writings

The People Who Hugged the Trees, illustrated by Birgitta Säflund, Roberts Rinehart (Niwot, CO), 1990.

Meredith's Mother Takes the Train, illustrated by Irene Trivas, Albert Whitman (Morton Grove, IL), 1991.

The Rose Horse, illustrated by Greg Shed, Harcourt (San Diego, CA), 1996.

Into the A, B, Sea: An Ocean Alphabet, illustrated by Steve Jenkins, Scholastic (New York, NY), 2000.

Birthday Zoo, illustrated by Lynn Munsinger, Albert Whitman (Morton Grove, IL), 2002.

One Nighttime Sea: An Ocean Counting Rhyme, illustrated by Steve Jenkins, Scholastic (New York, NY), 2003.

The Twelve Days of Kindergarten: A Counting Book, illustrated by Carey Armstrong-Ellis, Harry N. Abrams (New York, NY), 2003.

Ocean Babies, illustrated by Hiroe Nakata, National Geographic Society (Washington, DC), 2004.

The Twelve Days of Winter: A Counting Book, illustrated by Carey Armstrong-Ellis, Harry N. Abrams (New York, NY), 2006.

Contributor to *A Childhood Remembered,* Narada, 1991; *The ABCs of Writing for Children,* by Elizabeth Koehler-Pentacoff; and *Spark Your Child's Success in Math and Science.*

Author's work has been translated into German, French, Spanish, Danish, Norwegian, Chinese, Vietnamese, Cambodian, and Hmong.

Adaptations

The People Who Hugged the Trees was adapted for television and radio by the British Broadcasting Corporation.

Sidelights

Deborah Lee Rose was an experienced science writer as well as a speech writer before she made the decision to write books for young readers. Inspired by her experiences as a mother, as well as her interests in both science and history, Rose has produced a selection of books that include *The People Who Hugged the Trees, Into the A, B, Sea: An Ocean Alphabet,* and *The Rose Horse.* As a child, Rose dreamed of becoming a translator for the United Nations, and creating picture books for children is not so different from that dream, as she once explained to *SATA.* "Writing for children is a process of translating complex concepts into very accessible language," she explained.

The People Who Hugged the Trees, Rose's first picture book for children, is based on a centuries-old story from Rajasthan, India, that was adapted during the twentieth century to inspire India's Chipko environmental movement. Readers will recognize the story's messages about caring for the environment as both timeless and contemporary, both local and global. "I was particularly struck by this story of a young girl who grows up to lead her entire village in saving a forest," Rose once explained to *SATA.* "I hope, as my daughter grows up, she will also feel strongly about making the world a better place in some way."

In *The People Who Hugged the Trees* Amrita Devi grows up knowing that the trees growing near her village are crucial to her family's survival. In addition to shelter from the sun, they protect the village from the violent sandstorms of the surrounding desert. One day the Maharajah decides to build a new fort, and he sends his men to Amrita's village to cut the trees down. Armed with axes, the men approach, only to find each tree embraced by a villager as a form of resistance thought up by the young girl to save her beloved trees. A *Horn Book* reviewer complimented illustrator Birgitta Säflund's "delicate, detailed" images, and called the book "a successful, timely tale." *Growing Point* critic Margery Fisher termed *The People Who Hugged the Trees* "an impressive example of the way story can convey a general idea" to children.

Other picture books by Rose touch on both serious and lighthearted family themes that range from workday separations to birthday celebrations. *Meredith's Mother Takes the Train* focuses on the concerns of both parents and children regarding work-week day care. Meredith's mom boards the train every morning to commute to work and spends her day thinking about the time she will spend with her daughter once she gets home. Meanwhile, Meredith spends time at day care, busily playing with her friends yet anticipating her mother's welcome arrival to pick her up. Rose's rhyming text captures the feeling of a train along the track—a poetic device that makes the story appealing to very young, even preverbal children. In *Booklist,* Leone McDermott called the work "subtly reassuring" to young children.

The love she and her children share for ocean animals prompted Rose to write a picture book about the ocean that weaves together marine science and language arts. *Into the A, B, Sea* uses what *Booklist* contributor Gillian Engberg described as "rhymed couplets filled with appealing action words" to introduce young story-time audiences to the diversity of the world's oceans. *School Library Journal* reviewer Joy Fleishhacker called the book "a tantalizing, visually stunning invitation to explore a new frontier," and noted that the "breathtaking" cut-paper collage illustrations contributed by Steve Jenkins provide "a perfect medley of vibrant color and restless motion."

Rose got the idea for *Into the A, B, Sea* while writing alphabet letters in the sand with her young son. "It hit me," she once recalled to *SATA,* "that the ocean and the alphabet are both so vast and full of possibilities." Rose's text mimics the rhythm of the waves against the shore, and Jenkins' illustrations are complemented by factual details for each ocean creature, as well as a useful glossary of terms. Rose and Jenkins have also created a sequel, *One Nighttime Sea: An Ocean Counting Rhyme,* which sheds light on the little-seen habits of the ocean's nocturnal creatures.

The idea for *One Nighttime Sea* stemmed from the author's research for *Into the A, B, Sea,* as Rose told *California Readers* interviewer Bonnie O'Brian. "While visiting the Monterey Bay Aquarium," the author explained, "I discovered that there was an amazing change that came over the ocean after dark, called 'vertical migration'—where every night, billions of animals rise from the deep ocean up to the surface to feed, then return to the depths at sunrise. This got me wondering about all kinds of nocturnal animals in the ocean." Reviewing *One Nighttime Sea,* a contributor in *Publishers Weekly* praised the "lyrical text," and *School Library*

Deborah Lee Rose provides an alphabetical introduction to the underwater world in **Into the A, B, Sea,** *a picture book featuring cut-paper collage art by Steve Jenkins.* (Illustration © 2000 by Steve Jenkins. Reproduced by permission of Scholastic, Inc.)

Journal contributor Julie Roach remarked that the "enchanting counting book lulls its audience into the world beneath the waves."

In *Ocean Babies* Rose explores the wonders and diversity of marine life. Using rhyming text, Rose describes how ocean animals are born, how they learn to swim, and how they find food, among other things. In *Booklist*, Carolyn Phelan praised the author's sensitivity to her audience, stating that Rose's narrative "establishes an amiable tone, sometimes addressing children directly and sometimes simply presenting information." Kathleen Kelly MacMillan, writing in *School Library Journal*, commented that *Ocean Babies* "beautifully captures the magic of the ocean world," and a contributor in *Kirkus Reviews* described the work as "a touching look at birth and perfect for reminiscing about the births of loved ones."

Designed for beginning readers making the transition from picture books to novels, *The Rose Horse* opens a window onto the life of immigrants in New York City at the turn of the twentieth century. Inspired by the work of the great carousel carvers of Brooklyn's Coney Island, Rose delves into American history and lore to recreate a time long ago. Lily and her family find themselves on Coney Island following the premature birth of Lily's baby sister, for the only way the infant's "state-of-the-art" medical care can be paid for is with the coins paid by curious onlookers who flock to see the incubator baby "sideshow," where Lily's sister is being kept alive. Staying temporarily with a cousin's family, Lily learns more about her family's Eastern European Jewish traditions and the craft of woodcarving, for her cousin Samuel is a talented artisan at work on the animals for Coney Island's renowned carousels. Priscilla Wallace, writing in *Multicultural Review*, noted that *The Rose Horse* offers "a subtle story of strong family relationships" and "supplements the teaching of American history, immigration, folk art, and Hebrew traditions."

An unusual celebration is the subject of *Birthday Zoo*, a work Rose tells in verse. As a young boy's birthday approaches, the animals in the zoo, including a tamarin, an okapi, a sloth, a stingray, and an emu, prepare to host a party in his honor. The festivities include a lynx pouring drinks, bats wearing silly hats, and bears playing musical chairs. Laura Scott, writing in *School Library Journal*, predicted that Rose's "strong rhythm and rhymes will charm youngsters in a storytime," and *Horn Book* contributor Mary M. Burns described *Birthday Zoo* as an "infectious read-aloud, and great fun for youngsters who will enjoy adding to their vocabulary of unfamiliar beasts."

The Twelve Days of Kindergarten: A Counting Book, Rose's take on the popular holiday song "The Twelve Days of Christmas," centers on a small girl's adjustment to her harried new teacher and her uproarious classmates. As the busy first dozen days of school pass, the youngster enjoys a host of learning activities such as chanting the alphabet, planting seeds, drawing pictures, stringing beads, and feeding fish. According to a reviewer in *Publishers Weekly,* "classroom leaders with a sense of humor will enjoy sharing this book at circle time," and Hazel Rochman noted in *Booklist* that young readers "will find a story about learning, messing up a lot, and sometimes changing." The rambunctious kindergarteners and their frazzled teacher return in a companion volume, *The Twelve Days of Winter: A Counting Book.* The students again savor a variety of adventures, including a zoo trip involving an escaped penguin. In *School Library Journal,* Grace Oliff called the work "a surefire choice to spice up the dreariest winter day."

"Since I began writing children's books," Rose once told *SATA,* "I have learned to listen more closely to both the insightful and silly things my children and their friends say. I've had to look at things through their eyes, and as a result I've rediscovered things I missed, or forgot, in my own childhood." The character Rose admires most in children's books is Charlotte, the spider in E.B. White's *Charlotte's Web.* "Charlotte is a writer like I am," Rose observed. "She thinks a long time before she starts to write, she researches and checks her spelling with a little help from her friends, she likes to work when it's quiet, and she shows off her work in the best light possible. She loves words and understands they are powerful—they can teach, surprise, entertain, convince, and even save a life."

Rose, who creates exhibits and writes articles for the Lawrence Hall of Science, believes that children's literature has broadened her horizons. "Writing children's books has helped me discover so many new things, like ocean life, and rediscover old things, like my boundless love of reading," she told Patricia M. Newman in *California Kids.* "Through reading children's books I've had the joy of close times with my own children, and through writing children's books, I've shared a part of myself with children around the globe."

Biographical and Critical Sources

PERIODICALS

California Kids, March, 2001, Patricia M. Newman, "Who Wrote That? Featuring Deborah Lee Rose."

Booklist, February 15, 1991, Leone McDermott, review of *Meredith's Mother Takes the Train,* p. 1202; March 1, 1991, Kathleen T. Horning, review of *The People Who Hugged the Trees,* p. 1403; September 1, 1995, Hazel Rochman, review of *The Rose Horse,* p. 58; September 15, 2000, Gillian Engberg, review of *Into the A, B, Sea: An Ocean Alphabet,* p. 246; September 15, 2002, Cynthia Turnquest, review of *Birthday Zoo,* p. 242; August, 2003, Hazel Rochman, review of *The Twelve Days of Kindergarten: A Counting Book,* p. 1994; April 1, 2005, Carolyn Phelan, review of *Ocean Babies,* p. 1362.

An elementary-grade classroom presents some unusual challenges for the teacher in Rose's picture book The Twelve Days of Winter, *featuring artwork by Carey Armstrong-Ellis.* (Abrams Books for Young Readers, 2006. Illustration © 2006 by Carey Armstrong-Ellis. Reproduced by permission.)

Bulletin of the Center for Children's Books, November, 1995, Susan Dove Lempke, review of *The Rose Horse,* p. 104.

Childhood Education, winter, 2003, review of *One Nighttime Sea: An Ocean Counting Rhyme,* p. 90.

Growing Point, March, 1991, Margery Fisher, review of *The People Who Hugged the Trees,* p. 5495.

Horn Book, July-December, 1990, review of *The People Who Hugged the Trees,* p. 102; November-December, 2002, Mary M. Burns, review of *Birthday Zoo,* p. 738.

Junior Bookshelf, February, 1991, review of *The People Who Hugged the Trees,* p. 16.

Kirkus Reviews, July 15, 2002, review of *Birthday Zoo,* p. 1042; July 1, 2003, reviews of *One Nighttime Sea,* p. 913, and *The Twelve Days of Kindergarten,* p. 914; May 15, 2005, review of *Ocean Babies,* p. 595; September 15, 2006, review of *The Twelve Days of Winter: A Counting Book,* p. 965.

Multicultural Review, March, 1996, Priscilla Wallace, review of *The Rose Horse.*

Publishers Weekly, September 18, 2000, "From A to Z," p. 113; September 2, 2002, review of *Birthday Zoo,* p. 78; June 9, 2003, review of *The Twelve Days of Kindergarten,* p. 50; August 25, 2003, review of *One Nighttime Sea,* p. 66.

School Library Journal, March, 1991, Patricia Pearl, review of *Meredith's Mother Takes the Train,* p. 179; January, 1996, Marcia W. Posner, review of *The Rose Horse,* p. 94; October, 2000, Joy Fleishhacker, review of *Into the A, B, Sea,* p. 134; October, 2002, Laura Scott, review of *Birthday Zoo,* p. 126; August, 2003, Linda M. Kenton, review of *The Twelve Days of Kindergarten,* p. 151; September, 2003, Julie Roach, review of *One Nighttime Sea,* p. 206; June, 2005, Kathleen Kelly MacMillan, review of *Ocean Babies,* p. 144; October, 2006, Grace Oliff, review of *The Twelve Days of Winter,* p. 125.

ONLINE

California Readers Online, http://www.californiareaders.
org/ (December 1, 2007), Bonnie O'Brian, "Meet
Deborah Lee Rose."

Deborah Lee Rose Home Page, http://www.deborahlee
rose.com (December 1, 2007).

Scholastic Books Web site, http://content.scholastic.com/
(December 1, 2007), "Deborah Lee Rose."*

*   *   *

RUPP, Rebecca

Personal

Married; husband's name Randy; children: Josh, Ethan,
Caleb. *Education:* Ph.D. (cell biology).

Addresses

Home—Shaftsbury, VT. *E-mail*—RRrupp@aol.com.

Career

Freelance writer. Producer and host of homeschool television program.

Awards, Honors

Book Sense Picks for Children, 2006, for *Journey to
the Blue Moon.*

Writings

JUVENILE FICTION

The Dragon of Lonely Island, Candlewick Press (Cambridge, MA), 1998.

The Waterstone, Candlewick Press (Cambridge, MA),
2002.

The Return of the Dragon, Candlewick Press (Cambridge,
MA), 2005.

*Journey to the Blue Moon: In Which Time Is Lost and
Then Found Again,* Candlewick Press (Cambridge,
MA), 2006.

NONFICTION

*Blue Corn and Square Tomatoes: Unusual Facts about
Common Vegetables,* Storey Communications (Pownal,
VT), 1987.

*Red Oaks and Black Birches: The Science and Lore of
Trees,* Storey Communications (Pownal, VT), 1990.

Good Stuff: Learning Tools for All Ages, Home Education
Press (Tonasket, WA), 1993, revised edition, Holt/
CWS (Cambridge, MA), 1997.

Everything You Never Learned about Birds, illustrated by
Jeffrey C. Domm, Storey Communications (Pownal,
VT), 1995.

*Committed to Memory: How We Remember and Why We
Forget,* Crown (New York, NY), 1998, published as
How We Remember and Why We Forget, Three Rivers
Press (New York, NY), 1998.

*The Complete Home Learning Sourcebook: The Essential
Resource Guide for Homeschoolers, Parents, and Educators Covering Every Subject from Arithmetic to Zoology,* Three Rivers Press (New York, NY), 1998.

*Getting Started on Home Learning: How and Why to Teach
Your Kids at Home,* Three Rivers Press (New York,
NY), 1999.

*Home Learning Year by Year: How to Design a Home-
school Curriculum from Preschool through High
School,* Three Rivers Press (New York, NY), 2000.

Weather!: Watch How Weather Works, illustrated by Melissa Sweet and Dug Nap, Storey Kids (North Adams,
MA), 2003.

Rocks, Storey Kids (North Adams, MA), 2004.

Author of monthly column for *Home Education* magazine. Contributor to periodicals.

Sidelights

Rebecca Rupp, a nationally recognized advocate for
homemeschooling, is also the author of several fantasy
novels for middle-grade readers, including *The Dragon
of Lonely Island* and *The Waterstone.* Rupp, who has a
Ph.D. in cell biology, has also written books on natural
history and numerous journal articles on education.

Rupp published her debut work of fiction, *The Dragon
of Lonely Island,* in 1998. The fantasy centers on the
adventures of twelve-year-old Hannah, ten-year-old Za-
chary, and eight-year-old Sarah Emily, who venture to
their great-aunt Mehitabel's house on Lonely Island, a
remote isle off the coast of Maine. A cryptic message
from Mehitabel leads the trio to Fafnyr, a golden-scaled,
three-headed dragon with a penchant for telling stories.
Over the summer, the siblings learn how the tridrake
saved a Chinese girl from invading Mongols, rescued a
London orphan from pirates, and helped a timid youngster find strength after she became marooned on a desert
island. Although a *Publishers Weekly* reviewer felt that
Rupp's "narrative frame, which strives for a classic
timelessness, can feel overly tame or quaint," *Booklist*
contributors Chris Sherman and Jack Helbig praised the
"rich, sensory images" in the novel and called *The
Dragon of Lonely Island* "an entertaining fantasy for
preteen readers."

In a sequel, *The Return of the Dragon,* Hannah, Za-
chary, and Sarah Emily join forces to protect Fafnyr
from an unscrupulous billionaire. When the children
suspect that J.P. King plans to capture the tridrake and
use the creature for financial gain, they seek Fafnyr's

wisdom. The dragon shares three tales about a Greek shepherd, a young squire, and a slave child that, together, help the children learn the meaning of freedom. *The Return of the Dragon* "is a quick, easy read that goes down like warm milk," noted *School Library Journal* critic Walter Minkel, and a *Kirkus Reviews* critic remarked that Rupp's "fluent prose and savvy, lightly presented life advice make this as readable and thought provoking" as her earlier novel.

A young man attempts to save his dying world in *The Waterstone,* a book that takes readers on "an amazing journey of surprising proportions," according to a critic in *Kirkus Reviews.* As twelve-year-old Tad, a member of the Fisher tribe, notices that the water from a nearby pond is drying up, he begins having strange "rememberings": thoughts featuring people, places, and events that the boy does not recognize. Together with his father, Pondleweed, and younger sister, Birdie, Tad journeys beyond the pond to visit the other tribes living nearby, such as the Hunters and the Diggers. During his journey, Tad discovers that he holds the memories and powers of past Sagamores, beings charged with protecting an energy source called the Waterstone, which may be able to restore balance to the forest where Tad lives. *The Waterstone* "deceptively starts out as an adventure story and ends on a somewhat epic note," commented *School Library Journal* reviewer Lisa Prolman.

In *Journey to the Blue Moon: In Which Time Is Lost and Then Found Again* Rupp examines themes of loyalty and integrity. After eleven-year-old Alex loses his grandfather's antique pocket watch, he finds himself mysteriously losing track of time. During a chance meeting with an elderly woman, the boy learns that lost belongings can be found on a blue moon, Determined to go there, Alex and his dog, Zeke, set off in a rickety spaceship belonging to the Moon Rats. Upon arrival on the blue moon, Alex encounters a host of misplaced individuals people, including a woman who lost her heart in a failed romance and a medieval scholar who lost his train of thought. Alex also faces down Urd, a powerful wizard-like creature, as well as the terrifying Time Eaters. A *Kirkus Reviews* critic described *Journey to the Blue Moon* as a "fast-paced fantasy, dusted with humor, rife with danger and bulging with bizarre characters," and Todd Morning wrote in *Booklist* that Rupp "holds the reader's interest . . . with humor and some well-placed excitement."

Biographical and Critical Sources

PERIODICALS

American Forests, September-October, 1992, Wallace Kaufman, review of *Red Oaks and Black Birches: The Science and Lore of Trees,* p. 57.

Booklist, December 15, 1997, William Beatty, review of *Committed to Memory: How We Remember and Why We Forget,* p. 668; February 1, 1999, Chris Sherman and Jack Helbig, review of *The Dragon of Lonely Island,* p. 975; September 1, 2005, Kay Weisman, review of *The Return of the Dragon,* p. 135; December 1, 2006, Todd Morning, review of *Journey to the Blue Moon: In Which Time Is Lost and Then Found Again,* p. 48.

Bulletin of the Center for Children's Books, December, 1998, review of *The Dragon of Lonely Island,* p. 145.

Kirkus Reviews, July 1, 2002, review of *The Waterstone,* p. 962; July 1, 2005, review of *The Return of the Dragon,* p. 743; September 15, 2006, review of *Journey to the Blue Moon,* p. 965.

Library Journal, November 15, 1998, Terry Christner, review of *The Complete Home Learning Sourcebook: The Essential Resource Guide for Homeschoolers, Parents, and Educators Covering Every Subject from Arithmetic to Zoology,* p. 76.

Publishers Weekly, November 10, 1997, review of *How We Remember and Why We Forget,* p. 60; November 16, 1998, review of *The Dragon of Lonely Island,* p. 75.

School Library Journal, November, 2002, Lisa Prolman, review of *The Waterstone,* p. 174; May, 2004, Kathryn Kosiorek, review of *Weather!: Watch How Weather Works,* p. 173; December, 2005, Walter Minkel, review of *The Return of the Dragon,* p. 154; October, 2006, Walter Minkel, review of *Journey to the Blue Moon,* p. 168.

Smithsonian, June, 1991, Joe Sherman, review of *Red Oaks and Black Birches,* p. 137.

ONLINE

Candlewick Press Web site, http://www.candlewick.com/ (November 20, 2007), "Rebecca Rupp."

Homeschool Zone Web site, http://www.homeschoolzone. com/ (November 20, 2007), "Rebecca Rupp."*

S

SCHMIDT, Karen Lee 1953-

Personal

Born August 28, 1953, in Albuquerque, NM; daughter of Norman (an air force test pilot) and Marie (a teacher) Schmidt. *Education:* Attended University of California, Santa Barbara Art Institute, Art Students' League, National Academy of Design, and School of Visual Arts; Oregon College of Art/Oregon State College, B.A.

Addresses

Home and office—Seattle, WA. *E-mail*—karenlee-schmidt@earthlink.net.

Career

Illustrator and author. Visiting speaker at schools; also conducts workshops and interactive drawing demonstrations.

Writings

SELF-ILLUSTRATED

Carl's Nose, Harcourt (Orlando, FL), 2006.

ILLUSTRATOR

Thomas M. Disch, *The Brave Little Toaster: A Bedtime Story for Small Appliances,* Doubleday (New York, NY), 1986.
My First Book of Baby Animals, Platt & Munk (New York, NY), 1986.
Down by the Station, Bantam (New York, NY), 1987.
Marcia Leonard, *Little Fox's Best Friend,* Bantam (New York, NY), 1987.
Marcia Leonard, *Little Kitten Sleeps Over,* Bantam (New York, NY), 1987.

Karen Lee Schmidt (Reproduced by permission of Karen Lee Schmidt.)

Eve Merriam, *You Be Good and I'll Be Night: Jump-on-the-Bed Poems,* Morrow (New York, NY), 1988.
Mary Pope Osborne, compiler, *Bears, Bears, Bears: A Treasury of Stories, Songs, and Poems about Bears,* Silver Press (San Jose, CA), 1990.
Joanne Barkan, *Whiskerville Bake Shop,* Grosset & Dunlap (New York, NY), 1990.
Joanne Barkan, *Whiskerville Firehouse,* Grosset & Dunlap (New York, NY), 1990.
Joanne Barkan, *Whiskerville School,* Grosset & Dunlap (New York, NY), 1990.
Joanne Barkan, *Whiskerville Theater,* Grosset & Dunlap (New York, NY), 1991.

Joanne Barkan, *Whiskerville Toy Shop,* Grosset & Dunlap (New York, NY), 1991.

Joanne Barkan, *Whiskerville Train Station,* Grosset & Dunlap (New York, NY), 1991.

Joanne Barkan, *Whiskerville Grocery,* Grosset & Dunlap (New York, NY), 1991.

Elizabeth Lee O'Donnell, *The Twelve Days of Summer,* Morrow (New York, NY), 1991.

Iris Hiskey, *Hannah the Hippo's No Mud Day,* Simon & Schuster (New York, NY), 1991.

Pat Upton, *Who Lives in the Woods?,* Bell Books (Honesdale, PA), 1991.

Diane Patenaude, *The Monster Counting Book,* Doubleday (New York, NY), 1992.

Alan Benjamin, *A Nickel Buys a Rhyme,* Morrow (New York, NY), 1993.

Linda Glaser, *Stop That Garbage Truck,* Albert Whitman (New York, NY), 1993.

Maxine Meltzer, *Pups Speak Up,* Bradbury Press (Seattle, WA), 1994.

Pollita Tita (Chicken Little), Putnam (New York, NY), 1995.

Joanna Cole, *Monster and Muffin,* Putnam (New York, NY), 1996.

Peter Cottontail, Putnam (New York, NY), 1996.

Wee Puppy, Putnam (New York, NY), 1996.

Tom Paxton, *Going to the Zoo,* Morrow (New York, NY), 1996.

Kathryn Lasky, *Grace the Pirate,* Hyperion (New York, NY), 1997.

Barbara Ware Holmes, *My Sister the Sausage Roll,* Hyperion (New York, NY), 1997.

Kathleen Karr, *The Lighthouse Mermaid,* Hyperion (New York, NY), 1998.

Tom Paxton, *The Jungle Baseball Game,* Morrow (New York, NY), 1999.

Jonathan London, *What Do You Love?,* Harcourt (New York, NY), 2000.

Jerdine Nolen, *Max and Jax in Second Grade,* Harcourt (San Diego, CA), 2002.

Jane Yolen, *Hoptoad,* Harcourt (San Diego, CA), 2003.

Dandi Daley Mackall, *I Love You, Daddy,* Standard (Cincinnati, OH), 2006.

Dandi Daley Mackall, *I Love You, Mommy,* Standard (Cincinnati, OH), 2006.

Sidelights

On her home page, illustrator Karen Lee Schmidt described her childhood as full of animals. "We lived in the Mojave Desert, in California. . . .There were few houses and no fences so our yard played host to a wide variety of desert animals," the artist quipped. "Two large turtles took up residence in our cactus garden. Roadrunners and jackrabbits ventured into and out of the yard. There were legions of lizards and herds of horned toads, not to mention snakes and tarantulas." "My illustrations are populated by as wide a variety of animals as my youth was." Encouraged by her mother, a first-grade teacher, to create art at a young age, Schmidt became a "classroom art decorator," a role that gave her the courage she needed to leave California and travel to New York for college. There she discovered a passion for children's books and began illustrating for a number of well known writers, including Tom Paxton, Jane Yolen, and Mary Pope Osborne. Twenty years after illustrating her first children's book, Schmidt wrote one of her own: her self-illustrated title, *Carl's Nose.*

Schmidt's illustrations have been warmly praised for the colorful and humorous addition they make to story books for young children. *You Be Good and I'll Be Night: Jump-on-the-Bed Poems,* a tale by Eve Merriam, features humorous rhymes in a collection that, according to *New York Times Book Review* contributor Laurel Graeber, "allows the illustrator . . . to show off her talents to best advantage." Schmidt's "bouncy watercolor scenes" accompany each poem, observed Betsy Hearne in the *Bulletin of the Center for Children's Books,* and often feature "comically incongruous animals." Graeber went on to note that Schmidt's "sprightly pictures of creatures ranging from jigging pigs to cuddling crocodiles are the visual equivalents of the poems, right down to the hidden joke: carved fish on a bear's bed, for instance."

Another collection of rhyming poems, Alan Benjamin's *A Nickel Buys a Rhyme,* features Schmidt's "exuberant" and "dapper" interpretations of "silly and sweet, modern Mother Goose-style rhymes," according to Annie Ayres in *Booklist.* Benjamin's poems are accompanied by "Schmidt's lively, good-natured illustrations," making *A Nickel Buys a Rhyme* "an inviting book to share," according to a *Kirkus Reviews* critic. Jonathan London's rhyming text in *What Do You Love* is paired with double-page spreads featuring Schmidt's watercolors. The "illustrations are effective from a distance," according to Susan Hepler, the reviewer adding in her *School Library Journal* review that the book is good for group reading. Lauren Peterson, writing about the same title in *Booklist,* called the illustrations "adorable."

Tom Paxton's *Going to the Zoo* also benefits from Schmidt's "energetic" approach in the form of "exaggerated yet still somewhat realistic" illustrations, according to Lauren Peterson in *Booklist. The Jungle Baseball Game,* also by Paxton, finds monkeys playing hippos in a game of baseball. A *Publishers Weekly* critic noted that both baseball and jungle motifs are featured in the border illustrations Schmidt creates for each page, and found the "chubby hippos . . . particularly fetching." In *Booklist* John Peters was most attracted to the monkeys, noting that Schmidt "decorates the margins with capering, overconfident primates."

In *Hoptoad* Schmidt brings to life award-winning author Jane Yolen's tale of a near-disastrous encounter between a lizard, a turtle, a toad, and a truck. Though most might purchase the title based on Yolen's reputation, a *Kirkus Reviews* contributor noted that her "text is not the star here. Schmidt's watercolor-and-gouache, cartoon-skewed pictures are the real joy." The illustrator's "paintings get right down to road—and toad—level," Karin Snelson quipped in her *Booklist* review of Yolen's entertaining beginning reader.

Along with her picture books, Schmidt has also provided pencil illustrations for novels, including *The Lighthouse Mermaid,* and cartoon art for chapter books such as *Max and Jax in Second Grade.* Of the latter, a *Publishers Weekly* critic noted that the book's "boldly hued" illustrations "will serve as bait to lure beginning readers back for more." Louie Lahana, writing in *School Library Journal,* felt that "Schmidt's appealing artwork matches this tone perfectly."

Schmidt takes on the role of both author and illustrator in *Carl's Nose,* the story of a weather-dog named Carl. Carl's predictions for the weather near Old Man Mountain have always been accurate until one day, when his nose for the weather loses its knack. Ultimately, Carl's sense of self-worth is restored when he takes up a new profession: rescue dog. "Prose that begs to be read aloud abounds" in the picture book, according to Rita Hunt Smith in *School Library Journal.* A contributor to *Kirkus Reviews* noted that Schmidt's story is told as much through her artwork as through her text, writing that the author/illustrator "uses some sophisticated vocabulary and perspectives in her work."

A veteran of more than a decade of work with children's books, Schmidt frequently visits elementary schools to discuss her life and work as an illustrator. She also conducts workshops and interactive drawing demonstrations. "Children's books address universal themes—love, friendship, jealousy, loss, joy, sadness—often in poetic, humorous, or profound ways," she wrote on her home page. "As an artist I am able to give my own voice to these themes by playing off the words and building on them from page to page. . . . It is that variety I love—that, and being able to integrate my artistic training with themes that have occupied me since childhood."

Biographical and Critical Sources

PERIODICALS

Booklinks, July, 2005, Sue McCleaf Nespeca, review of *Going to the Zoo,* p. 19; March, 2006, Angela Leeper, review of *Max and Jax in Second Grade,* p. 46.

Booklist, July, 1993, Annie Ayres, review of *A Nickel Buys a Rhyme,* pp. 1968-1969; June 1, 1996, Lauren Peterson, review of *Going to the Zoo,* p. 1728; June 1, 1998, Ilene Cooper, review of *The Lighthouse Mermaid,* p. 1767; May 1, 1999, John Peters, review of *The Jungle Baseball Game,* p. 1600; January 1, 2001, Lauren Peterson, review of *What Do You Love?,* p. 967; June 1, 2002, Kathy Broderick, review of *Max and Jax in Second Grade,* p. 1724; May 15, 2003, Karin Snelson, review of *Hoptoad,* p. 1674.

Bulletin of the Center for Children's Books, October, 1988, Betsy Hearne, review of *You Be Good and I'll Be Night: Jump-on-the-Bed Poems,* p. 48; July, 1997, review of *My Sister the Sausage Roll,* p. 398; June, 1998, review of *The Lighthouse Mermaid,* p. 365.

Kirkus Reviews, March 1, 1993, review of *A Nickel Buys a Rhyme,* p. 297; March 1, 2002, review of *Max and Jax in Second Grade,* p. 342; May 15, 2003, review of *Hoptoad,* p. 758; September 15, 2006, review of *Carl's Nose,* p. 966.

New York Times Book Review, March 26, 1989, Laurel Graeber, review of *You Be Good and I'll Be Night,* p. 19.

Publishers Weekly, March 29, 1993, review of *A Nickel Buys a Rhyme,* p. 56; March 1, 1999, review of *The Jungle Baseball Game,* p. 67; May 10, 1999, Shannon Maughan, "Songs Spun into Books," p. 35; February 11, 2002, review of *Max and Jax in Second Grade,* p. 187.

School Library Journal, August, 1997, Carrie A. Guarria, review of *My Sister the Sausage Roll,* p. 135; August, 1998, Elaine Lesh Morgan, review of *The Lighthouse Mermaid,* p. 141; April, 1999, Jane Marino, review of *The Jungle Baseball Game,* p. 106; December, 2000, Susan Hepler, review of *What Do You Love?* p. 114; April, 2002, Louie Lahana, review of *Max and Jax in Second Grade,* p. 118; June, 2003, review of *Hoptoad,* p. 122; November, 2006, Rita Hunt Smith, review of *Carl's Nose,* p. 112.

ONLINE

Children's Literature Web site, http://www.childrenslit. com/ (December 2, 2007), "Karen Lee Schmidt."

Frostburg State University Web site, http://www.frostburg. edu/ (December 2, 2007), "Karen Lee Schmidt."

Karen Lee Schmidt Home Page, http://www.karenlee schmidt.net (December 2, 2007).

* * *

SCHRECK, Karen
See SCHRECK, Karen Halvorsen

* * *

SCHRECK, Karen Halvorsen 1962-
(Karen Schreck)

Personal

Born 1962; married Greg Halvorsen Schreck (a photographer), c. 1991; children: Magdalena, Teo (son). *Education:* Wheaton College, B.A.; State University of New York, Binghamton, M.A.; University of Illinois at Chicago, Ph.D. *Hobbies and other interests:* Gardening, hiking, camping, cross-country skiing, yoga, traveling, and attending movies, concerts, plays, and art gallery exhibitions.

Addresses

Home—Wheaton, IL. *E-mail*—k.schreck@comcast.net; karen@karenhalvorsenschreck.net.

Career

Writer, novelist, and educator. Taught writing and literature at State University of New York, Binghamton and University of Illinois at Chicago. Worked in publishing in Boston, MA, and as an advertising copywriter, editor, and proofreader.

Awards, Honors

Pushcart Prize; Illinois State Arts Council grant; Honor Book selection, Society of School Librarians, 2001, for *Lucy's Family Tree.*

Writings

Lucy's Family Tree (picture book), illustrated by Stephen Gassler III, Tilbury House (Gardiner, ME), 2001.
Dream Journal (young-adult novel), Hyperion Books for Children (New York, NY), 2006.

Sidelights

Karen Halvorsen Schreck is an educator and author of books for teens and young readers. In *Lucy's Family Tree* Lucy is a young Mexican girl who is adopted as a baby by an American family. When she is given an assignment at school to make her family tree, she worries that she will be unable to complete the project because her family is "different." In an effort to help Lucy realize the benefits of this difference, her teacher challenges her to make a family tree for three families that she believes are the same. Dora and Seth, she finds, have a stepfather. In Lucinda's family, her mother works to earn a living while her father stays home and cares for the children. Robert has two mothers who care for him a great deal. Soon, Lucy realizes that some families she thought were "typical" and "normal" are actually strengthened by their differences. Lucy renews her efforts on her class project, constructing a traditional Mexican Tree of Life with pictures of both her birth parents and her adopted mother and father. The material in *Lucy's Family Tree* helps "deliver a timely message to educators about the appropriateness of family-related assignments in today's world of diverse lifestyles," commented Thomas Pitchford in *School Library Journal.*

Livy, the sixteen-year-old protagonist of *Dream Journal,* is struggling to cope with the fact that her mother is dying of cancer. Her father is also terribly upset by the situation, but he has told her to not talk about these troubles outside of the family. Her father's rules mean that Livy is isolated and unable to share her concerns with friends or other adults who could help her. Because she has been staying home to care for her mother for months, Livy has drifted apart from her peers, including from best friend Ruth, daughter of the local pastor. As the story progresses, both Livy and Ruth are testing the limits of their teenage lives, their fathers' patience, and their own sense of self and morality. Concerned about their friendship, Ruth convinces Livy to accompany her and several members of the school football team on a cheerful outing. When the group goes to a local teen hangout the next day, a tragic accident injures a promising young musician, and Livy reacts by isolating herself from the world again. Facing her own maturation and the impending death of her mother, Livy must ultimately come to terms with her loneliness, her relationship with her father, and her own future.

The foundation of *Dream Journal* exists in a tragic event from Schreck's own life. Her mother was diagnosed with breast cancer when Schreck was in the fifth grade. Three years later, she stated on her home page, her mother died from the illness. "With *Dream Journal,* I wrote the book I wanted and needed to read when I was a girl," Schreck commented. "It took me several years and many drafts to complete the manuscript. But every minute I spent waiting for the angel was worth it. Through Livy I did things I wish I could have done when my mother was ill and dying. I understood things I'd never understood before. I had always heard writing could be healing. Now I experienced this first-hand."

Young-adult readers who have "lost someone close to them, or know that it's about to happen, will appreciate this sincere and thoughtful novel," commented Kelly Czarnecki in a *School Library Journal* review of the novel. In *Kliatt* reviewer Claire Rosser concluded that *Dream Journal* is "a poignant story that in essence is believable." Livy's "plight and her honesty will interest many YA readers," Rosser commented.

Biographical and Critical Sources

PERIODICALS

Kirkus Reviews, August 15, 2006, review of *Dream Journal,* p. 851.
Kliatt, September, 2005, Claire Rosser, review of *Dream Journal,* p. 17.
Publishers Weekly, June 11, 2001, review of *Lucy's Family Tree,* p. 85.
School Library Journal, January, 2002, Thomas Pitchford, review of *Lucy's Family Tree,* p. 109; November, 2006, Kelly Czarnecki, review of *Dream Journal,* p. 151.

ONLINE

Karen Halvorsen Schreck Home Page, http://www.karen halvorsenschreck.net (March 28, 2007).

Karen Halvorsen Schreck Web log, http://www.karenhal vorsenschreck.net/blogger.html (March 28, 2007).

Teenreads.com, http://www.teenreads.com/ (March 28, 2007), "Karen Halvorsen Schreck."*

*   *   *

SCHWABACH, Karen

Personal

Female. *Education:* Antioch College, B.A.; State University of New York at Albany, M.S. (teaching English to speakers of other languages).

Addresses

Home—Anchorage, AK.

Career

Educator and author. Administrator of English-as-a-second-language program at Yup'ik Inuit villages in Alaskan Bush until 2000; freelance writer.

Awards, Honors

Sidney Taylor Manuscript Award, 2001, for *A Pickpocket's Tale.*

Writings

Thailand: Land of Smiles, Dillon Press (Minneapolis, MN), 1991.
El Salvador on the Road to Peace, Dillon Press (Minneapolis, MN), 1999.
A Pickpocket's Tale, Random House (New York, NY), 2006.
The Hope Chest, Random House (New York, NY), 2006.

Sidelights

Raised in New York State, Karen Schwabach now makes her home in Alaska, where she works as a teacher among students from a variety of cultures and language backgrounds. Until 2000, she operated an English-as-a-second-language (ESL) program for Inuit students living in Alaska's remote bush. A move to Anchorage provided her with the opportunity to shift her concentration to her writing, and the historical novels *A Pickpocket's Tale* and *The Hope Chest* have been the result. Schwabach's novels feature adventurous young heroines who bravely journey into unfamiliar urban settings, In the first book, a preteen travels from England to New York City as part of the immigrant waves of the late 1800s, while the second finds a young runaway ending her journey in Nashville, Tennessee, as battle lines form for the 1919 fight for women's right to vote.

Praised by a *Kirkus Reviews* writer as "a first novel with lots of concrete and engaging historical detail," *A Pickpocket's Tale* introduces readers to a ten year old named Molly. An orphan, Molly has been living on the streets of 1730 London since her mother died of small-pox. When the girl is arrested for picking pockets, she is sent to America, her punishment being to become an indentured servant to a New York City family. In her new home with the Bell family, Molly has difficulty dealing with regular work as well as with her new culture, which includes regular baths, self-improvement through reading, and participating in the family's Jewish traditions. Ultimately, a meeting with a black slave shows the girl that her life could have been marked by far greater hardships, in a novel that features "an engaging protagonist" and "vividly detailed prose," according to *Booklist* contributor Shelle Rosenfeld. Although noting that some readers may wrestle with Molly's street-thief dialect, *School Library Journal* contributor Barbara Auerbach deemed *A Pickpocket's Tale* an "engaging tale about some lesser-known aspects of 18th-century life," and concluded that Schwabach's novel is filled "with memorable characters."

Cover of Karen Schwabach's novel **A Pickpocket's Tale,** *featuring a painting by Dan Craig.* (Illustration © 2006 by Dan Craig. Reproduced by permission of Random House Children's Books, a division of Random House, Inc.)

Biographical and Critical Sources

PERIODICALS

Booklist, November 15, 2006, Shelle Rosenfeld, review of *A Pickpocket's Tale,* p. 62.
Kirkus Reviews, October 15, 2006, review of *A Pickpocket's Tale,* p. 1080.
School Library Journal, November, 2006, Barbara Auerbach, review of *A Pickpocket's Tale,* p. 151.
Voice of Youth Advocates, December 2006, Rebecca Barnhouse, review of *A Pickpocket's Tale,* p. 432.

ONLINE

Association of Jewish Libraries Web site, http://www.jewishlibraries.org/ (June 23, 2002), Karen Schwabach, acceptance speech for Sydney Taylor Award.*

SHELDON, David (Quentin)

Personal

Married; wife's name Margit; children: William, Sarah, Christopher.

Addresses

Home—Asheville, NC. *Agent*—Ronnie Ann Herman, Herman Agency, 350 Central Park W., New York, NY 10025. *E-mail*—DQSheldon@Bellsouth.net.

Career

Illustrator and author. Presenter at schools.

Awards, Honors

Outstanding Science Trade Book designation, National Science Teachers' Association, 2007, for *Barnum Brown.*

David Sheldon profiles a unique individual with an unusual passion in his self-illustrated picture book **Barnum Brown: Dinosaur Hunter.** (Walker, 2006. Illustration © 2006 by David Sheldon. Reproduced by permission.)

Writings

SELF-ILLUSTRATED

Barnum Brown: Dinosaur Hunter, Walker (New York, NY), 2006.

(Under pseudonym Quentin) *Monster Halloween,* Harper-Festival (New York, NY), 2006.

(Under pseudonym Quentin) *Monster Friends,* HarperFestival (New York, NY), 2008.

Into the Wild: The Life of Naturalist, Explorer William Beebe, Charlesbridge (New York, NY), 2009.

ILLUSTRATOR

Pat Matuszak, *Spiders!* ("Bible Critters" series), Zonderkidz (Grand Rapids, MI), 2002.

Pat Matuszak, *Bugs!* ("Bible Critters" series), Zonderkidz (Grand Rapids, MI), 2002.

Diane Namm, *Guess Who?,* Children's Press (New York, NY), 2004.

Also illustrator of numerous books for educational publishers. Contributor of illustrations to periodicals, including *Weekly Reader* and *Ladybug.*

Sidelights

David Sheldon gained an early reputation as an artist when, in elementary school, his friends were entertained by his drawings of scary monsters. Eventually turning to illustration as a career, Sheldon spent several years creating artwork for educational materials published by major publishers such as Harcourt, Houghton Mifflin, and Scott-Foresman. With his interest in nature and science, he has also undertaken the role of author with the picture-book biography *Barnum Brown: Dinosaur Hunter,* while continuing to entertain children with his amusing monster drawings in the books *Monster Halloween* and *Monster Friends,* published under his pen name—and middle name—Quentin. Although he sometimes employs the computer in his art, Sheldon is most at home in traditional artistic media, such as water color, acrylics, colored pencil, and pen-and-ink.

The first of a planned series of illustrated biographies about famous naturalists, *Barnum Brown* focuses on the paleontologist who, in the late 1800s, discovered the fossil remains of T. Rex and founded the fossil collection at New York City's American Museum of Natural History. Sheldon's detailed illustrations, which follow Brown from childhood through his adult explorations, are paired with a clear and simple text "rich in specific detail," according to a *Kirkus Reviews* writer. Praising Sheldon's "evocative" images, Steven Engelfried concluded in *School Library Journal* that *Barnum Brown* is "a fun picture-book biography . . . with strong child appeal," and *Booklist* critic Ilene Cooper appreciated the "whimsical touches" that appear in Sheldon's art.

"When creating books for children," Sheldon told *SATA,* "I try to stay close to the child in me who loves exploring, discovering new things, and sharing those discover-

ies with others. I fill my books with big, colorful pictures full of life and imagination. It was that sort of illustration that kept me clutching my own favorite books when I was younger.

"In writing books for beginning readers, I bear in my mind the point of view of my reader who might be experiencing interesting words and concepts for the first time. I try to introduce those readers to words in a fun, imaginative way, hoping that this will help them get to know and love words for their own sake, to enjoy how words sound to the ear and how they feel rolling off the tongue, and to appreciate the sheer wonder of how words allow us to communicate ideas and stories.

"For slightly older readers, I try to fashion a story that communicates interesting ideas but is nevertheless manageable for children to read on their own, giving them a sense of pride in reading.

"For me, a truly good story is one that inspires readers of all ages to explore the world he or she lives in and to keep asking questions about it, thereby continuing the thrill of discovery."

Biographical and Critical Sources

PERIODICALS

Booklist, December 1, 2006, Ilene Cooper, review of *Barnum Brown: Dinosaur Hunter,* p. 62.

Bulletin of the Center for Children's Books, March, 2007, Elizabeth Bush, review of *Barnum Brown,* p. 309.

Kirkus Reviews, September 15, 2006, review of *Barnum Brown,* p. 967.

School Library Journal, July, 2004, review of *Guess Who?,* p. 75; November, 2006, Steven Engelfried, review of *Barnum Brown,* p. 124.

ONLINE

David Sheldon Home Page, http://www.davidquentinsheldon.com (December 20, 2007).

Herman Agency Web site, http://www.hermanagency.com/ (December 20, 2007), "David Sheldon."

*   *   *

SIEGEL, Siena Cherson 1967(?)-

Personal

Born c. 1967, in PR; daughter of Samuel B. and Rosana Cherson; married Mark Siegel (a graphic designer, illustrator, and publisher), June 5, 1999. *Education:* Attended American School of Ballet (New York, NY); Brown University, earned degree, 1990.

Addresses

Home—MA.

Career

Dancer and author. Agnès B. (clothing store), Boston, MA, former manager; American Ballet Theatre, New York, NY, currently manager of training program for teens.

Writings

To Dance: A Ballerina's Graphic Novel (memoir), illustrated by husband, Mark Siegel, Atheneum (New York, NY) 2006.

Sidelights

Siena Cherson Siegel joins her husband, graphic artist and illustrator Mark Siegel, to create the memoir *To Dance: A Ballerina's Graphic Novel*. Beginning with Siena's childhood dreams of becoming a ballerina, the book follows her development as a dancer. Dance lessons at age six in her native Puerto Rico lead to study at New York City's American School of Ballet, where she dances in productions at Lincoln Center under the direction of George Balanchine. Much of Siegel's book is set in the 1970s, a time when ballet featured prominently in the media due to the rise of stars such as Mikhail Baryshnikov. Siegel's memoir radiates the excitement the young dancer experienced sharing the stage with such talent, and readers share her profound loss when a severe ankle injury ends her dreams of a dancing career at age eighteen. Noting the challenges endured by young dancers, and the fact that their initial love and passion for their art often erodes with each new challenge, Mark Siegel explained to *Brown Alumni Magazine* online interviewer Lawrence Goodman that *To Dance* "is about rediscovering that love through all the hardships."

Reviewing *To Dance* in *Publishers Weekly,* a contributor praised Siena Siegel's text for being written in a "credible, youthful voice that conveys both confidence and innocence," while Mark Siegel's cartoon art "captur[es] . . . both the dancers' movements and their passion." In *Booklist,* Francisca Goldsmith dubbed the work an "insightful, accessible, and aesthetically engaging graphic novel," and in *School Library Journal* Carol Schene praised the memoir for providing young dancers with "an inspiring message about the dedication required" to pursue their dream." Calling *To Dance* "a bravura performance," a *Kirkus Reviews* writer predicted that the Siegels' book "will be . . . treasured by ballet lovers of all ages."

Biographical and Critical Sources

PERIODICALS

Booklist, September 1, 2006, Francisca Goldsmith, review of *To Dance: A Ballerina's Graphic Novel,* p. 127.

Bulletin of the Center for Children's Books, January, 2007, Deborah Stevenson, review of *To Dance,* p. 230.
Horn Book, November-December, 2006, Robin Brenner, review of *To Dance,* p. 737.
Kirkus Reviews, September 1, 2006, review of *To Dance,* p. 912.
Publishers Weekly, October 2, 2006, review of *To Dance,* p. 64.
School Library Journal, November, 2006, Carol Schene, review of *To Dance,* p. 168.
Voice of Youth Advocates, April, 2007, Snow Wildsmith, review of *To Dance,* p. 81.

ONLINE

Blogcritics Web site, http://blogcritics.org/ (April 18, 2007), Gina Ruiz, review of *To Dance.*
Brown Alumni Magazine Online, http://www.brownalumnimagazine.com/ (September 1, 2006), Lawrence Goodman, review of *To Dance.**

* * *

SIMMONS, Michael 1970-

Personal

Born 1970.

Addresses

Home—New York, NY.

Career

Writer. Previously worked at a publishing house.

Writings

YOUNG-ADULT NOVELS

Pool Boy, Roaring Brook Press (Brookfield, CT), 2003.
Finding Lubchenko, Razorbill (New York, NY), 2005.
The Rise of Lubchenko, Razorbill (New York, NY), 2006.
Vandal, Roaring Brook Press (New Milford, CT), 2006.

Sidelights

Young-adult novelist Michael Simmons did not set out to become an author, but he was eventually motivated to pursue the occupation while working at a publishing company. "I was . . . writing teaching guides for popular young adult novels," the author related on the Random House Web site. "I liked a lot of them, and thought I might be able to write one myself. I had published short stories in the past, but never a novel, so this was my first crack at a longer piece. But it seemed to fall into place pretty easily. As for teen audiences, the best way to write for them is to forget that they're teenagers. When books for young readers don't succeed, it's usually because the author is too conscious of his or her audience."

Debuting with *Pool Boy,* Simmons received wide praise for his realistic depiction of a teenager facing major changes in his life. Fifteen-year-old Brett is the son of a rich man and enjoys all the material privileges that go with wealth. Obnoxious and self-centered, he is shocked when his father goes to prison for insider trading. The family's fortunes quickly turn, and Brett finds himself living on the wrong side of the tracks and working as a pool boy. He even has to clean the pool at the house that used to belong to his family. Brett is supervised by Alfie, a poor man who also drives a bus for a living but who has a spirited perspective on life that is refreshing. Gradually, Brett warms up to Alfie, but soon faces another tragedy when the elderly Alfie is rushed to the hospital. "It's no mean feat, rendering a character who is both detestable and sympathetic," observed a *Kirkus Reviews* writer; "Simmons has done this." *School Library Journal* critic Hillias J. Martin called the author's portrayals "dead on" and praised Simmons for taking readers on a "humorous yet thought-provoking journey." Claudia Mody, writing in *Bookseller,* asserted that *Pool Boy* "shows surprisingly sharp insight for a first novel, and features the most engagingly arrogant antihero of the year."

Simmons followed *Pool Boy* with the teen thrillers *Finding Lubchenko* and *The Rise of Lubchenko.* Less serious in theme than *Pool Boy,* these books are about Evan, whose father heads a medical technology company. The smart-mouthed Evan takes advantage of this by occasionally stealing small pieces of equipment and selling them on eBay. This scheme backfires when Evan takes a laptop containing files that he later learns could clear his father of a murder charge. Instead of telling his father he has the information that can free him but land Evan in big trouble, the teen flies to Paris to find a man named Lubchenko who can also solve the case. Comparing Evan to Brett, *School Library Journal* critic Martin wrote that "Simmons once again masters the voice of a smart-alecky teenage boy." "This is a fast-paced comic thriller, with plenty of twists, turns, technology and good old adolescent fun," reported *Kliatt* reviewer Michele Winship.

The Rise of Lubchenko finds Evans once again in trouble. This time, the teenager receives a mysterious tip that his father's partner is trying to sell a sample of smallpox virus to terrorists and that his family is also being targeted by killers. "Reading like an action movie, this sequel packs just as much punch as the first book," remarked Michelle Roberts in *School Library Journal.*

A story with deeper psychological themes, *Vandal* introduces Will, an ordinary teen dealing with high school, a crush on a girl, and his efforts to make his Kiss tribute band succeed. A huge complication in Will's life is his delinquent older brother, Jason, who seems determined to wreak havoc everywhere he goes. Will, who still feels like he needs his brother's approval, invites Jason to be a roadie for his band, but the results are disastrous. Jason seems determined to pursue a path of self-destruction, but when he cripples his sister in a car accident, events come to a head. *Booklist* reviewer Jennifer Mattson described the characterization as "nuanced," adding that "the pacing is skillfully modulated, and the conclusion, free of nostrums about catharsis and rehabilitation, feels touching and true." Mary R. Hoffmann, writing in *School Library Journal,* was disappointed with the characters, however, writing that it seemed that no one learned any lessons from Jason's behavior. "Sadly, the characters are as flat as the ending, making it difficult to believe or care what happens," Hoffmann reported. Other critics found Simmons' portrayal of a family plagued by one destructive member to be convincingly realistic. Paula Rohrlick commented in *Kliatt* that in *Vandal* the author "conveys the complex mix of emotions Jason stirs up in Will poignantly and believably," and a *Publishers Weekly* writer lauded Simmons for offering "no easy answers."

Biographical and Critical Sources

PERIODICALS

Booklist, April 1, 2003, Hazel Rochman, review of *Pool Boy,* p. 1391; July 1, 2006, Jennifer Mattson, review of *Vandal,* p. 57; September 1, 2006, Debbie Carton, review of *The Rise of Lubchenko,* p. 112.

Bookseller, January 16, 2004, Claudia Mody, review of *Pool Boy,* p. 37.

Horn Book, September-October, 2005, Betty Carter, review of *Finding Lubchenko,* p. 589; July-August, 2006, Betty Carter, review of *Vandal,* p. 451.

Kirkus Reviews, May 15, 2003, review of *Pool Boy,* p. 757; May 15, 2005, review of *Finding Lubchenko,* p. 596; May 1, 2006, review of *Vandal,* p. 467.

Kliatt, July, 2003, Paula Rohrlick, review of *Pool Boy,* p. 18; May, 2005, Michele Winship, review of *Finding Lubchenko,* p. 18; May, 2006, Paula Rohrlick, review of *Vandal,* p. 15.

Publishers Weekly, May 5, 2003, review of *Pool Boy,* p. 222; April 24, 2006, review of *Vandal,* p. 62.

School Library Journal, April, 2003, Hillias J. Martin, review of *Pool Boy,* p. 168; June, 2005, Hillias J. Martin, review of *Finding Lubchenko,* p. 169; June, 2006, Mary R. Hofmann, review of *Vandal,* p. 166; September, 2006, Michelle Roberts, review of *The Rise of Lubchenko,* p. 218.

ONLINE

Random House Web site, http://www.randomhouse.com/ (February 25, 2007), interview with Simmons.*

SKELTON, Matthew 1971-

Personal

Born 1971, in Southampton, England. *Education:* University of Alberta, B.A., M.A.; Somerville College Oxford, D.Phil., 2000.

Addresses

Home—Alberta, Canada.

Career

Writer, 2001—. Visiting lecturer, University of Mainz, Germany, 2001.

Writings

Endymion Spring (novel), Delacorte Press (New York, NY), 2006.

Adaptations

Endymion Spring was optioned for film by Warner Brothers.

Sidelights

Hailed as "'*The Da Vinci Code* for kids,'" aaccording to a *Teen Reads.com* contributor, Matthew Skelton's novel *Endymion Spring* tells the story of a powerful book that is rumored to contain all the world's knowledge. The book is discovered in Oxford University's famous Bodleian Library by Blake, the son of a visiting professor. In his novel, Skelton details not only Blake's story, but also that of Endymion Spring, an apprentice to innovative fifteenth-century printer Johann Gutenberg. Endymion has to keep the singular book out of the hands of Gutenberg's patron, the evil Fust. Like Endymion, Blake also "finds himself prey to dark forces," declared Caroline Sanderson in *Bookseller,* "who will stop at nothing to get their hands on The Last Book." "Allusions to legends and poetry mix with the appeal of a magical book that only answers questions in riddles," stated a *Kirkus Reviews* contributor. Noting the novel's appeal to "book lovers in particular," a *Publishers Weekly* reviewer concluded that readers "will savor [the] . . . palpable whiff of musty shelves and dusty volumes" that emanates from Skelton's fiction debut.

Biographical and Critical Sources

PERIODICALS

Booklist, June 1, 2006, Jennifer Mattson, review of *Endymion Spring,* p. 64.

Bookseller, November 18, 2005, Caroline Sanderson, "The Stuff of Dreams," p. 30.
Guardian (London, England), March 25, 2006, Philip Ardagh, "Matthew Skelton's Bookish Historical Tale, *Endymion Spring,* Doesn't Quite Grab."
Kirkus Reviews, June 15, 2006, review of *Endymion Spring,* p. 637.
Publishers Weekly, July 17, 2006, review of *Endymion Spring,* p. 159.
School Library Journal, September, 2006, Tim Wadham, review of *Endymion Spring,* p. 218.

ONLINE

Powells Web site, http://www.powells.com/ (January 3, 2007), interview with Skelton.
Random House Web site, http://www.randomhouse.com/ (January 3, 2007), "A Conversation with Matthew Skelton."
Teen Reads.com http://www.teenreads.com/ (November 1, 2006), interview with Skelton.*

*   *   *

SONNENBLICK, Jordan 1969-

Personal

Born July 4, 1969, in Fort Leonard Wood, MO; married; children: two. *Education:* University of Pennsylvania, B.A. (English), 1991.

Addresses

Home—Bethlehem, PA. *Office*—P.O. Box 20070, Lehigh Valley, PA 18002-0070. *E-mail*—jordansonnenblick@rcn.com.

Career

Author and educator. Taught middle school in NJ and elementary school in PA.

Awards, Honors

Book Sense Picks for Teens, 2004 and 2005, Borders Original Voices selection, and Popular Paperbacks for Young Adults selection, American Library Association, 2007, all for *Drums, Girls & Dangerous Pie.*

Writings

YOUNG-ADULT NOVELS

Drums, Girls & Dangerous Pie, DayBue Insights (Ketchum, ID), 2004.
Notes from the Midnight Driver, Scholastic Press (New York, NY), 2006.

Zen and the Art of Faking It, Scholastic Press (New York, NY), 2007.

Dodger and Me, Feiwel and Friends (New York, NY), 2008.

Sidelights

Jordan Sonnenblick is the author of a number of critically acclaimed novels for young adults, including *Drums, Girls & Dangerous Pie* and *Zen and the Art of Faking It.* A former middle-school English teacher, Sonnenblick often bases his works on events from his own life. When the younger brother of one of his students was diagnosed with cancer, Sonnenblick tried to locate a book that would help her understand the disease and cope with her fears. "I couldn't find a book to help her, so I decided to write one," he recalled to *BookPage* contributor Heidi Henneman. This decision resulted in Sonnenblick's fiction debut, *Drums, Girls & Dangerous Pie.*

Sonnenblick wrote the manuscript for his first novel in only twelve weeks, as he told interviewer Cynthia Leitich Smith for *Cynsations* online. "The research task was massive; I wanted to write about cancer realistically enough that the book would stand up to the most intense scrutiny from people who knew EVERYTHING

Cover of Jordan Sonnenblick's young-adult novel Drums, Girls & Dangerous Pie, *featuring artwork by Istvan Banyai.* (Illustration © 2006 by Istvan Banyai. Reproduced by permission of Scholastic, Inc.)

about cancer," he recalled. "Fortunately, my childhood best friend is a pediatric oncologist, so he was my research guru." *Drums, Girls & Dangerous Pie* focuses on Steven Alper, a smart, well-adjusted eighth grader whose life revolves around school, jazz band, and his pursuit of the lovely Renée Albert. When Steven's five-year-old brother, Jeffrey, is diagnosed with leukemia, the teen's life takes an unexpected and dramatic turn. According to *Horn Book* reviewer Claire E. Gross, Sonnenblick's "novel wisely avoids a resolution of Jeffrey's illness, focusing instead on the family's painful process of adjustment." The author "perceptively records the struggle within Steven to lash out against his parents for feeling neglected and to feel compassion for his brother," a critic observed in *Publishers Weekly,* and Ilene Cooper wrote favorably in *Booklist* about the "reality, rawness, and the wit Sonnenblick infuses into Steven's first-person voice." *Drums, Girls & Dangerous Pie* "does not miss a single emotional beat," Joel Shoemaker concluded in *School Library Journal.*

Like *Drums, Girls & Dangerous Pie, Notes from the Midnight Driver* was also inspired by an episode from Sonnenblick's teaching career. After his class behaved poorly for a substitute teacher, Sonnenblick asked the students to write letters explaining their behavior; they responded to the exercise with apathy. "They were flippant, self-serving, non-responsible, blaming notes—so much so that I couldn't even send them to the parents," he told Henneman. The theme of responsibility is at the center of *Notes from the Midnight Driver,* "a funny, bittersweet tour de force," according to *Booklist* contributor Frances Bradburn. Alex Gregory, the novel's sixteen-year-old narrator, is assigned to one hundred hours of community service after he gets drunk, steals his mom's car, and destroys his neighbor's lawn gnome. While working of his penance at a local nursing home, Alex meets grumpy Solomon Lewis, and the pair forges an unlikely friendship through their love of music. According to *Kliatt* reviewer Paula Rohrlick, *Notes from the Midnight Driver* is "genuinely heartwarming and entertaining, in the best senses of the words." James Blasingame, writing in the *Journal of Adolescent & Adult Literacy,* called the work "touching, hysterical, and insightful, sometimes even on the same page."

In *Zen and the Art of Faking It,* eighth-grader San Lee, an adopted Chinese teen whose father sits in prison, creates an unusual persona to help him fit in at his new school. Using his limited knowledge of Buddhism and Taoism, San convinces his classmates, including the adorable Woody, that he is a Zen master. "The story moves at a brisk clip, and San's first-person narrative . . . is filled with funny asides," noted Cooper. "San and his predicament are a delight," observed Paula Rohrlick in *Kliatt,* the critic adding that Sonnenblick "manages to make them both feel completely real."

Although Sonnenblick's stories deal with serious themes, they are also infused with humor. "I basically think the world is a hard place, so people have to be good to each other," the author told *Publishers Weekly* interviewer Jennifer M. Brown. "I've learned from [writer] Frank McCourt, partly because he was my high school writing teacher and also from *Angela's Ashes,* that the funniest parts of life are often wrapped around the saddest parts. It's the bonus that makes life livable."

Biographical and Critical Sources

PERIODICALS

Booklist, September 15, 2005, Ilene Cooper, review of *Drums, Girls & Dangerous Pie,* p. 63; October 1, 2006, Frances Bradburn, review of *Notes from the Midnight Driver,* p. 52; October 1, 2007, Ilene Cooper, review of *Zen and the Art of Faking It,* p. 68.

Bulletin of the Center for Children's Books, November, 2005, Deborah Stevenson, review of *Drums, Girls & Dangerous Pie,* p. 156; January, 2007, Karen Coats, review of *Notes from the Midnight Driver,* p. 231.

Horn Book, January-February, 2006, Claire E. Gross, review of *Drums, Girls & Dangerous Pie,* p. 89; September-October, 2006, Claire E. Gross, review of *Notes from the Midnight Driver,* p. 597; November-December, 2007, Christine M. Heppermann, review of *Zen and the Art of Faking It,* p. 686.

Journal of Adolescent & Adult Literacy, November, 2006, James Blasingame, review of *Notes from the Midnight Driver,* p. 238, and interview with Sonnenblick, p. 240.

Kirkus Reviews, September 1, 2005, review of *Drums, Girls & Dangerous Pie,* p. 983; September 15, 2006, review of *Notes from the Midnight Driver,* p. 968; September 1, 2007, review of *Zen and the Art of Faking It.*

Kliatt, September, 2005, Claire Rosser, review of *Drums, Girls & Dangerous Pie,* p. 15; November, 2006, review of *Notes from the Midnight Driver,* p. 15; September, 2007, Paula Rohrlick, review of *Zen and the Art of Faking It,* p. 18.

Publishers Weekly, December 12, 2005, review of *Drums, Girls & Dangerous Pie,* p. 68; September 18, 2006, Jennifer M. Brown, interview with Sonnenblick and review of *Notes from the Midnight Driver,* both p. 55; October 8, 2007, review of *Zen and the Art of Faking It,* p. 55.

School Library Journal, October, 2004, Joel Shoemaker, review of *Drums, Girls & Dangerous Pie,* p. 178; October, 2006, Shannon Seglin, review of *Notes from the Midnight Driver,* p. 173.

Voice of Youth Advocates, December, 2004, review of *Drums, Girls & Dangerous Pie,* p. 396.

ONLINE

Bookpage.com, http://www.bookpage.com/ (November 20, 2007), Heidi Henneman, "Self-serving Students Inspire a Teacher's Teen Novel."

Cynsations, http://cynthialeitichsmith.blogspot.com/ (December 22, 2005), Cynthia Leitich Smith, interview with Sonnenblick.

Jordan Sonnenblick Home Page, http://www.jordanson nenblick.com (November 20, 2007).

*   *   *

SORRA, Kristin

Personal

Born July 2, in Baltimore, MD; married Dennis Calero (a comic artist). *Education:* Pratt Institute, B.F.A. (illustration).

Addresses

Home—Southern NY. *Agent*—Libby Ford, Kirchoff/Wohlberg, 866 United Nations Plaza, No. 525, New York, NY 10017. *E-mail*—kristin@kristinsorra.com.

Career

Illustrator, animation developer, and graphic designer. Atomic Paintbrush, cofounder with husband, Dennis Calero; animation artist and book illustrator.

Member

Society of Children's Book Writers and Illustrators.

Illustrator

Lynea Bowdish, *One Glad Man,* Children's Press (New York, NY), 1999.

Betsy Franco, *Shells,* Children's Press (New York, NY), 2000.

Cheryl Ware, *Venola in Love,* Orchard Books (New York, NY), 2000.

Dana Meachen Rau, *So Many Sounds,* Children's Press (New York, NY), 2001.

Katy Hall and Lisa Eisenberg, *Turkey Riddles,* Dial Books (New York, NY), 2002.

Geof Smith, *City Tales,* Scholastic (New York, NY), 2002.

Cathrene Valente Youngquist, *The Three Billygoats Gruff and Mean Calypso Joe,* Atheneum (New York, NY), 2002.

Aaron Shepard, *King o' the Cats,* Atheneum (New York, NY), 2004.

Barbara Gregorich, *Waltur Buys a Pig in a Poke, and Other Stories* Houghton Mifflin (Boston, MA), 2006.

Barbara Gregorich, *Waltur Paints Himself into a Corner, and Other Stories* Houghton Mifflin (Boston, MA), 2007.

Biographical and Critical Sources

PERIODICALS

Booklist, August, 2002, Susan Dove Lempke, review of *The Three Billygoats Gruff and Mean Calypso Joe,* p. 1969; September 1, 2002, Stephanie Zvirin, review of

Turkey Riddles, p. 140; October 15, 2004, Carolyn Phelan, review of *King o' the Cats,* p. 408; June 1, 2006, Hazel Rochman, review of *Waltur Buys a Pig in a Poke, and Other Stories,* p. 82.

Kirkus Reviews, May 15, 2002, review of *The Three Billygoats Gruff and Mean Calypso Joe,* p. 746; July 1, 2004, review of *King o' the Cats,* p. 636; June 15, 2006, review of *Waltur Buys a Pig in a Poke, and Other Stories,* p. 633.

Publishers Weekly, November 6, 2000, review of *Venola in Love,* p. 91; November 4, 2002, review of *The Three Billygoats Gruff and Mean Calypson Joe,* p. 83; June 19, 2006, review of *Waltur Buys a Pig in a Poke, and Other Stories,* p. 63.

School Library Journal, October, 2000, Amy Stultz, review of *Venola in Love,* p. 174; November, 2002, Carol Ann Wilson, review of *The Three Billygoats Gruff and Mean Calypso Joe,* p. 151; August, 2004, Margaret Bush, review of *King o' the Cats,* p. 114; July, 2006, Carol L. MacKay, review of *Waltur Buys a Pig in a Poke, and Other Stories,* p. 78.

ONLINE

Kristin Sorra Blog site, http://www.kristinsorra.blogspot.com/ (December 5, 2007).
Kristin Sorra Home Page, http://www.kristinsorra.com (December 5, 2007).

*   *   *

SPAIN, Susan Rosson

Personal

Children: four daughters. *Ethnicity:* "Estonian/British/Irish/German." *Education:* Attended college in MD; attended Institute of Children's Literature. *Hobbies and other interests:* SCUBA diving, biking, gardening, running, yoga, every sort of needle art.

Addresses

Home and office—Conyers, GA. *E-mail*—susan@susan-spain.com.

Career

Author. Worked as a licensed optician for eight years; former optical superstore manager; former vision therapy coordinator for private optical practice. Presenter at schools and writer's workshops.

Member

Society of Children's Book Writers and Illustrators.

Writings

The Deep Cut, Marshall Cavendish (Tarrytown, NY), 2006.

Susan Rosson Spain (Courtesy of Susan Rosson Spain.)

Sidelights

Even as an adult, Susan Rosson Spain enjoys reading children's literature, and while raising her four daughters she often read the same books her daughters were reading. At some point, Spain decided to turn from reader to author, and in 2006 her first book, the middle-grade novel *The Deep Cut,* was published. *The Deep Cut* was inspired by one of Spain's ancestors, a mentally challenged boy named Lonzo who lived during the late nineteenth century. As Spain commented on her home page, she was "intrigued" by Lonzo's story, particularly by one possible scenario: During the 1800s how "could a boy with numerous disabilities find a way to make his mark?"

Cited by critics for its moving story and credible main character, *The Deep Cut* takes place during the U.S. Civil War and introduces a boy named Lonzo, who is deemed "slow." Spain's story begins when Lonzo is sent to live with his Aunt Mariah, a woman who has two sons fighting in the Army of the Confederacy. Lonzo personally does not believe in war and it is from his perspective that Spain tells her story. *The Deep Cut* follows the boy as he witnesses and experiences how war affects his own world as well as the world of those around him. Anne O'Malley, in her review of *The Deep Cut* for *Booklist,* dubbed the book a "fine first novel" that features "well wrought characters, vivid historical details, and nuanced themes." A *Kirkus Reviews* critic applauded Spain for introducing readers to an unusual young protagonist, calling Lonzo a "believable and admirable character."

"I've always loved to write," Spain told *SATA,* "but I first realized I wanted to write for young people when I

Cover of Spain's **The Deep Cut,** *featuring artwork by Vince Natale.* (Illustration © 2006 by Vince Natale. Reproduced by permission.)

was involved in vision therapy. I came into contact with children and teens every day who were dealing with various struggles, physical ones such as strabismus and amblyopia, combined with the usual difficulties every child encounters. I saw in those young people hope, determination, and even heroism. These are the qualities I believe essential to interesting, realistic characters as well."

Biographical and Critical Sources

PERIODICALS

Booklist, December 1, 2006, review of *The Deep Cut,* p. 45.

Kirkus Reviews, September 15, 2006, review of *The Deep Cut,* p. 968.

School Library Journal, December, 2006, Nancy P. Reeder, review of *The Deep Cut,* p. 156.

Voice of Youth Advocates, December, 2006, Steven Kral, review of *The Deep Cut,* p. 434.

ONLINE

Adams Literary Agency Web site, http://www.adamsliterary.com/ (November 18, 2007), "Susan Rosson Spain."

Children's Bookwatch Web site, http://www.midwestbookreview.com/ (November 18, 2007), review of *The Deep Cut.*

Susan Rosson Spain Home Page, http://susanspain.com (November 18, 2007).

T-Y

TASCHEK, Karen 1956-
(Karen Bentley)

Personal

Born March 12, 1956, in Columbia, MO; son of Robert (a botanist) and Barbara (an English professor) McDermott; married (marriage ended); married John Taschek (an environmental consultant), December 19, 1997; children: (first marriage) David Bentley. *Education:* Franklin & Marshall College, B.A., 1978. *Hobbies and other interests:* Horseback riding and training, hiking, rafting.

Addresses

Home—Corvales, NM. *E-mail*—ktaschek@aol.com.

Career

Writer. *Scientific American,* New York, NY, former editorial assistant; Random House Children's Books, New York, NY, former copy chief; University of New Mexico Press, Albuquerque, editor; copyeditor for Alloy Entertainment.

Writings

(Under name Karen Bentley) *The Unsers,* Chelsea House Publishers (New York, NY), 1996, new edition with Jeff Gluck, 2006.
Horse of Seven Moons, illustrated by Mina Yamashita, University of New Mexico Press (Albuquerque, NM), 2005.
Death Stars, Weird Galaxies, and a Quasar-spangled Universe: The Discoveries of the Very Large Array Telescope University of New Mexico Press (Albuquerque, NM), 2006.
The Real Story of Bats: Vampires, Movie Stars, and in Your Belfry, University of New Mexico Press (Albuquerque, NM), 2008.

Sidelights

Karen Taschek told *SATA:* "I've always wanted to be a children's book writer, mostly because I enjoyed reading so much as a child. I grew up in the golden age of children's books, the 1960s, when editor Ursula Nordstrom at Harper acquired E.B. White (the author of *Charlotte's Web* and *Stuart Little*), Louise Fitzhugh (author of *Harriet the Spy* and *The Long Secret*), and Maurice Sendak (*Where the Wild Things Are*). As a kid, I would pick up a book, read a sentence or two, and then spin off my own stories, sometimes for hours.

"I moved to New York City after college to find a job in the publishing field and became an editorial assistant at *Scientific American* magazine. There perfection was the order of the day, and I learned splendid science editing and writing skills. Later, as copy chief at Random House Children's Books, I crossed paths with Random House author Dr. Seuss at the end of his career.

"I now write horse books and science books for children. The University of New Mexico Press plans to publish a new science series for children aged nine to fourteen, starting with my book *The Real Story of Bats: Vampires, Movie Stars, and in Your Belfry,* and including titles on cell phones, horses, and dinosaurs."

Biographical and Critical Sources

PERIODICALS

Booklist, May 1, 2006, Jennifer Mattson, review of *Death Stars, Weird Galaxies, and a Quasar-spangled Universe: The Discoveries of the Very Large Array Telescope,* p. 79.
Kliatt, September, 2005, Edna Boardman, review of *Horse of Seven Moons,* p. 24.
School Library Journal, May, 2006, Patricia Manning, review of *The Unsers,* p. 142; July, 2006, Linda Wadleigh, review of *Death Stars, Weird Galaxies, and a Quasar-spangled Universe,* p. 124.
Science Books and Film, September-October, 2006, Bradley W. Carroll, review of *Death Stars, Weird Galaxies, and a Quasar-spangled Universe,* p. 213.

Voice of Youth Advocates, April, 2007, Amy Sisson, review of *Death Stars, Weird Galaxies, and a Quasar-spangled Universe,* p. 82.

ONLINE

University of New Mexico Web site, http://www.unmpress. com/ (December 10, 2007).*

* * *

von BUHLER, Cynthia

Personal

Married Russell Farhang (a jazz musician). *Education:* Art Institute of Boston, B.F.A.; attended Richmond College, London. *Hobbies and other interests:* Rescuing cats, raising doves, finding unique locations for film and television.

Addresses

Home and office—Staten Island, NY; Stratford, CT. *E-mail*—cvb@acynthiavonbuhler.com.

Career

Artist, author, illustrator, and performer. Gallery owner. *Exhibitions:* Artwork exhibited at Nassau County Museum of Art, Staten Island Museum, Museum of American Illustration, Norman Rockwell Museum, University of Toronto, Opera Company of Philadelphia, and Dana Farber Cancer Institute.

Member

Society of Illustrators, Cat Writer's Association.

Awards, Honors

Gold, Silver, and Bronze medals, Society of Illustrators, Los Angeles; Gold Medal, Visual Club; New York Public Library One Hundred Titles for Reading and Sharing designation, 2002, for *They Called Her Molly Pitcher* by Anne Rockwell; Teacher's Pick, *Parent & Child,* 2006, and Children's Pick, Booksense, 2007, both for *The Cat Who Wouldn't Come Inside.*

Writings

SELF-ILLUSTRATED

The Cat Who Wouldn't Come Inside: Based on a True Story, Houghton Mifflin (New York, NY), 2006.

ILLUSTRATOR

Nicholas B.A. Nicholson, *Little Girl in a Red Dress with Cat and Dog,* Viking (New York, NY), 1998.

Cynthia von Buhler (Self-portrait in clay, 2006. Courtesy of Cynthia von Buhler.)

Martha Stewart and others, *Once upon a Fairy Tale: Four Favorite Stories,* Viking (New York, NY), 2001.

Anne Rockwell, *They Called Her Molly Pitcher,* Alfred A. Knopf (New York, NY), 2002.

Dennis Brindell Fradin, *Nicolaus Copernicus: The Earth Is a Planet,* Mondo Publishing (New York, NY), 2003.

Dennis Brindell Fradin, *Tell Us a Tale, Hans!: The Life of Hans Christian Andersen,* Mondo Publishing (New York, NY), 2006.

Contributor of illustrations to various magazines.

Sidelights

A sculptor, painter, performance artist, and children's book author, Cynthia von Buhler has been recognized across a number of creative mediums. As she notes on her home page, von Buhler's art "require[s] the viewer to get involved," whether it be emotionally or physically. Her interest in writing and illustrating children's books was inspired by her own desire to get involved with the children that will comprise future generations. In an interview with Joan Anderman for the *Boston Globe* online, von Buhler explained that, as an author, she hopes to "teach children when they're young, so they turn into better adults."

Von Buhler's first self-illustrated picture book, *The Cat Who Wouldn't Come Inside: Based on a True Story,* is based on von Buhler's experience befriending a feral cat. The narrator of the story makes an attempt to invite a stray cat into her home, but each time she does, the cat runs away. The cat eventually warms up to the narrator, who by now has offered gifts of warm milk, yarn, and toys to tempt the homeless puss. A *Kirkus Reviews* critic noted that "von Buhler builds the cumulative tale, adding ever more elaborate items" as the story reaches its surprising conclusion. The author's illustrations for the story are also unexpected, retelling the story in a series of dioramas that include clay figures, found objects, and photography. A *Publishers Weekly* reviewer commented that "von Buhler's 3-D settings and characters work considerable magic" but found her photographs less than intriguing. In contrast, Julie Roach remarked in a review for *School Library Journal* that the book's "photographs are a delight to pore over." In *California Bookwatch* a contributor remarked that *The Cat Who Wouldn't Come Inside* will delight children as a "very different book of friendship and trust."

Biographical and Critical Sources

PERIODICALS

Booklist, December 15, 1997, Hazel Rochman, review of *Little Girl in a Red Dress with Cat and Dog,* p. 704; April 15, 2002, Carolyn Phelan, review of *They Called Her Molly Pitcher,* p. 1400; April 1, 2004, review of *Nicolaus Copernicus: The Earth Is a Planet,* p. 1361.

Bulletin of the Center for Children's Books, June, 2002, review of *They Called Her Molly Pitcher,* p. 381; April, 2004, Elizabeth Bush, review of *Nicolaus Copernicus,* p. 326.

Cat Fancy, April, 2007, Laura Lee Bloor, interview with von Buhler.

Communication Arts, March-April, 2002, Lisa L. Cyr, "Cynthia von Buhler."

Horn Book, March-April, 1998, Ann A. Flowers, review of *Little Girl in a Red Dress with Cat and Dog,* p. 216; May-June, 2002, Susan P. Bloom, review of *They Called Her Molly Pitcher,* p. 349.

Instructor, November-December, 2002, Judy Freeman, review of *They Called Her Molly Pitcher,* p. 57.

Kirkus Reviews, April 1, 2002, review of *They Called Her Molly Pitcher,* p. 498; September 1, 2006, review of *The Cat Who Wouldn't Come Inside: Based on a True Story,* p. 914.

New York Times Book Review, October 20, 2002, review of *They Called Her Molly Pitcher,* p. 22.

Parent and Child, November, 2006, Carolyn Rogalsky, profile of von Buhler.

Publishers Weekly, December 15, 1997, review of *Little Girl in a Red Dress with Cat and Dog,* p. 57; April

Anne F. Rockwell's biographical picture book **They Called Her Molly Pitcher** *features von Buhler's folk-inspired art.* (Illustration © 2002 by Cynthia von Buhler. Used by permission of Alfred A. Knopf, an imprint of Random House Children's Books, a division of Random House, Inc.)

Von Buhler's intricate diorama art brings to life a story about a stray cat and a lonely woman in The Cat Who Wouldn't Come Inside. (Illustration ©
2006 by Cynthia von Buhler. Reprinted by permission of Houghton Mifflin Company. All rights reserved.)

29, 2002, review of *They Called Her Molly Pitcher,* p.
71; February 16, 2004, review of *Nicolaus Coperni-cus,* p. 172; September 18, 2006, review of *The Cat
Who Wouldn't Come Inside,* p. 53.

Reading Teacher, November, 2003, review of *They Called
Her Molly Pitcher,* p. 276.

School Library Journal, February, 1998, Heide Piehler, review of *Little Girl in a Red Dress with Cat and Dog,*
p. 89; June, 2002, Anne Chapman, review of *They
Called Her Molly Pitcher,* p. 124; June, 2004, Donna
Cardon, review of *Nicolaus Copernicus,* p. 126; November, 2006, Julie Roach, review of *The Cat Who
Wouldn't Come Inside,* p. 115.

Tribune Books (Chicago, IL), July 14, 2002, review of
They Called Her Molly Pitcher, p. 5.

ONLINE

Boston Globe Online, http://www.boston.com/ (March 3,
2000), Joan Anderman, "Original Cynthia: Multital-
ented and Eccentric, von Buhler Reigns in the Underground."

California Bookwatch Web site, http://www.midwest
bookreview.com/ (November, 2006), review of *The
Cat Who Wouldn't Come Inside.*

Cynthia von Buhler Home Page, http://www.cynthiavon
buhler.com (November 18, 2007).

Woman Rock Web site, http://womanrock.com/ (June,
1999), Amy Steele, interview with von Buhler.*

*   *   *

WRONGO, I.B.
See KATZ, Alan

*   *   *

WYATT, David 1968-

Personal

Born November 28, 1968, in England. *Education:* Attended art college. *Hobbies and other interests:* Playing
guitar.

Addresses

Home—Dartmoor, England. *E-mail*—David.Wyatt@
btinternet.com.

Career

Illustrator. Formerly performed as part of a rock band.

Illustrator

Terry Deary, *True Monster Stories,* Hippo (London, England), 1992.

Philip Pullman, *The Wonderful Story of Aladdin and the Enchanted Lamp,* Scholastic (London, England), 1993.

Terry Deary, *True Horror Stories,* Hippo (London, England), 1993, new edition, Scholastic (London, England), 2006.

Terry Deary, *True Crime Stories,* Hippo (London, England), 1994.

Terry Deary, *True Ghost Stories,* Hippo (London, England), 1995, Puffin (New York, NY), 1996.

Terry Deary, *True Shark Stories,* Hippo (London, England), 1995.

Ian Waugh and Linda Straker, *Castles of Puzzles,* Hippo (London, England), 1995.

Terry Deary, *True Survival Stories,* Scholastic (London, England), 1995, Puffin (New York, NY), 1997.

Terry Deary, *True UFO Stories,* Hippo (London, England), 1997.

Terry Deary, *True War Stories,* Hippo (London, England), 1997.

Herbie Brennan, *Seriously Weird True Stories,* Hippo (London, England), 1997.

Terry Deary, *Teary Deary's True Stories: Monster, Horror, Ghost,* Scholastic (London, England), 1998.

Terry Deary, *True Spy Stories,* Scholastic (London, England), 1998.

Herbie Brennan, *Seriously Weird True Stories 2,* Scholastic (London, England), 1998.

Ann Pilling, *Black Harvest,* Collins (London, England), 1999.

Pete Johnson, *Eyes of the Alien,* Corgi Yearling (London, England), 1999.

Andrew Donkin, *Space Stories That Really Happened,* Hippo (London, England), 1999.

Terry Deary, *True Disaster Stories,* Scholastic (New York, NY), 1999.

Diana Wynne Jones, *Fire and Hemlock,* new edition, Collins (London, England), 2000.

Diana Wynne Jones, *A Tale of Time City,* new edition, Collins (London, England), 2000.

Pete Johnson, *The Creeper,* Corgi Yearling (London, England), 2000.

Terry Deary, *True Mystery,* Scholastic (London, England), 2000.

Theresa Breslin, *Dream Master Nightmare!,* Doubleday (London, England), 2000.

Neil Tonge, *A World in Flames: World War II on Land,* Macmillan Children's (London, England), 2001.

Neil Tonge, *A World in Flames: Civilians,* Macmillan Children's (London, England), 2001.

K.M. Peyton, *Stealaway,* Macmillan Childrens (London, England), 2001, Cricket Books (Chicago, IL), 2004.

Pete Johnson, *The Frighteners,* Corgi Yearling (London, England), 2001.

Peter Hepplewhite, *At Sea* ("World in Flames" series), Macmillan Children's (London, England), 2001.

Peter Hepplewhite, *World War II in the Air* ("World in Flames" series), Macmillan Children's (London, England), 2001.

Michael Molloy, *The Witch Trade,* Scholastic (New York, NY), 2001.

Cherith Baldry, *The Silver Horn* ("Eaglesmount Trilogy"), Macmillan Children's (London, England), 2001, Mondo (New York, NY), 2002.

Cherith Baldry, *The Emerald Throne* ("Eaglesmount Trilogy"), Macmillan Children's (London, England), 2001, Mondo (New York, NY), 2003.

Cherith Baldry, *The Lake of Darkness* ("Eaglesmount Trilogy"), Macmillan Children's (London, England), 2001, Mondo (New York, NY), 2004.

Adèle Geras, *Goodbye, Tommy Blue,* Macmillan Children's (London, England), 2003.

Theresa Breslin, *Dream Master Gladiator,* Doubleday (London, England), 2003.

Erik L'Homme, *Quadehar the Sorcerer,* Scholastic (New York, NY), 2003.

Michael Molloy, *The Time Witches,* Scholastic (New York, NY), 2003.

Maggie Pearson, reteller, *Taliesin: The Boy Wizzard,* A. & C. Black (London, England), 2004.

Pete Johnson, *Avenger,* Corgi Yearling (London, England), 2004.

Theresa Breslin, *Arabian Nights,* Doubleday (London, England), 2004.

Charles Butler, *Death of a Ghost,* HarperCollins (London, England), 2006.

Philip Reeve, *Larklight; or, The Revenge of the White Spider!; or, To Saturn's Rings and Back!: A Rousing Tale of Dauntless Pluck in the Farthest Reaches of Space,* Bloomsbury Children's Books (New York, NY), 2006.

Geraldine McCaughrean, *Peter Pan in Scarlet,* Oxford University Press (Oxford, England), 2006.

Teary Deary, *Flight of the Fire Thief,* Kingfisher (Boston, MA), 2007.

Philip Reeve, *Starcross: A Stirring Adventure of Spies, Time Travel, and Curious Hats* (sequel to *Larklight*), Bloomsbury Children's Books (New York, NY), 2007.

Julia Golding, *The Secret of the Sirens* ("Companions Quartet"), Marshall Cavendish (New York, NY), 2007.

Franzeska G. Ewart, reteller, *William Shakespeare's The Tempest,* A. & C. Black (London, England), 2007.

Dean Lorey, *Nightmare Academy,* HarperCollins (New York, NY), 2007.

Julia Golding, *Mines of the Minotaur* ("Companions Quartet"), Marshall Cavendish (New York, NY), 2008.

Julia Golding, *The Chimera's Curse* ("Companions Quartet"), Marshall Cavendish (New York, NY), 2008.

Contributor of illustration to comic-book series, including *Future Shock.* Illustrator of record albums and book covers.

Biographical and Critical Sources

PERIODICALS

Horn Book, November-December, 2006, Claire E. Gross, review of *Larklight,* p. 724.
Kirkus Reviews, October 1, 2001, review of *The Witch Trade,* p. 1428; September 15, 2006, review of *Larklight,* p. 965.
School Library Journal, December, 2001, Kathie Meizner, review of *The Witch Trade,* p. 139; August, 2003, John Peters, review of *The Time Witches,* p. 164; July, 2004, Mara Alpert, review of *The Lake of Darkness,* p. 66; December, 2004, Kelley Rae Unger, review of *Stealaway,* p. 117.

ONLINE

David Wyatt Home Page, http://www.david.wyatt.btinternet.com (December 15, 2007).*

*   *   *

YOUNG, Amy L.

Personal

Born in MA; married; husband's name Paul. *Education:* Attended Cleveland Institute of Art; Yale University, B.A.; Indiana University, M.F.A. (painting); Harvard University, J.D. *Hobbies and other interests:* Swimming, sailing, reading, tutoring, spending time with friends.

Addresses

Home—Spring Lake, MI.

Career

Author and illustrator. Practiced law for seven years; illustrator, beginning 1995. Worked variously as a waitress, construction worker, farm hand, and teaching assistant. Member of board, Harbor Humane Society.

Member

Society of Children's Book Writers and Illustrators.

Writings

SELF-ILLUSTRATED

Belinda the Ballerina, Viking (New York, NY), 2002.
Belinda in Paris, Viking (New York, NY), 2005.
Belinda and the Glass Slipper, Viking (New York, NY), 2006.
Belinda Begins Ballet, Viking (New York, NY), 2008.

ILLUSTRATOR

Heather Sellers, *Spike and Cubby's Ice Cream Island Adventure,* Henry Holt (New York, NY), 2004.
Cari Meister, *My Pony Jack,* Viking (New York, NY), 2005.
Cari Meister, *My Pony Jack at Riding Lessons,* Viking (New York, NY), 2005.
Cari Meister, *My Pony Jack at the Horse Show,* Viking (New York, NY), 2006.
Lynn Cullen, *Moi and Marie Antoinette,* Bloomsbury (New York, NY), 2006.

Sidelights

Amy L. Young took a rather unusual path to becoming a children's book author and illustrator: she started by getting her law degree and working as an attorney. Fortunately for young readers, her lifelong love of drawing and being creative won out, and in 1995 she left her law practice to become a full-time illustrator. Her first children's book, *Belinda the Ballerina,* which she both wrote and illustrated, was published seven years later. In addition to creating several more original stories that feature Belinda, Young has also created artwork for picture books by authors Heather Sellers, Cari Meister, and

Amy L. Young introduces readers to a dedicated young dancer with rather large feet in her self-illustrated Belinda and the Glass Slipper
(Illustration © 2006 by Amy L. Young. Reproduced by permission of Viking, a division of Penguin Putnam Books for Young Readers.)

Lynn Cullen. Praising *Belinda the Ballerina,* a *Kirkus Reviews* writer noted that "Young shows considerable potential in both her lively gouache paintings and her restrained, polished prose that captures the heart of a dancer."

Belinda is a girl whose love of ballet helps her overcome a rather significant impediment: two very large feet. The girl's story starts in *Belinda Begins Ballet,* when she is young and gets her first exposure to the dance. Cast in the role of a clown in the school talent show, Belinda finds the role a challenge because of the size of her feet. However, watching an older schoolmate rehearsing a ballet routine inspires Belinda to study each dance move and practice at home. *Belinda the Ballerina* finds the girl older but no less in love with ballet. Studying and practicing has improved her ability, but Belinda is still grounded to the stage by the same overly large feet. Rejected by the judges of the Spring Recital because of the size of her feet, Belinda tries to forget about dancing by working as a waitress at a local restaurant. When a trio performs during her shift waiting tables, Belinda cannot help it; she starts to dance and ultimately attracts the attention of a very special restaurant patron: the maestro of the city ballet! In *Publishers Weekly* a contributor cited Young's "optimistic" approach, calling *Belinda the Ballerina* a "tale of just deserts and an irrepressible urge to dance."

Audience acclaim quickly fuels Belinda's career as a prima ballerina, and in *Belinda in Paris* she is scheduled to appear on stage in Paris. However, her grandiose pink satin ballet shoes disappear during the trip, and readers join the dancer in worrying whether Belinda can replace them in time. Of course, Belinda is not the only dancer with talent, and in *Belinda and the Glass Slipper* she must deal with a jealous dance rival in the form of Miss Lola Mudge. When Belinda is scheduled to perform the leading role in the ballet *Cinderella,* Lola attempts to keep the star away from the state so that she can perform the role herself. Fortunately, Belinda's magical story also features a magical fairy godmother to save the day. Young's "droll text and . . . distinctive . . . gouache paintings . . . will make this witty book a pleasure to read aloud," Carolyn Phelan wrote in her *Booklist* review of *Belinda and the Glass Slipper.* Equally enthusiastic about *Belinda in Paris,* Phelan concluded of the work that it "features an engaging story, graceful illustrations, and, in Belinda, an instantly recognizable character who is simply magnifique." In *School Library Journal,* Carol Schene wrote that *Belinda in Paris* serves up "whimsy, humor, and an engaging glimpse of France."

On her home page, Young offered aspiring authors this advice: "Read as many children's books you can. Read the classics. Read the new ones. Read the good ones. Read the bad ones. Reread the good ones. Read them aloud. Read them to children. Read them to your goldfish. Develop that ear! Listen for the rhythm, the pacing, the syntax, the drama. Read!"

Biographical and Critical Sources

PERIODICALS

Booklist, March 1, 2003, Carolyn Phelan, review of *Belinda the Ballerina,* p. 1205; January 1, 2005, Carolyn Phelan, review of *Belinda in Paris,* p. 876; May 1, 2005, Gillian Engberg, review of *My Pony Jack,* p. 1592; October 15, 2005, Carolyn Phelan, review of *My Pony Jack at Riding School,* p. 57; October 1, 2006, Carolyn Phelan, review of *Belinda and the Glass Slipper,* p. 61; November 1, 2006, Shelle Rosenfeld, review of *Moi and Marie Antoinette,* p. 60.

Kirkus Reviews, February 15, 2003, review of *Belinda the Ballerina,* p. 318; January 15, 2005, review of *Belinda in Paris,* p. 127; August 1, 2006, review of *Belinda and the Glass Slipper,* p. 799; September 15, 2006, review of *Moi and Marie Antoinette,* p. 950.

Magpies, November, 2003, review of *Belinda the Ballerina,* p. 28.

Publishers Weekly, December 23, 2002, review of *Belinda the Ballerina,* p. 69; October 9, 2006, review of *Moi and Marie Antoinette,* p. 55.

School Library Journal, March, 2003, Susan Pine, review of *Belinda the Ballerina,* p. 210; April, 2005, Carol Schene, review of *Belinda in Paris,* p. 117; August, 2005, Melinda Piehler, review of *My Pony, Jack,* p. 103; October, 2005, Laurel L. Takovakis, review of *My Pony Jack at Riding School,* p. 122; October, 2006, Catherine Callegari, review of *Belinda and the Glass Slipper,* p. 131.

ONLINE

Amy L. Young Home Page, http://www.amylyoung.com (December 10, 2007).*

Illustrations Index

(In the following index, the number of the *volume* in which an illustrator's work appears is given *before* the colon, and the *page number* on which it appears is given *after* the colon. For example, a drawing by Adams, Adrienne appears in Volume 2 on page 6, another drawing by her appears in Volume 3 on page 80, another drawing in Volume 8 on page 1, and so on and so on. . . .)

YABC

Index references to *YABC* refer to listings appearing in the two-volume *Yesterday's Authors of Books for Children,* also published by Gale, Cengage Learning. *YABC* covers prominent authors and illustrators who died prior to 1960.

H

I

J

Q

Author Index

The following index gives the number of the volume in which an author's biographical sketch, Autobiography Feature, Brief Entry, or Obituary appears.

This index includes references to all entries in the following series, which are also published by The Gale Group.

YABC—*Yesterday's Authors of Books for Children: Facts and Pictures about Authors and Illustrators of Books for Young People from Early Times to 1960*
CLR—*Children's Literature Review: Excerpts from Reviews, Criticism, and Commentary on Books for Children*
SAAS—*Something about the Author Autobiography Series*

Author Index